Writing Arguments

Writing Arguments
A Rhetoric with Readings
Seventh Edition

John D. Ramage
Arizona State University

John C. Bean
Seattle University

June Johnson
Seattle University

PEARSON

Longman

New York   San Francisco   Boston
London   Toronto   Sydney   Tokyo   Singapore   Madrid
Mexico City   Munich   Paris   Cape Town   Hong Kong   Montreal

Publisher: Joseph Opiela
Acquisitions Editor: Lauren A. Finn
Development Editor: Marion B. Castellucci
Senior Marketing Manager: Sandra McGuire
Senior Supplements Editor: Donna Campion
Media Supplements Editor: Jenna Egan
Production Manager: Donna DeBenedictis
Project Coordination, Text Design, and Electronic Page Makeup: Elm Street Publishing
    Services, Inc.
Cover Design Manager: Wendy Ann Fredericks
Cover Designer: Kay Petronio
Cover Art: Balla, Giacomo (1871–1958). *Mercurio passa davanti al sole* (*Mercury passes before the sun*), 1914. Canvas,
    120 × 100 cm. Guggenheim Museum, Venice, Italy. Photo credit: Erich Lessing/Art Resource, NY. © ARS, NY.
Photo Researcher: Photosearch, Inc.
Senior Manufacturing Buyer: Alfred C. Dorsey
Printer and Binder: R.R. Donnelley & Sons Company, Harrisonburg
Cover Printer: Phoenix Color Corporation

For permission to use copyrighted material, grateful acknowledgment is made to the copyright holders on pp. 739 to 744, which are hereby made part of this copyright page.

Library of Congress Cataloging-in-Publication Data

Ramage, John D.
  Writing arguments : a rhetoric with readings / John D. Ramage, John C. Bean, June Johnson—7th ed.
      p. cm.
  Includes bibliographical references and index.
  ISBN 0-321-36466-X
  1. English language—Rhetoric.   2. Persuasion (Rhetoric) 3. College readers.   4. Report writing.
  I. Bean, John C.   II. Johnson, June.   III. Title.
PE1431.R33   2007
808'.0427—dc22
                                2005055229

Please visit us at http://www.ablongman.com/ramage

ISBN 0-321-36466-X (Complete Edition)
ISBN 0-321-41290-7 (Brief Edition)
ISBN 0-321-41289-3 (Concise Edition)

6 7 8 9 10—DOH—09 08

Brief Contents

Detailed Contents

Part One   Overview of Argument   1

---

1   Argument: An Introduction   3

3 Writing Arguments   50

Part Two   Principles of Argument   73

4 The Core of an Argument: A Claim with Reasons   75

7   Moving Your Audience: *Ethos, Pathos,* and *Kairos*   129

8   Accommodating Your Audience: Treating Differing Views   141

Part Three   Arguments in Depth: Six Types of Claims   193

10   An Introduction to the Types of Claims   195

12   Causal Arguments: X Causes (Does Not Cause) Y   242

14   Evaluation and Ethical Arguments: X Is (Is Not) a Good Y; X Is Right (Wrong)   289

Responses to Terrorism: Public Safety and Civil Liberties   484

Wal-Mart and the Public Good   561

Biotech Agriculture and the Ethics of Food Production   584

The Cultural Debate on Stem Cell Research and Cloning   610

In Search of Perfection: Steroids, Bionic Athletes, and Designer Children   634

Marriage and Family in the New Millennium   659

The Media and Public Responsibility: What Counts As News and Who Decides?   683

Gender and Technology in Advertising   708

Internet Controversies: Blogs, Hate Sites, and Spam   716

Color Plates
Following page 176

A. Council for Biotechnology Information, "Would It Surprise You to Know That Growing Soybeans Can Help the Environment?" (advocacy advertisement)

B. Tom Reese/*The Seattle Times,* Mosh Pit Crowd Surfer (news photo)

C. Alex Quesada/Matrix, Woman Crossing Bridge in Haitian Slum (news photo)

D. Save the Children, "She's the Best Qualified Teacher for Her Children" (advocacy advertisement)

E. Earthjustice Legal Defense Fund, "It's Just Not the Same without Bears" (advocacy advertisement)

F. Wal-Mart, "Mother Nature Does Her Most Stunning Work When You Give Her Some Space" (corporate image advertisement)

G. General Motors, "Creatures of the Evergreen Forest" (product advertisement)

H. America's Army, "Urban Assault #3" (video game image)

I. America's Army, "Village #5" (video game image)

J. Athletes Against Steroids (Web site)

Preface

As *Writing Arguments* enters its seventh edition, we continue to be gratified by the enthusiastic endorsement of its users. Appreciation for its comprehensive treatment of argument, its clear and flexible structure, its rhetorical focus, and its effective pedagogy has established *Writing Arguments* as the leading college textbook in argumentation. By focusing on argument as dialogue in search of solutions to problems instead of as pro-con debate with winners and losers, *Writing Arguments* treats argument as a process of inquiry as well as a means of persuasion. Users and reviewers have consistently praised the book for its teaching of critical thinking skills that help students *write* arguments: how to analyze the occasion for an argument; how to ground an argument in the values and beliefs of the targeted audience; how to develop and elaborate an argument; and how to respond sensitively to objections and alternative views. Available in three versions—a regular edition, which includes an anthology of readings; a brief edition, which offers the complete rhetoric without the anthology; and a concise edition with fewer readings and examples—*Writing Arguments* has been used successfully at every level, from first-year composition to advanced argumentation courses.

In this seventh edition, we have maintained the signature strengths of *Writing Arguments* while making significant improvements based on our evolving understanding of the theory and practice of argumentation. Furthermore, to counter the trend toward increasingly longer textbooks, we have made the seventh edition shorter than the sixth, even though we have added important new material. As in previous editions, our aim is to integrate a comprehensive study of argument with an effective pedagogy that engages students' interest, builds their confidence as writers and critical thinkers, and gives them tools for effective problem solving and advocacy in civic life. In both its treatment of argumentation and its approach to teaching writing, the text is rooted in current research and theory. Our emphasis throughout is on providing a student-friendly text that really works in the classroom.

What's New in the Seventh Edition?

The seventh edition retains all the features that have made earlier editions successful. In addition, the seventh edition has been improved in the following ways:

- **A new section on *kairos*—introduced in Chapter 4 and developed in Chapter 7.** Renewed interest in *kairos* in recent rhetorical scholarship has led us to appreciate its value in teaching argumentation. We have created a student-friendly explanation of this concept as part of our discussion of the classical appeals of *logos, ethos,* and *pathos.* The new title of Chapter 7 reflects this change: "Moving Your Audience: *Ethos, Pathos,* and *Kairos.*"

- **A new section on "hybrid arguments" in our introduction to stasis or claim-type theory (Chapter 10).** Showing how most arguments are hybrids or composites of different claim types, this new section helps students understand that arguments seldom illustrate a single stasis; rather, parts or sections developed from different stases work together as building blocks to support an overarching main claim.

- **A thoroughly updated and revised anthology** that continues our commitment, initiated in the sixth edition, to a wide range of argument genres including organizational white papers, op-ed pieces, speeches, documented scholarly articles, articles from public affairs magazines, interviews, and blogs; the anthology also includes an equally wide range of visual arguments such as advocacy advertisements, posters, news photographs, and political cartoons. (For a table of contents organized by genre, see the inside back cover.)

- **In the anthology, four engaging new topic areas chosen for their civic importance and student interest:** "Finding Soldiers: The Volunteer Army, Recruitment, and the Draft"; "Wal-Mart and the Public Good"; "In Search of Perfection: Steroids, Bionic Athletes, and Designer Children"; and "The Media and Public Responsibility: What Counts As News and Who Decides?" In many cases, the anthology units build on issues first introduced in the rhetoric portion of the text.

- **Many new professional readings throughout the stasis chapters, chosen for their illustrative power and student interest.** The issues addressed include the definition of bloggers (Are bloggers true journalists?), the role of government in helping the poor (using the stases of precedence and analogy), the possible causes of women's being underrepresented in math and science (by Olivia Judson, an evolutionary biologist), the morality of selling human organs, and a provocative proposal for solving the problem of illicit poppy/opium production in Afghanistan. Chapter 12 on causal arguments also contains an engaging new student argument analyzing the causes of credit card debt among college students.

- **A refocusing of Chapter 8 ("Accommodating Your Audience: Treating Differing Views").** Chapter 8 now emphasizes the continuum from "dialogic argument"—which seeks common ground with its audience, aims at reducing hostility, and takes a more inquiring or conciliatory stance—to the more adversarial approaches typified by summary and refutation of opposing views. These revisions help students better understand the varieties of dialogic arguments—such as delayed thesis or Rogerian argument—and explain more helpfully the rhetorical contexts in which a writer might consider a dialogic rather than an adversarial approach.

- **Updated treatment of visual argument (Chapter 9), based on four new color plates supplemented by new images throughout the text.** Images for analysis and discussion now include Army recruiting posters and video games, a Wal-Mart corporate image ad, and a Web page opposing steroids.

- **Many new examples and illustrations aimed at engaging students' interest by showing multiple perspectives on interesting issues.** For example, we have improved the introduction to visual rhetoric in Chapter 1 by using a striking Veterans Day photograph integrated into our discussion of explicit versus implicit arguments. In Chapter 5 we have replaced the Ramona and Professor Choplogic material with a lively new extended example of a cheerleading controversy sparked by the Texas legislature's attempt to ban "sexually suggestive dances" in high school cheerleading routines. And in Chapter 11 on definition arguments, a new extended discussion of "felonious taking of property" replaces the outdated sports car example featuring Oscar and Felix. ("Odd couple?" our students say. "Never heard of them.")

- **Frequent additions of explanatory material.** For example, in Chapter 1 we include a new graphic that helps students visualize the continuum from argument as truth seeking to argument as persuasion, while in Chapters 2 and 3 we add blogs and think tanks in our discussion of the genres and sources of argument. We have also improved the explanations of *pathos* (Chapter 7) by creating a new illustration based on an op-ed piece from the *New York Times* calling for sympathy for telemarketers.

- **A complete rewriting of Appendix One on informal fallacies to provide a fresh, updated, shorter, and more useful introduction to these reasoning problems.** The revised appendix includes a new opening section on syllogisms that better explains the difference between formal and informal fallacies. We continue to treat informal fallacies in a rhetorical rather than a positivistic way so that the borderline between sound and fallacious reasoning is always shifting, fuzzy, and dependent on the audience's degree of resistance to the writer's claim.

- **An improved "norming" exercise in Appendix Two (working in groups) that eliminates the sixth edition's outdated material about the fictitious Elwood Lunt.** The norming exercise now has a sequence of easy-to-follow steps that can be productively integrated into a classroom hour.

- **Tightened and streamlined prose throughout the rhetoric section** enables crisper reading, more cohesive instruction, shorter text, and livelier prose.

What Hasn't Changed? The Distinguishing Features of *Writing Arguments*

Building on earlier success, we have preserved the signature features of earlier editions praised by students, instructors, and reviewers:

- **Focus throughout on writing arguments.** Grounded in composition theory, this text combines explanations of argument with class-tested discussion tasks, exploratory writing tasks, and sequenced writing assignments aimed at developing skills of writing and critical thinking. This text builds students' confidence in their ability to enter the argumentative conversations of our culture, understand diverse points of view, synthesize ideas, and create their own persuasive texts.

- **Equal focus on argument as a rhetorical act, particularly on analyzing audience, on understanding the real-world occasions for argument, and on appreciating the rhetorical context and genre of arguments.** Focusing on both the reading and the writing of arguments, the text emphasizes the critical thinking that underlies effective arguments, particularly the skills of critical reading, of believing and doubting, of empathic listening, of active questioning, and of negotiating ambiguity and seeking synthesis.

- **Integration of four different approaches to argument:** The Toulmin system as a means of invention and analysis of arguments; the enthymeme as a logical structure rooted in the beliefs and values of the audience; the classical concepts of *logos*, *pathos*, and *ethos* as persuasive appeals; and stasis theory (called claim types) as an aid to inventing and structuring arguments through understanding of generic argumentative moves associated with different categories of claims.

- **Copious treatment of the research process,** including two student examples of documented research papers—one using the MLA system and one using the APA system.

- **Numerous "For Class Discussion" exercises and sequenced Writing Assignments and Microthemes** designed to teach critical thinking and build argumentative skills. All "For Class Discussion" exercises can be used either for whole-class discussions or for collaborative group tasks.

- **Numerous student and professional arguments** to illustrate argumentative strategies and stimulate discussion, analysis, and debate. Altogether, the seventh edition contains 86 essays and 38 visual arguments drawn from the public arena and 13 student essays and 2 student visual arguments.

- **An attractive design,** which includes eight pages of color plates, enhances the book's visual appeal, and supports an increased emphasis on visual rhetoric throughout the text. The color plates, along with other images and graphics interspersed throughout the text, highlight the function of political cartoons, advocacy ads, photographs, fliers, posters, and quantitative graphics as important genres of argument in contemporary culture.

Our Approaches to Argumentation

Our interest in argumentation grows out of our interest in the relationship between writing and thinking. When writing arguments, writers are forced to lay bare their thinking processes in an unparalleled way, grappling with the complex interplay between inquiry and persuasion, between issue and audience. In an effort to engage students in the kinds of critical thinking that argument demands, we draw on four major approaches to argumentation:

- **The enthymeme as a rhetorical and logical structure.** This concept, especially useful for beginning writers, helps students "nutshell" an argument as a claim with one or more supporting *because* clauses. It also helps them see how real-world arguments are rooted in assumptions granted by the audience rather than in universal and unchanging principles.

- **The three classical types of appeal—** *logos, ethos,* **and** *pathos.* These concepts help students place their arguments in a rhetorical context focusing on audience-based appeals; they also help students create an effective voice and style.

- **Toulmin's system of analyzing arguments.** Toulmin's system helps students see the complete, implicit structure that underlies an enthymeme and develop appropriate grounds and backing to support an argument's reasons and warrants. It also highlights the rhetorical, social, and dialectical nature of argument.

- **Stasis theory concerning types of claims.** This approach stresses the heuristic value of learning different patterns of support for different types of claims and often leads students to make surprisingly rich and full arguments.

Throughout the text these approaches are integrated and synthesized into generative tools for both producing and analyzing arguments.

Structure of the Text

The text has five main parts plus two appendixes. Part One gives an overview of argumentation. These first three chapters present our philosophy of argument, showing how argument helps writers clarify their own thinking and connect with the values and beliefs of a questioning audience. Throughout, we link the process of arguing—articulating issue questions, formulating propositions, examining alternative points of view, and creating structures of supporting reasons and evidence—with the processes of reading and writing.

Part Two examines the principles of argument. Chapters 4 through 6 show that the core of an effective argument is a claim with reasons. These reasons are often stated as enthymemes, the unstated premise of which must sometimes be brought to the surface and supported. In effective arguments, the reasons are audience-based so that the argument proceeds from underlying beliefs, values, or assumptions held by the intended audience. Discussion of Toulmin logic shows students how to discover both the stated and unstated premises of their arguments and how to provide audience-based structures of reasons and evidence to support them. Chapter 7 focuses on *ethos, pathos,* and *kairos* as means of persuasion, while Chapter

8 focuses on strategies for accommodating arguments to different kinds of audiences from sympathetic to neutral to hostile. Finally, Chapter 9 focuses on the theory and practice of visual arguments—both images and quantitative graphics—giving students the tools for analyzing visual arguments and for creating their own.

Part Three discusses six different types of argument: simple categorical arguments, definitional arguments, causal arguments, resemblance arguments, evaluation arguments including ethics, and proposal arguments. These chapters introduce students to two recurring strategies of argument that cut across the different category types: Criteria-match arguing in which the writer establishes criteria for making a judgment and argues whether a specific case does or does not meet those criteria, and causal arguing in which the writer shows that one event or phenomenon can be linked to others in a causal chain.

Part Four (Chapters 16 and 17) shows students how to incorporate research into their arguments including the skills of formulating a research question; understanding differences in the kinds of sources; conducting effective searches of online catalogs, electronic databases, and the Web; reading sources rhetorically to understand context and bias; evaluating sources according to one's purpose, audience, and genre; understanding the rhetoric of Web sites; incorporating sources into the writer's own argument using summary, paraphrase, and judicious quotation; and documenting sources according to MLA or APA conventions. Unlike standard treatments of the research paper, our discussion explains to students how the writer's meaning and purpose control the selection and shaping of source materials.

The appendixes provide important supplemental information useful for courses in argument. Appendix One gives an overview of informal fallacies while Appendix Two shows students how to get the most out of collaborative groups in an argument class. Appendix Two also provides a sequence of collaborative tasks that will help students learn to peer-critique their classmates' arguments in progress. The numerous "For Class Discussion" exercises within the text provide additional tasks for group collaboration.

Finally, Part Five, the anthology, provides a rich and varied selection of professional arguments arranged into twelve high-interest units including military recruitment and the draft, the image of women in technology advertisements, the use of steroids and other interventions to perfect the human body, and the role of the United States as the sole superpower. The anthology selections are grouped by topic rather than by issue question to encourage students to see that any conversation of alternative views gives rise to numerous embedded and intertwined issues. Formulating the issue question, targeting an audience, framing the issue as a claim, and determining the depth and complexity of the argument are all part of the writer's task. Many of the issues raised in the anthology are first raised in the rhetoric (Parts One through Four). For example, issues related to the war on terrorism or the United States as superpower are first raised in the rhetoric, as are issues related to genetic modification of food, marriage and family in the new millennium, the role of bloggers in the media, and military recruitment.

Writing Assignments

The text provides a variety of sequenced writing assignments. Parts One and Two include exploratory tasks for discovering and generating arguments, "microthemes" for practicing basic argumentative moves (for example, supporting a reason with evidence), and assignments calling for complete arguments (a classical argument for neutral audiences, a delayed-thesis or Rogerian argument for resistant audiences, and an advocacy ad or poster). Each chapter in Part Three on claim types includes a writing assignment based on the claim type covered in the chapter. (Chapter 15 includes both a practical proposal assignment and a researched policy proposal assignment.) Finally, Part Five, the anthology, provides case assignments focusing on problems related to each anthology unit. Instructors can also design anthology assignments requiring argument analysis. Thus, the text provides instructors with a wealth of options for writing assignments on which to build a coherent course.

The Instructor's Manual

The Instructor's Manual has been revised to make it more useful for teachers and writing program administrators. Written by Tim N. Taylor of St. Louis Community College at Meramec, the revised Instructor's Manual has the following features:

- Discussion of planning decisions an instructor must make in designing an argument course: for example, how to use readings; how much to emphasize Toulmin or claim-type theory; how much time to build into the course for invention, peer review of drafts, and other writing instruction; and how to select and sequence assignments.

- Three detailed syllabi showing how *Writing Arguments* can support a variety of course structures and emphases:

    Syllabus #1: This course emphasizes argumentative skills and strategies, uses readings for rhetorical analysis, and asks students to write on issues drawn from their own interests and experiences.

    Syllabus #2: This more rigorous course works intensely with the logical structure of argument, the classical appeals, the Toulmin schema, and claim-type theory. It uses readings for rhetorical analysis and for an introduction to the argumentative controversies that students will address in their papers.

    Syllabus #3: This course asks students to experiment with genres of argument (for example, op-ed pieces, visual arguments, white papers, and researched freelance or scholarly arguments) and focuses on students' choice of issues and claim types.

- For instructors who include Toulmin, an independent, highly teachable introductory lesson on the Toulmin schema, and an additional exercise giving students practice using Toulmin to generate argument frames.

- For new instructors, a helpful discussion of how to sequence writing assignments and how to use a variety of collaborative tasks in the classroom to promote active learning and critical thinking.

- Chapter-by-chapter responses to the For Class Discussion exercises.

- Numerous teaching tips and suggestions placed strategically throughout the chapter material, including several sample quizzes asking students to explain and apply argumentative concepts.

- For instructors who teach visual arguments, suggestions for encouraging students to explore how visual arguments have molded and continue to mold public thinking about issues and controversies.

- For instructors who like to use student essays in class exercises and discussions, a number of new student essays showing how students responded to assignments in the text. Several of these student pieces exemplify stages of revision.

- Helpful suggestions for using the exercises on critiquing readings in Part Three, "Arguments in Depth: Six Types of Claims." By focusing on rhetorical context as well as on the strengths and weaknesses of these arguments, our suggestions will help students connect their reading of arguments to their writing of arguments.

- At the end of each claim-type chapter in Part Three, a list of anthology readings that employ the same claim type, either as a major claim or as a substantial portion of the argument.

- An analysis of anthology readings that better connects the anthology to the rhetoric portion of the text. Using a bulleted, quick-reference format, each analysis briefly discusses (1) the core of the argument, (2) the major or dominant claims of the argument, (3) the argument's use of evidence and argumentative strategies, (4) the appeals to *ethos* and *pathos* in the argument, and (5) the argument's genre. This easy-to-scan format helps instructors select readings and provides good starting points for class discussion. Our analyses also point out striking connections among readings, suggesting how the readings participate in larger societal argumentative conversations.

Companion Website

The Companion Website to accompany the *Writing Arguments* series (http://www.ablongman.com/ramage), revised by Laurie Cubbison of Radford University, offers a wealth of resources for both students and instructors. Students will have access to reviews of the concepts in each chapter of the book, exploratory writing exercises, online activities, and Web resources to help them develop their skills of argumentation. In addition, instructors will find Web resources and a link to the Instructor's Manual available for download.

MyCompLab 2.0 (www.mycomplab.com)

Available at no extra charge when ordered packaged with *Writing Arguments*, MyCompLab 2.0 provides the best available online solutions to a wide variety of composition course needs—all in one easy-to-use place. The only online system to offer resources for grammar, writing, and research, MyCompLab 2.0 is a dynamic and comprehensive site that will engage students as it helps them to learn.

- **Grammar resources:** Diagnostics; ExerciseZone (over 3,600 self-grading practice exercises, including sentence and paragraph editing); ESL ExerciseZone; an online handbook; Web Links.
- **Writing resources:** Exchange (online peer review tool); Process; Activities (100 activities, some video- and image-based); Model Documents Gallery; Student Bookshelf; and Web Links.
- **Research resources:** ResearchNavigator (access to searchable databases of credible sources and access to Autocite, a bibliography-maker); Avoiding Plagiarism tutorials.
- **Other resources:** Students using MyCompLab receive complimentary access to **Longman's English Tutor Center.** Instructors who order a MyCompLab package for their course can receive a complimentary subscription to **MyDropBox,** a leading online plagiarism detection service.

MyCompLab 2.0 is available in four versions: Website with Grade Tracker, CourseCompass, Blackboard, and WebCT. Please contact your local Allyn & Bacon/Longman representative for more information.

Acknowledgments

We are happy for this opportunity to give public thanks to the scholars, teachers, and students who have influenced our approach to composition and argument. We especially thank three talented students who worked with us on new material for this text: Carlos Macias for his research and writing on credit card debt and Jean Bessette and Sarah Bean for their research contributions to several of the anthology units. We would also like to thank Michael Harker, a Ph.D. candidate at Ohio State University, whose manuscript "The Ethics of Argument: Rereading *Kairos* and Making Sense in a Timely Fashion" (forthcoming in *College Composition and Communication*) convinced us to include the concept of *kairos* in the seventh edition. Additionally, we are grateful to all our students whom we have been privileged to teach in our writing classes; several of their arguments from these classes appear in this text. Their insights and growth as writers have inspired our ongoing study of rhetoric and composition.

We thank too the many users of our texts who have given us encouragement about our successes and offered helpful suggestions for improvements. Particularly we thank the following scholars and teachers who reviewed this edition of *Writing Arguments* in its various stages.

Shanan Ballam, Utah State University
Greg Barnhisel, Duquesne University
Robin Barrow, University of Tennessee
Lee Bauknight, University of South Carolina, Columbia
Beverly Carmo, Community College of Allegheny
Heather Hicks, Arizona State University
Katharine Jackson, Old Dominion University
Jay Jordan, Penn State University Park
Linda Moore, University of West Florida
Brooke Rollins, University of South Carolina, Columbia
Liesl Smith, Lincoln Land Community College
Tim Taylor, St. Louis Community College, Meramec
Karin Westman, Kansas State University

Our deepest thanks to Eben Ludlow, our editor and friend for more than twenty years, who recently retired from publishing to the deep regret of his authors and his colleagues at Longman. Prior to his retirement, Eben conferred with us in the planning of this revision, offering us one last time his wisdom and knowledge of the field. Eben, we will miss you greatly. We thank Publisher Joe Opiela for providing a smooth transition following Eben's retirement, and we thank our new editor, Lauren Finn, whose supportive and professional expertise has cheered our spirits. Finally, we want to thank Marion Castellucci, our development editor, who has become indispensable to us through a number of revisions of this text and our others. Marion's expertise and professionalism as well as her wonderful competence and sense of humor have encouraged us and shepherded this project at every point.

As always, we want to conclude by thanking our families. John Bean thanks his wife, Kit, also a professional composition teacher and director of a writing center, and his children, Matthew, Andrew, Stephen, and Sarah, who have grown to adulthood since he first began writing textbooks. June Johnson thanks her husband, Kenneth Bube, a mathematics professor and researcher, who has been an invaluable supporter of this intellectual endeavor, offering his astute insights into the need for better understanding of science and logic in civic arguments, his knowledge of teaching and scientific writing, and his Internet expertise. She also thanks her daughter, Jane Ellen, who knows well how much time and work textbook writing takes and who has contributed her own critical thinking, wisdom, and delightful humor.

J. C. B.
J. J.

Overview of Argument

This political cartoon presents one of the major perspectives in the public controversy over genetically modified foods, an issue discussed in Chapter 2, pp. 23–49.

1 Argument

An Introduction

At the outset of a book on argument, we ought to explain what an argument is. Instead, we're going to explain why no simple definition is possible. Philosophers and rhetoricians have disagreed over the centuries about the meaning of the term and about the goals that arguers should set for themselves. This opening chapter introduces you to some of these controversies. Our goal is to introduce you to various ways of thinking about argument as a way of helping you become a more powerful arguer yourself.

We begin by asking what we mean by argument and then proceed to three defining features: *Argument* requires justification of its claims, it is both a product and a process, and it combines elements of truth seeking and persuasion. We then explore more deeply the relationship between truth seeking and persuasion by asking questions about the nature of "truth" that arguments seek. Finally, we give you an example of a successful arguing process.

What Do We Mean by Argument?

Let's begin by examining the inadequacies of two popular images of argument— fight and debate.

Argument Is Not a Fight or a Quarrel

To many, the word *argument* connotes anger and hostility, as when we say, "I just got in a huge argument with my roommate," or "My mother and I argue all the time." What we picture here is heated disagreement, rising pulse rates, and an urge to slam doors. Argument imagined as fight conjures images of shouting talk-show guests, flaming e-mailers, or fist-banging speakers.

But to our way of thinking, argument doesn't imply anger. In fact, arguing is often pleasurable. It is a creative and productive activity that engages us at high levels of inquiry and critical thinking, often in conversation with persons we like and respect. For your primary image of argument, we invite you to think not of a shouting match on cable news but of a small group of reasonable persons seeking the best solution to a problem. We will return to this image throughout the chapter.

Argument Is Not Pro-Con Debate

Another popular image of argument is debate—a presidential debate, perhaps, or a high school or college debate tournament. According to one popular dictionary, *debate* is "a formal contest of argumentation in which two opposing teams defend and attack a given proposition." While formal debate can develop critical thinking, its weakness is that it can turn argument into a game of winners and losers rather than a process of cooperative inquiry.

For an illustration of this weakness, consider one of our former students, a champion high school debater who spent his senior year debating the issue of prison reform. Throughout the year he argued for and against propositions such as "The United States should build more prisons" and "Innovative alternatives to prison should replace prison sentences for most crimes." We asked him, "What do you personally think is the best way to reform prisons?" He replied, "I don't know. I haven't thought about what I would actually choose."

Here was a bright, articulate student who had studied prisons extensively for a year. Yet nothing in the atmosphere of pro-con debate had engaged him in truth-seeking inquiry. He could argue for and against a proposition, but he hadn't experienced the wrenching process of clarifying his own values and taking a personal stand. As we explain throughout this text, argument entails a desire for truth; it aims to find the best solutions to complex problems. We don't mean that arguers don't passionately support their own points of view or expose weaknesses in views they find faulty. Instead, we mean that their goal isn't to win a game but to find and promote the best belief or course of action.

Arguments Can Be Explicit or Implicit

Before proceeding to some defining features of argument, we should note also that arguments can be either explicit or implicit. An *explicit* argument states directly a controversial claim and supports it with reasons and evidence. An *implicit* argument, in contrast, doesn't look like an argument. It may be a poem or short story, a photograph or cartoon, a personal essay or an autobiographical narrative. But like an explicit argument, it persuades its audience toward a certain point of

Source: Jim Mahoney/The Dallas Morning News.

FIGURE 1.1   *Veterans Day Photograph*

view. Consider how Wilfred Owen's poem "Dulce et Decorum Est" and the Veterans Day photograph shown in Figure 1.1 persuade us toward different conceptions of war and patriotism.

Dulce et Decorum Est

Wilfred Owen

Bent double, like old beggars under sacks,
Knock-kneed, coughing like hags, we cursed through sludge
Till on the haunting flares we turned our backs,
And towards our distant rest began to trudge.
Men marched asleep. Many had lost their boots,
But limped on, blood-shod. All went lame, all blind;
Drunk with fatigue; deaf even to the hoots
Of gas-shells dropping softly behind.

Gas! Gas! Quick, boys—An ecstasy of fumbling,
Fitting the clumsy helmets just in time,
But someone still was yelling out and stumbling
And flound'ring like a man in fire or lime.
Dim through the misty panes and thick green light,
As under a green sea, I saw him drowning.

In all my dreams before my helpless sight
He plunges at me, guttering, choking, drowning.

If in some smothering dreams, you too could pace
Behind the wagon that we flung him in,
And watch the white eyes writhing in his face,
His hanging face, like a devil's sick of sin,
If you could hear, at every jolt, the blood
Come gargling from the froth-corrupted lungs
Bitter as the cud
Of vile, incurable sores on innocent tongues,—
My friend, you would not tell with such high zest
To children ardent for some desperate glory,
The old lie: *Dulce et decorum est
Pro patria mori.**

Owen's poem makes an implicit argument against the premise that it is heroic
and ennobling to give up one's life for one's country. The poem's argument is conveyed by the horrible image of a soldier drowning in his own fluids from a mus-
tard gas attack. The poem urges us to regard war as so horrifying that it becomes
utterly meaningless, devoid of heroism or higher purpose.

In contrast, the Veterans Day photograph makes an implicit argument honoring service to one's country. By powerfully capturing the emotions of two generations of veterans, this photo urges us to find meaning and purpose in the sacrifice
of soldiers. War is not prettified; the Marine sergeant's artificial hand is shocking
and sad. But the photo captures the moving embrace of the younger Iraq veteran
by the older Pearl Harbor veteran, showing their expressions of grief, pride, and
comradeship. The tall Marine wears an impressive uniform decorated with
medals. The photograph is framed by an American flag on the left and by an up-
wardly gazing World War II veteran on the right, suggesting dedication to a high
mission carried on from generation to generation.

Neither the poem nor the photograph uses the conventions of explicit argument—an ordered structure of thesis, reasons, and evidence. But their effective
use of images and vivid details (whether verbal or visual) evokes powerful emotions that urge the reader or viewer to see patriotism and war from a particular
angle of vision.

---

*"How sweet and fitting it is to die for one's country." Wilfred Owen (1893–1918) was killed in World
War I and wrote many of his poems while in the trenches.

For Class Discussion

1. In your own words, how do explicit and implicit arguments differ?

2. The perspectives that photos take, the stories they tell, or the vivid details of place and time they display influence viewers literally to see a subject from a particular angle; however, visual images can be more fluid—less fixed—than fully developed written arguments. Some images are ambiguous, open to multiple interpretations, and can be enlisted in support of different arguments. Consider the image of the veterans in Figure 1.1. What other implicit arguments about war and military service might this image be used to support?

3. Imagine that you wanted to take a photograph that created an implicit argument persuading (1) the general public toward banning handguns; (2) the general public against banning handguns; (3) the general public toward building more freeways; (4) the general public toward building more public transportation; (5) teenagers toward taking chastity vows; or (6) teenagers toward practicing safe sex. You might imagine that your photograph would be part of a poster or a printed advocacy advertisement. Working individually or in small groups, describe a photograph you might take that would create an appropriate implicit argument.

Example: To create an implicit argument in favor of protecting endangered species, you might photograph a colorful tree frog perched on an exotic plant in a tropical rain forest.

Although implicit arguments can be powerful, the predominant focus of this text is on explicit argument. However, we continue to value implicit arguments because their strategies—especially the persuasive power of stories and narratives—can often be incorporated into explicit arguments (see especially the discussion of *pathos* in Chapter 7 and all of Chapter 9, which is devoted to visual argument).

The Defining Features of Argument

We turn now to examine argument in more detail. (From here on, when we say "argument," we mean "explicit argument.") This section examines three defining features.

Argument Requires Justification of Its Claims

To begin defining argument, let's turn to a humble but universal site of disagreement: the conflict between a parent and a teenager over rules. In what way and in what circumstances do such conflicts constitute arguments?

Consider the following dialogue:

YOUNG PERSON (*racing for the front door while putting coat on*):   Bye. See you later.

PARENT: Whoa! What time are you planning on coming home?

YOUNG PERSON (*coolly, hand still on doorknob*):   I'm sure we discussed this earlier. I'll be home around 2 A.M. (*The second sentence, spoken very rapidly, is barely audible.*)

PARENT (*mouth tightening*):   We did *not* discuss this earlier and you're *not* staying out till two in the morning. You'll be home at twelve.

At this point in the exchange, we have a quarrel, not an argument. Quarrelers exchange antagonistic assertions without any attempt to support them rationally. If the dialogue never gets past the "Yes-you-will/No-I-won't" stage, it either remains a quarrel or degenerates into a fight.

Let us say, however, that the dialogue takes the following turn:

YOUNG PERSON (*tragically*):   But I'm *sixteen years old!*

Now we're moving toward argument. Not, to be sure, a particularly well-developed or cogent one, but an argument all the same. It's now an argument because one of the quarrelers has offered a reason for her assertion. Her choice of curfew is satisfactory, she says, *because* she is sixteen years old, an argument that depends on the unstated assumption that sixteen-year-olds are old enough to make decisions about such matters.

The parent can now respond in one of several ways that will either advance the argument or turn it back into a quarrel. The parent can simply invoke parental authority ("I don't care—you're still coming home at twelve"), in which case argument ceases. Or the parent can provide a reason for his or her view ("You will be home at twelve because your dad and I pay the bills around here!"), in which case the argument takes a new turn.

So far we've established two necessary conditions that must be met before we're willing to call something an argument: (1) a set of two or more conflicting assertions and (2) the attempt to resolve the conflict through an appeal to reason.

But good argument demands more than meeting these two formal requirements. For the argument to be effective, an arguer is obligated to clarify and support the reasons presented. For example, "But I'm sixteen years old!" is not yet a clear support for the assertion "I should be allowed to set my own curfew." On the surface, Young Person's argument seems absurd. Her parent, of all people, knows precisely how old she is. What makes it an argument is that behind her claim lies an unstated assumption—all sixteen-year-olds are old enough to set their own curfews. What Young Person needs to do now is to support that assumption.* In doing

---

*Later in this text we will call the assumption underlying a line of reasoning its *warrant* (see Chapter 5).

so, she must anticipate the sorts of questions the assumption will raise in the minds of her parent: What is the legal status of sixteen-year-olds? How psychologically mature, as opposed to chronologically mature, is Young Person? What is the actual track record of Young Person in being responsible? and so forth. Each of these questions will force Young Person to reexamine and clarify her assumptions about the proper degree of autonomy for sixteen-year-olds. And her response to those questions should in turn force the parents to reexamine their assumptions about the dependence of sixteen-year-olds on parental guidance and wisdom. (Likewise, the parents will need to show why "paying the bills around here" automatically gives them the right to set Young Person's curfew.)

As the argument continues, Young Person and Parent may shift to a different line of reasoning. For example, Young Person might say: "I should be allowed to stay out until 2 A.M. because all my friends get to stay out that late." (Here the unstated assumption is that the rules in this family ought to be based on the rules in other families.) The parent might in turn respond, "But I certainly never stayed out that late when I was your age"—an argument assuming that the rules in this family should follow the rules of an earlier generation.

As Young Person and Parent listen to each other's points of view (and begin realizing why their initial arguments have not persuaded their intended audience), both parties find themselves in the uncomfortable position of having to examine their own beliefs and to justify assumptions that they have taken for granted. Here we encounter one of the earliest senses of the term *to argue,* which is "to clarify." As an arguer begins to clarify her own position on an issue, she also begins to clarify her audience's position. Such clarification helps the arguer see how she might accommodate her audience's views, perhaps by adjusting her own position or by developing reasons that appeal to her audience's values. Thus Young Person might suggest an argument like this:

> I should be allowed to stay out until two on a trial basis because I need enough space to demonstrate my maturity and show you I won't get into trouble.

The assumption underlying this argument is that it is good to give teenagers freedom to demonstrate their maturity. Because this reason is likely to appeal to her parent's own values (the parent wants to see his or her daughter grow in maturity) and because it is tempered by the qualifier "on a trial basis" (which reduces some of the threat of Young Person's initial demands), it may prompt productive discussion.

Whether or not Young Person and Parent can work out a best solution, the preceding scenario illustrates how argument leads persons to clarify their reasons and provide justifications that can be examined rationally. The scenario also illustrates two specific aspects of argument that we will explore in detail in the next sections: (1) Argument is both a process and a product. (2) Argument combines truth seeking and persuasion.

Argument Is Both a Process and a Product

As the preceding scenario revealed, argument can be viewed as a *process* in which two or more parties seek the best solution to a question or problem. Argument can also be viewed as a *product*, each product being any person's contribution to the conversation at a given moment. In an informal discussion, the products are usually short, whatever time a person uses during his or her turns in the conversation. Under more formal settings, an orally delivered product might be a short impromptu speech (say, during an open-mike discussion of a campus issue) or a longer, carefully prepared formal speech (as in a PowerPoint presentation at a business meeting or an argument at a public hearing for or against a proposed city project).

Similar conversations occur in writing. Roughly analogous to a small-group discussion is an e-mail discussion of the kind that occurs regularly through informal chat groups or professional listservs. In an online discussion, participants have more thinking time to shape their messages than they do in a real-time oral discussion. Nevertheless, messages are usually short and informal, making it possible over the course of several days to see participants' ideas shift and evolve as conversants modify their initial views in response to others' views.

Roughly equivalent to a formal speech would be a formal written argument, which may take the form of an academic argument for a college course; a grant proposal; a guest column for the op-ed* section of a newspaper, a legal brief, a letter to a member of congress; or an article for an organizational newsletter, popular magazine, or professional journal. In each of these instances, the written argument (a product) enters a conversation (a process)—in this case, a conversation of readers, many of whom will carry on the conversation by writing their own responses or by discussing the writer's views with others. The goal of the community of writers and readers is to find the best solution to the problem or issue under discussion.

Argument Combines Truth Seeking and Persuasion

In thinking about argument as a product, the writer will find herself continually moving back and forth between truth seeking and persuasion—that is, between questions about the subject matter (What is the best solution to this problem?) and about audience (What do my readers already believe or value? What reasons and evidence will most persuade them?). Back and forth she'll weave, alternately absorbed in the subject of her argument and in the audience for that argument.

---

*Op-ed stands for "opposite-editorial." It is the generic name in journalism for a signed argument that voices the writer's opinion on an issue, as opposed to a news story that is supposed to report events objectively, uncolored by the writer's personal views. Op-ed pieces appear in the editorial-opinion section of newspapers, which generally features editorials by the resident staff, opinion pieces by syndicated columnists, and letters to the editor from readers. The term *op-ed* is often extended to syndicated columns appearing in newsmagazines, advocacy Web sites, and online news services.

Neither of the two focuses is ever completely out of mind, but their relative importance shifts during different phases of the development of a paper. Moreover, different rhetorical situations place different emphases on truth seeking versus persuasion. We could thus place arguments on a kind of continuum that measures the degree of attention a writer gives to subject matter versus audience. (See Figure 1.2.) At the far truth-seeking end of the continuum might be an exploratory piece that lays out several alternative approaches to a problem and weighs the strengths and weaknesses of each with no concern for persuasion. At the other end of the continuum would be outright propaganda, such as a political campaign advertisement that reduces a complex issue to sound bites and distorts an opponent's position through out-of-context quotations or misleading use of data. (At its most blatant, propaganda obliterates truth seeking; it will do anything, including the knowing use of bogus evidence, distorted assertions, and outright lies, to win over an audience.) In the middle ranges of the continuum, writers shift their focuses back and forth between truth seeking and persuasion but with varying degrees of emphasis.

As an example of a writer focusing primarily on truth seeking, consider the case of Kathleen, who, in her college argument course, addressed the definitional question "Is American Sign Language (ASL) a 'foreign language' for purposes of meeting the university's foreign language requirement?" Kathleen had taken two years of ASL at a community college. When she transferred to a four-year college, the chair of the foreign languages department at her new college would not allow her ASL proficiency to count for the foreign language requirement. ASL isn't a "language," the chair said summarily. "It's not equivalent to learning French, German, or Japanese."

Kathleen disagreed, so she immersed herself in developing her argument. While doing research, she focused almost entirely on subject matter, searching for what linguists, neurologists, cognitive psychologists, and sociologists had said about the language of deaf people. Immersed in her subject matter, she was only tacitly concerned with her audience, whom she thought of primarily as her classmates and the professor of her argument class—persons who were friendly to her

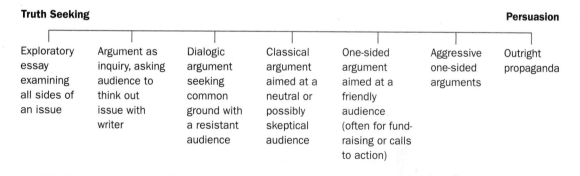

FIGURE 1.2 *Continuum of arguments from truth seeking to persuasion*

views and interested in her experiences with the deaf community. She wrote a well-documented paper, citing several scholarly articles, that made a good case to her classmates (and the professor) that ASL was indeed a distinct language.

Proud of the big red A the professor had placed on her paper, Kathleen returned to the chair of the foreign languages department with a new request to count ASL for her language requirement. The chair read her paper, congratulated her on her good writing, but said her argument was not persuasive. He disagreed with several of the linguists she cited and with the general definition of *language* that her paper assumed. He then gave her some additional (and to her, fuzzy) reasons why the college would not accept ASL as a foreign language.

Spurred by what she considered the chair's too-easy dismissal of her argument, Kathleen decided, for a subsequent assignment in her argument class, to write a second paper on ASL—but this time aiming it directly at the chair of foreign languages. Now her writing task falls closer to the persuasive end of our continuum. Kathleen once again immersed herself in research, but this time it focused not on subject matter (whether ASL is a distinct language) but on audience. She researched the history of the foreign language requirement at her college and discovered some of the politics behind it (an old foreign language requirement had been dropped in the 1970s and reinstituted in the 1990s, partly—a math professor told her—to boost enrollments in foreign language courses). She also interviewed foreign language teachers to find out what they knew and didn't know about ASL. She discovered that many teachers thought ASL was "easy to learn," so that accepting ASL would allow students a Mickey Mouse way to avoid the rigors of a "real" foreign language class. Additionally, she learned that foreign language teachers valued immersing students in a foreign culture; in fact, the foreign language requirement was part of her college's effort to create a multicultural curriculum.

This new understanding of her target audience helped Kathleen totally reconceptualize her argument. She condensed and abridged her original paper down to one line of reasoning in her new argument. She added sections showing the difficulty of learning ASL (to counter her audience's belief that learning ASL was easy), showing how the deaf community formed a distinct culture with its own customs and literature (to show how ASL met the goals of multiculturalism), and showing that the number of transfer students with ASL credits would be negligibly small (to allay fears that accepting ASL would threaten enrollments in language classes). She ended her argument with an appeal to her college's public emphasis (declared boldly in its mission statement) on eradicating social injustice and reaching out to the oppressed. She described the isolation of deaf people in a world where almost no hearing people learn ASL, and she argued that the deaf community on her campus could be integrated more fully into campus life if more students could "talk" with them. Thus the ideas included in her new argument—the reasons selected, the evidence used, the arrangement and tone—all were determined by her primary focus on persuasion.

Our point, then, is that all along the continuum writers are concerned both to seek truth and to persuade, but not necessarily with equal balance. Kathleen could not have written her second paper, aimed specifically at persuading the chair of foreign languages, if she hadn't first immersed herself in truth-seeking research that convinced her that ASL was indeed a distinct language. Nor are we saying that her second argument was better than her first. Both fulfilled their purposes and met the needs of their intended audiences. Both involved truth seeking and persuasion, but the first focused primarily on subject matter whereas the second focused primarily on audience.

Argument and the Problem of Truth

The tension that we have just examined between truth seeking and persuasion raises an ancient issue in the field of argument: Is the arguer's first obligation to truth or to winning the argument? And just what is the nature of the truth to which arguers are supposed to be obligated?

In Plato's famous dialogues from ancient Greek philosophy, these questions were at the heart of Socrates' disagreement with the Sophists. The Sophists were professional rhetoricians who specialized in training orators to win arguments. Socrates, who valued truth seeking over persuasion and believed that truth could be discovered through philosophic inquiry, opposed the Sophists. For Socrates, Truth resided in the ideal world of forms, and through philosophic rigor humans could transcend the changing, shadowlike world of everyday reality to perceive the world of universals where Truth, Beauty, and Goodness resided. Through his method of questioning his interlocutors, Socrates would gradually peel away layer after layer of false views until Truth was revealed. The good person's duty, Socrates believed, was not to win an argument but to pursue this higher Truth. Socrates distrusted rhetoricians because they were interested only in the temporal power and wealth that came from persuading audiences to the orator's views.

Let's apply Socrates' disagreement with the Sophists to a modern instance. Suppose your community is divided over the issue of raising environmental standards versus keeping open a job-producing factory that doesn't meet new guidelines for waste discharge. The Sophists would train you to argue any side of this issue on behalf of any lobbying group willing to pay for your services. If, however, you followed the spirit of Socrates, you would be inspired to listen to all sides of the dispute, peel away false arguments, discover the Truth through reasonable inquiry, and commit yourself to a Right Course of Action.

But what is the nature of Truth or Right Action in a dispute between jobs and the environment? The Sophists believed that truth was determined by those in power; thus they could enter an argument unconstrained by any transcendent beliefs or assumptions. When Socrates talked about justice and virtue, the Sophists could reply contemptuously that these were fictitious concepts invented by the weak to protect themselves from the strong. Over the years, the Sophists' relativist beliefs became so repugnant to people that the term *sophistry* became synonymous with trickery in argument.

However, in recent years the Sophists' critique of a transcendent Universal Truth has been taken seriously by many philosophers, sociologists, and other thinkers who doubt Socrates' confident belief that arguments, properly conducted, necessarily arrive at a single Truth. For these thinkers, as for the Sophists, there are often different degrees of truth and different kinds of truths for different situations or cultures. From this perspective, when we consider questions of interpretation or value, we can never demonstrate that a belief or assumption is true— not through scientific observation, not through reason, and not through religious revelation. We get our beliefs, according to these contemporary thinkers, from the shared assumptions of our particular cultures. We are condemned (or liberated) to live in a pluralistic, multicultural world with competing visions of truth.

If we accept this pluralistic view of the world, do we then endorse the Sophists' radical relativism, freeing us to argue any side of any issue? Or do we doggedly pursue some modern equivalent of Socrates' truth?

Our own sympathies are with Socrates, but we admit to a view of truth that is more tentative, cautious, and conflicted than his. For us, truth seeking does not mean finding the "Right Answer" to a disputed question, but neither does it mean a valueless relativism in which all answers are equally good. For us, truth seeking means taking responsibility for determining the "best answer" or "best solution" to the question for the good of the whole community when taking into consideration the interests of all stakeholders. It means making hard decisions in the face of uncertainty. This more tentative view of truth means that you cannot use argument to "prove" your claim, but only to make a reasonable case for your claim. One contemporary philosopher says that argument can hope only to "increase adherence" to ideas, not absolutely convince an audience of the necessary truth of ideas. Even though you can't be certain, in a Socratic sense, that your solution to the problem is the best one available, you must ethically take responsibility for the consequences of your claim and you must seek justice for stakeholders beyond yourself. You must, in other words, forge a personal stance based on your examination of all the evidence and your articulation of values that you can make public and defend.

To seek truth, then, means to seek the best or most just solution to a problem while observing all available evidence, listening with an open mind to the views of all stakeholders, clarifying and attempting to justify your own values and assumptions, and taking responsibility for your argument. It follows that truth seeking often means delaying closure on an issue, acknowledging the pressure of alternative views, and being willing to change one's mind. Seen in this way, learning to argue effectively has the deepest sort of social value: It helps communities settle conflicts in a rational and humane way by finding, through the dialectic exchange of ideas, the best solutions to problems without resorting to violence or to other assertions of raw power.

For Class Discussion

On any given day, newspapers provide evidence of the complexity of living in a pluralistic culture. Issues that could be readily decided in a completely homogeneous culture raise questions in a society that has fewer shared assumptions. Choose one of the following cases as the subject for a "simulation game" in which class members present the points of view of the persons involved.

CASE 1: MOSH PITS: IT'S NOT ALL FUN AND MUSIC

This news story begins with the case of a fourteen-year-old boy who suffered brain damage when he was dropped while crowd surfing at a Rage Against the Machine concert in Seattle. The article then discusses the controversy over crowd safety at grunge concerts:

> Most concerts do not result in injuries and deaths. But the increasing frequency of serious injuries—including broken bones, brain damage and paralysis—is shining a spotlight on what some critics see as fun and freedom pushed to irresponsible limits.
>
> The injuries have prompted a handful of U.S. cities and some bands to ban crowd surfing and stage diving, but there are no national standards for concert safety, and no one has exact numbers on how many people are injured in mosh pits every year. One survey cites at least 10 deaths and more than 1,000 injuries resulting from just 15 U.S. concerts last year.

Your task: Imagine a public hearing in which city officials are trying to develop a city policy on mosh pits at concerts. Should they be banned altogether? If not, how might they be regulated and who is responsible for injuries? Hold a mock hearing in which classmates present the views of the following: (a) a rock band that values crowd surfing and stage diving; (b) several concert fans who love mosh pits; (c) parents of a teenager seriously injured in a mosh pit accident; (d) a woman who was groped while crowd surfing; (e) local police; (f) concert promoters; (g) a venue owner fearing a liability lawsuit; (h) a city attorney fearing a liability lawsuit. To help stimulate your thinking, look at the crowd surfing photograph in Color Plate B.

CASE 2: HOMELESS HIT THE STREETS TO PROTEST PROPOSED BAN

> The homeless stood up for themselves by sitting down in a peaceful but vocal protest yesterday in [name of city].
>
> About 50 people met at noon to criticize a proposed set of city ordinances that would ban panhandlers from sitting on sidewalks, put them in jail for repeatedly urinating in public, and crack down on "intimidating" street behavior.
>
> "Sitting is not a crime," read poster boards that feature mug shots of [the city attorney] who is pushing for the new laws. [...] "This is city property; the police want to tell us we can't sit here," yelled one man named R. C. as he sat cross-legged outside a pizza establishment.

Your task: Imagine a public hearing seeking reactions to the proposed city ordinance. Hold a mock hearing in which classmates play the following roles: (a) a homeless person; (b) an annoyed merchant; (c) a shopper who avoids places with homeless people; (d) a citizen advocate for the homeless; (e) the city attorney.

A Successful Process of Argumentation: The Well-Functioning Committee

We have said that neither the fist-banging speaker nor the college debate team represents our ideal image of argument. The best image for us, as we have implied, is a well-functioning small group seeking a solution to a problem. In professional life such small groups usually take the form of committees.

We use the word *committee* in its broadest sense to indicate all sorts of important work that grows out of group conversation and debate. The Declaration of Independence is essentially a committee document with Thomas Jefferson as the chair. Similarly, the U.S. Supreme Court is in effect a committee of nine judges who rely heavily, as numerous books and articles have demonstrated, on small-group decision-making processes to reach their judgments and formulate their legal briefs.

To illustrate our committee or small-group model for argument, let's briefly consider the workings of a university committee on which coauthor John Ramage once served, the University Standards Committee. The Arizona State University (ASU) Standards Committee plays a role in university life analogous to that of the Supreme Court in civic life. It's the final court of appeal for ASU students seeking exceptions to various rules that govern their academic lives (such as registering under a different catalog, waiving a required course, or being allowed to retake a course for the third time).

The issues that regularly come before the committee draw forth all the argument types and strategies discussed throughout this text. For example, the different argument claim types discussed in Part Three regularly surface during committee deliberations, as shown in the following list:

- Definition issues: Is math anxiety a "learning disability" for purposes of exempting a student from a math requirement?
- Cause/consequence issues: What were the causes of this student's sudden poor performance during spring semester? What will be the consequences of approving or denying her appeal?
- Resemblance issues: How is this case similar to a case from the same department that we considered last semester?
- Evaluation issues: What criteria need to be met before we allow a student to graduate under a previous catalog?
- Proposal issues: Should we make it a policy to allow course X to substitute for course Y in the General Studies requirements?

On any given day, the committee's deliberations show how dialogue can lead to clarification of thinking. On many occasions, committee members' initial views shift as they study the specifics of individual cases and listen to opposing arguments from their colleagues. What allows this committee to function as well as it does is the fundamental civility of its members and their collective concern that their decisions be just. Because of the importance of these decisions to students' lives, committee members are willing to concede a point to another member in the name of reaching a better decision and to view the deliberations as an ongoing process of negotiation rather than a series of win-lose debates.

To give you firsthand experience at using argument as a process of clarification, we conclude this chapter with an actual case that came before the University Standards Committee in the early 1990s when Ramage was a member of the committee. We invite you to read the following letter, pretending that you are a member of the University Standards Committee, and then proceed to the exercises that follow.

Petition to Waive the University Mathematics Requirement

Standards Committee Members,

I am a 43-year-old member of the Pawnee Tribe of Oklahoma and a very nontraditional student currently pursuing Justice Studies at the Arizona State University (ASU) College of Public Programs. I entered college as the first step toward completion of my goal—becoming legal counsel for my tribe, and statesman. 1

I come before this committee in good faith to request that ASU suspend, in my special case, its mathematics requirement for undergraduate degree completion so I may enter the ASU college of Law during Fall 1993. The point I wish to make to this committee is this: I do not need algebraic skills; I will never use algebra in my intended profession; and, if forced to comply with ASU's algebra requirement, I will be needlessly prevented from graduating in time to enter law school next fall and face an idle academic year before my next opportunity in 1994. I will address each of these points in turn, but a few words concerning my academic credentials are in order first. 2

Two years ago, I made a vow of moral commitment to seek out and confront injustice. In September of 1990, I enrolled in college. Although I had only the benefit of a ninth grade education, I took the General Equivalency Diploma (GED) examination and placed in the top ten percent of those, nationwide, who took the test. On the basis of this score I was accepted into Scottsdale Community College (SCC). This step made me the first in my entire family, and practically in my tribe, to enter college. During my first year at SCC I maintained a 4.0 GPA, I was placed on the President's list twice, was active in the Honors Program, received the Honors Award of Merit in English Humanities, and was conferred an Honors Scholarship (see attached) for the Academic year of 1991–1992 which I declined, opting to enroll in ASU instead. 3

4   At the beginning of the 1991 summer semester, I transferred to ASU. I chose to graduate from ASU because of the courses offered in American Indian studies, an important field ignored by most other Universities but necessary to my commitment. At ASU I currently maintain a 3.6 GPA, although my cumulative GPA is closer to 3.9, I am a member of the Honors and Justice Colleges, was appointed to the Dean's List, and awarded ASU's prestigious Maroon and Gold Scholarship twice. My academic standing is impeccable. I will enter the ASU College of Law to study Indian and criminal law during the Fall of 1993—if this petition is approved. Upon successful completion of my juris doctorate I will return to Oklahoma to become active in the administration of Pawnee tribal affairs as tribal attorney and advisor, and vigorously prosecute our right to sovereignty before the Congress of the United States.

5   When I began my "college experience," I set a rigid time schedule for the completion of my goal. By the terms of that self-imposed schedule, founded in my belief that I have already wasted many productive years, I allowed myself thirty-five months in which to achieve my Bachelor of Science degree in Justice Studies, for indeed justice is my concern, and another thirty-six months in which to earn my juris doctorate—summa cum laude. Consistent with my approach to all endeavors, I fell upon this task with zeal. I have willingly assumed the burden of carrying substantial academic loads during fall, spring and summer semesters. My problem now lies in the fact that in order to satisfy the University's math requirement to graduate I must still take MAT-106 and MAT-117. I submit that these mathematics courses are irrelevant to my goals, and present a barrier to my fall matriculation into law school.

6   Upon consideration of my dilemma, the questions emerged: Why do I need college algebra (MAT-117)? Is college algebra necessary for studying American Indian law? Will I use college algebra in my chosen field? What will the University gain or lose, from my taking college algebra—or not? I decided I should resolve these questions.

7   I began my inquiry with the question: "Why do I need college algebra (MAT-117)?" I consulted Mr. Jim _____ of the Justice College and presented this question to him. He referred to the current ASU catalog and delineated the following answer: I need college algebra (1) for a minimum level of math competency in my chosen field, and (2) to satisfy the university math requirement in order to graduate. My reply to the first answer is this: I already possess ample math skills, both practical and academic; and, I have no need for algebra in my chosen field. How do I know this? During the spring 1992 semester at ASU I successfully completed introductory algebra (MAT-077), scoring the highest class grade on one test (see attached transcript and test). More noteworthy is the fact that I was a machine and welding contractor for fifteen years. I used geometry and algebra commonly in the design of many welded structures. I am proficient in the use of Computer Assisted Design (CAD) programs, designing and drawing all my own blueprints for jobs. My blueprints and designs are always approved by city planning departments. For example, my most recent job consisted of the manufacture, transportation and installation of one linear mile of anodized, aluminum handrailing at a luxury resort condo on Maui, Hawaii. I

applied extensive use of math to calculate the amount of raw materials to order, the logistics of mass production and transportation for both men and materials from Mesa to Maui, the job site installation itself, and cash flow. I have successfully completed many jobs of this nature—all without a mathematical hitch. As to the application of math competency in my chosen field, I can guarantee this committee that there will not be a time in my practice of Indian law that I will need algebra. If an occasion ever occurs that I need algebra, I will hire a mathematician, just as I would an engineer if I need engineering, or a surgeon if I need an operation.

I then contacted Dr. _____ of the ASU Mathematics Department and presented him with the same question: "Why do I need college algebra?" He replied: (1) for a well rounded education; (2) to develop creative thinking; and (3) to satisfy the university math requirement in order to graduate. Responding to the first answer, I have a "well rounded education." My need is for a specific education in justice and American Indian law. In fact, I do not really need the degree to practice Indian law as representative of my tribe, just the knowledge. Regarding the second, I do not need to develop my creative thinking. It has been honed to a keen edge for many years. For example, as a steel contractor, I commonly create huge, beautiful and intricate structures from raw materials. Contracting is not my only experience in creative thinking. For twenty-five years I have also enjoyed the status of being one of this country's foremost designers and builders of racebikes. Machines I have designed and brought into existence from my imagination have topped some of Japan and Europe's best engineering efforts. To illustrate this point, in 1984 I rode a bike of my own design to an international victory over Honda, Suzuki, Laverda, BMW and Yamaha. I have excelled at creative thinking my entire life—I called it survival. 8

Expanding on the question of why I need college algebra, I contacted a few friends who are practicing attorneys. All responded to my question in similar manner. One, Mr. Billy _____, Esq., whose law firm is in Tempe, answered my two questions as follows: "When you attended law school, were there any courses you took which required algebra?" His response was "no." "Have you ever needed algebra during the many years of your practice?" Again, his response was "no." All agreed there was not a single occasion when they had need for algebra in their professional careers. 9

Just to make sure of my position, I contacted the ASU College of Law, and among others, spoke to Ms. Sierra _____. I submitted the question "What law school courses will I encounter in which I will need algebra?" The unanimous reply was, they knew of none. 10

I am not proposing that the number of credit hours I need for graduation be lowered. In fact, I am more than willing to substitute another course or two in its place. I am not trying to get out of anything hard or distasteful, for that is certainly not my style. I am seeking only to dispose of an unnecessary item in my studies, one which will prevent me from entering law school this fall—breaking my stride. So little holds up so much. 11

I agree that a young adult directly out of high school may not know that he needs algebraic skills. Understandably, he does not know what his future holds—but I am not that young adult. I claim the advantage. I know precisely what my future holds and that future holds no possibility of my needing college algebra. 12

13   Physically confronting injustice is my end. On reservations where government apathy allows rapacious pedophiles to pose as teachers; in a country where a million and a half American Indians are held hostage as second rate human beings whose despair results in a suicide, alcohol and drug abuse rate second to no other people; in prisons where helpless inmates are beaten like dogs by sadistic guards who should be the inmates—this is the realm of my chosen field—the disenfranchised. In this netherworld, algebra and justice exist independently of one another.

14   In summary, I am convinced that I do not need college algebra for a minimum level of math competency in my chosen field. I do not need college algebra for a well rounded education, nor to develop my creative thinking. I do not need algebra to take the LSAT. I do not need algebra for any courses in law school, nor will I for any purpose in the practice of American Indian law. It remains only that I need college algebra in order to graduate.

15   I promise this committee that ASU's integrity will not be compromised in any way by approving this waiver. Moreover, I assure this committee that despite not having a formal accreditation in algebra, I will prove to be nothing less than an asset to this University and its Indian community, both to which I belong, and I will continue to set a standard for integrity, excellence and perseverance for all who follow. Therefore, I ask this committee, for all the reasons described above, to approve and initiate the waiver of my University mathematics requirement.

[Signed] Gordon Adams

For Class Discussion

1. Before class discussion, decide how you would vote on this issue. Should this student be exempted from the math requirement? Write out the reasons for your decision.

2. Working in small groups or as a whole class, pretend that you are the University Standards Committee, and arrive at a group decision on whether to exempt this student from the math requirement.

3. After the discussion, write for five to ten minutes in a journal or notebook describing how your thinking evolved during the discussion. Did any of your classmates' views cause you to rethink your own? Class members should share with each other their descriptions of how the process of argument led to clarification of their own thinking.

We designed this exercise to help you experience argument as a clarifying process. But we had another purpose. We also designed the exercise to stimulate thinking about a problem we introduced at the beginning of this chapter: the difference between argument as clarification and argument as persuasion. Is a good argument necessarily a persuasive argument? In our opinion, this student's letter to the committee is a *good* argument. The student writes well, takes a clear stand, offers good reasons for his position, and supports his reasons with effective evidence. To what extent, however, is the letter a *persuasive* argument? Did it win its case? You know how you and your classmates stand on this issue. But what do you think the University Standards Committee at ASU actually decided during its deliberations?

We will return to this case again in Chapter 5.

Conclusion

In this chapter we have explored some of the complexities of argument, showing you why we believe that argument is a matter not of fist banging or of win-lose debate but of finding, through a process of rational inquiry, the best solution to a problem or issue. What is our advice for you at the close of this introductory chapter? Briefly, to see the purpose of argument as truth seeking as well as persuasion. We suggest that throughout the process of argument you seek out a wide range of views, that you especially welcome views different from your own, that you treat these views respectfully, and that you see them as intelligent and rationally defensible. (Hence you must look carefully at the reasons and evidence on which they are based.)

Our goal in this text is to help you learn skills of argument. If you choose, you can use these skills, like the Sophists, to argue any side of any issue. Yet we hope you won't. We hope that, like Socrates, you will use argument for truth seeking and that you will consequently find yourselves, on at least some occasions, changing your position on an issue while writing a rough draft (a sure sign that the process of arguing has complicated your views). We believe that the skills of reason and inquiry developed through the writing of arguments can help you get a clearer sense of who you are. If our culture sets you adrift in pluralism, argument can help you take a stand, to say, "These things I believe." In this text we will not pretend to tell you what position to take on any given issue. But as a responsible being, you will often need to take a stand, to define yourself, to say, "Here are the reasons that choice A is better than choice B, not just for me but for you also." If this text helps you base your commitments and actions on reasonable grounds, then it will have been successful.

2 Reading Arguments

Why Reading Arguments Is Important for Writers

In the previous chapter we explained how argument is a social phenomenon in which communities search for the best answers to disputed questions. As you'll see in this chapter, we live in an environment saturated with oral, visual, print, and hypertext arguments. When we enter an argumentative conversation, we need to position ourselves as inquirers as well as persuaders, listening attentively to alternative points of view. Doing so, we will often be compelled not only to protest an injustice or work for change but also to reexamine our values, assumptions, and behaviors, perhaps even to change our views. Rhetorician Wayne Booth proposes that when we enter an argumentative conversation we should first ask, "When should I change my mind?" rather than "How can I change your mind?"*
In this chapter, we focus on reading arguments as a process of inquiry. We present five strategies that will help you listen to the arguments you encounter, resist simplistic answers, delve into multiple views, and emerge from your intellectual wrestling with informed, deepened, and supportable solutions to problems.

Because argument begins in disagreements within a social community, you should examine any argument as if it were only one voice in a larger conversation. We therefore recommend the following sequence of strategies:

1. Read as a believer.
2. Read as a doubter.
3. Explore how the rhetorical context and genre are shaping the argument.
4. Consider alternative views and analyze sources of disagreement.
5. Use disagreement productively to prompt further investigation.

---

*Wayne Booth raised these questions in a featured session with Peter Elbow entitled "Blind Skepticism vs. the Rhetoric of Assent: Implications for Rhetoric, Argument, and Teaching" at CCCC Convention, Chicago, Illinois, March 2002.

Let's now examine each of these strategies in turn.

Strategy 1: Reading as a Believer

When you read an argument as a believer, you practice what psychologist Carl Rogers calls *empathic listening.* Empathic listening requires that you see the world through the author's eyes, adopt temporarily the author's beliefs and values, and suspend your skepticism and biases long enough to hear what the author is saying.

Because empathic listening is such a vital skill, we soon will invite you to practice it on a brief argument opposing the genetic engineering of food. Before we ask you to read the argument, however, we want to introduce you to this issue. Since 1994, when genetically modified foods first appeared in supermarkets, they have become increasingly more prevalent, but not without resistance from some consumers. Antibiotechnology groups have labeled genetically modified foods "Frankenfoods" after the power-seeking scientist who created the monster in Mary Shelley's novel *Frankenstein.* This catchy and shrewd word "Frankenfoods" connotes God-playing scientists whose work backfires into an uncontrollable destructive force. The proponents of biotechnology, in contrast, see genetic engineering as beneficial and progressive, offering ways to create disease-resistant plants, more environmentally friendly agricultural methods, and more promising ways to feed the world. With this background, you are now ready to examine for yourself some of the controversies surrounding genetic engineering of food.

For Class Discussion

1. Suppose you are thumbing through a magazine and come across the advocacy advertisement shown in Figure 2.1. The ad is sponsored by three groups called "Citizens for Health," "The Center for Food Safety," and "Sustain." Working as a whole class or in small groups, respond to the following questions:

    a. What is the claim of this ad? Whom or what is it arguing against?

    b. How does this ad try to make you nervous about eating genetically modified foods? What aspects of the ad are most effective in influencing your response? (Consider both the text of the ad and its visual elements.)

2. Now suppose you saw in the op-ed section of your local newspaper the political cartoon shown at the beginning of Part One of this text (p. 1).

    a. What is the claim of this cartoon? Whom or what is it arguing against?

    b. How does this cartoon speak back to the "Keep Nature Natural" ad in Figure 2.1?

WHAT IF EVERYTHING WAS LABELED LIKE GENETICALLY ENGINEERED FOODS?

Genetically engineered (GE) fruits, vegetables and meats are on your dinner plate. Up to 70% of processed foods now contain GE ingredients. Yet, despite the fact that most Americans have indicated in national polls that they want to be able to identify these products, there is no label for GE foods, and no way for consumers to know whether the food they eat contains them.

Because the government doesn't require rigorous independent safety testing, no one can predict the long-term effects of these foods on our health, the environment, the economy, or the future of farming.

We believe that consumers have the right to know if their food has been genetically engineered. Join with us in asking the Food and Drug Administration to better regulate GE foods by requiring mandatory labeling and safety testing.

Take Action Today!

KEEP NATURE NATURAL   Learn more! 800-357-2211
www.keepnatural.org

FIGURE 2.1   *"Keep Nature Natural" advocacy ad. This ad ran in* Vegetarian Times *and the* Utne Reader.

3. What is your current view of genetically modified foods? (If you buy your food from supermarkets, you are probably eating some genetically modified ingredients. According to some sources, 33 percent of corn, 50 percent of soy, and 50 percent of cotton crops are genetically modified.)

4. Based on the "Keep Nature Natural" ad and the political cartoon, what do you think are the major arguments for and against genetically modified foods?

Now that you have done some thinking about genetic modification of food, read carefully the following article, which appeared in a health food magazine called *Better Nutrition* in June 2000.

Playing with Our Food
Genetic Engineering and Irradiation

Lisa Turner

It used to be that getting clean food wasn't so hard. A trip to the local health food store and a quick scan of food labels, and you could fill your 'fridge with whole, healthy foods. Now, even tofu is likely to be tainted with genetically modified organisms, and your favorite natural tabouli mix may contain irradiated herbs and spices. Is nothing sacred? Not in the brave new world of "biotech" foods.   1

GENETIC ENGINEERING WEIRD SCIENCE

Flounder genes in your pasta sauce? Insect genes in your mashed potatoes? Welcome to the high-tech process of artificially shuffling genes from one organism to another. Proponents of *genetic engineering* say it's a sure way to boost food supply, reduce pesticide use and possibly breed super-foods with extraordinary nutritional profiles. The problem is, no one really knows the long-term effects of such complex *genetic* manipulation—and the potential *dangers* to humans and the environment are substantial.   2

Don't think that *genetic engineering* is merely a stepped-up version of traditional cross-breeding techniques. It's a new, weird science that allows the insertion of genes from any plant or animal into any other organism. One example: an "antifreeze" gene that allows flounder to survive in very cold water is inserted into tomatoes to boost their tolerance to frost. Or insect-killing genes from bacteria may be inserted into corn or potatoes to up their defenses against pests.   3

Shuffling genes between species raises plenty of scary possibilities. The technology is new enough to be frighteningly imprecise, with generally uncertain   4 outcomes. And because no long-term safety tests have been conducted, no one really knows the full scope of potential health risks. According to an editorial in a 1996 issue of the *New England Journal of Medicine,* "Questions of safety vex federal regulators and industry as well as the public. The transfer of genes from microbes, plants or animals into foods raises issues about the unintended consequences of such manipulations."

5   Some of these consequences include the production of new allergens in foods and unexpected mutations in an organism, which can create new and higher levels of toxins. One example: in 1993, 37 people died and more than 1,500 people suffered partial paralysis from a disease called eosinophilia-myalgia, which was eventually linked to a tryptophan supplement made with genetically engineered bacteria.

6   Another worrisome possibility is that insects, birds and the wind can carry genetically altered seeds into neighboring fields and beyond, where they can cross-pollinate, threatening the future of wild crops, genetically natural crops and organic foods.

7   And once genetically modified organisms are introduced into the food supply, they can't be recalled. "Unlike pesticide use, *genetic engineering* introduces living organisms that will be replicated in other living organisms," says Susan Haeger, president/CEO of Citizens for Health, a non-profit consumer advocacy group based in Boulder, Colorado. "Once they're in the environment, there's no way to bring them back."

IRRADIATION: ZAPPING OUR FOOD

8   What happens when you cross a potato with 10,000 rads of ionizing radiation—more than 2,500,000 times the dose of a chest X-ray? Better find out before you eat your next order of french fries. Irradiation, used to extend shelf life and kill microorganisms in food, can also lower nutritional value, create environmental hazards, promote the growth of toxins and produce compounds called unique radiolytic products, which have been associated with a variety of biological abnormalities.

9   Food irradiation was proposed by the Atomic Energy Commission in the early 1950s as a way of dealing with a formidable nuclear waste problem from the manufacture of nuclear weapons, according to Michael Colby, editor of the *Food & Water Journal.* In the mid-1980s, the FDA began to approve a huge range of foodstuffs for irradiation, including meat, poultry, produce, herbs and spices. Since then, permissible levels of radiation have been dramatically increased, and the amount now allowed is substantial.

10   Proponents say irradiation destroys harmful microorganisms and may reduce outbreaks of salmonella and trichinosis from meat. It is also said that irradiation increases shelf life of various foods and can reduce the use of toxic chemicals as post-harvest fumigants. Absurd, say irradiation opponents. "Irradiation is destroying our food supply," says Gary Gibbs, D.O., author of *The Food That Would Last Forever.* "It is nothing more than a toxic band-aid approach to the problems."

11   Adequate cooking, sanitary handling and preparation and hygienic processing methods are better ways to reduce illness from microorganisms in meat. Shelf life is an unfounded concern in the United States, and the cost of irradiation in less-

developed countries would usually offset savings from extended shelf life. As for the argument that irradiation would reduce the need for post-harvest chemical fumigants, some say that irradiated foods are more prone to infection by certain fungi.

The FDA and irradiation proponents claim the process is safe, but compelling evidence to the contrary says otherwise. Meanwhile, considerable controversy exists regarding safety studies. Although 441 studies have been conducted on food irradiation, the FDA based their toxicity evaluation on only five animal studies, according to Gibbs. Of these five studies, two were found to be methodologically flawed, one suggested that irradiated food could have adverse effects on older animals and two investigated foods irradiated at doses well below FDA-approved levels.   12

Few human trials exist, because of obvious ethical considerations, but some small studies have raised concerns, suggesting that food irradiation can cause chromosomal abnormalities.   13

Irradiation of food can lead to cardiac disease, cancer, kidney disease, fetal malformations and a dramatic shortening of the life span, according to Gibbs. "A lot of studies have shown problems with the heart, specifically that irradiation causes bleeding in the heart," he says. "Also, when food is irradiated, it creates benzene and formaldehyde, which are known mutagens and suspected carcinogens."   14

Irradiation also appears to cause significant nutrient loss in foods, especially of vitamins A, B, C and E. Generally, the higher the amount of radiation, the greater the nutrient loss. Add to that environmental concerns, including hazards in transporting and handling radioactive isotopes, danger of exposure to workers and possible security problems at irradiation facilities. Right now, there are about 50 irradiation facilities in the United States, says Colby, but a huge increase is expected if irradiation is embraced in the marketplace. The result: a substantial increase in potential environmental disasters.   15

WHAT TO DO

Because biotech foods are still new, the core issues are safety testing and consumer awareness. "It may be that there are some positive aspects to biotech food," says Haeger. "We don't know. Our concern is that the commercialization of biotech foods and their integration in the food system is outpacing the science and is being promoted without the awareness of the public."   16

More stringent safety testing is critical, as are more comprehensive labeling requirements. Under current laws, irradiated foods must be labeled as such, with a written notice and a "radura"—the international irradiation symbol—but processed foods and foods prepared for restaurants, hospitals or school cafeterias are exempt from such labeling. Additionally, no labeling requirements exist for genetically engineered foods.   17

Some say *genetic engineering* and food irradiation should be banned. "This is beyond labeling considerations," says Gibbs. "It should be completely outlawed. We shouldn't even have to have conversations about labeling." It the meantime, the primary thrust is toward public awareness.   18

19   "Our main concern is for consumers to be aware of food manipulation," says Haeger. "We want to ensure that they are informed and have adequate information on what they're purchasing, so they can make their own choices."

References

Belongia, F.A., et al. "The eosinophilia-myalgia syndrome and tryptophan," *Annu Rev Nutr* 12: 235–56, 1992.

Bhaskaram, C., Sadasivan, G. "Effects of feeding irradiated wheat to malnourished children," *American Journal of Clinical Nutrition* 28(2): 130–35, 1975.

Hickman, J.R., McLean, L.A., Ley, F.J. "Rat feeding studies on wheat treated with gamma radiation," *Food and Cosmetic Toxicology* 2(2): 175–180, 1964.

Khattak, A.B., Klopfenstein, C.F. "Effects of gamma irradiation on the nutritional quality of grains and legumes," *Cereal Chemistry* 66(3): 171–72, 1989.

McGivney, W.T. "Preservation of food products by irradiation," *Seminars in Nuclear Medicine* 18: 36, 1998.

Nyhan, W.L., et al. "New approaches to understanding Lesch-Nyhan disease," *New England Journal of Medicine* 334(24): 1602–4, 1996.

Piccioni, R. "Food irradiation: Contaminating our food," *The Ecologist* 18(2): 48, 1988.

Radomski, J.L., et al. "Chronic toxicity studies in irradiated beef stew and evaporated milk," *Toxicology and Applied Pharmacology* 7(1): 113–21, 1965.

Raica, N., Scott, J., Nielson, N. "Nutritional quality of irradiated foods," *Radiation Research Review* 3(4): 447–57, 1972.

Shanghai Institute of Radiation Medicine and Shanghai Institute of Nuclear Research. "Safety evaluation of 35 kinds of irradiated human foods," *Chinese Medical Journal* 100(9): 715–18, 1987.

Summary Writing as a Way of Reading to Believe

Now that you have finished the article, ask yourself how well you "listened" to it. If you listened well, you should be able to write a summary of Turner's argument in your own words. A *summary* (also called an *abstract*, a *précis*, or a *synopsis*) presents only a text's major points and eliminates supporting details. Writers often incorporate summaries of other writers' views into their own arguments, either to support their own claims or to represent alternative views that they intend to address. Summaries can be any length, depending on the writer's purposes, but usually they range from several sentences to one or two paragraphs.

Practicing the following steps should help you be a better summary writer:

Step 1:   Read the argument first for general meaning. Don't judge it; put your objections aside; just follow the writer's meaning, trying to see the issue from the writer's perspective. Try to adopt the writer's values and belief system. Walk in the writer's shoes.

Step 2:   Read the argument slowly a second and a third time, writing in the margins brief *does* and *says* statements for each paragraph (or group of closely connected paragraphs). A *does* statement identifies a paragraph's function, such as "summarizes an opposing view," "introduces a supporting reason," "gives an example," or "uses statistics to support the previous point." A *says* statement summarizes a paragraph's content.

Your challenge in writing *says statements* is to identify the main point in each paragraph. This process may actually be easier with an academic article that uses long block paragraphs headed by topic sentences than it is for more informal journalistic articles like Turner's that use a string of shorter, less developed paragraphs. What follows are the *does* and *says* statements for the first six paragraphs of Turner's article.

DOES/SAYS ANALYSIS OF TURNER'S ARTICLE

Paragraph 1: *Does:* Introduces the problem of "the brave new world of 'biotech' foods." *Says:* It is becoming difficult today to find foods that have not been irradiated or genetically modified.

Paragraph 2: *Does:* Briefly sketches the benefits of genetic engineering and shifts to the potential dangers. *Says:* Advocates claim that biotechnology can increase the food supply, reduce the use of pesticides, and increase the nutritional value of foods, but no one knows the long-term effects of genetic engineering on humans or the environment.

Paragraph 3: *Does:* Elaborates on how genetic engineering works with some specific examples. *Says:* Genetic engineering alters plants and animals far beyond crossbreeding.

Paragraph 4: *Does:* Elaborates on the potential dangers of genetic engineering. *Says:* Imprecision and unpredictable long-term consequences make this biotechnology frightening.

Paragraph 5: *Does:* Offers examples of some of the dangerous consequences so far. *Says:* Genetic engineering created toxins that caused deaths and partial paralysis in 1993.

Paragraph 6: *Does:* States another problem of genetic engineering. *Says:* Cross-pollination can contaminate wild or organic plants.

For Class Discussion

Working individually or in groups, write *does* and *says* statements for the remaining paragraphs of Turner's article.

Step 3: Examine your *does* and *says* statements to determine the major sections of the argument, and create a list of major points and subpoints. If you are visually oriented, you may prefer to make a diagram, flowchart, or scratch outline of the sections of Turner's argument.

Step 4: Turn your list, outline, flowchart, or diagram into a prose summary. Typically, writers do this in one of two ways. Some start by joining all their *says* statements into a lengthy paragraph-by-paragraph summary and then prune it and streamline. They combine ideas into sentences and then revise those sentences to make them clearer and more tightly structured. Others start with a one-sentence summary of the argument's thesis and major supporting reasons and then flesh it out with more supporting ideas. Your goal is to be as neutral and as objective as possible by keeping your own responses to the writer's ideas out of your summary. To be fair to the writer, you also need to cover all the writer's main points and give them the same emphasis as in the original article.

Step 5: Revise your summary until it is the desired length and is sufficiently clear, concise, and complete. When you incorporate a summary of someone else's argument into your own essay, you must distinguish that author's words and ideas from your own by using *attributive tags* (expressions like "Turner says," "according to Turner," or "Turner further explains"), by putting any directly borrowed language in quotation marks, and by citing the original author using appropriate conventions for documenting sources.

As illustration, we will show our summaries of Turner's article—a one-paragraph version and a single-sentence version. In the one-paragraph version, we illustrate the MLA documentation system in which page numbers for direct quotations are placed in parentheses after the quotation and complete bibliographic information is placed in a Works Cited list at the end of the paper. See Chapter 17 for a complete explanation of the MLA and APA documentation systems.

ONE-PARAGRAPH SUMMARY OF TURNER'S ARGUMENT

Identification of author and source →

Insertion of short quotation; MLA documentation shows page numbers in parentheses

Attributive tags

Continued use of attributive tags

In an article, "Playing with Our Food," from the magazine Better Nutrition, health food advocate Lisa Turner warns readers that much of our food today is genetically modified or irradiated. She describes genetic engineering as artificial gene rearranging that differs completely from "traditional cross-breeding" (25). She argues that the potential, unforeseen, harmful consequences of this "new, weird science" (25) offset the possible benefits of increasing the food supply, reducing the use of pesticides, and boosting the nutritional value of foods. Turner asserts that genetic engineering is imprecise, untested, unpredictable, irreversible, and also uncontrollable due to animals, insects, and winds. She also objects to the use of irradiation to enable foods to stay fresh longer and to kill harmful microorganisms. Claiming that the FDA has not tested irradiation at the levels that it allows, she suggests that irradiation has many harmful effects: depleting vitamins in foods, causing cancer and cardiac problems, and increasing amounts of radioactive material in the environment. Turner concludes by saying that the marketing of these products has proceeded much more quickly than scientific knowledge about them warrants. If we don't ban genetic engineering and irradiation completely (a course that some people propose), Turner argues that at the very least more safety testing and labeling are needed. We consumers must know how our food has been manipulated. (220 words)

Correct citation of article in MLA format. (In a formal paper the "Works Cited" list begins a new page.)

Works Cited

Turner, Lisa. "Playing with Our Food." <u>Better Nutrition</u> June 2000: 56–59. Rpt. in <u>Writing Arguments: A Rhetoric with Readings</u>. John D. Ramage, John C. Bean, and June Johnson. 7th ed. New York: Longman, 2007.

ONE-SENTENCE SUMMARY OF TURNER'S ARGUMENT

In her article in <u>Better Nutrition</u>, health food writer Lisa Turner warns readers of the prevalence, risk, and potential health and environmental dangers of genetic modification and irradiation of food, arguing that these products should undergo more stringent testing for safety and should be labeled for consumer protection.

Whether you write a very short summary or a more detailed one, your goal should be to come as close as possible to a fair, accurate, and balanced condensation of the author's argument and to represent the relationships among the parts fairly and accurately. We don't want to pretend that summary writing is easy; often it's not, especially if the argument is complex and if the author doesn't explicitly highlight his or her thesis and main supporting reasons. Nonetheless, being able to summarize the arguments of others in your own words is an important skill for arguers.

Suspending Doubt: Willing Your Own Belief in the Writer's Views

Summarizing an argument is only the first step in your effort to believe it. You must also suspend doubt and will yourself to adopt the writer's view. Suspending doubt is easy if you already agree with the author. But if an author's views affront your own values, then "believing" can be a hard but valuable exercise. By struggling to believe strange, threatening, or unfamiliar views, we can grow as learners and thinkers.

To believe an author, search your mind for personal experiences, values, and beliefs that affirm his or her argument. Here is how one student wrote a journal entry trying to believe Turner's article.

JOURNAL ENTRY SHOWING STUDENT'S ATTEMPT TO BELIEVE TURNER

Although I had heard of genetic modification of plants and of hormones given to cows to produce more milk, I never thought about how I might be affected. Turner's article made me worry about how many of the things I eat have been produced by artificial genetic processes and how many have been treated with radiation. How much do scientists actually know about long-term effects of growing and eating biotech food? I know of lots of cases where scientists have tried to fix environmental problems, and their intervention has had disastrous results. My biology teacher told us about a failed scientific intervention involving cane toads brought into Australia to eat the beetles and grubs plaguing the sugar cane. The natural cycles of the grubs, beetles, and toads didn't match. Now the cane toads have proliferated out of control because they have no native predators. What's worse, they are poisonous! Ten years from now will genetic engineering be failed science in the category of "it seemed like a great idea at the time"? As it is, every year we read studies that say vitamin C or some food that we thought was good for us is actually harmful. Turner's article has made me want to know how the government is regulating what biotech foods are sold. Maybe I should spend more time reading the labels on all the food I buy. How much more will I have to pay to avoid foods that have been genetically modified or treated with radiation?

Strategy 2: Reading as a Doubter

Reading as a believer is an important part of being a powerful reader, but you must also learn to read as a doubter by raising objections, asking questions, expressing skepticism, and withholding your assent. When you read as a doubter, you also question what is *not* in the argument. What is glossed over, unexplained, or left out? In the margins of the text you add a new layer of notes demanding proof, doubting evidence, challenging the author's assumptions and values, and so forth. Because writing marginal notes helps you read a text actively—to follow the author's argument and speak back to it in your own voice—we show you an example of one reader's marginal notes for a section of Turner's text (Figure 2.2). Note how it is a mixture of believing and doubting commentary.

Some of these consequences include the production of new allergens in foods and unexpected mutations in an organism, which can create new and higher levels of toxins. One example: in 1993, 37 people died and more than 1,500 people suffered partial paralysis from a disease called eosinophilia-myalgia, which was eventually linked to a tryptophan supplement made with genetically engineered bacteria. [5]	This "eventual link" sounds weak. I need more explanation. Where did this case occur? What food was involved? What is a "tryptophan supplement"?
Another worrisome possibility is that insects, birds and the wind carry genetically altered seeds into neighboring fields and beyond, where they can cross-pollinate, threatening the future of wild crops, genetically natural crops and organic foods. [6]	Seems like a strong point. Supports what I've read about cross-pollination and organic farms.
And once genetically modified organisms are introduced into the food supply, they can't be recalled. "Unlike pesticide use, genetic engineering introduces living organisms that will be replicated in other living organisms," says Susan Haeger, president/CEO of Citizens for Health, a non-profit consumer advocacy group based in Boulder, Colorado. "Once they're in the environment, there's no way to bring them back." [7]	This quote not from scientist. Would scientists agree about dangers to the environment?

FIGURE 2.2   *Believing and doubting notes for Turner article*

For Class Discussion

Return now to Turner's article, reading skeptically. Raise questions, offer objections, and express doubts. Then, working as a class or in small groups, list all the doubts you have about Turner's argument.

Now that you have doubted Turner's article, compare your doubts to some raised by our students.

- In the third sentence of her article, Turner says that tofu is "likely to be tainted with genetically modified organisms." Her word "taint" suggests a strong bias against technology right from the start.

- She mentions the possible advantages of genetic engineering in only one sentence—boosting food supply, reducing needs for pesticides, and so forth. These seem like major advantages that should be investigated. How successful has biotechnology been at achieving its stated goals? What scientific breakthroughs has genetic engineering made? What good has it done so far?

- She gives no sources for her claim that an antifreeze gene from flounders is inserted into tomatoes. We would like to learn if this claim is true and see how scientists describe the purpose and results. There may be another side to this story.

- She doesn't claim that biotech foods are not safe. She just claims that they haven't been tested enough. The only negative evidence she provides is the 37 persons killed by a disease that was "linked" to genetically engineered bacteria. Why the weak word "linked"? Did scientists prove that the disease was caused by genetic engineering? Is this case exceptional? Is it good evidence to show that all genetically engineered foods are potentially harmful?

- The case against irradiation is not supported by evidence but by testimony from Gary Gibbs and Susan Haeger, whose scientific credentials aren't clearly stated. Turner claims that "compelling evidence" refutes the claim of the FDA that irradiation is safe. She doesn't provide or document this compelling evidence. She makes numerous frightening claims about irradiation without any evidence that the claims are true.

These are only some of the objections that might be raised against Turner's argument. Perhaps you and your classmates have other objections that are equally important. Our point is that you should practice "doubting" an argument as well as "believing" it. Both skills are essential. *Believing* helps you expand your view of the world or modify your arguments and beliefs in response to others. *Doubting* helps protect you from becoming overpowered by others' arguments and teaches you to stand back, consider, and weigh points carefully.

Strategy 3: Exploring How Rhetorical Context and Genre Shape the Argument

The strategies of believing and doubting an argument urge you toward further exploration and inquiry. In the next stage of analysis, you should consider the rhetorical context of the argument as well as its genre. In this section we'll explain these concepts and show you why they are important.

Understanding the Genres of Argument

Knowing the genre of an argument helps you understand how the writer's purpose, intended audience, and angle of vision or bias have shaped the argument. A "genre" is a recurring type or pattern of argument such as a letter to the editor, a scholarly journal article, or the home page of an advocacy Web site. Genres are often categorized by format, purpose, or type of publication; as we'll see, they place on writers certain demands (such as the need for a particular tone or kind of evidence) and constraints (such as limits on length).

When you read arguments anthologized in a textbook such as this one, you lose clues about the argument's original genre. (You should therefore note the information about genre provided in our introductions to readings.) You can also lose clues about genre when you download articles from the Internet or from licensed databases such as LexisNexis or ProQuest. (See Chapter 16 for explanations of these research tools.) When you do your own research, you therefore need to be aware of the original genre of what you are reading: Is this piece a newspaper editorial, an article from a magazine, an organizational white paper, an academic argument in a peer-reviewed journal, a student paper posted to a Web site, or something else?

In the following list, we identify most of the genres of argument through which readers and writers carry on the conversations of a democracy.

- *Personal correspondence.* This category includes letters or e-mail messages sent to specific decision makers in order to achieve the writer's purpose (complaint letter, request for a certain action). The style can range from a formal business letter to an informal note. The tone depends on purpose and audience.

- *Letters to the editor.* Letters to the editor provide an excellent forum for ordinary citizens to voice their views on public issues. Published in newspapers and some public affairs magazines, letters are aimed at the readers of the publication to influence opinion on recently discussed issues. They are very short (fewer than three hundred words) and time sensitive. They can sometimes be summaries of longer arguments, but often focus in "sound bite" style on one point. Their perspective or bias can vary widely since editors seek a wide range of opinions.

- *Newspaper editorials and op-ed columns.* Often written in response to a recent occurrence, political event, or social problem in the news, editorials and op-ed pieces are widely read, influential types of arguments. Editorials, which appear on the editorial page of a newspaper and promote the views of the editors, are short (usually fewer than five hundred words), and are written in a journalistic style, often without detailed evidence. They can range from conservative to liberal, depending on the political bias of the editors (see p. 380 in Chapter 16). Op-ed columns appear "opposite the editorial page" (hence the abbreviation "op-ed") and are usually written by syndicated columnists who are professional writers ranging in bias from ultraconservative to socialist (see p. 380 in Chapter 16). Op-ed columns typically average 500–1000 words and can vary from explicit thesis-driven arguments to implicit arguments with stylistic flair. Newspapers also publish "guest op-ed pieces" by local writers on a one-time or occasional basis when a person has particular expertise on an issue. Sometimes an especially good but overly long letter to the editor is published as an op-ed piece.

■ *Public affairs or niche magazine articles.* Public affairs magazines such as *National Review, New Republic, Atlantic Monthly,* or *The Progressive* are outlets for in-depth studies of current issues. Written by staff writers or freelancers, articles in public affairs magazines usually reflect the political bias of the magazine (see pp. 363–364 in Chapter 16). The articles often have a journalistic style with informal documentation, and they frequently include narrative elements rather than explicit thesis-and-reasons organization. Many of the best articles give well-researched coverage of various perspectives on a public issue. In contrast to public affairs magazines, niche magazines advocate for the interests of a particular profession or target audience. Niche magazines include trade publications such as *Automotive Week* or *Construction Marketing Today,* arts and entertainment magazines such as *Rolling Stone* or *Cinema,* and culture and society magazines aimed at particular audiences such as *The Advocate* (gay and lesbian issues) or *Minority Business Entrepreneur.*

■ *Scholarly journals.* Scholarly journals are nonprofit magazines subsidized by universities or scholarly societies. They publish academic articles that have been reviewed by scholars in the field. Although scholars try scrupulously to collect evidence in an unbiased way and analyze it objectively, their work necessarily reflects the biases, methods, and strategies associated with a specific school of thought or theory within a discipline. Scholarly articles usually employ a formal academic style and include academic documentation and bibliographies. When scholars write to influence public opinion on the basis of their research, they often use a more popular style and may seek outlets other than scholarly journals, such as a public affairs magazine or an academic Web site. (Student papers in an argument class often fit this genre—academic argument aimed at a popular audience on a public issue.)

■ *Organizational white papers.* This is perhaps the most common genre of argument in an organizational or professional setting. White papers are in-house documents written by individuals or committees to influence organization decisions or policies or to give informed advice to clients. Sometimes they are written for external audiences to influence public opinion favorable to the organization, in which case they reflect the organization's bias and perspective (external white papers are often posted on Web sites or sent to legislators). They are usually desktop published for use within an organization and written in a utilitarian style with thesis-and-reasons organization and formal documentation. They often include graphics and other visuals. They can vary in style from the dully bureaucratic (satirized in *Dilbert* cartoons) to the cogent and persuasive.

- *Proposals.*   Typed or desktop published, proposals identify a problem, propose a specific solution, and support the solution with a justifying argument. Proposals focus on the needs of the targeted audience, using the audience's values and desires to justify the writer's proposed solution. They are often used to seek grant funding or secure contracts with clients. Proposals are the lifeblood of organizations that depend on meeting the needs of clients for their livelihood.

- *Legal briefs and court decisions.*   Legal briefs are written by attorneys to support the position of one of the parties in a trial or judicial review. "Friends of the court" briefs are written by stakeholders in a case to influence appeals courts such as the U.S. Supreme Court. Briefs are usually written in legalese, but use a logical, well-organized reasons-and-evidence structure. Friends of the court briefs are serious reasons-and-evidence position papers reflecting the bias or perspective of the writer. Once a judge or court makes a decision, the "court decision" is often published to explain the judge's reasoning. Court decisions—particularly those of the U.S. Supreme Court—make fascinating reading; they reveal the complexities of the issue and the intricacies of the judges' thinking. They also include minority arguments if the decision was not unanimous.

- *Public affairs advocacy advertisements.*   Published as posters, fliers, Web pages, or paid advertisements, these condensed arguments try to influence public opinion on civic issues. Using a succinct "sound bite" style, these ads often employ document design, bulleted lists, and visual elements such as graphics, photographs, or drawings for rhetorical effect. They have an explicit bias and often ignore the complexities of an issue by focusing strongly on one view. During periods of civic debate, advocacy groups often purchase full-page newspaper ads to influence public opinion.

- *Advocacy Web sites.*   Often identified by the extension ".org" in the Web site address, advocacy Web sites support the views of the site owner on civic issues. Web sites by well-financed advocacy groups such as the NRA (National Rifle Association) or PETA (People for the Ethical Treatment of Animals) are professionally designed with extensive links to other sites supporting the same views. Well-designed sites use visuals and hyperlinked texts aimed at creating an immediate visceral response favorable to the site owner's views. Advocacy sites reflect the bias of the site owner; ethically responsible sites explicitly announce their bias and purpose in an "about us" or "Mission Statement" link on the home page. (For further discussion of reading and evaluating Web sites, see Chapter 16, pp. 381–386.)

- *Blogs and postings to chat rooms and electronic bulletin boards.*   Blogs, or Web logs, are informal commentaries that individuals write, usually on specific topics, in the form of online journals to influence the opinions of other participants and users of the Web. These blogs are established on Web sites that allow other "bloggers" to respond. Blogs can be personal, but many offer political analysis and hyperlinks to other related sites on the Web. As popular forums for civic dialogue, some blogs are gaining influence as alternative commentaries to the established media. Blogs and postings to chat rooms and electronic bulletin boards reflect a wide range of perspectives and can be a place to try out ideas-in-progress.

- *Visual arguments.*   Although seldom appearing by themselves without some accompanying text, photographs, drawings, political cartoons, and graphics can have an intense rhetorical impact (see Chapter 9). Visuals make strong emotional appeals, often reducing complex issues to one powerful perspective.

- *Speeches.*   Many of the important arguments in our culture, including those in print, begin initially as speeches—either formal speeches such as a presidential address or a keynote speech at a professional meeting, or more informal speeches such as presentations at hearings or interviews on talk shows. Often transcriptions of speeches are printed in newspapers or made available on the Web.

Now that you have a brief overview of the genres of argument, we can apply this knowledge to the issue we have been examining—the genetic engineering of food. As we did our own research on this issue, we found letters to editors, newspaper editorials, op-ed pieces, magazine articles in public affairs and niche magazines, scholarly academic articles, professional and scientific proposals, political speeches, advocacy ads and posters, and white papers presenting the views of organizations, advocacy groups, and governmental agencies. The public debate about genetic engineering of foods is thus being carried on across the total spectrum of argument genres.

Analyzing Rhetorical Context and Genre

Besides understanding an argument's genre, you need to reconstruct its rhetorical context—that is, learn more about the conversation the writer is joining and about the writer's credentials, purpose, audience, and motivation. Awareness of genre and rhetorical context can help you determine how much influence an argument should have on your own thinking about an issue. To explore the rhetorical context of an argument, you can use the following guide questions:

Questions about Rhetorical Context and Genre

1. Who is the author? What are the author's credentials and what is his/her investment in the issue?
2. What audience is he or she writing for?

3. What motivating occasion prompted this writing? What is the author's purpose?

4. What genre of argument is this? How do the conventions of that genre help determine the depth, complexity, and even appearance of the argument?

5. What information about the publication or source (magazine, newspaper, advocacy Web site) explains the angle of vision that shapes the argument?

Consider how we applied these questions to Lisa Turner's article "Playing with Our Food." We began by investigating the identity of the author and the kind of publication. Checking on Lisa Turner's background (by keyboarding her name into a Web search engine), we discovered that she specializes in alternative health therapies and has training in naturopathy, Chinese herbal medicine, yoga, and meditation techniques. She has written five books on nutrition and health published by presses associated with alternative medicine, regularly appears on talk shows to promote natural health, teaches cooking classes at Whole Foods Market (one of the biggest organic food chains), and owns a catering company called "The Healthy Gourmet." We learned that *Better Nutrition* is a niche magazine about consumer health and alternative therapies distributed primarily at health food stores. It is indexed in CINAHL, the main nursing index, but not in MEDLINE, one of the main medical indexes. (Its absence from MEDLINE means that mainstream medical researchers, who value the scientific method, don't regard the magazine as an outlet for serious scholarship.)

When we returned to the article "Playing with Our Food" and analyzed it rhetorically, we saw more clearly how Turner's background, the type of magazine, and her sense of audience shaped her argument. She is strongly biased toward organic foods and alternative approaches to medicine and health. Because *Better Nutrition* is a natural health magazine, Turner assumes that her audience will share her opposition to scientific intervention in farming and food processing. Although this article does include references, they are not the most current or the most exact. The two sources that she quotes directly—the CEO of the advocacy group Citizens for Health and the author of the book *The Food That Would Last Forever*—do not appear in her list of references. Her alarmist tone and vehement language as well as the scarcity of specific examples suggest that she is writing to an audience who may be uninformed but who nevertheless share her bias. We decided that this article represents a "health foods" point of view in the biotech foods controversy but provides only a starting point for inquiry into this complex issue.

Strategy 4: Seeking Out Alternative Views and Analyzing Sources of Disagreement

When you analyze an argument, you shouldn't isolate it from the general conversation of differing views that form its context. If you were an arbitrator, you wouldn't think of settling a dispute between A and B on the basis of A's testimony only. You would also insist on hearing B's side of the story (and perhaps also C's and D's if they are stakeholders in the dispute). In analyzing an argument, therefore, you should try to seek out the views of those who disagree with the author to appreciate the full context of the issue.

As you listen to differing views, try to identify sources of disagreement, which often fall into two categories: (1) disagreement about the facts or reality of the case and (2) disagreement about underlying values, beliefs, or assumptions, including assumptions about definitions or appropriate analogies. Let's look at each in turn.

Disagreement about Facts or Their Relevance

Often disputants in an argument disagree about facts in a case or about the relevance of certain facts. Consider the controversies over global warming. Although the majority of scientists believe that the earth is getting hotter and that at least some portion of this increase is caused by the emission of greenhouse gases, scientists have factual disputes about the rate of global warming, about its causes (How much is natural? How much is human-caused?), and about its environmental effects. Additionally, disputants can disagree on the significance or relevance of a fact. For example, global warming activists often cite the dramatic shrinking of the glacial ice cap on Africa's Mount Kilimanjaro as evidence of human-caused global warming. But some climatologists, who agree that Kilimanjaro's ice cap is shrinking, argue that nonhuman causes such as changes in solar output or natural climate variability may be the primary factors. In this case, a fact that urges one person to propose political action to combat global warming leaves another person unmoved. Other examples of disagreements about facts or reality include the following:

- In arguing whether silver-mercury amalgam tooth fillings should be banned, dental researchers disagree on the amount of mercury vapor released by older fillings; they also disagree on how much mercury vapor has to be present before it is harmful.

- In arguing about the legalization of drugs, writers disagree about the degree to which Prohibition reduced alcohol consumption; they also disagree on whether crack cocaine is "crimogenic" (has chemical properties that induce violent behavior).

Disagreement about Values, Beliefs, or Assumptions

A second source of disagreement concerns differences in values, beliefs, or assumptions. Here are some examples:

- Persons A and B might agree that a huge tax on gasoline would cut down on the consumption of petroleum. They might agree further that the world's supply of petroleum will eventually run out. Thus Persons A and B agree at the level of facts. But they might disagree about whether the United States should enact a huge gas tax. Person A might support the law in order to conserve oil. Person B might oppose it, perhaps because B believes that scientists will find alternative energy sources before the petroleum runs out or because B believes the short-term harm of such a tax outweighs distant benefits.

- Person A and Person B might agree that capital punishment deters potential murderers (an agreement on facts). Person A supports capital punishment for this reason, but Person B opposes it, believing that the taking of a human life is always wrong in principle even if the state does it legally (a disagreement about basic beliefs).

Sometimes differing beliefs or values present themselves as disagreements about definitions or appropriate analogies.

- Social Theorist A and Social Theorist B disagree about whether the covers of some women's magazines like *Cosmopolitan* are pornographic. This disagreement turns on the definition of *pornography*, with different definitions reflecting different underlying values and beliefs.
- In supporting a Texas law forbidding flag burning, Chief Justice William Rehnquist argued that desecration of a flag in the name of free speech is similar to desecrating the Washington Monument. He thus made this analogy: Just as we would forbid desecration of a national monument, so should we forbid desecration of the flag. Opposing justices did not think the analogy was valid.
- Person A and Person B disagree on whether it is ethically acceptable to have Down's syndrome children undergo plastic surgery to correct some of the facial abnormalities associated with this genetic condition. Person A supports the surgery, arguing that it is analogous to any other cosmetic surgeries done to improve appearance. Person B argues against such surgery, saying it is analogous to the racial self-hatred of some minority persons who have tried to change their ethnic appearance and become lily white. (The latter analogy argues that Down's syndrome is nothing to be ashamed of and that persons should take pride in their difference.)

We now invite you to consider a different view of biotechnology. Examine Color Plate A, which is an advocacy advertisement sponsored by the Council for Biotechnology Information. This ad, promoting biotech soybeans, appeared in a July 2002 issue of *Time* magazine. A similar ad, also by the Council for Biotechnology Information, appeared in an April 2002 issue of *Atlantic Monthly*. Then read this same organization's argument opposing consumer labels for genetically engineered foods. (We found the argument on the Council's Web site.) These pro-biotech arguments—in conversation with Turner's article and the "Keep Nature Natural" ad (Figure 2.1)—vividly exemplify the differing values and beliefs that compete for our allegiance in a pluralistic world.

Why Biotech Labeling Can Confuse Consumers
Council for Biotechnology Information

Consumers want food product labels with clear, meaningful information.   1

A grocery shopper, for example, finds a wealth of factual information on labels,   2
whether it's about nutrient and caloric content or specific health aspects of a food
product.

Should that same shopper also be able to read on the label whether those corn   3
chips or that bottle of cooking oil contains biotech ingredients? Some say yes. Given
the concerns raised by a few about biotech safety, there's an important "right to
know," they contend.

Others say there's no need to label foods with biotech ingredients that are the   4
same as foods with ingredients from conventional crops. Requiring a label for
biotech ingredients, they say, would confuse consumers, not inform them.

The U.S. Food and Drug Administration (FDA), which oversees food safety is-   5
sues in the United States, takes the second view. The agency performs exhaustive
safety tests on every biotech food entering the marketplace, and requires special labeling only when the new food product is significantly different from its conventional counterpart.

TESTED FOR SAFETY

Before they reach a farmer's field, biotech corn, soybeans and other genetically   6
enhanced foods undergo years of review by researchers, university scientists, farmers and other government agencies in addition to the FDA.

The results are unambiguous. Biotech crops are safe to eat. No studies or test   7
results have said otherwise. There hasn't been a single documented case of an illness caused by biotech foods.[1] A report issued in 2000 by the National Academy of
Sciences, an independent group of scientists and scholars, confirmed that all approved biotech products are as safe as their conventional counterparts.[2]

So safety is not at issue in labeling biotech food. Instead, the FDA considers   8
whether a biotech orange, for example, is "substantially equivalent" to a traditional
orange. Does it produce the same nutrients? If it does, there's no need for a label. If
it doesn't—if the orange has a higher or lower level of vitamin C—then the FDA requires a label.

Under this line of thinking, labeling *all* biotech foods would make a distinction   9
without a difference. Rather than communicating relevant health or safety information, it would merely explain the *process* by which the food was developed. And in so
doing it could sow confusion among consumers. Ninety-two percent of food industry
leaders, for example, believe that mandatory biotech food labeling—which proponents often position simply as an informational tool—will instead be perceived as a
"warning" by at least some consumers.[3]

10   The American Medical Association (AMA) has stated that "there is no scientific justification for special labeling of genetically modified foods, as a class."[4]

11   Statistics show that the current FDA policy—labeling biotech foods when there's a meaningful reason to do so—is what consumers want. When surveyed for their opinions, two-thirds to three-quarters consistently approve of the existing system once it's explained that biotech foods have been reviewed and found safe by experts, and would be specially labeled if the nutritional content has been significantly changed.[5]

12   When asked in an open-ended way what information they'd like more of on product labels, only 1 percent of consumers mentioned biotechnology. Three percent said ingredients, four percent nutrition and 75 percent said they wanted no additional information.[6]

COSTLY AND CONFUSING

13   Countries and trading blocs that want to require labels have had to develop a long list of exemptions and loopholes.[7] That's the case in Europe, which enacted labeling requirements and other restrictions. An article in the *Wall Street Journal* pointed out that the European system has "confused consumers" and "spawned a bewildering array of marketing claims, counterclaims and outright contradictions that only a food scientist possibly could unravel."[8]

14   Labeling requirements also increase costs. Keeping biotech commodity crops separate from traditional ones requires new expenses in the agricultural supply chain—in added handling measures, testing requirements, and so on—that inevitably will be passed on to consumers.

15   A Canadian study estimated that mandatory labeling would cost that country's consumers $700 million to $950 million annually[9]—arguably, a food tax on the majority to pay for the labeling demands of a few.[10]

16   An alternative is the voluntary labeling guidelines for biotech and nonbiotech products currently being developed by the FDA. Under this system, manufacturers can let consumers know if a food was developed using biotechnology to have a beneficial trait such as reduced saturated fat—or, conversely, if biotech ingredients were not used in making a food.[11]

17   Professor Thomas Hoban, director of the Center for Biotechnology in Global Society at North Carolina State University, points out that voluntary labeling can provide choice "without imposing costs on . . . the majority of consumers who support or have no objection to biotechnology."[12]

FOCUSING DEBATE

18   Biotechnology is a fast-changing science that's raising environmental, economic and ethical issues. Given the importance of food in a fast-growing world where about 840 million people go hungry, those issues deserve to be considered on their merits.

19   By raising questionable concerns in the minds of consumers, and introducing unnecessary costs, mandatory labeling requirements may only distract from what's

truly important: a rational, fact-informed debate about the risks of biotechnology, balanced against the benefits it offers.

Notes

[1]Aaron, David L., U.S. Undersecretary of Commerce for Trade, Reuters, September 16, 1999; also, "In Support of Biotechnology (Expert Views)" The Alliance for Better Foods, <www.betterfoods.org/Expert/Expert.htm>.

[2]Woo, Robin Y., "No Room for Politics on Food Labels," *Des Moines Register,* May 11, 2000, reprinted at <index.asp?id=1226&redirect=con508mid17%2Ehtml>.

[3]Hoban, Thomas J., "Market Acceptance of Agricultural Biotechnology," North Carolina State University, electronic multimedia presentation.

[4]"Genetically Modified Crops and Foods," American Medical Association (AMA), <www.ama-assn.org/ama/pub/article/2036-3604.html>.

[5]Hoban, Thomas J., "Biotechnology," *Forum,* Fourth Quarter 2000, p. 102.

[6]Hoban, Thomas J., "Biotechnology," *Forum,* Fourth Quarter 2000, p. 95.

[7]Chin, Mary Lee, "Confusing Customers," *Denver Post,* June 17, 2001.

[8]Stecklow, Steve, "Genetically Modified Label Confuses U.K. Shoppers," *The Wall Street Journal,* October 27, 1999.

[9]"Economic Impact Study: Potential Costs of Mandatory Labeling of Food Products Derived from Biotechnology in Canada," KPMG Consulting, December 1, 2000.

[10]"Labeling Biotechnology Foods and the Organic Lobby," Economic & Agricultural Trade 2000, <www.eat2k.org/issues/labeling_backgrounder.html>.

[11]"Guidance for Industry: Voluntary Labeling Indicating Whether Foods Have or Have Not Been Developed Using Bioengineering," U.S. Food and Drug Administration, January 2001, <www.cfsan.fda.gov/dms/biolabgu.html>.

[12]Hoban, Thomas J., "Biotechnology," *Forum,* Fourth Quarter 2000, p. 103.

For Class Discussion

Working as a whole class or in small groups, respond to the following questions about the readings and visual arguments you have just considered.

1. What claims about biotech foods does the soybean ad (Color Plate A) make?

2. Consider this ad in dialogue with Turner and the "Keep Nature Natural" ad (Figure 2.1). How does this ad try to allay the fears and answer the objections of the opponents of genetically engineered foods?

3. The genre of the advocacy ad requires brevity and strong, clear, audience-based appeals to a target audience. Why did the Council for Biotechnology Information choose to publish its ads in *Time* and *Atlantic Monthly?* What audiences is it trying to reach?

4. What does this advocacy ad do to establish its authority and credibility?

5. Now consider the Council's policy argument on biotech labeling. To what extent do Lisa Turner and the Council disagree about the basic facts concerning genetically engineered foods?

6. To what extent do Turner and the Council disagree about values, beliefs, and underlying assumptions?

Writing an Analysis of a Disagreement

A common writing assignment in argument courses asks students to analyze the sources of disagreement between two or more writers who take different positions on an issue. In writing such an analysis, you need to determine whether the writers disagree primarily about facts/reality or values (or both). Specifically, you should pose the following questions:

1. Where do the writers disagree about facts and/or the interpretation of facts?
2. Where do the writers disagree about underlying beliefs, values, or assumptions?
3. Where do the writers disagree about key definitions or about appropriate analogies? How do these differences imply differences in values, beliefs, or assumptions?

To illustrate how these three questions can help you write an analysis, we've constructed the following model: our own brief analysis of the disagreement between Turner and the Council for Biotechnology Information written as a short formal essay.

An Analysis of the Sources of Disagreement between Lisa Turner and the Council for Biotechnology Information

1   Lisa Turner and the Council for Biotechnology Information clash about facts and values in their arguments over the genetic engineering of food. Turner stresses the dangers of biotechnology while the Council stresses the value of scientific advancement

2   At the heart of their controversy is disagreement about facts. Have genetically engineered foods been appropriately tested for safety? "No," says Turner; "yes," says the Council. These antithetical views determine the stand each source takes on the need for biotech labeling. Turner argues that biotech foods are risky. Her strategy is to raise doubts about the safety of genetically engineered food, mainly by suggesting frightening hypothetical scenarios. She emphasizes the experimental quality of these modifications, arguing that they are imprecise, uncontrollable, and irreversible because they alter living things that pass on genetic modifications

when they propagate and affect natural cycles that involve other plants and animals. She mentions the creation of new allergens that could provoke dangerous allergic reactions. She cites one example of deaths and paralysis in 1993, but she does not explain what food product caused this response. (The Council states that no death or disease has ever resulted from biotech foods.) Her main point is that scientists, farmers, and marketers are foisting these entirely experimental foods on an uninformed public.

In contrast, the Council for Biotechnology Information assumes the safety of   3
genetically engineered foods. It has confidence in the U.S. Food and Drug Administration's declaration that biotech foods are safe and agrees with the FDA rule that labels are needed only when a biotech food substantially differs from its natural counterpart. The Council asserts that these biotech foods have undergone rigorous tests "by researchers, university scientists, farmers, and other government agencies in addition to the FDA" (paragraph 6). However, in the conclusion of the article, the Council does mention that "[b]iotechnology is a fast-changing science" (paragraph 18) and there is a need for "a rational, fact-informed debate about the risks of biotechnology" (paragraph 19).

The "facts" in these two arguments derive from the authors' dramatically dif-   4
ferent values and assumptions. Turner's article appeared in a health food magazine, and she writes to an audience who shares her distrust of technology. Turner reveals her angle of vision as a health and natural foods practitioner in her strong alarmist tone and her antagonism to genetic engineering, which come through her choice of language. Words such as "nothing sacred," "brave new world of 'biotech foods,'" "artificially shuffling genes," and "new, weird science" express her antitechnology bias (paragraphs 1–3). Clearly, she believes that plants, animals, and foods in their natural state are superior to anything that is artificially created.

In contrast, the Council for Biotechnology Information makes an effort to sound   5
balanced, rational, and knowledgeable, but this article also reveals its underlying values. The Council, which is an advocacy organization for the biotechnology industry, believes that biotechnology is a beneficent force that uses human ingenuity to improve nature. Its slogan "Good ideas are growing" (found on its Web site home page) encodes the idea that progress results when humans can manipulate natural processes. This article enhances its credibility by citing the American Medical Association's endorsement of the safety of genetically engineered foods and documenting its reputable sources. However, under the guise of concern for cost to consumers, the Council hides its pro-big business and pro-government bias. The hidden reality here is that the creation and marketing of genetically modified foods are highly profitable enterprises. It also assumes that the FDA and other government regulatory agencies are completely neutral and have consumers' well-being foremost in mind. Thus while Turner sees the labeling of biotech ingredients as a needed warning to consumers, the Council sees its costs as a tax on food brought about by a small minority.

These arguments sketch out in bold strokes two alternative views of geneti-   6
cally engineered foods, demonstrating how different values cause persons to perceive different realities and construct different facts.

Works Cited

Council for Biotechnology Information. "Biotech Labeling." 2002. 11 July 2002. <http://whybiotech.com/index.asp?id=1812>. Rpt. in <u>Writing Arguments: A Rhetoric with Readings</u>. John D. Ramage, John C. Bean, and June Johnson. 7th ed. New York: Longman, 2007.

Turner, Lisa. "Playing with Our Food." <u>Better Nutrition</u> June 2000: 56–59. Rpt. in <u>Writing Arguments: A Rhetoric with Readings</u>. John D. Ramage, John C. Bean, and June Johnson. 7th ed. New York: Longman, 2007.

Strategy 5: Using Disagreement Productively to Prompt Further Investigation

Our fifth strategy—using disagreement productively to prompt further investigation—is both a powerful strategy for reading arguments and a bridge toward constructing your own arguments. Our goal is to suggest ways to help you proceed when the experts disagree. Encountering divergent points of view, such as the disagreement between Turner and the Council, can create intense intellectual pressure. Inexperienced arguers sometimes opt for easy escape routes. Either they throw up their hands, claim that "everyone has a right to his own opinion," and leave the argumentative arena, or they latch on to one of the competing claims, defend it against all comers, and shut off opportunity for growth and change. What our fifth strategy invites you to do is stay in the argumentative arena. It urges you to become an active questioner and thinker—to seek answers where possible to disputed questions of fact and value and to articulate and justify your own beliefs and assumptions, which will ultimately inform the positions you take on issues.

As you sort through conflicting viewpoints, your goal is not to identify one of them as "correct" but to ask what is the best solution to the problems being debated here. You may eventually decide that one of the current viewpoints is indeed the best solution. Or you may develop a synthesis that combines strengths from several divergent viewpoints. In either case, you will emerge from the process with an enlarged, informed understanding. You will have developed the ability to remain intellectually flexible while listening to alternative viewpoints. Most important, you will have learned how to avoid falling into a valueless relativism. Responding productively to disagreement thus becomes part of your preparation for writing ethically responsible arguments.

To illustrate the process of responding to disagreements, we now show you how we responded to the disagreement between Turner and the Council for Biotechnology Information over genetically engineered food.

Accepting Ambiguity and Uncertainty

When confronted with conflicting positions, you must learn to cope with ambiguity. If there were no disagreements, of course, there would be no need for argument. It is important to realize that experts can look at the same data, can analyze the same arguments, can listen to the same authorities, and still reach different conclusions. Seldom will one expert's argument triumph over another's in a field of dissenting claims. More often, one expert's argument will modify another's and in turn will be modified by yet another. Accepting ambiguity is a way of suspending judgment as you enter the complexity of an issue. A willingness to live with ambiguity enables you to delve deeply into an issue and to resist easy answers.

Seeking Sources of Facts and More Complete Versions of Alternative Views

After analyzing the sources of disagreement between Turner and the Council for Biotechnology Information (see our essay on pp. 44–46), we pondered how we would continue our search for personal clarity on the issue. We decided to seek out alternative views through library and online research (see Part Four for instruction on research strategies), particularly exploring these questions:

- Are genetically engineered foods safe? What kinds of tests are currently used to verify short-term and long-term safety? How rigorous are they? How accurate are Turner's claims that these foods are potentially dangerous?

- What are the current regulations on the sale and labeling of genetically engineered crops and food? What legislation is being proposed?

- Among disinterested scientists who don't have contracts with the biotech industry, what is the view of the potential benefits and dangers of genetically modified foods? What is the view of the dangers and benefits to the environment?

- What are the achievements of genetic engineering of food so far? How extensive is genetic engineering? Have there been any catastrophes or near catastrophes?

- What is the feasibility and practicality of labeling foods with biotech ingredients?

- What are alternatives to using biotechnology?

When we began our research, we found major disagreement among scientists. For example, the Union of Concerned Scientists (www.ucsusa.org) gives a detailed list of the specific crops that have been modified, the corporations or companies that control the modification, and the traits that genetic engineers are trying to create. This organization raises questions about the safety of these food products, proposing a slower investigative process—basically calling for more science and less business in the whole biotech movement. On the other hand, the American Council on Science and Health (www.acsh.org), consisting of physicians, scientists, and policy advisers, actively campaigns for further implementation of what it considers to be highly advantageous and beneficial scientific processes. We discovered that other scientific groups such as the American Medical Association (www.ama-assn.org) take a middle position, praising current advances in genetic engineering of foods but recommending closer monitoring of these crops and more scientifically sound criteria for testing them.

The range of views on testing and labeling of genetically modified foods revealed to us the complexity of this issue. The arguments we found most useful acknowledged the potential value of genetic engineering of foods while realistically confronting the risks and calling for more pre-market testing. We were also drawn to arguments that exposed the profit-making motives driving much of the experimentation with biotech foods. We welcomed discussions of the real challenges of accurately and helpfully labeling these food products.

In addition, we discovered that recently scientists, environmentalists, and social activists have intensified the focus on alternatives to biotechnology. For example, "smart breeding" claims to be able to manipulate the genetic makeup of crops without introducing genes from other plants or animals. Scientists using this approach try, for example, to improve rice or wheat by looking for desired genes within different varieties of rice and wheat. By turning on and off certain genes that are part of a plant's genetic code, scientists hope to be able to cultivate traits such as increased vitamin content or resistance to drought. This new science sounded promising to us. We also realized the need to investigate the movement to keep these discoveries about gene manipulation freely available to the public instead of patented by corporations. Finally, our researching of the use of biotechnology in food production suggested that this field offers continuous developments that merit ongoing investigation.

Determining What Values Are at Stake for You and Articulating Your Own Values

In responding to disagreement, you need to articulate your own values and try to justify them by explaining the reasons you hold them. The authors of this text, for instance, support the pursuit of scientific knowledge but often question the motives and actions of big business. We believe in the value of strong oversight of scientific experimentation—both from peer review by disinterested scientists and from government regulatory agencies that represent the common good. We like the idea of health food stores, of organic farming, of small family farms, and of less commercialism, but we also appreciate inexpensive food and the convenience of supermarkets. Additionally, we are drawn to technologies that might help feed the world's poor. Therefore, we are trying to stake out our own positions within the complex middle ground on genetic engineering.

Considering Ways to Synthesize Alternative Views

As a final step in your evaluation of conflicting sources, you should consider what you have gained from the different perspectives. How do alternative views modify each other or otherwise "speak to each other"? How might we synthesize the apparently polarized views on genetic engineering of food?

Environmentalists and organic food supporters like Lisa Turner teach us the need for long-range thinking. They prompt us to be more active in exploring alternative solutions to agricultural problems. They advise society to weigh human health and well-being against profits, and they exhort us to be responsible, proactive citizens and knowledgeable, assertive consumers. At the same time, the Council for Biotechnology Information shows us that the "science as bad guy" view is much too simplistic and that science and technology may help us solve otherwise intractable problems. In trying to synthesize these divergent perspectives, we would look for ways to combine sensible caution and rigorous science.

When you try to synthesize points from conflicting views, as we begin to do here, you tap into the dialectical nature of argument, carefully reflecting when you should change your mind, questioning and modifying positions in response to new perspectives. Your ultimate goal is to find a position that is reasonable and responsible in light of the available facts and your own values.

Conclusion

This chapter has explained why reading arguments is crucially important to writers of arguments and has offered five main strategies for deep reading: (1) Read as a believer. (2) Read as a doubter. (3) Explore how rhetorical context and genre shape an argument. (4) Consider alternative views and analyze sources of disagreement. (5) Use disagreement productively to prompt further investigation. This chapter has also shown you how to summarize an article and incorporate summaries into your own writing through the use of attributive tags. It has explained who writes arguments and how writer, purpose, audience, and the genre of the argument are closely connected and must be considered in any thoughtful response to an argument.

In the next chapter we turn from the reading of arguments to the writing of arguments, suggesting ways that you can generate ideas for arguments, structure your arguments, and improve your own writing processes.

3 Writing Arguments

As the opening chapters suggest, when you write an argument, you try to achieve two goals: (1) to understand your issue thoroughly enough so that your stance reflects an ethical consideration of conflicting views and (2) to persuade your audience toward your stance on the issue. Because managing these tasks takes time, the quality of any argument depends on the quality of the thinking and writing processes that produced it. In this chapter, we suggest ways that you can improve these processes. We begin by looking at the social contexts that produce arguments, asking who writes arguments and why. We then present some writing tips based on the composing practices of experienced writers. Finally, we describe nuts-and-bolts strategies for generating ideas and organizing an argument for an intended audience, concluding with two sets of exploratory exercises that can be adapted to any kind of argumentative task.

Who Writes Arguments and Why?

In the previous chapter we described the genres of arguments ranging from letters to the editor to advocacy Web sites. To help you see further how writers operate in a social context—how they are spurred to write by a motivating occasion and by a desire to change the views of particular audiences—we begin this chapter by asking you to consider more fully why someone would produce an argument.

To illustrate the multiple contexts for persuasion, let's return to the issue of biotech foods that we used in Chapter 2. Who in our culture actually writes arguments on this issue? To whom are they writing and why? Here is a partial list of these writers and their contexts:

- *Lobbyists and advocacy groups.* Advocacy groups commit themselves to a cause, often with passion, and produce avidly partisan arguments aimed at persuading voters, legislators, or other targeted decision makers. We have seen how both proponents and opponents of biotechnology have formed well-established advocacy groups that buy advertisement space in magazines, maintain professional Web sites, and exert lobbying pressure on political candidates and elected officials. Opponents of biotech foods advocate for labeling of biotech ingredients in food, for family farms and local production of food, and for stricter, long-term safety testing of biotech products. Proponents lobby for research grants and for agricultural and world trade legislation conducive to the biotech industry.

■ *Legislators, political candidates, and government officials.*   Whenever new laws, regulations, or government policies are proposed, staffers do research and write white papers recommending positions on an issue. Because the production of biotech food is a highly contested national and world issue—along with related issues involving organic farming, pesticides, agribusiness, third-world development, and agricultural production in general—numerous staff researchers for legislators, political candidates, or government officials have produced white papers on food and agricultural issues. Often these white papers are available on the Web.

■ *Business professionals.*   Businesses devoted to organic foods, holistic medicine, family farming, and "natural" substances in diets and nutrition tend to oppose biotech foods, while those devoted to factory farming, scientific methods in agriculture, and biotech research support biotech foods. Executives and staff writers in all these organizations regularly produce arguments supporting their views for a variety of different audiences.

■ *Lawyers and judges.*   Many biotech issues have legal dimensions ranging from patent disputes to class action lawsuits. Lawyers write briefs supporting their clients' cases. Sometimes lawyers or legal experts not directly connected to a case, particularly law professors, file "friends of the court" briefs aimed at influencing the decision of judges. Finally, judges write court opinions explaining their decisions on a case.

■ *Media commentators.*   Whenever biotech issues get in the news, media commentators (journalists, editorial writers, syndicated columnists) write on the issue, filtering it through the perspective of their own political views.

■ *Professional freelance or staff writers.*   Some of the most thoughtful analyses of public issues are composed by freelance or staff writers for public forum magazines such as *Atlantic Monthly, The Nation, Ms., The National Review, Utne Reader,* and many others. Arguments on biotechnology surface whenever the topic seems timely to magazine editors.

■ *Think tanks.*   Because today many political, economic, and social issues are very complex, policymakers and commentators often rely on research institutions or think tanks to supply statistical studies and in-depth investigation of problems. These think tanks range across the political spectrum, from conservative and libertarian to centrist to liberal. They usually have many-layered Web sites that include background on their researchers, recent publications, and archives of past publications. These publications take the form of explorations and surveys as well as policy statements and white papers. You would probably find relevant research on the development, marketing, and environmental impact of genetically modified crops on the Web sites of any of the following think tanks: Hoover Institute, the Cato Institute, Heritage Foundation, Pew Research Center for the People and the Press, Brookings Institution, and WorldWatch Institute.

- *Scholars and academics.*   A key public role played by college professors comes from their scholarly research. Almost all public debates on science, technology, and social policy derive at least some data and analysis from the scholarship of college professors. Although no research can be purely objective—unshaped by the biases of the researcher—scholarly research differs substantially from advocacy argument in its systematic attempt to arrive at the best answers to questions based on the full examination of all relevant data. Much scholarship has been devoted to the biotechnology issue—primarily by agricultural scientists, nutritionists, economists, political scientists, and sociologists. Scholarly research is usually published in refereed academic journals rather than popular magazines. (Of course, scholars can also take personal positions on social issues and use their research for advocacy arguments.)

- *Citizens.*   Average citizens influence social policy through letters, contributions to advocacy Web sites, guest editorials for newspapers, blogs, speeches at public forums, or pieces in professional newsletters or other media. Biotech issues reach national consciousness when enough individuals make their views heard. The movement to label biotech ingredients on food products arose through grassroots efforts promoted by ordinary citizens.

Where do student writers fit on this list? As a student you are already a member of both the "citizen" group and the "scholars and academics" group. Moreover, you may often be given opportunities to role-play membership in other groups as well. As a professional-in-training, you can practice both advocacy arguments and inquiry-based research pieces. Some students taking argument courses in college publish their work as letters to the editor or guest editorials (in the case of advocacy pieces) or present their work at undergraduate research conferences (in the case of scholarly pieces). Others try to influence public opinion by writing persuasive letters to legislators, submitting proposals to decision makers in the workplace, or posting their arguments on Web sites.

What all these writers have in common is a deep engagement with their issues. They share a strong belief that an issue matters, that decisions have consequences, and that the stakes are often high. You can engage an issue either by having a strong position to advocate or by seeking to clarify your stand on a complex problem. What is important to note is how fluid a writer's position can be along this continuum from advocate to inquirer (analogous to the continuum between "persuasion" and "truth seeking" discussed in Chapter 1, pp. 10–13, Figure 1.2). An advocate, while writing an argument, might discover an issue's complexity and be drawn into inquiry. Likewise, an inquirer, in the course of studying an issue, might clarify her thinking, establish a strong claim, and become an advocate. It is also possible to write arguments from any position on the continuum: You can be a tentative advocate as well as an avidly committed one, or you can be a cautious skeptic. You can even remain an inquirer by arguing that no proposed solution to a problem is yet adequate.

So how do you become engaged? We suggest that you immerse yourself in the arguments of the communities to which you belong—your classroom community, your dorm or apartment community, your work community, your civic community—and look for points of entry into these conversations: either places where you can take a stand or places where you are puzzled and uncertain. By opening yourself to the conversations of your culture, and by initiating these conversations when you encounter situations you would like to change, you will be ready to write arguments.

Tips for Improving Your Writing Process

Once you are motivated to write, you can improve your arguing ability if you know something about the writing processes of experienced writers. Too often inexperienced writers cut this process short, producing undeveloped arguments that don't speak effectively to the needs of the intended audience. Although no two writers follow the same process, we can describe the evolution of an argument in a loose way and offer tips for making your writing processes more effective. You should regard the writing process we are about to describe as *recursive*, meaning that writers often loop back to earlier phases by changing their minds on an issue, by throwing out a draft and starting over, or by going back to do more research late in the process.

Starting Point, Exploration, and Research

Most writers of arguments start with an issue about which they are undecided or a claim they want to assert. Often they are motivated by a specific occasion. At the outset, they may pose questions such as these: What is at issue in this controversy? Who are the invested parties? Why do they disagree? What is at stake? The writer, in short, feels caught up in a problem—hooked into deeper reflection. Once engaged with a problem, writers typically explore it in depth through research and through their own critical thinking, trying to understand arguments on all sides. While investigating their issues, writers often discover that their own views evolve. During research, writers often do exploratory writing, sometimes drafting whole pieces of an argument.

Tips for Getting Started, Exploring, and Researching

- If you aren't already drawn into a controversy, discuss issues with friends and classmates. Talking about ideas in small groups may help you discover claims that you want to make or issues that you find significant yet perplexing. By questioning claims and presenting multiple points of view, groups can help you understand points of disagreement on an issue.

- Besides talking with friends and classmates, try using some of the exploratory exercises described later in this chapter. These exercises help you inventory issues within the communities to which you belong, find points of engagement, and articulate the values and consequences that are at stake for you.

- Read. A great number of issues emerge when you peruse the pages of a campus or city newspaper, read op-ed pieces or letters to the editor, and leaf through current affairs magazines. Readings from courses you are currently taking may engage you with disciplinary questions that invite argument. Finally, the readings presented in this text are designed to stimulate your own thinking about issues that matter. Chapter 2 shows you how to read arguments as a believer and a doubter to become a more powerful critical thinker.

- Find situations in your environment that you would like to see changed. You can often focus an argument by asking yourself who has the power to make the changes you desire. What obstacles constrain the actions of decision makers? How can these obstacles be overcome? How can you craft an argument that persuades decision makers to act on your proposals?

- Stay in conversation with others. Active discussion of your issue—especially with persons who don't agree with you—is a powerful way to explore an argument and find the best means of persuasion. As you talk through your argument, note where listeners look confused or skeptical and where they question your points. Skeptics may find holes in your reasoning, argue from different values, surprise you by conceding points you thought had to be developed at length, and challenge you by demanding more justification of your claim.

Writing a First Draft

At some point in the process, a writer's attention begins to shift away from gathering data and probing an issue to composing a first draft. The act of writing a draft forces deep and focused thinking, which may then send the writer back to do more research and exploration. Effective first drafts are likely to be jumbled, messy, and full of gaps. Ideas appear at the point the writer thought of them rather than where readers need them. The writer's tone and style may be inappropriate, needed evidence may be entirely missing, the audience's beliefs and values may not be adequately addressed, and the whole draft may be confusing to an outside reader. Moreover, writers may discover that their own views are still shifting and unstable. Nevertheless, such drafts are a crucial first step. They get your ideas onto paper and give you material to work with.

Tips for Writing a First Draft

- Try lowering your expectations. Writers can quickly create writer's block if they aim for perfection on the first draft. If you get blocked, keep writing. Don't worry about grammar, correctness, or polish. Just get ideas on paper.

- Rehearse your ideas orally. Working in pairs with another student, talk through your argument orally before you write it down. Make a scratch outline first to prompt you as you talk. Then let your partner question you to help you flesh out your argument with more details.

- For a first draft, try following the template for a "classical argument" described on pages 63–67. This strategy will help you consider and respond to opposing views as well as clarify the reasons and evidence that support your own claim.

- Do the exploration tasks entitled "Set 2: Exploration and Rehearsal" (pp. 70–71) prior to writing a first draft. These exercises will help you brainstorm most of the ideas you'll need for an initial draft.

Revising through Multiple Drafts

After completing a first draft, you have materials out on the table to work with. Most writers need multiple drafts to convert an early draft into a persuasive finished product. Sometimes writers revise their claims significantly during revision, having discovered hidden complexities in the issue while composing the first draft.

Tips for Revising

- Don't manicure your drafts; rebuild them. Cross out whole paragraphs and rewrite them from scratch. Move blocks of text to new locations. Make a mess. Inexperienced writers often think of revision as polishing and correcting rather than as making the kinds of substantial changes that writing teachers call "global revision." Revising means to rethink your whole argument. Some writers even throw away the first draft and start fresh.

- Improve your mechanical procedures. We recommend that you revise off double-spaced hard copy rather than off the computer screen. Leave lots of space between lines and in the margins on your drafts so that you have room to draw arrows and make pencil or pen deletions and inserts. When your draft becomes too messy, keyboard your changes back into the computer. If you manage all your drafts on computer, you may find that copying to a new file for each new draft gives you more freedom to experiment with changes (since you can always recover an earlier draft).

- As you revise, think of your audience. Many first drafts show why the writer believes the claim but not why the intended audience should believe it or act on it. As we explain later in this text (especially Chapters 5, 6, and 8), first drafts often contain "writer-based reasons" rather than "audience-based reasons." How can you hook into your audience's beliefs and values? Look also at the obstacles or constraints that keep your audience from adopting your beliefs or acting on your claim. How can you address those constraints in your revision?

- As you revise, also consider the image of yourself conveyed in your tone and style. Do you want to come across as angry? As sarcastic? As conciliatory and sympathetic? Also, to what extent do you want to appeal to readers' emotions and imagination as well as to their logical intellects? These concerns are discussed in Chapter 7 under the headings *ethos* and *pathos*.

- Exchange drafts with classmates. Ask classmates where your argument is not persuasive, where your tone is offensive, where they have doubts, where your writing is unclear or undeveloped. Ask your classmates to role-play your intended audience. Explain the values and beliefs of this audience and the constraints members face. Let them give you their reactions and advice. Classmates can also help you meet your readers' needs for effective organization, development, and style.
- Loop back to do more exploration and research. Revising your first draft may involve considerably more research and exploration.

Editing for Style, Impact, and Correctness

Writers now polish their drafts, rephrasing sentences, finding the precise word, and establishing links between sentences. At this point, you should turn to surface features such as spelling, punctuation, and grammar as well as to the appearance and form of the final manuscript.

Tips for Editing

- Read your draft out loud. Your ear can often pick up problems missed by the eye.
- Use your computer's spell check program. Remember, however, that spell checkers won't pick up mistakes with homonyms like *to/two/too, here/hear,* or *affect/effect.* Be skeptical of computerized grammar checkers, which cannot "read" with human intelligence but can only mechanically count, sort, and match. Your instructor can guide you on what grammar checkers can and cannot do.
- Use a good handbook for up-to-date advice on usage, punctuation, style, and manuscript form.
- Ask a classmate or friend to proofread your paper.
- Be prepared to loop back again to earlier stages. Sometimes thinking of a better way to word a sentence uncovers larger problems of clarity and meaning requiring you to rewrite a whole section of your argument.

Using Exploratory Writing to Discover Ideas and Deepen Thinking

What follows is a compendium of strategies to help you discover and explore ideas. None of these strategies works for every writer. But all of them are worth trying. Each requires practice, so don't give up on the strategy if it doesn't work at first. We recommend that you keep your exploratory writing in a journal or in easily identified files in your word processor so you can review it later and test the "staying power" of ideas produced by the different strategies.

Freewriting or Blind Writing

Freewriting is useful at any stage of the writing process. When you freewrite, you put pen to paper and write rapidly *nonstop,* usually ten to fifteen minutes at a stretch. The object is to think of as many ideas as possible without stopping to edit your work. On a computer, freewriters often turn off the monitor so that they can't see the text being produced. Such "blind writing" frees the writer from the urge to edit or correct the text and simply to let ideas roll forth. Some freewriters or blind writers achieve a stream-of-consciousness style, recording their ideas at the very moment they bubble into consciousness, stutters and stammers and all. Others produce more focused chunks, though without clear connections among them. You will probably find your initial reservoir of ideas running out in three to five minutes. If so, force yourself to keep writing or typing. If you can't think of anything to say, write "relax" or "I'm stuck" over and over until new ideas emerge.

Here is an example of a freewrite from a student named Jean, exploring her thoughts about hate speech following a class discussion of the "Machado Case" in which a Los Angeles man, Richard Machado, was convicted for sending e-mail death threats to fifty-nine Asian students at the University of California, Irvine. He sent the e-mails from a campus computer and signed them "Asian hater."

> I was really disturbed in class today when we talked about the Machado case of the man who made e-mail death threats to Asians saying that he would hunt them down and kill them if they did not leave the campus—I think it was in California somewhere—anyway I just shivered and shuddered to think about this creepy guy. I haven't heard anything like this on our campus but after 9/11 a lot of discussions have gotten really heated with people saying hateful things about Arabs and also about Jews. The whole Israeli/Palestinian conflict divides people and creates stereotypes that get really close to hate speech. Do I think hate speech ought to be banned? I don't know it is such a hard question because I can see both sides of this issue. I don't think people should be allowed to use hateful words for races or sexes in class discussions but just banning the words doesn't mean that people still don't feel the same hate. I wish people could just be nicer to each other, but that's relax relax relax what do I think about hate speech? A lot of hate speech can lead to violence it has the effect of making people want to fight and shout rather than conduct real conversations. Hate speech is like the Jerry Springer show instead of an intelligent discussion. But does that mean it should be banned? I don't know. I hope we get to discuss this more in class.

For Class Discussion

Individual task: Choose one of the following controversial claims (or another chosen by your instructor) and freewrite your response to it for five or ten minutes. **Group task:** Working in pairs, in small groups, or as a whole class, share your freewrite with classmates. Don't feel embarrassed if your freewrite is fragmentary or disjointed. Freewrites are not supposed to be finished products; their sole purpose is to generate a flow of thought. The more you practice the technique, the better you will become.

1. A student should report a fellow student who is cheating on an exam or plagiarizing an essay.
2. States should legalize marriages between homosexuals.
3. Sports records achieved by athletes known to have used steroids should be identified with an asterisk as "steroid-aided."
4. Spanking children should be considered child abuse.
5. State and federal governments should legalize hard drugs.
6. It should be illegal for credit card companies to issue credit cards to anyone under twenty-one years of age.
7. It is permissible to use racial profiling for airport screening.
8. Violent video games such as Soldier of Fortune should be made illegal.
9. Rich people are morally obligated to give part of their wealth to the poor.
10. Women should be assigned to combat duty equally with men.

Idea Mapping

Another good technique for exploring ideas is *idea mapping*. When you make an idea map, draw a circle in the center of the page and write some trigger idea (a broad topic, a question, or working thesis statement) in the center of the circle. Then record your ideas on branches and subbranches extending from the center circle. As long as you pursue one train of thought, keep recording your ideas on the branch. But when that line of thinking gives out, start a new branch. Often your thoughts jump back and forth between branches. That's a major advantage of "picturing" your thoughts; you can see them as part of an emerging design rather than as strings of unrelated ideas.

Idea maps usually generate more ideas, though less well-developed ones, than freewrites. Writers who practice both techniques report that each strategy causes them to think about their ideas very differently. When Jean, the student who produced the freewrite on hate speech (p. 57), decided to explore this issue further, she created the idea map shown in Figure 3.1.

For Class Discussion

Choose a controversial issue—national, local, or campus—that's interesting to the class. The instructor will lead a class discussion on the issue, recording ideas on an idea map as they emerge. Your goal is to appreciate the fluidity of idea maps as a visual form of idea generation halfway between an outline and a list.

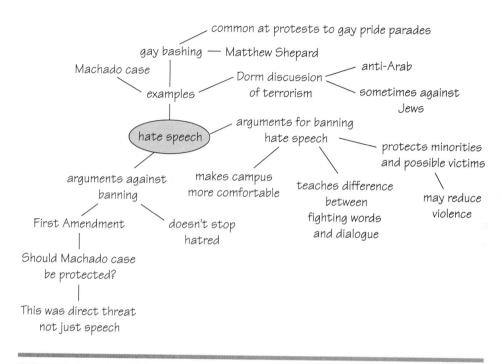

FIGURE 3.1   *Jean's idea map on hate speech*

Playing the Believing and Doubting Game

The believing/doubting game* is an excellent way to imagine views different from your own and to anticipate responses to those views.

As a believer, your role is to be wholly sympathetic to an idea, to listen carefully to it, and to suspend all disbelief. You must identify all the ways in which the idea might appeal to different audiences and all the reasons for believing the idea. The believing game is easy so long as you already accept an idea. But in dealing with ideas that strike you as shaky, false, or threatening, you will find that the believing game can be difficult, even frightening.

The doubting game is the opposite of the believing game. As a doubter, your role is to be judgmental and critical, to find faults with an idea. You do your best to find counterexamples and inconsistencies that undermine it. Again, it is easy to play the doubting game with ideas you reject, but doubting those you've invested in can be threatening.

When you play the believing and doubting game with an assertion, simply write two different chunks, one chunk arguing for the assertion (the believing

---

*A term coined by Peter Elbow, *Writing without Teachers* (New York: Oxford UP, 1973), 147–90.

game) and one chunk opposing it (the doubting game). Freewrite both chunks, letting your ideas flow without censoring. Or, alternatively, make an idea map with believing and doubting branches.

To illustrate the believing and doubting game, we ask you to consider the following classified ad seeking young college women to be egg donors for an infertile couple.

> Infertile professional couple seeks egg donor for artificial insemination. Donor should be slim, athletic, blue-eyed with 1400 SAT's or better. $50,000 and all medical expenses. Must be discrete and willing to sign documents giving up all legal rights to a baby that might be produced.

Here is how one student played the believing and doubting game in response to the assertion "Recent advances in reproductive technology, including the use of egg donors, are good for society."

BELIEVING EXAMPLE

The latest advances in reproductive technology are good for society. Up until now, infertile couples had only adoption to turn to if they wanted a child. Using egg donation enables the parents to feel like real parents because the mother does carry the child. The parents can be a bit more selective about the child they get because egg donors are carefully screened. I think egg donors are more stable and safe than women who carelessly or accidentally get pregnant and give up their babies for adoption. Egg donors can be smart, healthy young women, such as college students. These young women also get an opportunity to make some money. Another point is that women can preserve some of their own eggs from their youth and actually have a child much later in life when they are ready for such a commitment. I can see how egg donation can help infertile couples, young women, and older women.

DOUBTING EXAMPLE

While egg donation sounds promising, I think the supporters of it often leave out the dark side and the moral implications. The process is changing having babies from a natural experience to a completely commercial one. Eggs are bought and judged like any other product. The high prices reaching even tens of thousands of dollars mean that only rich couples will be able to afford the process. The fact that the preferred egg donors have common traits (are Ivy League students, are tall, blonde, and blue eyed) only serves to increase a certain elitism. The donor part has pitfalls too. I can understand the attraction of the large sums of money, but the medical process is not easy. The young women must take fertility drugs and injections to boost their egg production. These drugs may have side effects and long-term complications. I wouldn't want my girlfriend to undergo this process.

Although this writer condemns these medical advances in reproductive technology, he does a good job of trying to sympathize with women who are involved in them. Playing the believing and doubting game has helped him see the issue more complexly.

Return to the ten controversial claims in the For Class Discussion on page 58. **Individual task:** Choose one of the claims and play the believing and doubting game with it by freewriting for five minutes trying to believe the claim and then for five minutes trying to doubt the claim. Or, if you prefer, make an idea map by creating a believing spoke and a doubting spoke off the main hub. Instead of freewriting, enter ideas onto your idea map, moving back and forth between believing and doubting. **Group task:** Share what you produced with members of your group or with the class as a whole.

Repeat the exercise with another claim.

Brainstorming for Pro and Con *Because* Clauses

This activity is similar to the believing and doubting game in that it asks you to brainstorm ideas for and against a controversial assertion. In the believing and doubting game, however, you simply freewrite or make an idea map on both sides of the issue. In this activity, you try to state your reasons for and against the proposition as *because* clauses. The value of doing so is discussed in depth in Chapter 4, which shows how a claim with *because* clauses can form the core of an argument.

Here is an example of how you might create *because* clauses for and against the claim "The recent advances in reproductive technology, including the use of egg donors, are good for society."

PRO

The recent advances in reproductive technology, including the use of egg donors, are good for society.

- because this technology helps couples overcome infertility, which can create damaging stress within a marriage
- because children born through this technology will be really wanted and given loving homes
- because this technology restores hope, thereby supporting marriage and creating loving families
- because this technology gives couples some measure of control over their reproductive options

CON

The recent advances in reproductive technology, including the use of egg donors, are dangerous to society.

- because this technology could lead to situations in which persons have no idea to whom they are genetically related

- because the technology might harm persons such as the egg donors who do not know what the long-term consequences of tampering with their reproductive systems through the use of fertility drugs might be

- because using donor eggs is equivalent to "special ordering" children who may not live up to the parents' expectations (to be smart, tall)

- because the expense of reproductive technology (especially when it results in multiple births) is too large for individuals, insurance companies, or the state to bear

For Class Discussion

Generating *because* clauses like these is an especially productive discussion activity for groups. Once again return to the ten controversial claims in the For Class Discussion exercise on page 58. Select one or more of these claims (or others provided by your instructor) and, working in small groups, generate pro and con *because* clauses supporting and attacking the claim. Share your group's *because* clauses with those of other groups.

Brainstorming a Network of Related Issues

The previous exercise helps you see how certain issues can provoke strong pro-con stances. Occasionally in civic life, an issue is presented to the public in such a pro-con form, as when voters are asked to approve or disapprove a referendum or when a jury must decide the guilt or innocence of a defendant.

But in most contexts, the argumentative situation is more open-ended and fluid. You can easily oversimplify an issue by reducing it to two opposing sides. Because most issues are embedded in a network of subissues, side issues, and larger issues, seeing an issue in pro-con terms can often blind you to other ways to join a conversation. For example, a writer might propose a middle ground between adversarial positions, examine a subissue in more depth, connect an issue to a related side issue, or redefine an issue to place it in a new context.

Consider, for example, the assertion about reproductive technology. Rather than arguing for or against this claim, a writer might focus on reproductive technology in a variety of other ways:

- Who should determine the ethics of reproductive technology? Families? Doctors? Government?

- How can risky physical outcomes such as multiple births (mothers carrying seven and eight babies) be avoided?

- What effect will the new reproductive technologies have on our concepts of motherhood and family?

- In case of divorce, who has legal rights to frozen embryos and other genetic material?

- Will reproductive technology lead to control over the sex and genetic makeup of children? Should it?
- What is the difference between paying someone to donate a kidney (which is illegal) and paying a woman to donate her eggs (which is currently legal)?
- Currently many adopted children want to seek out their birth mothers. Would children born from donated eggs want to seek out their genetic mothers?
- Who should pay for reproductive technology?

For Class Discussion

Working as a whole class or in small groups, choose one or more of the controversial assertions on page 58. Instead of arguing for or against them, brainstorm a number of related issues (subissues, side issues, or larger issues) on the same general subject. For example, brainstorm a number of issues related to the general topics of cheating, gay marriage, women in combat, and so forth.

Shaping Your Argument: Classical Argument as a Planning Tool

We turn now from discovery strategies to organizing strategies. As you begin drafting, you need some sort of plan. How elaborate that plan is varies considerably from writer to writer. Some writers plan extensively before writing; others write extensively before planning. But somewhere along the way, all writers must decide on a structure. This section gives you an overview of a powerful template for initial planning—a structure often called "classical argument" because it follows the conventions of persuasive speeches as taught by ancient rhetoricians.

The Structure of Classical Argument

In traditional Latin terminology, classical argument has the following parts:

- the *exordium*, which gets the audience's attention
- the *narratio*, which provides needed background
- the *propositio*, which introduces the speaker's proposition or thesis
- the *partitio*, which forecasts the main parts of the speech
- the *confirmatio*, which presents arguments supporting the proposition
- the *confutatio*, which refutes opposing views
- the *peroratio*, which sums up the argument, calls for action, and leaves a strong last impression

In slightly homelier terms (see Figure 3.2), writers of classical argument typically begin with a dramatic story or a startling statistic that commands attention. Then they focus the issue, often by stating it directly as a question and perhaps by briefly summarizing opposing views. Next, they contextualize the issue by providing needed background, explaining the immediate context, or defining key terms. They conclude the introduction by presenting the thesis and forecasting the argument's structure.

The body of a classical argument has two major sections—one presenting the writer's own position and the other summarizing and critiquing alternative views. Figure 3.2 shows that the writer's own position comes first. But writers have the option of reversing that order. Where you place the opposing arguments depends on whether you picture an undecided audience who will listen openmindedly to your argument or a resistant audience initially hostile to your views. The more resistant your audience, the more it is advantageous to summarize and respond to opposing views before you present your own argument. Doing so reassures skeptics that you have thoughtfully considered alternative positions, thus reducing their initial hostility to your own argument. In contrast, undecided audiences often benefit from hearing your argument first, before you summarize and respond to alternative views. In Chapter 8, we explain these considerations in more detail and give you additional options for addressing resistant audiences.

Whether you place your own argument before or after your summary and critique of opposing views, this section is usually the longest part of a classical argument. Here writers present the reasons and evidence supporting their claims, typically choosing reasons that tie into their audience's values, beliefs, and assumptions (see the discussion of "warrants" and of "audience-based reasons" in Chapter 5, pp. 91–97, 102–108). Usually each reason is developed in its own paragraph or sequence of paragraphs. When a paragraph introduces a new reason, writers state the reason directly and then proceed to support it with evidence or a chain of ideas. Along the way, writers guide their readers with appropriate transitions.

When summarizing and responding to opposing views, writers have several options. If there are several opposing arguments, writers may summarize all of them together and then compose a single response, or they may summarize and respond to each argument in turn. As we will explain in Chapter 8, writers may respond to opposing views either by refuting them or by conceding to their strengths and shifting to a different field of values where these strengths seem less decisive.

Finally, in their conclusion, writers sum up their argument, often calling for some kind of action, thereby creating a sense of closure and leaving a strong final impression.

For all its strengths, the classical argument may not always be your best model. In some cases, for example, delaying your thesis or ignoring alternative views may be justified (see Chapter 8). Even in these cases, however, the classical argument is a useful planning tool. Its call for a thesis statement and a forecasting statement in the introduction helps you see the whole of your argument in miniature. And by requiring you to summarize and consider opposing views, classical

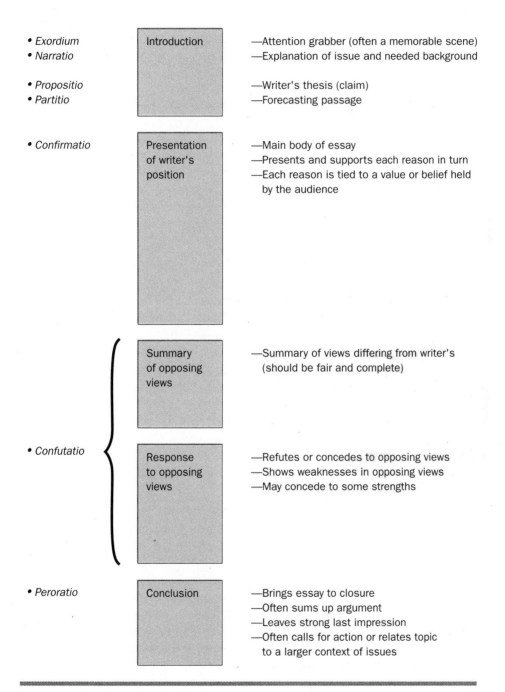

• *Exordium* • *Narratio*	Introduction	—Attention grabber (often a memorable scene) —Explanation of issue and needed background
• *Propositio* • *Partitio*		—Writer's thesis (claim) —Forecasting passage
• *Confirmatio*	Presentation of writer's position	—Main body of essay —Presents and supports each reason in turn —Each reason is tied to a value or belief held by the audience
	Summary of opposing views	—Summary of views differing from writer's (should be fair and complete)
• *Confutatio*	Response to opposing views	—Refutes or concedes to opposing views —Shows weaknesses in opposing views —May concede to some strengths
• *Peroratio*	Conclusion	—Brings essay to closure —Often sums up argument —Leaves strong last impression —Often calls for action or relates topic to a larger context of issues

FIGURE 3.2 *Diagram of a classical argument*

argument alerts you to the limits of your position and to the need for further reasons and evidence. Moreover, the classical argument is a particularly persuasive mode of argument when you address a neutral or undecided audience.

An Illustration of Classical Argument as a Planning Guide

Here is how Jean, the student whose freewrite and idea map on hate speech you have already read, used the structure of classical argument to plan an initial draft of her paper. Note how the classical argument template helps her create a flowchart for her initial ideas.

Jean's Planning Notes Based on Classical Argument

INTRODUCTION

Attention grabber	I'll think of a good opening story about hate speech—maybe the Machado example or the recent anti-gay case on my own campus.
Explanation of issue	I'll give some background on the controversy—how college campuses are trying to figure out ways to ban hate speech without infringing on free speech.
My claim	"Colleges should *not* try to ban hate speech."
Forecasting of structure	I don't know yet the exact structure, but when I do I may need to forecast the structure (I'll come back to this problem).

SUMMARY AND RESPONSE TO OPPOSING VIEWS

Summary of opposing views	I want to put the opposing views first because I picture an audience quite resistant to my views. I'll need to summarize the following arguments that support a ban on hate speech:

- Banning hate speech will lead to a safer environment (show how hate speech promotes violence, etc.).
- Banning hate speech raises consciousness about importance of manners, politeness, and civility in public dialogue.
- Banning hate speech will make life more comfortable for minorities and other potential victims.
- Banning hate speech shows importance of intelligent, reasoned argument, rather than ignorant name-calling, as central to the marketplace of ideas on a college campus.
- Anything else?

Response to opposing views	I'm not sure how I am going to refute these. I actually agree with these arguments. Maybe I can say that I concede to

these arguments, but they have one serious flaw: banning hate speech doesn't ban hate. It just drives hate underground. (I'll have to ask my peer response group if readers need more rebuttal.)

PRESENTATION OF MY OWN ARGUMENT

Development of my own reasons and evidence in support of my claim

So far I have two major reasons why I think campuses should not ban hate speech.

- Reason 1: Hate speech is protected by the First Amendment. (First Amendment protects all sorts of things we don't like such as Nazi marches. Banning hate speech could lead to more and more censorship based on views of those in power.)

- Reason 2: It doesn't help overcome hate (doesn't let people understand each other's anger; doesn't promote dialogue; doesn't help people learn to listen to each other; it's like putting your head in the sand instead of dealing with a problem).

Conclusion

There are better ways to deal with prejudice and hatred.

- Let the ugly incidents happen.
- Create discussions around the ugly incidents.

Once again it is important to understand that classical argument doesn't provide a rigid template for all arguments. Many times you will want to vary substantially from this kind of top-down, thesis-first structure. In some cases, for example, you might want to create a more implicit argument based on stories and personal narrative. In other cases, you might want to omit references to opposing views, or to blend rebuttals into your own argument, or to delay your thesis until the end. But as Jean discovered, the template of classical argument can guide you through the process of producing an argument—hooking your readers' initial interest, focusing your issue and presenting your claim, summarizing and responding to views different from your own, and presenting your own argument.

Discovering Ideas: Two Sets of Exploratory Writing Tasks

The following tasks use exploratory writing to help you generate ideas. The first set of tasks helps you gather ideas early in a writing project either by helping you think of issues to write about or by deepening and complicating your response to readings. The second set of tasks helps you think about your ideas systematically before you compose a first draft.

Set 1: Starting Points

Task 1: Make an Inventory of the Communities to Which You Belong and the Issues That Arise   All of us belong to a variety of communities. For example, you have a classroom community for each course you are taking. Each club or organization has its own community, as does the community where you live (dorm, apartment, your family). Beyond these small communities, you have your campus community and beyond that your city, state, region, nation, and world communities. You may also belong to a work or job community, to a church/ mosque/synagogue community, or to communities related to your hobbies or avocations.

The occasion for argument grows out of your life in these communities—your desire to make a difference on some issue that divides or troubles the community. As an arguer, you might tackle a big issue in your world community (What is the best way to prevent destruction of rain forests?) or a small issue in your dorm (Should quiet hours be enforced?). In your classroom community, you might tackle a practical problem (What should the instructor do about persons coming in late?) or intellectual issues in the discipline itself (Is Frankenstein's monster good or evil? Is gender socially constructed?).

For this task make a list of the communities to which you belong. Then brainstorm controversies in these communities—issues that are being debated or that you would like to see debated. You might find one or more of the following "trigger questions" helpful:

- Persons in my dorm (at work, in the state legislature, at the United Nations) disagree about. . . .
- Our campus (this dorm, my hometown, my worksite, our state, our country) would be a better place if. . . .
- Something that really makes me mad about this campus (my apartment life, city government, our society) is. . . .
- In the career I hope to pursue, X is a serious problem that needs to be addressed.
- Person X believes . . . ; however, I believe. . . .

Task 2: Make an Inventory of Issues That Interest You   The previous task can overwhelm students with the sheer number of issues that surround them. Once you broaden out to the large communities of city, state, nation, and world, the numbers of issues multiply rapidly. Moreover, each large issue has numerous subissues. For this task make an inventory of ten to fifteen possible issues that you would like to explore more deeply and possibly write about. Share your list with classmates, adding their ideas to yours.

Task 3: Choose Several Areas of Controversy for Exploration   For this task choose two or three possible controversies from the list above and explore them through freewriting or idea mapping. Try responding to the following questions: (a) What is my position on this issue and why? (b) What are opposing or alternative positions on this issue? (c) Why do people disagree about this issue? (Do they disagree about the facts of the case? About underlying values, assumptions, and beliefs?) (d) To argue a position on this issue, what evidence do I need to find and what further research will be required?

Task 4: Choose a Local Issue and Explore Its Rhetorical Context   For this task choose a local issue (some situation that you would like to see changed on your campus, in your place of work, or in your town or city) and explore its rhetorical context: (a) What is the situation you would like to change? (b) Who has the power to change that situation? (c) What are the values and beliefs of these decision makers? (d) What obstacles or constraints may prevent these decision makers from acting on your desires? (e) What reasons and evidence would exert the most pressure on these decision makers? (How can you make acting on your proposal a good thing for them?)

Task 5: Identify and Explore Issues That Are Problematic for You· A major assignment often given in argument courses is to write a research-based argument on an issue or problem initially puzzling to you. Perhaps you don't know enough about the issue (for example, establishing international controls on pesticides), or perhaps the issue draws you into an uncomfortable conflict of values (for example, assisted suicide, legalization of drugs, noncriminal incarceration of sexual predators). Your goal for this task is to identify several issues about which you are undecided, to choose one, and to explore your current uncertainty. Why can't you make up your mind on this issue?

Task 6: Deepen Your Response to Readings   This task requires you to read a collection of arguments on an issue and to explore them thoughtfully. As you read the arguments assigned by your instructor, annotate the margins with believing and doubting notes as explained in Chapter 2. Then respond to one or more of the following prompts, using freewriting or idea mapping:

- Why do the writers disagree? Are there disagreements about facts? About underlying values, beliefs, and assumptions?
- Identify "hot spots" in the readings—passages that evoke strong agreement or disagreement, anger, confusion, or any other memorable response—and explore your reaction to these passages.
- Explore the evolution of your thinking as you read and later review the essays. What new questions have they raised? How did your thinking change? Where do you stand now and why?
- If you were to meet one of the authors on a plane or at a coffee shop, what would you say to him or her?

Set 2: Exploration and Rehearsal

The following tasks are designed to help you once you have chosen a topic and begun to clarify your thesis. While these tasks may take two or more hours to complete, the effort pays off by helping you produce a full set of ideas for your rough draft. We recommend using these tasks each time you write an argument for this course.

Task 1   What issue do you plan to address in this argument? Try wording the issue as a one-sentence question. Reword your question in several different ways because each version will frame the issue somewhat differently. Then put a box around your best version of the question.

Task 2   Now write out your tentative answer to the question. This will be your beginning thesis statement or claim. Put a box around this answer. Next write out one or more different answers to your question. These will be alternative claims that a neutral audience might consider. If you don't know your position at this time and wish to use these tasks for thinking through the issue, you can return to Task 2 later.

Task 3   What personal interest do you have in this issue? What are the consequences for you if your argument succeeds or doesn't succeed? How does the issue affect you? Why do you care about it? (Knowing why you care about it might help you get your audience to care about it.)

Task 4   Why is this a controversial issue? Is there insufficient evidence to resolve the issue, or is the evidence ambiguous or contradictory? Are definitions in dispute? Do the parties disagree about basic values, assumptions, or beliefs?

Task 5   Who is the audience that you need to persuade? If your argument calls for an action, who has the power to act on your claim? Can you address these persons of power directly? Or do you need to sway others (such as voters) to exert pressure on persons in power? With regard to your issue, what are the values and beliefs of the audience you are trying to sway?

Task 6   What obstacles or constraints in the social or physical environment prevent your audience from acting on your claim or accepting your beliefs? What are some ways these obstacles can be overcome? If these obstacles cannot be overcome, should you change your claim?

Task 7   In this task you will rehearse the main body of your paper. Using freewriting or idea mapping, think of the main reasons and evidence you could use to sway your intended audience. Brainstorm everything that comes to mind that might help you support your case. Because this section will eventually provide the bulk of your argument, proceed rapidly without worrying whether your argument makes sense. Just get ideas on paper. As you generate reasons and evidence, you are likely to discover gaps in your knowledge. Where could your argument be bolstered by additional data such as statistics, examples, and expert testimony? Where and how will you do the research to fill these gaps?

Task 8   Now reread what you wrote for Tasks 5 and 6, in which you examined your audience's perspective. Role-playing that audience, imagine all the counterarguments members might make. Where does your claim threaten them or oppose their values? What obstacles or constraints in their environment are individuals likely to point to? ("I'd love to act on your claim, but we just don't have the money" or "If we grant your request, it will set a bad precedent.") Brainstorm all the objections your audience might raise to your argument.

Task 9   How can you respond to those objections? Take them one by one and brainstorm possible responses.

Task 10   Finally, explore again why this issue is important. What are its broader implications and consequences? What other issues does it relate to? Thinking of possible answers to these questions may prove useful when you write your introduction or conclusion.

WRITING ASSIGNMENTS
FOR CHAPTERS 1–3

OPTION 1: *An Argument Summary*   Write a 250-word summary of an argument selected by your instructor. Then write a one-sentence summary of the same argument. Use as models the summaries of Lisa Turner's argument on biotech foods in Chapter 2.

OPTION 2: *An Analysis of Sources of Disagreement in a Controversy*   Using as a model the analysis of the controversy between Turner and the Council for Biotechnology Information in Chapter 2, write an analysis of the sources of disagreement in any two arguments that take differing views on the same issue.

OPTION 3: *Evaluating Your Use of Exploratory Writing*   For this option your instructor will assign one or more of the exploratory exercises in Chapter 3 for you to do as homework. Do the tasks as well as you can, submitting your exploratory writing as an exhibit for evidence. Then write a reflective evaluation of how well the assignment worked for you. In your evaluation, address questions such as these:

   A. Did the exercise help you develop ideas? (Why or why not?)
   B. What are examples of some of the ideas you developed?
   C. What did the exercise teach you about the demands of good arguments?
   D. What did the exercise teach you about your own writing and thinking process?

OPTION 4: *Propose a Problem for a Major Course Project*   An excellent major project for an argument course is to research an issue about which you are initially undecided. Your final essay for the course could be an argument in which you take a stand on this issue. Choose one of the issues you listed in "Set 1: Starting Points," Task 5—"I am unable to take a stand on the issue of . . . "—and make this issue a major research project for the course. During the term keep a log of your research activities and be ready, in class discussion or in writing, to explain what kinds of arguments or evidence turned out to be most persuasive in helping you take a stand.

For this assignment, write a short letter to your instructor identifying the issue you have chosen, and explain why you are interested in it and why you can't make up your mind at this time.

Part Two

Principles of Argument

Appealing to the patriotism of citizens and soldiers, this poster for Armed Forces Day 2005, a holiday established in 1949 with the consolidation of all branches of the Armed Forces under the Department of Defense, pays tribute to Americans in military service. The For Class Discussion exercise on page 137 and the discussion of posters on page 176 explore this poster in depth.

4 The Core of an Argument

A Claim with Reasons

An Introduction to the Classical Appeals

Before we examine the structure of arguments, we should explain briefly their social context, which can be visualized as a triangle with interrelated points labeled *message, writer/speaker,* and *audience* (see Figure 4.1). Effective arguments consider all three points on this *rhetorical triangle*. As we will see in later chapters, when you alter one point of the triangle (for example, when you change the audience for whom you are writing), you often need to alter the other points (by restructuring the message itself and perhaps by changing the tone or image you project as writer/speaker). We have created a series of questions based on the "rhetorical triangle" to help you plan, draft, and revise your argument.

Each point on the triangle in turn corresponds to one of the three kinds of persuasive appeals that ancient rhetoricians named *logos, ethos,* and *pathos. Logos* (Greek for "word") refers primarily to the internal consistency and clarity of the message and to the logic of its reasons and support. The impact of *logos* on an audience is referred to as its *logical appeal.*

Ethos (Greek for "character") refers to the credibility of the writer/speaker. *Ethos* is often conveyed through the tone and style of the message, through the care with which the writer considers alternative views, and through the writer's investment in his or her claim. In some cases, it's also a function of the writer's reputation for honesty and expertise independent of the message. The impact of *ethos* on an audience is referred to as its *ethical appeal* or *appeal from credibility.*

Our third term, *pathos* (Greek for "suffering" or "experience"), is often associated with emotional appeal. But *pathos* appeals more specifically to an audience's imaginative sympathies—their capacity to feel and see what the writer feels and sees. Thus, when we turn the abstractions of logical discourse into a palpable and immediate story, we are making a pathetic appeal. While appeals to *logos* and *ethos* can further an audience's intellectual assent to our claim, appeals to *pathos* engage the imagination and feelings, moving the audience to deeper appreciation of the argument's significance.

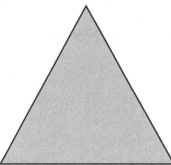

Message
(LOGOS: *How can I make the argument
internally consistent and logical?
How can I find the best reasons and
support them with the best evidence?*)

Audience
(PATHOS: *How can I make the reader
open to my message? How can I best
appeal to my reader's values and
interests? How can I engage my
reader emotionally and imaginatively?*)

Writer or Speaker
(ETHOS: *How can I present myself
effectively? How can I enhance my
credibility and trustworthiness?*)

FIGURE 4.1   *The rhetorical triangle*

A related rhetorical concept, connected to the appeals of *logos*, *ethos*, and *pathos*, is that of *kairos*, from the Greek word for "right time," "season," or "opportunity." This concept suggests that for an argument to be persuasive, its timing must be effectively chosen and its tone and structure in right proportion or measure. You may have had the experience of composing an argumentative e-mail and then hesitating before clicking the "send" button. Is this the right moment to send this message? Is my audience ready to hear what I'm saying? Would my argument be more effective if I waited for a couple of days? If I send this message now, should I change its tone and content? This attentiveness to the unfolding of time is what is meant by *kairos*. We will return to this concept in Chapter 7, when we consider *ethos* and *pathos* in more depth.

Given this background on the classical appeals, let's turn now to *logos*—the logic and structure of arguments.

Issue Questions as the Origins of Argument

At the heart of any argument is an issue, which we can define as a controversial topic area such as "the labeling of biotech foods" or "racial profiling," that gives rise to differing points of view and conflicting claims. A writer can usually focus an issue by asking an issue question that invites at least two alternative answers.

Within any complex issue—for example, the issue of abortion—there are usually a number of separate issue questions: Should abortions be legal? Should the federal government authorize Medicaid payments for abortions? When does a fetus become a human being (at conception? at three months? at quickening? at birth?)? What are the effects of legalizing abortion? (One person might stress that legalized abortion leads to greater freedom for women. Another person might respond that it lessens a society's respect for human life.)

Difference between an Issue Question and an Information Question

Of course, not all questions are issue questions that can be answered reasonably in two or more differing ways; thus not all questions can lead to effective arguments. Rhetoricians have traditionally distinguished between *explication,* which is writing that sets out to inform or explain, and *argumentation,* which sets out to change a reader's mind. On the surface, at least, this seems like a useful distinction. If a reader is interested in a writer's question mainly to gain new knowledge about a subject, then the writer's essay could be considered explication rather than argument. According to this view, the following questions about teenage pregnancy might be called information questions rather than issue questions:

> How does the teenage pregnancy rate in the United States compare with the rate in Sweden? If the rates are different, why?

Although both questions seem to call for information rather than for argument, we believe that the second one would be an issue question if reasonable people disagreed on the answer. Thus, different writers might agree that the teenage pregnancy rate in the United States is four times higher than the rate in Sweden. But they might disagree about why. One writer might emphasize Sweden's practical, secularized sex-education courses in the schools, leading to more consistent use of contraceptives among Swedish teenagers. Another writer might point to the higher use of oral contraceptives among teenage girls in Sweden (partly a result of Sweden's generous national health program) and to less reliance on condoms for preventing pregnancy. Another might argue that moral decay in the United States is at fault. Still another might argue that the American welfare system helps promote teenage pregnancy (a popular conservative argument in the late 1990s). Thus, underneath the surface of what looks like a simple explication of the "truth" is really a controversy.

You can generally tell whether a question is an issue question or an information question by examining your purpose in relationship to your audience. If your relationship to your audience is that of teacher to learner, so that your audience hopes to gain new information, knowledge, or understanding that you possess, then your question is probably an information question. But if your relationship to your audience is that of advocate to decision maker or jury, so that your audience needs to make up its mind on something and is weighing different points of view, then the question you address is an issue question.

Often the same question can be an information question in one context and an issue question in another. Let's look at the following examples:

- How does a diesel engine work? (This is probably an information question since reasonable people who know about diesel engines will probably agree on how they work. This question would be posed by an audience of new learners.)

- Why is a diesel engine more fuel-efficient than a gasoline engine? (This also seems to be an information question since all experts will probably agree on the answer. Once again, the audience seems to be new learners, perhaps students in an automotive class.)

- What is the most cost-effective way to produce diesel fuel from crude oil? (This could be an information question if experts agree and you are addressing new learners. But if you are addressing engineers and one engineer says process X is the most cost-effective and another argues for process Y, then the question is an issue question.)

- Should the present highway tax on diesel fuel be increased? (This is certainly an issue question. One person says yes; another says no; another offers a compromise.)

For Class Discussion

Working as a class or in small groups, try to decide which of the following questions are information questions and which are issue questions. Many of them could be either, depending on the rhetorical context. For such questions, create hypothetical contexts to show your reasoning.

1. What percentage of public schools in the United States are failing?
2. What is the cause of failing public schools in the United States?
3. Should states use high-stakes testing of students to motivate improvement of public schools?
4. What percentage of TV shows during prime-time hours depict violence?
5. What is the effect of violent TV shows on children?
6. What interrogation techniques are permitted for prisoners of war according to current military codes?
7. Is playing loud rap music twenty-four hours per day over prison loudspeakers an instance of torture?
8. Is genetically modified corn safe for human consumption?
9. Should a woman with a newly detected breast cancer opt for a radical mastectomy (complete removal of the breast and surrounding lymph tissue) or

a lumpectomy (removal of the malignant lump without removal of the whole breast)?

10. Is Simone de Beauvoir correct in calling marriage an outdated, oppressive, capitalist institution?

Difference between a Genuine Argument and a Pseudo-Argument

While every argument features an issue question with alternative answers, not every dispute over answers is a rational argument. Rational arguments require two additional factors: (1) reasonable participants who operate within the conventions of reasonable behavior and (2) potentially sharable assumptions that can serve as a starting place or foundation for the argument. Lacking one or both of these conditions, disagreements remain stalled at the level of pseudo-arguments.

Pseudo-Arguments: Fanatical Believers and Fanatical Skeptics

A reasonable argument assumes the possibility of growth and change; disputants may modify their views as they acknowledge strengths in an alternative view or weaknesses in their own. Such growth becomes impossible—and argument degenerates to pseudo-argument—when disputants are fanatically committed to their positions. Consider the case of the fanatical believer or the fanatical skeptic.

Fanatical believers believe that their claims are true because they say so, period. Often fanatical believers follow some party line with knee-jerk predictability, their ideological convictions often shaped by their favorite, not-to-be-disputed texts, Web sites, blogs, or radio shows. Once you've pushed their buttons on global warming, welfare, abortion, gun control, gay marriage, or some other issue, you can expect only a barrage of never-changing pronouncements. Disagreeing with a fanatical believer is like ordering the surf to quiet down. The only response is another crashing wave.

The fanatical skeptic, in contrast, dismisses the possibility of proving anything. So what if the sun has risen every day of recorded history? That's no proof that it will rise tomorrow. Short of absolute proof, which never exists, fanatical skeptics accept nothing. In a world where the most we can hope for is increased audience adherence to our ideas, the fanatical skeptic demands an ironclad, logical demonstration of our claim's rightness. In the presence of fanatical believers or skeptics, then, genuine argument is impossible.

Another Source of Pseudo-Arguments: Lack of Shared Assumptions

A reasonable argument is difficult to conduct unless the participants share common assumptions on which the argument can be grounded. Like axioms in geometry, these shared assumptions serve as the starting point for the argument. Consider the following conversation, in which Randall refuses to accept Rhonda's assumptions:

RHONDA: Smoking should be banned because it causes cancer.

RANDALL: So it causes cancer. What's so bad about that?

RHONDA: Don't be perverse, Randy. Cancer causes suffering and death.

RANDALL: Rhonda, my dear girl, don't be such a twinkie. Suffering and death are just part of the human condition.

RHONDA: But that doesn't make them desirable, especially when they can be avoided.

RANDALL: Perhaps in particular cases they're avoidable for a while, but in the long run, we all suffer and we all die, so who cares if smoking causes what's inevitable anyway?

This, we would suggest, is a doomed argument. Without any shared assumptions (for example, that cancer is bad, that suffering should be minimized and death delayed), there's no "bottom" to this argument, just an endless regress of reasons based on more reasons. While calling assumptions into question is a legitimate way to deepen and complicate our understanding of an issue, the unwillingness to accept any assumption makes argument impossible.

Lack of shared assumptions often dooms arguments about purely personal opinions—for example, someone's claim that opera is boring or that pizza is better than nachos. Of course, a pizza-versus-nachos argument might be possible if the disputants agreed on a criterion such as the value of balanced nutrition. For example, a nutritionist could argue that pizza is better than nachos because it provides more balanced nutrients per calorie. But if one of the disputants responds, "Nah, nachos are better than pizza because nachos taste better," then he makes a different assumption—"My sense of taste is better than your sense of taste." This is a wholly personal standard, an assumption that others are unable to share.

For Class Discussion

The following questions can all be answered in alternative ways. However, not all of them will lead to reasonable arguments. Try to decide which questions will lead to reasonable arguments and which will lead only to pseudo-arguments.

1. Are the *Star Wars* films good science fiction?
2. Is postmodern architecture beautiful?
3. Should cities subsidize professional sports venues?
4. Is this abstract oil painting by a monkey smearing paint on a canvas a true work of art?
5. Are nose rings and tongue studs attractive?

Frame of an Argument: A Claim Supported by Reasons

We said earlier that an argument originates in an *issue question*, which by definition is any question that provokes disagreement about the best answer. When you write an argument, your task is to take a position on the issue and to support it with reasons and evidence. The *claim* of your essay is the position you want your audience to accept. To put it another way, your claim is your essay's thesis statement, a one-sentence summary answer to your issue question. Your task, then, is to make a claim and support it with reasons.

What Is a Reason?

A *reason* (also called a *premise*) is a claim used to support another claim. In speaking or writing, a reason is usually linked to the claim with connecting words such as *because, since, for, so, thus, consequently,* and *therefore,* indicating that the claim follows logically from the reason.

Let's take an example. In one of our recent classes a woman naval ROTC student argued that women should be allowed to serve on submarines. A heated discussion quickly followed, expanding into the more general issue of whether women should be allowed to join military combat units. Here are frameworks the class developed for two alternative positions on that issue:

ONE VIEW

CLAIM: Women should be barred from joining military combat units.

REASON 1: Women for the most part don't have the strength or endurance for combat roles.

REASON 2: Women in close-knit combat units would hurt unit morale by introducing sexual jealousies.

REASON 3: Women haven't been socialized into fighters and wouldn't have the "Kill them with a bayonet" spirit that men can get.

REASON 4: Women would be less reliable to a combat unit if they became pregnant or had to care for infants or small children.

ALTERNATIVE VIEW

CLAIM: Women should be allowed to join combat units in the military.

REASON 1: Millions of women are stronger and more physically fit than most men; women selected for combat duty would have the strength and endurance for the job.

REASON 2:   The image of women as combat soldiers would help society overcome harmful gender stereotyping.

REASON 3:   Women are already seeing direct combat in the Iraq war, where there are no front lines.

REASON 4:   Women would have more opportunities for career advancement in the military if they could serve in combat units.

REASON 5:   Allowing women to serve in combat units promotes equal rights.

Formulating a list of reasons in this way breaks your argumentative task into a series of subtasks. It gives you a frame for building your argument in parts. In the previous example, the frame for the argument supporting women in combat suggests five different lines of reasoning a writer might pursue. A writer might use all five reasons or select only two or three, depending on which reasons would most persuade the intended audience. Each line of reasoning would be developed in its own separate section of the argument.

For example, you might begin one section of your argument with the following sentence: "Women should be allowed to join combat units because they are already seeing combat in the Iraq war, where there are no front lines." You would then provide examples of women engaged in heavy fighting in Iraq even though they are assigned to support units. You would also need to support the unstated assumption that if women are already seeing combat while assigned to support units, they should be allowed to join combat units. (How one articulates and supports the underlying assumptions of an argument will be developed in Chapter 5 when we discuss warrants and backing.) You would then proceed in the same way for each separate section of your argument.

To summarize our point in this section, the frame of an argument consists of a claim (the thesis statement of the essay), which is supported by one or more reasons, which are in turn supported by evidence or sequences of further reasons.

Advantages of Expressing Reasons in *Because* Clauses

Chances are that when you were a child the word *because* contained magical explanatory powers:

DOROTHY: I want to go home now.

TOMMY: Why?

DOROTHY: Because.

TOMMY: Because why?

DOROTHY: Just because.

Somehow *because* seemed decisive. It persuaded people to accept your view of the world; it changed people's minds. Later, as you got older, you discovered that *because* only introduced your arguments and that it was the reasons following *because* that made the difference. Still, *because* introduced you to the powers potentially residing in the adult world of logic.

Of course, there are many other ways to express the logical connection between a reason and a claim. Our language is rich in ways of stating *because* relationships:

- Women shouldn't be allowed to join combat units because they don't have the strength or endurance for combat roles.

- Women don't have the strength or endurance for combat roles. Therefore women should not be allowed to join combat units.

- Women don't have the strength or endurance for combat roles, so they should not be allowed to join combat units.

- One reason why women should not be allowed to join combat units is that they don't have the strength or endurance for combat roles.

- My argument that women should not be allowed to join combat units is based mainly on evidence that women don't have the strength or endurance for combat roles.

Even though logical relationships can be stated in various ways, writing out one or more *because* clauses seems to be the most succinct and manageable way to clarify an argument for oneself. We therefore suggest that sometime in the writing process you create a *working thesis statement* that summarizes your main reasons as *because* clauses attached to your claim.* Just when you compose your own working thesis statement depends largely on your writing process. Some writers like to plan out their whole argument from the start and often compose their working thesis statements with *because* clauses before they write their rough drafts. Others discover their arguments as they write. And sometimes it is a combination of both. For these writers, an extended working thesis statement is something they might write halfway through the composing process as a way of ordering their argument when various branches seem to be growing out of control. Or they might compose a working thesis statement at the very end as a way of checking the unity of the final product.

Whenever you write your extended thesis statement, the act of doing so can be simultaneously frustrating and thought provoking. Composing *because* clauses

---

*A working thesis statement for an argument opposing women in combat units might look like this: *Women should not be allowed to join combat units because they lack the strength, endurance, and "fighting spirit" needed in combat; because being pregnant or having small children would make them unreliable for combat at a moment's notice; and because women's presence would hurt morale of tight-knit combat units.* (A working thesis statement for an argument supporting women in combat is found on p. 85.)

You might not put a bulky thesis statement like this into your essay itself; rather, a working thesis statement is a behind-the-scenes way of summarizing your argument for yourself so that you can see it whole and clear.

can be a powerful discovery tool, causing you to think of many different kinds of arguments to support your claim. But it is often difficult to wrestle your ideas into the *because* clause shape, which sometimes seems to be overly tidy for the complex network of ideas you are trying to work with. Nevertheless, trying to summarize your argument as a single claim with reasons should help you see more clearly what you have to do.

For Class Discussion

Try this group exercise to help you see how writing *because* clauses can be a discovery procedure. Divide into small groups. Each group member should contribute an issue that he or she might like to explore. Discussing one person's issue at a time, help each member develop a claim supported by several reasons. Express each reason as a *because* clause. Then write out the working thesis statement for each person's argument by attaching the *because* clauses to the claim. Finally, try to create *because* clauses in support of an alternative claim for each issue. Recorders should select two or three working thesis statements from the group to present to the class as a whole.

Application of This Chapter's Principles to Your Own Writing

In Chapter 2 we discussed the difficulties of summarizing various types of arguments. Generally, an argument is easiest to summarize when the writer places her thesis in the introduction and uses explicit transitions to highlight the argument's reasons and structural frame. Such arguments are said to have a *self-announcing structure* because they announce their thesis (and sometimes supporting reasons) and forecast their shape at the outset. Such self-announcing arguments typically follow the conventional format of classical argument discussed in Chapter 3. The invention strategies set forth in this chapter—generating parallel *because* clauses and nutshelling them in a working thesis statement—lead naturally to a classical argument with a self-announcing structure. Each *because* clause, together with its supporting evidence, becomes a separate section of the argument.

An argument with an *unfolding structure,* in contrast, is considerably harder to summarize. In an unfolding structure, the thesis is delayed until the end or is unstated and left to be inferred by the reader from a narrative that may be both complex and subtle. As we explain in Chapter 8, unfolding structures can be especially effective for dealing with hostile audiences or with troubling or tangled issues. In contrast, classical arguments are often more effective for neutral or undecided audiences weighing alternative views on a clear-cut issue.*

---

*Instead of the terms *self-announcing* and *unfolding,* rhetoricians sometimes use the terms *closed form* and *open form. Closed-form* structures tell the reader in advance where the argument is headed. In choosing to use a closed form, which forecasts the structure in the introduction, the writer also chooses to follow through with that structure in a straightforward, undeviating way. In contrast, *open-form* structures are like stories or narratives, keeping the reader in suspense about the argument's final destination.

In writing classical arguments, students often ask how much of the argument to summarize in the introduction. Consider the following options. You might announce only your claim:

Women should be allowed to join combat units.

Or you could also forecast a series of parallel reasons:

Women should be allowed to join combat units for several reasons.

Or you could forecast the actual number of reasons:

Women should be allowed to join combat units for five reasons.

Or you could forecast the whole argument:

Women should be allowed to join combat units because they are physically capable of doing the job; because the presence of women in combat units would weaken gender stereotypes; because they are already seeing combat in Iraq; because opening combat units to women would expand their military career opportunities; and because it would advance the cause of civil rights.

Those, of course, are not your only options. If you choose to delay your thesis until the end (a typical kind of unfolding argument), you might place the issue question in the introduction without giving away your own position:

Is the nation well served by allowing women to join combat units?

No formula can tell you how much of your argument to forecast in the introduction. In Chapter 8, we discuss how stating your thesis in the introduction versus withholding it until later can affect your *ethos*. We also show how a delayed thesis argument may be a better option for hostile audiences. It is clear at this point, though, that the more you forecast, the clearer your argument is to your reader, whereas the less you forecast, the more surprising your argument will be. The only general rule is this: Readers sometimes feel insulted by too much forecasting. In writing a self-announcing argument, forecast only what is needed for clarity. In short arguments readers often need only your claim. In longer arguments, however, or in especially complex ones, readers appreciate your forecasting the complete structure of the argument (claim with reasons).

Application of This Chapter's Principles to the Reading of Arguments

When you read a complex argument that lacks explicit forecasting, it is often hard to discern its structural core, to identify its claim, and to sort out its reasons and evidence. The more "unfolding" its structure, the harder it is to see exactly how the writer makes his or her case. Moreover, extended arguments often contain digressions and subarguments. Thus there may be dozens of small interlinked arguments going on inside a slowly unfolding main argument.

When you feel yourself getting lost in an unfolding structure, try converting it to a self-announcing structure. (It might help to imagine that the argument's author must state the argument as a claim with *because* clauses. What working thesis statement might the writer construct?) Begin by identifying the writer's claim. Then ask yourself: What are the one, two, three, or four main lines of argument this writer puts forward to support that claim? State those arguments as *because* clauses attached to the claim. Then compare your *because* clauses with your classmates'. You can expect disagreement—indeed, disagreement can enrich your understanding of a text—because the writer has left it to you to infer her intent. You should, however, find considerable overlap in your responses.

Once you have converted the support for the claim to *because* clauses and reached consensus on them, you will find it much easier to analyze the writer's reasoning, underlying assumptions, and use of evidence.

Conclusion

This chapter has introduced you to the rhetorical triangle with its key concepts of *logos, ethos,* and *pathos.* It has also shown how arguments originate in issue questions, how issue questions differ from information questions, and how arguments differ from pseudo-arguments. At the heart of this chapter we explained that the frame of an argument is a claim supported by reasons. As you generate reasons to support your own arguments, it is often helpful to articulate them as *because* clauses attached to the claim. Finally, we explained how you can apply the principles of this chapter to your own writing and reading of arguments.

In the next chapter we will see how to support a reason by examining its logical structure, uncovering its unstated assumptions, and planning a strategy of development.

5 The Logical Structure of Arguments

In Chapter 4 you learned that the core of an argument is a claim supported by reasons and that these reasons can often be stated as *because* clauses attached to a claim. In the present chapter we examine the logical structure of arguments in more depth.

An Overview of *Logos:* What Do We Mean by the "Logical Structure" of an Argument?

As you will recall from our discussion of the rhetorical triangle, *logos* refers to the strength of an argument's support and its internal consistency. *Logos* is the argument's logical structure. But what do we mean by "logical structure"?

First of all, what we *don't* mean by logical structure is the kind of precise certainty you get in a philosophy class in formal logic. Logic classes deal with symbolic assertions that are universal and unchanging, such as "If all ps are qs and if r is a p, then r is a q." This statement is logically certain so long as p, q, and r are pure abstractions. But in the real world, p, q, and r turn into actual things, and the relationships among them suddenly become fuzzy. For example, p might be a class of actions called "Sexual Harassment," while q could be the class called "Actions That Justify Dismissal from a Job." If r is the class "Telling Off-Color Stories," then the logic of our p–q–r statement suggests that telling off-color stories (r) is an instance of sexual harassment (p), which in turn is an action justifying dismissal from one's job (q).

Now, most of us would agree that sexual harassment is a serious offense that might well justify dismissal from a job. In turn, we might agree that telling off-color stories, if the jokes are sufficiently raunchy and are inflicted on an unwilling audience, constitutes sexual harassment. But few of us would want to say categorically that all people who tell off-color stories are harassing their listeners and ought to be fired. Most of us would want to know the particulars of the case before making a final judgment.

In the real world, then, it is difficult to say that *r*s are always *p*s or that every instance of a *p* results in *q*. That is why we discourage students from using the word *prove* in claims they write for arguments (as in "This paper will prove that euthanasia is wrong"). Real-world arguments seldom *prove* anything. They can only make a good case for something, a case that is more or less strong, more or less probable. Often the best you can hope for is to strengthen the resolve of those who agree with you or weaken the resistance of those who oppose you.

A key difference, then, between formal logic and real-world argument is that real-world arguments are not grounded in abstract, universal statements. Rather, as we shall see, they must be grounded in beliefs, assumptions, or values granted by the audience. A second important difference is that in real-world arguments these beliefs, assumptions, or values are often unstated. So long as writer and audience share the same assumptions, it's fine to leave them unstated. But if these underlying assumptions aren't shared, the writer has a problem.

To illustrate the nature of this problem, consider one of the arguments we introduced in the last chapter.

> Women should be allowed to join combat units because the image of women in combat would help eliminate gender stereotypes.

On the face of it, this is a plausible argument. But the argument is persuasive only if the audience agrees with the writer's assumption that it is a good thing to eliminate gender stereotyping. The writer assumes that gender stereotyping (for example, seeing men as the fighters who are protecting the women and children back home) is harmful and that society would be better off without such fixed gender roles. But what if you believed that some gender roles are biologically based, divinely intended, or otherwise culturally essential and that society should strive to maintain these gender roles rather than dismiss them as "stereotypes"? If such were the case, you might believe as a consequence that our culture should socialize women to be nurturers, not fighters, and that some essential trait of "womanhood" would be at risk if women served in combat. If these were your beliefs, the argument wouldn't work for you because you would reject its underlying assumption. To persuade you with this line of reasoning, the writer would have to show not only how women in combat would help eliminate gender stereotypes but also why these stereotypes are harmful and why society would be better off without them.

The previous core argument ("Women should be allowed to join combat units because the image of women in combat would help eliminate gender stereotypes") is an incomplete logical structure called an *enthymeme*. Its persuasiveness depends on an unstated assumption or belief that the audience must accept. To complete the enthymeme and make it effective, the audience must willingly supply a missing premise—in this case, that gender stereotypes are harmful and should be eliminated. The Greek philosopher Aristotle showed how successful enthymemes, which he considered the main underlying structure of argument, root the speaker's argument in assumptions, beliefs, or values held by the audience. The word *enthymeme* comes from the Greek *en* (meaning "in") and *thumos* (meaning "mind"). Listeners or readers must have "in mind" an assumption, belief, or value that lets them willingly supply the missing premise. If the audience is unwilling to supply the missing premise, then the argument fails. Our point is that successful arguments depend both on what the arguer says and on what the audience already has "in mind."

To clarify the concept of "enthymeme," let's go over this same territory again more slowly, examining what we mean by "incomplete logical structure." The sentence "Women should be allowed to join combat units because the image of women in combat would help eliminate gender stereotypes" is an enthymeme. It combines a claim (women should be allowed to join combat units) with a reason expressed as a *because* clause (because the image of women in combat would help eliminate gender stereotypes). To render this enthymeme logically complete, the audience must willingly supply an unstated assumption—that gender stereotypes are harmful and should be eliminated. If your audience accepts this assumption, then you have a starting place on which to build an effective argument. If your audience doesn't accept this assumption, then you must supply another argument to support it, and so on until you find common ground with your audience.

To sum up:

1. Claims are supported with reasons. You can usually state a reason as a *because* clause attached to a claim (see Chapter 4).

2. A *because* clause attached to a claim is an incomplete logical structure called an enthymeme. To create a complete logical structure from an enthymeme, the unstated assumption (or assumptions) must be articulated.

3. To serve as an effective starting point for the argument, this unstated assumption should be a belief, value, or principle that the audience grants.

Let's illustrate this structure by putting the previous example—plus a new one—into schematic form.

INITIAL ENTHYMEME: Women should be allowed to join combat units because the image of women in combat would help eliminate gender stereotypes.

CLAIM: Women should be allowed to join combat units.

STATED REASON: because the image of women in combat would help eliminate gender stereotypes

UNSTATED ASSUMPTION: Gender stereotypes are harmful and should be eliminated.

INITIAL ENTHYMEME: Cocaine and heroin should be legalized because legalization would eliminate the black market in drugs.

CLAIM: Cocaine and heroin should be legalized.

STATED REASON: because legalization would eliminate the black market in drugs

UNSTATED ASSUMPTION: An action that eliminates the black market in drugs is good.

For Class Discussion

Working individually or in small groups, identify the claim, stated reason, and unstated assumption that completes each of the following enthymemic arguments.

EXAMPLE:

Rabbits make good pets because they are gentle.

CLAIM: Rabbits make good pets.

STATED REASON: because they are gentle

UNSTATED ASSUMPTION: Gentle animals make good pets.

1. We shouldn't elect Joe as committee chair because he is too bossy.
2. Drugs should not be legalized because legalization would greatly increase the number of drug addicts.
3. You should shop at Wal-Mart because they have consistently low prices.
4. You should not shop at Wal-Mart because they do not provide health benefits for most workers.
5. Airport screeners should use racial profiling because doing so will increase the odds of stopping terrorists.
6. Racial profiling should not be used by airport screeners because it violates a person's civil rights.
7. We should strengthen the Endangered Species Act because doing so will preserve genetic diversity on the planet.
8. The Endangered Species Act is too stringent because it severely damages the economy.

9. Embryonic stem cell research should be supported because such research may lead to the cures of devastating diseases.

10. Embryonic stem cell research is unethical because it violates the inherent dignity of human embryos.

Adopting a Language for Describing Arguments: The Toulmin System

Understanding a new field usually requires us to learn a new vocabulary. For example, if you were taking biology for the first time, you'd have to memorize dozens and dozens of new terms. Luckily, the field of argument requires us to learn a mere handful of new terms. A particularly useful set of argument terms, one we'll be using occasionally throughout the rest of this text, comes from philosopher Stephen Toulmin. In the 1950s, Toulmin rejected the prevailing models of argument based on formal logic in favor of a very audience-based courtroom model.

Toulmin's courtroom model differs from formal logic in that it assumes that (1) all assertions and assumptions are contestable by "opposing counsel" and that (2) all final "verdicts" about the persuasiveness of the opposing arguments will be rendered by a neutral third party, a judge or jury. Keeping in mind the "opposing counsel" forces us to anticipate counterarguments and to question our assumptions. Keeping in mind the judge and jury reminds us to answer opposing arguments fully, without rancor, and to present positive reasons for supporting our case as well as negative reasons for disbelieving the opposing case. Above all else, Toulmin's model reminds us not to construct an argument that appeals only to those who already agree with us. In short, it helps arguers tailor arguments to their audiences.

The system we use for analyzing arguments combines Toulmin's language with Aristotle's concept of the enthymeme. It builds on the system you have already been practicing. We simply need to add a few key terms from Toulmin. The first term is Toulmin's *warrant*, the name we will now use for the unstated assumption that turns an enthymeme into a complete logical structure. For example:

INITIAL ENTHYMEME: Women should be allowed to join combat units because the image of women in combat would help eliminate gender stereotypes.

CLAIM: Women should be allowed to join combat units.

STATED REASON: because the image of women in combat would help eliminate gender stereotypes

WARRANT: Gender stereotypes are harmful and should be eliminated.

INITIAL ENTHYMEME: Cocaine and heroin should be legalized because legalization would eliminate the black market in drugs.

CLAIM: Cocaine and heroin should be legalized.

STATED REASON: because legalization would eliminate the black market in drugs

WARRANT: An action that eliminates the black market in drugs is good.

Toulmin derives his term *warrant* from the concept of "warranty" or "guarantee." The warrant is the value, belief, or principle that the audience has to hold if the soundness of the argument is to be guaranteed or warranted. We sometimes make similar use of this word in ordinary language when we say, "That is an unwarranted conclusion," meaning one has leapt from information about a situation to a conclusion about that situation without any sort of general principle to justify or "warrant" that move. Thus if we argue that legalizing hard drugs is good because doing so will end the black market, we depend on our readers' supplying the warrant that "eliminating the black market is good." It is this underlying belief that warrants or guarantees the argument.

But arguments need more than claims, reasons, and warrants. These are simply one-sentence statements—the frame of an argument, not a developed argument. To flesh out our arguments and make them convincing, we need what Toulmin calls *grounds* and *backing*. Grounds are the supporting evidence—facts, data, statistics, testimony, or examples—that cause you to make a claim in the first place or that you produce to justify a claim in response to audience skepticism. Toulmin suggests that grounds are "what you have to go on" in an argument. In short, they are collectively all the evidence you use to support a reason. It sometimes helps to think of grounds as the answer to a "How do you know that . . . ?" question preceding a reason. (How do you know that letting women into combat units would help eliminate gender stereotypes? How do you know that legalizing drugs will end the black market?) Here is how grounds fit into our emerging argument schema.

CLAIM: Women should be allowed to join combat units.

STATED REASON: because the image of women in combat would help eliminate gender stereotypes

GROUNDS: data and evidence showing that a chief stereotype of women is that they are soft and nurturing whereas men are tough and aggressive. The image of women in combat gear packing a rifle, driving a tank, firing a machine gun from a foxhole, or radioing for artillery support would shock people into seeing women not as "soft and nurturing" but as equal to men.

CLAIM: Cocaine and heroin should be legalized.

STATED REASON: because legalization would eliminate the black market in drugs

GROUNDS: data and evidence showing how legalizing cocaine and heroin would eliminate the black market (statistics, data, and examples describing the size and effect of the current black market, followed by arguments showing how selling cocaine and heroin legally in state-controlled stores would lower the price and eliminate the need to buy them from drug dealers)

In many cases, successful arguments require just these three components: a claim, a reason, and grounds. If the audience already accepts the unstated assumption behind the reason (the warrant), then the warrant can safely remain in the background unstated and unexamined. But if there is a chance that the audience will question or doubt the warrant, then the writer needs to back it up by providing an argument in its support. *Backing* is the argument that supports the warrant. Backing answers the question "How do you know that . . . ?" or "Why do you believe that . . . ?" prefixed to the warrant. (Why do you believe that gender stereotyping is harmful? Why do you believe that the benefits of ending the black market outweigh the costs of legalizing cocaine and heroin?) Here is how *backing* is added to our schema:

WARRANT: Gender stereotypes are harmful and should be eliminated.

BACKING: arguments showing how the existing stereotype of soft and nurturing women and tough and aggressive men is harmful to both men and women (examples of how the stereotype keeps men from developing their nurturing sides and women from developing autonomy and power; examples of other benefits that come from eliminating gender stereotypes include more egalitarian society, no limits on what persons can pursue, deeper respect for both sexes)

WARRANT: An action that eliminates the black market in drugs is good.

BACKING: an argument supporting the warrant by showing why eliminating the black market in drugs is good (statistics and examples about the ill effects of the black market, data on crime and profiteering, evidence that huge profits make drug dealing more attractive than ordinary jobs, the high cost of crime created by the black market, the cost to taxpayers of waging the war against drugs, the high cost of prisons to house incarcerated drug dealers)

Toulmin's system next asks us to imagine how a resistant audience would try to refute our argument. Specifically, the adversarial audience might challenge our reason and grounds by showing how letting women become combat soldiers wouldn't do much to end gender stereotyping or how legalizing drugs would *not* end the black market. Or the adversary might attack our warrant and backing by showing how some gender stereotypes are worth keeping, or how the negative consequences of legalizing drugs might outweigh the benefit of ending the black market.

In the case of the argument supporting women in combat or of legalizing heroin and cocaine, an adversary might offer one or more of the following rebuttals:

CONDITIONS OF REBUTTAL

Rebutting the reasons and grounds: Evidence that letting women join combat units wouldn't overcome gender stereotyping (very few women would want to join combat units; those who did would be considered freaks; most girls would still identify with Barbie dolls, not with female infantry).

Rebutting the warrant and backing: Arguments showing that it is important to maintain gender role differences because they are biologically based, divinely inspired, or otherwise important culturally; women should be nurturers and mothers, not fighters; essential nature of "womanhood" sullied by putting women in combat.

Rebutting the reasons and grounds: Arguments showing that legalizing cocaine and heroin would not eliminate the black market in drugs (perhaps taxes on the drugs would keep the costs above black market prices; perhaps new kinds of illegal designer drugs would be developed and sold on the black market).

Rebutting the warrant and backing: Arguments showing that the costs of eliminating the black market outweigh the benefits: the number of new drug users and addicts would be unacceptably high; our social structure would have too many harmful changes; the health and economic costs of treating drug addiction would be too high; the consequences to families and communities resulting from addiction or erratic behavior during drug-induced "highs" would be too great.

As these examples show, adversaries can question an argument's reasons and grounds or its warrant and backing or sometimes both. Conditions of rebuttal remind writers to look at their arguments from the perspective of skeptical readers.

Toulmin's final term, used to limit the force of a claim and indicate the degree of its probable truth, is *qualifier*. The qualifier reminds us that real-world arguments almost never prove a claim. We may say things like "very likely," "probably," or "maybe" to indicate the strength of the claim we are willing to draw from our grounds and warrant. Thus if there are exceptions to your warrant or if your grounds are not very strong, you will have to qualify your claim. For example, you might say, "Except in rare cases, women should not be allowed in combat units," or "With full awareness of the potential dangers, I suggest we consider the option of legalizing drugs as a way of ending the ill effects of the black market."

Although the system just described might at first seem complicated, it is actually fairly easy to use after you've had some opportunity to practice. The following chart will help you review the terms:

ORIGINAL ENTHYMEME: your claim with *because* clause

CLAIM: the point or position you are trying to get your audience to accept

STATED REASON: your *because* clause;* your reasons are the subordinate claims you make in support of your main claim

GROUNDS: the evidence (data, facts, testimony, statistics, examples) supporting your stated reason

WARRANT: the unstated assumption behind your enthymeme; the statement of belief, value, principle, and so on, that, when accepted by an audience, warrants or underwrites your argument

BACKING: evidence or other argumentation supporting the warrant (if the audience already accepts the warrant, then backing is usually not needed, but if the audience doubts the warrant, then backing is essential)

CONDITIONS OF REBUTTAL: your acknowledgment of the ways that skeptics might challenge your argument, show its weaknesses, or identify conditions under which it does not hold; adversaries can question either your reason and grounds or your warrant and backing

QUALIFIER: words or phrases limiting the force of your claim

To help you practice using these terms, here is another example.

INITIAL ENTHYMEME: Women should be barred from combat duty because the presence of women would harm unit morale.

CLAIM: Women should be barred from combat duty.

STATED REASON: because the presence of women would harm unit morale

GROUNDS: evidence and examples of how the presence of women would lead to romantic or sexual relationships and create sexual competition and

---

*Most arguments have more than one *because* clause or reason in support of a claim. Each enthymeme thus develops only one line of reasoning, one piece of your whole argument.

jealousy; evidence that male bonding is difficult when women are present; fear that a woman wouldn't be strong enough to carry a wounded buddy off a battlefield, etc.; fear that men couldn't endure watching a woman with her legs blown off in a minefield

WARRANT: Combat units need high morale to function effectively.

BACKING: arguments supporting the warrant by showing that combat soldiers have to have an utmost faith in buddies to do their job; anything that disrupts male bonding will make the unit less likely to stick together in extreme danger or endure being prisoners of war; examples of how unit cohesion is what makes a fighting unit able to withstand battle

CONDITIONS OF REBUTTAL

Rebutting the reason and grounds: arguments that letting women join combat units would *not* harm unit morale (times are changing rapidly; men are used to working professionally with women; current Iraq war has women integrated into support units that actually see some combat; Iraq war has made men more used to the idea of wounded female soldiers; examples of successful mixed-gender sports teams and mountain-climbing teams; example of women astronauts working in close quarters with men; arguments that sexual and romantic liaisons would be forbidden and sexual activity punished; after a period of initial discomfort, men and women would overcome modesty about personal hygiene, etc.)

Rebutting the warrant and backing: arguments that unit morale is not as important for combat efficiency as are training and discipline; unit morale is not as important as promoting women's rights; men will have to learn to deal with the presence of women and treat them as fellow soldiers; men can learn to act professionally even if their morale is lower

QUALIFIER: In many cases the presence of women would hurt morale.

For Class Discussion

Working individually or in small groups, imagine that you have to write arguments developing the ten enthymemes listed in the For Class Discussion exercise on pages 90–91. Use the Toulmin schema to help you determine what you need to consider when developing each enthymeme. As an example, we have applied the Toulmin schema to the first enthymeme.

ORIGINAL ENTHYMEME: We shouldn't elect Joe as committee chair because he is too bossy.

CLAIM: We shouldn't elect Joe as committee chair.

STATED REASON: because he is too bossy

GROUNDS: various examples of Joe's bossiness; testimony about his bossiness from people who have worked with him

WARRANT: Bossy people make bad committee chairs.

BACKING: arguments showing that other things being equal, bossy people tend to bring out the worst rather than the best in those around them; bossy people tend not to ask advice, make bad decisions; etc.

CONDITIONS OF REBUTTAL: *Rebuttal of reason and grounds:* perhaps Joe isn't really bossy (counterevidence of Joe's cooperativeness and kindness; testimony that Joe is easy to work with; etc.)

Rebuttal of the warrant and backing: perhaps bossy people sometimes make good chairpersons (arguments showing that at times a group needs a bossy person who can make decisions and get things done); perhaps Joe has other traits of good leadership that outweigh his bossiness (evidence that, despite his bossiness, Joe has many other good leadership traits such as high energy, intelligence, charisma, etc.)

QUALIFIER: In most circumstances, bossy people make bad committee chairs.

Using Toulmin's Schema to Determine a Strategy of Support

Having introduced you to Toulmin's terminology for describing the logical structure of arguments, we can turn directly to a discussion of how to use these concepts for developing your own arguments. As we have seen, the claim, supporting reasons, and warrant form the frame for a line of reasoning. The majority of words in an argument, however, are devoted to grounds and backing—the supporting sections that develop the argument frame.

For an illustration of how a writer can use the Toulmin schema to generate ideas for an argument, consider the following case. In April 2005, the Texas house of representatives passed a bill banning "sexually suggestive" cheerleading. Across the nation, night show comics poked fun at the bill, while newspaper editorialists debated its wisdom and constitutionality. In one of our classes, however, several students, including one who had earned a high school varsity letter in competitive cheerleading, defended the bill by contending that provocative dance moves and skimpy uniforms hurt the athletic image of cheerleading that many female cheerleaders are trying to promote. In the following example, which draws on ideas developed in class discussion, we create a hypothetical student writer (we'll call her Chandale) who argues in defense of the Texas bill. Chandale wants to write a short newspaper editorial rebutting those who mocked the bill. Chandale's main line of reasoning is based on the following enthymeme:

> The Texas cheerleading bill to ban suggestive dancing should be supported because banning suggestive dancing will help promote a healthy view of female cheerleaders as athletes.

The grounds for this argument will be all the evidence that Chandale can muster to show that cheerleading is a rigorous athletic activity and that sexually suggestive dance routines hurt this athletic image. The warrant for this argument is that we should support the view of female cheerleaders as athletes. Here are Chandale's brainstorming notes using the Toulmin schema.

CHANDALE'S PLANNING NOTES USING THE TOULMIN SCHEMA

Claim: The Texas cheerleading bill to ban suggestive dancing should be supported.

Stated Reason: because banning suggestive dancing will help promote a healthy view of female cheerleaders as athletes

Grounds: What is my evidence here? What facts and observations can I draw on to show that cheerleading is an athletic activity?

- Cheerleaders at my high school are carefully chosen for their stamina and skill after exhausting two-week tryouts.
- We begin all practices with a mile run and an hour of grueling warm-up exercises—also expected to work out on our own for at least an hour on weekends and on days without practice.
- We learned all sorts of competitive routines and stunts consisting of lifts, tosses, flips, catches, and gymnastic moves. This requires athletic ability! We'd practice these stunts for hours each week.
- Throughout the year cheerleaders have to attend practices, camps, and workshops to learn new routines and stunts.
- Our squad competed in competitions around the state.
- Competitive cheerleading is a growing movement across the country—University of Maryland has made it a varsity sport for women.
- Skimpy uniforms and suggestive dance moves destroy this image—these moves make women eye candy like the Dallas Cowboys cheerleaders—entertaining objects to ogle.

Warrant: We should support the view of female cheerleaders as athletes.

Backing: How can I support this warrant? How can I make the case that it is good to see cheerleaders as athletes rather than as eye candy?

- Athletic competition builds self-esteem, independence, a powerful sense of achievement—contributes to health, strength, conditioning.

- Competitive cheerleading is one of the few sports where teams are made up of both men and women (Why is this good? Should I use this?).

- The suggestive dance moves turn women into sex objects whose function is to be gazed at by men—suggests that women's value is based on their beauty and sex appeal.

- We are talking about HIGH SCHOOL cheerleading—very bad early influence on girls to model themselves on Dallas Cowboys cheerleaders or sexy MTV videos of rock stars or popular film images of cheerleaders like those in *American Beauty* and *Bring It On.*

- Junior high girls want to do what senior high girls do—suggestive dance moves promote sexuality way too early.

Conditions of Rebuttal: Would anybody try to rebut my reasons and grounds that cheerleading is an athletic activity?

- No. I think it is obvious that cheerleading is an athletic activity once they see my evidence.

- However, they might not think of cheerleading as a sport. They might say that the University of Maryland just declared it a sport as a cheap way to meet Title IX federal rules to have more women's sports. I'll have to make sure that I show this is really a sport.

- They also might say that competitive cheerleading shouldn't be encouraged because it is too dangerous—lots of serious injuries including paralysis have been caused by mistakes in doing flips, lifts, and tosses. If I include this, maybe I could say that other sports are dangerous also—and it is in fact danger that makes this sport so exciting.

Would anyone doubt my warrant and backing that it is good to see female cheerleaders as athletes?

- Yes, all those people who laughed at the Texas legislature think that people are being too prudish and that banning suggestive dance moves violates free expression. I'll need to make my case that it is bad for young girls to see themselves as sex objects too early.

In her notes, the information Chandale lists under "grounds" is what she sees as the facts of the case—the hard data she will use as evidence to support her contention that cheerleading is an athletic activity. The paragraph that follows shows how this argument might look when placed into written form.

FIRST PART OF CHANDALE'S ARGUMENT

Claim and stated reason

Although critics have made fun of the Texas legislature's desire to ban "suggestive" dance moves from cheerleading routines, I applaud their action because skimpy outfits and provocative dance routines undermine a healthy view of female cheerleaders as athletes. I was lucky enough to attend a high school where cheerleading is a sport, and I earned a varsity letter as a cheerleader. To get

Grounds (evidence in support of stated reason)

on my high school's cheerleading squad, students have to go through an exhausting two-week tryout of workouts and instruction in the basic routines; then they are chosen based on their stamina and skill. Once on the squad, cheerleaders begin all practices with a mile run and an hour of grueling warm-up exercises and are expected to exercise on their own on weekends. As a result of this regimen, cheerleaders achieve and maintain a top level of physical fitness. In addition, to get on the squad, students must be able to do handstands, cartwheels, handsprings, high jumps, and the splits. Each year the squad builds up to its complex routines and stunts consisting of lifts, tosses, flips, catches, and gymnastic moves that only trained athletes can do. In tough competitions at the regional and state levels, the cheerleading squad demonstrates its athletic talent. This view of cheerleading as a competitive sport is also spreading to colleges. As reported recently in a number of newspapers, the University of Maryland has made cheerleading a varsity sport, and many other universities are following suit. Athletic performance of this caliber is a far cry from the sexy dancing that many high school girls often associate with cheerleading. By banning suggestive dancing in cheerleading routines, the Texas legislature creates an opportunity for schools to emphasize the athleticism of cheerleading.

As you can see, Chandale has plenty of evidence for arguing that competitive cheerleading is an athletic activity quite different from sexy dancing. But how effective is this argument as it stands? Is this all she needs? The Toulmin schema encourages writers to include—if needed for the intended audience—explicit development of their warrants and backing as well as attention to conditions for rebuttal. Because the overwhelming national response to the Texas law was ridicule at the perceived prudishness of the legislators, Chandale decides to expand her argument as follows:

CONTINUATION OF CHANDALE'S ARGUMENT

Warrant and backing

Whether we see cheerleading as a sport or as sexy dancing is an important issue, especially for women. The suggestive dance moves that many high school cheerleaders now try to incorporate into their routines show that these girls' role models are the Dallas Cowboys cheerleaders or the latest pop star singers in MTV videos. Popular films featuring high school cheerleaders such as *American Beauty* (1999) and *Bring It On* (2000) have also contributed to the image of young female cheerleaders entertaining guys and older men. It is unhealthy and demeaning for high school–age cheerleaders (and the junior high girls who emulate them) to learn to measure their own value by their beauty and sex appeal. The sexually saturated culture already pushes girls and women to this destructive self-image as we can see by the marketing of suggestive clothing to little girls. It would be far healthier, both physically and psychologically, if high school cheerleaders were identified as athletes, just like the athletes performing in the sports for which they are cheering. For women and men both, competitive cheerleading can build self-esteem, pride in teamwork, and a powerful sense of achievement, as well as promote health, strength, and fitness.

Response to conditions of rebuttal

Some people might object to competitive cheerleading by saying that cheerleading isn't really a sport. Some have accused the University of Maryland of making cheerleading a varsity sport only as a cheap way of meeting Title IX requirements. But anyone who has watched competitive cheerleading, and imagined what it would be like to be thrown thirty feet into the air, knows instinctively that this is a sport indeed. In fact, other persons might object to competitive cheerleading because it is too dangerous with potential for very severe injuries including paralysis. Obviously the sport is dangerous—but so are many sports, including football, gymnastics, diving, or trampoline. The danger and difficulty of the sport is part of its appeal. Part of what can make cheerleaders as athletes better role models for girls than cheerleaders as erotic dancers is the courage and training needed for success. Of course, the Texas legislators might not have had athleticism in mind when they banned suggestive dancing. They might only have been promoting their vision of morality. But at stake are the role models we set for young girls. I'll pick an athlete over a Dallas Cowboys cheerleader every time.

Our example suggests how a writer can use the Toulmin schema to generate ideas for an argument and to brainstorm possible kinds of evidence that constitutes the grounds (for the stated reason) or backing (for the warrant) of an argument. For evidence, Chandale drew primarily on her personal experiences as a cheerleader/athlete and on her cultural knowledge of the Dallas Cowboys cheerleaders, MTV videos, and popular films. She also drew on her reading of a newspaper article about the University of Maryland's making cheerleading a varsity sport. (In an academic paper rather than a newspaper editorial, she would need to document these sources through formal citations.)

In general, the evidence you use for support can come from your own personal experiences and observations, from field research such as interviews or questionnaires, or from reading and library or Internet research. Although many arguments depend on your skill at research, many can be supported wholly or in part from your own personal experiences, so don't neglect the wealth of evidence from your own life when searching for data. Chapter 6 is devoted to a more detailed discussion of evidence in arguments.

For Class Discussion

1. Working individually or in small groups, consider ways you could use evidence to support the stated reason in each of these following partial arguments.

   a. Another reason to oppose a state sales tax is that it is so annoying.

    b. Rap music has a bad influence on teenagers because it promotes disrespect for women.

    c. Professor X is an outstanding teacher because he (she) generously spends so much time outside of class counseling students with personal problems.

2. Now create arguments to support the warrants in each of the partial arguments in exercise 1. The warrants for each of the arguments are stated below.

    a. Support this warrant: We should oppose taxes that are annoying.

    b. Support this warrant: It is bad to promote disrespect for women.

    c. Support this warrant: Time spent counseling students with personal problems is an important criterion for identifying outstanding teachers.

3. Using Toulmin's conditions of rebuttal, work out a strategy for refuting either the stated reasons or the warrants or both in each of the arguments above.

The Power of Audience-Based Reasons

As we have seen, both Aristotle's concept of the enthymeme and Toulmin's concept of the warrant focus on the arguer's need to create what we will now call "audience-based reasons." Whenever you ask whether a given piece of writing is persuasive, the immediate rejoinder should always be "Persuasive to whom?" What seems like a good reason to you may not be a good reason to others. Finding audience-based reasons means finding arguments whose warrants the audience will accept—that is, arguments effectively rooted in your audience's beliefs and values.

Difference between Writer-Based and Audience-Based Reasons

To illustrate the difference between writer-based and audience-based reasons, consider the following hypothetical case. Suppose you believed that the government should build a dam on the nearby Rapid River—a project bitterly opposed by several environmental groups. Which of the following two arguments might you use to address environmentalists?

1. The government should build a dam on the Rapid River because the only alternative power sources are coal-fired or nuclear plants, both of which pose greater risk to the environment than a hydroelectric dam.

2. The government should build a hydroelectric dam on the Rapid River because this area needs cheap power to attract heavy industry.

Clearly, the warrant of Argument 1 ("Choose the source of power that poses least risk to the environment") is rooted in the values and beliefs of environmentalists, whereas the warrant of Argument 2 ("Growth of industry is good") is likely to make them wince. To environmentalists, new industry means more congestion, more smokestacks, and more pollution. However, Argument 2 may appeal to out-of-work laborers or to the business community, to whom new industry means more jobs and a booming economy.

From the perspective of logic alone, Arguments 1 and 2 are both sound. They are internally consistent and proceed from reasonable premises. But they will affect different audiences very differently. Neither argument proves that the government should build the dam; both are open to objection. Passionate environmentalists, for example, might counter Argument 1 by asking why the government needs to build any power plant at all. They could argue that energy conservation would obviate the need for a new power plant. Or they might argue that building a dam hurts the environment in ways unforeseen by dam supporters. Our point, then, isn't that Argument 1 will persuade environmentalists. Rather, our point is that Argument 1 will be more persuasive than Argument 2 because it is rooted in beliefs and values that the intended audience shares.

Let's consider a second example by returning to Chapter 1 and student Gordon Adams's petition to waive his math requirement. Gordon's central argument, as you will recall, was that as a lawyer he would have no need for algebra. In Toulmin's terms, Gordon's argument looks like this:

CLAIM: I should be exempted from the algebra requirement.

STATED REASON: because in my chosen field of law I will have no need for algebra

GROUNDS: testimony from lawyers and others that lawyers never use algebra

WARRANT: (largely implicit in Gordon's argument) General education requirements should be based on career utility (that is, if a course isn't needed for a particular student's career, it shouldn't be required).

BACKING: (not provided) arguments that career utility should be the chief criterion for requiring general education courses

In our discussions of this case with students and faculty, students generally vote to support Gordon's request, whereas faculty generally vote against it. And in fact, the University Standards Committee rejected Gordon's petition, thus delaying his entry into law school.

Why do faculty and students differ on this issue? Mainly they differ because faculty reject Gordon's warrant that general education requirements should serve students' individual career interests. Most faculty believe that general education courses, including math, provide a base of common learning that links us to the past and teaches us modes of understanding useful throughout life.

Gordon's argument thus challenges one of college professors' most cherished beliefs—that the liberal arts and sciences are innately valuable. Further, it threatens his immediate audience, the committee, with a possible flood of student requests to waive other general education requirements on the grounds of their irrelevance to a particular career choice.

How might Gordon have created a more persuasive argument? In our view, Gordon might have prevailed had he accepted the faculty's belief in the value of the math requirement and argued that he had fulfilled the "spirit" of that requirement through alternative means. He could have based his argument on an enthymeme like this:

> I should be exempted from the algebra requirement because my experience as a contractor and inventor has already provided me with equivalent mathematical knowledge.

Following this audience-based approach, he would drop all references to algebra's uselessness for lawyers and expand his discussion of the mathematical savvy he acquired on the job. This argument would honor faculty values and reduce the faculty's fear of setting a bad precedent. Few students are likely to have Gordon's background, and those who do could apply for a similar exemption without threatening the system. Again, this argument might not have won, but it would have gotten a more sympathetic hearing.

For Class Discussion

Working in groups, decide which of the two reasons offered in each instance would be more persuasive to the specified audience. Be prepared to explain your reasoning to the class. Write out the implied warrant for each *because* clause and decide whether the specific audience would likely grant it.

1. Audience: a beleaguered parent
   a. I should be allowed to stay out until 2 A.M. because all my friends do.
   b. I should be allowed to stay out until 2 A.M. because only if I'm free to make my own decisions will I mature.
2. Audience: a prospective employer
   a. I would be a good candidate for a summer job at the Happy Trails Dude Ranch because I have always wanted to spend a summer in the mountains and because I like to ride horses.
   b. I would be a good candidate for a summer job at the Happy Trails Dude Ranch because I am a hard worker, because I have had considerable experience serving others in my volunteer work, and because I know how to make guests feel welcome and relaxed.
3. Audience: people who oppose the present grading system on the grounds that it is too competitive

   a. We should keep the present grading system because it prepares people for the dog-eat-dog pressures of the business world.

   b. We should keep the present grading system because it tells students that certain standards of excellence must be met if individuals are to reach their full potential.

4. Audience: young people ages fifteen to twenty-five

   a. You should become a vegetarian because an all-vegetable diet is better for your heart than a meaty diet.

   b. You should become a vegetarian because that will help eliminate the suffering of animals raised in factory farms.

5. Audience: conservative proponents of "family values"

   a. Same-sex marriages should be legalized because doing so will promote public acceptance of homosexuality.

   b. Same-sex marriages should be legalized because doing so will make it easier for gay people to establish and sustain long-term, stable relationships.

Finding Audience-Based Reasons: Asking Questions about Your Audience

As the preceding exercise makes clear, reasons are most persuasive when linked to your audience's values. This principle seems simple enough, yet it is easy to forget. For example, employers frequently complain about job interviewees whose first concern is what the company will do for them, not what they might do for the company. Conversely, job search experts agree that most successful job candidates do extensive background research on a prospective company so that in an interview they can relate their own skills to the company's problems and needs. Successful arguments typically grow out of similar attention to audience needs.

To find out all you can about an audience, we recommend that you explore the following questions:

1. *Who is your audience?* Your audience might be a single, identifiable person. For example, you might write a letter to your student body president arguing for a change in intramural policies or to a vice president for research proposing a new research and development project for your company. Or your audience might be a decision-making body such as the University Standards Committee or a philanthropic organization to which you're writing a grant proposal. At other times your audience might be the general readership of a newspaper, church bulletin, magazine, Web site, or journal, or you might produce a flier to be handed out on street corners.

2. *How much does your audience know or care about your issue?* Are members of this audience currently part of the conversation on this issue, or do they need considerable background information? If you are writing to specific decision makers, are they currently aware of the problem or issue you are addressing, and do they care about it? If not, how can you get their attention? Your answers to these questions will especially affect your introduction and conclusion.

3. *What is your audience's current attitude toward your issue?*   Are members of this audience supportive of your position on the issue? Neutral or undecided? Skeptical? Strongly opposed? What other points of view besides your own will your audience be weighing? In Chapter 8, we will explain how your answers to these questions can help you decide the structure and tone of your argument.

4. *What will be your audience's likely objections to your argument?*   What weaknesses will audience members find? What aspects of your position will be most threatening to them and why? How are your basic assumptions, values, or beliefs different from your audience's? Your answers here will help determine the content of your argument and will alert you to extra research you may need.

5. *Finally, what values, beliefs, or assumptions about the world do you and your audience share?*   Despite differences of view on this issue, where can you find common links with your audience? How might you use these links to build bridges to your audience?

Suppose, for example, that you support racial profiling (rather than random selection) for determining persons to receive intensive screening at airports. It's important from the start that you understand and acknowledge the interests of those opposed to your position. Middle Eastern men, the most likely candidates for racial profiling, will object to your racial stereotyping, which lumps all persons of Arabic or Semitic appearance into the category "potential terrorists." African Americans and Hispanics, frequent victims of racial profiling by police in U.S. cities, may object to further extension of this hated practice. Also, most political liberals, as well as many moderates and conservatives, may object to the racism inherent in selecting persons for airport screening on the basis of ethnicity.

What shared values might you use to build bridges to those opposed to racial profiling at airports? Suppose that you are writing a guest op-ed column for a liberal campus newspaper and imagine readers repulsed by the notion of racial profiling. (Indeed you too feel repulsed by racial profiling.) You need to develop a strategy to reduce your audience's fears and to link your reasons to their values. Your thinking might go something like this:

> **Problem:** How can I create an argument rooted in shared values? How can I reduce fear that racial profiling in this situation endorses racism or will lead to further erosion of civil liberties?
>
> **Bridge-building goals:** I must try to show that my argument's goal is to increase airline safety by preventing terrorism like that of 9/11/01. My argument must show my respect for Islam and for Arabic and Semitic peoples. I must also show my rejection of racial profiling as normal police practice.

Possible strategies:
- Stress the shared value of protecting innocent people from terrorism.
- Show how racial profiling significantly increases the efficiency of secondary searches. (If searches are performed at random, then we waste time and resources searching persons who are statistically unlikely to be terrorists.)
- Argue that airport screeners must also use indicators other than race to select persons for searches (for example, traits that might indicate a domestic terrorist like Timothy McVeigh).
- Show my respect for Islam.
- Show sympathy for persons selected for searching via racial profiling and acknowledge that this practice would normally be despicable except for the extreme importance of airline security, which overrides personal liberties in this case.
- Show my rejection of racial profiling in situations other than airport screening—for example, stopping African Americans for traffic violations more often than whites and then searching their cars for drugs or stolen goods.
- Perhaps show my support of affirmative action, which is a kind of racial profiling in reverse.

These thinking notes allow you to develop the following plan for your argument.

Airport screeners should use racial profiling rather than random selection to determine which persons undergo intensive screening.

- because doing so will make more efficient use of airport screener's time, increase the odds of finding terrorists, and thus lead to greater airline safety (*WARRANT: increased airline safety is good;* or, at a deeper level: *The positive consequences of increasing airline safety through racial profiling outweigh the negative consequences*)
- because allowing racial profiling in this specific case does not mean allowing it in everyday police practices (*WARRANT: Racial profiling is unacceptable in everyday police practices*) nor does it imply disrespect for Islam or for Middle Eastern males (*WARRANT: It is wrong to show disrespect for Islam or Middle Eastern males*)

As this plan shows, your strategy is to seek reasons whose warrants your audience will accept. First, you will argue that racial profiling will lead to greater airline safety, allowing you to stress that safe airlines benefit all passengers. Your concern is the lives of hundreds of passengers as well as others who might be killed in a terrorist attack. Second, you plan to reduce adversaries' resistance to your proposal by showing that the consequences aren't as severe as they might fear. Using racial profiling in airports would not justify using it in urban police work (a practice you find despicable) and it would not imply disrespect for Islam or Middle Eastern males. As this example shows, your focus on audience—on the search for audience-based reasons—shapes the actual invention of your argument from the start.

For Class Discussion

Working individually or in small groups, plan an audience-based argumentative strategy for one or more of the following cases. Follow the thinking process used by the writer of the racial profiling argument: (1) State several problems that the writer must solve to reach the audience, and (2) develop possible solutions to those problems.

1. An argument for the right of software companies to continue making and selling violent video games: Aim the argument at parents who oppose their children's playing these games.

2. An argument to reverse grade inflation by limiting the number of A's and B's a professor can give in a course: Aim the argument at students who fear the results of getting lower grades.

3. An argument supporting a $1-per-gallon increase in gasoline taxes as an energy conservation measure: Aim your argument at business leaders who oppose the tax for fear it will raise the cost of consumer goods or at SUV owners who fear the hit to their family transportation budgets.

4. An argument supporting the legalization of cocaine: Aim your argument at readers of *Reader's Digest,* a conservative magazine that supports the current war on drugs.

Conclusion

Chapters 4 and 5 have provided an anatomy of argument. They have shown that the core of an argument is a claim with reasons that usually can be summarized in one or more *because* clauses attached to the claim. Often, it is as important to support the unstated assumptions in your argument as it is to support the stated reasons because a successful argument must eventually be rooted in beliefs and values held by your audience. In order to plan an audience-based argument strategy, arguers can use the Toulmin schema, which helps writers discover grounds, warrants, and backing for their arguments and to test them through conditions of rebuttal. Finally we showed how a search for audience-based reasons helps you keep your audience in mind from the start whenever you design a plan for an argument.

6 Using Evidence Effectively

In Chapters 4 and 5 we introduced you to the concept of *logos*—the logical structure of reasons and evidence in an argument—and showed you how an effective argument advances the writer's claim by linking its supporting reasons to one or more assumptions, beliefs, or values held by the intended audience. In this chapter, we turn to the uses of evidence in argument. By "evidence," we mean all the verifiable information a writer might use as support for an argument, such as facts, observations, examples, cases, testimony, experimental findings, survey data, statistics, and so forth. In Toulmin's terms, evidence is part of the "grounds" or "backing" of an argument in support of reasons or warrants.

In this chapter, we show you how to use evidence effectively. We begin by explaining some general principles for the persuasive use of evidence. Next we describe and illustrate various kinds of evidence and then present a rhetorical way to think about evidence, particularly the way writers select and frame evidence to support the writer's reasons while simultaneously guiding and limiting what the reader sees. By understanding the rhetorical use of evidence, you will better understand how to use evidence ethically, responsibly, and persuasively in your own arguments. We conclude the chapter by suggesting strategies to help you gather evidence for your arguments, including advice on conducting interviews and using questionnaires.

General Principles for the Persuasive Use of Evidence

Consider a target audience of educated, reasonable, and careful readers who approach an issue with healthy skepticism, open-minded but cautious. What demands would such readers make upon a writer's use of evidence? To begin to answer that question, let's look at some general principles for using evidence persuasively.

Apply the STAR Criteria to Evidence

Our open-minded but skeptical audience would first of all expect the evidence to meet what rhetorician Richard Fulkerson calls the STAR criteria:*

Sufficiency: Is there enough evidence?

Typicality: Is the chosen evidence representative and typical?

Accuracy: Is the evidence accurate and up-to-date?

Relevance: Is the evidence relevant to the claim?

Let's examine each in turn.

Sufficiency of Evidence   How much evidence you need is a function of your rhetorical context. In a court trial, opposing attorneys often agree to waive evidence for points that aren't in doubt in order to concentrate on contested points. The more a claim is contested or the more your audience is skeptical, the more evidence you may need to present. If you provide too little evidence, you may be accused of *hasty generalization* (see Appendix One), a reasoning fallacy in which a person makes a sweeping conclusion based on only one or two instances. On the other hand, if you provide too much evidence your argument may become overly long and tedious. You can guard against having too little or too much evidence by appropriately qualifying the claim your evidence supports.

> **Strong claim:** Working full time seriously harms a student's grade point average. (much data needed—probably a combination of examples and statistical studies)
>
> **Qualified claim:** Working full time often harms a student's grade point average. (a few representative examples may be enough)

Typicality of Evidence   Whenever you select evidence, readers need to believe the evidence is typical and representative rather than extreme instances. Suppose that you want to argue that students can combine full-time work with full-time college and cite the case of your friend Pam who pulled a straight-A grade average while working forty hours per week as a night receptionist in a small hotel. Your audience might doubt the typicality of Pam's case since a night receptionist can often use work hours for studying. What about more typical jobs, they'll ask, where you can't study while you work?

Accuracy of Evidence   Evidence can't be used ethically unless it is accurate and up-to-date, and it can't be persuasive unless the audience believes in the writer's credibility. As a writer, you must be scrupulous in using the most recent and accurate evidence you can find. We have already encountered a case of doubtful data in the two articles on biotech food in Chapter 2. Lisa Turner cites a 1993 case

---

*Richard Fulkerson, *Teaching the Argument in Writing* (Urbana, IL: National Council of Teachers of English, 1996), 44–53. In this section, we are indebted to Fulkerson's discussion.

in which thirty-seven people died from a rare disease allegedly linked to bioengineered food (see Chapter 2, p. 26), yet the Council for Biotechnology Information states, "There hasn't been a single documented case of an illness caused by biotech foods" (p. 41). One of these writers must be using inaccurate data—a problem the reader can unravel only through additional research. Faith in the accuracy of a writer's data is one function of *ethos*—the audience's confidence in the writer's credibility and trustworthiness (see Chapter 7, pp. 131–132).

Relevance of Evidence   Finally, evidence will be persuasive only if the reader considers it relevant to the contested issue. Consider the following student argument: "I deserve an A in this course because I worked exceptionally hard." The student then cites substantial evidence of how hard he worked—a log of study hours, copies of multiple drafts of papers, testimony from friends, and so forth. Such evidence is ample support for the claim "I worked very hard" but is irrelevant to the claim "I deserve an A." Although some instructors may give partial credit for effort, the criteria for grades usually focus on the quality of the student's performance, not the student's time spent studying.

Use Sources That Your Reader Trusts

Another way to enhance the persuasiveness of your evidence is to choose data, whenever possible, from sources you think your readers will trust. Because questions of fact are often at issue in arguments, readers may be skeptical of certain sources. When you research an issue, you soon get a sense of who the participants in the conversation are and what their reputations tend to be. Knowing the political biases of sources and the extent to which a source has financial or personal investment in the outcome of a controversy will also help you locate data sources that both you and your readers can trust. Citing a peer-reviewed scholarly journal is often more persuasive than citing an advocacy Web site. Similarly, citing a conservative magazine such as the *National Review* may be unpersuasive to liberal audiences, just as citing a Sierra Club publication may be unpersuasive to conservatives. (See Chapter 16 for further discussion of how to evaluate research sources from a rhetorical perspective.)

Rhetorical Understanding of Evidence

In the previous section we presented some general principles for the effective use of evidence. We now want to deepen your understanding of how evidence persuades by asking you to consider more closely the rhetorical context in which evidence operates. We'll look first at the kinds of evidence used in arguments and then show you how writers select and frame evidence for persuasive effect.

Kinds of Evidence

Writers have numerous options for the kinds of evidence they can use in an argument, ranging from personal experience data to research findings to hypothetical examples. To explain these options, we present a series of charts that categorize different kinds of evidence, illustrate how each kind might be worked into an argument, and comment on the strengths and limitations of each.

Data from Personal Experience   One powerful kind of evidence comes from personal experience:

EXAMPLE	STRENGTHS AND LIMITATIONS
Despite recent criticism that Ritalin is overprescribed for hyperactivity and attention deficit disorder, it can often seem like a miracle drug. My little brother is a perfect example. Before he was given Ritalin he was a terror in school. . . . [Tell the "before" and "after" story of your little brother.]	■ Personal experience examples help readers identify with writer; they show writer's personal connection to the issue. ■ Vivid stories capture the imagination. ■ Skeptics may sometimes argue that personal experience examples are insufficient (writer is guilty of hasty generalization), not typical, or not adequately scientific or verifiable.

Data from Observation or Field Research   You can also develop evidence by personally observing a phenomenon or by doing your own field research:

EXAMPLE	STRENGTHS AND LIMITATIONS
The intersection at Fifth and Montgomery is particularly dangerous because pedestrians almost never find a comfortable break in the heavy flow of cars. On April 29, I watched fifty-seven pedestrians cross the street. Not once did cars stop in both directions before the pedestrian stepped off the sidewalk onto the street. [Continue with observed data about danger.]	■ Field research gives the feeling of scientific credibility. ■ It increases typicality by expanding database beyond example of one person. ■ It enhances *ethos* of the writer as personally invested and reasonable. ■ Skeptics may point to flaws in how observations were conducted, showing how data are insufficient, inaccurate, or nontypical.

Data from Interviews, Questionnaires, Surveys   You can also gather data by interviewing stakeholders in a controversy, creating questionnaires, or doing surveys. (See pp. 122–124 for advice on how to conduct this kind of field research.)

EXAMPLE	STRENGTHS AND LIMITATIONS
In the first two months after the terrorist attacks on September 11, 2001, Muslim students on our campus suffered from anxiety at an especially severe rate. In a survey I conducted through the Student Affairs Office, 87 percent of Muslim students reported [give details of survey]. Additionally, in my interviews with three Muslim students—two international students from Saudi Arabia and one American student born and raised in Chicago—I discovered that [report interview data].	■ Interviews, questionnaires, and surveys enhance the sufficiency and typicality of evidence by expanding the database beyond the experiences of one person. ■ Quantitative data from questionnaires and surveys often increase the scientific feel of the argument. ■ Surveys and questionnaires often uncover local or recent data not available in published research. ■ Interviews can provide engaging personal stories enhancing *pathos*. ■ Skeptics can raise doubts about research methodology, questionnaire design, or typicality of interview subjects.

Data from Library or Internet Research For many arguments, evidence is derived from reading, particularly from library or Internet research. Part Four of this text helps you conduct effective research and incorporate research sources into your arguments:

EXAMPLE	STRENGTHS AND LIMITATIONS
The belief that a high carbohydrate–low fat diet is the best way to lose weight has been challenged by research conducted by Walter Willett and his colleagues in the department of nutrition in the Harvard School of Public Health. Willett's research suggests that complex carbohydrates such as pasta and potatoes spike glucose levels, increasing the risk of diabetes. Additionally, some fats—especially monounsaturated and polyunsaturated fats found in nuts, fish, and most vegetable oils—help lower "bad" cholesterol levels (45).*	■ Researched evidence is often powerful, especially when sources are respected by your audience; writers can spotlight source's credentials through attributive tags (see Chapter 17, pp. 390–391). ■ Researched data may take the form of facts, examples, quotations, summaries of research studies, and so forth (see Chapters 16 and 17). ■ Skeptics might doubt the accuracy of facts, the credentials of a source, or the research design of a study. They might also cite studies with different results. ■ Skeptics might raise doubts about sufficiency, typicality, or relevance of your research data.

---

*Parenthetical citations in this example and the next follow the MLA documentation system. See Chapter 17 for a full discussion of how to cite and document sources.

Testimony   Writers frequently use testimony when direct data are either unavailable or highly technical or complex. Testimonial evidence can come from research or from interviews:

<table>
<tr><td align="center">**EXAMPLE**</td><td align="center">**STRENGTHS AND LIMITATIONS**</td></tr>
<tr>
<td>Although the Swedish economist Bjorn Lomborg claims that acid rain is not a significant problem, many environmentalists disagree. According to David Bellamany, president of the Conservation Foundation, "Acid rain does kill forests and people around the world, and it's still doing so in the most polluted places, such as Russia" (qtd. in *BBC News*).</td>
<td>

- By itself, testimony is generally less persuasive than direct data.
- Persuasiveness can be increased if source has impressive credentials, which the writer can state through attributive tags introducing the testimony (see Chapter 17, pp. 390–391).
- Skeptics might undermine testimonial evidence by questioning credentials of source, showing source's bias, or quoting a countersource.

</td>
</tr>
</table>

Statistical Data   Many contemporary arguments rely heavily on statistical data, often supplemented by graphics such as tables, pie charts, and graphs. (See Chapter 9 for a discussion of the use of graphics in argument.)

<table>
<tr><td align="center">**EXAMPLE**</td><td align="center">**STRENGTHS AND LIMITATIONS**</td></tr>
<tr>
<td>Americans are delaying marriage at a surprising rate. In 1970, 85 percent of Americans between the ages of fifteen and twenty-nine were married. In 2000, however, only 54 percent were married (U.S. Census Bureau).</td>
<td>

- Statistics can give powerful snapshots of aggregate data from a wide database.
- They are often used in conjunction with graphics (see pp. 185–191).
- They can be calculated and displayed in different ways to achieve different rhetorical effects, so the reader must be wary (see pp. 187–189).
- Skeptics might question statistical methods, research design, and interpretation of data.

</td>
</tr>
</table>

Hypothetical Examples, Cases, and Scenarios   Arguments occasionally use hypothetical examples, cases, or scenarios, particularly to illustrate conjectured consequences of an event or to test philosophical hypotheses.

EXAMPLE	STRENGTHS AND LIMITATIONS
Consider what might happen if we continue to use biotech soybeans that are resistant to herbicides. The resistant gene, through cross-pollination, might be transferred to an ordinary weed, creating an out-of-control superweed that herbicides couldn't kill. Such a superweed could be an ecological disaster.	■ Scenarios have strong imaginative appeal. ■ They are persuasive only if they seem plausible. ■ A scenario narrative often conveys a sense of "inevitability," even if the actual scenario is unlikely; hence rhetorical effect may be illogical. ■ Skeptics might show the implausibility of the scenario or offer an alternative scenario.

Reasoned Sequence of Ideas   Sometimes arguments are supported with a reasoned sequence of ideas rather than with concrete facts or other forms of empirical evidence. The writer's concern is to support a point through a logical progression of ideas. Such arguments are conceptual, supported by linked ideas, rather than evidential. This kind of support occurs frequently in arguments and is often intermingled with evidentiary support.

EXAMPLE	STRENGTHS AND LIMITATIONS
Embryonic stem cell research, despite its promise in fighting diseases, may have negative social consequences. This research encourages us to place embryos in the category of mere cellular matter that can be manipulated at will. Currently we reduce animals to this category when we genetically alter them for human purposes, such as engineering pigs to grow more human-like heart valves for use in transplants. Using human embryos in the same way—as material that can be altered and destroyed at will—may benefit society materially, but this quest for greater knowledge and control involves a reclassifying of embryos that could potentially lead to a devaluing of human life.	■ These sequences are often used in causal arguments to show how causes are linked to effects or in definitional or values arguments to show links among ideas. ■ They have great power to clarify values and show the belief structure upon which a claim is founded. ■ They can sketch out ideas and connections that would otherwise remain latent. ■ Their effectiveness depends on the audience's acceptance of each link in the sequence of ideas. ■ Skeptics might raise objections at any link in the sequence, often by pointing to different values or outlining different consequences.

Angle of Vision and the Selection and Framing of Evidence

You can increase your ability to use evidence effectively—and to analyze how other arguers use evidence—by becoming more aware of a writer's rhetorical choices when using evidence to support a claim. Where each of us stands on an issue is partly a function of our own critical thinking, inquiry, and research—our search for the best solution to a problem. But it is also partly a function of who we are as persons—our values and beliefs as formed by the particulars of our existence such as our family history, our education, our gender and sexual orientation, our age, class, and ethnicity, and so forth. In other words, we don't enter the argumentative arena like disembodied computers arriving at our claims through a value-free calculus. We enter with our own ideologies, beliefs, values, and guiding assumptions.

These guiding assumptions, beliefs, and values work together to create a writer's "angle of vision." (Instead of "angle of vision," we could also use other words or metaphors such as *perspective, bias, lens,* or *filter*—all terms that suggest that our way of seeing the world is shaped by our values and beliefs.) A writer's angle of vision, like a lens or filter, helps determine what stands out for that writer in a field of data—that is, what data are important or trivial, significant or irrelevant, worth focusing on or worth ignoring.

To illustrate the concept of selective seeing, we ask you to consider how two hypothetical speakers might select different data about homeless persons when presenting speeches to their city council. The first speaker argues that the city should increase its services to the homeless. The second asks the city to promote tourism more aggressively. Their differing angles of vision will cause the two speakers to select different data about homeless persons and to frame these data in different ways. (Our use of the word "frame" derives metaphorically from a window frame or the frame of a camera's viewfinder. When you look through a frame, some part of your field of vision is blocked off, while the material appearing in the frame is emphasized. Through framing, a writer maximizes the reader's focus on some data, minimizes the reader's focus on other data, and otherwise guides the reader's vision and response.)

Because the first speaker wants to increase the council's sympathy for the homeless, she frames homeless people positively by telling the story of one homeless man's struggle to find shelter and nutritious food. Her speech focuses primarily on the low number of tax dollars devoted to helping the homeless. In contrast, the second speaker, using data about lost tourist income, might frame the homeless as "panhandlers" by telling the story of obnoxious, urine-soaked winos who pester shoppers for handouts. As arguers, both speakers want their audience to see the homeless from their own angles of vision. Consequently, lost tourist dollars don't show up at all in the first speaker's argument, while the story of a homeless man's night in the cold doesn't show up in the second speaker's argument. As this example shows, one goal writers have in selecting and framing evidence is to bring the reader's view of the subject into alignment with the writer's angle of vision. The writer selects and frames evidence to limit and control what the reader sees.

To help you better understand the concepts of selection and framing, we offer the following class discussion exercise to give you practice in a kind of controlled laboratory setting. As you do this exercise, we invite you to observe your own processes for selecting and framing evidence.

For Class Discussion

Suppose that your city has scheduled a public hearing on a proposed city ordinance to ban mosh pits at rock concerts. (See p. 15, where we introduced this issue.) Among the factual data available to various speakers for evidence are the following:

Possible Data for Mosh Pit Argument

- Some bands, like Nine Inch Nails, specify festival seating that allows a mosh pit area.

- A female mosher writing on the Internet says: "I experience a shared energy that is like no other when I am in the pit with the crowd. It is like we are all a bunch of atoms bouncing off of each other. It's great. Hey, some people get that feeling from basketball games. I get mine from the mosh pit."

- A student conducted a survey of fifty students on her campus who had attended rock concerts in the last six months. Of the respondents, 80 percent thought that mosh pits should be allowed at concerts.

- Narrative comments on these questionnaires included the following:

  - Mosh pits are a passion for me. I get an amazing rush when crowd surfing.

  - I don't like to be in a mosh pit or do crowd surfing. But I love festival seating and like to watch the mosh pits. For me, mosh pits are part of the ambience of a concert.

  - I know a girl who was groped in a mosh pit, and she'll never do one again. But I have never had any problems.

  - Mosh pits are dangerous and stupid. I think they should be outlawed.

  - If you are afraid of mosh pits just stay away. Nobody forces you to go into a mosh pit! It is ridiculous to ban them because they are totally voluntary. They should just post big signs saying "City assumes no responsibility for accidents occurring in mosh pit area."

- A 14-year-old boy suffered permanent brain damage from a mosh pit accident when he went to hear Rage Against the Machine in Seattle in 1996.

- A teenage girl suffered brain damage and memory loss at a 1998 Pearl Jam concert in Rapid City, South Dakota. According to her attorney, she hadn't intended to body surf or enter the mosh pit but "got sucked in while she was standing at its fringe."

- There were twenty-four concert deaths recorded in 2001, most of them in the area closest to the stage where people are packed in.

- A 21-year-old man suffered cardiac arrest at a Metallica concert in Indiana and is now in a permanent vegetative state. Because he was jammed into the mosh pit area, nobody noticed he was in distress.

Tasks: Working individually or in small groups, complete the following tasks:

1. Compose two short speeches, one supporting the proposed city ordinance to ban mosh pits and one opposing it. How you use these data is up to you, but be able to explain your reasoning in the way you select and frame them. Share your speeches with classmates.

2. After you have shared examples of different speeches, explain the approaches that different classmates employed. What principle of selection was used? If arguers included evidence contrary to their positions, how did they handle it, respond to it, minimize its importance, or otherwise channel its rhetorical effect?

3. In the first task, we assigned you two different angles of vision—one supporting the ordinance and one opposing it. If you had to create your own argument on a proposal to ban mosh pits and if you set for yourself a truth-seeking goal—that is, finding the best solution for the problem of mosh pit danger, one for which you would take ethical responsibility—what would you argue? How would your argument use the list of data we provided? What else might you add?

Rhetorical Strategies for Framing Evidence

What we hope you learned from the preceding exercise is that an arguer consciously selects evidence from a wide field of data and then frames these data through rhetorical strategies that emphasize some data, minimize others, and guide the reader's response. Now that you have a basic idea of what we mean by framing of evidence, here are some strategies writers can use to guide what the reader sees and feels.

Strategies for Framing Evidence

- *Controlling the space given to supporting versus contrary evidence:*   Depending on their audience and purpose, writers can devote most of their space to supporting evidence and minimal space to contrary evidence (or omit it entirely). Thus persons arguing in favor of mosh pits may have used lots of evidence supporting mosh pits, including enthusiastic quotations from concertgoers, while omitting (or summarizing very rapidly) the data about the dangers of mosh pits.

- *Emphasizing a detailed story versus presenting lots of facts and statistics:*   Often, writers can choose to support a point with a memorable individual case or with aggregate data such as statistics or lists of facts. A memorable story can have a strongly persuasive effect. For example, to create a negative view of mosh pits, a writer might tell the heartrending story of a teenager suffering permanent brain damage from being dropped on a mosh pit floor. In contrast, a supporter of mosh pits might tell the story of a happy music lover turned on to the concert scene by the rush of crowd surfing. A different strategy is to use facts and statistics rather than case narratives—for example, data about the frequency of mosh pit accidents, financial consequences of lawsuits, and so forth. The single-narrative case often has a more powerful rhetorical effect, but it is always open to the charge that it is an insufficient or nonrepresentative example. Vivid anecdotes make for interesting reading, but by themselves they may not be compelling logically. In contrast, aggregate data, often used in scholarly studies, can provide more compelling, logical evidence but sometimes make the prose wonkish and dense.

- *Providing contextual and interpretive comments when presenting data:* When citing data, writers can add brief contextual or interpretive comments that act like lenses over the readers' eyes to help them see the data from the writer's perspective. Suppose you want to support mosh pits, but want to admit that mosh pits are dangerous. You could make that danger seem irrelevant or inconsequential by saying: "It is true that occasional mosh pit accidents happen, just as accidents happen in any kind of recreational activity from swimming to weekend softball games." The concluding phrase frames the danger of mosh pits by comparing them to other recreational accidents that don't require special laws or regulations. The implied argument is this: Banning mosh pits because of an occasional accident would be as silly as banning recreational swimming because of occasional accidents.

- *Putting contrary evidence in subordinate positions:* Just as a photographer can place a flower at the center of a photograph or in the background, a writer can place a piece of data in a subordinate or main clause of a sentence. Note how the structure of the following sentence minimizes emphasis on the rarity of mosh pit accidents: "Although mosh pit accidents are rare, the danger to the city of multimillion-dollar liability lawsuits means that the city should nevertheless ban them for reasons of fiscal prudence." The factual data that mosh pit accidents are rare is summarized briefly and tucked away in a subordinate "*although* clause," while the writer's own position is elaborated in the main clause where it receives grammatical emphasis. A writer with a different angle of vision might say, "Although some cities may occasionally be threatened with a lawsuit, serious accidents resulting from mosh pits are so rare that cities shouldn't interfere with the desires of music fans to conduct concerts as they please."

- *Choosing labels and names that guide the reader's response to data:* One of the most subtle ways to control your readers' response to data is to choose labels and names that prompt them to see the issue as you do. If you like mosh pits, you might refer to the seating arrangements in a concert venue as "festival seating, where concertgoers have the opportunity to create a free-flowing mosh pit." If you don't like mosh pits, you might refer to the seating arrangements as "an accident-inviting use of empty space where rowdies can crowd together, slam into each other, and occasionally punch and kick." The labels you choose, along with the connotations of the words you select, urge your reader to share your angle of vision.

- *Using images (photographs, drawings) to guide the reader's response to data:*   Another strategy for moving your audience toward your angle of vision is to include a photograph or drawing that portrays a contested issue from your perspective. (See Chapter 9 for a complete discussion of the use of visuals in argument.) Consider the photograph of crowd surfing shown in Color Plate B. This photograph supports a positive view of mosh pits. The crowd looks happy and relaxed (rather than rowdy or out of control) and the young woman lifted above the crowd smiles broadly, her body relaxed, her arms extended.

- *Revealing the value system that determines the writer's selection and framing of data:* Ultimately, how a writer selects and frames evidence is linked to the system of values that organize his or her argument. If you favor mosh pits, you probably favor maximizing the pleasure of concertgoers, promoting individual choice, and letting moshers assume the risk of their own behavior. If you want to forbid mosh pits, you probably favor minimizing risks, protecting the city from lawsuits, and protecting individuals from the danger of their own out-of-control actions. Sometimes you can foster connections with your audience by openly addressing the underlying values that you hope your audience shares with you. You can often frame your selected data by stating explicitly the values that guide your argument.

Special Strategies for Framing Statistical Evidence

Numbers and statistical data can be framed in so many ways that this category of evidence deserves its own separate treatment. By recognizing how writers frame numbers to support the story they want to tell, you will always be aware that other stories are also possible. Ethical use of numbers means that you use reputable sources for your basic data, that you don't invent or intentionally distort numbers for your own purposes, and that you don't ignore alternative points of view. Here are some of the choices writers make when framing statistical data:

- *Raw numbers versus percentages.*   You can alter the rhetorical effect of a statistic by choosing between raw numbers or percentages. In the summer of 2002, many American parents panicked over what seemed like an epidemic of child abductions. If you cited the raw number of these abductions reported in the national news, this number, although small, could seem scary. But if you computed the actual percentage of American children who were abducted, that percentage was so infinitesimally small as to seem insignificant. You can apply this framing option directly to the mosh pit case. To emphasize the danger of mosh pits, you can say that twenty-four deaths occurred at rock concerts in the year 2001. To minimize this statistic, you could compute the percentage of deaths by dividing this number by the total number of persons who attended rock concerts during the year, certainly a number in the several millions. From the perspective of percentages, the death rate at concerts is extremely low.

- *Median versus mean.*   Another way to alter the rhetorical effect of numbers is to choose between the median and the mean. The mean is the average of all numbers on a list. The median is the middle number when all the numbers are arranged sequentially from high to low. In 1998 the mean annual income for retired families in the United States was $32,600—not a wealthy amount but enough to live on comfortably if you owned your own home. However, the median income was only $19,300, a figure that gives a much more striking picture of income distribution among older Americans. This median figure means that half of all retired families in the United States had annual incomes of $19,300 or less. The much higher mean income indicates that many retired Americans are extremely wealthy. This wealth raises the average of all incomes (the mean) but doesn't affect the median.

- *Unadjusted versus adjusted numbers.*   Suppose your boss told you that you were getting a 5 percent raise. You might be happy—unless inflation rates were running at 6 percent. Economic data can be hard to interpret across time unless the dollar amounts are adjusted for inflation. This same problem occurs in other areas. For example, comparing grade point averages of college graduates in 1970 versus 2006 means little unless one can somehow compensate for grade inflation.

- *Base point for statistical comparisons.*   In the summer of 2002, the stock market was in precipitous decline if one compared 2002 prices with 2000 prices. However, the market still seemed vigorous and healthy if one compared 2002 with 1990. One's choice of the base point for a comparison often makes a significant rhetorical difference.

For Class Discussion

A proposal to build a new ballpark in Seattle, Washington, yielded a wide range of statistical arguments. All of the following statements are reasonably faithful to the same facts:

- The ballpark would be paid for by raising the sales tax from 8.2 percent to 8.3 percent during a twenty-year period.
- The sales tax increase is one-tenth of 1 percent.
- This increase represents an average of $7.50 per person per year—about the price of a movie ticket.
- This increase represents $750 per five-person family over the twenty-year period of the tax.
- For a family building a new home in the Seattle area, this tax will increase building costs by $200.
- This is a $250 million tax increase for the residents of the Seattle area.

How would you describe the costs of the proposed ballpark if you opposed the proposal? How would you describe the costs if you supported the proposal?

Gathering Evidence

We conclude this chapter with some brief advice on ways to gather evidence for your arguments. We begin with a list of brainstorming questions that may help you think of possible sources for evidence. We then provide suggestions for conducting interviews and creating surveys and questionnaires, since these powerful sources are often overlooked by students. For help in conducting library and Internet research—the most common sources of evidence in arguments—see Part Four: "The Researched Argument."

Creating a Plan for Gathering Evidence

As you begin contemplating an argument, you can use the following checklist to help you think of possible sources for evidence.

A Checklist for Brainstorming Sources of Evidence

- What personal experiences have you had with this issue? What details from your life or the lives of your friends, acquaintances, or relatives might serve as examples or other kinds of evidence?
- What observational studies would be relevant to this issue?
- What persons could you interview to provide insights or expert knowledge on this issue?
- What questions about your issue could be addressed in a survey or questionnaire?
- What useful information on this issue might encyclopedias, specialized reference books, or the regular book collection in your university library provide? (See Chapter 16.)
- What evidence might you seek on this issue using licensed database indexing sources in magazines, newspapers, and scholarly journals? (See Chapter 16.)
- How might an Internet search engine help you research this issue? (See Chapter 16.)
- What evidence might you find on this issue from reliable statistical resources such as U.S. Census Bureau data, the Centers for Disease Control, or *Statistical Abstract of the United States?* (See Chapter 16.)

Gathering Data from Interviews

Conducting interviews is a useful way not only to gather expert testimony and important data but also to learn about alternative views. To make interviews as productive as possible, we offer these suggestions.

- *Determine your purpose.* Think out why you are interviewing the person and what information he or she is uniquely able to provide.

- *Do background reading.* Find out as much as possible about the interviewee before the interview. Your knowledge of his or her background will help establish your credibility and build a bridge between you and your source. Also, equip yourself with a good foundational understanding of the issue so that you will sound informed and truly interested in the issue.

- *Formulate well-thought-out questions but also be flexible.* Write out beforehand the questions you intend to ask, making sure that every question is related to the purpose of your interview. However, be prepared to move in unexpected directions if the interview opens up new territory. Sometimes unplanned topics can end up being the most illuminating and useful.

- *Come well prepared for the interview.* As part of your professional demeanor, be sure to have all the necessary supplies (notepaper, pens, pencils, perhaps a tape recorder, if your interviewee is willing) with you.

- *Be prompt and courteous.* It is important to be punctual and respectful of your interviewee's time. In most cases, it is best to present yourself as a listener seeking clarity on an issue rather than an advocate of a particular position or an opponent. During the interview, play the believing role. Save the doubting role for later, when you are looking over your notes.

- *Take brief but clear notes.* Try to record the main ideas and be accurate with quotations. Ask for clarification of any points you don't understand.

- *Transcribe your notes soon after the interview.* Immediately after the interview, while your memory is still fresh, rewrite your notes more fully and completely.

When you use interview data in your writing, put quotation marks around any direct quotations. In most cases, you should also identify your source by name and indicate his or her title or credentials—whatever will convince the reader that this person's remarks are to be taken seriously.

Gathering Data from Surveys or Questionnaires

A well-constructed survey or questionnaire can provide lively, current data that give your audience a sense of the popularity and importance of your views. To be effective and responsible, however, a survey or questionnaire needs to be carefully prepared and administered, as we suggest in the following guidelines.

- *Include both closed-response questions and open-response questions.* To give you useful information and avoid charges of bias, you will want to include a range of questions. Closed-response questions ask participants to check a box or number on a scale and yield quantitative data that you can report statistically, perhaps in tables or graphs. Open-response questions elicit varied responses and often short narratives that allow participants to offer their own input. These may contribute new insights to your perspective on the issue.

■ *Make your survey or questionnaire clear and easy to complete.*   Think out the number, order, wording, and layout of the questions in your questionnaire. Your questions should be clear and easy to answer. The neatness and overall formal appearance of the questionnaire will also invite serious responses from your participants.

■ *Explain the purpose of the questionnaire.*   Respondents are usually more willing to participate if they know how the information gained from the questionnaire will benefit others. Therefore, it is a good idea to state at the beginning of the questionnaire how it will be used.

■ *Seek a random sample of respondents in your distribution of the questionnaire.* Think out where and how you will distribute and collect your questionnaire to ensure a random sampling of respondents. For example, if a questionnaire about the university library went only to dorm residents, then you wouldn't learn how commuting students felt.

■ *Convert questionnaires into usable data by tallying and summarizing responses.* Tallying the results and formulating summary statements of the information you gathered will yield material that might be used as evidence.

Conclusion

Effective use of evidence is an essential skill for arguers. In this chapter we introduced you to the STAR criteria and other strategies for making your data persuasive. We showed you various kinds of evidence and then examined how a writer's angle of vision influences the selection and framing of evidence. We also described framing strategies for emphasizing evidence, de-emphasizing it, and guiding your reader's response to it. Finally we concluded with advice on how to gather evidence, including the use of interviews, surveys, and questionnaires.

WRITING ASSIGNMENTS
FOR CHAPTERS 4–6

OPTION 1: A Microtheme   Write a one- or two-paragraph argument in which you support one of the following enthymemes, using evidence from personal experience, field observation, interviews, or data from a brief questionnaire or survey. Most of your microtheme should support the stated reason with evidence. However, also include a brief passage supporting the implied warrant. The opening sentence of your microtheme should be the enthymeme itself, which serves as the thesis statement for your argument. (Note: If you disagree with the enthymeme's argument, recast the claim or the reason to assert what you want to argue.)

1. Reading fashion magazines can be detrimental to teenage girls because such magazines can produce an unhealthy focus on beauty.
2. Surfing the Web might harm your studying because it causes you to waste time.
3. Service-learning courses are valuable because they allow you to test course concepts within real-world contexts.
4. Summer internships in your field of interest, even without pay, are the best use of your summer time because they speed up your education and training for a career.
5. Any enthymeme (a claim with a *because* clause) of your choice that can be supported without library or Internet research. (The goal of this microtheme is to give you practice using data from personal experience or from brief field research.) You may want to have your instructor approve your enthymeme in advance.

OPTION 2: A Classical Argument   Write a classical argument that uses at least two reasons to support your claim. Classical argument is explained in detail in Chapter 3. As we explain further in Chapter 8, classical argument is particularly effective when you are addressing neutral or undecided audiences. It has a self-announcing or closed-form structure in which you state your claim at the end of the introduction, begin body paragraphs with clearly stated reasons, and use effective transitions throughout to keep your reader on track. In developing your own argument, place your most important reason last, where it will have the greatest impact on your readers. Typically, a classical argument also summarizes anticipated objections to the writer's argument and responds to them briefly. You can place this section either before or after you develop your main argument. (Chapter 8, pp. 145–152, gives a detailed explanation of how to respond to objections and alternative views.) See Chapter 3, pages 63–67, for further description of a classical argument, including a diagram of its typical structure.

The student essay that follows illustrates a classical argument. This essay grew out of a class discussion about alternative sports, conflicts between traditional sports and newer sports (downhill skiing and snowboarding), and middle-age prejudices against groups of young people.

"Half-Criminals" or Urban Athletes? A Plea for Fair Treatment of Skateboarders

David Langley (Student)

1   For skateboarders, the campus of the University of California at San Diego is a wide-open, huge, geometric, obstacle-filled, stair-scattered cement paradise. The signs posted all over campus read, "No skateboarding, biking, or rollerblading on campus except on Saturday, Sunday, and Holidays." I have always respected these signs at my local skateboarding spot. On the first day of 1999, I was skateboarding here with my hometown skate buddies and had just landed a trick when a police officer rushed out from behind a pillar, grabbed me, and yanked me off my board. Because I didn't have my I.D. (I had emptied my pockets so I wouldn't bruise my legs if I fell—a little trick of the trade), the officer started treating me like a criminal. She told me to spread my legs and put my hands on my head. She frisked me and then called in my name to police headquarters.

2   "What's the deal?" I asked. "The sign said skateboarding was legal on holidays."

3   "The sign means that you can only *roll* on campus," she said.

4   But that's *not* what the sign said. The police officer gave one friend and me a warning. Our third friend received a fifty-dollar ticket because it was his second citation in the last twelve months.

5   Like other skateboarders throughout cities, we have been bombarded with unfair treatment. We have been forced out of known skate spots in the city by store-owners and police, kicked out of every parking garage in downtown, compelled to skate at strange times of day and night, and herded into crowded skateboard parks. However, after I was searched by the police and detained for over twenty minutes in my own skating sanctuary, the unreasonableness of the treatment of skateboarders struck me. Where are skateboarders supposed to go? Cities need to change their unfair treatment of skateboarders because skateboarders are not antisocial misfits as popularly believed, because the laws regulating skateboarding are ambiguous, and because skateboarders are not given enough legitimate space to practice their sport.

6   Possibly because to the average eye most skateboarders look like misfits or delinquents, adults think of us as criminal types and associate our skateboards with antisocial behavior. But this view is unfair. City dwellers should recognize that skateboards are a natural reaction to the urban environment. If people are surrounded by cement, they are going to figure out a way to ride it. People's different environments have always produced transportation and sports to suit the conditions: bikes, cars, skis, ice skates, boats, canoes, surfboards. If we live on snow, we are going to develop skis or snowshoes to move around. If we live in an environment that has flat panels of cement for ground with lots of curbs and stairs, we are going to invent an ingeniously designed flat board with wheels. Skateboards are as natural to cement as surfboards are to water or skis to snow. Moreover, the result-

ing sport is as healthful, graceful, and athletic. A fair assessment of skateboarders should respect our elegant, nonpolluting means of transportation and sport, and not consider us hoodlums.

A second way that skateboarders are treated unfairly is that the laws that regulate skateboarding in public places are highly restrictive, ambiguous, and open to abusive application by police officers. My being frisked on the UCSD campus is just one example. When I moved to Seattle to go to college, I found the laws in Washington to be equally unclear. When a sign says "No Skateboarding," that generally means you will get ticketed if you are caught skateboarding in the area. But most areas aren't posted. The general rule then is that you can skateboard so long as you do so safely without being reckless. But the definition of "reckless" is up to the whim of the police officer. I visited the front desk of the Seattle East Precinct and asked them exactly what the laws against reckless skateboarding meant. They said that skaters are allowed on the sidewalk as long as they travel at reasonable speed and the sidewalks aren't crowded. One of the officers explained that if he saw a skater sliding down a handrail with people all around, he would definitely arrest the skater. What if there were no people around, I asked? The officer admitted that he might arrest the lone skater anyway and not be questioned by his superiors. No wonder skateboarders feel unfairly treated. 7

One way that cities have tried to treat skateboarders fairly is to build skateboard parks. Unfortunately, for the most part these parks are no solution at all. Most parks were designed by nonskaters who don't understand the momentum or gravity pull associated with the movement of skateboards. For example, City Skate, a park below the Space Needle in Seattle, is very appealing to the eye, but once you start to ride it you realize that the transitions and the verticals are all off, making it unpleasant and even dangerous to skate there. The Skate Park in Issaquah, Washington, hosts about thirty to fifty skaters at a time. Collisions are frequent and close calls, many. There are simply too many people in a small area. The people who built the park in Redmond, Washington, decided to make a huge wall in it for graffiti artists "to tag on" legally. They apparently thought they ought to throw all us teenage "half-criminals" in together. At this park, young teens are nervous about skating near a gangster "throwing up his piece," and skaters become dizzy as they take deep breaths from their workouts right next to four or five cans of spray paint expelling toxins in the air. 8

Of course, many adults probably don't think skateboarders deserve to be treated fairly. I have heard the arguments against skateboarders for years from parents, storeowners, friends, police officers, and security guards. For one thing, skateboarding tears up public and private property, people say. I can't deny that skating leaves marks on handrails and benches, and it does chip cement and granite. But in general skateboarders help the environment more than they hurt it. Skateboarding places are not littered or tagged up by skaters. Because skaters need smooth surfaces and because any small object of litter can lead to painful accidents, skaters actually keep the environment cleaner than the average citizen does. As for the population as a whole, skateboarders are keeping the air a lot cleaner 9 than many other commuters and athletes such as boat drivers, car drivers, and skiers on ski lifts. In the bigger picture, infrequent repair of curbs and benches is cheaper than attempts to heal the ozone.

10   We skateboarders aren't going away, so cities are going to have to make room for us somewhere. Here is how cities can treat us fairly. We should be allowed to skate when others are present as long as we skate safely on the sidewalks. The rules and laws should be clearer so that skaters don't get put into vulnerable positions that make them easy targets for tickets. I do support the opening of skate parks, but cities need to build more of them, need to situate them closer to where skateboarders live, and need to make them relatively wholesome environments. They should also be designed by skateboarders so that they are skater-friendly and safe to ride. Instead of being treated as "half-criminals," skaters should be accepted as urban citizens and admired as athletes; we are a clean population, and we are executing a challenging and graceful sport. As human beings grow, we go from crawling to walking; some of us grow from strollers to skateboards.

7 Moving Your Audience:
Ethos, Pathos, and *Kairos*

In Chapters 5 and 6 we focused on *logos*—the logical structure of reasons and evidence in argument. Even though we have treated *logos* in its own chapters, an effective arguer's concern for *logos* is always connected to *ethos* and *pathos* (see the rhetorical triangle introduced in Chapter 4, p. 76). By seeking audience-based reasons—so that an arguer connects her message to the assumptions, values, and beliefs of her audience—she appeals also to *ethos* and *pathos* by enhancing the reader's trust and by triggering the reader's sympathies and imagination. In this chapter, we turn specifically to *ethos* and *pathos*. We also introduce you to a related rhetorical concept, *kairos*, which concerns the timeliness, fitness, and appropriateness of an argument for its occasion.

Ethos and *Pathos* as Persuasive Appeals: An Overview

At first, one may be tempted to think of *logos, ethos,* and *pathos* as "ingredients" in an essay, like spices you add to a casserole. But a more appropriate metaphor might be that of different lamps and filters used on theater spotlights to vary lighting effects on a stage. Thus if you switch on a *pathos* lamp (possibly through using more concrete language or vivid examples), the resulting image will engage the audience's sympathy and emotions more deeply. If you overlay an *ethos* filter (perhaps by adopting a different tone toward your audience), the projected image of the writer as a person will be subtly altered. If you switch on a *logos* lamp (by adding, say, more data for evidence), you will draw the reader's attention to the logical appeal of the argument. Depending on how you modulate the lamps and filters, you shape and color your readers' perception of you and your argument.

Our metaphor is imperfect, of course, but our point is that *logos, ethos,* and *pathos* work together to create an impact on the reader. Consider, for example, the different impacts of the following arguments, all having roughly the same logical appeal.

1.   People should adopt a vegetarian diet because doing so will help prevent the cruelty to animals caused by factory farming.

2.   If you are planning to eat chicken tonight, please consider how much that chicken suffered so that you could have a tender and juicy meal. Commercial growers cram the chickens so tightly together into cages that they never walk on their own legs, see sunshine, or flap their wings. In fact, their beaks must be cut off to keep them from pecking each other's eyes out. One way to prevent such suffering is for more and more people to become vegetarians.

3.   People who eat meat are no better than sadists who torture other sentient creatures to enhance their own pleasure. Unless you enjoy sadistic tyranny over others, you have only one choice: Become a vegetarian.

4.   People committed to justice might consider the extent to which our love of eating meat requires the agony of animals. A visit to a modern chicken factory—where chickens live their entire lives in tiny, darkened coops without room to spread their wings—might raise doubts about our right to inflict such suffering on sentient creatures. Indeed, such a visit might persuade us that vegetarianism is a more just alternative.

Each argument has roughly the same logical core:

CLAIM: People should adopt a vegetarian diet.

STATED REASON: because doing so will help prevent the cruelty to animals caused by factory farming

GROUNDS: the evidence of suffering in commercial chicken farms, where chickens are crammed together, and lash out at each other; evidence that only widespread adoption of vegetarianism will end factory farming

WARRANT: If we have an alternative to making animals suffer, we should adopt it.

But the impact of each argument varies. The difference between Arguments 1 and 2, most of our students report, is the greater emotional power of Argument 2. Whereas Argument 1 refers only to the abstraction "cruelty to animals," Argument 2 paints a vivid picture of chickens with their beaks cut off to prevent their pecking each other blind. Argument 2 makes a stronger appeal to *pathos* (not necessarily a stronger argument), stirring feelings by appealing simultaneously to the heart and to the head.

The difference between Arguments 1 and 3 concerns both *ethos* and *pathos*. Argument 3 appeals to the emotions through highly charged words like *torture, sadist,* and *tyranny.* But Argument 3 also draws attention to its writer, and most of our students report not liking that writer very much. His stance is self-righteous and insulting. In contrast, Argument 4's author establishes a more positive *ethos.*

He establishes rapport by assuming his audience is committed to justice and by qualifying his argument with conditional terms such as *might* and *perhaps*. He also invites sympathy for his problem—an appeal to *pathos*—by offering a specific description of chickens crammed into tiny coops.

Which of these arguments is best? They all have appropriate uses. Arguments 1 and 4 seem aimed at receptive audiences reasonably open to exploration of the issue, whereas Arguments 2 and 3 seem designed to shock complacent audiences or to rally a group of True Believers. Even Argument 3, which is too abusive to be effective in most instances, might work as a rallying speech at a convention of animal liberation activists.

Our point thus far is that *logos, ethos,* and *pathos* are different aspects of the same whole, different lenses for intensifying or softening the light beam you project onto the screen. Every choice you make as a writer affects in some way each of the three appeals. The rest of this chapter examines these choices in more detail.

How to Create an Effective *Ethos:* The Appeal to Credibility

The ancient Greek and Roman rhetoricians recognized that an argument would be more persuasive if the audience trusted the speaker. Aristotle argued that such trust resides within the speech itself, not in the prior reputation of the speaker. In the speaker's manner and delivery, in the speaker's tone, word choice, and arrangement of reasons, in the sympathy with which he or she treats alternative views, the speaker creates a trustworthy persona. Aristotle called the impact of the speaker's credibility the appeal from *ethos.* How does a writer create credibility? We suggest three ways.

Be Knowledgeable about Your Issue

The first way to gain credibility is to *be* credible—that is, to argue from a strong base of knowledge, to have at hand the examples, personal experiences, statistics, and other empirical data needed to make a sound case. If you have done your homework, you will command the attention of most audiences.

Be Fair

Besides being knowledgeable about your issue, you need to demonstrate fairness and courtesy to alternative views. Because true argument can occur only where persons may reasonably disagree with one another, your *ethos* will be strengthened if you demonstrate that you understand and empathize with other points of view. There are times, of course, when you may appropriately scorn an opposing view. But these times are rare, and they mostly occur when you address audiences predisposed to your view. Demonstrating empathy to alternative views is generally the best strategy.

Build a Bridge to Your Audience

A third means of establishing credibility—building a bridge to your audience—has been treated at length in our earlier discussions of audience-based reasons. By grounding your argument in shared values and assumptions, you demonstrate your goodwill and enhance your image as a trustworthy person respectful of your audience's views. We mention audience-based reasons here to show how this aspect of *logos*—finding the reasons that are most rooted in the audience's values—also affects your *ethos* as a person respectful of your readers' views.

How to Create *Pathos:* The Appeal to Beliefs and Emotions

Before the federal government enacted its "do-not-call-list" outlawing unsolicited telephone marketing, newspapers around the country published a flurry of anti-telemarketing articles. Within this context, a worker in the communications department of the United Parcel Service wrote a *New York Times* op-ed piece entitled "Don't Hang Up, That's My Mom Calling." The writer, Bobbi Buchanan, begins her article this way:

> The next time an annoying sales call interrupts your dinner, think of my 71-year-old mother, LaVerne, who works as a part-time telemarketer to supplement her social security income. To those Americans who have signed up for the new national do-not-call list, my mother is a pest, a nuisance, an invader of privacy. To others, she's just another anonymous voice on the other end of the line. But to those who know her, she's someone struggling to make a buck, to feed herself and pay her utilities—someone who personifies the great American way.

Buchanan then describes her mother in an emotionally appealing way. Buchanan's rhetorical aim is to transfer the reader's anonymous, depersonalized image of telemarketers into the concrete image of "my mother, LaVerne"—"hard-working, first generation American; the daughter of a Pittsburgh steelworker; survivor of the Great Depression; the widow of a World War II veteran; a mother of seven, grandmother of eight, great grandmother of three. . . ." The intended effect is to alter our view of telemarketers through the positive emotions triggered by our identification with LaVerne.

By urging readers to think of LaVerne instead of an anonymous telemarketer, Buchanan illustrates the power of *pathos,* an appeal to the reader's emotions. Arguers create pathetic appeals whenever they connect their claims to readers' values, thus triggering positive or negative emotions depending on whether these values are affirmed or transgressed. Pro-life proponents appeal to *pathos* when they graphically describe the dismemberment of a fetus during an abortion; proponents of improved women's health and status in Africa do so when they describe the helplessness of wives forced to have unprotected sex with husbands likely infected with HIV; opponents of oil exploration in the Arctic National

Wildlife Refuge (ANWR) do so when they lovingly describe the calving grounds of caribou.

Are such appeals legitimate? Our answer is yes, if they intensify and deepen our response to an issue rather than divert our attention from it. Because understanding is a matter of feeling as well as perceiving, *pathos* can give access to non-logical, but not necessarily nonrational, ways of knowing. *Pathos* helps us see what is deeply at stake in an issue, what matters to the whole person. Appeals to *pathos* help readers walk in the writer's shoes. That is why arguments are often improved through the use of stories that make issues come alive or sensory details that allow us to see, feel, and taste the reality of a problem.

Appeals to *pathos* become illegitimate, we believe, when they confuse an issue rather than clarify it. Consider the case of a student who argues that Professor Jones ought to raise his grade from a D to a C, lest he lose his scholarship and leave college, shattering the dreams of his dear old grandmother. To the extent that students' grades should be based on performance or effort, the student's image of the dear old grandmother is an illegitimate appeal to *pathos* because it diverts the reader from rational to irrational criteria. The weeping grandmother may provide a legitimate motive for the student to study harder but not for the professor to change a grade.

Although it is difficult to classify all the ways that writers can create appeals from *pathos*, we will focus on four strategies: concrete language; specific examples and illustrations; narratives; and connotations of words, metaphors, and analogies. Each of these strategies lends "presence" to an argument by creating immediacy and emotional impact.

Use Concrete Language

Concrete language—one of the chief ways that writers achieve voice—can increase the liveliness, interest level, and personality of a writer's prose. When used in argument, concrete language typically heightens *pathos*. For example, consider the differences between the first and second drafts of the following student argument:

> *First draft:* People who prefer driving a car to taking a bus think that taking the bus will increase the stress of the daily commute. Just the opposite is true. Not being able to find a parking spot when in a hurry to work or school can cause a person stress. Taking the bus gives a person time to read or sleep, etc. It could be used as a mental break.

> *Second draft:* Taking the bus can be more relaxing than driving a car. Having someone else behind the wheel gives people time to chat with friends or cram for an exam. They can balance their checkbooks, do homework, doze off, read the daily newspaper, or get lost in a novel rather than foam at the mouth looking for a parking space.

In this revision, specific details enliven the prose by creating images that trigger positive feelings. Who wouldn't want some free time to doze off or to get lost in a novel?

Use Specific Examples and Illustrations

Specific examples and illustrations serve two purposes in an argument: They provide evidence that supports your reasons; simultaneously, they give your argument presence and emotional resonance. Note the flatness of the following draft arguing for the value of multicultural studies in a university core curriculum:

> *Early draft:* Another advantage of a multicultural education is that it will help us see our own culture in a broader perspective. If all we know is our own heritage, we might not be inclined to see anything bad about this heritage because we won't know anything else. But if we study other heritages, we can see the costs and benefits of our own heritage.

Now note the increase in "presence" when the writer adds a specific example:

> *Revised draft:* Another advantage of multicultural education is that it raises questions about traditional Western values. For example, owning private property (such as buying your own home) is part of the American dream and is a basic right guaranteed in our Constitution. However, in studying the beliefs of American Indians, students are confronted with a very different view of private property. When the U.S. government sought to buy land in the Pacific Northwest from Chief Sealth, he is alleged to have replied:
>
> > The president in Washington sends words that he wishes to buy our land. But how can you buy or sell the sky? The land? The idea is strange to us. If we do not own the freshness of the air and the sparkle of the water, how can you buy them? [. . .] We are part of the earth and it is part of us. [. . .] This we know: The earth does not belong to man, man belongs to the earth.
>
> Our class was shocked by the contrast between traditional Western views of property and Chief Sealth's views. One of our best class discussions was initiated by this quotation from Chief Sealth. Had we not been exposed to a view from another culture, we would have never been led to question the "rightness" of Western values.

The writer begins his revision by evoking a traditional Western view of private property, which he then questions by shifting to Chief Sealth's vision of land as open, endless, and unobtainable as the sky. Through the use of a specific example, the writer brings to life his previously abstract point about the benefit of multicultural education.

Use Narratives

A particularly powerful way to evoke *pathos* is to tell a story that either leads into your claim or embodies it implicitly and that appeals to your readers' feelings and imagination. Brief narratives—whether true or hypothetical—are particularly effective as opening attention grabbers for an argument. To illustrate how an introductory narrative (either a story or a brief scene) can create pathetic appeals, consider the following first paragraph to an argument opposing jet skis:

> I dove off the dock into the lake, and as I approached the surface I could see the sun shining through the water. As my head popped out, I located my cousin a few feet away in a rowboat waiting to escort me as I, a twelve-year-old girl, attempted to swim across the mile-wide, pristine lake and back to our dock. I made it, and that glorious summer day is one of my most precious memories. Today, however, no one would dare attempt that swim. Jet skis have taken over this small lake where I spent many summers with my grandparents. Dozens of whining jet skis crisscross the lake, ruining it for swimming, fishing, canoeing, row-boating, and even water-skiing. More stringent state laws are needed to control jet-skiing because it interferes with other uses of lakes and is currently very dangerous.

This narrative makes a case for a particular point of view toward jet skis by winning our identification with the writer's experience. She invites us to relive that experience with her while she also taps into our own treasured memories of summer experiences that have been destroyed by change.

Opening narratives to evoke *pathos* can be powerfully effective, but they are also risky. If they are too private, too self-indulgent, too sentimental, or even too dramatic and forceful, they can backfire on you. If you have doubts about an opening narrative, read it to a sample audience before using it in your final draft.

Choose Words, Metaphors, and Analogies with Appropriate Connotations

Another way of appealing to *pathos* is to select words, metaphors, or analogies with connotations that match your aim. We have already described this strategy in our discussion of the "framing" of evidence (Chapter 6, pp. 116–121). By using words with particular connotations, a writer guides readers to see the issue through the writer's angle of vision. Thus if you want to create positive feelings about a recent city council decision, you can call it "bold and decisive"; if you want to create negative feelings, you can call it "haughty and autocratic." Similarly, writers can use favorable or unfavorable metaphors and analogies to evoke different imaginative or emotional responses. A tax bill might be viewed as a "potentially fatal poison pill" or as "unpleasant but necessary economic medicine." In each of these cases, the words create an emotional as well as intellectual response.

For Class Discussion

Outside class, rewrite the introduction to one of your previous papers (or a current draft) to include more appeals to *pathos*. Use any of the strategies for giving your argument presence: concrete language, specific examples, narratives, metaphors, analogies, and connotative words. Bring both your original and your rewritten introductions to class. In pairs or in groups, discuss the comparative effectiveness of these introductions in trying to reach your intended audience.

Using Images for Emotional Appeal

One of the most powerful ways to engage an audience emotionally is to use photos or other images. (Chapter 9 focuses exclusively on visual rhetoric—the persuasive power of images.) While many written arguments do not lend themselves to visual illustrations, we suggest that when you construct arguments you consider the potential of visual support. Imagine that your argument were to appear in a newspaper or magazine where space would be provided for one or two visuals. What photographs or drawings might help persuade your audience toward your perspective?

When images work well, they are analogous to the verbal strategies of concrete language, specific illustrations, narratives, and connotative words. The challenge in using visuals is to find material that is straightforward enough not to require elaborate explanations, that is timely and relevant, and that clearly adds impact to a specific part of your argument. As an example, suppose you are writing an argument supporting fund-raising efforts to help third-world countries. To add a powerful appeal to *pathos*, you might consider incorporating into your argument the photograph shown in Color Plate C—a photograph of a Haitian woman walking on a rickety bridge over a vast garbage heap in a Haitian slum. This photograph, which appeared in the *New York Times* in the summer of 2002, creates an almost immediate emotional and imaginative response.

For Class Discussion

Working in small groups or as a whole class, share your responses to the following questions:

1. How would you describe the emotional/imaginative impact of Color Plate C (the photograph of a Haitian slum)?

2. Many appeals for helping third-world countries show pictures of big-bellied, starving children during a famine, often in Africa. How is your response to Color Plate C similar to or different from the commonly encountered pictures of starving children? How is Color Plate C's story about the ravages of poverty different from the stories of starving children?

3. Figures 7.1 and 7.2 show two photographs of John Walker Lindh, the "American Taliban" captured in Afghanistan as part of the U.S. military's response to the September 11 terrorist attacks in 2001. Figure 7.1 shows the photograph of Lindh taken by the Alexandria, Virginia, Sheriff's

FIGURE 7.1 *Sheriff's office photograph of John Walker Lindh*

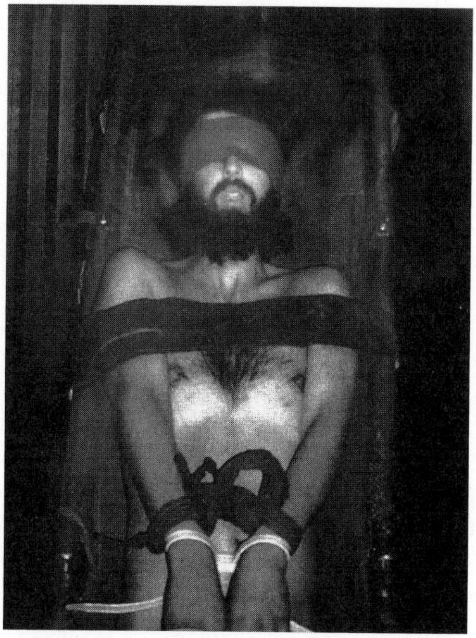

FIGURE 7.2 *Photograph of Lindh during incarceration in Afghanistan*

Department after Lindh was incarcerated in the United States, shaved, and placed in a prison uniform. This photograph was widely reproduced in arguments calling for Lindh's prosecution as a traitor. In late March 2002, the U.S. government was forced to release a photograph of Lindh (Figure 7.2) taken while he was held captive in Afghanistan before being transferred to the United States. This photograph was immediately used by Lindh's defense attorneys and by groups seeking Lindh's release.

a. How would you describe the emotional and intellectual impact of Figure 7.2? As a visual argument, what claim does it make?

b. Why would prosecuting attorneys favor Figure 7.1 while defense attorneys favor Figure 7.2?

4. Sometimes drawings as well as photographs can enhance an argument's emotional appeal. Consider the "America Supports You" poster (p. 73) that celebrates Armed Forces Day, May 21, 2005. How do the images of the little boy in the foreground, the sailor and his son in the top right-hand corner, and the soldiers advancing in combat gear in the bottom of the poster work with the verbal text to create an appeal to *pathos?*

Kairos: The Timeliness and Fitness of Arguments

To increase your argument's effectiveness, you need to consider not only its appeals to *logos, ethos,* and *pathos,* but also its *kairos*—that is, its timing, its appropriateness for the occasion. *Kairos* is one of those wonderful words, adopted from another language (in this case ancient Greek), that is impossible to define, yet powerful in what it represents. In Greek, *kairos* means "right time," "season," or "opportunity." It differs subtly from the ordinary Greek word for time, *chronos,* the root of our words "chronology" and "chronometer." You can measure *chronos* by looking at your watch, but you measure *kairos* by sensing the opportune time through psychological attentiveness to situation and meaning. To think *kairotically* is to be attuned to the total context of a situation in order to act in the right way at the right moment. By analogy, consider a skilled base runner who senses the right moment to steal second, a wise teacher who senses the right moment to praise or critique a student's performance, or a successful psychotherapist who senses the right moment to talk rather than listen in a counseling session. *Kairos* reminds us that a rhetorical situation is not stable and fixed, but evolves as events unfold or as audiences experience the psychological ebbs and flows of attention and care. Here are some examples that illustrate the range of insights contained by the term *kairos:*

- If you write a letter to the editor of a newspaper, you usually have a one- or two-day window before a current event becomes "old news" and is no longer interesting. An out-of-date letter will be rejected, not because it is poorly written or argued but because it misses its *kairotic* moment. (Similar instances of lost timeliness occur in class discussions: On how many occasions have you wanted to contribute an idea to class discussion, but the professor doesn't acknowledge your raised hand? When you finally are called on, the *kairotic* moment has passed.)

- Bobbi Buchanan's "Don't Hang Up, That's My Mom Calling," which we used to illustrate *pathos* (p. 132), could have been written only during a brief historical period when telemarketing was being publicly debated. Moreover, it could have been written only late in that period after numerous writers had attacked telemarketers. The piece was published in the *New York Times* because the editor received it at the right *kairotic* moment.

- After the July 7, 2005, suicide bombings in London, newspapers, magazines, and Internet news and advocacy sites were barraged with people's speculations about the cultural conditions that had converted some second- and third-generation British Muslims into terrorists. Europeans and British citizens and leaders judged that the *kairotic* moment was right to call on their Muslim citizens to be more active in condemning Islamic extremism. Discussions of homegrown Islamic militancy, previously ignored, suppressed, or politely not talked about, suddenly emerged in the British and European presses.

- A sociology major is writing a senior capstone paper for graduation. The due date for the paper is fixed, so the timing of the paper isn't at issue. But *kairos* is still relevant. It urges the student to consider what is appropriate for such a paper. What is the "right way" to produce a sociology paper at this moment in the history of the discipline? Currently, what are leading-edge versus trailing-edge questions in sociology? What theorists are now in vogue? What research methods would most impress a judging committee? How would a good capstone paper written in 2007 differ from one written a decade earlier?

■ A group of your friends has decided to protest your university's on-campus residency requirement for all students except seniors. This group has designed a poster—portraying the university administration as greedy corporate capitalists exploiting students—to be hung all over campus during a university fund-raising weekend when alumni and donors are likely to be touring the campus. The fund-raising weekend creates a *kairotic* moment for the posters, but some members of your group wonder if the poster is fair. After all, successful fund-raising benefits students as well as faculty and administrators. How could the poster be redesigned to emphasize student unhappiness with the residency requirement without creating such a negative view of university administrators? Here *kairos* concerns the appropriateness of the message for the moment, its being the right message at the right time.

As you can see from these examples, *kairos* concerns a whole range of questions connected to the timing, fitness, appropriateness, and proportions of a message within an evolving rhetorical context. There are no rules to help you determine the *kairotic* moment for your argument, but being attuned to *kairos* will help you "read" your audience and rhetorical situation in a dynamic way.

For Class Discussion

Your instructor will select an argument for analysis. We suggest an argument addressing a past event such as Charles Krauthammer's "This Isn't a 'Legal' Matter, This Is War," written soon after the September 11, 2001, terrorist attacks (pp. 236–238), or Daeha Ko's "The Monster That Is High School," written after the 1999 Columbine massacre (pp. 259–261). Working in small groups or as a whole class, analyze the assigned argument first from the perspective of *kairos* and then from the perspectives of *logos, ethos,* and *pathos.*

1. As you analyze the argument from the perspective of *kairos,* consider the following questions:

   a. What is the motivating occasion for this argument? That is, what causes this writer to put pen to paper or fingers to keyboard?

   b. What conversation is the writer joining? Who are the other voices in this conversation? What are these voices saying that compels the writer to add his or her own voice? How was the stage set to create the *kairotic* moment for this argument?

    c. Who is the writer's intended audience and why?

    d. What is the writer's purpose? Toward what view or action is the writer trying to persuade his or her audience?

    e. To what extent can various features of the argument be explained by your understanding of its *kairotic* moment?

2. Now analyze the same argument for its appeals to *logos, ethos,* and *pathos.* How successful is this argument in achieving its writer's purpose?

Conclusion

In this chapter, we have explored ways that writers can strengthen the persuasiveness of their arguments by creating appeals to *ethos* and *pathos* and by being attentive to *kairos.* Arguments are more persuasive if readers trust the credibility of the writer and if the argument appeals to readers' hearts and imaginations as well as to their intellects. Sometimes images such as drawings or photographs may reinforce the argument by evoking strong emotional responses, thus enhancing *pathos.* Finally, attentiveness to *kairos* keeps the writer attuned to the dynamics of a rhetorical situation in order to create the right message at the right time.

8 Accommodating Your Audience

Treating Differing Views

In the previous chapter we discussed strategies for moving your audience through the appeals of *ethos, pathos,* and *kairos.* In this chapter we focus on strategies for accommodating different kinds of audiences. Particularly, we discuss the problem of addressing opposing or alternative views—whether to omit them, refute them, concede to them, or incorporate them through compromise and conciliation. We show you how your choices about structure, content, and tone may differ depending on whether your audience is sympathetic, neutral, or resistant to your views. The strategies explained in this chapter will increase your flexibility as an arguer and enhance your chance of persuading a wide variety of audiences.

One-Sided, Multisided, and Dialogic Arguments

Arguments are sometimes said to be one-sided, multisided, or dialogic. A *one-sided* argument presents only the writer's position on the issue without summarizing and responding to alternative viewpoints. A *multisided* argument presents the writer's position, but also summarizes and responds to possible objections and alternative views. *One-sided* arguments and many *multisided* arguments often take an adversarial stance in that the writer regards alternative views as flawed or wrong and supports his own claim with a strongly persuasive intent. In contrast, *dialogic* arguments have a much stronger component of inquiry, where the writer presents himself as uncertain or searching, where the audience is considered a partner in the dialogue, and where the writer's purpose is to seek common ground perhaps leading to a consensual solution to a problem. (See our discussion in Chapter 1 of argument as truth seeking versus persuasion, pp. 10–13.) Although multisided arguments can be adversarial, they can also be made to feel dialogic, depending on the way the writer introduces and responds to alternative views.

At issue, then, is the writer's treatment of alternative views. Does the writer ignore them (one-sided argument), summarize them in order to rebut them (adversarial kind of multisided argument), or summarize them in order to acknowledge their validity, value, and force (a more dialogic kind of multisided argument)? Each of these approaches can be appropriate for certain occasions, depending on your purpose, your confidence in your own stance, and your audience's resistance to your views.

How can one determine the kind of argument that would be most effective in a given case? As a general rule, one-sided arguments are effective primarily for persons who already agree with the writer's claim. They tend to strengthen the convictions of those who are already in the writer's camp, but alienate those who aren't. For those initially opposed to a writer's claim, a multisided argument shows that the writer has considered other views and thus reduces some initial hostility. An especially interesting effect can occur with neutral or undecided audiences. In the short run, one-sided arguments are often persuasive to a neutral audience, but in the long run multisided arguments have more staying power. Neutral audiences who've heard only one side of an issue tend to change their minds when they hear alternative arguments. By anticipating and rebutting opposing views, a multisided argument diminishes the surprise and force of subsequent counterarguments. If we move from neutral to highly resistant audiences, adversarial approaches—even multisided ones—are seldom effective because they increase hostility and harden the differences between writer and reader. In such cases, more dialogic approaches have the best chance of establishing common ground for inquiry and consensus.

In the rest of this chapter we will show you how your choice of writing one-sided, multisided, or dialogic arguments is a function of how you perceive your audience's resistance to your views as well as your level of confidence in your own views.

Determining Your Audience's Resistance to Your Views

When you write an argument, you must always consider your audience's point of view. One way to imagine your relationship to your audience is to place it on a scale of resistance ranging from strong support of your position to strong opposition (see Figure 8.1). At the "Accord" end of this scale are like-minded people who basically agree with your position on the issue. At the "Resistance" end are those who strongly disagree with you, perhaps unconditionally, because their values, beliefs, or assumptions sharply differ from your own. Between "Accord" and "Resistance" lies a range of opinions. Close to your position will be those leaning in your direction but with less conviction than you have. Close to the re-

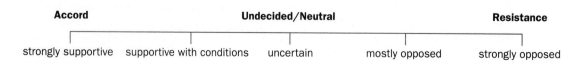

FIGURE 8.1   *Scale of resistance*

sistance position will be those basically opposed to your view but willing to listen to your argument and perhaps willing to acknowledge some of its strengths. In the middle are those undecided people who are still sorting out their feelings, seeking additional information, and weighing the strengths and weaknesses of alternative views.

Seldom, however, will you encounter an issue in which the range of disagreement follows a simple line from accord to resistance. Often resistant views fall into different categories so that no single line of argument appeals to all those whose views are different from your own. You have to identify not only your audience's resistance to your ideas but also the causes of that resistance.

Consider, for example, an issue that divided the state of Washington when the Seattle Mariners baseball team demanded a new stadium. A ballot initiative asked citizens to approve an increase in taxes to build a new retractable-roof stadium for the Mariners. Supporters of the initiative faced a complex array of resisting views (see Figure 8.2). Opponents of the initiative could be placed into four categories. Some simply had no interest in sports, cared nothing about baseball, and saw no benefit in building a huge sports facility in downtown Seattle. Another group loved baseball, perhaps followed the Mariners passionately, but was philosophically opposed to subsidizing rich players and owners with taxpayer money. This group argued that the whole sports industry needed to be restructured so that stadiums were paid for out of sports revenues. Still another group was opposed to tax hikes in general. It focused on the principle of reducing the size of government and of using tax revenues only for essential services. Finally, another powerful group supported baseball and supported the notion of public funding of a new stadium but opposed the kind of retractable-roof stadium specified in the initiative. This group wanted an old-fashioned, open-air stadium like Baltimore's Camden Yards or Cleveland's Jacobs Field.

Writers supporting the initiative found it impossible to address all these resisting audiences at once. If a supporter of the initiative wanted to aim an argument at sports haters, he or she could stress the spinoff benefits of a new ballpark (for example, the new ballpark would attract tourist revenue, renovate the deteriorating Pioneer Square neighborhood, create jobs, make sports lovers more likely to vote for public subsidies of the arts, and so forth). But these arguments

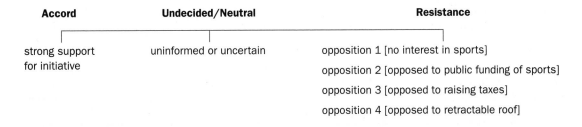

FIGURE 8.2   *Scale of resistance, baseball stadium issue*

were irrelevant to those who wanted an open-air stadium, who opposed tax hikes categorically, or who objected to public subsidy of millionaires.

Another kind of complexity occurs when a writer is positioned between two kinds of resisting views. Consider the position of student writer Sam, a gay man who wished to argue that gay and lesbian people should actively support legislation to legalize same-sex marriage (see Figure 8.3). Most arguments that support same-sex marriage hope to persuade conservative heterosexual audiences who tend to disapprove of homosexuality and stress traditional family values. But Sam imagined writing for a gay magazine such as the *Harvard Gay and Lesbian Review* or *The Advocate,* and he wished to aim his argument at liberal gay and lesbian activists who opposed traditional marriage on different grounds. These thinkers, critiquing traditional marriage for the way it stereotypes gender roles and limits the freedom of partners, argued that heterosexual marriage wasn't a good model for relationships in the gay community. These persons constituted an audience 180 degrees removed from the conservative proponents of family values who oppose same-sex marriage on moral and religious grounds.

In writing his early drafts, Sam was stymied by his attempt to address both audiences at once. Only after he blocked out the conservative "family values" audience and imagined an audience of what he called "liberationist" gays and lesbians was he able to develop a consistent argument. (You can read Sam's essay on pp. 308–310.)

The Mariners example and the same-sex marriage example illustrate the difficulty of adapting your argument to your audience's position on the scale of resistance. Yet doing so is important because you need a stable vision of your audience before you can determine an effective content, structure, and tone for your argument. As we showed in Chapter 5, an effective content derives from choosing audience-based reasons that appeal to your audience's values, assumptions, and beliefs. As we show in the rest of this chapter, an effective structure and tone are often a function of where your audience falls on the scale of resistance. The next sections show how you can adjust your arguing strategy depending on whether your audience is supportive, neutral, or hostile.

FIGURE 8.3   *Scale of resistance for same-sex marriage issue*

Appealing to a Supportive Audience: One-Sided Argument

Although arguing to a supportive audience might seem like preaching to the choir, such arguments are common. Usually, the arguer's goal is to convert belief into action—to inspire a party member to contribute to a senator's campaign or a bored office worker to sign up for a change-your-life weekend seminar.

Typically, appeals to a supportive audience are structured as one-sided arguments that either ignore opposing views or reduce them to "enemy" stereotypes. Filled with motivational language, these arguments list the benefits that will ensue from your donations to the cause and the horrors just around the corner if the other side wins. One of the authors of this text recently received a fund-raising letter from an environmental lobbying group declaring, "It's crunch time for the polluters and their pals on Capitol Hill." The "corporate polluters" and "anti-environment politicians," the letter continues, have "stepped up efforts to roll back our environmental protections—relying on large campaign contributions, slick PR firms and well-heeled lobbyists to get the job done before November's election." This letter makes the reader feel part of an in-group of good guys fighting the big business "polluters." Nothing in the letter examines environmental issues from business's perspective or attempts to examine alternative views fairly. Since the intended audience already believes in the cause, nothing in the letter invites readers to consider the issues more thoroughly. Rather, the goal is to solidify support, increase the fervor of belief, and inspire action. Most appeal arguments make it easy to act, ending with an 800 phone number to call, a Web site to visit, a tear-out postcard to send in, or a congressperson's address to write to.

Appealing to a Neutral or Undecided Audience: Classical Argument

The in-group appeals that motivate an already supportive audience can repel a neutral or undecided audience. Because undecided audiences are like jurors weighing all sides of an issue, they distrust one-sided arguments that caricature other views. Generally the best strategy for appealing to undecided audiences is the classical argument described in Chapter 3 (pp. 63–67).

What characterizes the classical argument is the writer's willingness to summarize opposing views fairly and to respond to them openly—either by trying to refute them or by conceding to their strengths and then shifting to a different field of values. Let's look at these strategies in more depth.

Summarizing Opposing Views

The first step toward responding to opposing views in a classical argument is to summarize them fairly. Follow the *principle of charity*, which obliges you to avoid loaded, biased, or "straw man" summaries that oversimplify or distort opposing arguments, making them easy to knock over.

Consider the difference between an unfair and a fair summary of Lisa Turner's "Playing with Our Food" (pp. 25–28), which we examined in Chapter 2.

UNFAIR SUMMARY

In a biased article lacking scientific understanding of biotechnology, natural foods huckster Lisa Turner parrots the health food industry's party line that genetically altered crops are Frankenstein's monsters run amuck. She ignorantly claims that consumption of biotech foods will lead to worldwide destruction, disease, and death ignoring the wealth of scientific literature showing that genetically modified foods are safe. Her misinformed attacks are scare tactics aimed at selling consumers on overpriced "health food" products to be purchased at boutique organic food stores.

This summary distorts and oversimplifies Turner's argument while continually interjecting the writer's own views rather than fairly summarizing Turner's views. It uses loaded phrases ("huckster," "parrots the health food industry's party line," "ignorantly," "scare tactics") and creates an *ad hominem* attack (see Appendix One for a definition of this reasoning fallacy) by implying that Turner is motivated by health food industry profits rather than genuine concern. The writer thus sets up a straw man that is easier to knock over than is Turner's original argument.

In contrast, consider the following more fair summary, which follows the principle of charity and tries to represent Turner's views as justly and accurately as possible. (For a longer summary of Turner's article, see Chapter 2, p. 30.)

FAIR SUMMARY

In an article appearing in a nutrition magazine, health food advocate Lisa Turner warns readers that much of our food today is genetically modified using gene-level techniques that differ completely from ordinary crossbreeding. She argues that the potential, unforeseen, harmful consequences of genetic engineering offset the possible benefits of increasing the food supply, reducing the use of pesticides, and boosting the nutritional value of foods. Turner asserts that genetic engineering is imprecise, untested, unpredictable, irreversible, and also uncontrollable due to animals, insects, and winds.

For Class Discussion

Suppose that you believe that ROTC courses ought to receive academic credit and thus you oppose the views of the student writer of "ROTC Courses Should Not Get College Credit" (see Appendix Two). Working individually or in groups, prepare two different summaries of this writer's views, as follows:

1. Unfair summary using loaded language or straw man oversimplification or distortion

2. Fair summary following the principle of charity

When you are finished, be prepared to read your summaries aloud to the class.

Refuting Opposing Views

Once you have summarized opposing views, you can either refute them or concede to their strengths. In refuting an opposing view, you attempt to convince readers that its argument is logically flawed, inadequately supported, or based on erroneous assumptions. In refuting an argument, you can rebut (1) the writer's stated reason and grounds, (2) the writer's warrant and backing, or (3) both. Put in less specialized language and you can rebut a writer's reasons and evidence or the writer's underlying assumptions. Suppose, for example, that you wanted to refute this argument:

> We shouldn't elect Joe as committee chair because he is too bossy.

One way to refute this argument is to rebut the stated reason that Joe is too bossy.

REBUTTAL OF REASON

I disagree with you that Joe is bossy. In fact, Joe is very unbossy. He's a good listener who's willing to compromise, and he involves others in decisions. The example you cite for his being bossy wasn't typical. It was a one-time circumstance that doesn't represent his normal behavior. [The writer could then provide examples of Joe's cooperative nature.]

Or you could concede that Joe is bossy but rebut the argument's warrant that bossiness is a bad trait:

REBUTTAL OF WARRANT

I agree that Joe is bossy, but in this circumstance bossiness is just the trait we need. This committee hasn't gotten anything done for six months and time is running out. We need a decisive person who can come in, get the committee organized, assign tasks, and get the job done.

Let's now illustrate these strategies in a more complex situation. Consider the controversy inspired by a *New York Times Magazine* article entitled "Recycling Is Garbage." Its author, John Tierney, argued that recycling is not environmentally sound and that it is cheaper to bury garbage in a landfill than to recycle it. In criticizing recycling, Tierney argued that recycling wastes money; he provided evidence that "every time a sanitation department crew picks up a load of bottles and cans from the curb, New York City loses money." In Toulmin's terms, one of Tierney's arguments is structured as follows:

CLAIM: Recycling is bad policy.

STATED REASON: because it costs more to recycle material than to bury it in a landfill

GROUNDS: evidence of the high cost of recycling [Tierney cites evidence that it costs New York City $200 more per ton to collect and dispose of recyclables than to bury them]

WARRANT: We should dispose of garbage in the least expensive way.

A number of environmentalists responded angrily to Tierney's argument, challenging either his reason, his warrant, or both. Those refuting the reason offered counterevidence showing that recycling isn't as expensive as Tierney claimed. Those refuting the warrant said that even if the costs of recycling are higher than burying wastes in a landfill, recycling still benefits the environment by reducing the amount of virgin materials taken from nature. These critics, in effect, offered a new warrant: Saving the earth's resources takes precedence over economic costs.

Strategies for Rebutting Evidence

Whether you are rebutting an argument's reasons or its warrant, you will frequently need to question a writer's use of evidence. Here are some strategies you can use:

- *Deny the truth of the data.*   Arguers can disagree about the facts of a case. If you have reasons to doubt a writer's facts, call them into question.
- *Cite counterexamples and countertestimony.*   You can often rebut an argument based on examples or testimony by citing counterexamples or countertestimony that denies the conclusiveness of the original data.
- *Cast doubt on the representativeness or sufficiency of examples.*   Examples are powerful only if the audience feels them to be representative and sufficient. Many environmentalists complained that John Tierney's attack on recycling was based too largely on data from New York City and that it didn't accurately take into account the more positive experiences of other cities and states. When data from outside New York City were examined, the cost-effectiveness and positive environmental impact of recycling seemed more apparent.
- *Cast doubt on the relevance or recency of the examples, statistics, or testimony.*   The best evidence is up-to-date. In a rapidly changing universe, data that are even a few years out-of-date are often ineffective. For example, as the demand for recycled goods increases, the cost of recycling will be reduced. Out-of-date statistics will skew any argument about the cost of recycling.
- *Call into question the credibility of an authority.*   If an opposing argument is based on testimony, you can undermine its persuasiveness if you show that a

person being cited lacks up-to-date or relevant expertise in the field. (This procedure is different from the *ad hominem* fallacy discussed in Appendix One because it doesn't attack the personal character of the authority but only the authority's expertise on a specific matter.)

■ *Question the accuracy or context of quotations.* Evidence based on testimony is frequently distorted by being either misquoted or taken out of context. Often scientists qualify their findings heavily, but these qualifications are omitted by the popular media. You can thus attack the use of a quotation by putting it in its original context or by restoring the qualifications accompanying the quotation in its original source.

■ *Question the way statistical data were produced or interpreted.* Chapter 6 provides fuller treatment of how to question statistics. In general, you can rebut statistical evidence by calling into account how the data were gathered, treated mathematically, or interpreted. It can make a big difference, for example, whether you cite raw numbers or percentages or whether you choose large or small increments for the axes of graphs.

Conceding to Opposing Views

In writing a classical argument, a writer must sometimes concede to an opposing argument rather than refute it. Sometimes you encounter portions of an argument that you simply can't refute. For example, suppose you support the legalization of hard drugs such as cocaine and heroin. Adversaries argue that legalizing hard drugs will increase the number of drug users and addicts. You might dispute the size of their numbers, but you reluctantly agree that they are right. Your strategy in this case is not to refute the opposing argument but to concede to it by admitting that legalization of hard drugs will promote heroin and cocaine addiction. Having made that concession, your task is then to show that the benefits of drug legalization still outweigh the costs you've just conceded.

As this example shows, the strategy of a concession argument is to switch from the field of values employed by the writer you disagree with to a different field of values more favorable to your position. You don't try to refute the writer's stated reason and grounds (by arguing that legalization will *not* lead to increased drug usage and addiction) or the writer's warrant (by arguing that increased drug use and addiction is not a problem). Rather, you shift the argument to a new field of values by introducing a new warrant, one that you think your audience can share (that the benefits of legalization—eliminating the black market and ending the crime, violence, and prison costs associated with procurement of drugs—outweigh the costs of increased addiction). To the extent that opponents of legalization share your desire to stop drug-related crime, shifting to this new field of values is a good strategy. Although it may seem that you weaken your own position by conceding to an opposing argument, you may actually strengthen it by increasing your credibility and gaining your audience's goodwill. Moreover, conceding to one part of an opposing argument doesn't mean that you won't refute other parts of that argument.

Example of a Student Essay Using Refutation Strategy

The following extract from a student essay is the refutation section of a classical argument appealing to a neutral or undecided audience. In this essay, student writer Marybeth Hamilton argues for continued taxpayer support of First Place, an alternative public school for homeless children that also provides job counseling and mental health services for families. Because running First Place is costly and because it can accommodate only 4 percent of her city's homeless children, Marybeth recognizes that her audience may object to continued public funding. Consequently, to reach the neutral or skeptical members of her audience, she devotes the following portion of her argument to summarizing and refuting opposing views.

From *"First Place: A Healing School for Homeless Children"*
Marybeth Hamilton (Student)

---

1   . . . As stated earlier, the goal of First Place is to prepare students for returning to mainstream public schools. Although there are many reasons to continue operating an agency like First Place, there are some who would argue against it. One argument is that the school is too expensive, costing many more taxpayer dollars per child than a mainstream school. I can understand this objection to cost, but one way to look at First Place is as a preventative action by the city to reduce the future costs of crime and welfare. Because all the students at First Place are at-risk for educational failure, drug and alcohol abuse, or numerous other long-term problems, a program like First Place attempts to stop the problems before they start. In the long run, the city could be saving money in areas such as drug rehabilitation, welfare payments, or jail costs.

2   Others might criticize First Place for spending some of its funding on social services for the students and their families instead of spending it all on educational needs. When the city is already making welfare payments and providing a shelter for the families, why do they deserve anything more? Basically, the job of any school is to help a child become educated and have social skills. At First Place, students' needs run deep, and their entire families are in crisis. What good is it to help just the child when the rest of the family is still suffering? The education of only the child will not help the family out of poverty. Therefore, First Place helps parents look for jobs by providing job search help including assistance with résumés. They even supply clothes to wear to an interview. First Place also provides a parent support group for expressing anxieties and learning coping skills. This therapy helps parents deal with their struggles in a productive way, reducing the chance that they will take out their frustration on their child. All these "extras" are an attempt to help the family get back on its feet and become self-supporting.

Another objection to an agency like First Place is that the short-term stay at First Place does no long-term good for the student. However, in talking with Michael Siptroth, a teacher at First Place, I learned that the individual attention the students receive helps many of them catch up in school quite quickly. He reported that some students actually made a three-grade-level improvement in one year. This improvement definitely contributes to the long-term good of the student, especially in the area of self-esteem. Also, the students at First Place are in desperate situations. For most, any help is better than no help. Thus First Place provides extended day care for the children so they won't have to be unsupervised at home while their parents are working or looking for work. For example, some homeless children live in motels on Aurora Avenue, a major highway that is overrun with fast cars, prostitutes, and drugs. Aurora Avenue is not a safe place for children to play, so the extended day care is important for many of First Place's students.

Finally, opponents might question the value of removing students from mainstream classrooms. Some might argue that separating children from regular classrooms is not good because it further highlights their differences from the mainstream children. Also, the separation period might cause additional alienation when the First Place child does return to a mainstream school. In reality, though, the effects are quite different. Children at First Place are sympathetic to each other. Perhaps for the first time in their lives, they do not have to be on the defensive because no one is going to make fun of them for being homeless; they are all homeless. The time spent at First Place is usually a time for catching up to the students in mainstream schools. When students catch up, they have one fewer reason to be seen as different from mainstream students. If the students stayed in the mainstream school and continued to fall behind, they would only get teased more.

First Place is a program that merits the community's ongoing moral and financial support. With more funding, First Place could help many more homeless children and their families along the path toward self-sufficiency. While this school is not the ultimate answer to the problem of homelessness, it is a beginning. These children deserve a chance to build their own lives, free from the stigma of homelessness, and I, as a responsible citizen, feel a civic and moral duty to do all I can to help them.

For Class Discussion

1. Individually or in groups, analyze the refutation strategies that Marybeth employs in her argument.

   a. Summarize each of the opposing reasons that Marybeth anticipates from her audience.

   b. How does she attempt to refute each line of reasoning in the opposing argument? Where does she refute her audience's stated reason? Where does she refute a warrant? Where does she concede to an opposing argument but then shift to a different field of values?

   c. How effective is Marybeth's refutation? Would you as a city resident vote for allotting more public money for this school? Why or why not?

2. Examine each of the following arguments, imagining how the enthymeme could be fleshed out with grounds and backing. Then attempt to refute each argument. Suggest ways to rebut the reason or the warrant or both, or to concede to the argument and then switch to a different field of values.

a. Signing the Kyoto treaty (pledging that the United States would substantially lower its emission of greenhouse gases) is a bad idea because reducing greenhouse emissions would seriously harm the American economy.

b. Majoring in engineering is better than majoring in music because engineers make more money than musicians.

c. The United States should reinstitute the draft because doing so is the only way to maintain a large enough military to preserve freedom in Iraq and still be able to defend American interests in other trouble spots in the world.

d. The United States should build more nuclear reactors because nuclear reactors will provide substantial electrical energy without emitting greenhouse gases.

e. People should be allowed to own handguns because owning handguns helps them protect their homes against potentially violent intruders.

Appealing to a Resistant Audience: Dialogic Argument

Whereas classical argument is effective for neutral or undecided audiences, it is often less effective for audiences strongly opposed to the writer's views. Because resistant audiences hold values, assumptions, or beliefs widely different from the writer's, they are often unswayed by classical argument, which attacks their worldview too directly. On many values-laden issues such as abortion, gun control, gay rights, or the role of religion in the public sphere, the distance between a writer and a resistant audience can be so great that dialogue seems impossible. In these cases the writer's goal may be simply to open dialogue by seeking common ground—that is, by finding places where the writer and audience agree. For example, pro-choice and pro-life advocates may never agree on a woman's right to an abortion, but they might share common ground in wanting to reduce teenage pregnancy. There is room, in other words, for conversation, if not for agreement.

Because of these differences in basic beliefs and values, the goal of dialogic argument is seldom to convert resistant readers to the writer's position. The best a writer can hope for is to reduce somewhat the level of resistance, perhaps by increasing the reader's willingness to listen as preparation for future dialogue. In fact, once dialogue is initiated, parties who genuinely listen to each other and have learned to respect each other's views might begin finding solutions to shared problems. A recent example of this process can be seen in former Louisiana

Senator John Breaux's call for a common-ground strategy for solving the U.S. health care crisis characterized by soaring medical costs and rising numbers of Americans without medical insurance. Breaux objects to cable news talk shows in which political opponents shout at each other. "Why not," he asked in an interview, "try a program where the moderator would invite people of opposing philosophies to seek common ground?"* Breaux hopes to address the health care crisis by bringing together liberals and conservatives, patients and insurance companies, doctors and pharmaceutical executives, hospital managers and nurses to find common ground upon which they can begin a dialogic search for solutions.

The dialogic strategies we explain in this section—the delayed-thesis strategy and Rogerian strategy—are aimed at promoting understanding between a writer and a resistant audience. They work to disarm hostility by showing the writer's respect for alternative views and by lessening the force with which the writer presents his or her own views.

Delayed-Thesis Argument

In many cases you can reach a resistant audience by using a *delayed-thesis* structure in which you wait until the end of your argument to reveal your thesis. Classical argument asks you to state your thesis in the introduction, support it with reasons and evidence, and then summarize and refute opposing views. Rhetorically, however, it is not always advantageous to tell your readers where you stand at the start of your argument or to separate yourself so definitively from alternative views. For resistant audiences, it may be better to keep the issue open, delaying the revelation of your own position until the end of the essay.

To illustrate the different effects of classical versus delayed-thesis arguments, we invite you to read a delayed-thesis argument by nationally syndicated columnist Ellen Goodman. The article appeared in 1985 shortly after the nation was shocked by a brutal gang rape in New Bedford, Massachusetts, in which a woman was raped on a pool table by patrons of a local bar.†

Minneapolis Pornography Ordinance
Ellen Goodman

Just a couple of months before the pool-table gang rape in New Bedford, Mass., 1
Hustler magazine printed a photo feature that reads like a blueprint for the actual crime. There were just two differences between *Hustler* and real life. In *Hustler,* the woman enjoyed it. In real life, the woman charged rape.

---

*David S. Broder, "Building Bipartisan Consensus on Health-Care Solutions," *Seattle Times* 14 July 2005, B8.

†The rape was later the subject of an Academy Award–winning movie, *The Accused,* starring Jodie Foster.

2   There is no evidence that the four men charged with this crime had actually read the magazine. Nor is there evidence that the spectators who yelled encouragement for two hours had held previous ringside seats at pornographic events. But there is a growing sense that the violent pornography being peddled in this country helps to create an atmosphere in which such events occur.

3   As recently as last month, a study done by two University of Wisconsin researchers suggested that even "normal" men, prescreened college students, were changed by their exposure to violent pornography. After just ten hours of viewing, reported researcher Edward Donnerstein, "the men were less likely to convict in a rape trial, less likely to see injury to a victim, more likely to see the victim as responsible." Pornography may not cause rape directly, he said, "but it maintains a lot of very callous attitudes. It justifies aggression. It even says you are doing a favor to the victim."

4   If we can prove that pornography is harmful, then shouldn't the victims have legal rights? This, in any case, is the theory behind a city ordinance that recently passed the Minneapolis City Council. Vetoed by the mayor last week, it is likely to be back before the Council for an overriding vote, likely to appear in other cities, other towns. What is unique about the Minneapolis approach is that for the first time it attacks pornography, not because of nudity or sexual explicitness, but because it degrades and harms women. It opposes pornography on the basis of sex discrimination.

5   University of Minnesota Law Professor Catherine MacKinnon, who co-authored the ordinance with feminist writer Andrea Dworkin, says that they chose this tactic because they believe that pornography is central to "creating and maintaining the inequality of the sexes. . . . Just being a woman means you are injured by pornography."

6   They defined pornography carefully as, "the sexually explicit subordination of women, graphically depicted, whether in pictures or in words." To fit their legal definition it must also include one of nine conditions that show this subordination, like presenting women who "experience sexual pleasure in being raped or . . . mutilated. . . ." Under this law, it would be possible for a pool-table rape victim to sue *Hustler.* It would be possible for a woman to sue if she were forced to act in a pornographic movie. Indeed, since the law describes pornography as oppressive to all women, it would be possible for any woman to sue those who traffic in the stuff for violating her civil rights.

7   In many ways, the Minneapolis ordinance is an appealing attack on an appalling problem. The authors have tried to resolve a long and bubbling conflict among those who have both a deep aversion to pornography and a deep loyalty to the value of free speech. "To date," says Professor MacKinnon, "people have identified the pornographer's freedom with everybody's freedom. But we're saying that the freedom of the pornographer is the subordination of women. It means one has to take a side."

8   But the sides are not quite as clear as Professor MacKinnon describes them. Nor is the ordinance.

9   Even if we accept the argument that pornography is harmful to women—and I do—then we must also recognize that anti-Semitic literature is harmful to Jews and

racist literature is harmful to blacks. For that matter, Marxist literature may be harmful to government policy. It isn't just women versus pornographers. If women win the right to sue publishers and producers, then so could Jews, blacks, and a long list of people who may be able to prove they have been harmed by books, movies, speeches or even records. The Manson murders, you may recall, were reportedly inspired by the Beatles.

We might prefer a library or book store or lecture hall without *Mein Kampf* or the Grand Whoever of the Ku Klux Klan. But a growing list of harmful expressions would inevitably strangle freedom of speech. 10

This ordinance was carefully written to avoid problems of banning and prior restraint, but the right of any woman to claim damages from pornography is just too broad. It seems destined to lead to censorship. 11

What the Minneapolis City Council has before it is a very attractive theory. What MacKinnon and Dworkin have written is a very persuasive and useful definition of pornography. But they haven't yet resolved the conflict between the harm of pornography and the value of free speech. In its present form, this is still a shaky piece of law. 12

Consider now how this argument's rhetorical effect would be different if Ellen Goodman had revealed her thesis in the introduction using the classical argument form. Here is how this introduction might have looked:

GOODMAN'S INTRODUCTION REWRITTEN IN CLASSICAL FORM

Just a couple of months before the pool-table gang rape in New Bedford, Mass., *Hustler* magazine printed a photo feature that reads like a blueprint for the actual crime. There were just two differences between *Hustler* and real life. In *Hustler*, the woman enjoyed it. In real life, the woman charged rape. Of course, there is no evidence that the four men charged with this crime had actually read the magazine. Nor is there evidence that the spectators who yelled encouragement for two hours had held previous ringside seats at pornographic events.

But there is a growing sense that the violent pornography being peddled in this country helps to create an atmosphere in which such events occur. One city is taking a unique approach to attack this problem. An ordinance recently passed by the Minneapolis City Council outlaws pornography not because it contains nudity or sexually explicit acts, but because it degrades and harms women. Unfortunately, despite the proponents' good intentions, the Minneapolis ordinance is a bad law because it has potentially dangerous consequences.

Even though Goodman's position can be grasped more quickly in this classical form, our students generally find the original delayed-thesis version more effective. Why is this?

Most people point to the greater sense of complexity and surprise in the delayed-thesis version, a sense that comes largely from the delayed discovery of the writer's position. Whereas the classical version immediately labels the ordinance a "bad law," the original version withholds judgment, inviting the reader to examine the law more sympathetically and to identify with the position of those who drafted it. Rather than distancing herself from those who see pornography as a violation of women's rights, Goodman shares with her readers her own struggles to think through these issues, thereby persuading us of her genuine sympathy for the ordinance and for its feminist proponents. In the end, her delayed thesis renders her final rejection of the ordinance not only more surprising but more convincing.

Clearly, then, a writer's decision about when to reveal her thesis is critical. Revealing the thesis early makes the writer seem more hardnosed, more sure of her position, more confident about how to divide the ground into friendly and hostile camps, more in control. Delaying the thesis, in contrast, complicates the issues, increases reader sympathy for more than one view, and heightens interest in the tension among alternative views and in the writer's struggle for clarity.

Rogerian Argument

An even more powerful strategy for addressing resistant audiences is a conciliatory strategy often called *Rogerian argument*, named after psychologist Carl Rogers, who used this strategy to help people resolve differences.* Rogerian argument emphasizes "empathic listening," which Rogers defined as the ability to see an issue sympathetically from another person's perspective. He trained people to withhold judgment of another person's ideas until after they listened attentively to the other person, understood that person's reasoning, appreciated that person's values, respected that person's humanity—in short, walked in that person's shoes. What Carl Rogers understood is that traditional methods of argumentation are threatening. Because Rogerian argument stresses the psychological as well as logical dimensions of argument, and because it emphasizes reducing threat and building bridges rather than winning an argument, it is particularly effective when dealing with emotionally laden issues.

Under Rogerian strategy, the writer reduces the sense of threat in her argument by showing that *both writer and resistant audience share many basic values.* Instead of attacking the audience as wrongheaded, the Rogerian writer respects the audience's views and demonstrates an understanding of the audience's position before presenting her own position. Finally, the Rogerian writer seldom asks the audience to capitulate entirely to the writer's side—just to shift somewhat toward the writer's views. By acknowledging that she has already shifted toward the audience's views, the writer makes it easier for the audience to accept compromise. All of this negotiation ideally leads to a compromise between—or better, a synthesis of—the opposing positions.

The key to successful Rogerian argument, besides the art of listening, is the ability to point out areas of agreement between the writer's and reader's posi-

---

*See Carl Rogers's essay "Communication: Its Blocking and Its Facilitation" in his book *On Becoming a Person* (Boston: Houghton Mifflin, 1961), 329–37. For a fuller discussion of Rogerian argument, see Richard Young, Alton Becker, and Kenneth Pike, *Rhetoric: Discovery and Change* (New York: Harcourt Brace, 1972).

tions. For example, if you support a woman's right to choose abortion and you are arguing with someone completely opposed to abortion, you're unlikely to convert your reader, but you might reduce the level of resistance. You begin this process by summarizing your reader's position sympathetically, stressing your shared values. You might say, for example, that you also value babies; that you also are appalled by people who treat abortion as a form of birth control; that you also worry that the easy acceptance of abortion diminishes the value society places on human life; and that you also agree that accepting abortion lightly can lead to lack of sexual responsibility. Building bridges like these between you and your readers makes it more likely that they will listen to you when you present your own position.

In its emphasis on establishing common ground, Rogerian argument has much in common with recent feminist theories of argument. Many feminists criticize classical argument as rooted in a male value system and tainted by metaphors of war and combat. Thus, classical arguments, with their emphasis on assertion and refutation, are typically praised for being "powerful" or "forceful." The writer "defends" his position and "attacks" his "opponent's" position using facts and data as "ammunition" and reasons as "big guns" to "blow away" his opponent's claim. According to some theorists, viewing argument as war can lead to inauthenticity, posturing, and game playing.

Writers who share this distrust of classical argumentation often find Rogerian argument appealing because it stresses self-examination, clarification, and accommodation rather than refutation. Rogerian argument is more in tune with win-win negotiation than with win-lose debate.

To illustrate a conciliatory or Rogerian approach to an issue, we show you student writer Rebekah Taylor's argument written in response to the assignment on page 160. Rebekah chose to write a Rogerian argument in the form of a letter. An outspoken advocate for animal rights on her campus, Rebekah addressed her letter to an actual friend, Jim, with whom she had had many long philosophical conversations when she attended a different college. Note how Rebekah "listens" empathically to her friend's position on eating meat and proposes a compromise action.

A Letter to Jim
Rebekah Taylor (Student)

Dear Jim,

    I decided to write you a letter today because I miss our long talks. Now that   1
I have transferred colleges, we haven't had nearly enough heated discussions to satisfy either of us. I am writing now to again take up one of the issues we vehemently disagreed on in the past—meat-based diets.

2   Jim, I do understand how your view that eating meat is normal differs from mine. In your family, you learned that humans eat animals, and this view was reinforced in school where the idea of the food pyramid based on meat protein was taught and where most children had not even heard of vegetarian options. Also, your religious beliefs taught that God intended humans to have ultimate dominion over all animals. For humans, eating meat is part of a planned cycle of nature. In short, you were raised in a family and community that accepted meat-based diets as normal, healthy, and ethically justifiable whereas I was raised in a family that cared very deeply for animals and attended a church that frequently entertained a vegan as a guest speaker.

3   Let me now briefly reiterate for you my own basic beliefs about eating animals. As I have shared with you, my personal health is important to me, and I, along with other vegetarians and vegans, believe that a vegetarian diet is much more healthy than a meat diet. But my primary motivation is my deep respect for animals. I have always felt an overpowering sense of compassion for animals and forceful sorrow and regret for the injuries that humans inflict upon them. I detest suffering, especially when it is forced upon creatures that cannot speak out against it. These deep feelings led me to become a vegetarian at the age of 5. While lying in bed one night, I looked up at the poster of a silky-white harbor seal that had always hung on my wall. As I looked at the face of that seal, I made a connection between that precious animal on my wall and the animals that had been killed for the food I ate every day. In the dim glow of my Strawberry Shortcake night light, I promised those large, dark seal eyes that I would never eat animals again. Seventeen years have passed now and that promise still holds true. Every day I feel more dedicated to the cause of animal rights around the world.

4   I know very well that my personal convictions are not the same as yours. However, I believe that we might possibly agree on more aspects of this issue than we realize. Although we would not be considered by others as allies on the issue of eating meat, we do share a common enemy—factory farms. Although you eat animal products and I do not, we both share a basic common value that is threatened by today's factory farms. We both disapprove of the unnecessary suffering of animals.

5   Though we might disagree on the morality of using animals for food at all, we do agree that such animals should not be made to suffer. Yet at factory farms, billions of animals across the world are born, live, and die in horribly cramped, dark, and foul-smelling barns. None of these animals knows the feeling of fresh air, or of warm, blessed sunlight on their backs. Most do not move out of their tight, uncomfortable pens until the day that they are to be slaughtered. At these factory farms, animals are processed as if they were inanimate objects, with no regard for the fact that they do feel fear and pain.

6   It is because of our shared opposition to animal suffering that I ask you to consider making an effort to buy meat from small, independent local farmers. I am told by friends that all supermarkets offer such meat options. This would be an easy and effective way to fight factory farms. I know that I could never con-

vince you to stop eating meat, and I will never try to force my beliefs on you. As your friend, I am grateful simply to be able to write to you so candidly about my beliefs. I trust that regardless of what your ultimate reaction is to this letter, you will thoughtfully consider what I have written, as I will thoughtfully consider what you write in return.

Sincerely,

Rebekah

For Class Discussion

1. In this letter, what shared values between writer and reader does the writer stress?
2. How is Rebekah's proposal—the action she asks of Jim—a compromise? How does this compromise show respect for Jim's values?
3. Imagine this letter rewritten as a classical argument. How would it be different?

Conclusion

This chapter has explained strategies for accommodating audiences according to their degree of resistance to the writer's view. In addressing supportive audiences, writers typically compose one-sided arguments with strong motivational appeals that whip up enthusiasm for the cause and promote action. Neutral or undecided audiences generally respond most favorably to classical arguments that set out strong reasons in support of the writer's position yet openly address alternative views, which are first summarized and then either rebutted or conceded to. Strongly resistant audiences typically respond most favorably to dialogic strategies, such as delayed-thesis or Rogerian argument, which seek common ground with an audience, aim at reducing hostility, and take a more inquiring or conciliatory stance.

WRITING ASSIGNMENT
FOR CHAPTERS 7 AND 8

The assignment for Chapters 7 and 8 has two parts. Part One is an actual argument you will write. Part Two is your own self-reflective analysis on how you chose to appeal to and accommodate your audience.

PART ONE: For this assignment, argue against a popular cultural practice or belief that you think is wrong, or argue for an action or belief that you think is right even though it will be highly unpopular. Your claim, in other words, must be controversial—going against the grain of popular actions, values, and beliefs—so that you can anticipate considerable resistance to your views. This essay invites you to stand up for something you believe in even though your view will be highly contested. Your goal is to persuade your audience toward your position.

In writing and revising your argument, draw upon appropriate strategies from Chapters 7 and 8. From Chapter 7 consider strategies for increasing your appeals to *ethos* and *pathos*. From Chapter 8 consider strategies for appealing to audiences according to their level of resistance. Choose the most resistant audience that you think you can sway to your point of view. Whether you use a refutation strategy, a delayed-thesis strategy, a Rogerian strategy, or some combination of these approaches is up to you.

PART TWO: Attach to your argument a self-reflective letter to your instructor and classmates explaining and justifying the choices you made for appealing to your audience and accommodating their views. In your letter address questions such as the following:

1. At the most resistant end of the spectrum, why are people opposed to your claim? How does your claim challenge their views and perhaps threaten their own value system?

2. Whom did you picture as the audience you were trying to sway? Where on the spectrum from "accord" to "resistance" did you address your argument? Why?

3. What strategies did you use for appealing to that audience?

4. What choices did you make in trying to accommodate differing views?

5. What challenges did this assignment present for you? How successful do you think you were in meeting those challenges?

9 Conducting Visual Arguments

In today's visually oriented culture, arguments increasingly use photographs, drawings, graphics, and innovative page and text design for persuasive effect. As we shall see, visuals can enhance the *logos, pathos,* and *ethos* of an argument by supporting or clarifying an argument's logical core, moving audiences imaginatively and emotionally, or enhancing the writer's credibility and authority. They can also substantially enliven a writer's argument, keeping readers hooked and engaged. In this chapter, we ask you to explore with us the enormous rhetorical potential of visual elements in arguments, particularly the way that visual and verbal elements can collaborate to achieve persuasive effects.

Using visuals in arguments also poses challenges. It places on arguers an even greater burden to understand their audience, to think through the effect visuals will have on that audience, and to make sure that the verbal and visual parts of an argument work together. In a public controversy between environmentalists and a Native American tribe, the Makah, over this tribe's right to hunt gray whales, a public relations expert advised, "One of the first things you want to do in public relations is control the picture. Whichever side has the better picture very often wins the argument." Before we examine visual design, we want to describe three recent examples of the powerful potential in using visuals.

- During the 2004 presidential campaign, the Republican party cast Democratic candidate John Kerry as a "flip-flopper" who constantly changed his position on issues. So powerful was this image that Republicans made campaign statements simply by holding up a pair of flip-flops or including a picture of flip-flops in anti-Kerry campaign ads. To counter the image of Kerry as indecisive or weak, his campaign managers highlighted Kerry's athletic image by showing him skiing or windsurfing. However, the strategy backfired. The Republicans seized on news coverage of Kerry's windsurfing off Nantucket to create their famous "zig zag" ad featuring aerial shots of Kerry on his windsurf board. Not only did Kerry flip-flop but he also zigged to the left and then zagged to the right. Republicans also insinuated that windsurfing was an elite sport for the rich and contrasted Kerry's windsurfing image with pictures of George Bush eating hot dogs at baseball games or working-class picnics.

■ Conflicts over news coverage of the Iraq war have focused on the use of images. While Al-Jazeera, the biggest Islamic news network in the Middle East, has extensively shown graphic images of civilian casualties in Iraq, American news networks have controlled all images of the war relayed to the American public. Consequently, when in April 2004 an Army contract worker in Kuwait, Tami Salicio, photographed a row of flag-draped coffins in the hold of a military cargo plane and the photograph was widely published in newspapers, Ms. Salicio was fired. Defenders of the policy to ban images of caskets coming home from the battlefield maintained that this photo was disrespectful to the soldiers' grieving families. Opponents of the Iraq war claimed that the real reason for the ban was the administration's desire to minimize public awareness of war casualties.

■ Reminding all arguers to choose their images carefully, in an article entitled "Sending the Right Message in Art Form," posted on the Web site of the Humane Society of the United States, the author warns local Humane Society chapters that poorly thought-out drawings and photos could undermine the organization's goals. To motivate people to care for their animals responsibly, the article proposes these guidelines: avoid showing any unneutered males or females with litters, dogs with prong collars or choke chains unless they are in training sessions, unsupervised dogs outside or cats outdoors, or dogs tied to trees, doghouses, or fences. Photos and drawings should show all dogs and cats with visible collars and ID tags and should depict mixed breeds as well as purebreds and mature animals as well as adorable puppies and kittens.

Each of these instances demonstrates the suggestive power of visual elements and the challenge of planning exactly how visuals should function in your argument.

With this background in mind, we turn now to explaining some basic components of visual design. We then examine several genres of visual argument such as posters and fliers, public affairs advocacy ads, political cartoons, and Web pages. The third section of the chapter explains how you can use visual elements in your own arguments and invites you to create your own poster or advocacy advertisement. In the final section, we explain how you can display numerical data graphically for rhetorical effect.

Understanding Design Elements in Visual Argument

To understand how visual images can produce an argument, you need to understand the design elements that work together to create a visual text. In this section we'll explain and illustrate the four basic components of visual design: use of type, use of space and layout, use of color, and use of images.

Use of Type

Type is an important visual element of written arguments. Variations in type, such as size, boldface, italics, or all caps, can direct a reader's attention to an argument's structure and highlight main points. In arguments designed specifically for visual impact, such as posters or advocacy advertisements, type is often used in eye-catching and meaningful ways. In choosing type, you need to consider the typeface or font style, the size of the type, and formatting options. The main typefaces or fonts are classified as serif, sans serif, and specialty type. Serif type has little extensions on the letters. (This text is set in serif type.) Sans serif type lacks these extensions. Specialty type includes script fonts and special symbols. In addition to font style, type comes in different sizes. It is measured in points, with one point equal to 1/72 of an inch. Most text-based arguments consisting mainly of body text are written in ten- to twelve-point type whereas more image-based arguments may use a mixture of type sizes that interact with the images for persuasive effect. Type can also be formatted using bold, italics, underlining, or shading for emphasis. Table 9.1 shows examples of type styles, as well as their typical uses.

The following basic principles for choosing type for visual arguments can help you achieve your overall goals of readability, visual appeal, and suitability.

Principles for Choosing Type for Visual Arguments

1. If you are creating a poster or advocacy advertisement, you will need to decide how much of your argument will be displayed in words and how much in images. For the text portions, choose *display type* (sans serif) or specialty fonts for titles, headings, and slogans and *body or text type* (serif) for longer passages of text.

TABLE 9.1 *Examples and uses of type fonts*

Font Style	Font Name	Example	Use
Serif fonts	Times New Roman Courier New Bookman Old Style	Use type wisely. Use type wisely. Use type wisely.	Easy to read; good for long documents, good for *body type*, or the main verbal parts of a document
Sans serif fonts	Arial Century Gothic	Use type wisely. Use type wisely.	Tiring to read for long stretches; good for *display type* such as headings, titles, slogans
Specialty fonts	Delphin BERMUDA	Use type wisely. USE TYPE WISELY.	Difficult to read for long stretches; effective when used sparingly for playful or decorative effect

2. Make type functional and appealing by using only two or three font styles per document.

3. Use consistent patterns of type (similar type styles, sizes, and formats) to indicate relationships among similar items or different levels of importance.

4. Choose type to project a specific impression (a structured combination of serif and sans serif type to create a formal, serious, or businesslike impression; sans serif and specialty type to create a casual, informal, or playful impression, and so forth).

Besides these general principles, rhetorical considerations of genre and audience expectations should govern decisions about type. Text-based arguments in scholarly publications generally use plain, conservative fonts with little variation whereas text-based arguments in popular magazines may use more variations in font style and size, especially in headings and opening leads. Visual arguments such as posters, fliers, and advocacy ads exploit the aesthetic potential of type.

Use of Space or Layout

A second component of visual design is layout, which is critical for creating the visual appeal of an argument and for conveying meaning. Even visual arguments that are mainly textual should use space very purposefully. By spacing and layout we mean all of the following points:

- Page size and type of paper
- Proportion of text to white space
- Proportion of text to image(s) and graphics
- Arrangement of text on page (space, margins, columns, size of paragraphs, spaces between paragraphs, justification of margins)
- Use of highlighting elements such as bulleted lists, tables, sidebars, boxes
- Use of headings and other means of breaking text into visual elements

In arguments that don't use visuals directly, the writer's primary visual concern is document design, where the writer tries to meet the conventions of a genre and the expectations of the intended audience. For example, Megan Matthews' researched argument on pages 418–425 is designed to meet the document conventions of the American Psychological Association (APA). Note the use of a plain, conventional typeface (for easy reading), double-spacing, and one-inch margins (to leave room for editorial marking and notations), and special title page, headers, and page number locations (to meet expectations of readers familiar with APA documents—which all look exactly the same).

But in moving from verbal-only arguments to visual arguments that use visual elements for direct persuasive effect—for example, posters, fliers, or advocacy ads—creative use of layout is vital. Here are some ideas to help you think about the layout of a visual argument.

Principles for Laying Out Parts of a Visual Text

1. Choose a layout that avoids clutter and confusion by limiting how much text and how many visual items you put on a page.
2. Focus on creating coherence and meaning with layout.
3. Develop an ordering or structuring principle that clarifies the relationships among the parts.
4. Use layout and spacing to indicate the importance of items and to emphasize key ideas. Because Western readers read from left to right and top to bottom, top and center are positions that readily draw readers' eyes.

An Analysis of a Visual Argument Using Type and Spatial Elements

To illustrate the persuasive power of type and layout, we ask you to consider Figure 9.1, which shows an advocacy ad sponsored by a coalition of organizations aimed at fighting illegal drugs.

This ad, warning about the dangers of the drug Ecstasy, uses different sizes of type and layout to present its argument. The huge word "Ecstasy" first catches the reader's attention. The first few words at the top of the ad, exuding pleasure, lull the reader with the congruence between the pleasurable message and the playful type. Soon, however, the reader encounters a dissonance between the playful type and the meaning of the words: "dehydrate," "hallucinate," "paranoid," and "dead" name unpleasant ideas. By the end of the ad, readers realize they have been led through a downward progression of ideas beginning with the youth culture's belief that Ecstasy creates wonderfully positive feelings and ending with the ad's thesis that Ecstasy leads to paranoia, depression, and death. The playful informality of the font styles and the unevenly scattered layout of the type convey the seductiveness and unpredictability of the drug. The ad concedes that the first effects are "falling in love with the world" but implies that what comes next is increasingly dark and dangerous. At the end of the ad, in the lines of type near the bottom, the message and typestyle are congruent again. The question "Does that sound harmless to you?" marks a shift in type design and layout. The designer composed this section of the ad in conventional fonts centered on the page in a rational, businesslike fashion. This type design signals a metaphoric move from the euphoria of Ecstasy to the ordered structure of everyday reality, where the reader can now consider rationally the drug's harm. The information at the bottom of the ad identifies the ad's sponsors and gives both a Web address and a telephone number to call for more information about Ecstasy and other illegal drugs.

For Class Discussion

This exercise asks you to examine Figure 9.2, an advocacy ad sponsored by Common Sense for Drug Policy. This ad also focuses on the drug Ecstasy and also uses type and layout to convey its points. (This ad appeared in the liberal

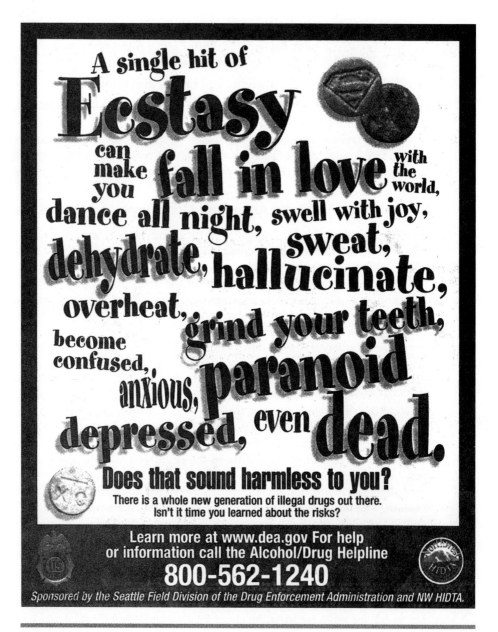

FIGURE 9.1   *Advocacy advertisement warning against Ecstasy*

magazine *The Progressive*.) Individually or in groups, study this advocacy ad and then answer the following questions.

1. What is the core argument of this ad? What view of drug use and what course of action is this ad promoting? What similarities and differences do

What We Know About Ecstasy

What is Ecstasy?

Ecstasy, MDMA,[1] is a semi-synthetic drug patented by Merck Pharmaceutical Company in 1914 and abandoned for 60 years. In the late 1970s and early 1980s psychiatrists and psychotherapists in the US used it to facilitate psychotherapy.[2] In 1985 its growing recreational use caused the DEA to criminalize it.

Ecstasy's effects last 3 to 6 hours. It is a mood elevator that produces feelings of empathy, openness and well-being. People who take it at all night "rave" dances say they enjoy dancing and feeling close to others. It does not produce violence or physical addiction.[3]

What are the greatest risks from Ecstasy?

Death is a possibility when using MDMA. According to coroner reports, there were nine Ecstasy-related deaths (three of these involved Ecstasy alone) in 1998.[4] Some of these deaths are related to overheating. MDMA slightly raises body temperature. This is potentially lethal in hot environments where there is vigorous dancing and the lack of adequate fluid replacement.[5] Many of these tragic deaths were preventable with simple harm reduction techniques such as having free water available and rooms where people can rest and relax.

One of the recent risks associated with Ecstasy is the possibility of obtaining adulterated drugs that may be more toxic than MDMA. Some of the reported deaths attributed to Ecstasy are likely caused by other, more dangerous drugs.[6] Deaths from adulterated drugs are another consequence of a zero tolerance approach. While we do not encourage Ecstasy use, we recommend that the drug be tested for purity to minimize the risk from adulterated drugs by those who consume it.[7] However, MDMA itself has risks. For example, it raises blood pressure and heart rate. Persons with known cardiovascular or heart disease should not take MDMA.

Recent studies have indicated that individuals who have used MDMA may have decreased performance in memory tests compared to nonusers. These studies are presently controversial because they involved people who used a variety of other drugs. Furthermore, it is difficult to rule out possible pre-existing differences between research subjects and controls.[8]

What is a rave?

Raves are all-night dance parties popular with young people that feature electronic music. A variety of drug use, from alcohol to nicotine, and including ecstasy, occurs at raves. Hysteria is leading to criminalization of raves, thus pushing them underground and into less safe and responsible settings.

Let's deal with legal and illegal drugs knowledgeably, understand their relative dangers, act prudently and avoid hysteria.

Kevin B. Zeese, President, Common Sense for Drug Policy, 3220 N Street, NW #141, Washington, DC 20007
www.csdp.org • www.DrugWarFacts.org • www.AddictintheFamily.org • info@csdp.org
202-299-9780 • 202-518-4028 (fax)

1, 3 & 4 - methylenedioxymethamphetamine.   2 - Greer G. and Tolbert R., A Method of Conducting Therapeutic Sessions with MDMA. In Journal of Psychoactive Drugs 30 (1998) 4:371.379. For research on the therapeutic use of MDMA see: www.maps.org. 3 - Beck J. and Rosenbaum M., Pursuit of Ecstasy: The MDMA Experience. Albany: State University of New York Press, 1994. 4 - Drug Abuse Warning Network, Office of Applied Studies, Substance Abuse and Mental Health Services Administration, Report of March 21, 2000. (This was a special report because the published report only includes drugs where there were over 10 deaths.) 5 - C.M. Milroy; J.C. Clark; A.R.W. Forrest, Pathology of deaths associated with "ecstasy" and "eve" misuse, Journal of Clinical Pathology Vol 49 (1996) 149-153. 6 - Laboratory Pill Analysis Program, DanceSafe. For results visit www.DanceSafe.org. See also, Byard RW et al., Amphetamine derivative fatalities in South Australia—is "Ecstasy" the culprit?, American Journal of Forensic Medical Pathology, 998 (Sep) 19(3): 261-5. 7 - DanceSafe provides testing equipment and a testing service which can be used to determine what a substance is. See www.DanceSafe.org. 8 - E. Gouzoulis-Mayfrank; J. Daumann; F. Tuchtenhagen; S. Pelz; S. Becker; H.J. Kunert; B. Fimm; H. Sass; Impaired cognitive performance in drug-free users of recreational ecstasy (MDMA), by Journal Neurol Neurosurg Psychiatry Vol 68, June 2000, 719-725; K.I.Bolla; U.D.; McCann; G.A. Ricaurte; Memory impairment in abstinent MDMA ('Ecstasy') users, by Neurology Vol 51, Dec 1998, 1532-1537.

FIGURE 9.2   *Common Sense for Drug Policy advocacy ad*

you see between the argument about Ecstasy in this ad and the ad in Figure 9.1?

2. What are the main differences in the type and layout of the two ads in Figures 9.1 and 9.2? To what extent do the ad makers' choices about type and layout match the arguments made in each ad?

3. How would you analyze the use of type and layout in Figure 9.2? How does this ad use typestyles to convey its argument? How does it use layout and spacing?

4. The ad in Figure 9.1 appeared in the weekly entertainment section of *The Seattle Times*, a newspaper with a large general readership, whereas the ad in Figure 9.2 appeared in a liberal news commentary magazine. In what ways is each ad designed to reach its audience?

Use of Color

A third important element of visual design is use of color, which can contribute significantly to the visual appeal of an argument and move readers emotionally and imaginatively. In considering color in visual arguments, writers are especially controlled by genre conventions. For example, academic arguments use color minimally whereas popular magazines often use color lavishly. The appeal of colors to an audience and the associations that colors have for an audience are also important. For instance, the psychedelic colors of 1960s rock concert posters would probably not be effective in poster arguments directed toward conservative voters. Color choices in visual arguments often have crucial importance, including the choice of making an image black and white when color is possible. As you will see in our discussions of color throughout this chapter, makers of visual arguments need to decide whether color will be primarily decorative (using colors to create visual appeal), functional (for example, using colors to indicate relationships), realistic (using colors like a documentary photo), aesthetic (for example, using colors that are soothing, exciting, or disturbing), or some intentional combination of these.

Use of Images and Graphics

The fourth design element includes images and graphics, which can powerfully condense information into striking and memorable visuals, clarify ideas, and add depth, liveliness, and emotion to your arguments. A major point to keep in mind when using images is that a few simple images may be more powerful than complicated and numerous images. Other key considerations are (1) how you intend an image to work in your argument (for example, convey an idea, illustrate a point, evoke an emotional response) and (2) how you will establish the relationship between the image or graphic and the verbal text. Because using images and graphics effectively is especially challenging, we devote the rest of this chapter to explaining how images and graphics can be incorporated into visual arguments.

We treat the use of photographs and drawings in the next main section and the use of quantitative graphics in the final section.

An Analysis of a Visual Argument Using All the Design Components

Before we discuss the use of images and graphics in detail, we would like to illustrate how all four of the design components—use of type, layout, color, and image—can reinforce and support each other to achieve a rhetorical effect. Consider the "Save the Children" advocacy ad appearing as Color Plate D. This advocacy ad combines type, layout, color, and image skillfully and harmoniously through its dominant image complemented by verbal text that interprets and applies the ideas conveyed by the image. The layout of the ad divides the page into three main parts, giving central focus to the image of the mother standing and looking into the eyes of the child she is holding in her arms. The blank top panel leads readers to look at the image. Two color panels, mauve behind the child and rose behind the mother, also highlight the two figures, isolate them in time and space, and concentrate the readers' attention on them. The large type in the black borders ("SHE'S THE BEST QUALIFIED TEACHER FOR HER CHILDREN." "IMAGINE IF SHE HAD AN EDUCATION.") frames the image, attracts readers' eyes, and plants the main idea in readers' minds: mothers should be equipped to teach their children.

This advocacy ad, which appeared in *Newsweek*, skillfully blends familiar, universal ideas—a mother's love for her child and the tenderness and strength of this bond—with unfamiliar, foreign associations—a mother and child from a third-world country, wearing the traditional clothing of their country depicted by the head scarf the mother is wearing and the elaborate design on her sleeve. In addition to the familiar-unfamiliar dynamic, a universal-particular dynamic also operates in this ad. This woman and baby are *every* mother and child (after all, we don't know exactly where she is from), but they are also from some specific third-world country. The two figures have been posed to conjure up Western paintings and statues of the Madonna and Christ child. With this pose, the ad intends that readers will connect with this image of motherly love and devotion and respond by supporting the "Every Mother/Every Child" campaign. Color in this ad also accents the warm, cozy, hopeful impression of the image; pink in Western culture is a feminine color often associated with women and babies. In analyzing the photographic image, you should note what is *not* shown: any surroundings, any indication of housing or scenery, any concrete sense of place or culture. The text of the ad interprets the image, provides background information, and seeks to apply the ideas and feelings evoked by the image to urging readers to action. The image, without either the large type or the smaller type, does convey an idea as well as elicit sympathy from readers, but the text adds meaning to the image and builds on those impressions and applies them.

The ad designer could have focused on poverty, illiteracy, hunger, disease, and high mortality rates but instead has chosen to evoke positive feelings of identification and to convey hopeful ideas. While acknowledging their cultural difference from this mother and child, readers recognize their common humanity and are moved to "give mothers and children the best chance to survive and thrive." The large amounts of blank space in this ad help to convey that the main points here are important, serious, elemental, but also simple—as if the ad has gotten to the heart of the matter. The bottom panel of the ad gives readers the logo and name of the organization "Save the Children" and a phone number and Web address to use to show their support.

The Compositional Features of Photographs and Drawings

Now that we have introduced you to the four major elements of visual design—type, layout, color, and images—we turn to an in-depth discussion of photographic images and drawings. Used with great shrewdness in product advertisements, photos and drawings can be used with equal shrewdness in posters, fliers, advocacy ads, and Web sites. When an image is created specifically for an argument, almost nothing is left to chance. Although such images are often made to seem spontaneous and "natural," they are almost always composed: Designers consciously select the details of staging and composition as well as manipulate camera techniques (filters, camera angle, lighting), and digital or chemical development techniques (airbrushing, merging of images). Even news photography can have a composed feel. For example, public officials often try to control the effect of photographs by creating "photo-ops" (photographing opportunities), wherein reporters are allowed to photograph an event only during certain times and from certain angles. Political photographs appearing in newspapers are often press releases officially approved by the politician's staff. (See the photographs of President Bush later in this chapter on p. 175)

To analyze a photograph or drawing, or to create visual images for your own arguments, you need to think both about the composition of the image and about the camera's relationship to the subject. Since drawings produce a perspective on a scene analogous to that of a camera, design considerations for photographs can be applied to drawings as well. The following list of questions can guide your analysis of any persuasive image.

- *Type of photograph or drawing:* Is the image documentary-like (representing a real event), fictionlike (intended to tell a story or dramatize a scene), or conceptual (illustrating or symbolizing an idea or theme)? The photo of a girl crowd surfing in a mosh pit in Color Plate B is a documentary photo capturing a real event in action. The drawing of the lizards in Color Plate E is both a fictional narrative telling a story and a conceptual drawing illustrating a theme.
- *Distance from the subject:* Is the image a close-up, medium shot, or long shot? Close-ups tend to increase the intensity of the image and suggest the importance of the subject; long shots tend to blend the subject into the background. In the Wal-Mart corporate ad shown in Color Plate F, the close-up of the eagle

draws the reader's eye immediately to this symbolic bird. In contrast, the photograph of the young woman crossing the bridge in the Haiti photograph (Color Plate C) is a long-range shot showing her blending into the poverty-stricken background, suggesting the devastating effect of poverty.

- *Orientation of the image and camera angle:* Is the camera (or artist) positioned in front of or behind the subject? Is it positioned below the subject, looking up (a low-angle shot)? Or is it above the subject, looking down (a high-angle shot)? Front-view shots, such as the one of the soldiers in Figure 1.1 (p. 5), tend to emphasize the persons being photographed. In contrast, rear-view shots often emphasize the scene or setting. A low-angle perspective tends to make the subject look superior and powerful, whereas a high-angle perspective can reduce the size—and by implication—the importance of the subject. A level angle tends to imply equality. The high-angle shot of the "American Taliban" John Lindh strapped naked to a stretcher (Figure 7.2, p. 137) emphasizes the superiority of the camera and the helplessness of Lindh. In contrast, the low-angle perspective of the lizards in Color Plate E emphasizes the power of the lizards and the inferiority of the viewer.

- *Point of view:* Does the camera or artist stand outside the scene and create an objective effect as in the Haiti photograph in Color Plate C? Or is the camera or artist inside the scene as if the photographer or artist is an actor in the scene, creating a subjective effect as in the drawing of the lizards in Color Plate E?

- *Use of color:* Is the image in color or in black and white? Is this choice determined by the restrictions of the medium (the publication can't afford color, as in many newspaper photographs) or is it the conscious choice of the photographer or artist? Are the colors realistic or muted? Have special filters been used (a photo made to look old through the use of brown tints)? The bright colors in the lizard and Goldilocks drawing in Color Plate E and in the forest scene in the Saturn VUE ad in Color Plate G resemble illustrations in books for children. The subdued colors in the soybean ad in Color Plate A are intended to look realistically natural and neutral.

- *Compositional special effects:* Is the entire image clear and realistic? Is any portion of it blurred? Is it blended with other realistic or nonrealistic images (a car ad that blends a city and a desert; a body lotion ad that merges a woman and a cactus)? Is the image an imitation of some other famous image such as a classic painting (as in parodies)? Both the Earthjustice ad in Color Plate E and the Saturn VUE ad in Color Plate G are conscious imitations of children's picture books.

- *Juxtaposition of images:* Are several different images juxtaposed, suggesting relationships between them? Juxtaposition can suggest sequential or causal relationships or can metaphorically transfer the identify of a nearby image or background to the subject (as when a bath soap is associated with a meadow). This technique is frequently used in public relations to shape viewers' perceptions of political figures as when President Bush is positioned in front of Mount Rushmore in Figure 9.5 (p. 175).

- *Manipulation of images:* Are staged images made to appear real, natural, documentary-like? Are images altered with airbrushing? Are images actually composites of a number of images (for instance, using images of different women's bodies to create one perfect model in an ad or film)? Are images cropped for emphasis? What is left out? Are images downsized or enlarged? For an example of a staged photo that is intended to look natural, see the "Save the Children" advocacy ad in Color Plate D. Note too how the figures in the "Save the Children" ad are silhouetted to remove all background. The photo for the Wal-Mart ad in Color Plate F resembles a scenic photo in a nature calendar.

- *Settings, furnishings, props:* Is the photo or drawing an outdoor or indoor scene? What is in the background and foreground? What furnishings and props, such as furniture, objects in a room, pets, and landscape features, help create the scene? What social associations of class, race, and gender are attached to these settings and props? Note, for example, how the designers of America's Army, the army video game, used a few simple props to create a gritty urban street fighting scene (Color Plate H). The burned-out vehicle hull suggests the aftermath of days of street fighting while the telephone or power poles in the middle of a narrow, deserted street suggest a poor city in a third-world country.

- *Characters, roles, actions:* Does the photo or drawing tell a story? Are the people in the scene models? Are the models instrumental (acting out real-life roles) or are they decorative (extra and included for visual or sex appeal)? What are the facial expressions, gestures, and poses of the people? What are the spatial relationships of the figures? (Who is in the foreground, center, and background? Who is large and prominent?) What social relationships are implied by these poses and positions? In the "Save the Children" advocacy ad shown in Color Plate D, the pose of the mother and child—each completely absorbed in adoration of the other—tells the story of the bonds of love between mothers and babies.

- *Presentation of images:* Are images separated from each other in a larger composition or connected to each other? Are the images large in proportion to verbal text? How are images labeled? How does the text relate to the image(s)? Does the image illustrate the text? Does the text explain or comment on the image? For example, the image of the soybean plant in Color Plate A dominates the right side of the advocacy ad, while attractively designed type dominates the left side of the ad. (You might consider why the ad maker places text on the left and image on the right instead of reversing the order or placing text on top and image on the bottom.) In contrast, the image of the coat hanger hook dominates the advocacy ad on page 178.

An Analysis of a Visual Argument Using Images

To show you how images can be analyzed, let's examine the advertisement for a Saturn VUE sport-utility vehicle (Color Plate G). At one level, the persuasive intent of this ad is to urge viewers to buy a Saturn VUE. But at a more subtle level, this advertisement participates in an international debate about SUVs and the environment. Whereas Europeans are buying smaller, more fuel-efficient cars, some

Americans are still buying SUVs that guzzle gas like trucks. Among their opponents, SUVs—whether fairly or unfairly—have become a worldwide symbol of Americans' greed for oil and their disdain for the environment.

How do car manufacturers fight back? Clearly, they can't make a logical argument that owning an SUV is good for the environment. But they can use psychological strategies that urge consumers to associate SUVs with pro-environment sentiments. So in this ad Saturn turns to visual argument. Using a carefully designed drawing, the advertisement shows the Saturn VUE blending into an "evergreen forest" scene. Surrounded by a moose, a porcupine, a bear, a squirrel, and other forest birds and animals, the SUV seems to belong in its forest home. The brilliance of the ad is the insert legend at the bottom left, where the forest creatures are identified by name. The ad teaches city dwellers who buy SUVs the names of the forest animals—not just "bird" but "Black-Capped Chickadee," not just "rabbit" but "Snowshoe Hare." (Because the ad was designed as a two-page magazine spread, we had to reduce its size in Plate G, making the animal names tiny. They are easily readable in the original.) The ad becomes a mini-lesson in identifying and naming the "Creatures of the evergreen forest"—Creature number one, of course, being the Saturn VUE.

To make the Saturn VUE blend harmoniously with the forest, this ad cleverly de-emphasizes the size of the vehicle, even though the dominant size of SUVs is part of their appeal to urban consumers. To compensate for this choice, the typical appeals of SUVs are rendered symbolically. For example, the VUE's power and agility, hinted at in the brief copy at the bottom right of the ad, are conveyed metaphorically in the image of the puma, "poised" like the Saturn, crouching and oriented in the same direction, like the car's guiding spirit. It enters the scene from the outside, the predator, silent and powerful—the main animal to be identified with the car itself. Other animals close to the car and facing the same direction as the car each stand for one of the car's attributes so that the VUE also possesses the speed of the hare, the brute size and strength of the bear, and the soaring freedom of the goshawk.

The whole ad works by association. The slogan "At home in almost any environment" means literally that the car can go from city to country, from desert to mountains, from snow to tropic heat. But so can any car. The slogan's purpose is to associate the car with the words *home* and *environment*—words that connote all the warm, fuzzy feelings that make you feel good about owning a Saturn VUE. In addition, the use of drawings and the identification of animals by numbers conjure up the delightful, instructive innocence of children's books: this car must be a good thing. And in its own special way, this ad has skillfully shifted consumers' attention away from global warming and environmental degradation.

For Class Discussion

1. The techniques for constructing photos come into play prominently in news photography. In this exercise, we ask you to examine three photographs of President Bush that accompanied news articles appearing in

the *New York Times* in summer 2002. These photographs were taken at photo-ops carefully staged by White House staff. Working individually or in groups, study Figures 9.3, 9.4, and 9.5 and then answer the following questions:

a. What are the most noticeable features of each photo?

b. What do you think is the dominant impression of Bush that each photo seeks to convey? In other words, what is the implicit argument?

c. What camera techniques and compositional features do you see in each photo?

d. What image of President Bush do these photographs attempt to create for citizens and voters?

2. Examine carefully Wal-Mart's corporate advertisement in Color Plate F. This ad was originally designed as a full-page newspaper spread. The ad has been reduced to fit on a book page, so the text that appears in the box under the photo image is hard to read and we reproduce it here. In this text, John Berry, the Executive Director of the National Fish and Wildlife Foundation, endorses Wal-Mart's environmental claims:

> Wal-Mart is making history today toward protecting and preserving America's natural habitats. Wal-Mart's *Acres For America* program will conserve an acre of natural habitat for every acre of land Wal-Mart uses to develop facilities. That's every developed acre of land Wal-Mart owns today and will build on for years to come. Wal-Mart is helping protect our natural resources so you, your kids and your grandkids can enjoy more wildlife and more natural areas. Wal-Mart is the first company to tie its footprint to land conservation, and we are proud to partner with Wal-Mart to build this premier land stewardship model.

Working individually or in groups, answer the following questions:

a. What camera techniques and compositional features do you see in this ad? What is striking or memorable about the visual features of this ad?

b. What is the proportion of verbal text to image? How would you describe the layout of this ad? How does the text relate to the image?

c. How would you state the ad's argument?

d. How does the ad use its visual design to reach its audience?

3. The images in Color Plates H and I are screen captures from the very popular and controversial PC action game America's Army, created by the U.S. Army. This "virtual soldiering" game, free to download from the Web site http://www.americasarmy.com, claims to "provide players with the most authentic military experience available."

FIGURE 9.3   *President Bush clearing brush from Texas ranch*

FIGURE 9.4   *President Bush greeting a crowd*

FIGURE 9.5   *President Bush delivering a speech at Mount Rushmore*

a. In these screen captures from the game, what is the effect of the camera's distance from the subject and the camera's point of view on the viewer/player?

b. How do color and composition affect the visual appeal of these images?

c. What impressions do settings, characters, and roles convey?

d. Based on these two scenes from the game, why do you think this game has provoked heated public discussion? How effective do you think this game is as a recruitment device?

The Genres of Visual Argument

We have already mentioned that verbal arguments today are frequently accompanied by photographs or drawings that contribute to the text's persuasive appeal. For example, a verbal argument promoting United Nations action to help AIDS victims in Africa might be accompanied by a photograph of a dying mother and child. However, some genres of argument are dominated by visual elements. In these genres, the visual design carries most of the argumentative weight; verbal text is used primarily for labeling, for focusing the argument's claim, or for commenting on the images. In this section we describe specifically these highly visual genres of argument.

Posters and Fliers

To persuade audiences, an arguer might create a poster designed for placement on walls or kiosks or a flier to be passed out on street corners. Posters dramatically attract and direct viewers' attention toward one subject or issue. They often seek to rally supporters, promote a strong stance on an issue, and call people to action. For example, during World War II, posters asked Americans to invest in war bonds and urged women to join the workforce to free men for active combat. During the Vietnam War, famous posters used slogans such as "Make Love Not War" or "Girls say yes to boys who say no" to increase national resistance to the war.

The hallmark of an effective poster is the way it focuses and encodes a complex meaning in a verbal-visual text, often with one or more striking images. These images are often symbolic—for example, using children to symbolize family and home, a soaring bird to symbolize freedom, or three firefighters raising the American flag over the World Trade Center rubble on September 11, 2001, to symbolize American heroism, patriotism, and resistance to terrorism. These symbols derive potency from the values they share with their target audience. Posters tend to use words sparingly, either as slogans or as short, memorable directives. This terse verbal text augments the message encoded in an eye-catching, dominant image.

As an example of a contemporary poster, consider the poster on page 73, which uses a collage of images to pay tribute to the men and women who are serv-

WOULD IT
SURPRISE YOU TO KNOW
THAT GROWING SOYBEANS CAN
HELP THE ENVIRONMENT?

Biotech soybeans have been widely
planted by American farmers and they
help preserve our natural resources.
Plant biotechnology makes it easier to
control weeds and plow soybean fields
less—which means less soil erosion.

But before those soybean seeds could
be planted, it took years of research and
testing to ensure that biotech crops
were safe for people and the environment. Extensive testing by scientists
shows foods derived from plant
biotechnology are as safe to eat as
traditional foods.

In fact, three government agencies
share the authority to evaluate the safety
of new biotech products from incep-
tion to approval—the U.S.
Department of Agriculture
(USDA), the Environmental Protection
Agency (EPA), and the Food and Drug
Administration (FDA). If you want to
learn more, we invite you to call or
visit our Web site.

WWW.WHYBIOTECH.COM
1-800-980-8660

Biotech
Soybean

COLOR PLATE A *Biotechnology advocacy ad (see Chapter 2).*

COLOR PLATE B *Crowd surfing at a rock concert (see Chapter 1).*

COLOR PLATE C *La Saline, a slum in Port-au-Prince, Haiti (see Chapter 7).*

COLOR PLATE D   *Save the Children advocacy ad (see Chapter 9).*

Just then, the three lizards came home and found Goldilocks eating their porridge...

IT'S JUST NOT THE SAME WITHOUT BEARS.

Once upon a time there were over 100,000 grizzly bears in the lower 48 states. Now, there are less than a thousand grizzly bears left. The health of the grizzly is dependent on vast, undisturbed, wild lands. When bears disappear, other species will follow. Bears are such an important part of our wilderness, history, and culture that it's hard to imagine a world without them in the picture.

Grizzly bears are a threatened species, protected by the Endangered Species Act. But some special interests are pushing the U.S. Fish and Wildlife Service to remove Yellowstone grizzlies from the endangered species list. Why? They want to open up wild lands around Yellowstone

National Park to destructive logging, mining, off-road vehicle use, and development.

You can help protect our wilderness and grizzly bears. Please take a moment to contact Secretary Bruce Babbitt, Department of Interior, 1849 C St. NW, Washington DC 20240, or email Bruce_Babbitt@os.doi.gov – Tell him to keep grizzly bears on the Endangered Species List and that grizzly bears need more protection, not less.

Earthjustice Legal Defense Fund is working tirelessly to protect the grizzly bears and the wilderness they stand for. If we all work together, the grizzly bears will live happily ever after.

HELP KEEP BEARS IN THE PICTURE

www.earthjustice.org

EARTHJUSTICE
LEGAL DEFENSE FUND
1-800-584-6460

designed by Sustain

COLOR PLATE E *Earthjustice advocacy ad (see Chapter 9).*

COLOR PLATE F *Wal-Mart corporate image ad (see Chapter 9).*

COLOR PLATE G *Saturn VUE ad (see Chapter 9).*

General Motors Corp. Used with permission, GM Media Archives.

COLOR PLATE H   *Urban assault scene, America's Army video game (see Chapter 9).*

COLOR PLATE I   *Village scene, America's Army video game (see Chapter 9).*

www.Athletes Against Steroids.org

"To help children make right choices, they need good examples. Athletics play such an important role in our society, but, unfortunately, some in professional sports are not setting much of an example. The use of performance-enhancing drugs like steroids in baseball, football and other sports is dangerous, and it sends the wrong message - that there are short cuts to accomplishment, and that performance is more important than character. So tonight I call on team owners, union representatives, coaches and players to take the lead, to send the right signal, to get tough and to get rid of steroids now."

George W. Bush, State of the Union Address, January 20, 2004

Home

AAS Goals

Steroid Side Effects

Ex-Steroid Users
Tell Their Stories

Nutrition
& Supplements

Are You Hooked On
Steroids?

A Special Plea
To Parents And
Coaches

The Gurus Are Dead
Long Live The Gurus

Interview With
IRONMAN Publisher
John Balik

News & Articles

'Drug Free Athlete'
e-Newsletter

Steroid Deaths

Press Releases

Feedback

Athletes Against Steroids

Organization Launched
To Fight Against Steroids

Our plan is to fight the problem through education, monthly newsletter, scientific research, nutritional alternatives, drug free athlete role models, addiction assistance, speaker's bureau.

Let's start by telling it like it is. The world has a HUGE steroid problem on its hands - and not just in bodybuilding. Young athletes everywhere are turning to performance enhancement drugs – playing steroid roulette with their lives in hopes of making it into the "big leagues." They're falling for the big lie that these drugs are safe and okay to use. And why shouldn't they? After all, aren't many of their favorite sports heroes juicing and getting paid millions of dollars a year for doing so?

But the truth is that steroids are **KILLERS... DESTROYERS... LIFE WRECKERS!** That's why this brand new anti-steroid organization has been formed called Athletes Against Steroids. The two main objectives of the organization are to discourage athletes from using dangerous bodybuilding drugs and to help those who have already developed a dependency on these pharmaceuticals to quit using them.

AAS has set up the following six-point plan
to help achieve these objectives:

(1) Educate amateur and professional athletes, students, coaches, personal trainers, sports researchers, nutritional companies, educators, magazine publishers, etc. on the dangers of steroids.

(2) Become a clearinghouse of information on the dangers of steroid usage while offering safe and effective options in training, nutrition, and

(4) Develop AAS local chapter support groups to help those athletes who have grown dependent on these drugs to stop using them. Offer cessation support through a phone-in line and the internet for those areas where there isn't yet a local chapter.

(5) Start a national speaker's bureau composed of AAS members who are willing to

---

COLOR PLATE J   *"About Us" page from Athletes Against Steroids web site (see Chapter 9).*

ing or have served in the U.S. military: a smiling African American sailor holding his son; five men in full military gear on a mission; and the large, light face of the blue-eyed boy waving the American flag. (The words mention women, but no women appear in the poster.) These positive figures set against the dark, dramatic, and ominous background send the message that our armed forces are protecting our country, especially our children. In fact, this poster, which draws the reader's eye to the little boy holding the flag, resembles the World War II posters' emphasis on America's precious children endangered by a hostile enemy. In color, this poster employs red, white, and blue in its background, lettering, and ribbon-heart icon. Expressing the country's gratitude to our troops, the poster seeks to ignite viewers' patriotism and encourage others to join the military and serve their country.

Fliers and brochures often use visual elements similar to those in posters. An image might be the top and center attraction of a flier or the main focus of the front cover of a brochure. However, unlike posters, fliers and brochures offer additional space for verbal arguments, which often present the writer's claim supported with bulleted lists of reasons. Sometimes pertinent data and statistics, along with testimony from supporters, are placed in boxes or sidebars.

Public Affairs Advocacy Advertisements

Public affairs advocacy advertisements share with posters an emphasis on visual elements, but they are designed specifically for publication in newspapers and magazines and, in their persuasive strategies, are directly analogous to product advertisements. Public affairs advocacy ads are usually sponsored by a corporation or an advocacy organization and often have a more time-sensitive message than do posters and a more immediate and defined target audience. Designed as condensed arguments aimed at influencing public opinion on civic issues, these ads are characterized by their brevity, audience-based appeals, and succinct, "sound bite" style. Often, in order to sketch out their claim and reasons clearly and concisely, they employ headings and subheadings, bulleted lists, different sizes and styles of type, and a clever, pleasing layout on the page. They usually have some attention-getting slogan or headline like "MORE KIDS ARE GETTING BRAIN CANCER. WHY?" or "STOP THE TAX REVOLT JUGGERNAUT!"

The balance between verbal and visual elements in an advocacy advertisement varies. Some advocacy ads are verbal only with visual concerns focused on document design (for example, an "open letter" from the president of a corporation appearing as a full-page newspaper ad). Other advocacy ads are primarily visual, using images and other design elements with the same shrewdness as advertisements. We looked closely at advocacy ads in Chapter 2, where we presented ads opposing and supporting genetically modified foods (The "Keep Nature Natural" ad on p. 24 and Color Plate A), and in this chapter in the ads on Ecstasy and "Save the Children."

As another example of a public affairs advocacy ad, consider Figure 9.6, which attempts to counter the influence of the pro-life movement's growing campaign against abortion. Sponsored by the Planned Parenthood Responsible

When
your right
to an abortion
is taken away,
what are you
going to
do

Reproductive rights are under attack. The Pro-Choice Public Education Project. It's pro-choice or no choice.
1(688)253-CHOICE or www.protect.choice.org

FIGURE 9.6   *Advocacy advertisement supporting a pro-choice stance*

Choices Action Network, this ad appeared in a variety of liberal magazines in the United States. The ad seems to have two targeted audiences in mind: The first audience is persons already committed to a pro-choice stance; the ad urges them to action. The second audience is neutral persons who may support women's rights but may be wavering on their stance toward abortion. Such an audience, the ad makers believe, might be startled into support of the pro-choice position by this stark reminder of the negative consequences of unsafe abortions.

As you can see, this ad is dominated by one stark image: a question mark formed by the hook of a coat hanger. The shape of the hanger hook draws the reader's eye to the concentrated type centered below it. The hanger hook carries most of the weight of the argument. Simple, bold, and harsh, the image of the hanger, tapping readers' cultural knowledge, evokes the dangerous experience of illegal abortions performed crudely by nonmedical people in the dark backstreets of cities. The ad wants viewers to think of the dangerous last resorts that desperate women would have to turn to if they could not obtain abortions legally.

The hanger itself creates a visual pun: As a question mark, it conveys the ad's dilemma about what will happen if abortions are made illegal. As a coat hanger, it provides the ad's frightening answer to the printed question—desperate women will return to backstreet abortionists who use coat hangers as tools. The further implied question is, "Will you help us prevent this bleak outcome?" The whole purpose of this ad is to motivate people to take action by contacting this organization. Note that in the small print below the image the word "choice" appears five times: in "pro-choice," in the organization's name, phone number, and Web site, and by itself to emphasize the organization's perspective that choice is an important, necessary right. The organization conveys that readers as citizens and voters need to choose to keep abortion legal, safe, and available so that women don't have to return to the era of back-alley abortions.

For Class Discussion

Examine the public affairs advocacy ad shown in Color Plate E. This ad, sponsored by Earthjustice, defends the presence of grizzly bears in Yellowstone National Park as well as other wilderness areas in the Rocky Mountains. In our classes, this ad has yielded rich discussion of its ingenuity and complexity.

Working individually or in groups, conduct your own examination of this ad using the following questions:

1. What visual features of this ad immediately attract your eyes? What principles for effective use of type, layout, and use of color and image does this ad exemplify?

2. What is the core argument of this ad?

3. Why did Earthjustice use the theme of Goldilocks? How do the lizards function in this ad? Why does the ad NOT have any pictures of grizzlies or bears of any kind?

4. How would you design an advocacy ad for the preservation of grizzly bears? What visuals would you use?

After discussing the Earthjustice advocacy ad, explore the rhetorical appeals of a product advertisement such as the one that appears on the opening page of Part 4 on page 357. The designers of this General Motors ad have also made key choices in the use of the main image, the lighthouse. How does this product ad work to convey its argument? Consider questions about its use of type, layout, and image, about the core of its argument, and about its appeals to *ethos, pathos,* and *kairos.*

Cartoons

An especially charged kind of visual argument is the political cartoon. Although you are perhaps not likely to create your own political cartoons, it is useful to understand how cartoonists use visual and verbal elements to convey their message. British cartoonist Martin Rowson calls himself "a visual journalist" who employs "humor to make a journalistic point." Political cartoons are often mininarratives, portraying an issue dramatically, compactly, and humorously. They employ images and a few well-chosen words to dramatize conflicts and problems. Using caricature, exaggeration, and distortion, cartoonists distill an issue down to an image that boldly reveals the creator's perspective and subsequent claim on a civic issue. The purpose of political cartoons is usually satirical, or, as cartoonist Rowson says, "about afflicting the comfortable and comforting the afflicted." Because they are so condensed and often connected to current affairs, political cartoons are particularly dependent on the audience's background knowledge of cultural and political events. When political cartoons work well, through their perceptive combination of image and words, they flash a brilliant, clarifying light on a perspective or open a new lens on an issue, often giving readers a shock of insight.

As an illustration, note the Benson cartoon in Figure 9.7, which first appeared in the *Arizona Republic.* The *kairotic* moment for this piece is the national debate about baseball players' using steroids to blast more home runs or add velocity to their fastballs. Some athletes and sports commentators have accepted the use of steroids, seeing them as logical outcomes of other performance enhancers such as Ritalin for concentration or botox for beauty. Others challenge the use of performance-enhancing drugs, citing health dangers to users, unfairness to nonusers, and loss of integrity to sports. In this wordless cartoon, Benson conjures up this controversy; the hefty batter and hypodermic needle substituting for a bat imply that this tampering with drugs and the great American tradition of baseball is abnormal, dangerous, and scary.

For Class Discussion

1. Cartoons can often sum up a worldview in a single image. The opening page of Part One (p. 1) shows a political cartoon on genetic engineering of food. The cartoon that opens Part Four (p. 357) responds to the problem of

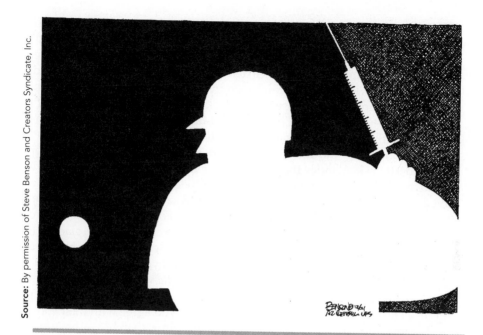

FIGURE 9.7   *Political cartoon protesting baseball players' use of steroids*

privacy and civil liberties versus national security. What mini-narrative does each convey? What is the cartoon arguing? How does the cartoon use caricature, exaggeration, or distortion to convey its perspective?

2. Cartoons can provide insight into how the public is lining up on issues. Choose a current issue such as athletes' use of steroids, homeland security, reforming Social Security, U.S. Army recruitment, or stem cell research. Then, using a cartoon index on the Internet such as Daryl Cagle's Professional Cartoonists Index (http://cagle.slate.msn.com) or a Web search of your own, find several cartoons that capture different perspectives on your issue. What is the mini-narrative, the main claim, and the use of caricature, exaggeration, or distortion in each? How is *kairos,* or timeliness, important to each cartoon?

Web Pages

So far we have only hinted at the influence of the World Wide Web in accelerating use of visual images in argument. The hypertext design of Web pages, along with its complex intermixture of text and image, has changed the way many writers think of argument. The home page of an advocacy site, for example, often has many features of a poster argument with hypertext links to galleries of images on the one hand, and to verbal arguments on the other. These verbal arguments themselves often contain photographs, drawings, and graphics. The strategies discussed in this chapter for analyzing and interpreting visual texts also apply to Web pages. Consider, for example, the "AAS Goals" page for Athletes Against Steroids (Color Plate J; http://www.athletesagainststeroids.org/pgs/aboutaas.shtml). This advocacy site announces its purpose in the black-and-red type in the center of the Web page. The bottom half of the page briefly summarizes the problem with steroids and then outlines the organization's objectives. The links on the left-hand side of the page announce the range, depth, and relevance of material on steroid use posted on this site. Under the masthead for the organization, the quotation from President Bush's 2004 State of the Union Address conveys that steroid use is a national problem needing immediate attention. Each page on this Web site follows the same basic design with subtle variations. For example, the "Steroid Side Effects" page features a tombstone with a skull and crossbones in place of the organizational shield, while the "Are You Hooked on Steroids?" page has an ominous close-up of scattered pills and a steroid needle. As you examine this whole page, how do the layout and use of color support the *ethos* of this site and its appeal to *pathos*? AAS could have made the page much more dramatic with scary pictures, but they chose this more understated design. Do you agree with their choice?

Because the Web is such an important tool in research, we have placed our main discussion of Web sites in Chapter 16, pages 381–386. On these pages you will find our explanations for reading, analyzing, and evaluating Web sites.

Constructing Your Own Visual Argument

The most common visual arguments you are likely to create are posters and fliers, public affairs advocacy ads, and possibly Web pages. You may also decide that in longer verbal arguments, the use of visuals or graphics could clarify your points while adding visual variety to your paper. The following guidelines will help you apply your understanding of visual elements to the construction of your own visual arguments.

Guidelines for Creating Visual Arguments

1. *Genre:* Determine where this visual argument is going to appear (bulletin board, passed out as a flier, imagined as a one-page magazine or newspaper spread, or as a Web page).

2. *Audience-based appeals:* Determine who your target audience is.

   - What values and background knowledge of your issue can you assume that your audience has?

   - What specifically do you want your audience to think or do after reading your visual argument?

   - If you are promoting a specific course of action (sign a petition, send money, vote for or against a bill, attend a meeting), how can you make that request clear and direct?

3. *Core of your argument:* Determine what clear claim and reasons will form the core of your argument; decide if this claim and these reasons will be explicitly stated or implicit in your visuals and slogans.

   - How much verbal text will you use?

   - If the core of your argument will be largely implicit, how can you still make it readily apparent and clear for your audience?

4. *Visual design:* What visual design and layout will grab your audience's attention and be persuasive?

   - How can font sizes and styles, layout, and color be used in this argument to create a strong impression?

   - What balance and harmony can you create between the visual and verbal elements of your argument? Will your verbal elements be a slogan, express the core of the argument, or summarize and comment on the image(s)?

5. *Use of images:* If your argument lends itself to images, what photo or drawing would support your claim or have emotional appeal? (If you want to use more than one image, be careful that you don't clutter your page and confuse your message. Simplicity and clarity are important.)

   - What image would be memorable and meaningful to your audience? Would a photo image or a drawing be more effective?

   - Will your image(s) be used to provide evidence for your claim or illustrate a main idea, evoke emotions, or enhance your credibility and authority?

As an example of a poster argument created by a student, consider Leah Johnson's poster in Figure 9.8. Intended for bulletin boards and kiosks around her college campus, Johnson's work illustrates how a writer can use minimal but well-chosen verbal text, layout, and images to convey a rhetorically effective argument. (That is Leah herself in the photograph.) In this ad, Leah is joining a national conversation about alcohol abuse on college campuses and is proposing a safe way of handling her university's weekly social get-together for older students, "Thirsty Thursdays." Notice how Leah in this visual argument has focused on her claim and reasons without seeing the need to supply evidence.

For Class Discussion

This exercise asks you to do the thinking and planning for a poster argument to be displayed on your college or university campus. Choose an issue that is controversial on your campus (or in your town or city), and follow the Guidelines for Creating Visual Arguments on pages 182–183 to envision the view you want to advocate on that issue. What might the core of your argument be? Who is your target audience? Are you representing a group, club, or other organization? What image(s)

> # Drink and Then Drive?
> # Jeopardize My Future?
>
> - Arrest
>   - Financial Problems (fines up to $8,125)
>   - Increased Insurance Rates
>   - License Suspension
>   - Criminal Conviction
>   - Incarceration
>   - Serious Injury or Death
>
> ## or
> # Designate a Driver?
>
> ## It's a no-brainer.
> Join your Senior Class at Thirsty Thursday, but
> # designate a driver.

FIGURE 9.8   *Student advocacy ad promoting the use of designated drivers*

might be effective in attracting and moving this audience? Possible topics for issues might be commuter parking; poor conditions in the computer lab; student reluctance to use the counseling center; problems with dorm life, financial aid programs, or intramural sports; ways to improve orientation programs for new students, work-study programs, or travel abroad opportunities; or new initiatives such as study groups for the big lecture courses or new service-learning opportunities.

Using Information Graphics in Arguments

Besides images in the form of photographs and drawings, writers often use quantitative graphics to support arguments using numbers. In Chapter 6 we introduced you to the use of quantitative data in arguments. We discussed the persuasiveness of numbers and showed you ways to use them responsibly in your arguments. With the advent of spreadsheet and presentation programs, today's writers often create and import quantitative graphics into their documents. These visuals—such as tables, pie charts, and line or bar graphs—can have great rhetorical power by making numbers tell a story at a glance. In this section, we'll show you how quantitative graphics can make numbers speak. We'll also show you how to incorporate graphics into your text and reference them effectively.

How Tables Contain a Variety of Stories

Data used in arguments usually have their origins in raw numbers collected from surveys, questionnaires, observational studies, scientific experiments, and so forth. Through a series of calculations, the numbers are combined, sorted, and arranged in a meaningful fashion, often in detailed tables. Some of the tables published by the U.S. Census Bureau, for example, contain dozens of pages. The more dense the table, the more their use is restricted to statistical experts who pore over them to analyze their meanings. More useful to the general public are mid-level tables contained on one or two pages that report data at a higher level of abstraction.

Consider, for example, Table 9.2, published by the U.S. Census Bureau in its document "America's Families and Living Arrangements: Population Characteristics" based on the 2000 census. This table shows the marital status of people fifteen years of age and older, broken into gender and age groupings, in March 2000. It also provides comparative data on the "never married" percent of the population in March 2000 and March 1970.

Take a few moments to peruse the table and be certain you know how to read it. You read tables in two directions: from top to bottom and from left to right. Always begin with the title, which tells you what the table contains and includes elements from both the vertical and horizontal dimensions of the table. In this case the vertical dimension presents demographic categories for people "15 years and over": for both sexes, for males, and for females. Each of these gender categories is subdivided into age categories. The horizontal dimension provides information about "marital status." Seven of the columns give total numbers (reported in thousands) for March 2000. The eighth column gives the "percent never married" for March 2000, while the last column gives the "percent never married" for March 1970. To make sure you know how to read the table, pick a couple of rows at random and say to yourself what each number means. For example, the first row under "Both sexes" gives total figures for the entire population of the United States ages fifteen and older. In March 2000 there were 213,773,000 persons fifteen and older (remember that the numbers are presented in thousands). Of these, 113,002,000 were married and living with their spouses.

TABLE 9.2 Marital status of people 15 years and over: March 1970 and March 2000 (In thousands)

Characteristic	Total	March 2000						Percent never married	March 1970 percent never married[a]
		Married spouse present	Married spouse absent	Separated	Divorced	Widowed	Never married		
Both sexes									
Total 15 years old and over..	213,773	113,002	2,730	4,479	19,881	13,665	60,016	28.1	24.9
15 to 19 years old	20,102	345	36	103	64	13	19,541	97.2	93.9
20 to 24 years old	18,440	3,362	134	234	269	11	14,430	78.3	44.5
25 to 29 years old	18,269	8,334	280	459	917	27	8,252	45.2	14.7
30 to 34 years old	19,519	11,930	278	546	1,616	78	5,071	26.0	7.8
35 to 44 years old	44,804	29,353	717	1,436	5,967	399	6,932	15.5	5.9
45 to 54 years old	36,633	25,460	492	899	5,597	882	3,303	9.0	6.1
55 to 64 years old	23,388	16,393	308	441	3,258	1,770	1,218	5.2	7.2
65 years old and over	32,620	17,827	485	361	2,193	10,484	1,270	3.9	7.6
Males									
Total 15 years old and over..	103,113	56,501	1,365	1,818	8,572	2,604	32,253	31.3	28.1
15 to 19 years old	10,295	69	3	51	29	3	10,140	98.5	97.4
20 to 24 years old	9,208	1,252	75	70	101	-	7,710	83.7	54.7
25 to 29 years old	8,943	3,658	139	170	342	9	4,625	51.7	19.1
30 to 34 years old	9,622	5,640	151	205	712	15	2,899	30.1	9.4
35 to 44 years old	22,134	14,310	387	585	2,775	96	3,981	18.0	6.7
45 to 54 years old	17,891	13,027	255	378	2,377	157	1,697	9.5	7.5
55 to 64 years old	11,137	8,463	158	188	1,387	329	612	5.5	7.8
65 years old and over	13,885	10,084	197	171	849	1,994	590	4.2	7.5
Females									
Total 15 years old and over..	110,660	56,501	1,365	2,661	11,309	11,061	27,763	25.1	22.1
15 to 19 years old	9,807	276	33	52	35	10	9,401	95.9	90.3
20 to 24 years old	9,232	2,110	59	164	168	11	6,720	72.8	35.8
25 to 29 years old	9,326	4,676	141	289	575	18	3,627	38.9	10.5
30 to 34 years old	9,897	6,290	127	341	904	63	2,172	21.9	6.2
35 to 44 years old	22,670	15,043	330	851	3,192	303	2,951	13.0	5.2
45 to 54 years old	18,742	12,433	237	521	3,220	725	1,606	8.6	4.9
55 to 64 years old	12,251	7,930	150	253	1,871	1,441	606	4.9	6.8
65 years old and over	18,735	7,743	288	190	1,344	8,490	680	3.6	7.7

[a]The 1970 percentages include 14-year-olds, and thus are for 14+ and 14–19.
- Represents zero or rounds to zero.
Source: U.S. Census Bureau, Current Population Survey, March 2000.

(If you have a pocket calculator handy, you can do your own arithmetic to determine that roughly 52 percent of people over fifteen are married and living with their spouses.) As you continue across the columns, you'll see that 2,730,000 persons were married but not living with their spouses (a spouse might be stationed overseas or in prison; or a married couple might be maintaining a "commuter marriage" with separate households in different cities). Continuing across the columns, you'll see that 4,479,000 persons were separated from their spouses, 19,881,000 were divorced, and 13,665,000 were widowed, and an additional 60,016,000 were never married. In the next to the last column, the number of never married persons is converted to a percentage: 28.1 percent (see for yourself that 60,016 divided by 213,773 is 28.1%). Finally, the last column shows the percentage of never married persons in 1970: 24.9%. These last two columns show us that the number of unmarried persons in the United States rose 3.2 percentage points since 1970.

Now that you know how to read the table, peruse it carefully to see the kinds of stories it tells. What does the table show you, for example, about the percentage of married persons ages 25–29 in 1970 versus 2000? What does it show about different age-related patterns of marriage in males and females? By showing you that Americans are waiting much later in life to get married, a table like this initiates many causal questions for analysis and argument. What has happened in American culture between 1970 and 2000 to explain the startling difference in the percentage of married persons within, say, the 20–24 age bracket? In 2000 only 22 percent of persons in this age bracket were married (we converted "unmarried" to "married" by subtracting 78.3 from 100). However, in 1970, 55 percent of persons in this age bracket were married.

Using a Graph to Tell a Story

Table 9.2, as we have seen, tells the story of how Americans are postponing marriage until later in life. However, one has to peruse the table carefully, poring over it like a sleuth, to tease out the story from the dense columns of numbers. To focus on a key story and make it powerfully immediate, you can create a graph.

Bar Graphs

Suppose, for example, that you are writing an argument in which you want to show that the percentage of married women in age groups 20–29 has dropped significantly since 1970. You could tell this story through a simple bar graph (Figure 9.9).

Bar graphs use bars of varying length, extending either horizontally or vertically, to contrast two or more quantities. As with any graphic presentation, you must create a comprehensive title. In the case of bar graphs, titles tell readers what is being compared to what. Most bar graphs also have "legends," which explain what the different features on the graph represent. Bars are typically distinguished from each other by use of different colors, shades, or patterns of cross-hatching. The special power of bar graphs is that they can help

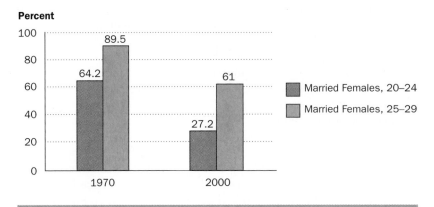

FIGURE 9.9   *Percentage of married females, ages 20–29, 1970 and 2000*
Source: U.S. Census Bureau, Current Population Survey, March 2000.

readers make quick comparisons between different groups across a variable such as time.

Pie Charts

Another vivid kind of graph is a pie chart, which depicts different percentages of a total (the pie) in the form of slices. Pie charts are a favorite way of depicting noteworthy patterns in the way parts of a whole are divided up. Suppose, for example, that you wanted your readers to notice the high percentage of widows among women 65 and older. To do so, you could create a pie chart (Figure 9.10) based on the data in the last row of Table 9.2. As you can see from Figure 9.10 a pie chart can demonstrate at a glance how the whole of something is divided into segments. The effectiveness of pie charts diminishes as you add more slices. In most cases, you'll begin to confuse readers if you include more than five or six slices.

Line Graphs

Another powerful quantitative graphic is a line graph, which converts numerical data into a series of points on a grid and connects them to create flat, rising, or falling lines. The result gives us a picture of the relationship between the variables represented on the horizontal and vertical axes.

Suppose you wanted to tell the story of the rising number of separated/divorced women in the U.S. population. Using Table 9.2, you can calculate the percent of separated/divorced females in 2000 by adding the number of separated females (2,661,000) and the number of divorced females (11,309,000) and dividing that sum by the total number of females (110,660,000). The result is 12.6 percent.

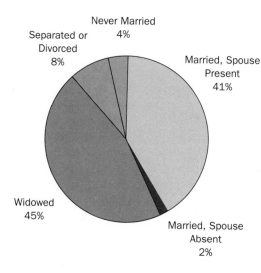

FIGURE 9.10   *Marital status of fe-males, age 65 and older, 2000*

Source: U.S. Census Bureau, Current Population Survey, March 2000.

You can make the same calculations for 1990, 1980, and 1970 by looking at U.S. census data from those years (available on the Web or in your library). The resulting line graph is shown in Figure 9.11.

To determine what this graph is telling you, you need to clarify what's represented on the two axes. By convention, the horizontal axis of a graph contains the predictable, known variable that has no surprises—what researchers call the "independent variable." In this case the horizontal axis represents the years 1970–2000 arranged predictably in chronological order. The vertical axis contains the unpredictable variable that forms the graph's story—what researchers call the "dependent variable"—in this case, the percentage of divorced females. The ascending curve tells the story at a glance.

Note that with line graphs the steepness of a slope (and hence the rhetorical effect) can be manipulated by the intervals chosen for the vertical axis. Figure 9.11 shows vertical intervals of 2 percent. The slope could be made less dramatic by choosing intervals of, say, 10 percent and more dramatic by choosing intervals of 1 percent.

Incorporating Graphics into Your Argument

Today writers working with quantitative data usually use graphing software that automatically creates tables, graphs, or charts from data entered into the cells of a spreadsheet. (It is beyond the scope of this textbook to explain how to use these graphing utilities.) For college papers, some instructors may allow you to make your graphs with pencil and ruler and paste them into your document.

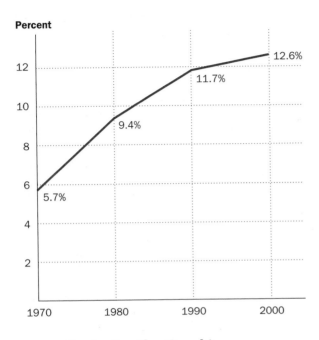

Percent

FIGURE 9.11   *Percentage of fe-males ages 15 and older who are separated or divorced, 1970–2000*

Source: U.S. Census Bureau, Current Population Survey, March 2000.

Designing the Graphic

When you design your graphic, your goal is to have a specific rhetorical effect on your readers, not to demonstrate all the bells and whistles available on your software. Adding extraneous data in the graph or chart or using such features as a three-dimensional effect can often call attention away from the story you are trying to tell. Keep the graphic as uncluttered and simple as possible and design it so that it reinforces the point you are making in your text.

Numbering, Labeling, and Titling the Graphic

In newspapers and popular magazines, writers often include graphics in boxes or sidebars without specifically referring to them in the text itself. However, in academic or professional workplace writing, graphics are always labeled, numbered, titled, and referred to directly in the text. By convention, tables are listed as "Tables," while line graphs, bar graphs, pie charts, or any other kinds of drawings or photographs are labeled as "Figures." Suppose you create a document that includes four graphics—a table, a bar graph, a pie chart, and an imported photograph. The table would be labeled as Table 1. The rest of the graphics would be labeled as Figure 1, Figure 2, and Figure 3.

In addition to numbering and labeling, every graphic needs a comprehensive title that explains fully what information is being displayed. Look back over the tables and figures in this chapter and compare their titles to the information in the graphics. In a line graph showing changes over time, for example, a typical title will identify the information on both the horizontal and vertical axes and the years covered. Bar graphs also have a "legend" explaining how the bars are coded if necessary. When you import the graphic into your own text, be consistent in where you place the title—either above the graphic or below it.

Referencing the Graphic in Your Text

Academic and professional writers follow a referencing convention called *independent redundancy*. The general rule is this: The graphic should be understandable without the text; the text should be understandable without the graphic; the text should repeat the most important information in the graphic. Suppose, for example, that you are writing an argument saying that social services for the elderly is a women's issue as well as an age issue and you want to use a pie chart that you have constructed. In your text, you would reference this chart and then repeat its key information as shown in Figure 9.12.

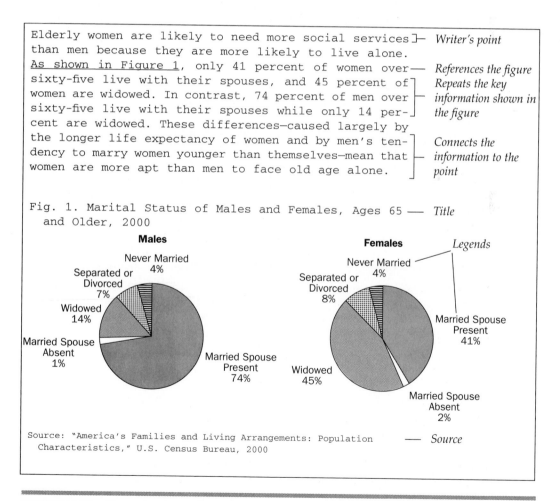

Elderly women are likely to need more social services]— *Writer's point*
than men because they are more likely to live alone.
As shown in Figure 1, only 41 percent of women over —— *References the figure*
sixty-five live with their spouses, and 45 percent of ⎤ *Repeats the key*
women are widowed. In contrast, 74 percent of men over ⎬ *information shown in*
sixty-five live with their spouses while only 14 per- ⎦ *the figure*
cent are widowed. These differences—caused largely by
the longer life expectancy of women and by men's ten- ⎤ *Connects the*
dency to marry women younger than themselves—mean that ⎬ *information to the*
women are more apt than men to face old age alone. ⎦ *point*

Fig. 1. Marital Status of Males and Females, Ages 65 —— *Title*
   and Older, 2000

Males

Never Married 4%
Separated or Divorced 7%
Widowed 14%
Married Spouse Absent 1%
Married Spouse Present 74%

Females   *Legends*

Never Married 4%
Separated or Divorced 8%
Married Spouse Present 41%
Widowed 45%
Married Spouse Absent 2%

Source: "America's Families and Living Arrangements: Population —— *Source*
   Characteristics," U.S. Census Bureau, 2000

FIGURE 9.12   *Example of a student text with a referenced graph*

Conclusion

In this chapter we have explained the challenge and power of using visuals in arguments. We have examined the components of visual design—use of type, layout, color, and images—and shown how these components can be used for persuasive effect in arguments. We have also described the argumentative genres that depend on effective use of visuals—posters and fliers, advocacy advertisements, cartoons, and Web pages—and invited you to produce your own visual argument. Finally, we showed you that graphics can tell a numeric story in a highly focused and dramatic way. Particularly we explained the functions of tables, bar graphs, pie charts, and line graphs, and showed you how to incorporate into and reference graphics in your own prose.

WRITING ASSIGNMENTS
FOR CHAPTER 9

OPTION 1: *A Poster Argument*   Working with the idea for a poster argument that you explored in the For Class Discussion on pages 183–184, use the visual design concepts and principles presented on pages 182–183 in this chapter, your understanding of the visual argument and the genre of poster arguments, and your own creativity to produce a poster argument that can be displayed on your campus or in your town or city. Try out the draft of your poster argument on people who are part of your target audience. Based on these individuals' suggestions for improving the clarity and impact of this visual argument, prepare a final version of your poster argument.

OPTION 2: *A Microtheme Using a Quantitative Graphic*   Write a short microtheme that tells a story based on data you select from Table 9.2 or from some other table provided by your instructor or located by you. Include in your microtheme at least one quantitative graphic (table, line graph, bar graph, pie chart), which should be labeled and referenced according to standard conventions. Use as a model the short piece shown in Figure 9.12 on page 191.

Part Three

Arguments in Depth

Six Types of Claims

A shortage of body organs and long waiting lists have motivated some people to make personal appeals to the public on billboards like this one. In Chapter 14, an introductory example, a reading, and the "Critiquing" exercise (on page 319) ask you to think about the evaluation and ethical issues involved in advertising for organs and in the selling and trading of body organs.

10 An Introduction to the Types of Claims

In Part One of this text, we discussed the reading and writing of arguments, linking argument to both persuasion and inquiry. In Part Two we examined the internal structure of arguments and showed how persuasive writers link their arguments to the beliefs and values of their audience. We also showed how writers can vary their content, structure, and style to reach audiences with varying degrees of resistance to the writer's views.

Now in Part Three we examine arguments in depth by explaining six types of claims and by showing how each type has its own characteristic patterns of development and support. Because almost all arguments use one or more of these types of claims as basic argumentative "moves" or building blocks, knowing how to develop each claim type will advance your skills in argument. The types of claims to be examined in Part Three are related to an ancient rhetorical concept called *stasis* from a Greek term meaning "stand" as in "to take a *stand* on something." There are many competing theories of stasis, so no two rhetoricians discuss stasis in exactly the same way. But all the theories have valuable components in common.

In Part Three we present our own version of stasis theory, or, to use more ordinary language, our own approach to argument based on the types of claims. The payoff for you will be threefold. First, understanding the types of claims will help you focus an argument and generate ideas for it. Second, a study of claim types teaches you characteristic patterns of support for each type, thereby helping you find a persuasive structure for your arguments. Finally, understanding claim types will help you increase your flexibility as an arguer by seeing how most arguments are hybrids of different claim types working together.

An Overview of the Types of Claims

To appreciate what a study of claim types can do, imagine one of those heated but frustrating arguments—let's suppose it's about gun control—where the question at issue keeps shifting. Everyone talks at cross-purposes, each speaker's point un-connected to the previous speaker's. The disputants start gesticulating at each other, faces contorted, voice levels rising. Sometimes such a discussion can get back on track if one person says, "Hold it for a moment. What are we actually dis-agreeing about here? Are we debating whether the government should enact gun control? Whether gun ownership prevents crime? Whether getting a gun license is like getting a car license? Let's figure out what we agree on and where we dis-agree because we can't debate all these questions at once." Whether she recog-nizes it or not, this person is applying the concept of claim types to get the argu-ment focused.

To understand how claim types work, let's return to the concept of stasis. A *stasis* is an issue or question that focuses a point of disagreement. You and your audience might agree on the answer to Question A and so have nothing to argue about. Likewise you might agree on the answer to Question B. But on Question C you disagree. Question C constitutes a *stasis* where you and your audience di-verge. It is the place where disagreement begins, where as an arguer you take a *stand* against another view. Thus you and your audience might agree that hand-gun ownership is legal. You might agree further that widespread ownership of handguns reduces crime. But if you ask the question "Is widespread handgun ownership a good thing?" you and your audience might disagree. This last ques-tion constitutes a *stasis*, the point where you and your audience part company.

Rhetoricians have discovered that the kinds of questions that divide people have classifiable patterns. In this text we identify six broad types of claims—each type originating in a different kind of question. To emphasize the structural pat-tern of each type, we will first use an X and a Y to represent slots so that you can focus on the structure rather than the content of the claim type. Then we'll move quickly to actual examples. Here is a brief overview of the six claim types.

Type 1: Simple Categorical Arguments (Is X a Y?, Where You and Your Audience Agree on the Meaning of Y)

A *categorical argument* occurs when persons disagree about the category (Y) that a given thing (X) belongs to. A categorical question is said to be simple if there is no dispute about the meaning of the Y term. Examples of questions leading to simple categorical arguments are the following:

Is President Bush a fiscal conservative?

Are manga (a style of Japanese comics) sexist?

Are painkillers made from synthetic opium addictive?

In these examples, we assume that the writer and audience agree on the meaning of "fiscal conservative," "sexist," and "addictive." At issue is whether President Bush, manga, or pain-killers made from synthetic opium belong to these categories.

The strategy for supporting a simple categorical argument is to provide examples or other evidence to show that X does or does not belong to category Y. No, President Bush is not a fiscal conservative (provide evidence of his government spending). Yes, manga are sexist (provide examples). No, these painkillers are not addictive (provide results of research studies). Simple categorical arguments are discussed in the first part of Chapter 11.

Type 2: Definitional Arguments (Is X a Y?, Where the Definition of Y Is Contested)

A categorical argument becomes more complex if you and your audience disagree about the meaning of the Y term. In this second type of claim, you have to define the Y term and defend your definition against objections and alternative definitions. Suppose, for example, you want to argue that using animals for medical research constitutes cruelty to animals. Here you would have to define what you mean by "cruelty to animals" and show how using animals for medical research fits your definition. Almost all legal disputes require definitional arguing because courts must determine whether an action meets or does not meet the criteria for a crime or civil tort as defined by a law, statute, or series of previous court rulings. Examples of questions leading to definitional arguments are the following:

Is occasional telling of off-color jokes in the workplace an instance of sexual harassment?

Is e-mail spam constitutionally protected free speech?

Is excessive online gaming a clinical addiction?

The general strategy for conducting a definitional argument is to define the second term and then argue whether the first term meets or does not meet the definition. We call this strategy *criteria-match arguing* because to define the second term you must specify the criteria that something must meet to fit the category. Then you must argue that your first term does or does not match these criteria. Definitional arguments are treated in depth in Chapter 11.

Type 3: Cause/Consequence Arguments (Does X Cause Y? Is Y a Consequence of X?)

Another major argument type entails cause and effect reasoning. Often such arguments arise from disagreements about the cause of an event or a trend. "What is causing the worldwide decline in frog populations?" or "What causes teenage males to become violent?" Just as frequently, causal arguments arise from speculations about the possible consequences of an action: "What would be the consequences of U.S. withdrawal from Iraq?" "Will gun control legislation reduce gang violence?"

The general strategy for conducting causal arguments is to describe the chain of events that lead from X to Y. If a causal chain cannot be directly established, you can argue indirectly, using inductive methods, statistical analyses, or analogies. Causal arguments are treated in detail in Chapter 12.

Type 4: Resemblance Arguments (Is X Like Y?)

A fourth argument type involves disputes about appropriate analogies or precedents. Suppose you disapproved of investing in the stock market and wanted to argue that stock market investing is like gambling. In showing the similarities between investing and gambling, you would be making a resemblance argument. Examples of questions that lead to resemblance arguing are the following:

> Was Slobodan Milosevic's policy of "ethnic cleansing" in Kosovo like Hitler's "final solution" against the Jews?
>
> Does pornography disparage women the way neo-Nazi propaganda disparages people of color? (Is pornography like racist propaganda?)
>
> Does J. K. Rowling's use of magic in her *Harry Potter* books more resemble the use of enchantment in Christian writer J. R. R. Tolkien's *The Lord of the Rings* trilogy or the occult magic in *Buffy the Vampire Slayer?*

The general strategy for resemblance arguments is to compare the first term to the second, pointing out similarities between them (if your goal is to make X like Y) or differences between them (if your goal is to make X unlike Y). Resemblance arguments are covered in Chapter 13.

Type 5: Evaluation Arguments (Is X Good or Bad? Is X a Good or Bad Y?)

Categorical, causal, and resemblance arguments (types 1–4) are often called reality or truth arguments. In such arguments, people question the way things are, were, or will be; they are disagreeing about the nature of reality. In contrast, evaluation and proposal arguments (types 5 and 6) deal with values, what people consider important, good, or worth doing. Although a person's values often begin as feelings founded on personal experience, they can nevertheless form the basis of reasonable argument in the public sphere if they are articulated and justified. When you articulate your values, explain their source (if necessary), and apply them consistently to specific cases, you make your values transpersonal and shareable and can use them to build coherent and reasonable arguments.

Evaluation arguments (type 5) ask questions about whether X is good or bad. Examples of evaluation questions are the following:

> Is a European-style, single-payer health insurance system a good policy for the United States to enact?

Is becoming a green company (making only hybrids and clean diesel vehicles) a good goal for a major American car manufacturer?

For purposes of her annual review, is the new office manager doing a good job?

The general strategy for evaluation arguments uses criteria-match arguing similar to that used for definitional arguments: You first establish your criteria for "good" in the specific case and then show how your first term does or does not meet the criteria. A special category of evaluation arguments deals with ethical or moral issues (for example, "Is it morally justifiable to spank children?" or "Is it ethical to use human embryonic stem cells for medical research?"). Evaluation arguments, including ethical evaluations, are covered in Chapter 14.

Type 6: Proposal Arguments (Should We Do X?)

Whereas argument types 1–5 all involve changing your audience's beliefs about something—whether about reality (types 1–4) or about the value of something (type 5)—proposal arguments call for action. Proposals ask your audience to *do* something, to act in some way. Typically, proposals use words like *should, ought,* or *must* followed by an action of some kind. The following questions all lead to proposal arguments:

Should the United States provide national health care for its citizens?

Should fast-food restaurants be required to help combat America's obesity problem?

Should the United Nations declare access to safe drinking water a human right?

The most typical strategy for making proposal arguments is to follow a problem-solution-justification structure whereby the opening section convinces the audience that a problem exists, the second section proposes a solution to solve the problem, and the last section justifies the solution by demonstrating that the benefits of acting on the proposal outweigh the costs or that the inherent "rightness" of the solution (on moral grounds) compels action. Proposal arguments are covered in Chapter 15.

For Class Discussion

Working as a whole class or in small groups, decide which claim type is represented by each of the following questions. Sometimes the argument categories overlap or blend together. For example, the question "Is airline travel safe?" might be considered either a simple categorical question or an evaluation question.

1. Should this state park allow overnight camping?

2. Are the chemicals in major brand-name cosmetics hazardous to your health?

3. Why is anorexia nervosa primarily a white, middle-class female disease?

4. Is depression in the elderly common in Asian cultures?

5. Were the terrorist attacks of September 11, 2001, like Pearl Harbor (an act of war) or like an earthquake (a natural disaster)?

6. How effective is acupuncture in reducing morning sickness?

7. How does acupuncture reduce morning sickness?

8. Should professional baseball impose a salary cap on its players?

9. Are Mattel toy factories sweatshops?

10. What are the primary causes of steroid use among teenage males?

How Knowledge of Claim Types Will Help You Focus an Argument and Generate Ideas

Having provided you with an overview of the types of claims, we now show you some of the benefits of this knowledge. First of all, understanding claim types will help you zero in on the argument you want to conduct. It will help you focus an argument by asking you to determine what's at stake between you and your audience. Where do you and your audience agree and disagree? What are the questions at issue? Second, it will help you generate ideas for your argument by suggesting the kinds of reasons, examples, and evidence you'll need.

To illustrate, let's take a hypothetical case—one Isaac Charles Little (affectionately known as I. C. Little), who desires to chuck his contact lenses and undergo the new lasik procedure to cure his nearsightedness. ("Lasik" is the common name for laser in-situ keratomileusis, a recent advance in surgical treatments for myopia. Sometimes known as "flap and zap" surgery, it involves using a laser to cut a layer of the corneal tissue thinner than a human hair and then flattening the cornea. It's usually not covered by insurance and is still quite expensive.) I. C. has two different arguments he'd like to make: (1) He'd like to talk his parents into helping him pay for the procedure, and (2) he'd like to join with others who are trying to convince insurance companies that the lasik procedure should be covered under standard medical insurance policies. In the discussions that follow, note how the six types of claims can help I. C. identify points of disagreement for each audience and simultaneously suggest lines of argument for persuading each one. Note, too, how the questions at issue vary for each audience.

First imagine what might be at stake in I. C.'s discussions with his parents.

Claim Type Analysis: Parents as Audience

■ *Simple categorical argument:* I. C.'s parents will be concerned about the safety and effectiveness of this procedure, especially for young adults. Is lasik a safe procedure? Is it an effective procedure? (These are the first questions at issue. I. C.'s mom has read about serious complications from lasik and has also heard that ophthalmologists prefer patients to be at least in their mid-twenties or older, so I. C. knows he will have to persuade her that lasik is safe and effective for twenty-year-olds.)

- *Definitional argument:* With parents as audience, I. C. will have to define what lasik surgery is so they won't have misconceptions about what is involved. However, he can't think of any arguments that would ensue over this definition, so he proceeds to the next claim type.

- *Causal argument:* Both parents will question I. C.'s underlying motivation for seeking this surgery. "What causes you to want this lasik procedure?" they will ask. (I. C.'s dad, who has worn eyeglasses all his adult life, will not be swayed by cosmetic desires. "If you don't like contacts," he will say, "just wear glasses.") Here I. C. needs to argue that permanently correcting his nearsightedness will improve his quality of life and even his academic and professional options. I. C. decides to emphasize his desire for an active, outdoor life, and especially his passion for water sports, where his need for contacts is a serious handicap. He is even thinking of majoring in marine biology, where lasik surgery would help him professionally. He says that wearing scuba equipment is easier without worrying about contact lenses or corrective goggles.

- *Resemblance argument:* I. C. can't think of any resemblance questions at issue.

- *Evaluation argument:* When the pluses and minuses are weighed, is lasik a good treatment for nearsightedness? Would the results of the surgery be beneficial enough to justify the cost and the risks? In terms of costs, I. C. might argue that even though the procedure is initially expensive (from $1,000 to $4,000), over the years he will save money by not needing glasses or contacts. The convenience of seeing well in the water and not being bothered by glasses or contacts while hiking and camping constitutes a major psychological benefit. (The cosmetic benefits—I. C. thinks he'll look cooler and feel more confident without glasses or contacts—he decides to leave out, since his dad thinks wearing glasses is fine.)

- *Proposal:* Should I. C. (or a young person in general) get this operation for treatment of myopia? (All the previous points of disagreement are subissues related to this overarching proposal issue.)

What this example should help you see is that the values arguments in the last two claim types (evaluation and proposal) depend on the writer's resolving related reality/truth questions in one or more of the first four types (simple categorical, definition, cause, resemblance). In this particular case, before convincing his parents that they should help him pay for the lasik procedure (I. C.'s proposal claim), I. C. would need to convince them that the procedure is safe and effective (simple categorical arguments), that there are significant recreational and professional benefits that would result from this surgery (causal argument), and that the benefits outweigh the costs (evaluation argument). Almost all arguments combine subarguments in this way so that lower-order claims provide supporting materials for addressing higher-order claims.

The previous illustration focused on parents as audience. If we now switch audiences, we can use our theory of claim types to identify different questions at issue. Let's suppose I. C. wants to persuade insurance companies to cover the lasik procedure. He imagines insurance company decision makers as his primary audience, along with the general public and state legislators, who may be able to influence them.

Claim Type Analysis: Insurance Decision Makers as Audience

- *Simple categorical argument:* No disagreements come immediately to mind. (This audience shares I. C.'s belief that lasik is safe and effective, although there may be some doubt about lasik for people under twenty-five.)

- *Definitional argument:* Should lasik be considered "cosmetic surgery" (as insurance companies contend) or as "medically justifiable surgery" (as I. C. contends)? This definitional question constitutes a major stasis. I. C. wants to convince his audience that lasik belongs in the category of "medically justifiable surgery" rather than "cosmetic surgery." He will need to define "medically justifiable surgery" in such a way that lasik can be included.

- *Causal argument:* What will be the consequences to insurance companies and to the general public of making insurance companies pay for lasik? Will there be an overwhelming crush of claims for lasik surgery? Will there be a corresponding decrease in claims for eye exams, contacts, and glasses? What will happen to the cost of insurance? Will optometrists and eyeglass manufacturers go out of business?

- *Resemblance argument:* Does lasik more resemble a face-lift (not covered by insurance) or plastic surgery to repair a cleft palate (covered by insurance)?

- *Evaluation argument:* Would it be good for society as a whole if insurance companies had to pay for lasik?

- *Proposal argument:* Should insurance companies be required to cover lasik?

As this analysis shows, the questions at issue change when you consider a different audience. Now the chief question at issue is definition: Is lasik cosmetic surgery or medically justifiable surgery? I. C. needs to spend no time arguing that the surgery is safe and effective (major concerns for his parents); instead he must establish criteria for "medically justifiable surgery" and then argue that lasik meets these criteria. Again note how the higher-order issues of value depend on resolving one or more lower-order issues of truth/reality.

So what can a study of claim types teach you about focusing an argument and generating ideas? First, it teaches you to analyze what's at stake between you and your audience by determining major points of disagreement. Second, it shows that you can make any of the claim types your argument's major focus.

Rather than tackle a values issue, you might tackle only a reality/truth issue. You could, for example, focus an entire argument on the simple categorical question "Is lasik safe?" (an argument requiring you to research the medical literature). Likewise you could write a causal argument focusing on what might happen to optometrists and eyeglass manufacturers if the insurance industry decided to cover lasik. The key insight here is that you may have to work through issues of reality and truth before you can figure out for yourself your own values position and before you can argue for change or action on an issue. Before you embark on writing an evaluation or proposal argument, consider whether you first need to resolve a lower-order claim based on reality/truth. Finally, a study of claim types helps you pose questions that generate ideas and suggest lines of reasoning.

For Class Discussion

Select an issue familiar to most members of the class—perhaps a current campus issue, an issue prominent in the local or national news, or an issue that the class has recently discussed—and analyze it using our sequence of claim types. Consider how a writer or speaker might address two different audiences on this issue. Hypothesizing the writer/speaker's perspective and claim, make a list of points of agreement and disagreement for both audiences, using as a pattern our claim-types analyses for lasik.

Hybrid Arguments: How Claim Types Work Together in Arguments

As you apply your knowledge of claim types to your reading and writing of arguments, you will see that most arguments are hybrids or composites of different claim types. These claim types work together as building blocks to support an overarching main claim. The reasons supporting the main claim operate as subarguments, and often these subarguments represent different kinds of claims. You can increase your flexibility as an arguer if you learn the typical "moves" that skilled arguers make to support different kinds of claims. Equipped with this insight, you will be able to muster appropriate support for these subarguments and increase your competence as an arguer.

Some illustrations will make this concept of hybrid arguments clearer. For example, a writer might develop a proposal argument with a causal subargument in one section, a resemblance subargument in another section, and an evaluation subargument in still another section. While the overarching proposal argument follows the typical structure of a proposal, each of the subsections follows a typical structure for its own claim type.

Some Examples of Hybrid Arguments

The following examples show how these combinations of claim types can play out in actual arguments.

> EVALUATION ARGUMENT DIRECTED TOWARD ENTERING
> COLLEGE STUDENTS
>
> *Evaluation claim:* Tutoring math and reading in urban elementary schools is a good way for college students to help children.
>
> *Reason:* because college students are positive role models for children (a *simple categorical claim*—provide examples of positive role models)
>
> *Reason:* because college students can dramatically improve children's motivation and foundational skills through one-on-one help (a *cause/consequence claim*—show causal links to explain how help leads to motivation, which sometimes leads to dramatic improvements; illustrate with examples)

> PROPOSAL ARGUMENT DIRECTED TOWARD REGIONAL
> NEWSPAPER READERSHIP
>
> *Proposal claim:* Our region should build a light-rail public transportation system.
>
> *Reason:* because light-rail would substantially reduce the number of cars on our overburdened road system (a *cause/consequence claim*—show causal links from building light-rail to reducing cars on the roads)
>
> *Reason:* because light-rail systems have been very successful in other parts of the country (a *resemblance claim*—provide evidence of success elsewhere; show how similar success will happen here)
>
> *Reason:* because light-rail is cost-effective and environmentally sound (an *evaluation claim:* use criteria-match structure by providing evidence showing how light-rail meets the evaluation criteria of being cost-effective and environmentally sound)

For more examples of these kinds of hybrid arguments, see Chapter 15, pages 326–331, where we explain how lower-order claims about truth/reality can support higher-order claims about values.

An Extended Example of a Hybrid Argument

As the previous examples illustrate, different claim types often serve as building blocks for larger arguments. We ask you now to consider a more extended example. Read the following op-ed piece arguing the proposal claim that "New York City should ban car alarms" and then read the analysis that follows. Note how the reasons are different claim-type subarguments that develop the overall proposal claim.

All That Noise for Nothing
Aaron Friedman

Early next year, the New York City Council is supposed to hold a final hearing 1
on legislation that would silence the most hated of urban noises: the car alarm.
With similar measures having failed in the past, and with Mayor Michael R.
Bloomberg withholding his support for the latest bill, let's hope the Council does
right by the citizens it represents.

Every day, car alarms harass thousands of New Yorkers—rousing sleepers, dis- 2
turbing readers, interrupting conversations and contributing to quality-of-life concerns that propel many weary residents to abandon the city for the suburbs.
According to the Census Bureau, more New Yorkers are now bothered by traffic
noise, including car alarms, than by any other aspect of city life, including crime or
the condition of schools.

So there must be a compelling reason for us to endure all this aggravation, 3
right? Amazingly, no. Many car manufacturers, criminologists and insurers agree
that car alarms are ineffective. When the nonprofit Highway Loss Data Institute
surveyed insurance-claims data from 73 million vehicles nationwide in 1997, they
concluded that cars with alarms "show no overall reduction in theft losses" compared with cars without alarms.

There are two reasons they don't prevent theft. First, the vast majority of blar- 4
ing sirens are false alarms, set off by passing traffic, the jostling of urban life or
nothing at all. City dwellers quickly learn to disregard these cars crying wolf; a recent national survey by the Progressive Insurance Company found that fewer than
1 percent of respondents would call the police upon hearing an alarm.

In 1992, a car alarm industry spokesman, Darrell Issa (if you know his name 5
that's because he would later spearhead the recall of Gov. Gray Davis in California),
told the New York City Council that an alarm is effective "only in areas where the
sound causes the dispatch of the police or attracts the owner's attention." In New
York, this just doesn't happen.

Car alarms also fail for a second reason: they are easy to disable. Most stolen 6
cars are taken by professional car thieves, and they know how to deactivate an
alarm in just a few seconds.

Perversely, alarms can encourage more crime than they prevent. The New York 7
Police Department, in its 1994 booklet "Police Strategy No. 5," explains how
alarms (which "frequently go off for no apparent reason") can shatter the sense of
civility that makes a community safe. As one of the "signs that no one cares," the
department wrote, car alarms "invite both further disorder and serious crime."

I've seen some of my neighbors in Washington Heights illustrate this by taking 8
revenge on alarmed cars: puncturing tires, even throwing a toaster oven through a
windshield. False alarms enrage otherwise lawful citizens, and alienate the very
people car owners depend on to call the police. In other words, car alarms work
about as well as fuzzy dice at deterring theft while irritating entire neighborhoods.

9   The best solution is to ban them, as proposed by the sponsors of the City Council legislation, John Liu and Eva Moskowitz. The police could simply ticket or tow offending cars. This would be a great improvement over the current laws, which include limiting audible alarms to three minutes—something that has proved to be nearly impossible to enforce.

10   Car owners could easily comply: more than 50 car alarm installation shops throughout the city have already pledged to disable alarms at no cost, according to a survey by the Center for Automotive Security Innovation.

11   And there is a viable alternative. People worried about protecting their cars can buy what are called silent engine immobilizers. Many European cars and virtually every new General Motors and Ford vehicle use the technology, in which a computer chip in the ignition key communicates with the engine. Without the key, the only way to steal the car is to tow it away, something most thieves don't have the time for. In the meantime, the rest of us could finally get some sleep.

The thesis of Friedman's op-ed piece is a proposal claim, and the article follows the typical problem-solution structure of proposal arguments. Although the whole argument follows a proposal shape, the individual pieces—the various subarguments that support the main argument—comprise different kinds of claim types with their own characteristic structures. If we break this argument down into subarguments, it looks like this:

Main proposal claim: New York City should ban car alarms (paragraph 1, repeated in paragraph 9).

- *Reason:* because car alarms are harassing (a simple *categorical claim*) developed with examples (paragraph 2)
- *Reason:* because car alarms are ineffective anti-theft devices (an *evaluation claim*) developed with two criteria—that car alarms go off for no reason and that they are easy to disable; data and evidence to show how car alarms match these criteria (paragraphs 3–6)
- *Reason:* because car alarms encourage crime (a *causal claim*) developed with causal links showing how a blaring car alarm leads to an outraged neighbor's smashing a toaster oven through the car's windshield (paragraphs 7–8)
- *Reason:* because banning car alarms is a workable solution (a *simple categorical claim*) supported by examples of what police and car owners can do (paragraphs 9–10)
- *Reason:* because car alarms have been successfully replaced in Europe with a better alternative—an ignition key with an embedded computer chip (a *precedent or resemblance claim*) (paragraph 11). Note that Friedman also uses a brief but undeveloped analogy (another kind of *resemblance claim*) that car alarms are about as effective as fuzzy dice at deterring theft (paragraph 8).

As you can see from this example, writers enlist other claim-type subarguments in building main arguments. This knowledge can help you increase your flexibility and effectiveness as an arguer. It encourages you to become skilled at four different kinds of arguers' "moves": (1) providing examples and evidence to support a simple categorical claim; (2) using a criteria-match strategy to support a definition or evaluation claim; (3) showing links in a causal chain to support a cause/consequence claim; or (4) using analogies and precedents to support a resemblance claim.

In the following chapters in Part Three, we discuss each of the claim types in more detail, showing you how they work and how you can develop skills and strategies for supporting each type of claim.

11 Categorical and Definitional Arguments

X Is (Is Not) a Y

CASE 1

The war against terrorism, first in Afghanistan and then in Iraq, led to the capture of many fighters or suspected al-Qaeda sympathizers, who were subsequently imprisoned at Abu Ghraib, Guantanamo Bay, or elsewhere. How to classify these persons gave rise to wrenching definitional questions. Was a captured fighter a "prisoner of war," in which case he was guaranteed certain rights by the Geneva Convention, including a right to a standard of food, health care, and shelter equivalent to that of U.S. troops and the right to be released and returned to his native country when the war was over? Or was a captured fighter an "unlawful combatant" still guaranteed humane treatment under the Geneva Convention but with fewer rights than a POW? Or was a captured fighter a "suspected terrorist" not entitled to any protection under the Geneva Convention? The U.S. executive branch argued that the Geneva Convention does not apply to a war against terrorism and that persons could be held indefinitely with no access to a lawyer. Critics of the U.S. policy, including The Human Rights Watch, argued that captured persons should be treated humanely and either released or brought to a fair trial with legal representation. Also at stake were definitional questions about torture. How much pain or psychological stress could be administered to prisoners before it should be classified as torture? Definitional issues such as these were bitterly debated in the media.

CASE 2

Recent developments in reproductive technology are creating complex definitional questions. For example, suppose an infertile couple conceives several embryos in a test tube and then freezes the fertilized embryos for future use. What category do those frozen embryos belong to when the couple divorces and disagrees about the disposition of the embryos? (In one actual case, the woman wanted to use the frozen embryos to try to get pregnant, and the man wanted to destroy the embryos.) What should be done with the embryos and who decides? Should frozen embryos be categorized as "persons," thus becoming analogous to children in custody arguments? Or should they be divided up as "property" with the man getting one half of the frozen embryos and the woman getting the other half? Or should a new legal category be created for them that regards them as more than property but less than actual persons? In one court case, the judge decided that frozen embryos "are not, strictly speaking, either 'persons' or 'property,' but occupy an interim category that entitles them to special respect because of their potential for human life."*

An Overview of Categorical Arguments

Categorical arguments are among the most common argument types you will encounter. They occur whenever you claim that any given X (a specific person, thing, event, or phenomenon) belongs in category Y (a more abstract or general term). Here are some examples of categorical claims: Piping loud rap music twenty-four hours a day into a prison cell is a form of torture. Even without the hidden sex scene, *Grand Theft Auto: San Andreas* merits an "Adults Only" rating. Graffiti is often art, not vandalism. My swerving off the road while trying to slap a bee on my windshield does not constitute "reckless driving."

We place items in categories all the time, and the categories we choose can have subtle but powerful rhetorical effects, creating implicit arguments. For example, if you don't like unsolicited e-mail, you might place it in the category "spam" and support legislation to make spam illegal. But people who make their livings through e-mail advertising place the same messages in the category "constitutionally protected free speech." If you favor biotech corn, you want to place it in the broad category "corn" and keep the term "biotech" off labels on cans. If you oppose it, you want to classify it as "Frankenfood." Or consider the competing categories proposed for whales in an international whaling controversy accelerated by the recent desires of whaling nations such as Japan to resume commercial whaling. What category does a whale belong to? Some arguers place whales in the category "sacred animals" that should never be killed because of their intelligence, beauty, grace, and power. Others categorize whales as a "renewable food resource" like tuna, crabs, cattle, and chickens. Others worry whether the specific kinds of whales being hunted are an "endangered species"—a concept that argues for the preservation of whale stocks but not necessarily for a ban on controlled hunting of individual whales once population numbers rise sufficiently. Each of these whaling arguments places whales within a different category that implicitly urges the reader to adopt that category's perspective on whaling.

---

*See Vincent F. Stempel, "Procreative Rights in Assisted Reproductive Technology: Why the Angst?" *Albany Law Review* 62 (1999), 1187.

Categorical claims shift from implicit to explicit arguments whenever the arguer supplies reasons and evidence to persuade us that X does (or does not) belong in category Y. In the rest of this chapter we discuss two kinds of categorical arguments: (1) simple categorical arguments in which the writer and an audience agree on the meaning of the Y term and (2) definitional arguments in which the meaning of the Y term is itself controversial.

Simple Categorical Arguments

A categorical argument can be said to be "simple" if there is no disagreement about the meaning of the Y term. For example, suppose you want to make the case that "David won't make a good committee chair because he is too bossy." Your supporting reason ("David is too bossy") is a simple categorical claim. You assume that everyone agrees what *bossy* means; the point of contention is whether David is or is not bossy. To support your claim, you would supply examples of David's bossiness. To refute it, someone else might supply counterexamples of David's cooperative and kind nature. As this example suggests, the basic procedural rule for developing a simple categorical claim is to supply examples and other data that show how X is (or is not) a member of category Y.

Difference between Facts and Simple Categorical Claims

Simple categorical claims are interpretive statements about reality. They claim that something does (or does not) exist or that something does (or does not) possess the qualities of a certain category. Often simple categorical claims look like facts, so it is important to distinguish between a fact and a simple categorical claim.

A *fact* is a statement that can be verified in some way, either by empirical observation or by reference to a reliable source (say, an encyclopedia) trusted by you and your audience. Here are some facts: Water freezes at 32 degrees. Boise is in Idaho, not Montana. The bald eagle is no longer on the EPA's endangered species list. These are all facts because they can be verified; no supporting arguments are needed or called for.

In contrast, a *simple categorical claim* is a contestable interpretation of facts. Consider the difference between these two sentences:

Fact: The bald eagle is no longer on the EPA's endangered species list.

Simple categorical claim: The bald eagle is no longer an endangered species.

The factual statement can be verified by looking at the list of endangered species published by the Environmental Protection Agency. We can see the date the bald eagle was placed on the list (1973) and the date it was removed (1995). The second statement is a claim. Imagine all the debates and arguments the EPA must have had as it pored over statistical data about eagle population numbers and over field reports from observers of eagles before deciding to remove the bald eagle from the list.

Often, it is difficult to draw the line between a fact and a claim. The acceptance or skepticism of a given audience can determine what passes as a fact or what becomes a claim that the arguer needs to support. Consider the statement "John F. Kennedy was killed by Lee Harvey Oswald." Most people call this statement a fact; to them, the report of the Warren Commission appointed to investigate the assassination is a reliable document that settles the issue. But conspiracy theorists, many of whom regard the Warren report as an unreliable rush to judgment, consider the statement above a highly contestable claim.

For Class Discussion

Working individually or in small groups, determine which of the following statements are facts and which are categorical claims. If you think a statement could be a "fact" for some audiences and a "claim" for others, explain your reasoning.

1. State sales taxes are not deductible on your federal income tax form.
2. State sales taxes are particularly burdensome for low-income families.
3. Nelly is a recording artist.
4. Nelly is a gangsta rapper.
5. Eleanor Roosevelt was a very unconventional woman.
6. Eleanor Roosevelt sometimes seemed anti-Semitic.
7. Eleanor Roosevelt was one of the drafters of the United Nations' Universal Declaration of Human Rights.

Variations in the Wording of Simple Categorical Claims

Simple categorical claims typically take the grammatical structure "X is a Y." Grammarians describe this structure as a subject followed by a linking verb (such as *to be* or *to seem*) followed by a predicate noun or adjective:

> David is bossy.
>
> State sales taxes are particularly burdensome for low-income families.
>
> Eleanor Roosevelt sometimes seemed anti-Semitic.

But other grammatical constructions can be used to make the same categorical claims:

> David frequently bosses people around. (He belongs to the category "people who are bossy.")

> Sales taxes particularly burden low-income families. (They belong to the category "things that are particularly burdensome.")
>
> On occasion, Eleanor Roosevelt made anti-Semitic remarks. (Eleanor Roosevelt belongs to the category "people who occasionally seem anti-Semitic.")

Almost any kind of interpretive statement about reality (other than causal statements, which are covered in Chapter 12) is a categorical claim of some kind. Here are a couple more examples of different kinds of categorical claims that can be translated into an "X is Y" format:

> Some teachers cheat during high-stakes testing by changing their students' answers. (Some teachers belong to the category of "cheaters.")
>
> Corporations often exaggerate the money they give to charities. (Corporate claims about their charitable giving are often exaggerated.)

Our point is to demonstrate that categorical claims are very common. Whether they are worded directly as "X is Y" statements or disguised in different grammatical structures, they assert that item X belongs in category Y or possesses the features of category Y.

Supporting Simple Categorical Claims: Supply Examples

The basic strategy for supporting a simple categorical claim is to give examples or other data showing how X belongs in category Y. If you want to argue that Sam is a party animal, provide examples of his partying behavior. If you want to argue that Eleanor Roosevelt sometimes seemed anti-Semitic, quote excerpts of anti-Semitic statements from her personal correspondence.* Because simple categorical arguments are common building blocks for longer, more complex arguments, they often take no more than one or two paragraphs inside a longer piece.

For an example of a simple categorical argument, consider the following passage from an article supporting regulated hunting of whales. The writer wants to contrast industrial countries without cultural ties to whaling with countries where whaling has deep cultural roots. The following passage supports the categorical claim that in Norway and Japan whaling is an "ancient occupation" worthy of respect and support:

> Things were different in other nations, especially Norway and Japan, where whaling is an ancient occupation worthy of the respect and support that Americans award to, say, the running of a farm. Norwegians view whaling as part of the hard, honorable life of a fisherman—a reliable slow-season activity that helps fishing communities to make it

---

*Roosevelt's biographer Blanche Wiesen Cook deals sensitively with this complex issue, largely exonerating Roosevelt from the charge of anti-Semitism. See *Eleanor Roosevelt*, vol. 2, *1933–38* (New York: Viking, 1999).

through the year. The Japanese who come from a long line of whalers have deeply held moral beliefs about maintaining their family tradition. To be prevented from honoring their ancestors in this manner is a source of shame. After the 1982 moratorium [on whaling] some Norwegian fishers went bankrupt. The same thing happened in Iceland. Given the abundance of the whale stocks, these nations ask, why can't such people be free to practice their traditional livelihood?*

Of course, a simple categorical claim can also be the thesis for a whole argument. We provide such an example in the argument from a Web health site that low-carb diets are unhealthy and potentially dangerous (pp. 231–234).

Refuting Simple Categorical Claims

If you wish to challenge or question someone else's simple categorical claim, you have three common strategies at your disposal:

- *Deny the accuracy or truth of the examples and data.* "You say that David is bossy. But you are remembering incorrectly. That wasn't David who did those bossy things; that was Paul."
- *Provide counterexamples that place X in a different category.* "Well, maybe David acted bossy on a few occasions. But more often he is kind and highly cooperative. For example . . ."
- *Raise definitional questions about the Y term.* "Well, that depends on what you mean by 'bossy.' What you call bossiness, I call decisiveness."

The last of these strategies shows how easily a simple categorical claim can slip into a definitional dispute. In the rest of this chapter we turn our attention to definitional arguments.

For Class Discussion

Working as a whole class or in small groups, prepare brief arguments in support of each of the following categorical claims. Then discuss ways that you might call these claims into question.

1. Americans today are obsessed with their appearance.
2. Professional athletes are overpaid.
3. The video games most enjoyed by children are extremely violent.

---

*William Aron, William Burke, and Milton Freeman. "Flouting the Convention." *Atlantic* May 1999, 26.

An Overview of Definitional Arguments

As we turn now to definitional arguments, it is important to distinguish between cases where definitions are needed and cases where definitions are *disputed*. Many arguments require a definition of key terms. If you are arguing, for example, that therapeutic cloning might lead to cures for various diseases, you would probably need to define "therapeutic cloning" and distinguish it from "reproductive cloning." Writers regularly define key words for their readers by providing synonyms, by citing a dictionary definition, by stipulating a definition, or by some other means. In the rest of this chapter, we focus on arguments in which the meaning of a key term is disputed. Consider, for example, the environmental controversy over the definition of *wetlands*. Section 404 of the federal Clean Water Act provides for federal protection of wetlands, but it leaves the task of defining wetlands to administrative agencies and the courts. Currently about 5 percent of the land surface of the contiguous forty-eight states is potentially affected by the wetlands provision, and 75 percent of this land is privately owned. Efforts to define wetlands have created a battleground between pro-environment and pro-development (or pro–private property rights) groups. Farmers, homeowners, and developers often want a narrow definition of wetlands so that more property is available for commercial or private use. Environmentalists favor a broad definition in order to protect different habitat types and maintain the environmental safeguards that wetlands provide (control of water pollution, spawning grounds for aquatic species, floodwater containment, and so forth). The problem is that defining wetlands is tricky. For example, one federal regulation defines a wetland as any area that has a saturated ground surface for twenty-one consecutive days during the year. But how would you apply this law to a pine flatwood ecosystem that was wet for ten days this year but thirty days last year? And how should the courts react to lawsuits claiming that the regulation itself is either too broad or too narrow? One can see why the wetlands controversy provides hefty incomes for lawyers and congressional lobbyists.

The Criteria-Match Structure of Definitional Arguments

As the wetlands example suggests, definitional arguments usually have a two-part structure—a definition part that tries to establish the meaning of the Y term (What do we mean by *wetland?*) and a match part that argues whether a given X meets that definition (Does this thirty-acre parcel of land near Swan Lake meet the criteria for a wetland?). We use the term *criteria-match* to describe this structure, which occurs regularly not only in definitional arguments but also, as we shall see in Chapter 14, in evaluation arguments of the type "X is (is not) a good Y." The *criteria* part of the structure defines the Y term by setting forth the criteria that must be met for something to be considered a Y. The *match* part examines whether the X term meets these criteria. Here are some examples:

- *Definitional issue:* In a divorce proceeding, is a frozen embryo a "person" rather than "property"?

  Criteria part: What criteria must be met for something to be a "person"?

  Match part: Does a frozen embryo meet these criteria?

- *Definitional issue:* For purposes of my feeling good about buying my next pair of running shoes, is the Hercules Shoe Company a socially responsible company?

  Criteria part: What criteria must be met for a company to be deemed "socially responsible"?

  Match part: Does the Hercules Shoe Company meet these criteria?

To show how a definitional issue can be developed into a claim with supporting reasons, let's look more closely at this second example. Let's suppose you work for a consumer information group that wishes to encourage patronage of socially responsible companies while boycotting irresponsible ones. Your group's first task is to define *socially responsible company*. After much discussion and research, your group establishes three criteria that a company must meet to be considered socially responsible:

> *Your definition:* A company is socially responsible if it (1) avoids polluting the environment, (2) sells goods or services that contribute to the well-being of the community, and (3) treats its workers justly.

The criteria section of your argument would explain and illustrate these criteria.

The match part of the argument would then try to persuade readers that a specific company does or does not meet the criteria. A typical thesis statement might be as follows:

> *Your thesis statement:* Although the Hercules Shoe Company is nonpolluting and provides a socially useful product, it is *not* a socially responsible company because it treats workers unjustly.

Here is how the core of the argument could be displayed in Toulmin terms (note how the criteria established in your definition serve as warrants for your argument):

INITIAL ENTHYMEME: The Hercules Shoe Company is not a socially responsible company because it treats workers unjustly.

CLAIM: The Hercules Shoe Company is *not* a socially responsible company.

STATED REASON: because it treats workers unjustly

GROUNDS: evidence that the company manufactures its shoes in East Asian sweatshops; evidence of the inhumane conditions in these shops; evidence of hardships imposed on displaced American workers

WARRANT: Socially responsible companies treat workers justly.

BACKING: arguments showing that just treatment of workers is right in principle and also benefits society; arguments that capitalism helps society as a whole only if workers achieve a reasonable standard of living, have time for leisure, and are not exploited

POSSIBLE CONDITIONS OF REBUTTAL: Opponents of this thesis might argue that justice needs to be considered from an emerging nation's standpoint: The wages paid workers are low by American standards but are above average by East Asian standards. Displacement of American workers is part of the necessary adjustment of adapting to a global economy and does not mean that a company is unjust.

As this Toulmin frame illustrates, the writer's argument needs to contain a criteria section (warrant and backing) showing that just treatment of workers is a criterion for social responsibility and a match section (stated reason and grounds) showing that the Hercules Shoe Company does not treat its workers justly. Your audience's initial beliefs determine how much emphasis you need to place on justifying each criterion and supporting each match. The conditions of rebuttal help the writer imagine alternative views and see places where opposing views need to be acknowledged and rebutted.

For Class Discussion

Consider the following definitional claims. Working individually or in small groups, identify the criteria issue and the match issue for each of the following claims.

EXAMPLE: A Honda assembled in Ohio is (is not) an American-made car.

CRITERIA PART: What criteria have to be met before a car can be called "American made"?

MATCH PART: Does a Honda assembled in Ohio meet these criteria?

1. American Sign Language is (is not) a "foreign language" for purposes of a college graduation requirement.
2. Burning an American flag is (is not) constitutionally protected free speech.
3. Bungee jumping from a crane is (is not) a "carnival amusement ride" subject to state safety inspections.

4. A Mazda Miata is (is not) a true sports car.

5. A race car driver is (is not) a true athlete.

Conceptual Problems of Definition

Before moving on to discuss ways of defining the Y term in a definitional argument, we should explore briefly some of the conceptual difficulties of definition. Language, for all its wonderful powers, is an arbitrary system that requires agreement among its users before it can work. And it's not always easy to get that agreement. In fact, the task of defining something can be devilishly complex.

Why Can't We Just Look in the Dictionary?

What's so hard about defining? you might ask. Why not just look in a dictionary? To get a sense of the complexity of defining something, consider again the word *wetland*. A dictionary can tell us the ordinary meaning of a word (the way it is commonly used), but it can't resolve a debate between competing definitions when different parties have interests in defining the word in different ways. For example, the *Webster's Seventh New Collegiate Dictionary* defines *wetland* as "land containing much soil moisture"—a definition that is hardly helpful in determining whether the federal government can prevent the development of a beach resort on some landowner's private property. Moreover, dictionary definitions rarely tell us such things as *to what degree* a given condition must be met before it qualifies for class membership. How wet does a wetland have to be before it is *legally* a wetland? How long does this wetness have to last? When is a wetland a mere swamp that ought to be drained rather than protected?

Definitions and the Rule of Justice: At What Point Does X Quit Being a Y?

For some people, all this concern about definition may seem misplaced. How often, after all, have you heard people accuse each other of getting bogged down in "mere semantics"? But how we define a given word can have significant implications for people who must either use the word or have the word used on them. Take, for example, what some philosophers refer to as the *rule of justice*. According to this rule, "Beings in the same essential category should be treated in the same way." Should an insurance company, for example, treat anorexia nervosa as a physical illness like diabetes (in which case treatment is paid for by the insurance company) or as a mental illness like paranoia (in which case insurance payments are minimal)? Or, to take another example, if a professor says that absences can be excused for emergencies only, is attending your best friend's wedding an "emergency"? How about attending an uncle's funeral? Could you make the case that in some instances attending a best friend's wedding or an uncle's funeral should count as an emergency while in other cases it should not count? What criteria would you set for "emergency"? These questions are all definitional issues involving arguments about what category a specific case belongs to and about what actions comply with the rule of justice, which demands that all cases in the same category be treated equally.

The rule of justice becomes even harder to apply when we consider Xs that grow, evolve, or otherwise change through time. When Young Person back in Chapter 1 argued that she could set her own curfew because she was mature, she raised the question "What are the attributes or criteria of a 'mature' person?" In this case, a categorical distinction between two separate kinds of things ("mature" versus "not mature") evolves into a distinction of degree ("mature enough"). So perhaps we should ask not whether Young Person is mature but whether she is "mature enough." At what point does a child become an adult? (When does a fetus become a human person? When does an Internet poker player become a compulsive gambler?)

Although we may be able arbitrarily to choose a particular point and declare, through stipulation, that "mature" means eighteen years old or that "human person" includes a fetus at conception, or at three months, or at birth, in the everyday world the distinction between child and adult, between egg and person, between Friday night poker playing and compulsive gambling seems an evolution, not a sudden and definitive step. Nevertheless, our language requires an abrupt shift between classes. In short, applying the rule of justice often requires us to adopt a digital approach to reality (switches are either on or off, either a fetus is a human person or it is not), whereas our sense of life is more analogical (there are numerous gradations between on and off, there are countless shades of gray between black and white).

As we can see by the preceding examples, the promise of language to fix what psychologist William James called "the buzz and confusion of the world" into an orderly set of categories turns out to be elusive. In most definitional debates, an argument, not a quick trip to the dictionary, is required to settle the matter.

For Class Discussion

Suppose your landlord decides to institute a "no pets" rule. The rule of justice requires that all pets have to go—not just your neighbor's barking dog, but also Mrs. Brown's cat, the kids' hamster downstairs, and your own pet tarantula. That is, all these animals have to go unless you can argue that some of them are not "pets" for purposes of a landlord's "no pets" rule.

1. Working in small groups or as a whole class, define *pets* by establishing the criteria an animal would have to meet to be included in the category "pets." Consider your landlord's "no pets" rule as the cultural context for your definition.

2. Based on your criteria, which of the following animals is definitely a pet that would have to be removed from the apartment? Based on your criteria, which animals could you exclude from the "no pets" rule? How would you make your argument to your landlord?

- a German shepherd dog
- a small housecat
- a tiny, well-trained lapdog
- a gerbil in a cage
- a canary
- a tank of tropical fish
- a tarantula

Kinds of Definitions

In this section we discuss two methods of definition commonly used in definitional arguments: Aristotelian and operational.

Aristotelian Definition

Aristotelian definitions, regularly used in dictionaries, define a term by placing it within the next larger class or category and then showing the specific attributes that distinguish the term from other terms within the same category. For example, according to a legal dictionary, *robbery* is "the felonious taking of property" (next larger category) that differs from other acts of theft because it seizes property "through violence or intimidation." Legal dictionaries often provide specific examples to show the boundaries of the term. Here is one example:

> There is no robbery unless force or fear is used to overcome resistance. Thus, surreptitiously picking a man's pocket or snatching something from him without resistance on his part is *larceny,* but not robbery.

Many states specify degrees of robbery with increasingly heavy penalties. For example, *armed robbery* involves use of firearms to threaten the victim. In all cases, *robbery* is distinguished from the lesser crime of *burglary* in which no force or intimidation is involved.

As you can see, an Aristotelian definition of a term identifies specific attributes or criteria that enable you to distinguish it from other members of the next larger class. We created an Aristotelian definition in our example about socially responsible companies. A socially responsible company, we said, is any company (next larger class) that meets three criteria: (1) It doesn't pollute the environment; (2) it creates goods or services that promote the well-being of the community; and (3) it treats its workers justly.

In constructing Aristotelian definitions, you may find it useful to employ the concept of accidental, necessary, and sufficient criteria. An *accidental criterion* is a usual but not essential feature of a concept. For example, armed robbers frequently wear masks, but wearing a mask is an accidental criterion because it has no bearing on the definition of *robbery.* In our example about socially responsible companies, "makes regular contributions to charities" might be an accidental criterion; most socially responsible companies contribute to charities, but some do not. And many socially irresponsible companies also contribute to charities—often as a public relations ploy.

A *necessary criterion* is an attribute that *must* be present for something to belong to the category being defined. To be guilty of robbery rather than burglary or larceny, a thief must have used direct force or intimidation. The use of force is thus a necessary criterion for robbery. However, for a robbery to occur another criterion must also be met: The robber must also take property from the victim. Together the use of force plus the taking of property are *sufficient criteria* for an act to be classified as robbery.

Consider again our defining criteria for a "socially responsible" company: (1) The company must avoid polluting the environment; (2) the company must create goods or services that contribute to the well-being of the community; and (3) the company must treat its workers justly. In this definition, each criterion is necessary, but none of the criteria alone is sufficient. In other words, to be defined as socially responsible, a company must meet all three criteria at once. It is not enough for a company to be nonpolluting (a necessary but not sufficient criterion); if that company makes a shoddy product or treats its workers unjustly, it fails to meet the other necessary criteria and can't be deemed socially responsible. Because no one criterion by itself is sufficient, all three criteria together must be met before a company can be deemed socially responsible.

In contrast, consider the following definition of *sexual harassment* as established by the U.S. Equal Employment Opportunity Commission in its 1980 guidelines:

> Unwelcome sexual advances, requests for sexual favors, and other verbal or physical conduct of a sexual nature constitute sexual harassment when (1) submission to such conduct is made either explicitly or implicitly a term or condition of an individual's employment, (2) submission to or rejection of such conduct by an individual is used as the basis for employment decisions affecting such individual, or (3) such conduct has the purpose or effect of unreasonably interfering with an individual's work performance or creating an intimidating, hostile, or offensive working environment.*

Here each of these criteria is sufficient but none is necessary. In other words, an act constitutes sexual harassment if any one of the three criteria is satisfied.

---

*Quoted by Stephanie Riger, "Gender Dilemmas in Sexual Harassment Policies and Procedures," *American Psychologist* 46 May 1991, 497–505.

For Class Discussion

Working individually or in small groups, try to determine whether each of the following is a necessary criterion, a sufficient criterion, an accidental criterion, or no criterion for defining the indicated concept. Be prepared to explain your reasoning and to account for differences in points of view.

CRITERION	CONCEPT TO BE DEFINED
presence of gills	fish
profane and obscene language	R-rated movie
line endings that form a rhyming pattern	poem
disciplining a child by spanking	child abuse
diet that excludes meat	vegetarian
killing another human being	murder
good sex life	happy marriage

Effect of Context and Authorial Purpose on Aristotelian Definitions

It is important to appreciate how the context of a given argument, as well as your own purpose, can affect your definition of a term. The question "Is a tarantula kept in the house a pet?" may actually have opposing answers, depending on the situation and your own goals. You may argue that your tarantula is or is not a pet, depending on whether you are trying to exclude it from your landlord's "no pets" rule or include it in your local talk show's "weird pet contest." Within one context you will want to argue that what your landlord really means by *pet* is an animal (next larger class) capable of disturbing neighbors or harming the landlord's property (criteria that distinguish it from other members of the class). Thus you could argue that your tarantula isn't a pet in your landlord's sense because it is incapable of harming property or disturbing the peace (assuming you don't let it loose!). In the other context you would argue that a pet is "any living thing" (note that in this context the "next larger class" is much larger) with which a human being forms a caring attachment and that shares its owner's domicile. In this case you might say, "Tommy Tarantula here is one of my dearest friends and if you don't think Tommy is weird enough, wait 'til I show you Vanessa, my pet Venus's-flytrap."

To apply the same principle to a different field of debate, consider whether obscene language in a student newspaper should be protected by the First Amendment. The purpose of school officials' suspending editors responsible for such language is to maintain order and decency in the school. The school officials thus hope to narrow the category of acts that are protected under the free-speech amendment in order to meet their purposes. In contrast, the American Civil Liberties Union (which has long defended student newspaper editors) is intent on avoiding any precedent that will restrict freedom of speech any more than is absolutely necessary. The different definitions of *free speech* that are likely to emerge thus reflect the different purposes of the disputants.

The problem of purpose shows why it is so hard to define a word out of context. Some people try to escape this dilemma by returning to the "original intent" of the authors of precedent-setting documents such as the Constitution. But if we try to determine the original intent of the writers of the Constitution on such matters as "free speech," "cruel and unusual punishment," or the "right to bear arms," we must still ask what their original purposes were in framing the constitutional language. If we can show that those original purposes are no longer relevant to present concerns, we have begun to undermine what would otherwise appear to be a static and universal definition to which we could turn.

Operational Definitions

In some rhetorical situations, particularly those arising in the physical and social sciences, writers need precise definitions that can be measured empirically and are not subject to problems of context and disputed criteria. Consider, for example, an argument involving the concept "aggression": "Do violent television programs increase the incidence of aggression in children?" To do research on this issue, a scientist needs a precise, measurable definition of *aggression*. Typically, a scientist might measure "aggression" by counting the number of blows or kicks a child gives to an inflatable bozo doll over a fifteen-minute period when other play options are available. The scientist might then define *aggressive behavior* as six or more blows to the bozo doll. In our wetlands example, a federal authority created an operational definition of *wetland*: A wetland is a parcel of land that has a saturated ground surface for twenty-one consecutive days during the year. Such definitions are useful because they are precisely measurable, but they are also limited because they omit criteria that may be unmeasurable but important. Many scientists, for example, object to definitions of *wetland* based on consecutive days of wetness. What is more relevant, they argue, is not the duration of wetness in any parcel of land but the kinds of plants and animals that depend on the wetland as a habitat. As another example, we might ask whether it is adequate to define a *superior student* as someone with a 3.5 GPA or higher or a *successful sex-education program* as one that results in a 25 percent reduction in teenage pregnancies. What important aspects of a superior student or a successful sex-education program are not considered in these operational definitions?

Strategies for Defining the Contested Term in a Definitional Argument

In constructing criteria to define your contested term, you can take two basic approaches—what rhetoricians call reportive and stipulative definitions. A *reportive definition* cites how others have used the term. A *stipulative definition* cites how you define the term. To put it another way, you can take a reportive approach by turning to standard or specialized dictionaries, judicial opinions, or expert testimony to establish a definition based on the authority of others. A lawyer defining a wetland based on twenty-one consecutive days of saturated ground surface would be using a reportive definition with a federal regulation as her source. The other approach is to use your own critical thinking to stipulate a definition, thereby defining the contested term yourself. Our definition of a socially responsible company, specifying three criteria, is an example of a stipulative definition. This section explains these approaches in more detail.

Reportive Approach: Research How Others Have Used the Term

When you take a reportive approach, you research how others have used the term, searching for authoritative definitions acceptable to your audience yet favorable to your case. Student writer Kathy Sullivan uses this approach in her argument that photographs displayed at the Oncore Bar are not obscene (see pp. 234–236). To define *obscenity*, she turns to *Black's Law Dictionary* and Pember's *Mass Media Laws.* (Specialized dictionaries are a standard part of the reference section of any library. See your reference librarian for assistance.) Other sources of specialized definitions are state and federal appellate court decisions, legislative and administrative statutes, and scholarly articles examining a given definitional conflict. Lawyers use this research strategy exhaustively in preparing court briefs. They begin by looking at the actual text of laws as passed by legislatures or written by administrative authorities. Then they look at all the court cases in which the laws have been tested and examine the ways courts have refined legal definitions and applied them to specific cases. Using these refined and elaborated definitions, lawyers then apply them to their own case at hand.

When research fails to uncover a definition favorable to the arguer's case, the arguer can sometimes adopt an *original intentions strategy.* For example, if a scientist is dissatisfied with definitions of *wetland* based on consecutive days of saturated ground surface, she might proceed as follows: "The original intention of the Congress in passing the Clean Water Act was to preserve the environment." What Congress intended, she could then claim, was to prevent development of those wetland areas that provide crucial habitat for wildlife or that inhibit water pollution. She could then propose an alternative definition (either a stipulative one that she develops herself or a reportive one that she uncovers in research) based on criteria other than consecutive days of ground saturation. (Of course, original intentions arguments can often be refuted by a "times have changed" strategy or by a "we can't know what they originally intended; we can only know what they wrote" strategy.)

Another way to make a reportive definition is to employ a strategy based on etymology, or *earlier meaning strategy.* Using an etymological dictionary or the *Oxford English Dictionary* (which traces the historical evolution of a word's meaning), an arguer can often unveil insights favorable to the writer's case. For example, if you wanted to argue that portrayal of violence in films is *obscene,* you could point to the etymology of the word, which literally means "offstage." The word derives from the practice of classical Greek tragedy, where violent acts occurred offstage and were only reported by a messenger. This strategy allows you to show how the word originally applied to violence rather than to sexual explicitness.

Stipulative Approach: Create Your Own Definition*

Often, however, you need to create your own definition of the contested term. An effective strategy is to establish initial criteria for your contested term by thinking of hypothetical cases that obviously fit the category you are trying to define and then by altering one or more variables until the hypothetical case obviously doesn't fit the category. You can then test and refine your criteria by applying them to borderline cases. For example, suppose you work at a homeless agency where you overhear street people discuss an incident that strikes you potentially as "police brutality." You wonder whether you should write to your local paper to bring attention to the incident.

CONTESTED CASE REGARDING POLICE BRUTALITY

Two police officers confront an inebriated homeless man who is shouting obscenities on a street corner. The officers tell the man to quiet down and move on, but he keeps shouting obscenities. When the officers attempt to put the man into the police car, he resists and takes a wild swing at one of the officers. As eyewitnesses later testified, this officer shouted obscenities back at the drunk man, pinned his arms behind his back in order to handcuff him, and lifted him forcefully by the arms. The man screamed in pain and was later discovered to have a dislocated shoulder. Is this officer guilty of police brutality?

To your way of thinking, this officer seems guilty: An inebriated man is too uncoordinated to be a threat in a fight, and two police officers ought to be able to arrest him without dislocating his shoulder. But a friend argues that because the man took a swing at the officer the police were justified in using force. The dislocated shoulder was simply an accidental result of using justified force.

To make your case, you need to develop a definition of "police brutality." You can begin by creating a hypothetical case that is obviously an instance of "police brutality":

CLEAR CASE OF POLICE BRUTALITY

A police officer confronts a drunk man shouting obscenities and begins hitting him in the face with his police baton. *[This is an obvious incidence of police brutality because the officer intentionally tries to hurt the drunk man without justification; hitting him with the baton is not necessary for making an arrest or getting the man into a police car.]*

---

*The defining strategies and collaborative exercises in this section are based on the work of George Hillocks and his research associates at the University of Chicago. See George Hillocks Jr., Elizabeth A. Kahn, and Larry R. Johannessen, "Teaching Defining Strategies as a Mode of Inquiry: Some Effects on Student Writing," *Research in the Teaching of English* 17 October 1983, 275–84. See also Larry R. Johannessen, Elizabeth A. Kahn, and Carolyn Calhoun Walter, *Designing and Sequencing Prewriting Activities* (Urbana, IL: NCTE, 1982).

You could then vary the hypothetical case until it is clearly *not* an instance of police brutality.

CASES THAT ARE CLEARLY NOT POLICE BRUTALITY

Case 1: The police officer handcuffs the drunk man, who, in being helped into the police car, accidentally slips on the curb and dislocates his arm while falling. *[Here the injury occurs accidentally; the police officer does not act intentionally and is not negligent.]*

Case 2: The police officer confronts an armed robber fleeing from a scene and tackles him from behind, wrestling the gun away from him. In this struggle, the officer pins the robber's arm behind his back with such force that the robber's shoulder is dislocated. *[Here aggressive use of force is justified because the robber was armed, dangerous, and resisting arrest.]*

Using these hypothetical cases, you decide that the defining criteria for police brutality are (1) *intention* and (2) use of *excessive force*—that is, force beyond what was required by the immediate situation. After more contemplation, you are convinced that the officer was guilty of police brutality and have a clearer idea of how to make your argument. Here is how you might write the "match" part of your argument.

MATCH ARGUMENT USING YOUR STIPULATED DEFINITION

If we define police brutality as the *intentional* use of *excessive* force, then the police officer is guilty. His action was intentional because he was purposefully responding to the homeless man's drunken swing and was angry enough to be shouting obscenities back at the drunk (according to an eyewitness). Second, he used excessive force in applying the handcuffs. A drunk man taking a wild swing hardly poses a serious danger to two police officers. Putting handcuffs on the drunk may have been justified, but lifting the man's arm violently enough to dislocate a shoulder indicates excessive force. The officer lifted the man's arms violently not because he needed to but because he was angry, and acting out of anger is no justification for that violence. In fact, we can charge police officers with "police brutality" precisely to protect us from being victims of police anger. It is the job of the court system to punish us, not the police's job. Because this officer acted intentionally and applied excessive force out of anger, he should be charged with police brutality.

The strategy we have demonstrated—developing criteria by imagining hypothetical cases that clearly do and do not belong to the contested category—gives you a systematic procedure for developing a stipulated definition for your argument.

For Class Discussion

1. Suppose you wanted to define the concept "courage." Working in groups, try to decide whether each of the following cases is an example of courage:

a. A neighbor rushes into a burning house to rescue a child from certain death and emerges, coughing and choking, with the child in his arms. Is the neighbor courageous?

b. A firefighter rushes into a burning house to rescue a child from certain death and emerges with the child in her arms. The firefighter is wearing protective clothing and a gas mask. When a newspaper reporter calls her courageous, she says, "Hey, this is my job." Is the firefighter courageous?

c. A teenager rushes into a burning house to recover a memento given to him by his girlfriend, the first love of his life. Is the teenager courageous?

d. A parent rushes into a burning house to save a trapped child. The fire marshal tells the parent to wait because there is no chance that the child can be reached from the first floor. The fire marshal wants to try cutting a hole in the roof to reach the child. The parent rushes into the house anyway and is burned to death. Was the parent courageous?

2. As you make your decisions on each of these cases, create and refine the criteria you use.

3. Make up your own series of controversial cases, like those above for "courage," for one or more of the following concepts:

a. cruelty to animals

b. child abuse

c. true athlete

d. sexual harassment

e. free speech protected by the First Amendment

Then, using the strategy of positive, contrastive, and borderline cases, construct a definition of your chosen concept.

Conducting the Match Part of a Definitional Argument

In conducting a match argument, you need to supply examples and other evidence showing that your contested case does (does not) meet the criteria you established in your definition. In essence, you support the match part of your argument in much the same way you would support a simple categorical claim.

For example, if you were developing the argument that the Hercules Shoe Company is not socially responsible because it treats its workers unjustly, your match section would provide evidence of this injustice. You might supply data about the percentage of shoes produced in East Asia, about the low wages paid these workers, and about the working conditions in these factories. You might also describe the suffering of displaced American workers when Hercules closed its American factories and moved operations to Asia, where the labor was nonunion and cheap. The match section should also summarize and respond to opposing views.

Writing a Definitional Argument

WRITING ASSIGNMENT
FOR CHAPTER 11

Write an argument that develops a definitional claim of the form "X is (is not) a Y," where Y is a controversial term with a disputed definition. Typically your argument will have a criteria section in which you develop an extended definition of your Y term and a match section in which you argue that your X does (does not) meet the criteria for Y.

Exploring Ideas

Ideally, in writing this argument you will join an ongoing conversation about a definitional issue that interests you. What cultural and social issues that concern you involve disputed definitions? In the public area, you are likely to find numerous examples simply by looking through a newspaper—the strategy used by student writer Kathy Sullivan, who became interested in the controversy over allegedly obscene photographs in a gay bar (see pp. 234–236). Others of our students have addressed definitional issues such as these: Is using TiVo to avoid TV commercials a form of theft? Is spanking a form of child abuse? Are cheerleaders athletes? Is flag burning protected free speech? Is a person who downloads instructions for making a bomb a terrorist? Are today's maximum security prisons "cruel and unusual punishment"? Is Wal-Mart a socially responsible company? Is Hillary Clinton a moderate or a liberal?

If you have trouble discovering a local or national issue that interests you, you can create fascinating definitional controversies among your classmates by asking whether certain borderline cases are "true" or "real" examples of some category: Are highly skilled video game players (race car drivers, synchronized swimmers, marbles players) true athletes? Is a gourmet chef (skilled furniture maker, tagger) a true artist? Is a chiropractor (acupuncturist, naturopathic physician) a "real doctor"? Working as a whole class or in small groups inside or outside of class, create an argumentative discussion on one or more of these issues. Listen to the various voices in the controversy, and then write out your own argument.

You can also stimulate definitional controversies by brainstorming borderline cases for such terms as *courage* (Is mountain climbing an act of courage?), *cruelty to animals* (Are rodeos [zoos, catch-and-release trout fishing, use of animals for medical research] cruelty to animals?), or *war crime* (Was the American firebombing of Tokyo in World War II a war crime?).

As you explore your definitional issue, try to determine how others have defined your Y term (a reportive procedure). If no stable definition emerges from your search, stipulate your own definition by deciding what criteria must be met for any X to be deemed a Y. Try using the strategy for creating criteria that we discussed on pages 224–226 with reference to police brutality. Once you have determined your criteria for your Y term, freewrite for five or ten minutes, exploring whether your X term meets each of the criteria. Before writing your first draft, you can explore your ideas further by doing the ten freewriting tasks on pages 70–71 in Chapter 3.

Organizing a Definitional Argument

As you compose a first draft of your essay, you may find it helpful to know a prototypical structure for definitional arguments. Here are several possible plans.

Plan 1 (Criteria and Match in Separate Sections)

- Introduce the issue by showing disagreements about the definition of a key term or about its application to a problematic case.
- State your claim.
- Present your definition of the key term.
  State and develop criterion 1.
  State and develop criterion 2.
  Continue with rest of criteria.
- Summarize and respond to possible objections to your definition.
- Restate your claim about the contested case (it does [does not] meet your definition).
  Apply criterion 1 to your case.
  Apply criterion 2 to your case.
  Continue the match argument.
- Summarize and respond to possible objections to your match argument.
- Conclude your argument.

Plan 2 (Criteria and Match Interwoven)

- Introduce the issue by showing disagreements about the definition of a key term or about its application to a problematic case.
- Present your claim.
  State criterion 1 and argue that contested case meets (does not meet) criterion.
  State criterion 2 and argue that contested case meets (does not meet) criterion.
  Continue with criteria-match sections for additional criteria.

- Summarize opposing views.
- Refute or concede to opposing views.
- Conclude your argument.

Revising Your Draft

Once you have written a discovery draft, your goal should be to make your argument more clear and persuasive to your audience. One way to strengthen your appeal to your readers is to use a Toulmin analysis to determine where your reasoning needs to be bolstered for your particular audience. In a definitional argument, the criteria established in your definition of the Y term are the warrants for your match argument. You might find it helpful at this time to summarize your argument as a claim with *because* clauses and to test it with Toulmin's schema. Here is how student writer Kathy Sullivan used Toulmin to analyze a draft of her essay examining the possible obscenity of photographs displayed in a gay bar in Seattle. The final version of this essay is printed on pages 234–236.

ENTHYMEME: The photographs displayed in the Oncore bar are not obscene because they do not violate the community standards of the patrons of the bar, because they do not appeal to prurient interest, because children are not likely to be exposed to them, and because they promote an important social value, safe sex, in order to prevent AIDS.

CLAIM: The photographs are not obscene.

STATED REASONS: (1) They don't violate community standards. (2) They do not appeal to prurient interests. (3) Children are not exposed to them. (4) They promote an important social purpose of preventing AIDS through safe sex.

GROUNDS: (1) evidence that most Oncore patrons are homosexual and that these photographs don't offend them (no complaints, etc.); (2) purpose of photographs is not prurient sexuality, they don't depict explicit sexual acts, the only thing complained about by the liquor board is visible body parts; (3) because this is a bar, children aren't allowed; (4) evidence that the purpose of these photographs is to promote safe sex, thus they have a redeeming social value

WARRANT: Things that don't violate community standards, do not appeal to prurient interests, don't come in view of children, and promote an important purpose are not obscene.

BACKING: These criteria come from the definition of *obscenity* in *Black's Law Dictionary*, which in turn is based on recent court cases. This is a very credible source. In addition, arguments showing why the community standard here should be that of the homosexual community rather than the community at large; arguments showing that the social importance of safe sex overrides other considerations.

CONDITIONS OF REBUTTAL: An opponent might say that the community standards should be those of the Seattle community at large, not those of the gay community. An opponent might say that photographs of male genitalia in a gay bar appeal to prurient interest.

QUALIFIER: Those photographs would be obscene if displayed anywhere but in a gay bar.

As a result of this analysis, Kathy revised her final draft considerably. By imagining where her arguments were weak ("conditions of rebuttal"), she realized that she needed to include more backing by arguing that the community standards to be applied in this case should be those of the homosexual community rather than the community at large. She also added a section arguing that visible genitalia in the photographs didn't make the photos obscene. By imagining how your readers might rebut your argument, you will see ways to strengthen your draft. Consequently, we close out this chapter by looking more carefully at the ways a definitional argument can be rebutted.

Questioning and Critiquing a Definitional Argument

Another powerful way to stimulate revision of a draft is to role-play a skeptical audience. The following means of questioning a definitional argument can be applied to your own draft to help you strengthen it or to someone else's definitional argument as a means of critiquing it closely. In critiquing a definitional argument, you need to appreciate its criteria-match structure. Your critique can question the argument's criteria, the match, or both.

Questioning the Criteria

- *Might a skeptic claim that your criteria are not the right ones?* This is the most common way to attack a definitional argument. Skeptics might say that one or more of your argument's criteria are only accidental criteria, not necessary or sufficient ones. Or they might argue for different criteria or point out crucial missing criteria.

- *Might a skeptic point out possible bad consequences of accepting your argument's criteria?* Here a skeptic could raise doubts about your definition by showing how it would lead to unintended bad consequences.

- *Might a skeptic cite extraordinary circumstances that weaken your argument's criteria?* Skeptics might argue that your criteria are perfectly acceptable in ordinary circumstances but are rendered unacceptable by extraordinary circumstances.

- *Might a skeptic point out a bias or slant in your definition?* Writers create definitions favorable to their case. By making this slant visible, a skeptic may be able to weaken the persuasiveness of your definition.

Questioning the Match

A match argument usually uses examples and other evidence to show that the contested case meets (does not meet) the criteria in the definition. The standard methods of refuting evidence apply (see pp. 148–149). Thus skeptics might ask one or more of the following questions:

- Are your examples out-of-date or too narrow and unrepresentative?
- Are your examples inaccurate?
- Are your examples too extreme?
- Are there existing counterexamples that alter the case?

By using these questions to test your own argument, you can reshape and develop your argument to make it thought provoking and persuasive for your audience.

Readings

Our first reading makes the simple categorical claim that low-carb diets are "imbalanced and potentially dangerous," or, more scientifically, that the diet is "ketogenic." The writer of this article takes a strong anti-low-carb stance in a national debate about the effectiveness and safety of the Atkins diet and other similar diets that have experienced cycles of popularity since 1972 when Dr. Robert C. Atkins first introduced his approach to weight loss. This article can be found on the Web site of the "Wellness Center" (http://atoz.iquhealth.com), which is a subsidiary of HealthAtoZ.com. The author of the article is unidentified.

Low-Carb Diets Unhealthy Trend

Low-carbohydrate diet books have been topping best-sellers' lists lately, but doctors and dietitians warn that low-carb, high-protein diets are imbalanced and potentially dangerous.   1

Sheila Kelly, clinical dietitian at Providence Hospital, Washington, D.C., says Americans are always looking for the "quick fix" diet plans. The allure of the low-carbohydrate diets, she says, is that they tend to promise rapid weight loss while allowing dieters to load up on proteins and fatty foods.   2

3   Under the Atkins diet, perhaps the most famous of all the low-carbohydrate, high-protein diets, a dieter might have a ham and cheese omelet with sides of bacon and sausage for breakfast, a hamburger for lunch (no bun) and a steak for dinner.

4   "It's a seductive concept," Kelly says. "Watch the pounds melt away while you eat all of the high-fat foods you want. Even better, don't bother watching your caloric intake or worrying about regaining your weight. All you have to do is avoid 'poison' carbohydrates."

5   Americans spend $33 billion a year on the diet industry but aren't getting any thinner. According to the Journal of the American Medical Association, there are 50 percent more obese people in America today than there were eight years ago.

6   Dr. Robert C. Atkins' low-carbohydrate diet first became a hit back in 1972. Now, almost 30 years later, he re-released his diet book with the title "Dr. Atkins' New Diet Revolution" and, like the first, this sequel has become a national bestseller.

7   According to Atkins, the problem is that people eat too many carbohydrates. He contends that Americans love to think that fat is making them fat when carbohydrates converted to fat by excess insulin is what really makes them fat.

8   People will lose weight on the near-elimination of carbohydrates from the diet, but the weight loss is the result of unhealthy eating, according to Kelly. The American Heart Institute and the National Institutes of Health both recommend a balanced diet that includes 250 grams to 300 grams of carbohydrates a day (15 times what Atkins allows).

9   Carbohydrates, essential nutrients that come in the form of starches and sugars, have the most effect on blood sugar. Carbohydrates are found in fruits, vegetables, beans, dairy foods and starchy foods such as breads and sweets. The Atkins diet not only requires that all sweets (cookies, pies, soda and ice cream) be avoided but it also severely restricts breads, pastas, beans, fruits and vegetables.

10   At its core, Kelly says, the Atkins diet is "nothing more than a garden-variety ketogenic diet."

11   Ketosis occurs when carbohydrates are not available to the body for energy. When the body doesn't get enough carbohydrates, it starts to reduce the blood sugar (glycogen) reserves in the liver. The body then starts to extract glycogen from muscle tissue, thus breaking it down and depleting water from the muscles at the same time. In the initial stages of the diet, the first seven to nine pounds a person loses are water, according to Kelly, presenting a real danger of dehydration and mineral deficiencies.

12   After the body has depleted the reserves of blood sugar in the muscles, it then starts to expand its production of ketone bodies, which many cells ultimately use for energy in lieu of glucose. That, indeed, is fat burning, Kelly says. But it is also dangerous.

13   Ketones, acid by-products of fat digestion, build up in the blood and make the blood acidic—a condition called ketosis. If ketones build up in the body long enough, they can cause serious illness and coma, Kelly explains.

14   Another potentially harmful feature of the low-carbohydrate, high-protein diets, such as Atkins', is that they generally are low in fiber and high in fat. "The Atkins'

paltry 3 to 5 grams of fiber per day falls far short of the recommended daily allowance of 25 to 30 grams per day," Kelly says.

Low-fiber diets have been linked to constipation, diverticulosis and cancers of the colon, breast and prostate. Some dieters may take fiber supplements to compensate, but supplements do not provide the same fiber mix and content as that found in foods, Kelly says.

15

The high total fat and saturated fat content of the Atkins diet is also cause for concern, she says. High total and saturated fat diets have been linked conclusively to heart disease. Research also shows that high saturated fat intakes are pro-inflammatory, and numerous studies implicate a high total-fat diet in cancers of the breast, prostate and lung.

16

"Perhaps the most worrisome aspect of this diet is its relative lack of fruits and vegetables," Kelly says. Atkins suggests that dieters compensate for the vitamin and mineral deficiencies expected from a low-carbohydrate diet by taking up to 30 vitamin supplements per day.

17

However, Kelly states research indicates that it is not the vitamins and minerals in fruits and vegetables that are protective against cancer, heart disease and oxidative injury but the carotenoid compounds, phytochemicals and other "nutraceuticals" that researchers are beginning to investigate. "A lifelong shunning of these foods deprives the body of disease-fighting weapons," she says.

18

Complete carbohydrate deprivation also appears to have a damaging psychological effect, according to Kelly. The permanent removal of favorite bingeing foods, such as chocolate, cookies, ice cream and desserts, leads to "obsessive cravings and ultimate capitulation to temptation." Recent studies seem to bear this out, with one estimating the weight regain from the Atkins diet to be 96 percent.

19

Critiquing "Low-Carb Diets Unhealthy Trend"

1. According to this article, what are the unhealthy and potentially dangerous consequences of low-carb diets? What evidence does this article use to support its claims?

2. How would you evaluate the writer's *ethos* in this article? You might note that the writer appears to be a journalist who relies extensively on testimony from clinical dietician Sheila Kelly. To what extent would you use this article in an academic research paper? In analyzing the writer's *ethos*, you might also examine the Web site from which we obtained this article (http://atoz.iquhealth.com) as well as the Web site of its sponsor (www.HealthAtoZ.com).

3. Not all studies support this article's claim that a low-carb diet is dangerous. Two studies in May 2003 in the *New England Journal of Medicine* showed that low-carb diets increased blood levels of "good cholesterol" and improved lipid profiles as compared to the same measures in dieters following a low-fat and low-calorie regimen. However, these studies lasted

only twelve weeks and did not consider possible long-term dangers. To what extent does this article focus on possible long-term as opposed to short-term risks?

The second reading, by student Kathy Sullivan, was written for the definition assignment on page 227. The definitional issue that she addresses—"Are the Menasee photographs obscene?"—became a local controversy in the state of Washington when the state liquor control board threatened to revoke the liquor license of a Seattle gay bar, the Oncore, unless it removed a series of photographs that the board deemed obscene.

Oncore, Obscenity, and the Liquor Control Board

Kathy Sullivan (student)

1   In early May, Geoff Menasee, a Seattle artist, exhibited a series of photographs with the theme of "safe sex" on the walls of an inner city, predominantly homosexual restaurant and lounge called the Oncore. Before hanging the photographs, Menasee had to consult with the Washington State Liquor Control Board because, under the current state law, art work containing material that may be considered indecent has to be approved by the board before it can be exhibited. Of the almost thirty photographs, six were rejected by the board because they partially exposed "private parts" of the male anatomy. Menasee went ahead and displayed the entire series of photographs, placing Band-Aids over the "indecent" areas, but the customers continually removed the Band-Aids.

2   The liquor control board's ruling on this issue has caused controversy in the Seattle community. The *Seattle Times* has provided news coverage, and a "Town Meeting" segment was filmed at the restaurant. The central question is this: Should an establishment that caters to a predominantly homosexual clientele be enjoined from displaying pictures promoting "safe sex" on the grounds that the photographs are obscene?

3   Before I can answer this question, I must first determine whether the art work should truly be classified as obscene. To make that determination, I will use the definition of obscenity in *Black's Law Dictionary:*

> Material is "obscene" if to the average person, applying contemporary community standards, the dominant theme of material taken as a whole appeals to prurient interest, if it is utterly without redeeming social importance, if it goes substantially beyond customary limits of candor in description or representation, if it is characterized by patent offensiveness, and if it is hard core pornography.

An additional criterion is provided by Pember's *Mass Media Laws:* "A work is obscene if it has a tendency to deprave and corrupt those whose minds are open to such immoral influences (children for example) and into whose hands it might happen to fall" (394). The art work in question should not be prohibited from display at predominantly homosexual establishments like the Oncore because it does not meet the above criteria for obscenity.

First of all, to the average person applying contemporary community standards, the predominant theme of Menasee's photographs is not an appeal to prurient interests. The first element in this criterion is "average person." According to Rocky Breckner, manager of the Oncore, 90 percent of the clientele at the Oncore is made up of young white homosexual males. This group therefore constitutes the "average person" viewing the exhibit. "Contemporary community standards" would ordinarily be the standards of the Seattle community. However, this art work is aimed at a particular group of people—the homosexual community. Therefore, the "community standards" involved here are those of the gay community rather than the city at large. Since the Oncore is not an art museum or gallery, which attracts a broad spectrum of people, it is appropriate to restrict the scope of "community standards" to that group who voluntarily patronize the Oncore.

Second, the predominant theme of the photographs is not "prurient interest" nor do the photographs go "substantially beyond customary limits of candor." There are no explicit sexual acts found in the photographs; instead, their theme is the prevention of AIDS through the practice of safe sex. Homosexual displays of affection could be viewed as "prurient interest" by the larger community, but same-sex relationships are the norm for the group at whom the exhibit is aimed. If the exhibit were displayed at McDonald's or even the Red Robin it might go "substantially beyond customary limits of candor," but it is unlikely that the clientele of the Oncore would find the art work offensive. The manager stated that he received very few complaints about the exhibit and its contents.

Nor is the material pornographic. The liquor control board prohibited the six photographs based on their visible display of body parts such as pubic hair and naked buttocks, not on the basis of sexual acts or homosexual orientation. The board admitted that the photographs depicted no explicit sexual acts. Hence, it can be concluded that they did not consider the suggestion of same-sex affection to be hard-core pornography. Their sole objection was that body parts were visible. But visible genitalia in art work are not necessarily pornographic. Since other art work, such as Michelangelo's sculptures, explicitly depict both male and female genitalia, it is arguable that pubic hair and buttocks are not patently offensive.

It must be conceded that the art work has the potential of being viewed by children, which would violate Pember's criterion. But once again the incidence of minors frequenting this establishment is very small.

But the most important reason for saying these photographs are not obscene is that they serve an important social purpose. One of Black's criteria is that obscene material is "utterly without redeeming social importance." But these photographs have the explicit purpose of promoting safe sex as a defense against AIDS. Recent statistics reported in the *Seattle Times* show that AIDS is now the leading cause of death of men under forty in the Seattle area. Any methods that can promote the message of safe sex in today's society have strong redeeming social significance.

9   Those who believe that all art containing "indecent" material should be banned or covered from public view would most likely believe that Menasee's work is obscene. They would disagree that the environment and the clientele should be the major determining factor when using criteria to evaluate art. However, in the case of this exhibit I feel that the audience and the environment of the display are factors of overriding importance. Therefore, the exhibit should have been allowed to be displayed because it is not obscene.

Critiquing "Oncore, Obscenity, and the Liquor Control Board"

1. Kathy Sullivan here uses a reportive approach for defining her Y term "obscenity." Based on the definitions of *obscenity* in *Black's Law Dictionary* and Pember's *Mass Media Laws*, what criteria for obscenity does Kathy use?

2. How does she argue that the Menasee photographs do *not* meet the criteria?

3. Working as a whole class or in small groups, share your responses to the following questions: (a) If you find Kathy's argument persuasive, which parts were particularly influential or effective? (b) If you are not persuaded, which parts of her argument do you find weak or ineffective? (c) How does Kathy shape her argument to meet the concerns and objections of her audience? (d) How might a lawyer for the liquor control board rebut Kathy's argument?

Our third reading, by conservative syndicated columnist Charles Krauthammer, was published on September 13, 2001, two days after the September 11 terrorist attacks. The United States, still reeling from the attacks, was entering the first phase of a national debate on how to respond. Krauthammer's article helped shape that debate, influencing President Bush's military response that eventually came to be called the "war" against terrorism. In this op-ed piece, Krauthammer argues that the terrorist attacks belong in the category "act of war" rather than the category "crime" and that the U.S. response should be shaped appropriately.

This Isn't a "Legal" Matter, This Is War
Charles Krauthammer

1   This is not crime. This is war. One of the reasons there are terrorists out there capable and audacious enough to carry out the deadliest attack on the United

States in its history is that, while they have declared war on us, we have in the past responded (with the exception of a few useless cruise missile attacks on empty tents in the desert) by issuing subpoenas.

Secretary of State Colin Powell's first reaction to the day of infamy was to pledge to "bring those responsible to justice." This is exactly wrong. Franklin Roosevelt did not respond to Pearl Harbor by pledging to bring the commander of Japanese naval aviation to justice. He pledged to bring Japan to its knees. 2

You bring criminals to justice; you rain destruction on combatants. This is a fundamental distinction that can no longer be avoided. The bombings of Sept. 11, 2001, must mark a turning point. War was long ago declared on us. Until we declare war in return, we will have thousands of more innocent victims. 3

We no longer have to search for a name for the post–Cold War era. It will henceforth be known as the age of terrorism. Organized terror has shown what it can do: execute the single greatest massacre in American history, shut down the greatest power on the globe, and send its leaders into underground shelters. All this, without even resorting to chemical, biological or nuclear weapons of mass destruction. 4

This is a formidable enemy. To dismiss it as a bunch of cowards perpetrating senseless acts of violence is complacent nonsense. People willing to kill thousands of innocents while they kill themselves are not cowards. They are deadly, vicious warriors and need to be treated as such. Nor are their acts of violence senseless. They have a very specific aim. To avenge alleged historical wrongs and to bring the great American satan to its knees. 5

Nor is the enemy faceless or mysterious. We do not know for sure who gave the final order but we know what movement it comes from. The enemy has identified itself in public and openly. Our delicate sensibilities have prevented us from pronouncing its name. 6

Its name is radical Islam. Not Islam as practiced peacefully by millions of the faithful around the world. But a specific fringe political movement, dedicated to imposing its fanatical ideology on its own societies and destroying the society of its enemies, the greatest of which is the United States. 7

Israel, too, is an affront to radical Islam, and thus of course must be eradicated. But it is the smallest of fish. The heart of the beast—with its military in Saudi Arabia, Kuwait, Turkey and Persian Gulf; with a culture that "corrupts" Islamic youth; with an economy and technology that dominates the world—is the United States. That is why we were struck so savagely. 8

How do we know? Who else trains cadres of fanatical suicide murderers who go to their deaths joyfully? And the average terrorist does not coordinate four hijackings within one hour. Nor fly a plane into the tiny silhouette of a single building. For that you need skilled pilots seeking martyrdom. That is not a large pool to draw from. 9

These are the shock troops of the enemy. And the enemy has many branches. Hezbollah in Lebanon, Hamas and Islamic Jihad in Israel, the Osama bin Laden organization headquartered in Afghanistan, and various Arab "liberation fronts" based in Damascus. And then there are the governments: Iran, Iraq, Syria and Libya among them. Which one was responsible? We will find out soon enough. 10

11   But when we do, there should be no talk of bringing these people to "swift justice," as Karen Hughes* dismayingly promised mid-afternoon Tuesday. An open act of war demands a military response, not a judicial one.

12   Military response against whom? It is absurd to make war on the individuals who send these people. The terrorists cannot exist in a vacuum. They need a territorial base of sovereign protection. For 30 years we have avoided this truth. If bin Laden was behind this, then Afghanistan is our enemy. *Any* country that harbors and protects him is our enemy. We must carry *their* war to them.

13   We should seriously consider a congressional declaration of war. That convention seems quaint, unused since World War II. But there are two virtues to declaring war: It announces our seriousness both to our people and to the enemy, and it gives us certain rights as belligerents (of blockade, for example).

14   The "long peace" is over. We sought this war no more than we sought war with Nazi Germany and Imperial Japan or cold war with the Soviet Union. But when war was pressed upon the greatest generation, it rose to the challenge. The question is: Will we?

Critiquing "This Isn't a 'Legal' Matter, This Is War"

1. In your own words, why does Krauthammer consider the terrorist attacks an "act of war" rather than a "crime"?

2. What criteria about the "enemy" have to be met, according to Krauthammer, in order for the United States to declare war against that enemy? How do the terrorists meet these criteria?

3. On September 10, 2002, on the eve of the first anniversary of the terrorist attacks, *New York Times* columnist Paul Krugman says that the United States made a mistake by placing the terrorist attacks in the category "war":

> Yet a year later there is great uneasiness in this nation. Corporate scandals, dropping stocks and rising unemployment account for much of the malaise. But part of what makes us uneasy is that we still don't know how to think about what happened to us. Our leaders and much of the media tell us that we're a nation at war. But that was a bad metaphor from the start, and looks worse as time goes by.†

   Why might Krugman object to calling the fight against terrorism a war? What makes the fight against terrorism different from World War II or other wars? What might be the bad consequences of the United States's declaring itself in a state of "war" against terrorism?

---

*Karen Hughes was an adviser to President Bush and often a spokesperson for the administration at the time of the terrorist attacks.
†Paul Krugman, "The Long Haul," *New York Times,* 10 September 2002, 431.

Our final article shows how definitional issues often intersect with other kinds of issues to create complex public controversies. In this op-ed piece published in the *New York Times* in 2004, blog writer Eugene Volokh, a professor of law at UCLA, focuses initially on the issue of whether journalists should be granted legal privilege to protect the identity of their sources. He then raises a definitional issue: If journalistic privilege is granted, how do we define "journalist"?

You Can Blog, But You Can't Hide
Eugene Volokh

Say that an I.R.S. agent leaks a politician's income tax return to a newspaper reporter, an act that is a federal felony. The newspaper may have a First Amendment right to publish the information, especially since it bears on a matter of public interest. The government, meanwhile, is entitled to punish the agent, to protect citizens' privacy and ensure a fair and efficient tax system.   1

To punish the agent, prosecutors may need to get the leaker's name from the reporter; but if the reporter refuses to testify because of a "journalist's privilege" to protect confidential sources, the agent may never be caught. Such a pattern is evident in the Valerie Plame matter,* where an independent prosecutor is trying to learn who leaked the name of Ms. Plame, a C.I.A. operative, to the press. Uncooperative journalists, including those at The Times, may face jail.   2

The fate of the reporters involved in the Plame affair—and that of the reporter in Providence, R.I., who was convicted of criminal contempt last month for refusing to disclose who, in violation of a court order, gave him a tape of a city official accepting a bribe—will of course turn on questions particular to their cases. But the solution to the larger problem turns on other questions: Should there be a journalist's privilege? What should its scope be? And who exactly qualifies as a journalist?   3

Thirty-two years ago, the Supreme Court held that the First Amendment does not create a journalist's privilege: like anyone else, journalists must testify when ordered to do so. But Justice Lewis Powell, in a cryptic three-paragraph concurrence, wrote that there should be a modest privilege protecting journalists from unnecessary harassment by law enforcement. In such cases, he wrote, journalists should be allowed to claim the privilege, and courts should try to strike "a proper balance between freedom of the press and the obligation of all citizens to give relevant testimony with respect to criminal conduct."   4

---

*In the Valerie Plame matter, Robert Novak, a journalist, revealed Plame's identity as a CIA operative in a newspaper column on July 14, 2003. He cited unnamed sources within the Bush administration. Although it was legal for newspapers to publish the story, it was illegal and potentially dangerous to national security for these "unnamed sources" to reveal the CIA operative. The ensuing Justice Department investigation led to an indictment against Scooter Libby, a high-level administration official, in 2005, and still continues.

5   Lower courts are now split on whether the privilege exists. Legislatures likewise disagree; about two-thirds of the states have recognized a journalist's privilege of varying strengths, but the remaining states and the federal government have not. Senator Christopher Dodd has introduced a bill that would establish the privilege in federal court.

6   So the situation is a mess—and it's getting messier. Because of the Internet, anyone can be a journalist. Some so-called Weblogs—Internet-based opinion columns published by ordinary people—have hundreds of thousands of readers. I run a blog with more than 10,000 daily readers. We often publish news tips from friends or readers, some of which come with a condition of confidentiality.

7   The First Amendment can't give special rights to the established news media and not to upstart outlets like ours. Freedom of the press should apply to people equally, regardless of who they are, why they write or how popular they are.

8   Yet when everyone is a journalist, a broad journalist's privilege becomes especially costly. The I.R.S. agent, for example, no longer needs to risk approaching many mainstream journalists, some of whom may turn him in. He can just ask a friend who has a blog and a political ax to grind. The friend can then post the leaked information and claim the journalist's privilege to prevent the agent from being identified. If the privilege is upheld, the friend and the agent will be safe—but our privacy will be lost.

9   What's the answer? On the one hand, tips from confidential sources often help journalists (print or electronic) uncover crime and misconduct. If journalists had to reveal such sources, many of these sources would stop talking. On the other hand, some tips are rightly made illegal.

10   The best solution may be to borrow a principle from other privileges, like those for confidential communications to lawyers, psychotherapists and spouses. The law has generally recognized that protecting the confidentiality of such communications is more important than forcing a person's testimony.

11   But it has also limited the privilege. Communications that facilitate crime or fraud, for example, are not protected. I may confess my crimes to a lawyer, but if I try to hire him to help me commit my crime, he may be obligated to testify against me.

12   Maybe a journalist's privilege should likewise be limited. Lawmakers could pass legislation that protects leakers who lawfully reveal information, like those who blow the whistle on governmental or corporate misconduct. But if a leaker tries to use a journalist as part of an illegal act—for example, by disclosing a tax return or the name of a C.I.A. agent so that it can be published—then the journalist may be ordered to testify.

13   Such a rule may well deter some sources from coming forward. But they will be the very sources that society should want to deter, to protect privacy and safety. In any event, the rules should be the same for old media and new, professional and amateur. Any journalist's privilege should extend to every journalist.

Critiquing "You Can Blog, But You Can't Hide"

1. The first issue raised by Volokh is whether journalists should have the legal privilege to protect the names of confidential sources. Consider Volokh's opening example. Although the newspaper has First Amendment rights to publish the politician's income tax return, the government also has the right to punish the IRS agent who leaked the information. At issue is whether the journalist has the right not to disclose the name of the agent. Currently many states grant journalistic privilege in such cases, but the federal government does not. What is your stand on this issue? What is Volokh's stand?

2. If the federal courts or the legislature establish a journalist's privilege, then who counts as a journalist? What are Volokh's answers to the following questions?

   a. Should bloggers be counted as journalists?

   b. If so, what special problems may result from granting journalistic privilege to bloggers?

   c. How could these special problems be solved?

3. How might you make the case that bloggers should not be counted as journalists? In other words, how might you define "journalist" so that bloggers are excluded?

12 Causal Arguments
X Causes (Does Not Cause) Y

CASE 1

Beginning in the 1990s, the crime rate in the United States began dropping precipitously. For example, the number of murders in New York City dropped from 2,245 in 1990 to 596 in 2003. Similar reductions in the rates for all kinds of crime, ranging from murders to assaults to auto thefts, were reported all across the nation. What caused this sudden and unexpected decline? Many causal theories were debated in social science journals and the popular media. Among the proposed causes were innovative policing strategies, increased incarceration of prisoners, aging of the population, tougher gun control laws, a strong economy, and an increased number of police. In 2001, however, economist Steven Levitt published a controversial paper arguing that the primary cause was *Roe v. Wade,* the 1973 Supreme Court decision that legalized abortion.* According to Levitt, the crime rate began dropping in the 1990s because the greatest source of criminals—unwanted children entering their teens and twenties—were largely absent from the cohort of young people coming of age in the 1990s: They had been aborted rather than brought up in the crime-producing conditions of unstable families, poverty, and neglect.

CASE 2

Consider the hypothetical case of Robert, an exceptionally shy teenager whose older brother is a party animal extrovert. What caused Robert, but not his brother, to become shy? Was it something in the family dynamics—perhaps related to birth order or to changes in his parents' marriage—that caused his parents to treat Robert differently from his brother? Was it the result of some bad early childhood experience when Robert was made fun of

---

*Steven D. Levitt and Stephen J. Dubner, "Where Have All the Criminals Gone?," *Freakonomics: A Rogue Economist Explores the Hidden Side of Everything* (New York: Harper Collins, 2005), 117–144.

or mocked? Is it perhaps genetic, in which case Robert, unlike his brother, inherited a "shyness" gene? Or might Robert's shyness be related to brain chemistry? Starting in the late 1990s, psychiatrists began treating shyness with selected antidepressants, often with encouraging success. Soon pharmaceutical companies began targeting shy people in their advertisements. The ads identified shyness as a symptom of "social anxiety disorder" and promised pills that could get shy persons out of their houses and into the social whirl. The result was a stunning increase in the sale of antidepressants as shy people by the droves redefined their shyness as a treatable brain condition rather than a personality trait. Critics of the drug companies complained about the power of advertising to cause perfectly normal (and mentally healthy) shy people to believe they had a personality disorder requiring drugs. Meanwhile psychiatrists explained how debilitating severe cases of shyness can be, robbing afflicted persons of a full life.

An Overview of Causal Arguments

We encounter causal issues all the time. What caused the sudden decline in the U.S. crime rate in the 1990s? What is the cause of shyness? Why did rap music become popular? What caused young women in Fiji, starting in the mid-1990s, to start feeling fat? (One proposed answer: American TV programs became available in Fiji.) Why are many frog species disappearing? Why did the major TV news networks devote fifty times more coverage to the Michael Jackson child molestation trial than they did to the Darfur genocide crisis in Sudan? In addition to causal questions, we can ask consequence questions: What might be the consequences of legalizing drugs, of privatizing Social Security, or of closing our borders to immigrants? What were the consequences—expected or unexpected—of *Roe v. Wade,* of invading Iraq, or of allowing drug companies to advertise?

Cause or consequence arguments are often used in support of proposal arguments, either to show the causes of a problem to which a writer wants to propose a solution or to support (or attack) a proposed solution by showing that it will lead to good (or bad) consequences. Convincing readers that you have analyzed the causes of a problem and that your proposed solution will have more benefits than costs thus bears on the success of many proposal arguments.

Because causal arguments require close analysis of phenomena, effective causal arguing is closely linked to critical thinking. Studies of critical thinking show that good problem solvers systematically explore the causes of a problem before proposing a solution. Equally important, before making a decision, good problem solvers predict and weigh the consequences of alternative solutions to a problem, trying to determine a solution that produces the greatest benefits with the least cost. Adding to the complexity of causal arguing is the way a given event can have multiple causes and multiple consequences. In an effort to save salmon, for example, environmentalists have proposed the elimination of several dams on the Snake River above Lewiston, Idaho. Will the removal of these dams save the

salmon? Nobody knows for sure, but three universally agreed-upon consequences of removing the dams will be the loss of several thousand jobs in the
Lewiston area, the loss of some hydroelectric power, and the shift in wheat transportation from river barges to overland trucks and trains. So the initial focus on
consequences to salmon soon widens to include consequences to jobs, to power
generation, and to agricultural transportation.

The Nature of Causal Arguing

Typically, causal arguments try to show how one event brings about another. The
scientific method used in both the physical and social sciences attempts to uncover the chains of causality behind observable phenomena. When causal investigation focuses on material objects, the notion of causality appears fairly straightforward. However, even the classical illustration of causality—one billiard ball
striking another—has been questioned by philosophers such as David Hume,
who argued that the notion of causality is a human construct, not a property of
billiard balls.

When humans become the focus of a causal argument, the definition of causality becomes more vexing. If we say that a given factor X "caused" a person to do Y,
what do we mean? Do we mean that X "forced her to do Y," thereby negating her
free will (as in, an undiagnosed brain tumor caused her to act erratically), or do we
mean more simply that X "motivated her to do Y" (as in, her desire to embarrass
her boyfriend caused her to act erratically)? When we argue about causality in human beings, we must guard against confusing these two senses of "cause" or assuming that human behavior can be predicted or controlled in the same way that
nonhuman behavior can. A rock dropped from a roof will always fall at thirty-two
feet per second squared, and a rat zapped for turning left in a maze will always
quit turning left. But if we raise interest rates, will consumers save more? If so, how
much? This is the sort of question we debate endlessly.

Fortunately, most causal arguments can avoid the worst of these scientific and
philosophical quagmires. As human beings, we share a number of assumptions
about what causes events in the observable world, and we can depend on the
goodwill of our audiences to grant us most of these assumptions. Most of us, for
example, would be satisfied with the following explanation for why a car went
into a skid: "In a panic the driver locked the brakes of his car, causing the car to go
into a skid."

panic → slamming brake pedal → locking brakes → skid

We probably do not need to defend this simple causal chain because the audience
will grant the causal connections between events A, B, C, and D. The sequence
seems reasonable according to our shared assumptions about psychological
causality (panic leads to slamming brake pedal) and physical causality (locked
brakes lead to skid).

But if you are an attorney defending a client whose skidding car damaged an upscale boutique, you might see all sorts of additional causal factors. ("Because the stop sign at that corner was obscured by an untrimmed willow tree, my client innocently entered what he assumed was an open intersection only to find a speeding beer truck bearing down on him. My client braked responsibly. His car skidded because of the improperly maintained, oil-slicked roadway, causing him to slide into the boutique's bow windows—windows that extruded into the walkway eleven full inches beyond the limit allowed by city code.") Okay, now what's the cause of the crash, and who's at fault?

As the previous example shows, explaining causality entails creating a plausible chain of events linking a cause to its effect. Let's take another example—this time a real rather than hypothetical one. Consider an argument put forward by syndicated columnist John Leo as an explanation for the Columbine High School massacre in Littleton, Colorado, in 1999.* Leo attributes part of the cause to the desensitizing effects of violent video games. After suggesting that the Littleton killings were partly choreographed on video game models, Leo suggests the following causal chain:

> Many youngsters are left alone for long periods of time → they play violent video games obsessively → their feelings of resentment and powerlessness "pour into the killing games" → the video games break down a natural aversion to killing, analogous to psychological techniques employed by the military → realistic touches in modern video games blur the "boundary between fantasy and reality" → youngsters begin identifying not with conventional heroes but with sociopaths who get their kicks from blowing away ordinary people ("pedestrians, marching bands, an elderly woman with a walker") → having enjoyed random violence in the video games, vulnerable youngsters act out the same adrenaline rush in real life.

Describing a Causal Argument in Toulmin Terms

Because causal arguments can involve lengthy or complex causal chains, they are often harder to summarize in *because* clauses than are other kinds of arguments. Likewise, they are not as likely to yield quick analysis through the Toulmin schema. Nevertheless, a causal argument can usually be stated as a claim with *because* clauses. Typically, a *because* clause for a causal argument pinpoints one or two key elements in the causal chain rather than tries to summarize every link. Leo's argument could be summarized in the following claim with a *because* clause:

> Violent video games may have been a contributing cause to the Littleton massacre because playing these games can make random, sociopathic violence seem pleasurable.

Once stated as an enthymeme, the argument can be analyzed using Toulmin's schema. (It is easiest to apply Toulmin's schema to causal arguments if you think

---

*John Leo, "Kill-for-Kicks Video Games Desensitizing Our Children," *Seattle Times* 27 Apr. 1999, B4.

of the grounds as the observable phenomena at any point in the causal chain and the warrants as the shareable assumptions about causality that join links together.)

CLAIM: Violent video games may have been a contributing cause to the Littleton massacre.

STATED REASON: because playing these games can make random, sociopathic violence seem pleasurable

GROUNDS: evidence that the killers, like many young people, played violent video games; evidence that the games are violent; evidence that the games involve random, sociopathic violence (not heroic cops against aliens or gangsters, but a killer blowing away ordinary people—marching bands, little old ladies, and so forth); evidence that young people derive pleasure from these games

WARRANT: If youngsters derive pleasure from random, sociopathic killing in video games, then they can transfer this pleasure to real life, thus leading to the Littleton massacre.

BACKING: testimony from psychologists; evidence that violent video games desensitize persons to violence; analogy to military training where video game strategies are used to "make killing a reflex action"; evidence that the distinction between fantasy and reality becomes especially blurred for unstable children.

CONDITIONS OF REBUTTAL: *Questioning the reason and grounds:* Perhaps the killers didn't play video games; perhaps the video games are no more violent than traditional kids' games (such as cops and robbers); perhaps the video games do not feature sociopathic killing.

Questioning the warrant and backing: Perhaps kids are fully capable of distinguishing fantasy from reality; perhaps the games are just fun with no transference to real life; perhaps these video games are substantially different from military training strategies.

QUALIFIER: (Claim is already qualified by *may* and *contributing cause*)

For Class Discussion

1. Working individually or in small groups, create a causal chain to show how the item mentioned in the first column could help lead to the item mentioned in the second.

   a. invention of the automobile   redesign of cities

   b. invention of the automobile   changes in sexual mores

    c. invention of the telephone   loss of sense of community in neighborhoods

    d. origin of rap in black urban music scene   the popularity of rap spreads from urban black audiences to white middle-class youth culture

    e. development of way to prevent rejections in transplant operations   liberalization of euthanasia laws

2. For each of your causal chains, compose a claim with an attached *because* clause summarizing one or two key links in the causal chain. For example, "The invention of the automobile helped cause the redesign of cities because automobiles made it possible for people to live farther away from their places of work."

Three Methods for Arguing That One Event Causes Another

One of the first things you need to do when preparing a causal argument is to note exactly what sort of causal relationship you are dealing with. Are you concerned with causes or consequences of a specific one-time event (such as the *Columbia* Space Shuttle disaster, the firing of a popular teacher at your university, or your friend's unexpected decision to join the Army), of a recurring phenomenon (such as eating disorders, road rage, or homelessness), or of a puzzling trend (such as the rising popularity of extreme sports, the decline in U.S. crime rates, or recent increases in the occurrence of autism or diabetes)?

With recurring phenomena or with trends, you have the luxury of being able to study multiple cases over long periods of time and establishing correlations between suspected causal factors and effects. In some cases you can even intervene in the process and test for yourself whether diminishing a suspected causal factor results in a lessening of the effect or whether increasing the causal factor results in a corresponding increase in the effect. Additionally, you can spend a good deal of time exploring just how the mechanics of causation might work.

But with a one-time occurrence your focus is on the details of the event and specific causal chains that may have contributed to the event. Sometimes evidence has disappeared or changed its nature. You often end up in the position more of a detective than of a scientific researcher, and your conclusion will have to be more tentative as a result.

Having briefly stated these words of caution, let's turn now to the various ways you can argue that one event causes another.

First Method: Explain the Causal Mechanism Directly

The most convincing kind of causal argument identifies every link in the causal chain, showing how X causes A, which causes B, which in turn causes C, which finally causes Y. In some cases, all you have to do is fill in the missing links. In other cases—when your assumptions about causality may seem questionable to your audience—you have to argue for the causal connection with more vigor.

A careful spelling out of each step in the causal chain is the technique used by science writer Robert S. Devine in the following passage from his article "The Trouble with Dams."* Although the benefits of dams are widely understood (cheap, pollution-free electricity; flood control; irrigation; barge transportation), the negative effects are less commonly known and understood. In this article, Devine tries to persuade readers that dams have serious negative consequences. In the following passage, he explains how dams reduce salmon flows by slowing the migration of smolts (newly hatched young salmon) to the sea.

CAUSAL ARGUMENT DESCRIBING A CAUSAL CHAIN

Such transformations lie at the heart of the ongoing environmental harm done by dams. Rivers are rivers because they flow, and the nature of their flows defines much of their character. When dams alter flows, they alter the essence of rivers.

Consider the erstwhile river behind Lower Granite [a dam on Idaho's Snake River]. Although I was there in the springtime, when I looked at the water it was moving too slowly to merit the word "flow"—and Lower Granite Lake isn't even one of the region's enormous storage reservoirs, which bring currents to a virtual halt. In the past, spring snowmelt sent powerful currents down the Snake during April and May. Nowadays hydropower operators of the Columbia and Snake systems store the runoff behind the dams and release it during the winter, when demand—and the price—for electricity rises. Over the ages, however, many populations of salmon have adapted to the spring surge. The smolts used the strong flows to migrate, drifting downstream with the current. During the journey smolts' bodies undergo physiological changes that require them to reach salt water quickly. Before dams backed up the Snake, smolts coming down from Idaho got to the sea in six to twenty days; now it takes from sixty to ninety days, and few of the young salmon reach salt water in time. The emasculated current is the single largest reason that the number of wild adult salmon migrating up the Snake each year has crashed from predevelopment runs of 100,000–200,000 to what was projected to be 150–75 this year.

This tightly constructed passage connects various causal chains to explain the decline of salmon runs:

Smolts use river flow to reach the sea → dams restrict flow of river → a trip that before development took 6–20 days now takes 60–90 days → migrating smolts undergo physiological changes that demand quick access to salt water → delayed migration time kills the smolts.

Describing each link in the causal chain—and making each link seem as plausible as possible—is the most persuasive means of convincing readers that X causes Y.

---

*Robert S. Devine, "The Trouble with Dams," *Atlantic* Aug. 1995, 64–75. The example quotation is from page 70.

Second Method: Use Various Inductive Methods to Establish a High Probability of a Causal Link

If we can't explain a causal link directly, we often employ a reasoning strategy called *induction*. Through induction we infer a general conclusion based on a limited number of specific cases. For example, if on several occasions you got a headache after drinking red wine but not after drinking white wine, you would be likely to conclude inductively that red wine causes you to get headaches. However, because there are almost always numerous variables involved, because there are exceptions to most principles arrived at inductively, and because we can't be certain that the future will always be like the past, inductive reasoning gives only probable truths, not certain ones.

When your brain thinks inductively, it sorts through data looking for patterns of similarity and difference. But the inductive process does not explain the causal mechanism itself. Thus, through induction you know that red wine gives you a headache, but you don't know how the wine actually works on your nervous system—the causal chain itself.

In this section we explain three kinds of inductive reasoning: informal induction, scientific experimentation, and correlation.

Informal Induction   *Informal induction* is our term for the habitual kind of inductive reasoning we do all the time. Toddlers think inductively when they learn the connection between flipping a wall switch and watching the ceiling light come on. They hold all variables constant except the position of the switch and infer inductively a causal connection between the switch and the light. Typical ways that the mind infers causality described by the nineteenth-century philosopher John Stuart Mill include looking for a common element that can explain a repeated circumstance. For example, psychologists attempting to understand the causes of anorexia have discovered that many anorexics (but not all) come from perfectionist, highly work-oriented homes that emphasize duty and responsibility. This common element is thus a suspected causal factor leading to anorexia. Another of Mill's methods is to look for a single difference. When infant death rates in the state of Washington shot up in July and August 1986, one event stood out making these two months different: increased radioactive fallout from the Chernobyl nuclear meltdown in the Ukraine. This single difference led some researchers to suspect radiation as a possible cause of infant deaths. Informal induction typically proceeds from this kind of "common element" or "single difference" reasoning.

Largely because of its power, informal induction can often lead you to wrong conclusions. You should be aware of two common fallacies of inductive reasoning that can tempt you into erroneous assumptions about causality. (Both fallacies are treated more fully in Appendix One.)

The *post hoc, ergo propter hoc* fallacy ("after this, therefore because of this") mistakes precedence for cause. Just because event A regularly precedes event B doesn't mean that event A causes event B. The same reasoning that tells us that flipping a switch causes the light to go on can make us believe that low levels of radioactive fallout from the Chernobyl nuclear disaster caused a sudden rise in infant death rates in the state of Washington. The nuclear disaster clearly preceded the rise in death rates. But did it clearly *cause* it? Our point is that precedence alone is no proof of causality and that we are guilty of this fallacy whenever we are swayed to believe that X causes Y primarily because X precedes Y. We can guard against this fallacy by seeking plausible link-by-link connections showing how X causes Y.

The *hasty generalization* fallacy occurs when you make a generalization based on too few cases or too little consideration of alternative explanations: You flip the switch, but the lightbulb doesn't go on. You conclude—too hastily—that the lightbulb has burned out. (Perhaps the power has gone off or the switch is broken.) How many trials does it take before you can make a justified generalization rather than a hasty generalization? It is difficult to say for sure. Both the *post hoc* fallacy and the hasty generalization fallacy remind us that induction requires a leap from individual cases to a general principle and that it is always possible to leap too soon.

Scientific Experimentation   One way to avoid inductive fallacies is to examine our causal hypotheses as carefully as possible. When we deal with a recurring phenomenon such as cancer, we can create scientific experiments that give us inductive evidence of causality with a fairly high degree of certainty. If, for example, we were concerned that a high-fat diet might increase the risk for colon cancer, we could test our hypothesis experimentally in rat populations by giving an experimental group of rats a high-fat diet and a control group a low-fat diet. After a specified time period, we could test both groups for the presence of colon cancer. If cancer appeared with a significantly greater frequency in the high-fat group, we could conclude that our hypothesis was supported.

Correlation   Still another method of induction is *correlation,* which expresses a statistical relationship between X and Y. A correlation between X and Y means that when X occurs, Y is likely to occur also, and vice versa. To put it another way, correlation establishes a possibility that an observed link between an X and a Y is a causal one rather than a mere coincidence. The existence of a correlation, however, does not tell us whether X causes Y, whether Y causes X, or whether both are caused by some third phenomenon. For example, there is a fairly strong correlation between nearsightedness and intelligence. (That is, in a given sample of nearsighted people and people with normal eyesight, a higher percentage of the nearsighted people will be highly intelligent. Similarly, in a sample of high-intelligence people and people with normal intelligence, a higher percentage of the high-intelligence group will be nearsighted.) But the direction of causality isn't clear. It could be that high intelligence causes people to read more, thus ruining their eyes (high intelligence causes nearsightedness). Or it could be that nearsightedness causes people to read more, thus raising their intelligence (nearsightedness causes high intelligence). Or it could be that some unknown phenomenon inside the brain causes both nearsightedness and high intelligence.

In recent years, correlation studies have been made stunningly sophisticated through the power of computerized analyses. For example, the link between high-fat diets and colon cancer was first discovered in correlation studies among populations that eat lots of fats and those that don't. One study, reported in *The Archives of Internal Medicine* in 2003, asked 76,402 women to record their diets over a ten-year period. The women's diets fell into what the researchers called the "Western pattern" (lots of red meats, processed meats, pastas, and fried foods) and the "prudent pattern" (lots of fruits, vegetables, fish, and very little red meat). During the time of the study, 445 of the women developed colon cancer. After factoring out other differences in lifestyle, climate, genetic inheritance, and so forth, the researchers discovered that women who followed the Western pattern developed colon cancer at a 50 percent higher rate than those who followed the prudent pattern. Factoring out variables is one of the complex feats that modern statistical analyses attempt to accomplish. But the fact remains that the most sophisticated correlation studies still cannot tell us for certain that a causal relationship exists. (For example, in the high-fat diet study only 0.6 percent of the women developed colon cancer.)

Conclusion about Inductive Methods   Induction, then, can tell us within varying degrees of certainty whether X causes Y. It does not, however, explain the causal mechanism itself. Typically, the *because* clause structure of an inductive argument would take one of the following three shapes: (1) "Although we cannot explain the causal mechanism directly, we believe that X and Y are very probably causally linked because we have repeatedly observed their conjunction"; (2) ". . . because we have demonstrated the linkage through controlled scientific experiments"; or (3) ". . . because we have shown that they are statistically correlated and have provided a plausible hypothesis concerning the causal direction."

For Class Discussion

Working individually or in small groups, develop plausible causal chains that might explain the correlations between the following pairs of phenomena:

a. A person who registers a low stress level on an electrochemical stress meter — does daily meditation

b. A white female teenager — is seven times more likely to smoke than a black female teenager

c. A person who grew up in a house with two bathrooms — is more likely to have higher SAT scores than a person who grew up in a one-bathroom home

d. A person who buys lots of ashtrays — is more likely to develop lung cancer

e. A member of the National Rifle Association — supports the death penalty

Third Method: Argue by Analogy or Precedent

Another common method of causal arguing is through analogy or precedent. (See also Chapter 13, which deals in more depth with the strengths and weaknesses of this kind of arguing.) When you argue through resemblance, you try to find a case that is similar to the one you are arguing about but is better known and less controversial to the reader. If the reader agrees with your view of causality in the similar case, you then try to transfer this understanding to the case at issue. In the following example, the writer tries to explain the link between environmental and biological factors in the creation of teen violence. In this analogy, the biological predisposition for violent behavior is compared to some children's biological predisposition for asthma. Cultural and media violence is then compared to air pollution.

CAUSAL ARGUMENT BY ANALOGY

To deny the role of these influences [bad parenting, easy access to guns, violence in the media] is like denying that air pollution triggers childhood asthma. Yes, to develop asthma a child needs a specific, biological vulnerability. But as long as some children have this respiratory vulnerability—and some always will—then allowing pollution to fill our air will make some children wheeze, and cough, and die. And as long as some children have a neurological vulnerability [to violent behavior]—and some always will—then turning a blind eye to bad parenting, bullying, and the gun culture will make other children seethe, and withdraw, and kill.*

Causal arguments by analogy and precedent are logically weaker than arguments based on causal chains or scientific induction. Although they can be powerfully persuasive, you should be aware of their limits. If any two things are alike in some ways (analogous), they are different in others (disanalogous), and these differences shouldn't be ignored. Consider the following example:

A huckster markets a book called *30 Days to a More Powerful Brain.* The book contains logical puzzles and other brain-teasing exercises that he calls "weight training for the mind."

This argument depends on the warrant that the brain is like a muscle. Because the audience accepts the causal belief that weight training strengthens muscles, the marketer hopes to transfer that same belief to the field of mental activity (mind exercises strengthen the brain). However, cognitive psychologists have shown that the brain does *not* work like a muscle, so the analogy is false. Although the argument seems powerful, you should realize that the warrant that says X is like Y is almost always vulnerable.

All resemblance arguments, therefore, are in some sense "false analogies." But some analogies are so misleading that logicians have labeled them "fallacious"—the fallacy of *false analogy.* The false analogy fallacy covers those truly blatant cases where the differences between X and Y are too great for the analogy

---

*Sharon Begley, "Why the Young Kill," *Newsweek* 3 May 1999, 35.

to hold. An example might be the following: "Putting red marks all over students' papers causes great emotional distress just as putting knife marks over their palms would cause great physical distress." It is impossible to draw a precise line, however, between an analogy that has true clarifying and persuasive power and one that is fallacious. Whether the analogy works in any situation depends on the audience's shared assumptions with the arguer.

Glossary of Terms Encountered in Causal Arguments

Because causal arguments are often easier to conduct if writer and reader share a few specialized terms, we offer the following glossary for your convenience.

- *Fallacy of Oversimplified Cause:*   One of the great temptations when establishing causal relationships is to look for *the* cause of something. Most phenomena, especially the ones we argue about, have multiple causes. Thus it would be a mistake to say that high-fat diets are *the* cause of colon cancer or that a certain gene is *the* cause of shyness. A number of different factors must often work together to create a complex effect. But though we know all this, we still long to make the world less complex by looking for *the* cause of a puzzling phenomenon.

- *Universal/Existential Quantifier:*   Closely related to the fallacy of the single cause is the tendency to confuse what logicians call the universal quantifier (*all*) and the existential quantifier (*some*). For example, to say that *all* the blame for recent school shootings comes from the shooters' playing violent video games is to claim that violent video games are *the* cause of school shootings—a universal statement. An argument will be stronger and more accurate if the arguer makes an existential statement: *Some* of the blame for school shootings can be attributed to violent video games. Arguers sometimes deliberately mix up these quantifiers to misrepresent and dismiss opposing views. For example, someone might argue that because violent video games aren't the sole cause of students' violent behavior, they are not an influential factor at all. Something that is not a total cause can still be a partial cause.

- *Immediate/Remote Causes:*   Every causal chain links backward indefinitely into the past. An immediate cause is the closest in time to the event being examined. Consider the public analysis of the well-publicized plane crash of John F. Kennedy, Jr., in July 1999. When Kennedy's plane crashed at night into the Atlantic Ocean south of Martha's Vineyard, experts speculated that the *immediate* cause was Kennedy's becoming disoriented in the night haze, losing visual control of the plane, and sending the plane into a fatal dive. A slightly less immediate cause was his decision to make an overwater flight at night without being licensed for instrument flying. (He and his wife needed to get to Hyannis Port quickly to attend a wedding.) Further back in time were all the factors that made Kennedy the kind of risk taker who took chances with his own life. For example, several months earlier he had broken his ankle in a hang gliding accident. Many commentators said that the numerous tragedies that befell the Kennedy family helped shape his risk-taking personality. Such causes going back into the past are considered *remote causes*.

■ *Precipitating/Contributing Causes:*   These terms are similar to *immediate* and *remote* causes but don't designate a temporal link going into the past. Rather, they refer to a main cause emerging out of a background of subsidiary causes. If, for example, a husband and wife decide to separate, the *precipitating cause* may be a stormy fight over money, after which one of the partners (or both) says, "I've had enough." In contrast, *contributing causes* would be all the background factors that are dooming the marriage—preoccupation with their respective careers, disagreement about priorities, in-law problems, and so forth. Note that contributing causes and the precipitating cause all coexist simultaneously in time—none is temporally more remote than another.

■ *Constraints:*   Sometimes an effect occurs not because X happened but because another factor—a *constraint*—is removed. In other words, the presence of a constraint may keep a certain effect from occurring. For example, in the marriage we have been discussing, the presence of children in the home might be a constraint against divorce; as soon as the children graduate from high school and leave home, the marriage may well dissolve.

■ *Necessary/Sufficient Causes:*   A *necessary cause* is one that has to be present for a given effect to occur. For example, fertility drugs are necessary to cause the conception of septuplets. Every couple who has septuplets must have used fertility drugs. In contrast, a *sufficient cause* is one that always produces or guarantees a given effect. Smoking more than a pack of cigarettes per day is sufficient to raise the cost of one's life insurance policy. This statement means that if you are a smoker, life insurance companies will always place you in a higher risk bracket and charge you more for life insurance. In some cases, a single cause can be both necessary and sufficient. For example, lack of ascorbic acid is both a necessary and a sufficient cause of scurvy. (Think of all those old sailors who didn't eat fruit for months.) It is a necessary cause because you can't get scurvy any other way except through absence of ascorbic acid; it is a sufficient cause because the absence of ascorbic acid always causes scurvy.

For Class Discussion

The terms in the preceding glossary can be effective brainstorming tools for thinking of possible causes of an event. For the following events, try to think of as many causes as possible by brainstorming possible *immediate causes, remote causes, precipitating causes, contributing causes,* and *constraints:*

1. Working individually, make a list of different kinds of causes/constraints for one of the following:

   a. your decision to attend your present college

    b. an important event in your life or your family (a job change, a major move, etc.)

    c. a personal opinion you hold that is not widely shared

2. Working as a group, make a list of different kinds of causes/constraints for one of the following:

    a. why women's fashion and beauty magazines are the most frequently purchased magazines in college bookstores

    b. why American students consistently score below Asian and European students in academic achievement

    c. why the number of babies born out of wedlock has increased dramatically in the last thirty years

Writing Your Causal Argument

WRITING ASSIGNMENT
FOR CHAPTER 12

Choose an issue about the causes or consequences of a trend, event, or other phenomenon. Write an argument that persuades an audience to accept your explanation of the causes or consequences of your chosen phenomenon. Within your essay you should examine alternative hypotheses or opposing views and explain your reasons for rejecting them. You can imagine your issue either as a puzzle or as a disagreement. If a puzzle, your task will be to create a convincing case for an audience that doesn't have an answer to your causal question already in mind. If a disagreement, your task will be more overtly persuasive since your goal will be to change your audience's views.

Exploring Ideas

Arguments about causes and consequences abound in public, professional, or personal life, so you shouldn't have difficulty finding a causal issue worth investigating and arguing. Angered by media explanations for the Columbine High School massacre, student writer Daeha Ko contributed his own argument to the conversation by blaming popular cliques and the school establishment that supports them (see pp. 259–262). Student writer Carlos Macias, puzzled by the ease with which college students are issued credit cards, wrote a researched argument disentangling the factors leading young people to bury themselves in debt (see pp. 266–269). Others of our students have focused on causal issues such as these: What causes some first-year students to develop better study habits in the first few months of college than other students? Why do kids join gangs? What causes anorexia? What are the consequences of violent video games on children? What are the consequences of mandatory drug testing (written by a student who has to take amphetamines for narcolepsy)? What are the causes of different sexual orientations? Why did the university fire a favorite assistant dean in a student affairs office? What has happened since 1970 to cause young people to delay getting married? (This question was initiated by the student's interest in the statistical table in Chapter 9, p. 186.) Why did this promising football season end so miserably for the university team? What effect will the Navy's low-frequency sonar system for finding enemy submarines have on whales and other marine mammals? (The student who posed this question eventually wrote the researched proposal argument on pp. 418–425.)

If you have trouble finding a causal issue to write about, you can often create provocative controversies among your classmates through the following strategies:

- *Make a list of unusual likes and dislikes.*   Think about unusual things that people like or dislike. We find it really strange, for example, that so many people like professional wrestling or dislike writing notes in margins while they read. You could summarize the conventional explanations that persons give for an unusual pleasure or aversion and then argue for a surprising or unexpected cause. Why do people like playing the lottery? What attracts people to extreme sports? What causes math phobia? How do you explain the popularity of the Hummer or the tricked-out Cadillac Escalade as dream cars for urban youth?

- *Make a list of puzzling events or trends.*   Another strategy is to make a list of puzzling phenomena and try to explain their causes. Start with one-time events (a cheating scandal at your school; the failure or passage of a controversial initiative at your city or state level; the public's puzzling first reaction to a film, book, or new TV show). Then list puzzling recurring events (failure of knowledgeable teenagers to practice safe sex; use of steroids among athletes). Finally, list some recent trends (growth of naturopathic medicine; teen interest in the gothic; hatred of women in much gangsta rap). Engage classmates in discussions of one or more of the items on your list. Look for places of disagreement as entry points into the conversation.

- *Brainstorm consequences of a recent or proposed action.*   Arguments about consequences are among the most interesting and important of causal disputes. If you can argue for an unanticipated consequence of a real, hypothetical, or proposed action—for example, a bad consequence of an apparently positive event or a good consequence of an apparently negative event—you can make an important contribution to the conversation. What might be the consequences, for example, of some of the following: requiring a passing grade on a high-stakes test for graduation from high school; depleting the world's oil supply; legalizing marijuana; overturning *Roe v. Wade*; requiring school uniforms; allowing a small number of corporations to own most of the nation's newspapers and radio and TV stations; greatly increasing public searches on subways, buses, trains, and ferries as a means of fighting terrorism; any similar recent, hypothetical, or proposed event?

Organizing a Causal Argument

At the outset, it is useful to know some of the standard ways that a causal argument can be organized. Later, you may decide on a different organizational pattern, but these standard ways will help you get started.

Plan 1

When your purpose is to describe and explain all the links in a causal chain:

- Introduce phenomenon to be explained and show why it is problematical.
- Present your thesis in summary form.
- Describe and explain each link in the causal chain.

Plan 2

When your purpose is to explore the relative contribution of a number of causes to a phenomenon or to explore multiple consequences of a phenomenon:

- Introduce the phenomenon to be explained and suggest how or why it is controversial.
- Devote one section to each possible cause/consequence and decide whether it is necessary, sufficient, contributory, remote, and so forth. (Arrange sections so that those causes most familiar to the audience come first and the most surprising ones come last.)

Plan 3

When your purpose is to argue for a cause or consequence that is surprising or unexpected to your audience:

- Introduce a phenomenon to be explained and show why it is controversial.
- One by one, examine and reject the causes or consequences your audience would normally assume or expect.
- Introduce your unexpected or surprising cause or consequence and argue for it.

Plans 2 and 3 are similar in that they examine numerous possible causes or consequences. Plan 2, however, tries to establish the relative importance of each cause or consequence, whereas plan 3 aims at rejecting the causes or consequences normally assumed by the audience and argues for an unexpected surprising cause or consequence.

Plan 4

When your purpose is to change your audience's mind about a cause or consequence:

- Introduce the issue and show why it is controversial.
- Summarize your opponent's causal argument and then refute it.
- Present your own causal argument.

Plan 4 is a standard structure for all kinds of arguments. This is the structure you would use if you were the attorney for the person whose car skidded into the boutique (pp. 244–245). The opposing attorney would blame your client's reckless driving. You would lay blame on a poorly signed intersection, a speeding beer truck, and violation of building codes.

Questioning and Critiquing a Causal Argument

Because of the strenuous conditions that must be met before causality can be proven, causal arguments are vulnerable at many points. The following strategies will generally be helpful.

If you described every link in a causal chain, would skeptics point out weaknesses in any of the links? Describing a causal chain can be a complex business. A skeptic can raise doubts about an entire argument simply by questioning one of the links. Your best defense is to make a diagram of the linkages and role-play a skeptic trying to refute each link in turn. Whenever you find possible arguments against your position, see how you can strengthen your own argument at that point.

If your argument is based on a scientific experiment, could skeptics question the validity of the experiment? The scientific method attempts to demonstrate causality experimentally. If the experiment isn't well designed, however, the demonstration is less likely to be acceptable to skeptical audiences. Here are ways to question and critique a scientific argument:

- *Question the findings.*   Skeptics may have reason to believe that the data collected were not accurate or representative. They might provide alternative data or simply point out flaws in the way the data were collected.

- *Question the interpretation of the data.*   Many research studies are divided into "findings" and "discussion" sections. In the discussion section the researcher analyzes and interprets the data. A skeptic might provide an alternative interpretation of the data or otherwise argue that the data don't support what the original writer claims.

- *Question the design of the experiment.*   A detailed explanation of research design is beyond the scope of this text, but we can give some typical examples of how critics question the design of experiments. To counter a study showing that genetically modified corn was lethal to Monarch butterflies, skeptics argued that the study used unnaturally concentrated doses of corn pollen and applied it to butterfly larvae in ways that would rarely occur in nature. Along a similar vein, skeptics often question the applicability to humans of medical research done on lab animals or the applicability to women, minorities, or children of research done with white adult males as subjects. Skeptics of social science research based on questionnaires often point out poorly worded or misleading questions or subjective or ambiguous response scales. In sum, there are any number of ways that experiments can have design weaknesses.

If you have used correlation data, could skeptics argue that the correlation is much weaker than you claim or that you haven't sufficiently demonstrated causality?   As we discussed earlier, correlation data tell us only that two or more phenomena are likely to occur together. They don't tell us that one phenomenon caused the other. Thus correlation arguments are usually accompanied by hypotheses about causal connections between the phenomena. Correlation arguments can often be refuted as follows:

- Find problems in the statistical methods used to determine the correlation.
- Weaken the correlation by pointing out exceptions.
- Provide an alternative hypothesis about causality.

If you have used an analogy argument, could skeptics point out disanalogies? Although among the most persuasive of argumentative strategies, analogy arguments are also among the easiest to refute. The standard procedure is to counter your argument that X is like Y by pointing out all the ways that X is *not* like Y. Once again, by role-playing an opposing view, you may be able to strengthen your own analogy argument.

Could a skeptic cast doubt on your argument by reordering your priority of causes? Up to this point we've focused on refuting the claim that X causes Y. However, another approach is to concede that X helps cause Y but that X is only one of several contributing causes and not the most significant one at that.

Readings

The following essay, by student writer Daeha Ko, appeared as an op-ed piece in the *University of Washington Daily* on May 9, 1999, several weeks after the Columbine High School massacre in Littleton, Colorado. Daeha's motivation for writing is his anger at media attempts to explain the massacre—none of which focuses on the cliquish social structure of high school itself.

The Monster That Is High School
Daeha Ko (student)

In the past weeks, intensive media coverage has surrounded the shooting incident in Littleton, Colorado, where 12 students and a teacher died, along with 23 wounded. Yet people forget the real victims of the Littleton massacre are Dylan Klebold and Eric Harris.   1

What they did was against the law, but let's face it—the incident was waiting to   2
happen. And there's nothing surprising about it.

3   The social priorities of high school are to blame. In truth, high school is a place where jocks, cheerleaders and anyone associated with them can do whatever they want and get away with it. Their exploits are celebrated in pep rallies, printed in school papers and shown off in trophy cases. The popular cliques have the most clout, and are—in a sense—local celebrities. If they ever run into disciplinary problems with the school or police, they get let off the hook under the guise that they are just kids.

4   Public schools claim to support all students, but in reality choose to invest their priorities in activities associated with popular cliques. Schools are willing to go to any means necessary to support the sports teams, for example. They care less about students who don't belong to popular cliques, leaving them almost nothing. School becomes less about getting a good education, instead priding itself on the celebration of elite cliques.

5   The popular cliques are nice to their own but spit out extremely cruel insults to those who don't fit in. As noted in *Time,* jocks admitted they like to pick on unpopular kids "because it's just fun to do." Their insulting words create deep emotional wounds, while school authorities ignore the cruelty of the corrupt high-school social system.

6   Schools refuse to accept any accountability and point to parents instead. While it is the job of parents to condition their kids, it is impossible for them to supervise their kids 24 hours a day.

7   As an outcast, I was harassed on an everyday basis by jocks, and received no help from school authorities. It got so bad that I attempted suicide.

8   Yes, I did (and still do) wear all black, play Doom and listen to raucous heavy metal, punk and Goth music. I was into the occult and had extensive knowledge on guns and how to build bombs.

9   I got into several fights, including one where I kicked the shit out of a basketball player. The only reason why I didn't shoot him and his jock cronies is because I lacked access to guns. I would've blown every single one of them away and not cared.

10   To defend myself, I carried around a 7-inch blade. If anyone continued to mess with me, I sent them anonymous notes with a big swastika drawn on them. I responded to harassment with "Yeah, heil Hitler," while saluting.

11   They got the hint. Eventually, I found some friends who were also outcasts. We banded together and didn't judge each other by the way we looked or what we liked. But I still held contempt for jocks whom I believed should be shot and fed to the sharks.

12   Even in their deaths, Klebold and Harris are still treated like outcasts. How dare *Time* call them "The Monsters Next Door." News analysis poured over the "abnormal" world of "Goth" culture, Marilyn Manson, violent computer games and gun control. It also targeted other outcast students as trenchcoat-goth, submerged, socially challenged kids who fail to fit the "correct" image of American teens.

13   The popular cliques have their likeness reinforced through the images of trashy teen media as seen on MTV, *90210,* and *Dawson's Creek.* It's heard in the bubblegum pop of Britney Spears and Backstreet Boys, along with their imitators.

Magazines like *YM* and *Seventeen* feature pretty-looking girls, offering advice on the latest trends in dress, makeup and dating.

Media coverage was saturated with memorials and funeral services of the deceased. Friends and family remembered them as "good kids." Not all those killed knew or made fun of Klebold or Harris. Obviously there were members of the popular cliques who made fun of them and escaped harm. But innocent people had to die in order to bring injustices to light that exist in our society.   14

It's tragic, but perhaps that's the price that had to be paid. Perhaps they are shocked by the fact that some "nerds" have actually defeated them for once because teasing isn't fun and games anymore.   15

With the last of the coffins being laid to rest, people are looking for retribution, someone to prosecute. Why? The two kids are dead—there is no sense in pursuing this problem any further. But lawyers are trying to go after those who they believe influenced Harris and Klebold: namely their parents, gun dealers, and the Trenchcoat Mafia. Police heavily questioned Harris' girlfriend about the guns she gave them and arrested one person.   16

The families of the deceased, lawyers and the police need to get a clue and leave the two kids' families and friends alone. They are dealing with just as much grief and do not need to be punished for someone else's choices. Filing lawsuits will drag on for years, burdening everyone and achieving little.   17

It's not like you can bring your loved ones back to life after you've won your case.   18

What we need is bigger emphasis on academic discipline and more financing toward academic programs. Counselors and psychiatrists need to be hired to attend to student needs. People need practical skills, not the pep-rally fluff of popular cliques.   19

The people of Littleton need to be at peace with the fate of their town and heal wounds instead of prying them open with lawsuits.   20

Critiquing "The Monster That Is High School"

1. Summarize Daeha Ko's argument by creating a plausible causal chain leading from popular high school cliques to the Littleton massacre. How persuasive is Daeha's argument?

2. Part of the *kairotic* moment shaping Daeha Ko's anger was the *Time* magazine article that characterized Klebold and Harris as "the monsters next door." How would you characterize Daeha's *ethos* in this piece? Do you see him as "monstrous" himself? Or does his *ethos* help create sympathy for social outcasts in high school culture?

3. Daeha presents his causal argument as a contribution to the frantic, contentious social conflict that raged among social scientists, columnists, and other media commentators after the shootings at Columbine High School in Littleton, Colorado. Which alternative explanations for the shooting does Daeha address? What strategy does he use to rebut alternative causal

arguments? Do you regard Daeha's argument as a valuable contribution to the controversy? Why or why not?

4. How does *kairos* help explain the claims and vehemence of this argument? Do you think this piece gains or loses impact as an argument when it is read at some time after its *kairotic* moment?

Our second reading (Figure 12.1) is an advocacy advertisement seeking donations to the "Community Safety Net Fund" of the United Way organization in a major American city. It consists of an intriguing visual image accompanied by a one-sentence statistic.

Critiquing the United Way Advocacy Ad

1. What techniques of visual argument (see pp. 162–180) are used by this advocacy ad? Do you find the visual images effective? Why or why not?

2. The verbal text for this ad consists of a single statistic. The ad maker invites its target audience to fill in the gaps in order to convert this statistic into an argument. What is the argument that this ad makes?

Kids who do not participate in after-school activities are 37% more likely to become teen parents than kids who do.

Your gift to the Community Safety Net Fund helps bring together the people and resources to identify and address the challenges that face our community. Call (206) 461-GIVE or log on to unitedwayofkingcounty.org.

UNITED WAY
of KING COUNTY

BE PART OF THE ANSWER.

FIGURE 12.1   *United Way advocacy ad*

3. What values does this ad appeal to? How does the ad use the strategy of "audience-based reasons" (see pp. 102–108)? This ad could have used either a boy or a girl of any ethnicity (white, African American, Asian) and appearance (hairstyle, for example, or body piercings) participating in any after-school activity (music, art, debate team). Why do you think the ad makers chose a pony-tailed white female teenager playing basketball? (Note that the statistic lumps together males and females—it talks about teen "parents" rather than teen "mothers.")

4. The statistic cited implies a cause and effect relationship between after-school activities and reduced likelihood for teenage parenthood. How might you argue that this statistic simply shows a correlation rather than a cause and effect?

Our third reading, by evolutionary biologist Olivia Judson at Imperial College in London, was published during intense public debate about the underrepresentation of women in science. The controversy was initiated by the remarks of Lawrence Summers, president of Harvard, at a January 2005 academic conference in which he suggested that there might be fewer women than men on prestigious science faculties because women have less innate talent for science and math. A furious reaction ensued. The Web site of the Women in Science and Engineering Leadership Institute has extensive coverage of the controversy, including Summers' original speech (http://wiseli.engr.wisc.edu/news/Summers.htm). In the following causal argument, published as an op-ed piece in the *New York Times*, a distinguished woman scientist looks at the scientific evidence bearing on Summers' remarks.

Different but (Probably) Equal

Olivia Judson

Hypothesis: males and females are typically indistinguishable on the basis of their behaviors and intellectual abilities. 1

This is not true for elephants. Females have big vocabularies and hang out in herds; males tend to live in solitary splendor, and insofar as they speak at all, their conversation appears mostly to consist of elephant for "I'm in the mood, I'm in the mood . . ." 2

The hypothesis is not true for zebra finches. Males sing elaborate songs. Females can't sing at all. A zebra finch opera would have to have males in all the singing roles. 3

And it's not true for green spoon worms. This animal, which lives on the sea floor, has one of the largest known size differences between male and female: the male is 200,000 times smaller. He spends his whole life in her reproductive tract, fertilizing eggs by regurgitating sperm through his mouth. He's so different from his 4 mate that when he was first discovered by science, he was not recognized as being a green spoon worm; instead, he was thought to be a parasite.

5   Is it ridiculous to suppose that the hypothesis might not be true for humans either?

6   No. But it is not fashionable—as Lawrence Summers, president of Harvard University, discovered when he suggested this month that greater intrinsic ability might be one reason that men are overrepresented at the top levels of fields involving math, science and engineering.

7   There are—as the maladroit Mr. Summers should have known—good reasons it's not fashionable. Beliefs that men are intrinsically better at this or that have repeatedly led to discrimination and prejudice, and then they've been proved to be nonsense. Women were thought not to be world-class musicians. But when American symphony orchestras introduced blind auditions in the 1970's—the musician plays behind a screen so that his or her gender is invisible to those listening—the number of women offered jobs in professional orchestras increased.

8   Similarly, in science, studies of the ways that grant applications are evaluated have shown that women are more likely to get financing when those reading the applications do not know the sex of the applicant. In other words, there's still plenty of work to do to level the playing field; there's no reason to suppose there's something inevitable about the status quo.

9   All the same, it seems a shame if we can't even voice the question. Sex differences are fascinating—and entirely unlike the other biological differences that distinguish other groups of living things (like populations and species). Sex differences never arise in isolation, with females evolving on a mountaintop, say, and males evolving in a cave. Instead, most genes—and in some species, all genes—spend equal time in each sex. Many sex differences are not, therefore, the result of *his* having one gene while *she* has another. Rather, they are attributable to the way particular genes behave when they find themselves in *him* instead of *her.*

10   The magnificent difference between male and female green spoon worms, for example, has nothing to do with their having different genes: each green spoon worm larva could go either way. Which sex it becomes depends on whether it meets a female during its first three weeks of life. If it meets a female, it becomes male and prepares to regurgitate; if it doesn't, it becomes female and settles into a crack on the sea floor.

11   What's more, the fact that most genes occur in both males and females can generate interesting sexual tensions. In male fruit flies, for instance, variants of genes that confer particular success—which on Mother Nature's abacus is the number of descendants you have—tend to be detrimental when they occur in females, and vice versa. Worse: the bigger the advantage in one sex, the more detrimental those genes are in the other. This means that, at least for fruit flies, the same genes that make a male a Don Juan would also turn a female into a wallflower; conversely, the genes that make a female a knockout babe would produce a clumsy fellow with the sex appeal of a cake tin.

12   But why do sex differences appear at all? They appear when the secret of success differs for males and females: the more divergent the paths to success, the more extreme the physiological differences. Peacocks have huge tails and strut

about because peahens prefer males with big tails. Bull elephant seals grow to five times the mass of females because big males are better at monopolizing the beaches where the females haul out to have sex and give birth.

Meanwhile, the crow-like jackdaw has (as far as we can tell) no obvious sex differences and appears to lead a life of devoted monogamy. Here, what works for him also seems to work for her, though the female is more likely to sit on the eggs. So by studying the differences—and similarities—among men and women, we can potentially learn about the forces that have shaped us in the past.   13

And I think the news is good. We're not like green spoon worms or elephant seals, with males and females so different that aspiring to an egalitarian society would be ludicrous. And though we may not be jackdaws either—men and women tend to look different, though even here there's overlap—it's obvious that where there are intellectual differences, they are so slight they cannot be prejudged.   14

The interesting questions are, is there an average intrinsic difference? And how extensive is the variation? I would love to know if the averages are the same but the underlying variation is different—with members of one sex tending to be either superb or dreadful at particular sorts of thinking while members of the other are pretty good but rarely exceptional.   15

Curiously, such a result could arise even if the forces shaping men and women have been identical. In some animals—humans and fruit flies come to mind—males have an X chromosome and a Y chromosome while females have two X's. In females, then, extreme effects of genes on one X chromosome can be offset by the genes on the other. But in males, there's no hiding your X. In birds and butterflies, though, it's the other way around: females have a Z chromosome and a W chromosome, and males snooze along with two Z's.   16

The science of sex differences, even in fruit flies and toads, is a ferociously complex subject. It's also famously fraught, given its malignant history. In fact, there was a time not so long ago when I would have balked at the whole enterprise: the idea there might be intrinsic cognitive differences between men and women was one I found insulting. But science is a great persuader. The jackdaws and spoon worms have forced me to change my mind. Now I'm keen to know what sets men and women apart—and no longer afraid of what we may find.   17

Critiquing "Different but (Probably) Equal"

1. The controversy sparked by Harvard President Lawrence Summers' remarks was a highly politicized version of the classic nature/nurture problem. Liberal commentators claimed that women were underrepresented in science because of cultural practices that discouraged young girls from becoming interested in math and science and that blocked women Ph.D.s from advancing in their scientific careers. In contrast, conservative commentators—praising Summers' courage for raising a politically incorrect subject—took the "nature" side of this argument by citing studies pointing to innate cognitive differences between human males and females. How would you characterize Judson's position in this controversy?

2. What parts of Judson's article tend to support the "nurture" view that cultural practices account for women's underrepresentation in math and science? What parts tend to support the "nature" view?

3. Judson's argument relies heavily on analogies between humans and the animal world. In your own words, explain why the green spoon worm and the jackdaw (crow) are important to Judson's argument. Why does she say that the interesting questions involve "average intrinsic difference" and the extensiveness of "variation"?

4. How would you characterize Judson's *ethos* in this article? Pay particular attention to the narrative embedded in the last paragraph—her claim that she is no longer afraid of what we might find. How important is it that we know the author is a woman?

Our final causal argument, by student writer Carlos Macias, examines the phenomenon of credit card debt among college students. Note how Macias intermixes personal experiences and research data in order to make his case.

"The Credit Card Company Made Me Do It!"—The Credit Card Industry's Role in Causing Student Debt

Carlos Macias

1   One day on spring break this year, I strolled into a Gap store. I found several items that I decided to buy. As I was checking out, the cute female clerk around my age, with perfect hair and makeup, asked if I wanted to open a GapCard to save 10 percent on all purchases I made at Gap, Banana Republic, and Old Navy that day. She said I would also earn points toward Gap gift certificates in the future. Since I shop at the Gap often enough, I decided to take her up on her offer. I filled out the form she handed me, and within seconds I—a jobless, indebted-from-student-loans, full-time college student with no substantial assets or income whatsoever—was offered a card with a $1000 credit line. Surprised by the speed in which I was approved and the amount that I was approved for, I decided to proceed to both Banana Republic and Old Navy that day to see if there was anything else I might be interested in getting (there was). By the end of the day, I had rung up nearly $200 in purchases.

2   I know my $200 shopping spree on credit is nothing compared to some of the horror stories I have heard from friends. One of my friends, a college sophomore, is carrying $2000 on a couple of different cards, a situation that is not unusual at all. According to a May 2005 study, students with credit cards carry average balances of just under $3000 by the time they are seniors (Nellie Mae 2). The problem is that most students don't have the income to pay off their balances, so they become

hooked into paying high interest rates and fees that enrich banks while exploiting students who have not yet learned how to exercise control on their spending habits.

Who is to blame for this situation? Many people might blame the students 3 themselves, citing the importance of individual responsibility and proclaiming that no one forces students to use credit cards. But I put most of the blame directly on the credit card companies. Credit cards are enormously profitable; according to a New York Times article, the industry made $30 billion in pretax profits in 2003 alone (McGeehan). Hooking college students on credit cards is essential for this profit, not only because companies make a lot of money off the students themselves, but because hooking students on cards creates a habit that lasts a lifetime. Credit card companies' predatory lending practices—such as using exploitive advertising, using credit scoring to determine creditworthiness, disguising the real cost of credit, and taking advantage of U.S. government deregulation—are causing many unwitting college students to accumulate high levels of credit card debt.

First of all, credit card companies bombard students with highly sophisticated 4 advertising. College students, typically, are in an odd "in-between" stage where they are not necessarily teens anymore, provided for by their parents, but neither are they fully adults, able to provide entirely for themselves. Many students feel the pressures from family, peers and themselves to assume adult roles in terms of their dress and jobs, not relying on mom or dad for help. Card companies know about these pressures. Moreover, college students are easy to target because they are concentrated on campuses and generally consume the same media. I probably get several mailings a month offering me a pre-approved credit card. These advertisements are filled with happy campus scenes featuring students wearing just the right clothes, carrying their books in just the right backpack, playing music on their iPods or opening their laptop computers. They also appeal to students' desire to feel like responsible adults by emphasizing little emergencies that college students can relate to such as car breakdowns on a road trip. These advertisements illustrate a point made by a team of researchers in an article entitled "Credit Cards as Lifestyle Facilitators": The authors explain how credit card companies want consumers to view credit cards as "lifestyle facilitators" that enable "lifestyle building" and "lifestyle signaling" (Bernthal, Crockett, and Rose). Credit cards make it easy for students to live the lifestyle pictured in the credit card ads.

Another contributing cause of high credit card debt for college students is the 5 method that credit card companies use to grant credit—through credit scoring that does not consider income. It was credit scoring that allowed me to get that quadruple-digit credit line at the Gap while already living in the red. The application I filled out never asked my income. Instead, the personal information I listed was used to pull up my credit score, which is based on records of outstanding debts and payment history. Credit scoring allows banks to grant credit cards based on a person's record of responsibility in paying bills rather than on income. According to finance guru Suze Orman, "Your FICO (credit) score is a great tool to size up how good you will be handling a new loan or credit card" (21). Admittedly, credit scoring has made the lending process as a whole much fairer, giving individuals such as minorities and women the chance to qualify for credit even if they have minimal incomes. But when credit card companies use credit scoring to determine college students' creditworthiness, many students are unprepared to handle a credit line that greatly exceeds their ability to pay based on income. In fact, the Center for Responsible Lending, a consumer advocacy organization in North Carolina, lobbied Congress in September 2003 to require credit card companies to secure proof of adequate income for college-age customers before approving credit card applications ("Credit Card Policy Recommendations"). If Congress passed such legislation, credit card companies would not be able to as easily take advantage of college students who have not yet learned how to exercise control on their spending habits. They would have to offer students credit lines commensurate to their incomes. No wonder these companies vehemently opposed this legislation.

6   Yet another contributing cause of high levels of credit card debt is the high cost of having this debt, which credit card companies are especially talented at disguising. As credit card debt increases, card companies compound unpaid interest, adding it to the balance that must be repaid. If this balance is not repaid, they charge interest on unpaid interest. They add exorbitant fees for small slip-ups like making a late payment or exceeding the credit limit. While these costs are listed on statements when first added to the balance, they quickly vanish into the "New Balance" number on all subsequent statements, as if these fees were simply past purchases that have yet to be repaid. As the balance continues to grow, banks spike interest rates even higher. In his 2004 article "Soaring Interest Is Compounding Credit Card Pain for Millions," Patrick McGeehan describes a "new era of consumer credit, in which thousands of Americans are paying millions of dollars each month in fees that they did not expect . . . lenders are doubling or tripling interest rates with little warning or explanation." These rate hikes are usually tucked into the pages of fine print that come with credit cards, which many consumers are unable to fully read, let alone understand. Usually, a credit card company will offer a very low "teaser rate" that expires after several months. While this industry practice is commonly understood by consumers, many do not understand that credit card companies usually reserve the right to raise the rate at any time for almost any reason, causing debt levels to rise further.

7   Admittedly, while individual consumers must be held accountable for any debt they accumulate and should understand compound and variable interest and fees, students' ignorance is welcomed by the credit card industry. In order to completely understand how the credit card industry has caused college students to amass high amounts of credit card debt, it is necessary to explain how this vicious monster was let loose during banking deregulation over the past 30 years. In 1978, the Supreme Court opened the floodgates by ruling that the federal government could not set a cap on interest rates that banks charged for credit cards; that was to be left to the states. With Uncle Sam no longer protecting consumers, Delaware and South Dakota passed laws that removed caps on interest rates, in order to woo credit card companies to conduct nationwide business there (McGeehan). Since then, the credit card industry has become one of the most profitable industries ever. Credit card companies were given another sweet deal from the U.S. Supreme Court in 1996, when the Court deregulated fees. Since then, the average late fee has risen from $10 or less, to $39 (McGeehan). While a lot of these fees and finance charges are avoidable if the student pays the balance in full, on time, every month, for college

students who carry balances for whatever reason, these charges are tacked on, further adding to the principal on which they pay a high rate of compounded interest. (79% of the students surveyed in the Nellie Mae study said that they regularly carried a balance on their cards [8].) Moreover, the U.S. government has refused to step in to regulate the practice of universal default, where a credit card company can raise the rate they charge if a consumer is late on an unrelated bill, like a utility payment. Even for someone who pays his or her bills in full, on time, 99% of the time, one bill-paying slip-up can cause an avalanche of fees and frustration, thanks to the credit card industry.

Credit card companies exploit college students' lack of financial savvy and security. It is no secret that most full-time college students are not independently wealthy; many have limited means. So why are these companies so willing to issue cards to poor college students? Profits, of course! If they made credit cards less available to struggling consumers such as college students, consumers would have a more difficult time racking up huge balances, plain and simple. It's funny that Citibank, one of the largest, most profitable credit card companies in the world, proudly exclaims "Live richly" in its advertisements. At the rate that it and other card companies collect interest and fees from their customers, a more appropriate slogan would be "Live poorly." 8

Works Cited

Bernthal, Matthew J., David Crockett, and Randall L. Rose. "Credit Cards as Lifestyle Facilitators." Journal of Consumer Research 32.1 (June 2005): 130–45. Research Library Complete. ProQuest. Multiple Databases. A.A. Lemieux Lib., Seattle U. 18 June 2005 <http://proquest.umi.com>.

"Credit Card Policy Recommendations." Center for Responsible Lending. Sept. 2003. 1p. 18 June 2005 <http://www.responsiblelending.org/pdfs/Card_website.PDF>.

McGeehan, Patrick. "Soaring Interest Is Compounding Credit Card Pain for Millions." New York Times 21 Nov. 2004. 3 July 2005 <http://www.nytimes.com>.

Nellie Mae. Undergraduate Students and Credit Cards in 2004: An Analysis of Usage Rates and Trends. 2005. 3 July 2005 <http://www.nelliemae.com/library/ccstudy_2005.pdf>.

Orman, Suze. The Money Book for the Young, Fabulous and Broke. New York: Riverhead, 2005.

Critiquing "The Credit Card Company Made Me Do It!"

1. How effective is Macias' argument that the predatory practices of banks and credit card companies are the primary cause of credit card debt among college students?

2. Suppose that you wanted to join this conversation by offering a counter-view with a thesis something like this: "Although Macias is partially correct that banks and credit card companies play a role in producing credit card debt among college students, he underestimates other important factors." What would you emphasize as the causes of credit card debt? How would you make your case?

13 Resemblance Arguments
X Is (Is Not) Like Y

CASE 1

Following the September 11, 2001, terrorist attacks on the World Trade Center and the Pentagon, media analysts tried to make sense of the horror by comparing it to different kinds of previous events. Some commentators likened it to Timothy McVeigh's bombing of the Alfred P. Murrah Federal Building in Oklahoma City in 1995—an argument that framed the terrorists as criminals who must be brought to justice. Others compared it to the 1941 Japanese attack on Pearl Harbor, an argument suggesting that the United States should declare war on some as-yet-to-be-defined enemy. (Charles Krauthammer makes this argument in "This Isn't a 'Legal' Matter, This Is War" on pp. 236–238.) Still others likened the event to an earthquake or an epidemic. This analogy argues that terrorists will continue to exist as long as the right conditions breed them and that it is useless to fight them using the strategies of conventional war. Under this analogy, the "war on terror" is a metaphorical war like the "war on poverty" or the "war against cancer." Clearly each of these resemblance arguments has high-stakes consequences. The Bush administration chose the Pearl Harbor argument and went to war, first against the Taliban in Afghanistan and then against Saddam Hussein in Iraq. Critics of the war continue to say that these were inappropriate strategies for fighting the "disease of terrorism."

CASE 2

Abuse of prescription drugs is becoming increasingly common among college students, especially analeptic drugs like Ritalin or Adderall to enhance concentration while studying for a final exam or pulling an all-nighter to finish a term paper. Many of the new "pushers" for these drugs are students diagnosed with attention-deficit hyperactivity disorder (ADHD) or students who can fake the symptoms of ADHD at the student health center. These students can then sell their extra pills for a nice profit. Although analeptics are safer than cocaine or methamphetamines, they entail a number of risks. But the chief complaint made by nonusing students concerns fairness and equity. Adderall is the student's steroid, some students say. Taking Adderall is cheating. To level the playing field, nonusers feel they must start taking performance-enhancing drugs themselves, sparking a vicious spiral.*

An Overview of Resemblance Arguments

Resemblance arguments support a claim by comparing one thing to another with the intention of transferring the audience's understanding of (or feelings about) the second thing back to the first. Sometimes an entire argument can be devoted to a resemblance claim. More commonly, brief resemblance arguments are pieces of a larger argument devoted to a different stasis. Thus, those who oppose taking analeptic drugs like Adderall or Ritalin compare analeptics to steroids, thus hoping to transfer the audience's ethical disapproval of steroids in athletic competition to analeptics in the competition for grades. Whether prescription drugs like Adderall are really analogous to steroids is the subject of intense debate.

The persuasive power of resemblance arguments comes from their ability to clarify an audience's conception of contested issues while conveying powerful emotions. Resemblance arguments typically take the form X is (is not) like Y. Resemblance arguments work best when the audience has a clear (and sometimes emotionally charged) understanding of the Y term. The writer then hopes to transfer this understanding, along with accompanying emotions, to the X term. The risk of resemblance arguments, as we shall see, is that the differences between the X and Y terms are often so significant that the resemblance argument may collapse under close examination.

Like most other argument types, resemblance arguments can be analyzed using the Toulmin schema. Suppose you want to find a startling way to warn teenage girls away from excessive dieting. Simultaneously, you want to argue that excessive dieting is partially caused by a patriarchal construction of beauty that keeps women submissive and powerless. You decide to create a resemblance argument claiming that women's obsessive dieting is like foot-binding in ancient China. This argument can be displayed in Toulmin terms as follows:

ENTHYMEME: Women's obsessive dieting in America serves the same harmful function as foot-binding in ancient China because both practices keep women childlike, docile, dependent, and unthreatening to men.

GROUNDS: evidence that both obsessive dieting and foot-binding lead to childlike subordination: Both practices involve women's painful attempts to meet patriarchal standards of beauty in which men are powerful agents and women are beautiful objects; women, in attempting to imitate society's image of the "perfect woman," damage themselves (Chinese women are physically

---

*Andrew Jacobs, "The Adderall Advantage," *New York Times Education Life* 31 July 2005, Section 4A, 16.

maimed; American women are psychologically maimed and often weakened by inadequate diet or constant worry about being fat); both practices make women childlike rather than grown-up (men call beautiful women "babes" or "dolls"; anorexia stops menstruation); women obsessed with beauty end up satisfied with less pay and subordinate positions in society as long as they are regarded as feminine and pretty.

WARRANT: We should reject practices that are like Chinese foot-binding.

BACKING: arguments that the subordinate position of women evidenced in both foot-binding and obsession with weight is related to patriarchal construction of women's roles; further arguments for why women should free themselves from patriarchal views

CONDITIONS OF REBUTTAL: All the ways that dieting and concern for weight are not like Chinese foot-binding. For example, skeptics might say that women who diet are concerned with health, not pursuit of beauty; concern for healthy weight is "rational," not "obsessive"; thin women are often powerful athletes, not at all like Chinese victims of foot-binding who can hardly walk; dieting does not cause crippling deformity; a concern for beauty does not make a woman subordinate or satisfied with less pay; dieting is a woman's choice—not something forced on her as a child.

QUALIFIER: Perhaps the writer should say "*Under certain conditions* obsessive dieting can even seem like Chinese foot-binding."

For many audiences, the comparison of women's dieting to Chinese foot-binding will have an immediate and powerful emotional effect, perhaps causing them to see attitudes toward weight and food from a new, unsettling perspective. The analogy invites them to transfer their understanding of Chinese foot-binding—which seems instantly repulsive and oppressive of women—to their understanding of obsessive concern for losing weight. Whereas social controls in ancient China were overt, the modern practice uses more subtle kinds of social control, such as the influence of the fashion and beauty industry and peer pressure. But in both cases women feel forced to mold their bodies to a patriarchal standard of beauty—one that emphasizes soft curves, tiny waists, and daintiness rather than strength and power.

But this example also illustrates the dangers of resemblance arguments, which often ignore important differences or *disanalogies* between the terms of comparison. As the "conditions of rebuttal" show, there are many differences between dieting and foot-binding. For example, the practice of foot-binding was not a conscious choice of young Chinese girls, who were forced to have their feet wrapped at an early age. Dieting, on the other hand, is something one chooses, and it may reveal a healthy and rational choice rather than an obsession with appearance. When the practice degenerates to anorexia or bulimia, it becomes a mental disease, not a physical deformity forced on a girl in childhood. Thus a resemblance argument is usually open to refutation if a skeptic points out important disanalogies.

We now turn to the two types of resemblance arguments: analogy and precedent.

Arguments by Analogy

The use of *analogies* can constitute the most imaginative form of argument. If you don't like your new boss, you can say that she's like a Marine drill sergeant, the cowardly captain of a sinking ship, or a mother hen. Each of these analogies suggests a different management style, clarifying the nature of your dislike while conveying an emotional charge. The ubiquity of analogies undoubtedly stems from their power to clarify the writer's understanding of an issue through comparisons that grip the audience.

Of course, this power to make things clear comes at a price. Analogies often clarify one aspect of a relationship at the expense of other aspects. For example, in nineteenth-century America, commentators were fond of justifying certain negative effects of capitalism (such as the squalor of the poor) by comparing economic processes to Darwin's survival of the fittest. In particular, they fastened on one aspect of evolution, competition, and spoke darkly of life as a cutthroat struggle for survival. However, even though market economies have some parallels to Darwinian evolution, whereby entrepreneurs compete for limited resources, territories, and markets and the weak get eaten by the strong, Darwin's theory isn't just about competition. The ability to dominate an environment is less important to long-term survival of the species than is the ability to adapt to the environment. Thus the mighty dinosaur disappeared while the lowly cockroach continues to thrive.

The use of evolutionary analogies to stress the competitive nature of human existence fit the worldview (and served the interests) of those who were most fond of invoking them—the factory owners, the robber barons, and other Social Darwinists. But in overlooking other dimensions of evolution, especially adaptation and cooperation, the analogy created a great deal of mischief.

So analogies have the power to get an audience's attention like virtually no other persuasive strategy. But seldom are they sufficient in themselves to provide full understanding. At some point with every analogy you need to ask yourself, "How far can I legitimately go with this? At what point are the similarities between the two things I am comparing going to be overwhelmed by their dissimilarities?" They are useful attention-getting devices, but they can conceal and distort as well as clarify.

With this caveat, let's look at the uses of both undeveloped and extended analogies.

Using Undeveloped Analogies

Typically, writers will use short, *undeveloped analogies* to drive home a point (and evoke an accompanying emotion) and then quickly abandon the analogy before the reader's awareness of disanalogies begins to set in. Thus columnist James

Kilpatrick, in arguing that it is not unconstitutional to require drug testing of federal employees, compares giving a urine specimen when applying for a federal job to going through an airport metal detector when flying:

> The Constitution does not prohibit all searches and seizures. It makes the people secure in their persons only from "unreasonable" searches and seizures. [. . .] A parallel situation may be observed at every airport in the land. Individuals may have a right to fly, but they have no right to fly without having their persons and baggage inspected for weapons. By the same token, the federal worker who refuses a urine specimen [has no right to a federal job].

Kilpatrick wants to transfer his audience's general approval of weapons searches as a condition for airplane travel to drug testing as a condition for federal employment. But he doesn't want his audience to linger too long on the analogy. (Is a urine specimen for employment really analogous to a weapons search before an airplane trip?)

Using Extended Analogies

Sometimes writers elaborate an analogy so that it takes on a major role in the argument. As an example of a claim based on an *extended analogy*, consider the following excerpt from a professor's argument opposing a proposal to require a writing proficiency exam for graduation. In the following portion of his argument, the professor compares development of writing skills to the development of physical fitness.

> A writing proficiency exam gives the wrong symbolic messages about writing. It suggests that writing is simply a skill, rather than an active way of thinking and learning. It suggests that once a student demonstrates proficiency then he or she doesn't need to do any more writing.
>
> Imagine two universities concerned with the physical fitness of their students. One university requires a junior-level physical fitness exam in which students must run a mile in less than 10 minutes, a fitness level it considers minimally competent. Students at this university see the physical fitness exam as a one-time hurdle. As many as 70 percent of them can pass the exam with no practice; another 10–20 percent need a few months' training; and a few hopeless couch potatoes must go through exhaustive remediation. After passing the exam, any student can settle back into a routine of TV and potato chips having been certified as "physically fit."
>
> The second university, however, believing in true physical fitness for its students, is not interested in minimal competency. Consequently, it creates programs in which its students exercise 30 minutes every day for the entire four years of the undergraduate curriculum. There is little doubt which university will have the most physically fit students. At the second university, fitness becomes a way of life with everyone developing his or her full potential. Similarly, if we want to improve our students' writing abilities, we should require writing in every course throughout the curriculum.

If you choose to write an extended analogy such as this, you will focus on the points of comparison that serve your purposes. The writer's purpose in the preceding case is to support the achievement of mastery rather than minimalist standards as the goal of the university's writing program. Whatever other disanalogous elements are involved (for example, writing requires the use of intellect, which may or may not be strengthened by daily exercise), the comparison reveals vividly that a commitment to mastery involves more than a minimalist test. Typically, then, in developing your analogy, you are not developing all possible points of comparison so much as you are bringing out those similarities consistent with the point you are trying to make.

For Class Discussion

The following is a two-part exercise to help you clarify for yourself how analogies function in the context of arguments. Part 1 is to be done outside class; part 2 is to be done in class.

PART 1   Think of an analogy that expresses your point of view toward each of the following topics. Your analogy can urge your readers toward either a positive view of the topic or a negative view, depending on the rhetorical effect you seek. Write your analogy in the following one-sentence format:

> X is like Y: A, B, C . . . (where X is the main topic being discussed; Y is the analogy; and A, B, and C are the points of comparison).

EXAMPLES:

Topic: Cramming for an exam

Negative analogy: Cramming for an exam is like pumping iron for ten hours straight to prepare for a weight-lifting contest: exhausting and counterproductive

Positive analogy: Cramming for an exam is like carbohydrate loading before a big race: it gives you the mental food you need for the exam, such as a full supply of concepts and details all fresh in your mind.

1. Using spanking to discipline children
2. Using racial profiling for airport security
3. Using steroids to increase athletic performance
4. Paying college athletes
5. Eating at fast-food restaurants

An effective analogy should influence both your audience's feelings toward the issue and your audience's understanding of the issue. For example, the writer of the negative analogy in the "cramming for an exam" illustration obviously believes that pumping iron for ten hours before a weight-lifting match is stupid. This feeling of stupidity is then transferred to the original topic—cramming for an exam. But the analogy also clarifies understanding. The writer imagines the mind as a muscle (which gets exhausted after too much exercise and which is better developed through some exercise every day rather than a lot all at once) rather than as a large container (into which lots of stuff can be "crammed").

PART 2   Bring your analogies to class and compare them to those of your classmates. Select the best analogies for each of the topics and be ready to say why you think they are good.

Arguments by Precedent

Precedent arguments are like analogy arguments in that they make comparisons between an X and a Y. In precedent arguments, however, the Y term is usually a past event where some sort of decision was reached, often a moral, legal, or political decision. An argument by precedent tries to show that a similar decision should be (should not be) reached for the present issue X because the situation of X is (is not) like the situation of Y. For example, if you wanted to argue that your college or university could increase retention by offering seminars for first-year students, you could point to the good results at other colleges that have instituted first-year seminars. If you wanted to argue that antidrug laws will never eradicate drug use, you could point to the failure of alcohol prohibition in the United States in the 1920s.

A good example of a precedent argument is the following excerpt from a speech by President Lyndon Johnson in the early years of the Vietnam War:

> Nor would surrender in Vietnam bring peace because we learned from Hitler at Munich that success only feeds the appetite of aggression. The battle would be renewed in one country and then another country, bringing with it perhaps even larger and crueler conflict, as we have learned from the lessons of history.

Here the audience knows what happened at Munich: France and Britain tried to appease Hitler by yielding to his demand for a large part of Czechoslovakia, but Hitler's armies continued their aggression anyway, using Czechoslovakia as a staging area to invade Poland. By arguing that surrender in Vietnam would lead to the same consequences, Johnson brings to his argument about Vietnam the whole weight of his audience's unhappy knowledge of World War II. Administration white papers developed Johnson's precedent argument by pointing toward the similarity of Hitler's promises with those of the Viet Cong: You give us this and we will ask for no more. But Hitler didn't keep his promise. Why should the Viet Cong?

Johnson's Munich precedent persuaded many Americans during the early years of the war and helps explain U.S. involvement in Southeast Asia. Yet many scholars attacked Johnson's reasoning. Let's analyze the Munich argument, using Toulmin's schema:

ENTHYMEME: The United States should not withdraw its troops from Vietnam because conceding to the Viet Cong will have the same disastrous consequences as did conceding to Hitler in Munich.

CLAIM: The United States should not withdraw its troops from Vietnam.

STATED REASON: because conceding to the Viet Cong will have the same disastrous consequences as did conceding to Hitler in Munich

GROUNDS: evidence of the disastrous consequences of conceding to Hitler at Munich: Hitler's continued aggression; his using Czechoslovakia as a staging area to invade Poland

WARRANT: What happened in Europe will happen in Southeast Asia.

BACKING: evidence of similarities between 1939 Europe and 1965 Southeast Asia (for example, similarities in political philosophy, goals, and military strength of the enemy; similarities in the nature of the conflict between the disputants)

CONDITIONS OF REBUTTAL: acknowledged differences between 1939 Europe and 1965 Southeast Asia that might make the outcomes different

Laid out like this, we see that the persuasiveness of the comparison depends on the audience's acceptance of the warrant, which posits close similarity between 1939 Europe and 1965 Southeast Asia. But many critics of the Vietnam War attacked this warrant.

During the Vietnam era, historian Howard Zinn attacked Johnson's argument by claiming three crucial differences between Europe in 1939 and Southeast Asia in 1965: First, Zinn argued, the Czechs were being attacked from outside by an external aggressor (Germany), whereas Vietnam was being attacked from within by rebels as part of a civil war. Second, Czechoslovakia was a prosperous, effective democracy, whereas the official Vietnam government was corrupt and unpopular. Third, Hitler wanted Czechoslovakia as a base for attacking Poland, whereas the Viet Cong and North Vietnamese aimed at reunification of their country as an end in itself.*

The Munich example shows again how arguments of resemblance depend on emphasizing the similarities between X and Y and playing down the dissimilarities. One could try to refute the counterargument made by Zinn by arguing first that the Saigon government was more stable than Zinn thinks and second that the

---

*Based on the summary of Zinn's argument in J. Michael Sproule, *Argument: Language and Its Influence* (New York: McGraw-Hill, 1980), 149–50.

Viet Cong and North Vietnamese were driven by goals larger than reunification of Vietnam, namely, communist domination of Asia. Such an argument would once again highlight the similarities between Vietnam and prewar Europe.

For Class Discussion

1. Consider the following claims of precedent, and evaluate how effective you think each precedent might be in establishing the claim. How would you develop the argument? How would you cast doubt on it?

   a. Gays should be allowed to serve openly in the U.S. military because they are allowed to serve openly in the militaries of most other Western countries.

   b. Gun control will reduce violent crime in the United States because many countries that have strong gun control laws (such as Japan and England) have low rates of violent crime.

   c. Post-war democracy can be created successfully in Iraq because it was created successfully in Germany and Japan following World War II.

2. Advocates for "right to die" legislation legalizing active euthanasia under certain conditions often point to the Netherlands as a country where acceptance of euthanasia works effectively. Assume for the moment that your state has a ballot initiative legalizing euthanasia. Assume further that you are being hired as a lobbyist for (against) the measure and have been assigned to do research on euthanasia in the Netherlands. Working in small groups, make a list of research questions you would want to ask. Your long-range rhetorical goal is to use your research to support (attack) the ballot initiative by making a precedence argument focusing on the Netherlands.

Writing a Resemblance Argument

WRITING ASSIGNMENT
FOR CHAPTER 13

Write a letter to the editor of your campus or local newspaper or a slightly longer guest editorial in which you try to influence public opinion on some issue through the use of a persuasive analogy or precedent. Megan Matthews' argument against the Navy's use of low-frequency sonar to locate submarines is a student piece written for this assignment (see pp. 280–281).

Exploring Ideas

Because letters to the editor and guest editorials are typically short, writers often lack space to develop full arguments. Because of their clarifying and emotional power, arguments from analogy or precedent are often effective in these situations.

Newspaper editors usually print letters or guest editorials only on current issues or on some current problem to which you can draw attention. For this assignment look through the most recent back issues of your campus or local newspaper, paying particular attention to issues being debated on the op-ed pages. Join one of the ongoing conversations about an existing issue, or draw attention to a current problem or situation that annoys you. In your letter or guest editorial, air your views. As part of your argument, include a persuasive analogy or precedent.

Organizing a Resemblance Argument

The most typical way to develop a resemblance argument is as follows:

- Introduce the issue and state your claim.
- Develop your analogy or precedent.
- Draw the explicit parallels you want to highlight between your claim and the analogy or precedent.
- Anticipate and respond to objections (optional depending on space and context).

Of course, this structure can be varied in many ways, depending on your issue and rhetorical context. Sometimes writers open an argument with the analogy, which serves as an attention grabber.

Questioning and Critiquing a Resemblance Argument

Once you have written a draft of your letter or guest editorial, you can test its effectiveness by role-playing a skeptical audience. What follows are some typical questions audiences will raise about arguments of resemblance.

Will a skeptic say I am putting too much persuasive weight on my analogy or precedent? The most common mistake people make with resemblance arguments is expecting them to do too much. Too often, an analogy is mistakenly treated as a logical proof rather than a playful figure suggesting tentative but significant insights. The best way to guard against this charge is to qualify your argument and to find other means of persuasion to supplement an analogy or precedent argument.

Will a skeptic point out disanalogies in my resemblance argument? To refute a resemblance argument, you can highlight significant differences between the two things being compared rather than similarities. As one example, we have already shown you how Howard Zinn identified disanalogies between Europe in 1939 and Southeast Asia in 1965. Here is another example. When the United States was debating the Twenty-sixth Amendment, which lowered the voting age from twenty-one to eighteen, supporters of the amendment often argued, "If you are old enough to fight for your country in a war, you are old enough to vote." But conservative rhetorician Richard Weaver claimed that this analogy was true "only if you believe that fighting and voting are the same kind of thing which I, for one, do not. Fighting requires strength, muscular coordination and, in a modern army, instant and automatic response to orders. Voting requires knowledge of men, history, reasoning power; it is essentially a deliberative activity. Army mules and police dogs are used to fight; nobody is interested in giving them the right to vote. The argument rests on a false analogy."*

Readings

Our first reading is a letter to the editor by student Megan Matthews, written for the assignment on page 278. The letter responds to a news story in her local paper about whales damaged by Navy sonar. Notice how Megan uses an analogy to help readers imagine the effect of human-produced sea noise on marine mammals. Megan later used this analogy in the introduction to her researched argument shown on pages 418–425.

Whales Need Silence
Megan Matthews (student)

1   Re: "Whales beach themselves following NATO exercise" (news story, September 26). Imagine that you are forced to live in an apartment located next to Interstate 5 with its constant roar of engines and tires against concrete, its blaring horns and piercing sirens. When you open your windows in the summer, you have to shout to be heard. What if you had to leave your windows open all the time? What if your only housing alternatives were next to other freeways?

2   Seems impossible? Not for whales, dolphins, and other marine mammals. Jacques Cousteau's "world of silence" has been turned into an underwater freeway by the rumbling of cargo ships, the explosions of undersea mineral explorations, and the cacophony of the blasting devices used by fisheries. Now the Navy is adding a more powerful and dangerous source of sound with its low-frequency active sonar (LFA) for detecting enemy submarines. Low-frequency waves travel farther than high-frequency waves, which is why the bumping bass of a car stereo reverberates after the car passes you. In this case, 215 dB "pings" reflect off submarines—and

---

*Richard M. Weaver, "A Responsible Rhetoric," *The Intercollegiate Review,* Winter 1976–1977, 86–87.

whales—hundreds of miles away. The recent beaching incident in the Canary Islands reflects the danger that Navy sonar systems pose to whales.

Marine mammals depend on sound to avoid predators, to communicate across great distances between pods and prospective mates, and to establish mother-calf bonds. The extreme noise of Navy sonar apparently kills whales outright, while background "freeway" noise throughout the oceans may be threatening their ability to survive as communities.   3

Congress should not fund further implementation of LFA, which springs from an outdated Cold War model of warfare; the risks to our *environmental* security are too great.   4

Critiquing "Whales Need Silence"

1. What is the analogy in this piece?

2. How effective is this analogy? Does the analogy succeed in moving the readers toward a positive identification with the plight of whales and a negative view of low-frequency sonar?

3. The letter to the editor genre requires very short arguments that usually focus on one main point, but sometimes include brief summaries of more developed arguments. Compare Megan's letter to the editor with her researched argument on pages 418–425. What is the main point that Megan wishes to drive home in her letter to the editor? Where in the letter does she summarize portions of her longer argument? Based on your reading of Megan's researched argument, what other strategies might Megan have used to write a letter to the editor?

Our second reading, by liberal political analyst and syndicated columnist Matthew Miller, aims to persuade political conservatives to support progressive social policies such as health coverage for children and better safety nets for the unemployed. The article appeared in newspapers around the country during the last weeks in August 2004, just after Hurricane Charley had devastated parts of Florida.

It Shouldn't Take a Disaster to Help America's Blameless
Matthew Miller

It may seem odd to look for the silver lining in a cloud as dark as Hurricane Charley.   1

But if you listen closely, the reaction to the storm that has inflicted more than $10 billion in damage and upended countless lives offers a clue about our collective possibilities.   2

3   Why? Because when a natural disaster like Charley strikes, the proper role of government is unambiguous.

4   "We are here to help you," runs Gov. Jeb Bush's refrain as he tours the devastation. "There will be ramifications for many families . . . and we are prepared to provide support."

5   "This is God's way of telling us that he's almighty and we're mortal," Bush remarked at another stop.

6   "You can't plan for the unforeseen," Bush added. "And these are powerful storms that don't behave in any kind of way that you can say with certainty where they're going to go."

7   Over and over, as Gov. Bush and other officials struggle to cope, two related elements are cited to justify our communal response—things so obvious they hardly need to be articulated.

8   First, the forces at work are beyond anyone's control. Second, the people who have suffered from the storm are blameless victims of some very bad luck.

9   When these two conditions are present, even conservative Republicans stand instinctively ready to redistribute money (and help) to those who have been hurt by the storm.

10   See where I'm headed?

11   Oh, I can hear conservatives grumbling already. Isn't it just like a liberal to take a disaster like Charley and try to convert it into some fable about redistribution! Are you so sick and twisted, my mail will soon read, that you have to politicize this tragedy?

12   Well, that certainly doesn't sound like a question one should answer in the affirmative, but I suppose I'm guilty. You have to seize your teachable moments where you find them.

13   If we don't pause to parse our empathy in the wake of Charley, and ask ourselves, "If we're prepared to act here, where else does that mean we should be prepared to act," we're not doing right by our best instincts.

14   To take one example, poor children are about as blameless as you can get. Yet millions of these kids lack health coverage and decent schools.

15   Why can we agree to help Charley victims and let these kids languish?

16   It turns out that asking such questions isn't just grist for policy wonks like me. According to Michele Landis Dauber of Stanford Law School, the analogy to "disaster relief" has driven advances in social policy throughout American history.

17   In a smart book due out next year, *The Sympathetic State,* Dauber debunks the "false narrative" according to which America remained a nation of "rugged individualists" right up until the New Deal. Instead, Dauber's research shows that from the late 18th century onward, the federal government consistently stepped in to redistribute wealth, often via the politically popular vehicle of "disaster relief."

18   Such relief was legislated for the usual earthquakes, floods and fire. It also eased the pain of collateral damage in armed conflict, from the Whiskey Rebellion to the War of 1812 to the Civil War. It was this tradition and this metaphor that FDR's shrewd lawyers called on during the Depression to make their case for bold efforts to help the unemployed, and eventually to craft Social Security.

"They expanded the definition of what could count as a 'disaster' and who   19
could be eligible for relief as a 'blameless victim,'" Dauber explains.

Unemployment, for example, had never been seen as an external "disaster" be-   20
fore; you were jobless because of something wrong with your character. The
Depression let unemployment be recast as a macroeconomic version of Jeb Bush's
"powerful storms that don't behave in any kind of way that you can say with certainty where they're going to go."

Seen this way, the task for progressives in every era may be to push America's   21
compassion toward a new consensus that broadens the meaning of unmerited "disaster" and appropriate "relief."

Charley and this history of social progress offer hope by reminding us that deep   22
down, many conservatives are merely liberals waiting to be awakened. They just
need a little help connecting the dots when the accident of birth or hand of fate is
less dramatically (but no less truly) a "disaster."

Critiquing "It Shouldn't Take a Disaster to Help America's Blameless"

1. Miller's analogy argument asks conservatives such as Florida's Governor
   Jeb Bush the following question: If you believe it is the government's responsibility to help victims of a natural disaster such as Hurricane
   Charley, why don't you believe it is the responsibility of government to
   provide health insurance for children or aid to the unemployed? How
   does Miller support this analogy? What similarities does he find between
   victims of a hurricane and the additional people he would like conservatives to support?

2. What are the disanalogies that Miller keeps in the background? What significant differences are there between a hurricane victim and an unemployed person or a child without health insurance?

3. In addition to the analogy argument (the unemployed are like hurricane
   victims), Miller also makes a precedent argument through his summary of
   a new book, Dauber's *The Sympathetic State*. What precedents does Miller
   use to support his argument?

4. Miller's resemblance argument finally leads to a definitional argument
   about whether we should adopt a narrow or expanded definition of "disaster." How does Jeb Bush define "disaster"? How does Miller propose we
   define "disaster"?

5. How convincing do you find Miller's argument? Why or why not?

The third reading, a political cartoon by Sven Van Assche from the *Darien
Times*, enters into the public controversy over Internet censorship and the protection of children (see Figure 13.1). It speaks to the number of cases where chat

FIGURE 13.1

room correspondence between children and strangers has resulted in abduction, rape, and murder.

Critiquing the Internet Chat Room Cartoon

1. What is the analogy in this cartoon?
2. Consider the simplicity of the scene and the figure of the little girl in this cartoon. What is significant about the way the scene and the girl are depicted? What cultural associations do the words and the pictures in this cartoon draw on?
3. How effective do you think the analogy in this cartoon is in influencing readers' views of the problems of chat rooms?

Our last reading is from feminist writer Susan Brownmiller's *Against Our Will: Men, Women, and Rape.* First published in 1975, Brownmiller's book was chosen by the *New York Times Book Review* as one of the outstanding books of the year. In the following excerpt, Brownmiller makes an argument from resemblance, claiming that pornography is "anti-female propaganda."

From *Against Our Will: Men, Women, and Rape*

Susan Brownmiller

Pornography has been so thickly glossed over with the patina of chic these days in the name of verbal freedom and sophistication that important distinctions between freedom of political expression (a democratic necessity), honest sex education for children (a societal good) and ugly smut (the deliberate devaluation of the role of women through obscene, distorted depictions) have been hopelessly confused. Part of the problem is that those who traditionally have been the most vigorous opponents of porn are often those same people who shudder at the explicit mention of any sexual subject. Under their watchful, vigilant eyes, frank and free dissemination of educational materials relating to abortion, contraception, the act of birth, the female biology in general is also dangerous, subversive and dirty. (I am not unmindful that frank and free discussion of rape, "the unspeakable crime," might well give these righteous vigilantes further cause to shudder.) Because the battle lines were falsely drawn a long time ago, before there was a vocal women's movement, the antipornography forces appear to be, for the most part, religious, Southern, conservative and right-wing, while the pro-porn forces are identified as Eastern, atheistic and liberal.

But a woman's perspective demands a totally new alignment, or at least a fresh appraisal. The majority report of the President's Commission on Obscenity and Pornography (1970), a report that argued strongly for the removal of all legal restrictions on pornography, soft and hard, made plain that 90 percent of all pornographic material is geared to the male heterosexual market (the other 10 percent is geared to the male homosexual taste), that buyers of porn are "predominantly white, middle-class, middle-aged married males" and that the graphic depictions, the meat and potatoes of porn, are of the naked female body and of the multiplicity of acts done to that body.

Discussing the content of stag films, "a familiar and firmly established part of the American scene," the commission report dutifully, if foggily, explained, "Because pornography historically has been thought to be primarily a masculine interest, the emphasis in stag films seems to represent the preferences of the middle-class American male. Thus male homosexuality and bestiality are relatively rare, while lesbianism is rather common."

The commissioners in this instance had merely verified what purveyors of porn have always known: hard-core pornography is not a celebration of sexual freedom; it is a cynical exploitation of female sexual activity through the device of making all such activity, and consequently all females, "dirty." Heterosexual male consumers of pornography are frankly turned on by watching lesbians in action (although never in the final scenes, but always as a curtain raiser); they are turned off with a sudden swiftness of a water faucet by watching naked men act upon each other. One study quoted in the commission report came to the unastounding conclusion that "seeing a stag film in the presence of male peers bolsters masculine esteem." Indeed. The men in groups who watch the films, it is important to note, are *not* naked.

5   When male response to pornography is compared to female response, a pronounced difference in attitude emerges. According to the commission, "Males report being more highly aroused by depictions of nude females, and show more interest in depictions of nude females than [do] females." Quoting the figures of Alfred Kinsey, the commission noted that a majority of males (77 percent) were "aroused" by visual depictions of explicit sex while a majority of females (68 percent) were not aroused. Further, "females more often than males reported 'disgust' and 'offense.' "

6   From whence comes this female disgust and offense? Are females sexually backward or more conservative by nature? The gut distaste that a majority of women feel when we look at pornography, a distaste that, incredibly, it is no longer fashionable to admit, comes, I think, from the gut knowledge that we and our bodies are being stripped, exposed and contorted for the purpose of ridicule to bolster that "masculine esteem" which gets its kick and sense of power from viewing females as anonymous, panting playthings, adult toys, dehumanized objects to be used, abused, broken and discarded.

7   This, of course, is also the philosophy of rape. It is no accident (for what else could be its purpose?) that females in the pornographic genre are depicted in two cleanly delineated roles: as virgins who are caught and "banged" or as nymphomaniacs who are never sated. The most popular and prevalent pornographic fantasy combines the two: an innocent, untutored female is raped and "subjected to unnatural practices" that turn her into a raving, slobbering nymphomaniac, a dependent sexual slave who can never get enough of the big, male cock.

8   There can be no "equality" in porn, no female equivalent, no turning of the tables in the name of bawdy fun. Pornography, like rape, is a male invention, designed to dehumanize women, to reduce the female to an object of sexual access, not to free sensuality from moralistic or parental inhibition. The staple of porn will always be the naked female body, breasts and genitals exposed, because as man devised it, her naked body is the female's "shame," her private parts the private property of man, while his are the ancient, holy, universal, patriarchal instrument of his power, his rule by force over *her.*

9   Pornography is the undiluted essence of anti-female propaganda. Yet the very same liberals who were so quick to understand the method and purpose behind the mighty propaganda machine of Hitler's Third Reich, the consciously spewed-out anti-Semitic caricatures and obscenities that gave an ideological base to the Holocaust and the Final Solution, the very same liberals who, enlightened by blacks, searched their own conscience and came to understand that their tolerance of "nigger" jokes and portrayals of shuffling, rolling-eyed servants in movies perpetuated the degrading myths of black inferiority and gave an ideological base to the continuation of black oppression—these very same liberals now fervidly maintain that the hatred and contempt for women that find expression in four-letter words used as expletives and in what are quaintly called "adult" or "erotic" books and

movies are a valid extension of freedom of speech that must be preserved as a Constitutional right.

To defend the right of a lone, crazed American Nazi to grind out propaganda calling for the extermination of all Jews, as the ACLU has done in the name of free speech, is, after all, a self-righteous and not particularly courageous stand, for American Jewry is not currently threatened by storm troopers, concentration camps and imminent extermination, but I wonder if the ACLU's position might change if, come tomorrow morning, the bookstores and movie theaters lining Forty-second Street in New York City were devoted not to the humiliation of women by rape and torture, as they currently are, but to a systematized commercially successful propaganda machine depicting the sadistic pleasures of gassing Jews or lynching blacks? 10

Is this analogy extreme? Not if you are a woman who is conscious of the ever-present threat of rape and the proliferation of a cultural ideology that makes it sound like "liberated" fun. The majority report of the President's Commission on Obscenity and Pornography tried to pooh-pooh the opinion of law enforcement agencies around the country that claimed their own concrete experience with offenders who were caught with the stuff led them to conclude that pornographic material is a causative factor in crimes of sexual violence. The commission maintained that it was not possible at this time to scientifically prove or disprove such a connection. 11

But does one need scientific methodology in order to conclude that the antifemale propaganda that permeates our nation's cultural output promotes a climate in which acts of sexual hostility directed against women are not only tolerated but ideologically encouraged? A similar debate has raged for many years over whether or not the extensive glorification of violence (the gangster as hero; the loving treatment accorded bloody shoot-'em-ups in movies, books and on TV) has a causal effect, a direct relationship to the rising rate of crime, particularly among youth. Interestingly enough, in this area—nonsexual and not specifically related to abuses against women—public opinion seems to be swinging to the position that explicit violence in the entertainment media does have a deleterious effect; it makes violence commonplace, numbingly routine and no longer morally shocking. 12

More to the point, those who call for a curtailment of scenes of violence in movies and on television in the name of sensitivity, good taste and what's best for our children are not accused of being pro-censorship or against freedom of speech. Similarly, minority group organizations, black, Hispanic, Japanese, Italian, Jewish, or American Indian, that campaign against ethnic slurs and demeaning portrayals in movies, on television shows and in commercials are perceived as waging a just political fight, for if a minority group claims to be offended by a specific portrayal, be it Little Black Sambo or the Frito Bandito, and relates it to a history of ridicule and oppression, few liberals would dare to trot out a Constitutional argument in theoretical opposition, not if they wish to maintain their liberal credentials. Yet when it comes to the treatment of women, the liberal consciousness remains fiercely obdurate, refusing to be budged, for the sin of appearing square or prissy in the age of the so-called sexual revolution has become the worst offense of all. 13

Critiquing the Passage from *Against Our Will: Men, Women, and Rape*

1. Summarize Brownmiller's argument in your own words.

2. Brownmiller states that pornography degrades and humiliates women the same way that anti-Semitic literature degrades and humiliates Jews or that myths of black inferiority degrade and humiliate blacks. According to Brownmiller, how does pornography degrade and humiliate women?

3. What disanalogies might a skeptic point out between pornography and anti-Semitic or other racist propaganda?

4. One reviewer of Brownmiller's book said, "Get into this book and hardly a single thought to do with sex will come out the way it was." How does this passage from Brownmiller contribute to a public conversation about sexuality? What is thought provoking about this passage? How does it cause you to view sex differently?

14 Evaluation and Ethical Arguments

X Is (Is Not) a Good Y; X Is Right (Wrong)

CASE 1

A young engineer has advanced to the level of a design group leader. She is now being considered for promotion to a management position. Her present supervisor is asked to write a report evaluating her as a prospective manager. He is asked to pay particular attention to four criteria: technical competence, leadership, interpersonal skills, and communication skills.

CASE 2

Currently in the United States there are some 87,000 sick people waiting as much as six years for an organ transplant, with a portion of these dying before they can receive a transplant. The problem of organ shortages raises two kinds of evaluation issues. First, doctors are reevaluating the criteria by which they judge a "good organ"—that is, a good lung, kidney, or liver suitable for transplanting. Formerly, people who were elderly or obese or who had engaged in risky behaviors or suffered heart failure or other medical conditions were not considered sources of good organs. Now doctors are reconsidering these sources as well as exploring the use of organs from pigs. Second, the shortage of organs for donation has raised numerous ethical issues: Is it ethical for people to bypass the national waiting list for organs by advertising on billboards and Web sites? Is it morally right for people to sell their organs? Is it right for patients and families to buy organs or remunerate in any way living organ donors? Some states are passing laws that allow some financial compensation to living organ donors. (See an example of a billboard advertisement for a liver in the photo on p. 193.)

An Overview of Evaluation Arguments

In our roles as citizens and professionals, we are continually expected to make difficult evaluations and to persuade others to accept them. In this chapter we explain strategies for conducting two different kinds of evaluation arguments. First, we examine categorical evaluations of the kind "X is (is not) a good Y."* (Is Ramon a good committee chair? Is Design Approach A or Design Approach B the better solution to this engineering problem?) In such an evaluation, the writer determines the extent to which a given X meets or fulfills the qualities or standards of category Y. As we explain, these qualities or standards are usually based on the purposes of category Y. Second, we examine ethical arguments of the kind "X is right (wrong)." (Was it a right or wrong action to drop an atomic bomb on Hiroshima and Nagasaki? On a job application is it ethical to omit a briefly held job from which I was fired?) In these arguments, the writer evaluates a given X from the perspective of some system of morality or ethics.

Criteria-Match Structure of Categorical Evaluations

A categorical evaluation follows the same criteria-match structure that we examined in definitional arguments (see Chapter 11). A typical claim for such an argument has the following structure:

> X is (is not) a good Y because it meets (fails to meet) criteria A, B, and C.

The main conceptual difference between this kind of evaluation argument and a definition argument involves the Y term. In a definition argument, one argues whether a particular Y term is the correct class or category in which to place X. (Does this swampy area qualify as a *wetland?* For purposes of federal fuel-efficiency regulations, is an SUV a *truck* or a *car?*) In a categorical evaluation argument, we know the Y term—that is, what class or category to put X into. For example, we know that this 2002 Ford Escort is a *used car.* For a categorical evaluation, the question is whether this 2002 Ford Escort is a *good used car.* Or, to place the question within a rhetorical context, Is this Ford Escort a *good used car for me to buy for college?*

As an illustration of the criteria-match structure of a categorical evaluation, let's continue with the Ford Escort example. Suppose you get in a debate with Parent or Significant Other about the car you should buy for college. Let's say that Parent or Significant Other argues that the following criteria are particularly important: (1) value for the initial money, (2) dependability, (3) safety, and (4) low maintenance costs. (If you are into muscle cars, coolness, or driving excitement, you might shudder at these criteria!) Here is how an argument supporting the first criterion could be analyzed using the Toulmin system. Note that in evaluation arguments, as in definition arguments, warrants are the criteria for the evalu-

---

*In addition to the term *good*, a number of other evaluative terms involve the same kind of thinking— *effective, successful, workable, excellent, valuable*, and so forth.

ation while the stated reasons and grounds assert that the specific case meets these criteria.

Toulmin Analysis for Criterion 1: High Value for the Initial Money

ENTHYMEME: This 2002 Ford Escort is a good used car for you at college because it provides the most value for the initial money.

CLAIM: This 2002 Ford Escort is a good used car for you at college.

STATED REASON: because it provides the most value for the initial money

GROUNDS: Used Ford Escorts give high value at less cost because they are basically boring but dependable cars that don't have high demand in the used car market; this lack of demand means that you can get a 2002 Escort for $5,000 less than a comparable 2002 Honda Civic with similar mileage; this particular Escort has only 65,000 miles; a 2002 Honda Civic for the same price would have 120,000 miles or more. This 2002 Ford Escort thus gives you a low mileage car at a reasonable price—high value for the initial money.

WARRANT: High value for the initial money is an important criterion for buying your college car.

BACKING: Arguments showing why it is important to get high value for the money: money saved on the car can be used for other college expenses; low initial mileage means you can get years of dependable use without having to rebuild an engine or transmission; buying in this conservative and wise way meets our family's image of being careful, utilitarian shoppers.

CONDITIONS OF REBUTTAL: *Attacking stated reason and grounds:* Perhaps this 2002 Ford Escort isn't as good a value as it seems; my research suggests it has high projected maintenance costs after 60,000 miles; initial savings may be blown on high maintenance costs.

Attacking warrant and backing: Other criteria are more important to me: I value great handling and acceleration, the fun of driving, and the status of having a cool car. The Ford Escort doesn't meet these criteria.

As this Toulmin schema shows, Parent or Significant Other needs to argue that getting high value for the initial money is an important consideration (the criterion argument) and that this 2002 Ford Escort meets this criterion better than competing choices (the match argument). If you can't see yourself driving a Ford Escort, you've either got to argue for other criteria (attack the warrant) or accept the criterion but argue that the Ford Escort's projected maintenance costs undermine its initial value (attack the reason and grounds).

Conducting a Categorical Evaluation Argument

Now that you understand the basic criteria-match structure of a categorical evaluation, let's consider the thinking strategies used for determining criteria and for arguing that your given X meets or does not meet the criteria.

Determining Criteria for a Categorical Evaluation Argument

How do you develop criteria for a categorical evaluation? What distinguishes a successful manager from a poor one, a good studying place from a bad one, or a more effective treatment for obesity from a less effective treatment? In this section we turn to the practical problem of finding criteria you'll need for conducting your categorical evaluation argument.

Step 1: Determine the Category in Which the Object Being Evaluated Belongs In determining the quality or value of any given X, you must first figure out the category in which X belongs. For example, if you asked one of your professors to write you a letter of recommendation for a summer job, what class of things should the professor put you into? Is he or she supposed to evaluate you as a student? a budding scholar in the field? a mentor to younger students? a leader? a team player? or what? This is an important question because the criteria for excellence in one class (budding scholar in the field) may be very different from criteria for excellence in another class (leader or team player).

To write a useful, effective letter, your professor needs to think beyond the general class "summer job holder" and focus on your qualifications in the context of the smallest applicable class of candidates: not "summer job holder," but "lab assistant," "law office intern," "camp counselor," or "recreation planner at a resort." Clearly, each of these subclasses has very different criteria for excellence that your professor needs to address.

We thus recommend placing X into the smallest relevant class because of the apples-and-oranges law. That is, to avoid giving a mistaken rating to a perfectly good apple, you need to make sure you are judging an apple under the class "apple" and not under the next larger class "fruit" or a neighboring class "orange." And to be even more precise, you may wish to evaluate your apple in the class "eating apple" as opposed to "pie apple" because the latter class is supposed to be tarter and the former class juicier and sweeter.

Step 2: Determine the Purpose or Function of This Class Once you have located X in its appropriate class, you should next determine what the purpose or function of this class is. Let's suppose that the summer job you are applying for is tour guide at the city zoo. The function of a tour guide is to make people feel welcome, to give them interesting information about the zoo, to make their visit pleasant, and so forth. Consequently, you wouldn't want your professor's evaluation to praise your term paper on Napoleon Bonaparte or your successful synthesis of some compound in your chemistry lab. Rather, the professor should highlight your dependability, your neat appearance, your good speaking skills, and your ability to work with groups. But if you were applying for graduate school, then your term paper on Bonaparte or your chem lab wizardry would be relevant. In other words, the professor has to evaluate you according to the class "tour guide," not "graduate student," and the criteria for each class derive from the purpose or function of the class.

Let's take another example. Suppose that you are the chair of a committee charged with evaluating the job performance of Lillian Jones, director of the admissions office at a small, private college. Ms. Jones has been a controversial manager because several members of her staff have filed complaints about her management style. In making your evaluation, your first step is to place Ms. Jones into an appropriate class, in this case, the general class "manager," and then the more specific class "manager of an admissions office at a small, private college." You then need to identify the purpose or function of these classes. You might say that the function of the general class "managers" is to "oversee actual operations of an organization so that the organization meets its goals as harmoniously and efficiently as possible," whereas the function of the specific class "manager of an admissions office at a small, private college" is "the successful recruitment of the best students possible."

Step 3: Determine Criteria Based on the Purposes or Function of the Class to Which X Belongs Once you've worked out the purposes of the class, you are ready to work out the criteria by which you judge all members of the class. Criteria for judgment will be based on those features of Y that help it achieve the purposes of its class. For example, once you determine the purpose and function of the position filled by Lillian Jones, you can develop a list of criteria for managerial success:

1. Criteria related to "efficient operation"
   - articulates priorities and goals for the organization
   - is aggressive in achieving goals
   - motivates fellow employees
   - is well organized, efficient, and punctual
   - is articulate and communicates well
2. Criteria related to "harmonious operation"
   - creates job satisfaction for subordinates
   - is well groomed, sets good example of professionalism
   - is honest, diplomatic in dealing with subordinates
   - is flexible in responding to problems and special concerns of staff members

3. Criteria related to meeting specific goals of a college admissions office
   - creates a comprehensive recruiting program
   - demonstrates that recruiting program works

Step 4: Give Relative Weightings to the Criteria Even though you have established criteria, you must still decide which of the criteria are most important. In the case of Lillian Jones, is it more important that she bring in lots of students or that she create a harmonious, happy office? These sorts of questions are at the heart of many evaluative controversies. Thus a justification for your weighting of criteria may well be an important part of your argument.

Determining Whether X Meets the Criteria

Once you've established your criteria, you've got to figure out how well X meets them. You proceed by gathering evidence and examples. In the Lillian Jones case, the success of the college's recruiting program can probably be measured empirically, so you gather statistics about applications to the college, SAT scores of applicants, number of acceptances, academic profiles of entering freshmen, and so forth. You might then compare those statistics to those compiled by Ms. Jones's predecessor or to her competitors at other, comparable institutions.

You can also look at what the recruiting program actually does—the number of recruiters, the number of high school visits, the quality of admissions brochures and other publications. You can also look at Ms. Jones in action, searching for specific incidents or examples that illustrate her management style. For example, you can't measure a trait such as diplomacy empirically, but you can find specific instances where the presence or absence of this trait was demonstrated. You could turn to examples where Ms. Jones may or may not have prevented a potentially divisive situation from occurring or where she offered or failed to offer encouragement at psychologically the right moment to keep someone from getting demoralized. As with criteria-match arguments in definition, one must provide examples of how the X in question meets each of the criteria that have been set up.

Your final evaluation of Ms. Jones, then, might include an overview of her strengths and weaknesses along the various criteria you have established. You might say that Ms. Jones has done an excellent job with recruitment (an assertion you can support with data on student enrollments over the last five years) but was relatively poor at keeping the office staff happy (as evidenced by employee complaints, high turnover, and your own observations of her rather abrasive management style). Nevertheless, your final recommendation might be to retain Ms. Jones for another three-year contract because you believe that an excellent recruiting record is the most important criterion for her position. You might justify this heavy weighting of recruiting on the grounds that the institution's survival depends on its ability to attract adequate numbers of good students.

For Class Discussion

The following small-group exercise can be accomplished in one or two class hours. It gives you a good model of the process you can go through in order to write your own categorical evaluation. Working in small groups, suppose that you are going to evaluate a controversial member of one of the following classes:

a. an athlete, a coach, a component of an athletic team (for example, the offensive line of a football team) or a whole team; a politician or officeholder; a teacher or administrator

b. a proposed or current law, a government regulation, or a government policy

c. a student service provided by your school, or any school policy or regulation; a school newspaper, a radio station, an intramural program, or a student government policy or service

d. a teaching method, your school's plagiarism policy, a homework assignment, a library orientation, or some other controversial academic policy or method

e. a play, a film, a music video, or a Web site; an actor, a director, a dancer, or other performer

f. an advertising campaign or a specific advertisement, a store, or a customer service department

g. an employer, a boss, a work policy, or a particular work environment

h. a day care center or school; a physician, dentist, or health care agency or policy

i. a restaurant, a college hangout, a vacation spot, or a study place

j. any controversial X of your choice

1. Choose a controversial member within one of these classes as the specific person, thing, or event you are going to evaluate (your school's Computer Services Help Desk, the Invite-a-Professor-to-Lunch program in your dormitory, a recent controversial film, Harvey's Hamburger Haven).

2. If not already apparent, stipulate a rhetorical context that gives importance to the issue, focuses the argument, and places the controversial X within the smallest relevant class. (Do you want to evaluate Harvey's Hamburger Haven in the broad category of *restaurants,* in the narrow category of *hamburger joints,* or in a different narrow category such as *late-night study places?* If you are evaluating a recent film, are you evaluating it as an *action film for guys,* as a possible *Academy Award nominee,* or as a *political filmmaking statement against corporate greed?*)

3. Make a list of the purposes or functions of that class, and then list the criteria that a good member of that class would need to have in order to accomplish

the purpose or function. (What is the purpose or function of a Computer Services Help Desk, an action film for guys, or a late-night study place? What criteria for excellence can you derive from these purposes or functions?)

4. If necessary, rank your criteria in order to show that X is superior (inferior) to a close competitor. (For a late-night study place, what is more important: good music to study by or cheap coffee? An Internet connection or convenience of the location?)

5. Evaluate your X by matching X to each of the criteria. (As a late-night study place, Harvey's Hamburger Haven has the best lighting, the shortest walk from campus, the least expensive coffee, and the best music to study by, but it doesn't offer Internet access and sometimes has too many rowdies. Therefore it ranks second to Carol's Coffee Closet.)

An Overview of Ethical Arguments

A second kind of evaluation argument focuses on moral or ethical issues, which can often merge or overlap with categorical evaluations. For example, many apparently straightforward categorical evaluations can turn out to have an ethical dimension. Consider again the criteria for buying a car. Most people would base their evaluations on cost, safety, comfort, stylishness, and so forth. But some people might feel morally obligated to buy the most fuel-efficient car (perhaps even an electric or hybrid car despite the extra cost), or not to buy a car from a manufacturer whose investment or labor policies they find morally repugnant. Depending on how large a role ethical considerations play in the evaluation, we might choose to call this an ethical argument based on moral considerations rather than a categorical evaluation based on the purposes of a class or category.

It is uncertainty about "purpose" that makes ethical evaluations particularly complex. In making a categorical evaluation, we assume that every class or category of being has a purpose, that the purpose should be defined as narrowly as possible, and that the criteria for judgment derive directly from that purpose. For example, the purpose of a computer repairperson is to analyze the problem with my computer, to fix it, and to do so in a timely and cost-efficient manner. Once I formulate this purpose, it is easy for me to define criteria for a good computer repairperson.

In ethics, however, the place of purpose is much fuzzier. Just what is the purpose of human beings? Before I can begin to determine what ethical duties I have to myself and to others, I'm going to have to address this question. What is my purpose in life? What kind of life do I want to lead? In ethical discussions we don't ask what a "manager" or a "judge" or a "point guard" is supposed to do in situations relevant to the respective classes. Who persons are or what their social function is makes no difference to our ethical assessment of their actions or traits of character. A morally bad person may be a good judge, and a morally good person may be a bad manager and a worse point guard.

As the discussion so far has suggested, disagreements about ethical issues often stem from different systems of values that make the issue irresolvable. It is precisely this problem—the lack of shared assumptions about value—that makes it so important to confront issues of ethics with rational deliberation. The arguments you produce may not persuade others to your view, but they should make others think seriously about it, and they should help you work out more clearly the reasons and warrants for your own beliefs. By writing about ethical issues, you see more clearly what you believe and why you believe it. Although the arguments demanded by ethical issues require rigorous thought, they force us to articulate our most deeply held beliefs and our richest feelings.

Two Major Ethical Systems

When we are faced with an ethical issue, we must move from arguments of good or bad to arguments of right or wrong. The terms *right* and *wrong* are clearly different from the terms *good* and *bad* when the latter terms mean simply "effective" (meets purposes of class, as in "This is a good stereo system") or "ineffective" (fails to meet purposes of class, as in "This is a bad cookbook"). But *right* and *wrong* often also differ from what seems to be a moral use of the terms *good* and *bad*. We might say, for example, that sunshine is good because it brings pleasure and that cancer is bad because it brings pain and death, but that is not quite the same thing as saying that sunshine is "right" and cancer is "wrong." It is the problem of "right" and "wrong" that ethical arguments confront.

For example, from a nonethical standpoint, you could say that certain persons are "good terrorists" in that they fully realize the purpose of the class "terrorist": They cause great anguish and damage with a minimum of resources, and they bring much attention to their cause. However, if we want to condemn terrorism on ethical grounds, we have to say that terrorism is wrong. The ethical question is not whether a person fulfills the purposes of the class "terrorist," but whether it is wrong for such a class to exist.

There are many schools of ethical thought—too many to cover in this brief overview—so we'll limit ourselves to two major systems: arguments from consequences and arguments from principles.

Consequences as the Base of Ethics

Perhaps the best-known example of evaluating acts according to their ethical consequences is utilitarianism, a down-to-earth philosophy that grew out of nineteenth-century British philosophers' concern to demystify ethics and make it work in the practical world. Jeremy Bentham, the originator of utilitarianism, developed the goal of the greatest good for the greatest number, or "greatest happiness," by which he meant the most pleasure for the least pain. John Stuart Mill, another British philosopher, built on Bentham's utilitarianism, using predicted consequences to determine the morality of a proposed action.

Mill's consequentialist approach allows you readily to assess a wide range of acts. You can apply the principle of utility—which says that an action is morally right if it produces a greater net value (benefits minus costs) than any available alternative action—to virtually any situation, and it will help you reach a decision. Obviously, however, it's not always easy to make the calculations called for by the principle, since, like any prediction of the future, an estimate of consequences is conjectural. In particular, it's often very hard to assess the long-term consequences of any action. Too often, utilitarianism seduces us into a short-term analysis of a moral problem simply because long-term consequences are very difficult to predict.

Principles as the Base of Ethics

Any ethical system based on principles will ultimately rest on moral tenets that we are duty bound to uphold, no matter what the consequences. Sometimes the moral tenets come from religious faith—for example, the Ten Commandments. At other times, however, the principles are derived from philosophical reasoning, as in the case of German philosopher Immanuel Kant. Kant held that no one should ever use another person as a means to his own ends and that everyone should always act as if his acts were the basis of universal law. In other words, Kant held that we are duty bound to respect other people's sanctity and to act in the same way that we would want all other people to act. The great advantage of such a system is its clarity and precision. We are never overwhelmed by a multiplicity of contradictory and difficult-to-quantify consequences; we simply make sure we are not violating a principle of our ethical system and proceed accordingly.

Conducting an Ethical Argument

To show you how to conduct an ethical argument, let's now apply these two strategies to an example. In general, you can conduct an ethical evaluation by using the frame for either a principles-based argument or a consequences-based argument or a combination of both.

> *Principles-Based Frame:* X is right (wrong) because it follows (violates) principles A, B, and C.
>
> *Consequences-Based Frame:* X is right (wrong) because it will lead to consequences A, B, and C, which are good (bad).

To illustrate how these frames might help you develop an ethical argument, let's use them to develop arguments for or against capital punishment.

Constructing a Principles-Based Argument

A principles-based argument looks at capital punishment through the lens of one or more guiding principles. Kant's principle that we are duty bound not to violate the sanctity of other human lives could lead to arguments opposing capital punishment. One might argue as follows:

> *Principles-based argument opposing capital punishment:* The death penalty is wrong because it violates the principle of the sanctity of human life.

You could support this principle either by summarizing Kant's argument that one should not violate the selfhood of another person or by pointing to certain religious systems such as Judeo-Christian ethics, where one is told "Vengeance is Mine, saith the Lord" or "Thou shalt not kill." To develop this argument further, you might examine two exceptions where principles-based ethicists may allow killing—self-defense and war—and show how capital punishment does not fall in either category.

Principles-based arguments can also be developed to support capital punishment. You may be surprised to learn that Kant himself—despite his arguments for the sanctity of life—actually supported capital punishment. To make such an argument, Kant evoked a different principle about the suitability of the punishment to the crime:

> There is no sameness of kind between death and remaining alive even under the most miserable conditions, and consequently there is no equality between the crime and the retribution unless the criminal is judicially condemned and put to death.

Stated as an enthymeme, Kant's argument is as follows:

> *Principles-based argument supporting capital punishment:* Capital punishment is right because it follows the principle that punishments should be proportionate to the crime.

In developing this argument, Kant's burden is to show why the principle of proportionate retribution outweighs the principle of the supreme worth of the individual. Our point is that a principles-based argument can be made both for or against capital punishment. The arguer's duty is to make clear what principle is being evoked and then to show why this principle is more important than opposing principles.

Constructing a Consequences-Based Argument

Unlike a principles-based argument, which appeals to certain guiding maxims or rules, a consequences-based argument looks at the consequences of a decision and measures the positive benefits against the negative costs. Here is the frame that an arguer might use to oppose capital punishment on the basis of negative consequences:

Consequences-based argument opposing capital punishment: Capital punishment is wrong because it leads to the following negative consequences:

- The possibility of executing an innocent person
- The possibility that a murderer who might repent and be redeemed is denied that chance
- The excessive legal and political costs of trials and appeals
- The unfair distribution of executions so that one's chances of being put to death are much greater if one is a minority or is poor

To develop this argument, the reader would need to provide facts, statistics, and other evidence to support each of the stated reasons.

A different arguer might use a consequences-based approach to support capital punishment:

Consequences-based argument supporting capital punishment: Capital punishment is right because it leads to the following positive consequences:

- It may deter violent crime and slow down the rate of murder.
- It saves the cost of lifelong imprisonment.
- It stops criminals who are menaces to society from committing more murders.
- It helps grieving families reach closure and sends a message to victims' families that society recognizes their pain.

It should be evident, then, that adopting an ethical system doesn't lead to automatic answers to one's ethical dilemmas. A system offers a way of proceeding—a way of conducting an argument—but it doesn't relieve you of personal responsibility for thinking through your values and taking a stand. When you face an ethical dilemma, we encourage you to consider both the relevant principles and the possible consequences the dilemma entails. In many arguments, you can use both principles-based and consequences-based reasoning as long as irreconcilable contradictions don't present themselves.

For Class Discussion

Working as individuals or in small groups:

1. Formulate a consequences-based argument in favor of biotech agriculture (see the readings and discussion in Chapter 2, pp. 25–28 and 41–43).

2. Now formulate a consequences-based argument opposing biotech agriculture.

3. How might a principles-based argument be constructed for or against biotech agriculture? For or against therapeutic or reproductive cloning?

4. When people argue about owning SUVs or hybrid cars, the controversies can be either categorical or ethical or both.

a. How would you make a categorical evaluation argument that SUVs are good (bad) cars for families in urban environments?

b. How would you make an ethical argument that it is morally right or wrong to buy an SUV?

c. How would you make a categorical evaluation argument that hybrids are good (bad) commuter cars?

d. How would you make an ethical argument that it is morally right or wrong for the government to pressure car companies into converting all their manufacturing to hybrids and fuel-efficient cars?

Common Problems in Making Evaluation Arguments

When conducting evaluation arguments (whether categorical or ethical), writers can bump up against recurring problems that are unique to evaluation. In some cases these problems complicate the establishment of criteria; in other cases they complicate the match argument. Let's look briefly at some of these common problems.

- *The problem of standards—What's commonplace versus what's ideal:* To appreciate this problem, consider again Young Person's archetypal argument with Parent about her curfew (see Chapter 1, pp. 8–9). She originally argued that staying out until 2 A.M. is fair "because all the other kids' parents let their kids stay out late," to which Parent might respond: "Well, *ideally*, all the other parents should not let their kids stay out that late." Young Person based her criterion for fairness on what is *commonplace*; her standards arose from common practices of a social group. Parent, however, argued from what is *ideal*, basing her or his criterion on some external standard that transcends social groups. We experience this dilemma in various forms all the time. Is it fair to get a ticket for going 70 mph on a 65-mph freeway when most of the drivers go 70 mph or higher? (Does what is *commonplace*—going 70—override what is *ideal*—obeying the law?) Is it better for high schools to pass out free contraceptives to students because students are having sex anyway (what's *commonplace*), or is it better not to pass them out in order to support abstinence (what's *ideal*)?

- *The problem of mitigating circumstances:* This problem occurs when an arguer claims that unusual circumstances should alter our usual standards of judgment. Ordinarily, it is fair for a teacher to reduce a grade if you turn in a paper late. But what if you were up all night taking care of a crying baby? Does that count as a *mitigating circumstance* to waive the ordinary criterion? What about your annual performance evaluation during a year when you had chronic back pain or were going through a divorce? When you argue for mitigating circumstances, you will likely assume an especially heavy burden of proof. People assume the rightness of usual standards of judgment unless there are compelling arguments for abnormal circumstances.

- *The problem of choosing between two goods or two bads:* Often an evaluation issue forces us between a rock and a hard place. Should we cut pay or cut people? Put our parents in a nursing home or let them stay at home where they have become a danger to themselves? Take the road trip I had planned across the United States or take the new job offer? In such cases one has to weigh conflicting criteria, knowing that the choices are too much alike—either both bad or both good.

- *The problem of seductive empirical measures:* The need to make high-stakes evaluations has led many persons to seek quantifiable criteria that can be weighed mathematically. Thus we use grade point averages to select scholarship winners, student evaluation scores to decide merit pay for teachers, SAT scores and GPAs for college admissions, and combined scores of judges to rank figure skaters. In some cases, empirical measures can be quite acceptable, but they are often dangerous because they discount important nonquantifiable traits. The problem with empirical measures is that they seduce us into believing that complex judgments can be made mathematically, thus rescuing us from the messiness of alternative points of view and conflicting criteria.

- *The problem of cost:* A final problem that can crop up in evaluations is cost. X may be the best of all possible Ys, but if X costs too much, we have to go for second or third best. We can avoid this problem somewhat by placing items into different classes on the basis of cost. For example, a Mercedes will exceed a Hyundai on almost any criterion, but if we can't afford more than a Hyundai, the comparison is pointless. It is better to compare a Mercedes to a Lexus and a Hyundai to an equivalent Ford. Whether costs are expressed in dollars, personal discomfort, moral repugnance, or some other terms, our final evaluation of X must take cost into account.

Writing an Evaluation Argument

WRITING ASSIGNMENT
FOR CHAPTER 14

Write an argument in which you try to change someone's mind about the value of X. The X you choose should be controversial or at least problematic. By *controversial* or *problematic*, we mean that people are likely to disagree with your evaluation of X, that they are surprised at your evaluation, or that you are somehow opposing the common or expected view of X. By choosing a controversial or problematic X, you will be able to focus on a clear issue. Somewhere in your essay you should summarize alternative views and either refute them or concede to them (see Chapter 8).

Note that this assignment asks you to do something different from a typical movie review, restaurant review, or product review in a consumer magazine. Many reviews are simply informational or analytical; the writer's purpose is to describe the object or event being reviewed and explain its strengths and weaknesses. In contrast, your purpose here is persuasive. You must change someone's mind about the evaluation of X.

Exploring Ideas

Evaluation issues are all around us. Some have high stakes involving long-term commitments or investments of time and money: Is criminal justice a better major for me than creative writing? Is this food bank a good program to support financially with our club's earnings? Is this private driving school a good place to refer international students who need to learn to drive? Other evaluation arguments entail interpretations and insights that can indirectly have real-world impacts: Is *War of the Worlds* a "good science fiction film"? Is it a "good film adapted from a novel" (by H. G. Wells)? Note that this topic becomes more provocative when we place X in an unexpected class. Is *War of the Worlds* a "good political commentary on contemporary global insecurity"?

If you are not currently involved in an organization, job, or community faced with the need to conduct an evaluation and make decisions, you could try brainstorming using the following categories: *people* (athletes, political leaders, musicians, clergy, entertainers, businesspeople); *science and technology* (weapons systems, word-processing programs, spreadsheets, automotive advancements, treatments for diseases); *media* (a newspaper, a magazine or journal, a TV program, a radio station, a Web site, an advertisement); *government and world affairs* (an economic policy, a Supreme Court decision, a law or legal practice, a government custom or practice, a foreign policy); *the arts* (a movie, a book, a building, a painting, a piece of music); *your college or university* (a course, a teacher, a textbook, a curriculum, an administrative policy, the financial aid system); *world of work* (a job, a company operation, a dress policy, a merit pay system, a hiring policy, a supervisor); or any other categories of your choice.

Then brainstorm possibilities for controversial Xs that might fit into the categories you have listed. As long as you can imagine disagreement about how to evaluate X, you have a potentially good topic for this assignment.

Once you have found an issue and have taken a tentative position on it, explore your ideas by freewriting your responses to the ten guided tasks in Chapter 3 (pp. 70–71).

Organizing an Evaluation Argument

As you write a draft, you might find useful the following prototypical structures for evaluation arguments. Of course, you can always alter these plans if another structure better fits your material.

Plan 1 (Criteria and Match in Separate Sections)

- Introduce the issue by showing disagreements about how to evaluate a problematic X (Is X a good Y? Is X right or wrong?).
- State your claim.
- Present your criteria for making the evaluation.

  State and develop criterion 1.

  State and develop criterion 2.

  Continue with the rest of your criteria.

- Summarize and respond to possible objections to your criteria.
- Restate your claim, asserting that X is (is not) a good member of class Y or that X is right (wrong).

  Apply criterion 1 to your case.

  Apply criterion 2 to your case.

  Continue the match argument.

- Summarize and respond to possible objections to your match argument.
- Conclude your argument.

Plan 2 (Criteria and Match Interwoven)

- Introduce the issue by showing disagreements about how to evaluate a problematic X (Is X a good Y? Is X right or wrong?).
- Present your claim.

  State criterion 1 and argue that your X meets (does not meet) this criterion.

  State criterion 2 and argue that your X meets (does not meet) this criterion.

  Continue with criteria-match sections for additional criteria.

- Summarize opposing views.
- Refute or concede to opposing views.
- Conclude your argument.

Revising Your Draft

Once you have written a rough draft, your goal is to make it clearer and more persuasive to your audience. Where might your audience question your claim, demand more evidence, or ask for further clarification and support of your criteria? One way to evaluate your draft's persuasiveness is to analyze it using the Toulmin schema.

Imagine that you are on a committee to determine whether to retain or fire Ms. Lillian Jones, the director of admissions in the example we examined on page 293. You have been asked to submit a written argument to the committee. Here is how you might use Toulmin to suggest revision strategies for making your argument more persuasive (your thinking processes are indicated in italics):

ENTHYMEME: Despite some weaknesses, Ms. Jones has been a good manager of the admissions office because her office's recruiting record is excellent.

CLAIM: Ms. Jones has been a good manager of the admissions office.

STATED REASON: Her office's recruitment record is excellent.

GROUNDS: *My draft has statistical data showing the good results of Ms. Jones's recruiting efforts. Can I get more data? Do I need more data? Would other grounds be useful such as testimony from other college officials or comparison with other schools?*

WARRANT: Successful recruitment is the most important criterion for rating job performance of the director of admissions.

BACKING: *In my draft I don't have any backing. I am just assuming that everyone will agree that recruiting is the most important factor. But a lot of people are angry at Ms. Jones for personnel problems in her office. How can I argue that her recruitment record is the most important criterion? I could mention that maintaining a happy, harmonious staff serves no purpose if we have no students. I could remind people of how much tuition dollars drive our budget; if enrollments go down, we're in big trouble.*

CONDITIONS OF REBUTTAL: *How could committee members who don't like Ms. Jones question my reason and grounds? Could they show that her recruitment record isn't that good? Might they argue that plenty of people in the office could do the same good job of recruitment—after all, this college sells itself—without stirring up any of the personnel problems that Ms. Jones has caused? Maybe I should add to the draft the specific things that Ms. Jones has done to improve recruiting.*
Will anyone attack my warrant by arguing that staff problems in Ms. Jones's office are severe enough that we ought to search for a new director? How can I counter that argument?

QUALIFIER: *I will need to qualify my general rating of an excellent record by acknowledging Ms. Jones's weaknesses in staff relations. But I want to be definite in saying that recruitment is the most important criterion and that she should definitely keep her job because she meets this criterion fully.*

Questioning and Critiquing an Evaluation Argument

To strengthen your draft, you can role-play a skeptic in order to probe weaknesses in your ideas and develop ways to overcome them.

Critiquing a Categorical Evaluation Argument

Here is a list of questions you can use to critique a categorical evaluation argument:
Will a skeptic accept my criteria? Many evaluative arguments are weak because the writers have simply assumed that readers will accept their criteria. Whenever

your audience's acceptance of your criteria is in doubt, you will need to make your warrants clear and provide backing in their support.

Are my criteria based on the "smallest applicable class" for X? For example, the 1999 film *The Blair Witch Project* will certainly be a failure if you evaluate it in the general class "movies," in which it would have to compete with *Citizen Kane* and other great classics. But if you evaluated it as a "horror film" or a "low-budget film," it would have a greater chance for success and hence of yielding an arguable evaluation.

Will a skeptic accept my general weighting of criteria? Another vulnerable spot in an evaluation argument is the relative weight of the criteria. How much anyone weights a given criterion is usually a function of his or her own interests relative to the X in question. You should always ask whether some particular group affected by the quality of X might not have good reasons for weighting the criteria differently.

Will a skeptic question my standard of reference? In questioning the criteria for judging X, we can also focus on the standard of reference used—what's commonplace versus what's ideal. If you have argued that X is bad because it doesn't live up to what's ideal, you can expect some readers to defend X on the basis of what's common. Similarly, if you argue that X is good because it is better than its competitors, you can expect some readers to point out how short it falls from what is ideal.

Will a skeptic criticize my use of empirical measures? The tendency to mistake empirical measures for criteria is a common one that any critic of an argument should be aware of. As we have discussed earlier, what's most measurable isn't always significant when it comes to assessing the essential traits needed to fulfill whatever function X is supposed to fulfill. A 95-mph fastball is certainly an impressive empirical measure of a pitcher's ability—but if the pitcher doesn't get batters out, that measure is a misleading gauge of performance.

Will a skeptic accept my criteria but reject my match argument? The other major way of testing an evaluation argument is to anticipate how readers might object to your stated reasons and grounds. Will readers challenge you by finding sampling errors in your data or otherwise find that you used evidence selectively? For example, if you think your opponents will emphasize Lillian Jones's abrasive management style much more heavily than you did, you may be able to undercut their arguments by finding counterexamples that show Ms. Jones acting diplomatically. Be prepared to counter objections to your grounds.

Critiquing an Ethical Argument

Perhaps the first question you should ask in setting out to analyze your draft of an ethical argument is "To what extent is the argument based on consequences or on ethical principles?" If it's based exclusively on one of these two forms of ethical thought, then it's vulnerable to the sorts of criticism discussed here. A strictly principled argument that takes no account of the consequences of its position is vulnerable to a simple cost analysis. What are the costs in the case of adhering to this principle? There will undoubtedly be some, or else there would be no real argument. If the argument is based strictly on consequentialist grounds, we should ask if the position violates any rules or principles, particularly such commandments as the Golden Rule—"Do unto others as you would have others do unto you"—which most members of our audience adhere to. By failing to mention these alternative ways of thinking about ethical issues, we undercut not only our argument but our credibility as well.

Let's now consider a more developed examination of the two positions, starting with some of the more subtle weaknesses in a position based on principle. In practice people will sometimes take rigidly "principled" positions because they live in fear of "slippery slopes"; that is, they fear setting precedents that might lead to ever more dire consequences. Consider, for example, the slippery slope leading from birth control to euthanasia if you have an absolutist commitment to the sanctity of human life. Once we allow birth control in the form of condoms or the pill, the principled absolutist would say, then we will be forced to accept birth control "abortions" in the first hours after conception (IUDs, "morning after" pills), then abortions in the first trimester, then in the second or even the third trimester. And once we have violated the sanctity of human life by allowing abortions, it is only a short step to euthanasia and finally to killing off all undesirables.

One way to refute a slippery-slope argument of this sort is to try to dig a foothold into the side of the hill to show that you don't necessarily have to slide all the way to the bottom. You would thus have to argue that allowing birth control does not mean allowing abortions (by arguing for differences between a fetus after conception and sperm and egg before conception), or that allowing abortions does not mean allowing euthanasia (by arguing for differences between a fetus and a person already living in the world).

Consequentialist arguments have different kinds of difficulties. As discussed before, the crucial difficulty facing anyone making a consequentialist argument is to calculate the consequences in a clear and reliable way. Have you considered all significant consequences? If you project your scenario of consequences further into the future (remember, consequentialist arguments are frequently stronger over the short term than over the long term, where many unforeseen consequences can occur), can you identify possibilities that work against the argument?

As also noted, consequentialist arguments carry a heavy burden of empirical proof. What evidence can you offer that the predicted consequences will in fact come to pass? Do you offer any evidence that alternative consequences won't occur? And just how do you prove that the consequences of any given action are a net good or evil?

In addition to the problems unique to each of the two positions, ethical arguments are vulnerable to the more general sorts of criticism, including consistency, recency, and relevance of evidence. Obviously, however, consequentialist arguments will be more vulnerable to weaknesses in evidence, whereas arguments based on principle are more open to questions about consistency of application.

Readings

Our first reading, by student writer Sam Isaacson, was written for the assignment on page 302. It joins a conversation about whether the legalization of same-sex marriage would be good for our society. However, Isaacson, a gay writer, limits the question to whether legalization of same-sex marriage would be *good for the gay community*. Earlier in this text (see Chapter 8, p. 144), we discussed Isaacson's rhetorical choices as he considered the audience for his essay. Isaacson's decision was to address this paper to the readers of a gay magazine such as *Harvard Gay and Lesbian Review* or *The Advocate*.

Would Legalization of Gay Marriage Be Good for the Gay Community?

Sam Isaacson (student)

---

1   For those of us who have been out for a while, nothing seems shocking about a gay pride parade. Yet at this year's parade, I was struck by the contrast between two groups—the float for the Toys in Babeland store (with swooning drag queens and leather-clad, whipwielding, topless dykes) and the Northwest chapters of Integrity and Dignity (Episcopal and Catholic organizations for lesbians and gays), whose marchers looked as conservative as the congregation of any American church.

2   These stark differences in dress are representative of larger philosophical differences in the gay community. At stake is whether or not we gays and lesbians should act "normal." Labeled as deviants by many in straight society, we're faced with various opposing methods of response. One option is to insist that we are normal and work to integrate gays into the cultural mainstream. Another response is to form an alternative gay culture with its own customs and values; this culture would honor deviancy in response to a society which seeks to label some as "normal" and some as "abnormal." For the purposes of this paper I will refer to those who favor the first response as "integrationists" and those who favor the second response as "liberationists." Politically, this ideological clash is most evident in the issue of whether legalization of same-sex marriage would be good for the gay community. Nearly all integrationists would say yes, but many liberationists would say no. My belief is that while we must take the objections of the liberationists seriously, legalization of same-sex marriage would benefit both gays and society in general.

3   Let us first look at what is so threatening about gay marriage to many liberationists. Many liberationists fear that legalizing gay marriage will reinforce current social pressures that say monogamous marriage is the normal and right way to live. In straight society, those who choose not to marry are often viewed as self-indulgent, likely promiscuous, and shallow—and it is no coincidence these are some of the same stereotypes gays struggle against. If gays begin to marry, married life will

be all the more the norm and subject those outside of marriage to even greater marginalization. As homosexuals, liberationists argue, we should be particularly sensitive to the tyranny of the majority. Our sympathies should lie with the deviants—the transsexual, the fetishist, the drag queen, and the leather-dyke. By choosing marriage, gays take the easy route into "normal" society; we not only abandon the sexual minorities of our community, we strengthen society's narrow notions of what is "normal" and thereby further confine both straights and gays.

Additionally, liberationists worry that by winning the right to marry gays and   4
lesbians will lose the distinctive and positive characteristics of gay culture. Many gay writers have commented on how as a marginalized group gays have been forced to create different forms of relationships that often allow for a greater and often more fulfilling range of life experiences. Writer Edmund White, for instance, has observed that there is a greater fluidity in the relationships of gays than straights. Gays, he says, are more likely than straights to stay friends with old lovers, are more likely to form close friendships outside the romantic relationship, and are generally less likely to become compartmentalized into isolated couples. It has also been noted that gay relationships are often characterized by more equality and better communication than are straight relationships. Liberationists make the reasonable assumption that if gays win the right to marry they will be subject to the same social pressure to marry that straights are subject to. As more gays are pressured into traditional life patterns, liberationists fear the gay sensibility will be swallowed up by the established attitudes of the broader culture. All of society would be the poorer if this were to happen.

I must admit that I concur with many of the arguments of the liberationists that   5
I have outlined above. I do think if given the right, gays would feel social pressure to marry; I agree that gays should be especially sensitive to the most marginalized elements of society; and I also agree that the unique perspectives on human relationships that the gay community offers should not be sacrificed. However, despite these beliefs, I feel that legalizing gay marriage would bring valuable benefits to gays and society as a whole.

First of all, I think it is important to put the attacks the liberationists make on   6
marriage into perspective. The liberationist critique of marriage claims that marriage in itself is a harmful institution (for straights as well as gays) because it needlessly limits and normalizes personal freedom. But it seems clear to me that marriage in some form is necessary for the well-being of society. Children need a stable environment in which to be raised. Studies have shown that children whose parents divorce often suffer long-term effects from the trauma. Studies have also shown that people tend to be happier in stable long-term relationships. We need to have someone to look over us when we're old, when we become depressed, when we fall ill. All people, gay or straight, parents or nonparents, benefit from the stabilizing force of marriage.

Second, we in the gay community should not be too quick to overlook the real   7
benefits that legalizing gay marriage will bring. We are currently denied numerous legal rights of marriage that the straight community enjoys: tax benefits, insurance benefits, inheritance rights, and the right to have a voice in medical treatment or funeral arrangements for a dying partner.

8   Further, just as important as the legal impacts of being denied the right to marriage is the socially symbolic weight this denial carries. We are sent the message
that while gay sex in the privacy of one's home will be tolerated, gay love will not be
respected. We are told that it is not important to society whether we form long-term
relationships or not. We are told that we are not worthy of forming families of our
own. By gaining the same recognitions by the state of our relationships and all the
legal and social weight that recognition carries, the new message will be that gay
love is just as meaningful as straight love.

9   Finally, let me address what I think is at the heart of the liberationist argument
against marriage—the fear of losing social diversity and our unique gay voice. The
liberationists are wary of society's normalizing forces. They fear that if gays win the
right to marry gay relationships will simply become imitations of straight relationships—the richness gained through the gay experience will be lost. I feel, however,
this argument unintentionally plays into the hands of conservatives. Conservatives
argue that marriage is, by definition, the union between man and woman. As a consequence, to the broad culture gay marriage can only be a mockery of marriage. As
gays and lesbians we need to argue that conservatives are imposing arbitrary standards on what is normal and not normal in society. To fight the conservative
agenda, we must suggest instead that marriage is, in essence, a contract of love
and commitment between two people. The liberationists, I think, unwittingly feed
into conservative identification and classification by pigeonholing gays as outsiders.
Reacting against social norms is simply another way of being held hostage by them.

10   We need to understand that the gay experience and voice will not be lost by
gaining the right to marry. Gays will always be the minority by simple biological fact
and this will always color the identity of any gay person. But we can only make our
voice heard if we are seen as full-fledged members of society. Otherwise we will remain an isolated and marginalized group. And only when we have the right to marry
will we have any say in the nature and significance of marriage as an institution.
This is not being apologetic to the straight culture, but is a demand that we not be
excluded from the central institutions of Western culture. We can help merge the
fluidity of gay relationships with the traditionally more compartmentalized married
relationship. Further, liberationists should realize that the decision *not* to marry
makes a statement only if one has the ability to choose marriage. What would be
most radical, most transforming, is two women or two men joined together in the
eyes of society.

Critiquing "Would Legalization of Gay Marriage Be Good for the Gay Community?"

1. Who is the audience that Sam Isaacson addresses in this argument?

2. Ordinarily when we think of persons opposing gay marriage, we imagine
   socially conservative heterosexuals. However, Sam spends little time addressing the anti-gay marriage arguments of straight society. Rather, he addresses the antimarriage arguments made by "liberationist" gay people.
   What are these arguments? How well does Sam respond to them?

3. What are the criteria Sam uses to argue that legalizing gay marriage would be good for the gay community?

4. How persuasive do you think Sam's argument is to the various audiences he addresses?

Our second reading, by student writer Tiffany Anderson, developed out of discussions of hip-hop music. Tiffany was torn between a general dislike of rap combined with a growing admiration for certain female rappers. This evaluation argument took shape once she formulated her issue question: What makes a good female hip-hop artist?

A Woman's View of Hip-Hop
Tiffany Anderson (student)

Is there anything good about hip-hop? If you had asked me this question several years ago, I would have said no. I probably disliked hip-hop as much as any typical middle-aged white suburbanite does. I found the aggressive, ego-driven, star-powered, competitive male image of hip-hop devoid of value, especially the beat and the strong language. I also disliked many of the themes explored in gangster rap, such as the derogatory terms for blacks, the treatment of women as sex objects, and the equation of power and money. When some boys at summer camp six years ago first introduced me to hip-hop, we listened to artists like Bone Thugs-n-Harmony, Tupak Shakur, and Biggie Smalls. These boys who liked rap were also sniffing markers and gave me my first encounter with drugs. In my sheltered white world, I associated rap with drugs and gangs, and I gravitated toward the comfort of alternative rock and punk instead.

But my view of rap began to change when I started listening to the female rappers introduced to me by my friends. During my sophomore year in high school I remember going home because of a bomb threat, and we danced to *The Miseducation of Lauryn Hill* in my living room. I liked what Lauryn was saying. Women hip-hop artists have something different to offer in a male-dominated industry, and it has been women artists who have converted me into a hip-hop fan, not the men. What exactly do these women have to offer that is so compelling? What makes a good female hip-hop artist? While many female rappers merely follow in the footsteps of male rappers by rapping about money, sex, or violence, the truly great female artists provide female listeners with a sense of self-empowerment and identity, they offer a woman's perspective on many topics, and they often create a hopeful message that counters the negativity of male rap. Through their songs, good female rappers spread positive, unique messages that not only benefit African Americans, but females of every race.

Very few male artists are able to provide women with a sense of self-empowerment or identity through their music. But excellent female hip-hop artists like

Lauryn Hill address women's sense of self, as Hill does in her song "Doo Wop (That Thing)." In the first verse she criticizes a woman who loses her self-respect by doing what men want her to do ("It's silly when girls sell their souls because it's in"). She encourages women who "ain't right within" to take pride in themselves, regain their self-respect, and be true to themselves. The encouragement Lauryn offers her female audience is uplifting in an industry where women are often reduced to sex objects as scantily clad dancers, back-up singers, and eye candy in music videos. Rapper Trina, in her song "Take Me," criticizes the idea that females have to be sex objects: "I wanna go to a world where I ain't gotta be a freak ho / just so I can be noticed by people." Perhaps through such urging, girls can take pride in themselves and rebel against stereotypes. Foxy Brown addresses stereotypes in an entirely different, but equally effective, way. She uses her explicitly sexual lyrics to objectify men in her songs, where her heroine is always the dominant one. Her songs help break female sexual inhibitions, reverse the typical roles of the sexes, and allow us to be proud of our sexuality. These songs can be a cathartic release in a world that is all too often dominated by men. Female artists should address the reality of derogatory stereotypes and work to foster a positive female image; if this were left to the male rappers of the industry, females would not be as positively represented in the hip-hop industry.

4   Another mark of a good female hip-hop artist is that she makes songs that give a woman's perspective on the world or her songs include topics not usually addressed in hip-hop songs at all. For example, my favorite song by Lauryn Hill, "To Zion," is about how her world changed after the birth of her son, Zion. When she sings, "Now the joy of my world is Zion," I am filled with pride that I am a woman and have the ability to give birth. How often do male artists, like Nelly or DMX, sing about the joys of parenthood? It is refreshing to hear songs about the miracles of life, as opposed to the death, drugs, and destruction that are often the topics in typical rap songs. On *Eve-olution,* Eve's most recent album, she criticizes our world where she "can't trust the air," an allusion to an oncoming ecological crisis. Hip-hop artists are rarely concerned with problems that affect the entire world, but focus more on their communities. Eve shows her scope as an artist in addressing ecological problems. Another topic not often explored in hip-hop songs is religion. In her song "Confessions," Lady of Rage asks for forgiveness and calls for appreciation of the Lord: "Forgive me, God, for I have forsaken thee / I'm not gonna say that it's the devil that's makin' me." Hip-hop is so often used to name all the evils in the world and lay blame, so hearing an artist take responsibility for her actions and explore a religious theme in her music is refreshing. When a female rap artist can offer her listeners something that they don't often hear, she is truly great.

5   Most importantly, the best female rappers often see some kind of hope in life. Some people might argue that the negativity so blatant in much hip-hop music actually conveys important social and political messages, addressing racial profiling, police brutality, gun control, violence, the glorification of money and sex, and problems with education and welfare reform. These people might say that this influential urban folk art exposes economic and social realities that America needs to confront. I agree that sometimes male artists will reveal a heartbreaking perspective

on this empty world by communicating how urban youth struggle with self-hatred, poverty, lack of education, hopelessness, discrimination, and injustice. For example, in Outkast's song "Git Up, Git Out," the lyrics speak of never-ending cycles of drugs, negativity, and lack of education that hold African Americans back: "I don't recall, ever graduatin' at all / Sometimes I feel I'm just a disappointment to y'all . . . Every job I get is cruel and demeanin' / Sick of taking trash out and toilet bowl cleanin' / But I'm also sick and tired of strugglin' / I never ever thought I'd have to resort to drug smugglin'." While male hip-hop often offers a unique, chilling perspective on the problems of urban America, their music often only serves to strengthen the cycles of despair and self-hatred. Where is hope in songs that often spend verse after verse on the negative aspects of life and the forces that hold people back?

In contrast, female hip-hop artists do identify the problems, but sometimes suggest ways to overcome the difficulties of their lives. For example, Eve's song "Heaven Only Knows" talks about the trouble she faced until she overcame her devastating situation by finding peace through music: "Do positive and positive will happen / Stay positive and positive was rapping / It was like my brain was clouded with unnecessary shit / But I chose to see through the negative and make hits." "Heaven Only Knows" demonstrates the power of rap music to heal. Through her songs, Eve encourages her listeners in new paths and reinforces the importance of overcoming the negative aspects of being an African American. In the title track of *The Miseducation of Lauryn Hill*, Lauryn deftly addresses the problems and offers her own personal story of how she overcame life's setbacks: "I look at my environment / And wonder where the fire went / What happened to everything we used to be / I hear so many cry for help / Searching outside themselves / Now I know His strength is within me / And deep in my heart the answer it was in me / And I made up my mind to find my own destiny." Lauryn sings about how she rejected what was expected of her from outside sources, turned to God, and found everything she needed in herself. To impoverished people of urban America, finding inner strength and self-empowerment could be encouraging. Although Lauryn and Eve usually direct their songs to an African American audience, their words of wisdom apply to all races. Every woman alive can benefit from knowing that we can find our "own destiny" within ourselves, as Lauryn raps about.

Because the lyrics of rap are its heart and soul, what a rapper says conveys a powerful worldview. The worldview of male rap for me is too violent, negative, and antiwoman, but female rap often conveys the same gritty sense of urban life without succumbing to hopelessness and without reducing women to sex objects. The best female rappers are able to arouse a sense of pride and self-worth through their thoughtful lyrics, offer a woman's perspective on the world, and include hopeful messages among the harsh realities of urban life. Female artists like Lauryn Hill, Eve, or Trina have taught me that not all hip-hop is bad, and that sometimes, I can even learn a little something from a song. I found hip-hop a surprising source of feminist pride, diversity, and hope, and this discovery served as a reminder that even in a male- and African American–dominated industry, any white girl can find something to relate to and learn from.

Critiquing "A Woman's View of Hip-Hop"

1. Controversies about popular culture can sometimes become purely subjective discussions about likes and dislikes. How effective is Tiffany Anderson at moving her evaluation of hip-hop from the purely private realm into the public arena where reasoned discussion can take place? Whose views of hip-hop do you think Tiffany wants to change?

2. What criteria does she use to evaluate the music of female hip-hop artists? Do you accept these criteria? What other criteria might an arguer offer to evaluate female hip-hop music? Can you think of good hip-hop music by a female artist that doesn't meet Tiffany's criteria?

3. For her categorical evaluation, Tiffany evaluates specific female artists within the category of "women's rap" as opposed to "men's rap." (Her criteria focus primarily on differences between women's and men's rap.) Within what other categories could you evaluate female rappers?

4. Does Tiffany effectively anticipate alternative views? If so, which alternative views does she address?

5. How effective do you find her argument? Why?

FIGURE 14.1 *Military recruitment cartoon*

Our third reading is a political cartoon by Mike Luckovich that joins the public controversy over supplying the military with enough soldiers to carry out U.S. foreign policy commitments (see Figure 14.1). Currently, U.S. Army standards require recruits to be between the ages of seventeen and thirty-four, to score well on the applicant aptitude test, and to be free of drug use and chronic physical problems. However, the *kairotic* moment of this cartoon is the growing problem of unmet recruitment quotas. The Army and Marines are exploring various incentives and options to increase the number of available soldiers.

Critiquing the Military Recruitment Cartoon

1. Through the use of image and text, political cartoons can powerfully condense a complex argument into a brief statement with a claim and implied line of reasoning. In your own words, what is the claim and implied supporting argument made by this cartoon?

2. How do the drawing, action, and words of the old soldier help convey the argument?

3. What background knowledge about Wal-Mart's hiring practices and wages for employees does this cartoon draw on?

4. What are the implied criteria for "good soldiers" in this cartoon? How does the imagined revision of Army recruitment standards fail to meet these criteria?

Our fourth reading is an op-ed piece that appeared in the *New York Times* on April 22, 2004. Its author, Geoffrey Johnson, coordinates programs for Green Life, a nonprofit organization that seeks to use "education, outreach and advocacy" to "support a demand-driven movement toward sustainable consumption" (from its "About Us" link on its Web site). The occasion for this piece is the annual April Earth Day celebration, a global movement that began in 1970 "to protect our planet, our children, and our future" (from Earth Day Network, www.earthday.net).

Marking Earth Day Inc.

Geoffrey Johnson

Welcome to Earth Day 2004, brought to you by petroleum powers, big-box developers, old-growth loggers and chemically dependent coffee companies trying to paint their public image green. 1

Let's start with Sierra Pacific, a benefactor of northern Nevada's celebration of Earth Day. The timber company is involved in a lawsuit aimed at weakening the Sierra Nevada Framework, which protects the region's forests. Marathon Oil is Earth Day's sponsor down in Houston. Behind closed doors in Texas, Marathon 2 worked on voluntary emissions regulations that have helped give Houston some of the worst air quality in the country.

3   The Earth Day cleanup and restoration program held by the California State Parks Foundation is financed by corporations with poor environmental records in the state: ChevronTexaco, which recently agreed to a $275 million settlement over air pollution from five of its California refineries; Wal-Mart, which lobbied unsuccessfully for a ballot initiative in Inglewood to exempt a proposed supercenter from environmental restrictions; and Pacific Gas and Electric, whose illegal dumping of carcinogenic chemicals near the town of Hinkley was memorialized in the movie *Erin Brockovich.*

4   In New York City and other areas, Starbucks has its own events, centered around its latest slogan, "More than our logo is green." Yet the company will neither label nor remove genetically modified ingredients in its products. And while it promotes its "origins" line of coffees as a symbol of its commitment to sustainable coffee farming, the origins varieties account for just a sliver of the coffee that Starbucks sells.

5   Some might argue that there is nothing wrong with corporations acting as a friend of Earth Day, no matter how unfriendly their everyday operations may be. Perhaps they are just showing solidarity with the millions of Americans who support Earth Day each year to combat the necessary environmental evils of their year-round lifestyles. But the reality is that sponsorship is often intended not as atonement for misdeeds against nature, but as a distraction from them.

6   Through concerted marketing and public relations campaigns, these "green-washers" attract eco-conscious consumers and push the notion that they don't need environmental regulations because they are already environmentally responsible; Greenwashing appears in misleading product labels like "all natural" and "eco-friendly"; in television commercials showing S.U.V.'s rolling peacefully through the wilderness; and in the co-opting of environmental buzzwords like "sound science" and "sustainability"—which corporate executives render meaningless through relentless repetition.

7   Earth Day events are select venues for greenwashers, allowing them to communicate with their target audience of green consumers. They also amount to a public relations bargain. BP spent $200 million rebranding itself from British Petroleum to "beyond petroleum." Major corporations pay hundreds of thousands of dollars for environmentally themed advertisements in high-circulation magazines like National Geographic and Time. In contrast, at most Earth Day festivities, a few hundred to a few thousand dollars will get a company marquee exhibition space and a prominent place for its logo on publicity materials.

8   It would be a shame to let the high-flying banners of greenwashers distract Earth Day participants from the environmental advocates, community associations and government agencies that work to protect the environment throughout the year. But it is also incumbent upon those same groups—many of which are in the position of choosing who sponsors these events—to adopt a strict screening process to separate the genuinely green businesses from the greenwashers. Finally,

let's not forget the most charitable patron of all. Earth Day, like every day, is brought to us by the generosity of none other than the planet itself.

Critiquing "Marking Earth Day Inc."

1. What ethical claim does Geoffrey Johnson make about big companies' sponsorship of Earth Day?
2. Does Johnson argue primarily from principles or consequences in this ethical argument?
3. How does Johnson respond to alternative views?
4. How convincing is this argument?

Our final reading was posted on the Web site of the Ayn Rand Institute in July 2005. The Ayn Rand Institute in Irvine, California, is an educational organization dedicated to the philosophy of novelist-philosopher Ayn Rand, who believed in "reason, rational self-interest, individual rights and free-market capitalism" (from the Web site, www.aynrand.org). This institute seeks to educate the public about Rand's philosophy, called Objectivism, and to promote a culture informed by its values. The author of this piece, David Holcberg, works for the institute as a media research specialist. In this argument, Holcberg joins the national and global debate about trading and selling human organs.

Human Organs for Sale?
David Holcberg

As athletes who have received organ transplants gathered for the 2005 World Transplant Games in the city of London, Canada, a record 87,000 individuals who did not share these athletes' good fortune stood on the U.S. national waiting list for organs. Of the 82,000 waiting for kidneys or livers, about 6,000 will die in the next twelve months. Yet no one is considering a simple way to save many of these people: legalize trade in human organs.

Let's consider it.

Millions of Americans have exercised their right to give away their organs by signing organ donation cards. But very few made the legal arrangements necessary to ensure that their organs can be harvested after death. Many more would make such arrangements if their families were to be paid for the donated organs. It may work as a type of life insurance for the benefit of the deceased's family and would create a mutually advantageous situation: the deceased's family gets needed money while the transplant patient gets a vital organ.

4   A few people, on the other hand, may choose to sell an organ (or part of one) during their lifetime. This may seem like a radical idea, but it need not be an irrational one.

5   According to the Mayo Clinic, the extraction of a section of liver, for example, carries a risk to the donor's life of less than 1 percent—not negligible, but not overwhelming. In the case of a kidney donation, the *New England Journal of Medicine* reports that the risk to the donor's life is even smaller; just 0.03 percent. Moreover, liver donors can usually count on their healthy liver's ability to regenerate and regain full function. And donors of kidneys usually live normal lives with no reduction of life expectancy.

6   A person may reasonably decide, after considering all the relevant facts (including the pain, risk and inconvenience of surgery), that selling an organ is actually in his own best interest. A father, for example, may decide that one of his kidneys is worth selling to pay for the best medical treatment available for his child.

7   But those who object to a free market in organs would deny this father the right to act on his own judgment. Poor people, they claim, are incapable of making rational choices and so must be protected from themselves. The fact, however, is that human beings (poor or rich) do have the capacity to reason, and should be free to exercise it. So long as a person respects the rights of others, he ought to be free to live his life and use his mind and body as he judges best, without interference from the government or anybody else.

8   Of course, the decision to sell an organ (or part of an organ) is a very serious one, and should not be taken lightly. That some people might make irrational choices, however, is no reason to violate the rights of everyone. If the law recognizes our right to give away an organ, it should also recognize our right to sell an organ.

9   The objection that people would murder to sell their victims' organs should be dismissed as the scaremongering that it is. (Indeed, the financial lure of such difficult-to-execute criminal action is today far greater than it would be if patients could legally and openly buy the organs they need.)

10   Opponents of a free market in organs argue as well that it would benefit only those who could afford to pay—not necessarily those in most desperate need. This objection should also be rejected. Need does not give anyone the right to damage the lives of other people, by prohibiting a seller from getting the best price for his organ, or a buyer from purchasing an organ to further his life. Those who can afford to buy organs would benefit at no one's expense but their own. Those unable to pay would still be able to rely on charity, as they do today. And a free market would enhance the ability of charitable organizations to procure organs for them.

11   Ask yourself: if your life depended on getting an organ, say a kidney or a liver, wouldn't you be willing to pay for one? And if you could find a willing seller, shouldn't you have the right to buy it from him?

12   The right to buy an organ is part of your right to life. The right to life is the right to take all actions a rational being requires to sustain and enhance his life. Your right to life becomes meaningless when the law forbids you to buy a kidney or liver that would preserve your life.

If the government upheld the rights of potential buyers and sellers of organs, many of the 87,000 people now waiting for organs would be spared hideous suffering and an early death. How many?   13

Let's find out.   14

Critiquing "Human Organs for Sale?"

1. In this piece, the proposal to legalize the sale of human organs accompanies an ethical argument about the morality of such a law. What reasoning from principles and consequences does David Holcberg offer in support of the legitimacy of this view?

2. What objections does Holcberg address? How well does he refute these opposing views?

3. How does this argument reflect the values of its sponsoring organization?

4. How does Holcberg use appeals to *pathos?* How would Holcberg respond to the billboard advertisement in the photo on page 193? What do you find persuasive about this argument?

15 Proposal Arguments

We Should (Should Not) Do X

CASE 1

In summer 2005 the U.S. Army had missed its recruitment goals for four consecutive months, leading to a deepening crisis in supplying enough soldiers for the Iraq war while maintaining backup forces to meet conflicts in other parts of the world. Long deployments to Iraq and a strengthening job market at home reduced what the Army calls the "propensity to enlist." The sluggish flow of enlistments meant that Army boot camps were less than half full. To address this crisis, analysts proposed a number of possible solutions: increase the number of Army recruiters; improve recruitment methods; expand the pool of possible recruits by lowering standards or increasing the upper age limit; double the size of enlistment bonuses for prized recruits from $20,000 to $40,000; eliminate the ban on gay soldiers; keep more first-term soldiers by reducing the discharge rate for drug abuse, poor conduct, or failure to meet fitness standards; reinstitute a lottery draft; or mandate a period of national service for all Americans upon graduation from high school (with military service one of the options).

CASE 2

A pressing world problem is the need to reduce oil consumption. In the United States, numerous methods have been tried. For example, Congress mandated that auto manufacturers make their cars more fuel-efficient, but the plan was thwarted by SUVs, which are classified as trucks rather than cars. Taking a different tack, some conservationists have wondered if market forces, rather than federal regulations, might be used to stimulate purchase of more fuel-efficient cars. One proposal is to institute "feebates," which is a combination of a fee and a rebate. When purchasing gas, drivers would be charged different prices depending on the type of vehicle being fueled. A computerized system would give drivers of fuel-efficient cars an immediate rebate, reducing the price per gallon of gas. In contrast, drivers of fuel-inefficient cars would be charged a fee, increasing the price per gallon of gas. This proposal would give car buyers a market incentive for buying more fuel-efficient cars.

An Overview of Proposal Arguments

Although proposal arguments are the last type we examine, they are among the most common arguments that you will encounter or be called on to write. Their essence is that they call for action. In reading a proposal, the audience is enjoined to make a decision and then to act on it—to *do* something. Proposal arguments are sometimes called *should* or *ought* arguments because those helping verbs express the obligation to act: "We *should* do X" or "We *ought* to do X."

For instructional purposes, we will distinguish between two kinds of proposal arguments, even though they are closely related and involve the same basic arguing strategies. The first kind we will call *practical proposals,* which propose an action to solve some kind of local or immediate problem. A student's proposal to change the billing procedures for scholarship students would be an example of a practical proposal, as would an engineering firm's proposal for the design of a new bridge being planned by a city government. The second kind we will call *policy proposals,* in which the writer offers a broad plan of action to solve major social, economic, or political problems affecting the common good. An argument that the United States should adopt a national health insurance plan or that the electoral college should be abolished would be examples of policy proposals.

The primary difference is the narrowness versus breadth of the concern. *Practical* proposals are narrow, local, and concrete; they focus on the nuts and bolts of getting something done in the here and now. They are often concerned with the exact size of a piece of steel, the precise duties of a new person to be hired, or a close estimate of the cost of paint or computers to be purchased. *Policy* proposals, in contrast, are concerned with the broad outline and shape of a course of action, often on a regional, national, or even international issue. What government should do about overcrowding of prisons would be a problem addressed by policy proposals. How to improve the security alarm system for the county jail would be addressed by a practical proposal.

Learning to write both kinds of proposals is valuable. Researching and writing a *policy* proposal is an excellent way to practice the responsibilities of citizenship, which require the ability to understand complex issues and to weigh positive and negative consequences of policy choices. In your professional life, writing *practical* proposals may well be among your most important duties on the job. Effective proposal writing is the lifeblood of many companies and also constitutes one of the most powerful ways you can identify and help solve problems.

The Structure of Proposal Arguments

Proposal arguments, whether practical proposals or policy proposals, generally have a three-part structure: (1) description of a problem, (2) proposed solution, and (3) justification for the proposed solution. In the justification section of your proposal argument, you develop *because* clauses of the kinds you have practiced throughout this text.

Special Concerns for Proposal Arguments

In their call for action, proposal arguments entail certain emphases and audience concerns that you don't generally face with other kinds of arguments. Let's look briefly at some of these special concerns.

The Need for Presence

Your audience might agree with your proposal on an intellectual level, but how can you move them to *act* on your proposal, especially if the personal cost of acting may be high? Urging action often requires you to engage your audience's emotions as well as their intellects. Thus proposal arguments often require more attention to *pathos* than do other kinds of arguments (see pp. 132–135).

In most cases, convincing people to act means that an argument must have presence as well as intellectual force. By *presence* we mean an argument's ability to grip the readers' hearts and imaginations as well as their intellects. You can give presence to an argument through the effective use of details, provocative statistics, dialogue, illustrative narratives, and compelling examples that show the reader the seriousness of the problem you are addressing or the consequences of not acting on your proposal. You can also use figurative language such as metaphor and analogy to make the problem being addressed more vivid or real to your audience.

The Need to Overcome People's Natural Conservatism

Another difficulty faced by a proposal maker is the innate conservatism of all human beings, whatever their political persuasion. One philosopher refers to this conservatism as the *law of inertia*, the tendency of all things in the universe, including human beings, to remain at rest if possible. The popular adage "If it ain't broke, don't fix it" is one expression of this tendency. Proposers of change face an extraordinary burden of proof. They have to prove that something needs fixing, that it can be fixed, and that the cost of fixing it will be outweighed by the benefits of fixing it.

The difficulty of proving that something needs fixing is compounded by the fact that frequently the status quo appears to be working. So sometimes when writing a proposal, you can't argue that what we have is bad, but only that what we could have would be better. Often, then, a proposal argument will be based not on present evils but on the evils of lost potential. And getting an audience to accept lost potential may be difficult indeed, given the inherently abstract nature of potentiality.

The Difficulty of Predicting Future Consequences

Further, most proposal makers will be forced to predict consequences of a given act. As we've seen in our earlier discussions of causality, it is difficult enough to argue backward from event Y in order to establish that X caused Y. Think how much harder it is to establish that X will, in the future, cause certain things to occur. We all know enough of history to realize that few major decisions have led neatly to their anticipated results. This knowledge indeed accounts for much of our conservatism. All the things that can go wrong in a causal argument can go wrong in a proposal argument as well; the major difference is that in a proposal argument we typically have less evidence for our conjectures.

The Problem of Evaluating Consequences

A final difficulty faced by all proposal arguments concerns the difficulty of evaluating the consequences of the proposal. In government and industry, managers often turn to a tool known as *cost-benefit analysis* to calculate the potential consequences of a given proposal. As much as possible, a cost-benefit analysis tries to reduce all consequences to a single scale for purposes of comparison. Most often, the scale will be money. Although this scale may work well in some circumstances, it can lead to grotesquely inappropriate conclusions in other situations.

Just how does one balance the money saved by cutting Medicare benefits against the suffering of the people denied benefits? How does one translate the beauty of a wilderness area into a dollar amount? On this score, cost-benefit analyses often run into a problem discussed in the previous chapter: the seductiveness of empirical measures. Because something can't be readily measured doesn't mean it can be safely ignored. And finally, what will be a cost for one group will often be a benefit for others. For example, if Social Security benefits are cut, those on Social Security will suffer, but current workers who pay for it with taxes will take home a larger paycheck.

These, then, are some of the general difficulties facing someone who sets out to argue in favor of a proposal. Although these difficulties may seem daunting, the rest of this chapter offers strategies to help you overcome them and produce a successful proposal.

Developing a Proposal Argument

Writers of proposal arguments must focus in turn on three main phases or stages of the argument: showing that a problem exists, explaining the proposed solution, and offering a justification.

Convincing Your Readers That a Problem Exists

There is one argumentative strategy generic to all proposal arguments: calling your reader's attention to a problem. In some situations, your intended audience might already be aware of the problem and may have even asked persons to offer solutions. In such cases, you do not need to develop the problem extensively or motivate your audience to solve it. But in most situations, awakening your readers to the existence of a problem—a problem they may well not have recognized before—is your first important challenge. You must give your problem presence through anecdotes, telling statistics, or other means that show readers how the problem affects people or otherwise has important stakes. Your goal is to gain your readers' intellectual assent to the depth, range, and potential seriousness of the problem and thereby motivate them to want to solve it.

Typically, the arguer develops the problem in one of two places in a proposal argument—either in the introduction prior to the presentation of the arguer's proposal claim or in the body of the paper as the first main reason justifying the proposal claim. In the second instance the writer's first *because* clause has the following structure: "We should do X *because* we are facing a serious problem that needs a solution."

Here is how one student writer gave presence to a proposal, addressed to the chair of the mathematics department at her school, calling for the redesign of the introductory math curriculum.

> My own experience in the Calculus 134 and 135 sequence last year showed me that it was not the learning of calculus that was difficult for me. I was able to catch on to the new concepts. The problem for me was in the fast pace. Just as I was assimilating new concepts and feeling the need to reinforce them, the class was on to a new topic before I had full mastery of the old concept. [. . .] Part of the reason for the fast pace is that calculus is a feeder course for computer science and engineering. If prospective engineering students can't learn the calculus rapidly, they drop out of the program. The high dropout rate benefits the Engineering School because they use the math course to weed out an overabundance of engineering applicants. Thus the pace of the calculus course is geared to the needs of the engineering curriculum, not to the needs of someone like me who wants to be a high school mathematics teacher and who believes that my own difficulties with math—combined with my love for it—might make me an excellent math teacher.

By describing the fast pace of the math curriculum from the perspective of a future math teacher rather than an engineering student, this writer illuminates a problem invisible to others. What before didn't look like a problem (it is good to weed out weak engineering majors) suddenly became a problem (it is bad to weed out future math teachers). Establishing herself as a serious student genuinely interested in learning calculus, she gave presence to the problem by calling attention to it in a new way.

Showing the Specifics of Your Proposal

Having decided that there is a problem to be solved, you should lay out your thesis, which is a proposal for solving the problem. Your goal now is to stress the feasibility of your solution, including costs. The art of proposal making is the art of the possible. To be sure, not all proposals require elaborate descriptions of the implementation process. If you are proposing, for example, that a local PTA chapter buy new tumbling mats for the junior high gym classes, the procedures for buying the mats will probably be irrelevant. But in many arguments the specifics of your proposal—the actual step-by-step methods of implementing it—may be instrumental in winning your audience's support.

You will also need to show how your proposal will solve the problem either partially or wholly. Sometimes you may first need to convince your reader that the problem is solvable, not something intractably rooted in "the way things are," such as earthquakes or jealousy. In other words, expect that some members of your audience will be skeptical about the ability of any proposal to solve the problem you are addressing. You may well need, therefore, to "listen" to this point of view in your refutation section and to argue that your problem is at least partially solvable.

In order to persuade your audience that your proposal can work, you can follow any one of several approaches. A typical approach is to lay out a causal argument showing how one consequence will lead to another until your solution is effected. Another approach is to turn to resemblance arguments, either analogy or precedent. You try to show how similar proposals have been successful elsewhere. Or, if similar things have failed in the past, you try to show how the present situation is different.

The Justification: Convincing Your Readers That Your Proposal Should Be Enacted

The justification phase of a proposal argument will need extensive development in some arguments and minimal development in others, again depending on your particular problem and the rhetorical context of your proposal. If your audience already acknowledges the seriousness of the problem you are addressing and has simply been waiting for the right solution to come along, then your argument will be successful so long as you can convince your audience that your solution will work and that it won't cost too much. Such arguments depend on the clarity of your proposal and the feasibility of its being implemented.

But what if the costs are high? What if your readers don't think the problem is serious? What if they don't appreciate the benefits of solving the problem or the bad consequences of not solving it? In such cases you have to develop persuasive reasons for enacting your proposal. You may also have to determine who has the power to act on your proposal and apply arguments directly to that person's or agency's immediate interests. You need to know to whom or to what your power source is beholden or responsive and what values your power source holds that can be appealed to. You're looking, in short, for the best pressure points.

Proposal Arguments as Advocacy Posters or Advertisements

A frequently encountered kind of proposal argument is the one-page newspaper or magazine advertisement often purchased by advocacy groups to promote a cause. Such arguments also appear as Web pages or as posters or fliers.

These condensed advocacy arguments are marked by their bold, abbreviated, tightly planned format. The creators of these arguments know they must work fast to capture our attention, give presence to a problem, advocate a solution, and enlist our support. Advocacy advertisements frequently use photographs, images, or icons that appeal to a reader's emotions and imagination. In addition to images, they often use different type sizes and styles. Large-type text in these documents frequently takes the form of slogans or condensed thesis statements written in an arresting style. To outline and justify their solutions, creators of advocacy ads often put main supporting reasons in bulleted lists and sometimes enclose carefully selected facts and quotations in boxed sidebars. To add an authoritative *ethos,* the arguments often include fine-print footnotes and bibliographies. (For more detailed discussion of how advocacy posters and advertisements use images and arrange text for rhetorical effect, see Chapter 9 on visual argument.)

Another prominent feature of these condensed, highly visual arguments is their appeal to the audience through a direct call for a course of action: go to an advocacy Web site to find more information on how to support a cause; cut out a postcard-like form to send to a decision maker; vote for or against the proposition or the candidate; write a letter to a political representative; or donate money to a cause.

An example of a student-produced advocacy advertisement is shown in Figure 15.1. Here student Lisa Blattner joins a heated debate in her city on whether to close down all-ages dance clubs. Frustrated because the evening dance options for under-twenty-one youth were threatened in Seattle, Lisa directed her ad toward the general readership of regional newspapers with the special intention of reaching adult voters and parents. Lisa's ad uses three documentary-like, emotionally loaded, and disturbing photographs to give immediacy and presence to the problem. The verbal text in the ad states the proposal claim and provides three reasons in support of the claim. Notice how the reasons also pick up the ideas in the three photo images. The final lines of text memorably reiterate the claim and call readers to action. The success of this ad derives from the collaboration of layout, photos, and verbal text in conveying a clear, direct argument.

Now that you have been introduced to the main elements of a proposal argument, including condensed visual arguments, we explain in the next two sections two invention strategies you can use to generate persuasive reasons for a proposal argument and to anticipate your audience's doubts and reservations. We call these the "claim-type strategy" and the "stock issues strategy."

Using the Claim-Type Strategy to Develop a Proposal Argument

In Chapter 10 we explained how claim-type theory can help you generate ideas for an argument. Specifically, we explained how values claims often depend for their supporting reasons on the reality claims of category, cause, or resemblance.

What Is Left for Teenagers to Do When the Teen Ordinance Bans Them from Dance Clubs?

Take Ecstasy   Drink at Places with   Roam the Streets
at Raves   No Adult Supervision

Is There an Answer to These Problems?

Yes! Through your support of the All Ages Dance Ordinance, teens will have a safe place to go where:

• **No hard drugs, like ecstasy and cocaine, are present**
• **Responsible adults are watching over everyone**
• **All of their friends can hang out in one place indoors, instead of outside with drug dealers, criminals, and prostitutes**

Give Your Child a Safe Place to Have Fun at Night

**Let the Seattle City Committee Know
That You Support the
All Ages Dance Ordinance**

FIGURE 15.1   *Student advocacy advertisement*

This principle leads to a powerful idea-generating strategy that can be schematized as follows:

Overview of Claim-Type Strategy

We should do X (proposal claim)

■ because X is a Y (categorical claim)

- because X will lead to good consequences (causal claim)
- because X is like Y (resemblance claim)

With each of those *because* clauses, the arguer's goal is to link X to one or more goods the audience already values. For a specific example, suppose that you wanted insurance companies to pay for long-term psychological counseling for anorexia. The claim-type strategy could help you develop arguments such as these:

Insurance companies should pay for long-term psychological counseling for anorexia (proposal claim)
- because paying for such counseling is a demonstration of commitment to women's health (categorical claim)
- because paying for such counseling might save insurance companies from much more extensive medical costs at a later date (causal claim)
- because paying for anorexia counseling is like paying for alcoholism or drug counseling, which is already covered by insurance (resemblance claim)

Proposal arguments using reality claims as reasons are very common. Here is another example, this time from a famous art exhibit controversy in the early 1990s when conservatives protested government funding for an exhibition of homoerotic photographs by artist Robert Mapplethorpe:

Taxpayer funding for the Mapplethorpe exhibit should be withdrawn (proposal claim)
- because the photographs are pornographic (a categorical claim linking the photographs to pornography, which the intended audience opposes)
- because the exhibit promotes community acceptance of homosexuality (a causal claim linking the exhibit to acceptance of homosexuality, which the intended audience opposes)
- because the photographs are more like political statements than art (a resemblance claim linking the exhibit to politics rather than art, a situation that the intended audience would consider unsuitable for arts funding)

Whatever you might think of this argument, it shows how the supporting reasons for a proposal claim can be drawn from claims of category, cause, and resemblance. Each of these arguments attempts to appeal to the value system of the audience. Each tries to show how the proposed action is within the class of things that the audience already values, will lead to consequences desired by the audience, or is similar to something the audience already values. The invention procedure can be summarized in the boxes and examples that follow.

> **Argument from Category**
>
> To discover reasons by using this strategy, conduct the following kind of search:
>
> We should (should not) do X because X is _____.
>
> Try to fill in the blank with an appropriate noun or adjective that appeals in some way to your audience's values. <u>Noun examples</u>: ... because X is *murder, torture, a violation of conservative principles, an act of love, an example of courage, cheating.* <u>Adjective examples</u>: ... because X is *ugly, beautiful, inflationary, too liberal, mean-spirited, unjust.* Your goal is to show that X belongs to the named or implied class or category.

Here are examples:

Using a "Category" Search to Generate Reasons

- Our university should abolish fraternities and sororities *because they are elitist* (or "racist" or "sexist" or "an outdated institution" or whatever).

- The public should support genetically modified foods *because they are safe* (or "healthy," or "nutritious," or "improvements over current products").

> **Argument from Consequence**
>
> To discover reasons by using this category, conduct the following kind of search:
>
> We should (should not) do X because X leads to these good (bad) consequences: _____, _____, _____, _____.
>
> Then think of consequences that your audience will agree are good (bad) as your argument requires.

Here are examples, using the same claims as before:

Using a "Consequence" Search to Generate Reasons

- Our university should abolish fraternities and sororities *because eliminating the Greek system will improve our school's academic reputation* (or "fill our dormitories," "allow us to experiment with new living arrangements," "replace rush with a better first-year orientation," "reduce the campus drinking problem," and so forth).

■ The public should support genetically modified foods *because these biotech crops can reduce world hunger* (or "reduce the need for pesticides" or "increase medical advancements through related genetic research").

Argument from Resemblance

To discover supporting reasons by using this strategy, conduct the following kind of search:

We should (should not) do X because doing X is like _____.

Then think of analogies or precedents that are similar to doing X but currently have greater appeal to your audience. Your task is then to transfer to X your audience's favorable (unfavorable) feelings toward the analogy/precedent.

Here are examples:

Using a "Resemblance" Search to Generate Reasons

■ Our university should abolish fraternities and sororities *because other universities that have eliminated the Greek system have reported good results* (or "because eliminating the Greek system is like leveling social classes to promote more democracy and individualism," and so forth).

■ The public should support genetically modified foods *because genetic modification is like natural crossbreeding* (or "because supporting biotechnology in agriculture is like supporting scientific advancements in other fields").

These three kinds of searches—supporting a proposal claim from the perspectives of category, consequence, and resemblance—are powerful means of invention. In selecting among these reasons, choose those most likely to appeal to your audience's assumptions, beliefs, and values.

For Class Discussion

1. Working individually or in small groups, use the strategies of category, consequence, and resemblance to create *because* clauses that support each of the following claims. Try to have at least one *because* clause from each of the categories, but generate as many reasons as possible. Don't worry about whether any individual reason exactly fits the category. The purpose is to stimulate thinking, not fill in the slots.

Example

CLAIM: People should not own pit bulls.

REASON FROM CATEGORY: because pit bulls are vicious

REASON FROM CONSEQUENCE: because owning a pit bull leads to conflicts with neighbors

REASON FROM RESEMBLANCE: because owning a pit bull is like having a shell-shocked roommate—mostly they're lovely companions but they can turn violent if startled

a. Marijuana should be legalized.

b. Division I college athletes should receive salaries.

c. High schools should pass out free contraceptives.

d. Violent video games should be made illegal.

e. Parents should be heavily taxed for having more than two children.

2. Repeat the first exercise, taking a different position on each issue.

Using the "Stock Issues" Strategy to Develop a Proposal Argument

Another effective way to generate ideas for a proposal argument is to ask yourself a series of questions based on the "stock issues" strategy. Suppose, for example, you wanted to develop the following argument: "In order to solve the problem of students who won't take risks with their writing, the faculty should adopt a pass/fail method of grading in all writing courses." The stock issues strategy invites the writer to consider "stock" ways (that is, common, usual, frequently repeated ways) that such arguments can be conducted.

Stock issue 1: *Is there really a problem here that needs to be solved?*   Is it really true that a large number of student writers won't take risks in their writing? Is this problem more serious than other writing problems such as undeveloped ideas, lack of organization, and poor sentence structure? This stock issue invites the writer to convince her audience that a true problem exists. Conversely, an opponent to the proposal might argue that a true problem does not exist.

Stock issue 2: *Will the proposed solution really solve this problem?*   Is it true that a pass/fail grading system will cause students to take more risks with their writing? Will more interesting, surprising, and creative essays result from pass/fail grading? Or will students simply put less effort into their writing? This stock issue prompts a supporter to demonstrate that the proposal will solve the problem; in contrast, it prompts the opponent to show that the proposal won't work.

Stock issue 3: *Can the problem be solved more simply without disturbing the status quo?*   An opponent of the proposal might agree that a problem exists and that the proposed solution might solve it. However, the opponent might say, "Are there not less radical ways to solve this problem? If we want more creative and risk-taking student essays, can't we just change our grading criteria so that we reward risky papers and penalize conventional ones?" This stock issue prompts supporters to show that *only* the proposed solution will solve the problem and that no minor tinkering with the status quo will be adequate. Conversely, opponents will argue that the problem can be solved without acting on the proposal.

Stock issue 4: *Is the proposed solution really practical? Does it stand a chance of actually being enacted?*   Here an opponent to the proposal might agree that the proposal would work but that it involves pie-in-the-sky idealism. Nobody will vote to change the existing system so radically; therefore, it is a waste of our time to debate it. Following this prompt, supporters would have to argue that pass/fail grading is workable and that enough faculty members are disposed to it that the proposal is worth debating. Opponents might argue that the faculty is so traditional that pass/fail has utterly no chance of being accepted, despite its merits.

Stock issue 5: *What will be the unforeseen positive and negative consequences of the proposal?*   Suppose we do adopt a pass/fail system. What positive or negative consequences might occur that are different from what we at first predicted? Using this prompt, an opponent might argue that pass/fail grading will reduce the effort put forth by students and that the long-range effect will be writing of even lower quality than we have now. Supporters would try to find positive consequences—perhaps a new love of writing for its own sake rather than the sake of a grade.

For Class Discussion

The following collaborative task takes approximately two class days to complete. The exercise takes you through the process of creating a proposal argument.

1. In small groups, identify and list several major problems facing students in your college or university.

2. Decide among yourselves which are the most important of these problems and rank them in order of importance.

3. Take your group's number one problem and explore answers to the following questions. Group recorders should be prepared to present your group's answers to the class as a whole:

    a. Why is the problem a problem?

    b. For whom is the problem a problem?

    c. How will these people suffer if the problem is not solved? (Give specific examples.)

    d. Who has the power to solve the problem?

    e. Why hasn't the problem been solved up to this point?

    f. How can the problem be solved? (That is, create a proposal.)

    g. What are the probable benefits of acting on your proposal?

    h. What costs are associated with your proposal?

    i. Who will bear those costs?

    j. Why should this proposal be enacted?

    k. Why is it better than alternative proposals?

4. As a group, draft an outline for a proposal argument in which you

    a. describe the problem and its significance.

    b. propose your solution to the problem.

    c. justify your proposal by showing how the benefits of adopting that proposal outweigh the costs.

5. Recorders for each group should write their group's outline on the board and be prepared to explain it to the class.

Writing a Proposal Argument

WRITING ASSIGNMENT
FOR CHAPTER 15

OPTION 1: *A Practical Proposal Addressing a Local Problem* Write a practical proposal offering a solution to a local problem. Your proposal should have three main sections: (1) description of the problem, (2) proposed solution, and (3) justification. You may include additional sections or subsections as needed. Longer proposals often include an *abstract* at the beginning of the proposal to provide a summary overview of the whole argument. (Sometimes called the *executive summary*, this abstract may be the only portion of the proposal read by high-level managers.) Sometimes proposals are accompanied by a *letter of transmittal*—a one-page business letter that introduces the proposal to its intended audience and provides some needed background about the writer.

    Document design is important in practical proposals, which are aimed at busy people who have to make many decisions under time constraints. Because the writer of a practical proposal usually produces the finished document (practical proposals are seldom submitted to newspapers or magazines for publication), the writer must pay particular attention to the attractive design of the document. An effective design helps establish the writer's *ethos* as a quality-oriented professional and helps make the reading of the proposal as easy as possible. Document design includes effective use of headings and subheadings, attractive typeface and layout, flawless editing, and other features enhancing the visual appearance of the document. For a student example of a practical proposal, see Laurel Wilson's argument on pages 339–343.

OPTION 2: *A Policy Proposal as a Guest Editorial*   Write a two- to three-page policy proposal suitable for publication as a feature editorial in a college or city newspaper or in some publication associated with a particular group or activity such as a church newsletter or employee bulletin. The voice and style of your argument should be aimed at general readers of your chosen publication. Your editorial should have the following features:

1. The identification of a problem (Persuade your audience that this is a genuine problem that needs solving; give it presence.)
2. A proposal for action that will help alleviate the problem
3. A justification of your solution (the reasons why your audience should accept your proposal and act on it)

OPTION 3: *A Researched Argument Proposing Public Policy*   Write an eight- to twelve-page proposal argument as a formal research paper, using research data for development and support. In business and professional life, this kind of research proposal is often called a "white paper," which recommends a course of action internally within an organization or externally to a client or stakeholder. An example of a researched policy proposal is student writer Mark Bonicillo's "A Proposal for Universal Health Insurance in the United States" on pages 344–350.

OPTION 4: *A One-Page Advocacy Advertisement*   Using the strategies of visual argument discussed in Chapter 9 and on pages 325–327 of this chapter, create a one-page advocacy advertisement urging action on a public issue. Your advertisement should be designed for publication in a newspaper or for distribution as a poster or flier. An example of a student-produced advocacy advertisement is shown in Figure 15.1 on page 327.

Exploring Ideas

Since *should* or *ought* issues are among the most common sources of arguments, you may already have ideas for proposal issues. To think of ideas for practical proposals, try making an idea map of local problems you would like to see solved. For initial spokes, try trigger words such as the following:

- problems at my university (dorms, parking, registration system, financial aid, campus appearance, clubs, curriculum, intramural program, athletic teams)

- problems in my city or town (dangerous intersections, ugly areas, inadequate lighting, parks, police policy, public transportation, schools)

- problems at my place of work (office design, flow of customer traffic, merchandise display, company policies)

- problems related to my future career, hobbies, recreational time, life as a consumer, life as a homeowner

If you can offer a solution to the problem you identify, you may make a valuable contribution to some phase of public life.

To find a topic for policy proposals, stay in touch with the news, which will keep you aware of current debates on regional and national issues. Also, visit the Web sites of your congressional representatives to see what issues they are currently investigating and debating. You might think of your policy proposal as a white paper for one of your legislators.

Once you have decided on a proposal issue, we recommend you explore it by trying one or more of the following activities:

- *Explore ideas by using the claim-type strategy.*   Briefly, this strategy invites you to find supporting reasons for your proposal (we should do X) by arguing that (1) X is a Y that the audience values; (2) doing X will lead to good consequences; and (3) doing X has been tried with good results elsewhere, or doing X is like doing Y, which the audience values.

- *Explore ideas by using the "stock issues" strategy.*   You will raise vital ideas for your argument by asking the stock questions: (1) Is there really a problem here that has to be solved? (2) Will the proposed solution really solve this problem? (3) Can the problem be solved in a simpler way without disturbing the status quo? (4) Is the proposed solution practical enough that it really stands a chance of being acted on? (5) What will be the positive and negative consequences of the proposal? A fuller version of the stock questions is the eleven questions (a–k) in the third For Class Discussion exercise on pages 332–333.

- *Explore ideas for your argument by completing the ten exploratory tasks in Chapter 3 (pp. 70–71).*   These tasks help you generate enough material for a rudimentary rough draft.

Organizing a Proposal Argument

When you write your draft, you may find it helpful to have at hand some plans for typical ways of organizing a proposal argument. What follow are two common methods of organization. Option 1 is the plan most typical for practical proposals. Either Option 1 or Option 2 is effective for a policy proposal.

Option 1

- Presentation of a problem that needs solving:
  Description of problem
  Background, including previous attempts to solve problem
  Argument that the problem is solvable (optional)
- Presentation of writer's proposal:
  Succinct statement of the proposed solution serves as thesis statement.
  Explain specifics of proposed solution.
- Summary and rebuttal of opposing views (in practical proposals, this section is often a summary and rejection of alternative ways of solving the problem)
- Justification persuading reader that proposal should be enacted:
  Reason 1 presented and developed.
  Reason 2 presented and developed.
  Additional reasons presented and developed.
- Conclusion that exhorts audience to act:
  Give presence to final sentences.

Option 2

- Presentation of issue, including background
- Presentation of writer's proposal
- Justification
  Reason 1: Show that proposal addresses a serious problem.
  Reason 2: Show that proposal will solve problem.
  Reason 3: Give additional reasons for enacting proposal.
- Summary and refutation of opposing views
- Conclusion that exhorts audience to act

Revising Your Draft

As you revise your draft based on peer reviews and on your own assessment of its problems and strengths, consider using a Toulmin analysis to test your argument's persuasiveness. Recall that Toulmin is particularly useful for helping you link each of your reasons to your audience's beliefs, assumptions, and values.

Suppose that there is a debate at your university about whether to banish fraternities and sororities. Suppose further that you are in favor of banishing the Greek system. One of your arguments is that eliminating the Greek system will improve your college's academic reputation. Here is how you might use the Toulmin system to make this line of reasoning as persuasive as possible.

CLAIM: Our university should eliminate the Greek system.

STATED REASON: because doing so will improve our academic reputation

GROUNDS: *I've got to provide evidence that eliminating the Greek system will improve our academic reputation. I have shown that last year the GPA of students in fraternities and sororities was 20 percent lower than the GPA of non-Greek students. What else can I add? I can talk about the excessive party atmosphere of some Greek houses, about the emphasis placed on social life rather than studying, about how new pledges have so many house duties that their studies suffer, about how new students think about rush more than about the academic life.*

WARRANT: It is good for our university to achieve a better academic reputation.

BACKING: *I see that my draft doesn't have any backing for this warrant. How can I argue that it would be good to have a better academic reputation? We would attract more serious students; the university's prestige would rise; it might attract and retain better faculty; the college would be a more intellectually interesting place; the long-range careers of our students might improve with a better education.*

CONDITIONS OF REBUTTAL: *How would skeptics doubt my reason and grounds? Might they say that I am stereotyping Greeks? Might they argue that some of the brightest and best students on campus are in fraternities and sororities? Might they argue that only a few rowdy houses are at fault? Might they point to very prestigious institutions that have fraternities and sororities? Might they say that the cause of a poor academic reputation has nothing to do with fraternities and sororities and point instead to other causes? How can I respond to these arguments?*

How could they raise doubts about my warrant and backing? They probably wouldn't argue that it is bad to have a good academic reputation. They will probably argue instead that eliminating sororities and fraternities won't improve the university's academic reputation but will hurt its social life and its wide range of living options. To respond to these arguments, maybe I should do some research into what happened at other colleges when they eliminated the Greek system.

QUALIFIER: *Should I add a "may" by saying that eliminating the Greek system* may *help improve our academic reputation?*

As this example shows, thinking systematically about the grounds, warrant, backing, and conditions of rebuttal for each of your reasons can help you generate additional ideas to strengthen your first draft.

Designing a One-Page Advocacy Advertisement

As an alternative to a traditional written argument, your instructor might ask you to create a one-page advocacy advertisement. The first stage of your invention process should be the same as for a longer proposal argument. Choose a controversial public issue that needs immediate attention or a neglected issue about which you want to arouse public passion. As with a longer proposal argument, consider your audience in order to identify the values and beliefs on which you will base your appeal.

When you construct your argument, the limited space available demands efficiency in your choice of words and in your use of document design. Your goal is to have a memorable impact on your reader in order to promote the action you advocate. The following questions may help you design and revise your advocacy ad.

1. How could photos or other graphic elements establish and give presence to the problem?

2. How can type size, style, and layout be used to present the core of your proposal, including the justifying reasons, in the most powerful way for the intended audience?

3. Can any part of this argument be presented as a slogan or memorable catchphrase? What key phrases could highlight the parts or the main points of this argument?

4. How can document design clarify the course of action and the direct demand on the audience this argument is proposing?

5. How can use of color enhance the overall impact of your advocacy argument? (Note: One-page advertisements are expensive to reproduce in color, but you might make effective use of color if your advocacy ad were to appear as a poster or Web page.)

Questioning and Critiquing a Proposal Argument

As we've suggested, proposal arguments need to overcome the innate conservatism of people, the difficulty of anticipating all the consequences of a proposal, and so forth. What questions, then, can we ask about proposal arguments to help us anticipate these problems?

Will a skeptic deny that my problem is really a problem? The first question to ask of your proposal is "What's so wrong with the status quo that change is necessary?" The second question is "Who loses if the status quo is changed?" Be certain not to overlook this second question. Most proposal makers can demonstrate that some sort of problem exists, but often it is a problem only for certain groups of people. Solving the problem will thus prove a benefit to some people but a cost to others. If audience members examine the problem from the perspective of the potential losers rather than the winners, they can often raise doubts about your proposal.

Will a skeptic doubt the effectiveness of my solution? Assuming that you've convinced your audience that a significant problem exists and is worth solving, you then have to convince readers that your solution will work. Skeptics are apt to raise at least two kinds of questions about your proposed solution. First, they may doubt that you have adequately identified the cause of the problem. Perhaps you have mistaken a symptom for a cause or confused two commonly associated but essentially unlinked phenomena for a cause-effect relationship. For example, will paying teachers higher salaries improve the quality of teaching or merely attract greedier rather than brighter people? Maybe more good teachers would be attracted and retained if they were given some other benefit (fewer students? fewer classes? more sabbaticals? more autonomy? more prestige?). Second, skeptics are apt to invoke the phenomenon of unintended consequences—solving one problem merely creates a sequence of new problems. ("Now that we've raised teachers' salaries, we don't have enough tax dollars for highway maintenance; not only that, now firefighters and police are demanding higher salaries also.") As you anticipate audience objections, look again at the potential negative consequences of your proposed solution.

Will a skeptic think my proposal costs too much? The most commonly asked question of any proposal is simply, "Do the benefits of enacting the proposal outweigh the costs?" As we saw above, you can't foresee all the consequences of any proposal. It's easy, before the fact, to underestimate the costs and exaggerate the benefits of a proposal. So, in asking how much your proposal will cost, we urge you to make an honest estimate. Will your audience discover costs you hadn't anticipated—extra financial costs or unexpected psychological or environmental or aesthetic costs? As much as you can, anticipate these objections.

Will a skeptic suggest counterproposals? Once you've convinced readers that a problem exists, they are apt to suggest alternative solutions different from yours. If readers acknowledge the seriousness of the problem, yet object to your proposal, they are faced with a dilemma: Either they have to offer their own counterproposals or they have to argue that the problem is simply in the nature of things and hence unsolvable. So, given the likelihood that you'll be faced with a counterproposal, it only makes sense to anticipate it and to work out a refutation of it before you have it thrown at you. And who knows, you may end up liking the counterproposal better and changing your mind about what to propose!

Readings

Our first reading, by student writer Laurel Wilson, is a practical proposal addressing the problem of an inequitable tipping policy for hosts in a national brewpub restaurant chain.* ("Hosts" are the persons who greet you when you enter a restaurant and escort you to a table.) As a practical proposal, it uses headings and

---

*Laurel Wilson wrote this proposal to an actual company; with the author's permission, we have changed the names of the manager and brewpub and disguised the location.

other elements of document design aimed to give it a finished and professional appearance. When sent to the intended audience, it is accompanied by a single-spaced letter of transmittal following the conventional format of a business letter.

Paul Smithson
CEO, Stone's End Restaurant and Brewery
1422 Stone Avenue
Certain City, Certain State, Zip

Dear Mr. Smithson:

Enclosed is a proposal that addresses Stone's End corporate policy forbidding hosts from receiving tips from servers. My proposal shows the problems associated with this rule and suggests a workable solution.

The enclosed proposal suggests a modest plan for tipping hosts that would make their wages more fair. Currently hosts earn only half as much as servers, and yet are expected not only to work as hard as servers, but also to wear dressy clothes that are quite expensive. Rewarding hosts for their important work in a job that is far from easy should be supported by management and servers, who benefit from hosts who go above and beyond the call of duty.

As a former host at Stone's End, I often felt unappreciated by both servers and management. I worked very hard and was not compensated for providing excellent service. I eventually found a different job because I could not afford to work there without the extra compensation of tips. I later discovered that many other restaurants not only tipped their hosts, but also gave them a clothing allowance. I hope my idea is received well and considered as a viable option. A change in corporate policy regarding the tipping of hosts might make Stone's End restaurants even more successful than they are now because hosts would feel like appreciated members of the restaurant team.

Thank you for your time.

Sincerely,

Laurel Wilson

A PROPOSAL TO PROVIDE TIPS FOR HOSTS AT STONE'S END
Submitted for Consideration by the Stone's End Corporate Office
by
Laurel Wilson, former Stone's End Host in _____
(Address and Phone Number)

If this were the actual proposal, the first page would begin on a new page following the cover page.

PROBLEM

Because the "no tips" policy for hosts at Stone's End restaurants keeps their wages significantly below those of servers, hosts often feel unnoticed and unappreciated. Hosts at Stone's End currently make a flat wage of $9.00 per hour without tips. Servers make $6.25 per hour plus tips, which range between $50 and $150 per shift. On a busy night, a server can make as much as $31.25 per hour for a four-hour shift if one adds $100 of tips to four hours of wages (6.25 × 4 + 100 divided by 4). Hosts usually have a six-hour shift making $9 per hour. In a four-hour shift a server typically makes $125, while a host makes $54 for a six-hour shift.

Some people might think that hosts shouldn't be tipped because their job is less stressful than that of servers. However, the host's job entails many things that keep the restaurant running smoothly. A host organizes the dining room in a way that accommodates all parties with no customers having to wait more than fifteen minutes for their tables. The host also has to make sure that servers do not have more than one party being seated in their section at the same time. There are usually nine servers in the dining room during the evening shift, each having five tables in his or her section. A good host will clear and wipe down tables of servers who are swamped in order to give them more time and to keep the restaurant running smoothly. At any given time a host will be dealing with cranky customers, answering a four-line phone, taking "to go" orders, trying to organize a dining room that seats over 200 people, and often clearing tables for overwhelmed servers. This is a highly stressful and active job which requires hard work and is often misunderstood by those who do not know all the duties a host performs.

PROPOSAL

I propose that servers give 1 percent of their tips to the host. As it is now, servers give 2 percent of their tips to the bartenders and 1 percent to the expediters (the expo brings the food out to the tables and arranges the servers' trays). If the servers contribute another 1 percent to their host, the cost to servers would average about one dollar per shift to their host. If you add $1 from each server (usually nine) that adds $9 to the host's pay for the shift, raising it from the $54 we figured earlier (based on six hours at $9 per hour) to $63. On a busy night, the host might get $1.50 or even $2.00 from each server—an amount that would help the host immensely while being barely a dent in the server's take-home pay for the shift.

JUSTIFICATION

Some persons might have objections to this proposal. Owners, in setting corporate policy for the national chain of Stone's End restaurants, have most likely researched all aspects of the restaurant business and decided that the "no tips" rule for hosts was the best policy. They probably have reasons for the "no tips" policy that hosts don't understand. But perhaps the owners don't currently recognize the disadvantages of this policy, which leads to disgruntled hosts and a high turnover. Running a successful restaurant hinges on the happiness of all employees. The hosts' contributions are currently disregarded, even though they are a valuable asset to the restaurant. Corporate owners would be caught in a tailspin if they spent just one night doing the job of a host.

Others might point to the plight of the servers. Servers work incredibly hard for their tips and rely on those tips to pay their bills. On a slow night (which is rare), servers might make minimal tips (maybe only $40 per shift). Taking even a small percentage out of their tips might seem painful. Also servers' shifts last about four hours whereas a host usually works a six-hour shift, sometimes even eight. Servers might argue that the host's extra hours, paid at a higher hourly rate than servers receive, give the hosts an adequate income. However, even on a very slow night in which the server makes only $40 in tips, their hourly wage is still $16.25 per hour, more than $7 per hour higher than the host's wage.

Despite the objections that might be raised by owners or servers, the hosts at Stone's End perform a difficult and thankless job that deserves recognition by both servers and the corporate office. My proposal should be enacted for the following reasons:

- Paying a small tip to hosts is a fair way to reward their contributions. As I have noted, the hosts' job entails many tasks that make the server's job more bearable. Moreover, the host makes the first impression on the customer and sets the mood for the customer's experience in the restaurant. Having to wear dressy clothes—a considerable extra expense—is only one part of the host's important job of setting a good first impression for the restaurant. During busy times, a host who goes above and beyond the call of duty helps out the servers by clearing and wiping tables and ensuring the smooth operation of the dining room.

- The current "no tips" policy set by the corporate office places local managers in the unpleasant position of having to defend a corporate policy that they don't personally support. At the Stone's End where I worked (in _____), the manager agreed with the hosts' desire to receive tips as did the servers, who agreed that hosts should be rewarded for all the help they provide servers with their hectic jobs. But the manager had to back the corporate office's "no tips for hosts" rule, making it difficult for the manager to keep every employee happy. The manager thus had to bear the brunt of the hosts' complaints without having power to change the situation.

- Finally, tipping hosts would make Stone's End more competitive with other restaurants in cities such as _____, where tipping hosts is common practice. For example, in _____, restaurants such as II Fornaio and Pallamino's pay their hosts the same wage as Stone's End, but require that servers tip the hosts. Moreover, each of these restaurants has a clothing allowance for their hosts. Not only do their hosts look nice, but they are happy with their jobs as well.

CONCLUSION

Asking servers to tip hosts at the low rate of 1 percent of tip income would show Stone's End hosts that they are respected and appreciated by their coworkers and part of the restaurant team whose livelihood depends on happy, satisfied customers. The host works hard to keep everyone happy including servers, managers, and customers. They do not make the money they deserve. In order to keep hosts happy and Stone's End competitive with surrounding restaurants, this policy would provide a satisfactory solution to a significant problem. I believe that corporate owners would be highly pleased with the all-around benefits of having happy hosts.

Critiquing "A Proposal to Provide Tips for Hosts at Stone's End"

1. In your own words, summarize briefly the problem that Laurel Wilson addresses, her proposed solution, and her justifying reasons.

2. Laurel addresses her proposal to the CEO of Stone's End restaurants because the CEO has the power to change policy. To what extent does Laurel develop audience-based reasons for this CEO audience? How effectively does she anticipate and respond to objections her audience might raise?

3. How does Laurel establish a positive *ethos* in this argument and a meaningful picture of the problem?

4. How effective is Laurel's proposal?

Our second reading, by student writer Mark Bonicillo, is a researched public policy proposal written for the "Option 3" assignment on page 334. Bonicillo's argument is based on research he conducted into the problem of Americans without health insurance. You will note that he supplemented library and Internet research with information from a personal interview he conducted with a leading local authority on health insurance issues. Bonicillo's argument is formatted as a formal research paper using the documentation style of the Modern Language Association (MLA). A full explanation of this format is given in Chapter 17.

Mark Bonicillo

Professor Scharf

Humanities Seminar 300

June 15, 2002

A Proposal for Universal Health Insurance in the United States

1   Ian, a twenty-three-year-old college graduate and the son of one of my professors, hasn't yet found a career-type job in the current slow economy. He currently works as a waiter at a downtown restaurant that offers minimum wage plus tips with no health insurance. A few weeks ago, Ian hurt his back in a recreational soccer game, and the pain is getting worse. Unfortunately, he has no doctor to go to. Like many recent college graduates, he is no longer covered by his student insurance policy, nor can he be covered on his parents' health insurance now that he has graduated from college. He can't afford to buy health insurance on his waiter's pay (the premiums would be $300 per month), and in any case his back injury wouldn't be covered because it is a "pre-existing condition." Now he is trying to pay for food and rent on his waiter's earnings, while also paying off his student loans. Meanwhile his back is killing him.

2   Ian's frightening situation is common in the United States. According to a study from the Employee Benefit Research Institute, 32.8% of Americans ages 21–24 and 22.5% of Americans ages 25–35 do not have health insurance (Fronstin 22). But it's not just young adults who don't have health insurance. The working poor and unemployed constitute the majority of the uninsured. Based on statistical research, recent estimates suggest that almost 39 million Americans do not have any form of health insurance (Kaiser Commission on Medicaid and the Uninsured).

3   These uninsured Americans lead sicker lives than insured Americans and create an unnecessary financial drain on the health care industry. If they are sick, they have to go to hospital emergency rooms, hassle with the subsequent unpaid bills, and hope that the hospital will eventually write them off as charity expense. (This is what Ian plans to do with his bad back.) According to a recent study by the Institute of Medicine, uninsured Americans are less likely than insured Americans to get regular checkups or receive preventative care. They have higher mortality rates and sickness rates. Moreover, treating these persons in emergency rooms is extremely expensive. It costs more to amputate the leg of a seriously ill diabetic than it would to diagnose the disease, prescribe insulin, and provide regular care (Institute of Medicine 1).

Bonicillo 2

Why do so many Americans lack health insurance? The answer lies in the way that insurance is paid for in the United States. In most European countries and in Canada, medicine is socialized so that the government pays for medical care and citizens pay the government through higher taxes. In such a system, coverage is universal. But in the United States, medical insurance is linked to employment. Employers pay for health insurance, which they purchase from competing insurance companies. Generally, the employer pays a significant percentage of the insurance costs as a fringe benefit of employment. This system works fine as long as (1) you are employed; (2) your employer is a large enough company to be required to purchase health insurance (many small companies don't have to provide insurance); and (3) you have a long-term, full-time position in the company (many companies don't provide benefits for temporary or other low-wage workers). If you don't have employer-provided insurance, you can purchase individual policies (assuming that you aren't already ill with disqualifying pre-existing conditions), but the premiums are very expensive and they are rated according to your health risk. People with illnesses such as diabetes often can't buy private insurance at any price.

For those who are retired or are low-income earners—and therefore do not have access to employer-provided insurance or cannot afford individual insurance—the federal or state governments try to help. The federal government provides Medicare for citizens over sixty-five and Medicaid for poor people who meet certain federal poverty guidelines. Additionally, some states provide subsidized health care plans for certain categories of people near the poverty line who are not covered by Medicaid. However, as shown in Figure 1 (based on data from the Kaiser Commission on Medicaid and the Uninsured), a significant number of Americans—16% of the adult population under sixty-five years of age—have no insurance.

Furthermore, two additional problems are connected to this employer-based system. First, insured Americans can quickly lose their insurance if they lose their jobs. When the economy is in recession, the number of uninsured increases significantly. Diane Rowland, Executive Director of the Kaiser Commission on Medicaid and the Uninsured, estimates that "for every 100 workers added to the unemployment rolls, 85 people will join the ranks of the uninsured" (10). She cites a study that showed when unemployment rose from 4% in December 2000 to 5.8% in December 2001, the number of uninsured Americans increased by 2.2 million. As we can see, the current U.S. policy of distributing health insurance through employers leaves Americans in jeopardy of losing their health insurance at any time.

Bonicillo 3

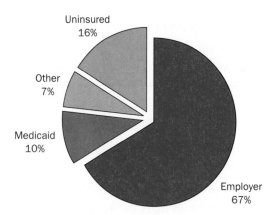

Fig. 1. Health insurance coverage in U.S., 2001, adult Americans under 65.

7   The second major problem with employer-provided insurance is that the attempts of the federal and state governments to create safety nets for the uninsured are underfunded and full of gaps. For example, Medicare certainly helps the elderly, but many persons fear that Medicare funding will collapse in the near future as baby boomers retire. Moreover, Medicare in some states is so poorly funded that many doctors will no longer take Medicare patients because the reimbursement payments are too low. According to a news report in the <u>Seattle Times</u>, some doctors in the state of Washington have even refused to accept new Medicare patients (Ostrom A1). In addition, the systems adopted by the states to provide insurance for persons at the poverty level are unevenly administered and burdened with red tape. In a personal interview I conducted with Randy Revelle, the director of health policy for the Washington State Hospital Association, I learned that in 1998 over fifteen thousand uninsured children in the state of Washington were eligible for state-subsidized insurance, but they and their parents did not know it because of inadequate advertising and red tape. Similar problems occur in other states. According to Rowland, even with the knowledge that one is eligible for government-sponsored health insurance, long and burdensome application forms and language problems discourage many uninsured Americans from even applying for government health insurance (7). And so, many uninsured Americans who could have had public health insurance are still left uninsured.

8   Finally, we must ask why the American people haven't demanded a change from this employer-based system. Why hasn't this problem already been solved?

Bonicillo 4

I think there are three basic reasons. First, because the majority of Americans 9
have employer-provided insurance, they don't give this problem a high priority.
Second, the general public is unwilling to support any real health care reform
because they think it might lead to "socialized medicine," which raises the fearful
specter of demoralized doctors, faceless patients, and long waiting lists for needed
services. Finally, insurance companies, doctors, and drug companies benefit from
the present system and lobby heavily to persuade politicians from adopting health
care reform that might cut into their profits.

The solution to the problem of the uninsured is to dismantle the current 10
employer-provided system without leading to European- or Canadian-style
socialized medicine that doesn't fit American values or business structures. Based
on my research, the best approach is a compromise between liberals and
conservatives, evidenced in a series of interviews conducted by journalist Matthew
Miller with two U.S. representatives—a liberal, Democrat Jim McDermott of
Washington, who personally favors a European-style government-as-single-payer
system, and a conservative, Republican Jim McCrery of Louisiana, who supports
insurance companies and free markets for health care. The common ground
between these two political opponents, evident in the interviews, leads to a
possible solution. Based on my reading of these interviews, I offer the following
three policy recommendations.

First, the federal government should break the linkage between health 11
insurance and employment. Instead, according to Rep. McCrery's suggestion, the
government should mandate that all adult citizens purchase individual or family
health insurance (Miller 84). This mandate would guarantee that all Americans
would be insured. To help pay for this insurance, McCrery suggests that the
insurance subsidies currently provided by employers as a fringe benefit could be
passed on to employees as increased salary (Miller 86). Therefore employed persons
would pay no additional costs under this system.

Second, McCrery and McDermott agree that the government should help 12
unemployed or low-income people buy health insurance by providing tax subsidies
on a sliding scale. The government would thus buy insurance for those at the
poverty line and subsidize insurance on a sliding scale for those above it (Miller 86).

Third, McCrery and McDermott both agree that to make health insurance 13
affordable for all, insurance companies must base their premiums on a community

rating spread across all buyers instead of charging higher rates for persons with illnesses or identifiable risk factors. Because young, healthy Americans would be required to buy insurance, these persons would help fund the system by paying in more than they draw out and yet be fully covered if they need medical care (Miller 84).

14   These three policy recommendations would solve most of the problems with the current system and fit the American structure of business. An advantage of this proposal is that it does not eliminate insurance companies or interfere with a free-market approach to medicine. As Miller explains, insurance companies would still compete with each other for customers (85). The major change would be that health insurance companies would market to individuals rather than to employers in the same way that car and life insurance companies do. Also, drug companies would not be frightened by the prospect of the government setting prices for drugs.

15   A second advantage is that the majority of Americans would need no government subsidy because their increased insurance costs would be covered by a transfer into salary of the insurance benefit currently paid by the employer. At the same time employers would benefit by no longer having to undergo the hassles of negotiating for and providing insurance for their employees (Miller 85).

16   Third, this system provides a safety net for employed Americans who risk losing their jobs in times of recession. The government would immediately step in to help pay for insurance based on the sliding scale need of the unemployed person.

17   Finally, this system brings health care to low-wage workers who do not currently receive employer-subsidized insurance and to all currently ill or at-risk persons whose pre-existing conditions disqualify them for self-pay insurance. Because a community rating spreads the risk across all Americans, the many young and healthy people paying into the system (the ones who today are apt not to buy insurance because they aren't sick) help subsidize the health care needed by others (Miller 84).

18   Undoubtedly many problems with this proposal need to be worked out— including the procedures for mandating every adult to buy insurance as well as the political battle of determining how new taxes will be assessed to pay for the substantial costs of subsidizing insurance for the poor and the unemployed. But this proposal attacks the problem of the uninsured and the U.S. health care system at its core. This nation has tried many different solutions, and they have all failed. While genuine reform is painful and politically difficult, it is the only way to heal our

sickening health care system that leaves 39 million Americans without health insurance. Under this system, Ian would have had government-subsidized health insurance. He could have gone to a doctor when he first hurt his back instead of waiting a month to go to a hospital emergency room and plead poverty.

Bonicillo 7

Works Cited

Fronstin, Paul. <u>Sources of Health Insurance and Characteristics of the Uninsured: Analysis of the March 1997 Current Population Survey</u>. Employee Benefit Research Institute Issue Brief 192. Washington, DC: EBRI, Dec. 1997.

Institute of Medicine. <u>Care Without Coverage: Too Little, Too Late</u>. New York: Natl. Acad. P., 2002.

Kaiser Commission on Medicaid and the Uninsured. "The Uninsured and Their Access to Health Care." Feb. 2002. <u>Henry J. Kaiser Family Foundation</u>. 2 pp. 26 May 2002 <http://www.kff.org/content/2002/142003/142003.pdf>.

Miller, Matthew. "Health Care: A Bolt of Civic Hope." <u>Atlantic Monthly</u> Oct. 2000: 77–87.

Ostrom, Carol M. "Doctors Fleeing Medicare, Medicaid." <u>Seattle Times</u> 12 Mar. 2002: A1.

Revelle, Randy. Personal interview. 9 May 2002.

Rowland, Diane. "The New Challenge of the Uninsured: Coverage in the Current Economy." Kaiser Commission on Medicaid and the Uninsured 28 Feb. 2002. <u>Henry J. Kaiser Family Foundation</u>. 24 pp. 23 May 2002 <http://www.kff.org/content/2002/4042/4042.pdf>.

Critiquing "A Proposal for Universal Health Insurance in the United States"

1. In your own words, sum up the problem that Mark Bonicillo addresses and his proposed solution to the problem.

2. Although the problem of being sick and uninsured is immediately vivid, the details of the American health care system are often tedious and wonkish. When President Clinton in 1994 proposed a sweeping reform of the health care system—led by First Lady Hillary Clinton—the insurance industry defeated his proposals using the "Harry and Louise" television ad campaign, which portrayed the Clinton plan as costly, bureaucratic socialized medicine that would prevent Americans from choosing their own doctors.

   a. To what extent is Mark successful in explaining the problems of health insurance in the United States? Does his argument become too wonkish? Unclear?

   b. To what extent does his proposed solution address Americans' fear of "socialized medicine"?

3. What rhetorical strategies does Mark use to make his argument as compelling as possible? How does he try to create presence? How does he appeal to *ethos* and *pathos* as well as *logos?* How effective is his use of quantitative graphics?

4. Overall, how effective do you find Mark's argument?

Our third reading (see Figure 15.2) is a one-page paid advocacy advertisement appearing in newspapers in 2002. This is the second in a series of ads produced by the Center for Children's Health and the Environment located at Mount Sinai School of Medicine in New York. The ads were intended to work in concert with the organization's Web site www.childenvironment.org, which provides backup documentation including access to the scientific studies on which the ads' arguments are based. All the ads can be downloaded in pdf format from the Web site. The ads' purpose is to call public attention to environmental dangers to children and to urge public action.

Critiquing the Advocacy Ad from the Center for Children's Health and the Environment

1. A difficulty faced by many proposal writers is awakening the audience to the existence of the problem. The doctors and researchers who founded the Center for Children's Health and the Environment felt that a series of full-page newspaper ads was the best way to awaken the public to a problem that Americans either denied or didn't know existed.

   a. In your own words, what is the problem that this proposal addresses?

   b. How does the ad give presence to the problem?

#2 IN A SERIES

More kids are getting brain cancer.
Why?

Toxic chemicals appear linked to rising rates of some cancers.

As scientists and physicians, we've seen a drop in the death rates of many adult and childhood cancers because of earlier detection and better treatment. But we are also seeing a disturbing rise in the reported *incidence* of cancer among young children and adolescents, especially brain cancer, testicular cancer, and acute lymphocytic leukemia. In fact, after injuries and violence, cancer is the leading cause of death in our children.

The increase in childhood cancers may be explained in part by better detection or better access to medical care. But evidence suggests the rise in these childhood cancers, as well as in cancers like non-Hodgkin's lymphoma and multiple myeloma among adults, may also be partially explained by exposure to chemicals in the environment, chemicals found in many products, from paints and pesticides to dark-colored hair dyes.

What We Know

Pound for pound, kids are exposed to more toxic chemicals in food, air, and water than adults, because children breathe twice as much air, eat three to four times more food, and drink as much as two to seven times more water. Recent epidemiologic studies have shown that as children's exposures to home and garden pesticides increase, so does their risk of non-Hodgkin's lymphoma, brain cancer, and leukemia. Yet, right now, you can go to your hardware store and buy lawn pesticides, paint thinner and weed killers, all containing toxic chemicals linked to these diseases.

In both children and adults, the incidence rate for non-Hodgkin's lymphoma has increased thirty percent since 1950. The disease has been linked to industrial chemicals, chemicals found in agricultural, home, and garden pesticides, as well as dark hair dyes.

Studies have shown that Vietnam veterans and chemical workers exposed to Agent Orange, a phenoxy herbicide, are especially at risk for non-Hodgkin's lymphoma. American farmers who use phenoxy herbicides have an increased risk of the cancer. A Swedish study showed that among the general population, the risk of non-Hodgkin's lymphoma rises with increased exposure to these herbicides. And, a study in Southern California found that children of parents who use home pesticides have seven times the risk of non-Hodgkin's lymphoma. Multiple myeloma, a bone marrow cancer, is also associated with toxic chemicals. Its incidence has tripled since 1950. Farmers are especially at risk: a recent analysis of thirty-two studies worldwide showed "consistent, positive findings" of an association between farming and multiple myeloma.

What We Can Do

There is much that parents can do to protect their children from carcinogenic chemicals, beginning with the elimination of many pesticides both outside and in the home. And, of course, the cessation of smoking. There are more suggestions on our website, www.childenvironment.org.

But more needs to be done. As a society, we've done much to protect people, especially children, from the toxic chemicals in cigarettes. But too many toxic chemicals are being marketed without adequate testing. We should demand that new chemicals undergo the same rigorous testing as medicines before being allowed on the market. And we should phase out those chemicals linked with a wide range of health problems from neurological impairment to cancer in children.

A summary of the supporting scientific evidence, and a list of scientific endorsers, can be found at www.childenvironment.org.

Center for Children's Health and the Environment

MOUNT SINAI SCHOOL OF MEDICINE

Box 1043, One Gustave Levy Place, New York, NY 10029 • **www.childenvironment.org**

FIGURE 15.2

2. How does this ad use the strategies of visual argument (use of images, arrangement of text, type size, and so forth) discussed in Chapter 9? The ad makers probably had available thousands of pictures to use in this ad. Why did they choose this photograph? Try to reconstruct the thinking of the ad makers when they decided on their use of type sizes and fonts. How is the message in different parts of the ad connected to the visual presentation of the words?

3. How effective is the actual verbal argument of this advertisement? Why does it place "Toxic chemicals appear linked to rising rates of some cancers" in boldface type at the beginning of the text?

4. Most of this ad is devoted to presentation of the problem. What does the ad actually propose?

5. Overall, how effective do you find this advocacy advertisement? If you were thumbing through a newspaper, would you stop to read this ad? If so, what would hook you?

Our last reading, by Maia Szalavitz, proposes a solution to the problem of black-market opium production in Afghanistan. Historically, Afghan poppy growers have produced more than 70 percent of the world's black-market opium. In 2000, however, the Taliban made poppy growing illegal and effectively shut down the country's illicit opium industry. The defeat of the Taliban as part of the U.S. war on terrorism has led to the rapid regrowth of the industry. In this op-ed piece, published in the *New York Times* in July 2005, Szalavitz proposes a solution. Maia Szalavitz is a senior fellow at STATS, a media watchdog group. She is also a freelance writer specializing in health, science, and public policy. In 1990, she was nominated for a Pulitzer Prize for an autobiographical article published in *The Village Voice* detailing her own struggles with IV drug use and addiction.

Let a Thousand Licensed Poppies Bloom
Maia Szalavitz

Even as Afghanistan's immense opium harvest feeds lawlessness and instability, finances terrorism and fuels heroin addiction, the developing world is experiencing a severe shortage of opium-derived pain medications, according to the World Health Organization. Developing countries are home to 80 percent of the world's population, but they consume just 6 percent of the medical opioids. In those countries, most people with cancer, AIDS and other painful conditions live and die in agony.

The United States wants Afghanistan to destroy its potentially merciful crop, which has increased sevenfold since 2002 and now constitutes 60 percent of the country's gross domestic product. But why not bolster the country's stability and end both the pain and the trafficking problems by licensing Afghanistan with the International Narcotics Control Board to sell its opium legally?

3   The Senlis Council, a European drug-policy research institution, has proposed this truly winning solution. Adopting it would improve the Afghan economy, deprive terrorists of income and keep heroin away from dealers and addicts, all while offering pain relief to the third world.

4   The United Nations estimated that Afghanistan produced more than 4,200 tons of opium last year; cultivation jumped to 323,701 acres from 197,680 acres in 2003. Ten percent of the Afghan population is believed to be involved in the trade, which supplies nearly 90 percent of the world's illegal heroin. Clearly, this drug war is not being won.

5   The global pain crisis is just as daunting. The World Health Organization has said that opioids are "absolutely necessary" for treating severe pain. But half the world's countries use them only rarely if at all even for the dying, and even though research shows that addiction is exceedingly uncommon among pain patients without a history of it.

6   Here in the United States, only half of all dying patients receive adequate relief, and those suffering from chronic non-cancer pain are even more likely to be under-medicated. Senlis estimates that meeting the global need for pain medications would require 10,000 tons of opium a year—more than twice Afghanistan's current production.

7   This shortfall is in part attributable to misguided regulation. Restrictions aimed at preventing diversion to the illegal market are so severe that in some countries, medical use of opioids is practically prohibited. Often, the rich retain access to expensive synthetic opioids like OxyContin, while those who cannot afford brand-name drugs receive no treatment at all. Generic morphine and codeine, made from Afghan opium, could help.

8   Because farmers aren't the ones who make the big bucks in the illegal drug trade, purchasing their poppies at competitive rates should be possible. But even if we paid exactly what the drug lords do, the entire crop would cost only about $600 million—less than the $780 million the United States planned to spend on eradication in Afghanistan this year.

9   Besides, eradication efforts have never eliminated a drug crop. Cocaine continues to be widely available, despite the roughly $3 billion that the United States has spent on coca eradication in Colombia over the last five years. And that is only the most recent example.

10   India's thriving generic drug industry suggests that there is plenty of money to be made in the marketing of generic pain relievers. But even if returns are modest, generating any profit at all is better than stamping out the major driver of an unstable country's economy. Legal products are also safer and easier to regulate than illegal drugs.

11   Of course, the Senlis plan does present serious logistical problems. Warlords would not relinquish profits without a fight, and their attempts to undermine the proposal could be formidable.

But think of it this way: what's an easier sell with farmers, hard cash now or pesticide spraying and potentially empty promises of economic assistance? Few Afghans begrudge farmers' efforts to feed their families—but many would turn against greedy planters who continued supplying drug lords despite adequate alternatives. 12

The real barriers here are political, not practical. The Afghan government initially appeared open to the proposal: its counternarcotics minister spoke at a Senlis meeting in Vienna in March. But another minister later dismissed the idea in front of foreign reporters and Hamid Karzai ducked the question in a March meeting with Secretary of State Condoleezza Rice. 13

The Bush administration has criticized Mr. Karzai's "leadership" on opium (despite his call for "jihad on drugs") but refuses to support measures beyond eradication. Responding to the Senlis proposal, one former State Department official who had been working on narcotics and law enforcement told *The Christian Science Monitor*: "Anything that went about legalizing an opiate in that market would send exactly the wrong message. It would suggest that there is something legitimate to growing." 14

But there is: countries like India are licensed by the International Narcotics Control Board to grow opium because modern medicine cannot find anything better than opioids to relieve pain. And think of the goodwill such a gesture could produce, a message that we literally want to assuage the world's suffering—not to mention that of the 30 million to 50 million Americans who endure chronic pain. 15

The Senlis Council is holding a conference in Kabul this September to secure support from drug policy experts for a feasibility study of its proposal. As Afghanistan seems to grow increasingly unstable by the day, let's hope that proposal receives the backing it deserves. 16

Critiquing "Let a Thousand Licensed Poppies Bloom"

1. Szalavitz's proposal addresses two problems rather than one. What are the two problems and how are they connected? How effective is Szalavitz at giving these problems presence?

2. Skeptics often criticize proposals by saying, "It is a good idea in theory, but it won't work." Where does Szalavitz anticipate these objections and address them?

3. Why does Szalavitz say that the "real barriers here are political, not practical"?

4. Based on Szalavitz's argument, what seem to be the benefits of the Senlis Council's proposal? What seem to be the costs?

5. How persuasive do you find this proposal? How would you analyze this article from the perspectives of *logos, ethos, pathos,* and *kairos*?

The Researched Argument

16   Finding and Evaluating Sources

17   Using, Citing, and Documenting Sources

Source: Kirk Anderson, www.kirktoons.com

Reminding viewers of the inconvenience of heightened airport security since 9/11, this political cartoon humorously suggests that the war on terrorism may have compromised our civil liberties. The For Class Discussion exercise on page 180 calls for analysis of this cartoon.

16 Finding and Evaluating Sources

Although the "research paper" is a common writing assignment in college, students are often baffled by their professor's expectations. The problem is that students often think of research writing as presenting information rather than as creating an argument. One of our business school colleagues calls these sorts of research papers "data dumps": The student backs a truckload full of fresh data up to the professor's desk, dumps it, and says: "Here's your load of info on 'world poverty,' Prof. You make sense of it."

But a research paper shouldn't be a data dump. Like any other argument, it should use its information to support a contestable claim. Formal researched arguments have much in common with arguments that freelancers might write in a popular magazine. However, there is one major difference between a formal research paper and an informal magazine article—the presence of citations and a bibliography. In academic research, the purpose of in-text citations and a complete bibliography is to enable readers to follow the trail of the author's research. The proper formats for citations and bibliographic entries are simply conventions within an academic discipline to facilitate the reader's retrieval of the original sources.

Fortunately, you will find that writing an argument as a formal research paper draws on the same argumentation skills you have been using all along—the ability to pose a good question at issue within a community, to formulate a contestable claim, and to support your claim with audience-based reasons and evidence. What special skills are required? The main ones are these:

- The ability to use your research effectively to frame your issue and to support your claim, revealing your reputable *ethos* and knowledge of the issue. Sources should be woven seamlessly into your argument, which is written in your own voice throughout. Writers should avoid a pastiche of block quotations.
- The ability to tap the resources of libraries, online databases, and the World Wide Web.

■ The ability to evaluate sources for credibility, bias, and accuracy. Special care is needed to evaluate anything retrieved from the "free-access" portion of the World Wide Web.

■ The ability to summarize, quote, or paraphrase sources and to avoid plagiarism through citations and attributive tags such as "according to Jones" or "Peterson says."

■ The ability to cite and document sources according to appropriate conventions.

This chapter and the next should help you to develop these skills. In Chapter 16 we focus on posing a research question, on unlocking the resources of your library and the Internet, and on developing the rhetorical skills for evaluating sources effectively. In Chapter 17 we explain the more nitty-gritty details of how to incorporate that information into your writing and how to document it properly.

Formulating a Research Question

The best way to avoid writing a data dump is to begin with a good research question—the formulation of a problem or issue that your essay will address. The research question, usually in the form of an issue question, will give you a guiding purpose in doing your library research. Let's say you are interested in how toys affect the development of gender identity in children. You can see that this topic is big and unfocused. Your library research will be much easier if you give yourself a clear direction through a focused research question. For example, you might formulate a specific question like one of these:

■ Why have Barbie dolls been so continuously popular?

■ Does the Barbie doll reinforce traditional ideas of womanhood or challenge them?

■ Is culture or biology the stronger force in making little boys interested in trucks and guns?

■ Do boys' toys such as video games, complex models, electronic gadgets, and science sets develop intellectual and physical skills more than girls' toys do?

The sooner you can settle on a research question, the easier it will be to find the source materials you need in a time-saving, efficient manner. The exploration methods we suggested in Chapter 3 can help you find a research topic that interests you.

A good way to begin formulating a research question is to freewrite for ten minutes or so, reflecting on recent readings that have stimulated your interest, on recent events that have sparked arguments, or on personal experiences that might open up onto public issues. If you have no idea for a topic, try starting with the trigger question "What possible topics am I interested in?" If you already have an idea for a topic area, explore why you are interested in it. Search for the personal connections or the particular angles that most intrigue you. When student writer Megan Matthews began brainstorming possible issues for a research project, she was initially interested in the problem of storing nuclear waste, but in the middle of a freewrite she switched her focus to a newspaper article she had seen on how the hearing of whales may be threatened by the Navy's sonar technology for detecting enemy submarines. After a few hours of research, both in the library and on the Web, Megan produced the following freewrite in her research notebook:

A FREEWRITE FROM MEGAN'S RESEARCH NOTEBOOK

I'm really becoming interested in the whale issue. The Navy has its own site with a Q&A that contradicts some of its earlier findings, and NOAA [National Oceanic and Atmospheric Administration] issued approval for the military to "harass and disturb" marine mammals despite expressing earlier reservations. Hmmm. Very interesting. Is this new sonar really necessary for security? No one seems to answer that! How many whales could suffer? How dangerous to whales is this sonar? Have they really done enough testing?

Note how Megan has moved from a topic orientation (I am researching whales and Navy sonar) to a question orientation (I am doing research to find the answers to questions that I have posed). Once you get engaged with questions, then your research has a purpose guided by your own critical thinking. To emphasize the importance of questions, we'll show you one more excerpt from Megan's research notebook. Note Megan's intense desire to find answers to her questions:

ANOTHER FREEWRITE FROM MEGAN'S RESEARCH NOTEBOOK

Oh, I am so annoyed. The Navy Web site conveniently lists a lot of general information without the documents I need to evaluate their claims. For example, they justify the need for this sonar by claiming that "there are 224 non-allied subs in operation." Who falls under the category of "non-allied"? Russia? Iran? African nations with which we have no real relationships yet? Also, what's the breakdown for the 224? But when I tried to e-mail them, their mailbox was full; no phone numbers were listed anywhere on the site, nor could I find an address. . . . So, a dilemma: I want to dig deeper into this to really evaluate the argument; as it is, I have some great info from environmental organizations and some so-so stuff from the Navy. I think I'm going to have to read through all of the science and policy documents on the government sites to try getting "between the lines" to see if they've omitted anything. I'm very upset by the fact that studies were only conducted on four species of whales/dolphins, when fish, turtles, pinnapeds, and other marine/aquatic animals might be affected as well.

Megan is now caught up in the research process. We'll return to her story occasionally throughout this chapter and the next. Her final argument is reprinted in full at the end of Chapter 17.

Understanding Differences in the Kinds of Sources

Once you begin researching an issue, you will encounter many different kinds of sources ranging from articles posted on Web sites to scholarly books. To be an effective researcher, you need to understand the differences among the many kinds of books, articles, and Web sites you are apt to encounter. In this section, we explain these different kinds of resources. We summarize our points in two handy tables labeled "A rhetorical overview of print sources" (Table 16.1) and "A rhetorical overview of Web sites" (Table 16.2). By the term "rhetorical overview," we indicate a way of looking at sources that makes you fully conscious of the writer's context, bias, and intentions: For any given piece, what is the writer's purpose and who is the intended audience? What is the writer's bias, perspective, or angle of vision? What is being *left out* of this source as well as included? Once you are aware of the many kinds of sources available—and of the kinds of library or Web search strategies needed to find them—you will be a savvy and responsible researcher.

Books versus Periodicals versus Web Sites

When you conduct library research, you often leave the library with an armload of books and a stack of articles that you have either photocopied from journals or magazines or downloaded from a computer and printed out. At home, you will have no trouble determining who wrote the books and for what purpose, but your photocopied or downloaded articles can pose problems. What is the original source of the article in your hands? If you photocopied the articles from actual journals or magazines in your library, then you can be sure that they are "periodical print sources" (*periodical* means a publication, such as a scholarly journal or magazine, issued at regular intervals—that is, periodically). If you downloaded them from a computer—which may have been connected either to a licensed database leased by the library or to the World Wide Web—they may be electronic copies of periodical print sources or they may be material posted on the Web but never published in a print periodical.

When you download a print article from a computer, you should be aware that you lose many contextual clues about the author's purpose and bias—clues that you can pick up from the original magazine or journal itself by its appearance, title, advertisements (if any), table of contents, and statement of editorial policy. When you download something from the Web that has never appeared in print, you have to be wary about its source. Because print publications are costly to produce, print articles generally go through some level of editorial review. In contrast, anyone can post almost anything on the Web. You need to become savvy at recognizing these distinctions in order to read sources rhetorically and to document them accurately in your bibliography.

Scholarly Books versus Trade Books

Note in Table 16.1 the distinction between scholarly books, which are peer reviewed and published by nonprofit academic presses, and trade books, which are

TABLE 16.1   *A rhetorical overview of print sources*

Genre and Publisher	Author and Angle of Vision	How to Recognize Them
Books		
SCHOLARLY BOOKS • University/academic presses • Nonprofit • Selected through peer review	**Author:** Professors, researchers **Angle of vision:** Scholarly advancement of knowledge	• University press on title page • Specialized academic style • Documentation and bibliography
TRADE BOOKS (NONFICTION) • Commercial publishers (for example, Penguin Putnam) • Selected for profit potential	**Author:** Journalists, freelancers, scholars aiming at popular audience **Angle of vision:** Varies from informative to persuasive; often well researched and respected, but sometimes shoddy and aimed for quick sale	• Covers designed for marketing appeal • Popular style • Usually documented in an informal rather than academic style
REFERENCE BOOKS—MANY IN ELECTRONIC FORMAT • Publishers specializing in reference material • For-profit through library sales	**Author:** Commissioned scholars **Angle of vision:** Balanced, factual overview	• Titles containing words such as *encyclopedia*, *dictionary*, or *guide* • Found in reference section of library or online through library Web site
Periodicals		
SCHOLARLY JOURNALS • University/academic presses • Nonprofit • Articles chosen through peer review • Examples: *Journal of Abnormal Psychology, Review of Metaphysics*	**Author:** Professors, researchers, independent scholars **Angle of vision:** Scholarly advancement of knowledge; presentation of research findings; development of new theories and applications	• Not sold on magazine racks • No commercial advertising • Specialized academic style • Documentation and bibliography • Cover often has table of contents
PUBLIC AFFAIRS MAGAZINES • Commercial, "for-profit" presses • Manuscripts reviewed by editors • Examples: *Harper's, Commonweal, National Review*	**Author:** Staff writers, freelancers, scholars, for general audiences **Angle of vision:** Aims to deepen public understanding of issues; magazines often have political bias of left, center, or right	• Long, well-researched articles • Ads aimed at upscale professionals • Often has reviews of books, theater, film, and the arts

(continued)

TABLE 16.1 *continued*

Genre and Publisher	Author and Angle of Vision	How to Recognize Them
	Periodicals (continued)	
TRADE MAGAZINES • Commercial, "for-profit" presses • Focused on a profession or trade • Examples: *Advertising Age, Automotive Rebuilder, Farm Journal*	**Author:** Staff writers, industry specialists **Angle of vision:** Informative articles for practitioners; advocacy for the profession or trade	• Title indicating trade or profession • Articles on practical job concerns • Ads geared toward a particular trade or profession
NEWSMAGAZINES AND NEWSPAPERS • Newspaper chains and publishers • Examples: *Time, Newsweek, Washington Post, Los Angeles Times*	**Author:** Staff writers and journalists; occasional freelance pieces **Angle of vision:** News reports aimed at balance and objectivity; editorial pages reflect perspective of editors; op-ed pieces reflect different perspectives	• Readily familiar by name, distinctive cover style • Widely available on newsstands and by subscription • Ads aimed at broad, general audience
POPULAR NICHE MAGAZINES • Large conglomerates or small presses with clear target audience • Focused on special interests of target audience • Examples: *Seventeen, People, TV Guide, Car and Driver, Golf Digest*	**Author:** Staff or freelance writers **Angle of vision:** Varies—in some cases content and point of view are dictated by advertisers or the politics of publisher	• Glossy paper, extensive ads, lots of visuals • Popular, often distinctive style • Short, undocumented articles • Credentials of writer often not mentioned

published by for-profit presses with the intention of making money. By "peer reviewed," which is a highly prized concept in academia, we mean the selection process by which scholarly manuscripts get chosen for publication. When manuscripts are submitted to an academic publisher, the editor sends them for independent review to experienced scholars who judge the rigor and accuracy of the research and the significance and value of the argument. The process is highly competitive and weeds out much shoddy or trivial work.

In contrast, trade books are not peer reviewed by independent scholars. Instead, they are selected for publication by editors whose business is to make a profit. Fortunately, it can be profitable for popular presses to publish superbly researched and argued intellectual material because college-educated people, as lifelong learners, create a demand for intellectually satisfying trade books written for the general reader rather than for the highly specialized reader. These can be excellent sources for undergraduate research, but you need to separate the trash

TABLE 16.2   *A rhetorical overview of Web sites*

Type of Site	Author/Sponsor and Angle of Vision	Characteristics
.COM OR .BIZ (A COMMERCIAL SITE CREATED BY A BUSINESS OR CORPORATION)		
▪ Either of these suffixes signals a for-profit operation; this group includes major periodicals and publishers of reference materials ▪ Purpose is to enhance image, attract customers, market products and services, provide customer service ▪ Creators are paid by salary or fees and often motivated by desire to design innovative sites ▪ Also in the business category: specialized suffixes .aero (for sites related to air travel), .pro (for professionals—doctors, lawyers, accountants)	**Author:** Difficult to identify individual writers; sponsoring company often considered the author **Angle of vision:** Purpose is to promote the point of view of the corporation or business; links are to sites that promote same values	▪ Links are often to other products and services provided by company ▪ Photographs and other visuals used to enhance corporate image
.ORG (NONPROFIT ORGANIZATIONS OR ADVOCACY GROUPS)		
▪ Note: Sites with the ".museum" suffix have similar purposes and feel. ▪ Sometimes purpose is to provide accurate, balanced information (for example, the American Red Cross site) ▪ May function as a major information portal, such as NPR.org, PBS.org, a think tank, or a museum (for example, the Heritage Foundation, the Art Institute of Chicago, or the Museum of Modern Art) ▪ Frequently, purpose is to advocate for or explain the organization (for example, the Ford Foundation or local charity sites); thus, advocacy for fund-raising or political views is likely (for example, Persons for the Ethical Treatment of Animals [PETA] site or blog portals [Cursor.org])	**Author:** Often hard to identify individual writers; sponsoring organization often considered the author; some sites produced by amateurs with passionate views; others produced by well-paid professionals **Angle of vision:** Purpose is to promote views of sponsoring organization and influence public opinion and policy; many encourage donations through the site	▪ Advocacy sites sometimes don't announce purpose on home page ▪ You may enter a node of an advocacy site through a link from another site and not realize the political slant ▪ Facts/data selected and filtered by site's angle of vision ▪ Often uses visuals for emotional appeal
.EDU (AN EDUCATIONAL SITE ASSOCIATED WITH A COLLEGE OR UNIVERSITY)		
▪ Wide range of purposes ▪ Home page aimed at attracting prospective students and donors ▪ Inside the site are numerous subsites devoted to research, pedagogy, libraries, student employment, and so forth	**Author:** Professors, staff, students **Angle of vision:** Varies enormously from personal sites of professors and students to organizational sites of research centers and libraries; can vary from scholarly and objective to strong advocacy on issues	▪ Often an .edu site has numerous "subsites" sponsored by the university library, art programs, research units ▪ Links to .pdf documents may make it difficult to determine where you are in the site—e.g., professor's course site, student site, administrative site

(continued)

TABLE 16.2   *continued*

Type of Site	Author/Sponsor and Angle of Vision	Characteristics
.GOV OR .MIL (SPONSORED BY GOVERNMENT AGENCIES OR MILITARY UNITS)		
• Provides enormous range of basic data about government policy, bills in Congress, economic forecasts, and so forth • Aims to create good public relations for agency or military unit	**Author:** Development teams employed by the agency; sponsoring agency is usually considered the author **Angle of vision:** Varies—informational sites publish data and government documents with an objective point of view; agency sites also promote agency's agenda—e.g., Dept. of Energy, Dept. of Labor	• Typical sites (for example, www.energy.gov, the site of the U.S. Dept. of Energy) are extremely layered and complex and provide hundreds of links to other sites • Valuable for research • Sites often promote values/assumptions of sponsoring agency
PERSONAL WEB SITES (.NAME OR .NET)		
• An individual contracts with server to publish the site; many personal Web sites have .edu affiliation • Promotes hobbies, politics; provides links according to personal preferences	**Author:** Anyone can create a personal Web site **Angle of vision:** Varies from person to person	• Credentials/bias of author often hard to determine • Irresponsible sites might have links to excellent sites; tracing links is complicated • Probably not designed for fast download
.INFO (INFORMATION PROVIDERS—UNRESTRICTED, SO BECOMING A CATCHALL)		
• Libraries and library information materials • Regulations, hours, procedures, resources from local governments (e.g., www.lowermanhattan.info) • Publicity brochures for local organizations (e.g., Celtic Heritage Society, hobby groups) • Consumer alerts • Lodging, restaurants, bike rental, hiking trails, or other travel advice from tourist bureaus • Privately authored materials	**Author:** Varies widely from small public and private offices with an information mandate to individuals or groups with an ax to grind **Angle of vision:** Varies from genuinely helpful (Where can bicycles be loaded onto the ferry?) to business motives (Where can you find books or movies about bicycles?) to thinly disguised advocacy (e.g., "Debunking the Myths about Gun Control")	• Makes some information easier to find through advanced searches that specify the domain type • If author is identified, credentials difficult to determine • Information will be filtered through author(s) and sponsor(s) • Quality of editing and fact-checking will vary

from the treasure. Trade books are aimed at many different audiences and market segments and can include sloppy, unreliable, and heavily biased material.

Scholarly Journals versus Magazines

Like scholarly books, scholarly journals are academic, peer-reviewed publications. Although they may look like magazines, they almost never appear on newsstands; they are nonprofit publications subsidized by universities for disseminating high-level research and scholarship.

In contrast, magazines are intended to make a profit through sales and advertising revenues. Fortunately for researchers, a demand exists for intellectually satisfying magazines, just as for sophisticated trade books. Many for-profit magazines publish highly respectable, useful material for undergraduate or professional researchers, but many magazines publish shoddy material. As Table 16.1 shows, magazines fall in various categories aimed at different audiences.

Print Sources versus Cyberspace Sources

Another crucial distinction exists between print sources and cyberspace sources. Much of what you can retrieve from a computer was originally published in print. What you download is simply an electronic copy of a print source, either from a library-leased database or from someone's Web site. (The next section shows you how to tell the difference.) In such cases, you often need to consider the article's original print origins for appropriate cues about its rhetorical context and purpose. But much cyberspace material, having never appeared in print, may never have undergone either peer review or editorial review. To distinguish between these two kinds of cyberspace sources, we call one kind a "print/cyberspace source" (something that has appeared in print and is made available on the Web or through library-leased databases) and the other a "cyberspace-only source." When you use a cyberspace-only source, you've got to take special care in figuring out who wrote it, why, and for what audience. Also, you document cyberspace-only material differently from print material retrieved electronically.

For Class Discussion

Your instructor will bring to class a variety of sources—different kinds of books, scholarly journals, magazines, and downloaded material. Working individually or in small groups, try to decide which category in Tables 16.1 and 16.2 each piece belongs to. Be prepared to justify your decisions on the basis of the cues you used to make your decision.

Finding Books: Searching Your Library's Online Catalog

Your library's holdings are listed in its online catalog. Most of the entries are for books, but an academic library also has a wealth of other resources such as periodical collections, government records and reports, newspapers, videos and cassettes, maps, encyclopedias, and hundreds of specialized reference works that your reference librarian can help you use.

Indexed by subject, title, and author, the online catalog gives you titles of books and other library-owned resources relevant to your research area. Note that the catalog lists the titles of journals and magazines in the library's periodical collection (for example, *Journal of Abnormal Psychology, Atlantic Monthly*), but does *not* list the titles of individual articles within these periodicals. As we explain next, you can search the contents of periodicals by using a licensed database. Methods of accessing and using online catalogs vary from institution to institution, so you'll need to learn the specifics of your library's catalog through direct experience.

Finding Print Articles: Searching a Licensed Database

For many research projects, useful sources are print articles from your library's periodical collection, including scholarly journals, public affairs magazines, newspapers or newsmagazines, and niche magazines related to your research area. Some of these articles are available free on the World Wide Web, but most of them are not. Rather, they may be located physically in your library's periodical collection (or in that of another library and available through interlibrary loan) or located electronically in vast databases leased by your library.

What Is a Licensed Database?

Electronic databases of periodical sources are produced by for-profit companies that index articles in thousands of periodicals and construct engines that can search the database by author, title, subject, keyword, date, genre, and other characteristics. In most cases the database contains an abstract of each article, and in many cases it contains the complete text of the article that you can download and print. These databases are referred to by several different generic names: "licensed databases" (our preferred term), "general databases," or "subscription services." Because access to these databases is restricted to fee-paying customers, they can't be searched through Web engines like Yahoo! or Google. Most university libraries allow students to access these databases from a remote computer by using a password. You can therefore use the Internet to connect your computer to licensed databases as well as to the World Wide Web (see Figure 16.1).

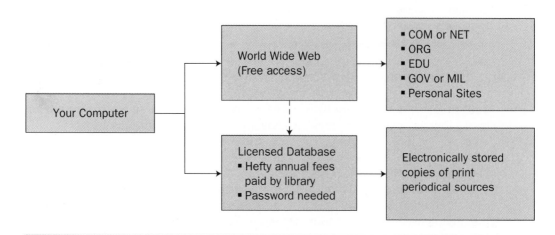

FIGURE 16.1   *Licensed database versus free-access portions of Internet*

Although the methods of accessing licensed databases vary from institution to institution, we can offer some widely applicable guidelines. Most likely your library has online one or more of the following databases:

- *EBSCOhost:*   Includes citations and abstracts from journals in most disciplines as well as many full-text articles from over three thousand journals; its *Academic Search Elite* function covers material published as long ago as the early 1980s.

- *UMI ProQuest Direct:*   Gives access to the full text of articles from journals in a variety of subject areas; includes full-text articles from newspapers.

- *InfoTrac:*   Is often called "Expanded Academic Index," and is similar to EBSCOhost and UMI ProQuest in its coverage of interdisciplinary subjects.

- *FirstSearch Databases:*   Incorporate multiple specialized databases in many subject areas, including WorldCat, which contains records of books, periodicals, and multimedia formats from libraries worldwide.

- *LexisNexis Academic Universe:*   Is primarily a full-text database covering current events, business, and financial news; includes company profiles and legal, medical, and reference information.

Generally, one of these databases is the "default database" chosen by your library for most article searches. Your reference librarian will be able to direct you to the most useful licensed database for your purpose.

Keyword Searching

To use an online database, you need to be adept at keyword searching. When you type a word or phrase into a search box, the computer will find sources that contain the same words or phrases. If you want the computer to search for a phrase, put it in quotation marks. Thus if you type *"street people"* using quotation marks, the computer will search for those two words occurring together. If you type in *street people* without quotation marks, the computer will look for the word *street* and the word *people* occurring in the same document but not necessarily together. Use your imagination to try a number of related terms. If you are researching gendered toys and you get too many hits using the keyword *toys,* try *gender toys, Barbie, G.I. Joe, girl toys, boy toys, toys psychology,* and so forth. You can increase the flexibility of your searches by using Boolean terms to expand, narrow, or limit your search (see Table 16.3 for an explanation of Boolean searches).

Illustration of a Database Search

As an illustration of a database search, we'll draw again on Megan's process as she researched the effect of Navy sonar on whales. Using the database EBSCOhost, Megan entered the keywords *Navy sonar* AND *whales,* which revealed the six articles shown in Figure 16.2 on page 371. As this Results list shows, EBSCOhost carries the full text for the first three records: "Baffling Boing Identified," "US Navy

TABLE 16.3   *Boolean search commands*

Command and Function	Research Example	What to Type	Search Result
X OR Y (Expands your search)	You are researching Barbie dolls and decide to include G.I. Joe figures.	"Barbie doll" OR "GI Joe"	Articles that contain either phrase
X AND Y (Narrows your search)	You are researching the psychological effects of Barbie dolls and are getting too many hits under *Barbie dolls*.	"Barbie dolls" AND psychology	Articles that include both the phrase "Barbie dolls" and the word *psychology*
X NOT Y (Limits your search)	You are researching girls' toys and are tired of reading about Barbie dolls. You want to look at other popular girls' toys.	"girl toys" NOT Barbie	Articles that include the phrase "girl toys" but exclude *Barbie*

Sonar Blocked," and "Sonic Blast." The Results list also notes that the Lemieux Library (the name of her college's library) subscribes to all the listed periodicals except for *Science Now* (Record 1) and *Ecologist* (Record 2). Thus Megan had access to all six articles, either from her college's periodical collection or from the online database. Because she wanted to decide whether the *New Scientist* article (Record 6) was worth tracking down, she clicked on its title "Noises Off," which revealed the screen shown in Figure 16.3 on page 372. This screen provides an abstract of the article, indicates that it is four pages long, and includes a graph and four color photographs or drawings.

After you've identified articles you'd like to read, locate physically all those available in your library's periodical collection. (This way you won't lose important contextual cues for reading them rhetorically.) For those unavailable in your library, print them from the database, if possible, or order them from interlibrary loan.

Finding Cyberspace Sources: Searching the World Wide Web

Another valuable resource is the World Wide Web. In this section we begin by explaining in more detail the logic of the Internet—the difference between restricted portions of the Internet, such as licensed databases, and the amorphous, ever changing, "free-access" portion, commonly called the "World Wide Web" (see again Figure 16.1). We then offer suggestions for searching the Web.

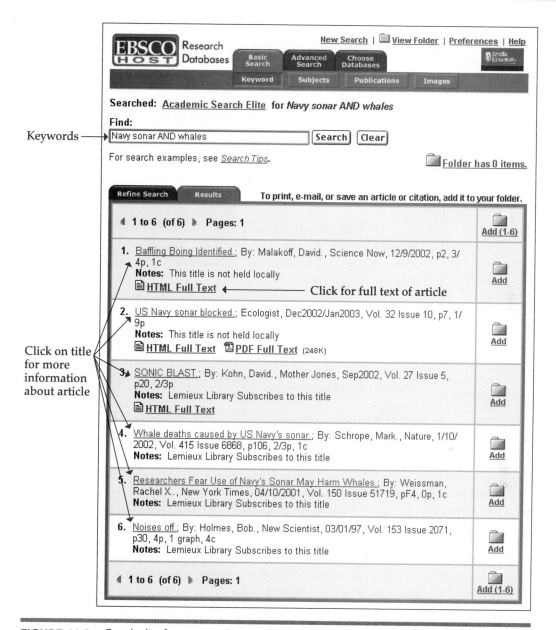

FIGURE 16.2   *Results list from a search using EBSCOhost*

The Logic of the Internet

To understand the logic of Web search engines, you need to know that the Internet is divided into restricted sections open only to those with special access rights and a "free-access" section. Web engines such as Yahoo! or Google search only the free-access portion of the Internet. When you type keywords into a Web search

Click on author; you'll get a
complete list of this person's
other publications in this database

Article is
4 pages long

Article
contains
1 graph

Article contains
4 color images

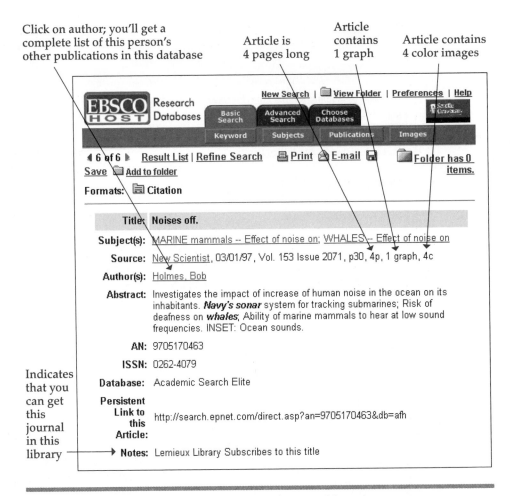

Indicates
that you
can get
this
journal
in this
library

FIGURE 16.3   *Sample full display for an article on EBSCOhost*

engine, it searches for matches in material made available on the Web by all the
users of the world's network of computers—government agencies, corporations,
advocacy groups, information services, individuals with their own Web sites, and
many others.

The following example will quickly show you the difference between a licensed database search and a Web search. When Megan entered the keywords
Navy sonar AND *whales* into EBSCOhost, she received six "hits"—the titles of six
articles on this subject appearing in print periodicals. In contrast, when she entered the same keywords into the Web search engine Yahoo!, she received 5,180
hits; when she tried the search engine Google, she got even more—6,220. The
Web search engines are picking up, in addition to print articles that someone
may have posted on the Web, all the references to Navy sonar and whales that

may appear in advocacy Web sites, government publications, newspapers, chat rooms, course syllabi posted by professors, student papers posted on the Web, and so forth.

For Class Discussion

Figure 16.4 shows the first screen of hits for the keywords *Navy sonar* and *whales* retrieved by the search engine Yahoo!. Working in small groups or as a whole class, compare these items with those retrieved from the equivalent search using the licensed database EBSCOhost (Figure 16.2).

1. Explain in your own words why the results for the Web search are different from those of the licensed database search.

2. What do you suspect would be the bias or angle of vision for the first record under the Yahoo! search—"NRDC: Spread of Active Sonar Threatens Whales. . . "?

3. What do you suspect would be the bias or angle of vision of the *Mother Jones* article and the *New Scientist* article identified in the EBSCOhost search? How could looking at the actual magazines in your college library help you determine the bias?

Using Web Search Engines

Although the hits you receive from a Web search frequently include useless, shoddy, trivial, or irrelevant material, the Web's resources for researchers are breathtaking. At your fingertips you have access to government documents and statistics, legislative and corporate white papers, court cases, persuasive appeals of advocacy groups, consumer information—the list is almost endless.

The World Wide Web can be searched by a variety of engines that collect and categorize individual Web files and search them for keywords. Most of these engines will find not only text files but also graphic, audio, and video files. Some look through the titles of files, whereas others scan the entire text of documents. Different engines search the Web in different ways, so it is important that you try a variety of search engines when you look for information. Again, if you are in doubt, your reference librarian can help you choose the most productive search engine for your needs.

Determining Where You Are on the Web

As you browse the Web looking for resources, clicking from link to link, try to figure out what site you are actually in at any given moment. This information is crucial, both for properly documenting a Web source and for reading the source rhetorically.

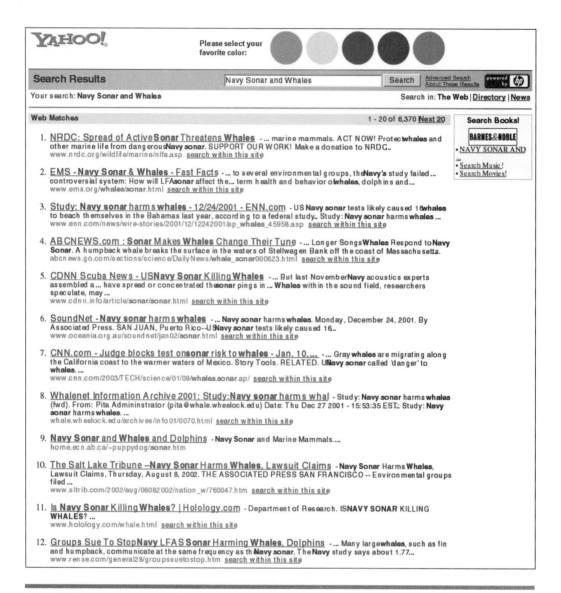

FIGURE 16.4   *First screen of hits from Yahoo!*

To know where you are on the Web, begin by recognizing the codes contained in a site's URL (uniform resource locator). The generic structure of a typical URL looks like this:

http://www.servername.domain/directory/subdirectory/filename.filetype

Here is a specific example:

The file named "resources" is linked through a series of directories and subdirectories to the home page of the National Education Association (www.nea.org).

Often, when you click on a link in one site, you will be sent to a totally different site. To determine the home page of this new site, simply note the root URL immediately following the "www."* To view the home page directly, delete the codes to the right of the initial home page URL in your computer's location window and hit Enter. You will then be linked directly to the site's home page. As you will see later in this chapter and in Chapter 17, being able to examine a site's home page helps you read the site rhetorically and document it properly.

Reading Your Sources Rhetorically

Even when you have a research question that interests you, it's easy to feel overwhelmed when you return from a library with a stack of books and magazine or journal articles. How do you begin reading all this material? There is no one right answer to this question. At times you need to read slowly with analytical closeness, as we discussed in Chapter 2. At other times you can skim a source, looking only for its gist or for a needed piece of information.

Reading with Your Own Goals in Mind

How you read a source depends to a certain extent on where you are in the research process. Early in the process, when you are in the thesis-seeking, exploratory stage, your goal is to achieve a basic understanding about your research problem. You need to become aware of different points of view, learn what is unknown or controversial about your research question, see what values or assumptions are in conflict, and build up your store of background knowledge.

Given these goals, at the early stages of research you should select, where possible, easy-to-read, overview kinds of sources to get you into the conversation.

---

*Not all URLs begin with "www" after the first set of double slashes. Our description doesn't include variations from the most typical URL types. You can generally find the home page of any site by eliminating all codes to the right of the first slash mark following the initial set of double slashes.

In some cases, even an encyclopedia or specialized reference work can be a good start for getting general background.

As you get deeper into your research, your questions become more focused, and the sources you read become more specialized. Once you formulate a thesis and plan a structure for your paper, you can determine more clearly the sources you need and read them with purpose and direction.

Reading with Rhetorical Awareness

To read your sources rhetorically, you should keep two basic questions in mind: (1) What was the source author's purpose in writing this piece? And (2) What might be my purpose in using this piece? Table 16.4 sums up the kinds of questions a rhetorical reader typically considers.

This chart reinforces a point we've made throughout this text: All writing is produced from an angle of vision that privileges some ways of seeing and filters

TABLE 16.4   *Questions asked by rhetorical readers*

What was the source author's purpose in writing this piece?	What might be my purpose in using this piece in my own argument?
• Who is this author? What are his or her credentials and affiliations?	• How has this piece influenced or complicated my own thinking?
• What audience was this person addressing?	• How does this piece relate to my research question?
• What is the genre of this piece? (If you downloaded the piece from the World Wide Web, did it originally appear in print?)	• How will my own intended audience react to this author?
• If this piece appeared in print, what is the reputation and bias of the journal, magazine, or press? Was the piece peer reviewed?	• How might I use this piece in my own argument?
	▪ Is it an opposing view that I might summarize?
• If this piece appeared only on the Web, who or what organization sponsors the Web site (check the home page)? What is the reputation and bias of the sponsor?	▪ Is it an alternative point of view that I might compare to other points of view?
• What is the author's thesis or purpose?	• Does it have facts and data that I might use?
• How does this author try to change his or her audience's view?	• Would a summary of all or part of this argument support or oppose one or more of my own points?
• What is this writer's angle of vision or bias?	
• What is omitted or censored from this text?	• Could I use this author for testimony? (If so, how should I indicate this author's credentials?)
• How reliable and credible is this author?	
• What facts, data, and other evidence does this author use and what are the sources of these data?	• If I use this source, will I need to acknowledge the author's bias and angle of vision?
• What are this author's underlying values, assumptions, and beliefs?	

out other ways. You should guard against reading your sources as if they present hard, undisputed facts or universal truths. For example, if one of your sources says that "Saint-John's-wort [a herb] has been shown to be an effective treatment for depression," some of your readers might accept that statement as fact; but many wouldn't. Skeptical readers would want to know who the author is, where his views have been published, and what he uses for evidence. Let's say the author is someone named Samuel Jones. Skeptical readers would ask whether Jones is relying on published research, and if so, whether the studies have been peer reviewed in reputable, scholarly journals and whether the research has been replicated by other scientists. They would also want to know whether Jones has financial connections to companies that produce herbal remedies and supplements. Rather than settling the question about Saint-John's-wort as a treatment for depression, a quotation from Jones might open up a heated controversy about medical research.

Reading rhetorically is thus a way of thinking critically about your sources. It influences the way you take notes, evaluate sources, and shape your argument.

Taking Effective Notes

Taking good research notes serves two functions: First, it encourages you to read actively because you must summarize your sources' arguments, record usable information, and extract short quotations. Second, taking notes encourages you to do exploratory thinking—to write down ideas as they occur to you, to analyze sources as you read them, and to join your sources in conversation.

There are many ways to take notes, but we can offer several techniques that have worked especially well for other writers. First of all, you can try using a double-entry journal. Divide a page in half, entering your informational notes on one side and your exploratory writing on the other. Another system is to record notes on index cards or in a computer file and then write out your exploratory thinking in a separate research journal. Still another method is to record informational notes on your computer in a regular font and then to use a boldfaced font for exploratory writing. Your objective here is to create a visual way to distinguish your informational notes from your exploratory thinking.

A common practice of beginning researchers—one that experienced researchers almost never use—is *not* taking notes as they read and *not* doing any exploratory writing. We've seen students photocopy a dozen or more articles, but then write nothing as they read (sometimes they highlight passages with a marker), planning to rely later on memory to navigate through the sources. This practice reduces your ability to synthesize your sources and create your argument. When you begin drafting your paper, you'll have no notes to refer to, no record of your thinking-in-progress. Your only recourse is to revisit all your sources, thumbing through them one at a time—a practice that leads to passive cutting and pasting.

TABLE 16.5   *Note taking according to purpose*

How Source Might Be Used in Your Paper	Notes to Take
Background information about research problem or issue	Summarize the information; record specific data.
Part of a section reviewing different points of view on your question	Summarize the source's argument; note its bias and perspective. In exploratory notes, jot down ideas on how and why different sources disagree.
As an opposing view that you must summarize and respond to	Summarize the argument fully and fairly. In exploratory notes, speculate about why you disagree with the source and whether you can refute the argument, concede to it, or compromise with it.
As data, information, or testimony to be used as evidence to support your thesis	Record the data or information; summarize or paraphrase the supporting argument with occasional quotations of key phrases; directly quote short passages for supporting testimony; note the credentials of the writer or person quoted. In exploratory notes, record new ideas as they occur to you.
As data, information, or testimony that counters your position or raises doubts about your thesis	Take notes on counterevidence. In exploratory notes, speculate on how you might respond to the counterevidence.

To make your notes purposeful, you need to imagine how a given source might be used in your research paper. Table 16.5 shows how notes are a function of your purpose.

When you use a source's exact words, be meticulous in copying them exactly and marking the quoted passage with prominent quotation marks. If you record information without directly quoting it, be sure that you restate it completely in your own words to avoid later problems with plagiarism. Next, check that you have all the bibliographic information you may need for a citation including the page numbers for each entry in your notes. (Citing page numbers for articles downloaded from the Web or a licensed database is problematic—see Chapter 17, p. 398.)

Evaluating Sources

When you read sources for your research project, you need to evaluate them as you go along. As you read each potential source, ask yourself questions about the author's angle of vision, degree of advocacy, reliability, and credibility.

Angle of Vision

By "angle of vision," we mean the way that a piece of writing gets shaped by the underlying values, assumptions, and beliefs of the author so that the text reflects a certain perspective, worldview, or belief system. The angle of vision is revealed by internal factors such as the author's word choice (especially notice the connotations of words), selection and omission of details, overt statements, figurative language, and grammatical emphasis; and by external factors such as the politics of the author, the genre of the source, the politics of the publisher, and so forth. When reading a source, see whether you can detect underlying assumptions or beliefs that suggest a writer's values or political views: Is this writer conservative or liberal? Predisposed toward traditional "family values" or new family structures? Toward technology or toward the simple life? Toward free markets or regulatory controls on the economy? Toward business interests or labor? Toward the environment or jobs? Toward order or freedom?

You can also get useful clues about a writer's angle of vision by looking at external data. What are the writer's credentials? Is the writer affiliated with an advocacy group or known for a certain ideology? (If you know nothing about an author who seems important to your research, try typing the author's name into a Web search engine. You might discover useful information about the author's other publications or about the writer's reputation in various fields.) Also pay attention to publishing data. Where was this source originally published? What is the reputation and editorial slant of the publication in which the source appears? For example, editorial slants of magazines can range from very liberal to very conservative. Likewise, publications affiliated with advocacy organizations (the Sierra Club, the National Rifle Association) will have a clear editorial bias.* Table 16.6 shows our own assessment of the political biases of various popular magazines and media commentators.

Degree of Advocacy

By "degree of advocacy" we mean the extent to which an author unabashedly takes a persuasive stance on a contested position as opposed to adopting a more neutral, objective, or exploratory stance. When a writer strongly advocates a position, you need to weigh carefully the writer's selection of evidence, interpretation of data, and fairness to opposing views. Although objectivity is itself an "angle of vision" and no one can be completely neutral, it is always useful to seek out authors who offer a balanced assessment of the evidence. Evidence from a more detached and neutral writer may be more trusted by your readers than the arguments of a committed advocate. For example, if you want to persuade corporate executives of the dangers of global warming, evidence from scholarly journals may be more persuasive than evidence from an environmentalist Web site or from a freelance writer in a leftist popular magazine like *Mother Jones*.

---

*If you are uncertain about the editorial bias of a particular magazine or newspaper, consult the *Gale Directory of Publications and Broadcast Media* or *Magazines for Libraries,* which, among other things, identify the intended audience and political biases of a wide range of magazines and newspapers.

TABLE 16.6   *Angles of vision in U.S. media and think tanks: A sampling across the political spectrum*

Commentators

Left	Left Center	Center	Right Center	Right
Barbara Ehrenreich	E.J. Dionne	David Broder	David Brooks	Pat Buchanan
Al Franken	Ellen Goodman	Amitai Etzioni	Midge Decter	Tucker Carlson
Bob Herbert	Nicholas Kristof	Thomas Friedman	Charles Krauthammer	Linda Chavez
Molly Ivins	Paul Krugman	Kathleen Hall Jamieson	William Kristol	Ann Coulter
Michael Moore	William Raspberry	Kevin Phillips	William Safire	John Leo
Bill Moyers	Mark Shields	Leonard Pitts	Andrew Sullivan	Rush Limbaugh
Salim Muwakkil	Fareed Zakaria	William Saletan	George Will	Bill O'Reilly
Daniel Schorr		Bob Woodward		Kathleen Parker
Gloria Steinem				Cal Thomas

Newspapers and Magazines[*]

Left/Liberal	Center	Right/Conservative
The American Prospect	*Atlantic Monthly*	*American Enterprise*
Harper's	*Business Week*	*American Spectator*
Los Angeles Times	*Christian Science Monitor*	*Fortune*
Mother Jones	*Commentary*	*National Journal*
The Nation	*Commonweal*	*National Review*
The New Yorker	*Foreign Affairs*	*Reader's Digest*
New York Times	*New Republic*	*Reason*
Salon	*Slate*	*Wall Street Journal*
Sojourners	*Washington Post*	*Washington Times*
Utne		*Weekly Standard*

Think Tanks

Left/Liberal	Center	Right/Conservative
Center for Defense Information	The Brookings Institution	American Enterprise Institute
Center for Media and Democracy (sponsors *Disinfopedia.org*)	Carnegie Endowment for International Peace	Cato Institute (Libertarian)
Institute for Policy Studies	Council on Foreign Relations	Center for Strategic and International Studies
Institute for Women's Policy Research	Jamestown Foundation	Heritage Foundation (sponsors *Townhall.com*)
Open Society Institute (Soros Foundation)	National Bureau of Economic Research	Project for the New American Century
Urban Institute	Progressive Policy Institute	Rand Corporation

[*]Newspapers are categorized according to positions they take on their editorial page; any reputable newspaper strives for objectivity in news reporting and includes a variety of views on its op-ed pages. Magazines do not claim and are not expected to present similar breadth and objectivity.

Reliability

"Reliability" refers to the accuracy of factual data in a source as determined by external validation. If you check a writer's "facts" against other sources, do you find that the facts are correct? Does the writer distort facts, take them out of context, or otherwise use them unreasonably? In some controversies, key data are highly disputed—for example, the number of homeless people in the United States, the frequency of date rape, or the risk factors for many diseases. A reliable writer acknowledges these controversies and doesn't treat disputed data as fact. Furthermore, if you check out the sources used by a reliable writer, they'll reveal accurate and careful research—respected primary sources rather than hearsay or secondhand reports.

Credibility

"Credibility" is similar to "reliability" but is based on internal rather than external factors. It refers to the reader's trust in the writer's honesty, goodwill, and trustworthiness and is apparent in the writer's tone, reasonableness, fairness in summarizing opposing views, and respect for different perspectives (what we have called "*ethos*"). Audiences differ in how much credibility they will grant to certain authors. Nevertheless a writer can achieve a reputation for credibility, even among bitter political opponents, by applying to issues a sense of moral courage, integrity, and consistency of principle.

Understanding the Rhetoric of Web Sites

In the previous section we focused on reading sources rhetorically by asking questions about a source's angle of vision, degree of advocacy, reliability, and credibility. In this section we turn to the skills of effectively evaluating and using Web sources by understanding the special rhetoric of Web sites.

The Web as a Unique Rhetorical Environment

Although many Web sites are highly professional and expensive to produce, the Web is also a great vehicle for democracy, giving voice to the otherwise voiceless. Anyone with a cause and a rudimentary knowledge of Web page design can create a Web site. Before the invention of the Web, people with a message had to stand on street corners passing out fliers or put money into newsletters or advocacy advertisements. The Web, in contrast, is cheap. The result is a rhetorical medium that differs in significant ways from print.

Analyzing the Purpose of a Site and Your Own Research Purpose

When you conduct research on the Web, your first question should be, Who placed this piece on the Web and why? You can begin answering this question by analyzing the site's home page, where you will often find navigational buttons linking to "Mission," "About Us," or other identifying information about the site's sponsors. You can also get hints about the site's purpose by asking, What kind of Web site is it? As we explained earlier, different kinds of Web sites have different purposes, often revealed by the domain identifier following the server name (.com, .net, .org, .gov, .mil). As you evaluate the Web site, also consider your own purpose for using it. For instance, are you trying to get an initial understanding of various points of view on an issue, or are you looking for reliable information? An advocacy site may be an excellent place for researching a point of view but a doubtful source of data and evidence for your own argument.

Sorting Sites by Domain Type

One powerful research strategy for reading Web sites rhetorically is to use the "advanced search" feature of a search engine to sort sites by domain type. As an example, consider again Megan's research dilemma when she plugged *Navy sonar* AND *whales* into Google and received 6,220 "hits." How could she begin to navigate through such a huge number? Using Google's "advanced search" feature, Megan first sorted through her hits by selecting only .com sites (2,790 hits). These, she discovered, were primarily the sites of newspapers, news services, and tourist sites catering to "whale watching"—a billion-dollar business, she discovered from one source. These sites tended to repeat the same news stories and offer superficial coverage. She next looked at .org sites (1,400 hits). These were primarily the sites of environmental advocacy groups—organizations such as the National Resources Defense Council, the Sierra Club, the Humane Society, the League for Coastal Protection, the Cetacean Society International, the Ocean Futures Society, and so forth—all dedicated to protecting marine life. These advocacy sites were strongly pro-whale; in their arguments against Navy sonar they either discounted or ignored issues of national security. Next she looked at .edu sites (449 hits), which were primarily references to course descriptions and syllabi that included this controversy as a source of study. She didn't find these helpful. Finally, she sorted by .gov (348 hits) and .mil (138 hits). The .gov sites revealed documents on whales and sonar submitted to congressional hearings; it also revealed the sites of two key government agencies involved in the sonar dispute: the National Marine Fisheries Service and the National Oceanic and Atmospheric Administration. The .mil sites gave access to white papers and other documents provided by the Navy to justify its use of low-frequency sonar.

This overview of the territory helped Megan understand the angle of vision or bias of different sources. The .org sites focused on protecting marine life. In contrast, the .mil and the .gov sites helped her understand the national security issue. In the middle, trying to balance the competing demands of the environment, national security, and preservation of commerce, were the sites of government agencies not directly connected to the military. All of these sites provided valuable information and most of them included links to scientific and research studies.

Evaluating a Web Site

Given this overview of the territory, Megan still had to decide which specific sites to use for her research. One of the most challenging parts of using the Web is determining whether a site offers gold or glitter. Sometimes the case may not be clear-cut. How do you sort out reliable, worthwhile sites from unreliable ones? We offer the following criteria developed by scholars and librarians as points to consider when you are using Web sites.

Criterion 1: Authority

- Is the author or sponsor of the Web site clearly identified?
- Does the site identify the occupation, position, education, experience, and credentials of the site's authors?
- Does the introductory material reveal the author's or sponsor's motivation for publishing this information on the Web?
- Does the site provide contact information for the author or sponsor such as an e-mail or organization address?

Criterion 2: Objectivity or Clear Disclosure of Advocacy

- Is the site's purpose (to inform, explain, or persuade) clear?
- Is the site explicit about declaring its author's or sponsor's point of view?
- Does the site indicate whether authors are affiliated with a specific organization, institution, or association?
- Does the site indicate whether it is directed toward a specific audience?

Criterion 3: Coverage

- Are the topics covered by the site clear?
- Does the site exhibit suitable depth and comprehensiveness for its purpose?
- Is sufficient evidence provided to support the ideas and opinions presented?

Criterion 4: Accuracy

- Are the sources of information stated? Can you tell whether this information is original or taken from someplace else?
- Does the information appear to be accurate? Can you verify this information by comparing this source with other sources in the field?

Criterion 5: Currency

- Are dates included in the Web site?
- Do the dates apply to the material itself or to its placement on the Web? Is the site regularly revised and updated?

■ Is the information current, or at least still relevant, for the site's purpose?

To illustrate how these criteria can help you evaluate a site, consider how they could be applied to the article "Spread of Active Sonar Threatens Whales," found on the site of the National Resources Defense Council. The first screen of this article is shown in Figure 16.5. The site is clearly from an advocacy group, as indicated by the boxed text on the right side urging readers to "ACT NOW!" and "SUPPORT OUR WORK!" The article is four pages long and gives a detailed overview of the history of Navy sonar and its negative impact on whales and other marine mammals. However, no author is identified. Is the article trustworthy and reliable or is it from a fringe environmental group apt to suppress or distort evidence? Using the criteria for evaluating Web sites, Megan was able to identify the strengths and weaknesses of this site in light of her research purpose.

The site does very well against the criteria "authority" and "clear disclosure of advocacy." Megan located the home page of the site, clicked on "About Us," and discovered that the National Resources Defense Council has been around for more than thirty years and established its first Web site in 1995. It is a large national organization with three regional offices, puts out numerous publications, and does extensive lobbying on environmental issues. The "About Us" section states:

> NRDC uses law, science, and the support of more than 500,000 members nationwide to protect the planet's wildlife and wild places and to ensure a safe and healthy environment for all living things. . . . We work to foster the fundamental right of all people to have a voice in decisions that affect their environment. We seek to break down the pattern of disproportionate environmental burdens borne by people of color and others who face social or economic inequities. Ultimately, NRDC strives to help create a new way of life for humankind, one that can be sustained indefinitely without fouling or depleting the resources that support all life on Earth.

The site provides contact information, the addresses of regional and national offices, and lists of phone numbers and e-mail addresses.

In terms of coverage (criteria 3), the site is unusually broad and deep. It covers hundreds of different environmental issues and has fun features for children as well as in-depth technical articles written for specialists. Megan also determined that the site was accurate (criteria 4). Technical articles had bibliographies, and references to factual data throughout the site had notes about sources. She discovered that information on this site corroborated well with references to the same data from other sites. Finally, the site was current (criteria 5). The home page has a "tip of the day," updated daily, and items within the site have clear indications of dates. This is an active, ongoing site.

Megan concluded that the site was an excellent source for both arguments and data from a pro-environmental perspective. She could use the site to understand potential dangers of Navy sonar to whales and other marine life. However, the site

Wildlife & Fish
Animals & Birds
Fish
• Whales & Marine
Animals

In Brief

In Depth

Related Links

Habitat
Preservation

○ Clean Air &
Energy

○ Global Warming

○ Clean Water &
Oceans

◉ Wildlife & Fish

○ Parks, Forests &
Wildlands

○ Toxic Chemicals
& Health

○ Nuclear Weapons
& Waste

○ Cities &
Green Living

○ Environmental
Legislation

Magazine
Reference/Links
Publications
Fun Features
Subscribe
Media Center
En Español
Site Map
Contact Us

Wildlife & Fish: Whales & Marine Animals: In Brief: News

✉ **Email This Article**

Spread of Active Sonar Threatens Whales

The U.S. Navy wants to flood the world's oceans and coastal waters with sonar technology that deafens -- and kills -- whales and other marine mammals.

Around the globe, nations are testing and beginning to deploy "active sonar" technology, which uses extremely loud sound to detect submarines. The problem? Active sonar can injure and even kill marine mammals. It has been conclusively linked to the deaths of seven whales in the Bahamas in March 2000, and is thought to have caused a 1996 mass stranding of beaked whales on the west coast of Greece.

ACT NOW!
Protect whales and
other marine life from
dangerous Navy sonar.

**SUPPORT OUR
WORK!**
Make a donation to
NRDC.

The U.S. Navy has led the push toward use of active sonar. In full knowledge of the disastrous effects that active sonar's intense noise may have on whale populations all over the world, the Navy has also conducted testing in complete secrecy and has consistently evaded and violated environmental law.

In July 2002, despite strong concerns from many leading scientists, the Bush administration issued a long-sought permit allowing the Navy to use the biggest gun in its active-sonar arsenal, the SURTASS LFA system, in as much as 75 percent of the world's oceans. (NRDC has filed a lawsuit to stop deployment of the system.) In addition, the Navy is attempting to expand its active-sonar program into U.S. coastal waters, and wants to do so without conducting the environmental analysis required by law.

The Bahamas Whale Deaths

In March 2000, four different species of whales and dolphins were stranded on beaches in the Bahamas after a U.S. Navy battle group used active sonar in the area. Despite efforts to save the whales, seven of them died. The Navy initially denied that active sonar was to blame, but its own investigation later found hemorrhaging around the dead whales' eyes and ears, indicating severe acoustic trauma. The government's study of the incident established with virtual certainty that the strandings in the Bahamas had been caused by mid-frequency active sonar used by Navy ships passing through the area. Since the

Of the 13 beaked whales that stranded in the Bahamas in March 2000 after exposure to active sonar, seven died, including this one.
Center for Whale Research

incident, the area's population of beaked whales has disappeared, leading researchers to conclude that they abandoned their habitat or died at sea. Scientists are concerned that, under the right circumstances, even the transient use of high-intensity active sonar can have a severe impact on populations of marine mammals.

FIGURE 16.5 *First screen from article on NRDC Web site*

was not helpful for understanding the Navy's reasons for needing low-frequency sonar or for understanding the role of this sonar in the war against terrorism.

Conclusion

Our discussion of the rhetoric of Web sites concludes this chapter's introduction to college-level research. We have talked about the need to establish a good research question; to understand the key differences among different kinds of sources; to use purposeful strategies for searching libraries, databases, and Web sites; to use your rhetorical knowledge when you read and evaluate sources; and to understand the rhetoric of Web sites. In the next chapter we focus on how to integrate research sources into your own prose and how to cite and document them appropriately.

17 Using, Citing, and Documenting Sources

The previous chapter helped you pose a good research question and begin unlocking some of the resources of your library and the Internet. This chapter teaches you how to use sources in your own argument—how to incorporate them into your own prose through summary, paraphrase, or quotation; how to cite them using attributive tags and in-text citations; and how to document them using the style and format of the Modern Language Association or the American Psychological Association.

Using Sources for Your Own Purposes

To illustrate the purposeful use of sources, we will use the following short argument from the Web site of the American Council on Science and Health—a conservative organization of doctors and scientists devoted to providing scientific information on health issues and to exposing health fads and myths. Please read the argument carefully in preparation for the discussions that follow.

IS VEGETARIANISM HEALTHIER THAN NONVEGETARIANISM?

Many people become vegetarians because they believe, in error, that vegetarianism is uniquely conducive to good health. The findings of several large epidemiologic studies indeed suggest that the death and chronic-disease rates of vegetarians—primarily vegetarians who consume dairy products or both dairy products and eggs—are lower than those of meat eaters. . . .

The health of vegetarians may be better than that of nonvegetarians partly because of nondietary factors: Many vegetarians are health-conscious. They exercise regularly, maintain a desirable body weight, and abstain from smoking. Although most epidemiologists have attempted to take such factors into account in their analyses, it is possible that they did not adequately control their studies for nondietary effects.

People who are vegetarians by choice may differ from the general population in other ways relevant to health. For example, in Western countries most vegetarians are more affluent than nonvegetarians and thus have better living conditions and more access to medical care.

An authoritative review of vegetarianism and chronic diseases classified the evidence for various alleged health benefits of vegetarianism:

- The evidence is "strong" that vegetarians have (a) a lower risk of becoming alcoholic, constipated, or obese and (b) a lower risk of developing lung cancer.
- The evidence is "good" that vegetarians have a lower risk of developing adult-onset diabetes mellitus, coronary artery disease, hypertension, and gallstones.
- The evidence is "fair to poor" that vegetarianism decreases risk of breast cancer, colon cancer, diverticular disease, kidney-stone formation, osteoporosis, and tooth decay.

For some of the diseases mentioned above, the practice of vegetarianism itself probably is the main protective factor. For example, the low incidence of constipation among vegetarians is almost certainly due to their high intakes of fiber-rich foods. For other conditions, nondietary factors may be more important than diet. For example, the low incidence of lung cancer among vegetarians is attributable primarily to their extremely low rate of cigarette smoking. Diet is but one of many risk factors for most chronic diseases.

What we want to show you is that the way you use this article depends on your own research question and purpose. Sometimes you may decide to summarize a source completely—particularly if the source represents an opposing or alternative view that you intend to address. (See Chapter 2 for a detailed explanation of summary writing; see also Chapter 8, pp. 145–147, for the difference between a fair summary and an unfair summary or "strawman.") At other times you may choose to use only parts of a source. To illustrate how your rhetorical purpose governs your use of a source, we show you three different hypothetical examples:

- *Writer 1, arguing for alternative approaches for reducing risk of alcoholism:* On some occasions, you will draw details from a source for use in a different context.

  Another approach to fighting alcoholism is through naturopathy, holistic medicine, and vegetarianism. Vegetarians generally have better health than the rest of the population and particularly have, according to the American Council on Science and Health, "a lower risk of becoming alcoholic."* This lower risk has been borne out by other studies showing that the benefits of the holistic health movement are particu-

---

*If the writer had found this quotation in a print source such as a book or magazine, the page number would be placed in parentheses immediately after the quotation, as explained on pages 395–396 later in this chapter. Because the writer found this passage in a Web site, no page citation is possible. In a research paper, readers would find full information about the source in the bibliography at the end. In this case, the author would be listed as "American Council on Science and Health," indicated in the attributive tag preceding the quotation.

larly strong for persons with addictive tendencies. . . . [goes on to other arguments and sources]

■ *Writer 2, arguing for the value of vegetarianism:* Sometimes you can use part of a source for direct support of your own claim. In this case, a summary of relevant parts of the argument can be used as evidence.

> Not only will a vegetarian diet help stop cruelty to animals, but it is also good for your health. According to the American Council on Science and Health, vegetarians have longer life expectancy than nonvegetarians and suffer from fewer chronic diseases. The Council summarizes evidence from the scientific literature strongly showing that vegetarians have reduced risk of lung cancer, obesity, constipation, and alcoholism. They also cite good evidence that they have a reduced risk of adult-onset diabetes, high blood pressure, gallstones, or hardening of the arteries. Although the evidence isn't nearly as strong, vegetarianism may also lower the risk of certain cancers, kidney stones, loss of bone density, and tooth decay.

■ *Writer 3, arguing for a skeptical view of vegetarianism:* Here Writer 3 uses portions of the article consciously excluded by Writer 2.

> The link between vegetarianism and death rates is a classic instance of correlation rather than causation. While it is true that vegetarians have a longer life expectancy than nonvegetarians and suffer from fewer chronic diseases, the American Council on Science and Health has shown that the causes can mostly be explained by factors other than diet. As the Council suggests, vegetarians are apt to be more health conscious than nonvegetarians and thus get more exercise, stay slender, and avoid smoking. The Council points out that vegetarians also tend to be wealthier than nonvegetarians and see their doctors more regularly. In short, they live longer because they take better care of themselves, not because they avoid meat.

For Class Discussion

Each of the hypothetical writers uses this short argument in different ways for different purposes. Working individually or in groups, respond to the following questions; be prepared to elaborate on and defend your answers.

1. How does each writer use the original article differently and why?
2. If you were the author of the article from the American Council on Science and Health, would you think that your article was used fairly and responsibly in each instance?
3. Suppose your goal were simply to summarize the argument from the American Council on Science and Health. Write a brief summary of the argument and then explain how your summary is different from the partial summaries used by Writers 2 and 3.

Creating Rhetorically Effective Attributive Tags

In the previous examples we used attributive tags to signal to readers which ideas are the writer's own and which ideas are being taken from another source, in this case the article from the American Council on Science and Health. Attributive tags can also be used rhetorically to shape your reader's response to a source.

Using Attributive Tags to Separate Your Ideas from Your Source's

Attributive tags are phrases such as "according to the American Council on Science and Health . . . ," "Smith claims that . . . ," or "the author continues. . . . " Such phrases signal to the reader that the material immediately following the tag is from the cited source. Sometimes writers indicate a source only by citing it in parentheses at the end of the borrowed material—a particularly common practice in the social sciences. The more preferred practice when writing to general audiences is to indicate a source with attributive tags. Parentheses after a quotation or at the end of the borrowed material are then used only to indicate page numbers from a print text. The use of attributive tags is generally clearer and often more rhetorically powerful.

> LESS PREFERRED: INDICATING SOURCE THROUGH PARENTHETICAL CITATION
>
> Vegetarians are apt to be more health-conscious than nonvegetarians (American Council on Science and Health).*
>
> MORE PREFERRED: INDICATING SOURCE THROUGH ATTRIBUTIVE TAG
>
> As the American Council on Science and Health has shown, vegetarians are apt to be more health-conscious than nonvegetarians.

Creating Attributive Tags to Shape Reader Response

When you introduce a source for the first time, you can use an attributive tag not only to introduce the source but also to shape your readers' attitude toward the source. For example, if you wanted your readers to respect the expertise of a source, you might say "according to noted chemist Marjorie Casper. . . . " If you wanted your readers to discount Casper's views, you might say "according to Marjorie Casper, an industrial chemist on the payroll of a major corporate polluter. . . ."

When you compose an initial tag, you can add to it any combination of the kinds of information in the following table, depending on your purpose, your audience's values, and your sense of what the audience already knows or doesn't know about the source:

---

*This parenthetical citation is in MLA form. If this had been a print source rather than a Web source, page numbers would also have been given as follows: (American Council on Science and Health 43). APA form also indicates the date of the source: (American Council on Science and Health, 2002). We explain MLA and APA styles for citing and documenting sources later in this chapter.

Add to Attributive Tag	Example
Author's credentials or relevant specialty (enhances credibility)	Civil engineer David Rockwood, a noted authority on stream flow in rivers,
Author's lack of credentials (decreases credibility)	City council member Dilbert Weasel, a local politician with no expertise in international affairs,
Author's political or social views	Left-wing columnist Alexander Cockburn [has negative feeling]; Alexander Cockburn, a longtime champion of labor [has positive feeling],
Title of source if it provides context	In her book *Fasting Girls: The History of Anorexia Nervosa*, Joan Jacobs Brumberg shows that [establishes credentials for comments on eating disorders]
Publisher of source if it adds prestige or otherwise shapes audience response	Dr. Carl Patrona, in an article published in the prestigious *New England Journal of Medicine*,
Historical or cultural information about a source that provides context or background	In his 1960s book popularizing the hippie movement, Charles Reich claims that
Indication of source's purpose or angle of vision	Feminist author Naomi Wolfe, writing a blistering attack on the beauty industry, argues that

Our point here is that you can use attributive tags rhetorically to help your readers understand the significance and context of a source when you first introduce it and to guide your readers' attitudes toward the source.

Working Sources into Your Own Prose

As a research writer, you need to incorporate sources gracefully into your own prose. One option is simply to draw factual data from a source. More complex options occur when you choose to summarize the whole or part of an argument, paraphrase a portion of an argument, or quote directly from the source. Let's look at these last three options in more detail.

Summarizing

Writing a summary of your source's argument (either of the whole argument or of a relevant section) is an appropriate strategy when the source represents an opposing or alternative view or when it supports or advances one of your own points. Summaries can be as short as a single sentence or as long as a paragraph. (See Chapter 2, pp. 28–32.)

Paraphrasing

Unlike a summary, which is a condensation of a source's whole argument, a paraphrase translates a short passage from a source into the writer's own words. You often paraphrase when you want to use specific information from a brief passage in the source and don't want to interrupt the flow of your own voice with a needless quotation. Of course, you must still acknowledge the source through an attributive tag or parenthetical citation. When you paraphrase, be careful to avoid the original writer's grammatical structure and syntax. If you mirror the original sentence structure while replacing occasional words with synonyms, you are *plagiarizing* rather than paraphrasing. (See pp. 395–396 for an explanation of plagiarism.) Here is an acceptable paraphrase of a short passage from the vegetarian article:

Original

- The evidence is "strong" that vegetarians have (a) a lower risk of becoming alcoholic, constipated, or obese and (b) a lower risk of developing lung cancer.
- The evidence is "good" that vegetarians have a lower risk of developing adult-onset diabetes mellitus, coronary artery disease, hypertension, and gallstones.

Paraphrase

The Council summarizes strong evidence from the scientific literature showing that vegetarians have reduced risk of lung cancer, obesity, constipation, and alcoholism. They also cite good evidence that they have a reduced risk of adult-onset diabetes, high blood pressure, gallstones, or hardening of the arteries.

[Note that to avoid plagiarism, the writer has changed the sentence structure substantially. However, the writer still acknowledges the original source with the attributive tag "The Council summarizes."]

Quoting

Occasionally, you will wish to quote an author's words directly. Avoid quoting too much because the effect, from your reader's perspective, is to move from an argument to a sequence of cut-and-pasted quotations. Quote only when doing so strengthens your argument. Here are some occasions when a direct quotation is appropriate:

- When the quotation comes from a respected authority and, in a pithy way, supports one of your points. (Your use of the quotation is like expert testimony in a trial.)
- When you are summarizing an opposing or alternative view and want to use brief quotations to show you have listened carefully and accurately.

- When you want to give readers the flavor of a source's voice, particularly if the language is striking or memorable.
- When you want to analyze the writer's choice of words or metaphors. (You would first quote the passage and then begin your analysis.)

When you quote, you must be meticulous in copying the passage *exactly*, including punctuation. When the quoted material takes up more than four lines in your paper, use the block quotation method by indenting the quoted material ten spaces (one inch) in MLA style or five spaces in APA style. When using the block method, do not use quotation marks because the block indentation itself signals a quotation.

When you insert quotations into your own sentences, how you punctuate depends on whether the inserted quotation is a complete sentence or a part of a sentence.

Inserted Quotation When Quotation Is Complete Sentence

> *Example:* According to the American Council on Science and Health, "Many people become vegetarians because they believe, in error, that vegetarianism is uniquely conducive to good health."

Explanation

- Because the quotation is a complete sentence, it starts with a capital letter and is separated from the introductory phrase by a comma.
- If the inserted quotation were taken from a print source, the page number would be indicated in parentheses between the ending quotation mark and the ending punctuation: ". . . conducive to good health" (43).

Inserted Quotation When Quotation Is Not a Complete Sentence

> *Example:* The American Council on Science and Health argues that the cause of vegetarians' longer life may be "nondietary factors." The Council claims that vegetarians are more "health-conscious" than meat eaters and that they "exercise regularly, maintain a desirable body weight, and abstain from smoking."

Explanation

- Because the material quoted is not a complete sentence, it is worked into the grammar of the writer's own sentence.
- No comma introduces the quotation; commas should be used to fit the grammatical structure of the writer's own sentence.
- If the inserted quotation were taken from a print source, the page number would be indicated in parentheses between the ending quotation mark and the period.

Use Brackets to Indicate Changes in a Quotation

Example: The American Council on Science and Health hypothesizes that vegetarians maintain better health by "exercis[ing] regularly, maintain[ing] a desirable body weight, and abstain[ing] from smoking."

Example: According to the American Council on Science and Health, "They [vegetarians] exercise regularly, maintain a desirable body weight, and abstain from smoking."

Explanation

- In the first example, brackets indicate where the grammar of the original passage has been modified to fit the grammar of the writer's own sentence.

- In the second example, the word "vegetarians" has been added inside brackets to explain what "they" refers to.

Use Ellipses to Indicate Omissions from a Quotation

The ellipsis, which consists of three spaced periods, indicates words omitted from the original. When an omission occurs at the end of a sentence, include a fourth period to mark the end of the sentence.

Example: According to the American Council on Science and Health, "people who are vegetarians by choice may differ . . . in other ways relevant to health. For example, in Western countries most vegetarians are more affluent than nonvegetarians. . . . "

If you wish to insert a parenthetical citation into the last sentence, insert a space before the first period and place the parentheses in front of the last period, which marks the end of the sentence. Note that the end quotation mark comes before the page number.

Example: "For example, in Western countries most vegetarians are more affluent than nonvegetarians . . . " (43).

Use Double and Single Quotation Marks to Indicate a Quotation within a Quotation

Example: According to the American Council on Science and Health, "The evidence is 'strong' that vegetarians have (a) a lower risk of becoming alcoholic, constipated, or obese and (b) a lower risk of developing lung cancer."

Explanation

- The original passage has quotation marks around "strong." To indicate those marks within the quotation, the writer has changed the original double marks to single marks.

Avoiding Plagiarism

Plagiarism, a form of academic cheating, is always a serious academic offense. You can plagiarize in one of two ways: (1) by borrowing another person's ideas without indicating the borrowing with attributive tags in the text and a proper citation or (2) by borrowing another person's language without putting the borrowed language in quotation marks or using a block indentation. The first kind of plagiarism is usually outright cheating; the writer usually knows he is stealing material and tries to disguise it.

The second kind of plagiarism, however, often begins in a hazy never-never land between paraphrasing and copying. We refer to it in our classes as "lazy cheating" and still consider it a serious offense, like stealing from your neighbor's vegetable garden because you are too lazy to do your own planting, weeding, and harvesting. Anyone who appreciates how hard it is to write and revise even a short passage will appreciate why it is wrong to take someone else's language ready-made. Thus, in our classes, we would fail a paper that included the following passage. (Let's call the writer Writer 4.)

> The link between vegetarianism and death rates is a classic instance of correlation rather than causation. While it is true that vegetarians have a longer life expectancy than nonvegetarians and suffer from fewer chronic diseases, the American Council on Science and Health has shown that the health of vegetarians may be better than that of nonvegetarians partly because of nondietary factors. Many vegetarians are very conscious of their health. They exercise regularly, keep a desirable body weight, and abstain from smoking. The Council points out that in Western countries most vegetarians are more affluent than nonvegetarians and thus have better living conditions and more access to medical care. In short, they live longer because they take better care of themselves, not because they avoid meat.

For Class Discussion

Do you think it was fair to flunk Writer 4's essay? He claimed he wasn't cheating because he used attributive tags to indicate his source throughout this passage, and he listed the American Council on Science and Health article accurately in his "Works Cited" list (bibliography) at the end of his paper. Before answering, compare Writer 4's passage with the original article on pages 387–388; also compare the passage with Writer 3's passage on page 389. What justification is there for giving a high grade to Writer 3 and a failing grade to Writer 4?

The best way to avoid plagiarism is to be especially careful at the note-taking stage. If you copy from your source, copy exactly, word for word, and put quotation marks around the copied material or otherwise indicate that it is not your own wording. If you paraphrase or summarize material, be sure that you don't borrow any of the original wording. Also be sure to change the grammatical structure of the original. Lazy note taking, in which you follow the arrangement and grammatical structure of the original passage and merely substitute occasional synonyms, leads directly to plagiarism.

Also remember that you cannot borrow another writer's ideas without citing them. If you summarize or paraphrase another writer's thinking about a subject, you should indicate in your notes that the ideas are not your own and be sure to record all the information you need for a citation. If you do exploratory reflection to accompany your notes, then the distinction between other writers' ideas and your own should be easy to recognize when it's time to incorporate the source material into your paper.

Understanding Parenthetical Citation Systems with Bibliographies

Not too many years ago, most academic disciplines used footnotes or endnotes to document sources. Today, however, both the MLA (Modern Language Association) system, used primarily in the humanities, and the APA (American Psychological Association) system, used primarily in the social sciences, use parenthetical citations instead of footnotes or endnotes.* Before we examine the details of MLA and APA styles, we want to explain the logic of parenthetical citation systems with concluding bibliographies.

In both the MLA and APA systems, the writer places a complete bibliography at the end of the paper. In the MLA system this bibliography is called "Works Cited." In the APA system it is called "References." The bibliography is arranged alphabetically by author or by title (if an author is not named). The key to the system's logic is this:

- Every source in the bibliography must be mentioned in the body of the paper.
- Conversely, every source mentioned in the body of the paper must be listed in the bibliography.
- There must be a one-to-one correspondence between the first word in each bibliographic entry (usually, but not always, an author's last name) and the name used to identify the source in the body of the paper.

Suppose a reader sees this phrase in your paper: "According to Debra Goldstein. . . ." The reader should be able to turn to your bibliography and find

---

*Our discussion of MLA style is based on Joseph Gibaldi, *MLA Handbook for Writers of Research Papers,* 6th ed. (New York: Modern Language Association of America, 2003). Our discussion of APA style is based on the *Publication Manual of the American Psychological Association,* 5th ed. (Washington, DC: American Psychological Association, 2001).

an alphabetized entry beginning with "Goldstein, Debra." Similarly, suppose that in looking over your bibliography, your reader sees an article by "Guillen, Manuel." This means that the name "Guillen" has to occur in your paper in one of two ways:

- As an attributive tag: "Economics professor Manuel Guillen argues that. . . ."
- As a parenthetical citation, often following a quotation: ". . . changes in fiscal policy" (Guillen 43).

Understanding MLA Style

From this point on, we separate our discussions of the MLA and APA systems. We begin with the MLA system because it is the one most commonly used in writing courses. We then explain the APA system.

The MLA Method of In-Text Citation

To cite sources in your text using the MLA system, place the author's last name and the page reference in parentheses immediately after the material being cited. If an attributive tag already identifies the author, give only the page number in parentheses. Once you have cited the author and it is clear that the same author's material is being used, you need cite only the page references in parentheses. The following examples show parenthetical documentation with and without an attributive tag. Note that the citation precedes the period. If you are citing a quotation, the parenthetical citation follows the quotation mark but precedes the final period.

> The Spanish tried to reduce the status of Filipina women who had been able to do business, get divorced, and sometimes become village chiefs (Karnow 41).
>
> According to Karnow, the Spanish tried to reduce the status of Filipina women who had been able to do business, get divorced, and sometimes become village chiefs (41).
>
> "And, to this day," Karnow continues, "women play a decisive role in Filipino families" (41).

A reader who wishes to look up the source will find the bibliographic information in the "Works Cited" section by looking for the entry under "Karnow." If more than one work by Karnow was used in the paper, the writer would include in the in-text citation an abbreviated title of the book or article following Karnow's name.

> (Karnow, "In Our Image" 41)

Special Case 1: Citing from an Indirect Source   Occasionally you may wish to use a quotation that you have seen cited in one of your sources. You read Jones, who has a nice quotation from Smith, and you want to use Smith's quotation.

What do you do? Whenever possible, find the quotation in its original source and cite that source. But if the original source is not available, cite the source indirectly by using the terms "qtd. in"; and list only the indirect source in your "Works Cited" list. In the following example, the writer wishes to quote a Buddhist monk, Thich Nhat Hanh, who has written a book entitled *Living Buddha, Living Christ*. However, the writer is unable to locate the actual book and instead has to quote from a review of the book by newspaper critic Lee Moriwaki. Here is how he would make the in-text citation:

> A Buddhist monk, Thich Nhat Hanh, stresses the importance of inner peace: "If we can learn ways to touch the peace, joy, and happiness that are already there, we will become healthy and strong, and a resource for others" (qtd. in Moriwaki C4).

The "Works Cited" list will have an entry for "Moriwaki" but not for "Thich Nhat Hanh."

Special Case 2: Citing Page Numbers for Downloaded Material   There is no satisfactory solution to the problem of citing page numbers for sources retrieved electronically from a database or the Web. Because different computers and printers will format the same source in different ways, the page numbers on a printout won't be consistent from user to user. Sometimes, a downloaded article will indicate page numbers from the original print source (for example, in .pdf files), in which case you can cite page numbers in the ordinary way. At other times downloaded material will have numbered paragraphs, in which case you can cite the paragraph number (preceded by *par.*) or numbers (preceded by *pars.*): (Jones, pars. 22–24). Most typically, however, downloaded sources will indicate neither page nor paragraph numbers. In such cases, MLA says to omit page references from the parenthetical citation. They assume that researchers can locate the source on a computer and then use a search engine to find a specific quotation or passage.

MLA Format for the "Works Cited" List

In the MLA system, you place a complete bibliography, titled "Works Cited," at the end of the paper. The list includes all the sources that you mention in your paper. However, it does not include works you read but did not use. Entries in the Works Cited list are arranged alphabetically by author, or by title if there is no author.

If you have more than one entry by the same author, begin the second and subsequent entries by typing three hyphens followed by a period rather than the author's name. Begin the list on a new sheet of paper with the words "Works Cited" centered one inch from the top of the page. Entries should use a "hanging indentation" so that the first line is flush with the left margin and succeeding lines are indented one-half inch or five spaces. For an example of how to format a "Works Cited" page in MLA style, see the last page of Mark Bonicillo's researched argument (p. 350).

The remaining pages in this section show examples of MLA formats for different kinds of sources.

MLA Citations

Books

General Format for Books
Author. <u>Title</u>. City of Publication: Publisher, year of publication.

One Author
Brumberg, Joan J. <u>The Body Project: An Intimate History of American Girls</u>. New
    York: Vintage, 1997.

Two or More Authors
Dombrowski, Daniel A., and Robert J. Deltete. <u>A Brief, Liberal, Catholic Defense of
    Abortion</u>. Urbana: U of Illinois P, 2000.
Belenky, Mary, et al. <u>Women's Ways of Knowing: The Development of Self, Voice,
    and Mind</u>. New York: Basic, 1986.

If there are four or more authors, you have the choice of listing all the authors in
the order in which they appear on the title page or using "et al." (meaning "and
others") to replace all but the first author.

Second, Later, or Revised Edition
Montagu, Ashley. <u>Touching: The Human Significance of the Skin</u>. 3rd ed. New York:
    Perennial, 1986.

**Republished Book (For Example, a Paperback Published after the Original
Hardback Edition or a Modern Edition of an Older Work)**
Hill, Christopher. <u>The World Turned Upside Down: Radical Ideas During the
    English Revolution</u>. 1972. London: Penguin, 1991.
Wollstonecraft, Mary. <u>The Vindication of the Rights of Woman, with Strictures on
    Political and Moral Subjects</u>. 1792. Rutland: Tuttle, 1995.

Multivolume Work
Churchill, Winston S. <u>A History of the English-Speaking Peoples</u>. 4 vols. New York:
    Dodd, 1956–58.
Churchill, Winston S. <u>The Great Democracies</u>. New York: Dodd, 1957. Vol. 4 of <u>A
    History of the English-Speaking Peoples</u>. 4 vols. 1956–58.

Use the first method when you cite the whole work; use the second method when
you cite one specific volume of the work.

Article in Familiar Reference Work

"Mau Mau." <u>The New Encyclopædia Britannica</u>. 15th ed. 2002.

Article in Less Familiar Reference Work

Ling, Trevor O. "Buddhism in Burma." <u>Dictionary of Comparative Religion</u>. Ed. S. G. F. Brandon. New York: Scribner's, 1970.

Translation

De Beauvoir, Simone. <u>The Second Sex</u>. Trans. H. M. Parshley. New York: Bantam, 1961.

Corporate Author (A Commission, Committee, or Other Group)

American Red Cross. <u>Standard First Aid</u>. St. Louis: Mosby Lifeline, 1993.

Anonymous Author

<u>The New Yorker Cartoon Album: 1975–1985</u>. New York: Penguin, 1987.
[Alphabetize under "n."]

Edited Anthologies

Citing the Editor

O'Connell, David F., and Charles N. Alexander, ed. <u>Self Recovery: Treating Addictions Using Transcendental Meditation and Maharishi Ayur-Veda</u>. New York: Haworth, 1994.

Citing an Individual Article

Royer, Ann. "The Role of the Transcendental Meditation Technique in Promoting Smoking Cessation: A Longitudinal Study." <u>Self Recovery: Treating Addictions Using Transcendental Meditation and Maharishi Ayur-Veda</u>. Ed. David F. O'Connell and Charles N. Alexander. New York: Haworth, 1994. 221–39.

In these examples, O'Connell and Alexander are the editors of the anthology. Ann Royer is the author of the article on smoking cessation. When you cite an individual article, the inclusive page numbers for the article come at the end of the citation.

Articles in Scholarly Journals Accessed in Print

When citing scholarly journals, you need to determine how the journal numbers its pages. Typically, separate issues of a journal are published four times per year.

The library then binds the four separate issues into one "annual volume." Some journals restart the page numbering with each issue, which means that during the year there would be four instances of, say, page 31. Other journals number the pages consecutively throughout the year. In such a case, the fall issue might begin with page 253 rather than page 1. When pages are numbered sequentially throughout the year, you need to include only the volume number in the volume slot (for example, "25"). When page numbering starts over with each issue, you need to include in the volume slot both the volume and the issue number, separated by a period (for example, "25.3").

General Format for Scholarly Journals

Author. "Article Title." <u>Journal Title</u> volume number.issue number (year): page numbers.

Scholarly Journal That Numbers Pages Continuously

Barton, Ellen L. "Evidentials, Argumentation, and Epistemological Stance." <u>College English</u> 55 (1993): 745–69.

Scholarly Journal That Restarts Page Numbering with Each Issue

Pollay, Richard W., Jung S. Lee, and David Carter-Whitney. "Separate, but Not Equal: Racial Segmentation in Cigarette Advertising." <u>Journal of Advertising</u> 21.1 (1992): 45–57.

Articles in Magazines and Newspapers Accessed in Print

Magazine and newspaper articles are easy to cite. If no author is identified, begin the entry with the title or headline. Distinguish between news stories and editorials by putting the word "Editorial" after the title. If a magazine comes out weekly or biweekly, include the complete date (27 Sept. 1998). If it comes out monthly, then state the month only (Sept. 1998).

General Format for Magazines and Newspapers

Author. "Article Title." <u>Magazine Title</u> [day] Month year: page numbers.

Note: If the article continues in another part of the magazine or newspaper, add "+" to indicate the nonsequential pages.

Magazine Article with Named Author

Snyder, Rachel L. "A Daughter of Cambodia Remembers: Loung Ung's Journey." <u>Ms</u>. Aug.–Sept. 2001: 62–67.

Hall, Stephen S. "Prescription for Profit." <u>New York Times Magazine</u> 11 Mar. 2001:
40–45+.

Anonymous Magazine Article

"Daddy, Daddy." <u>New Republic</u> 30 July 2001: 2–13.

Review of Book, Film, or Performance

Schwarz, Benjamin. "A Bit of Bunting: A New History of the British Empire
Elevates Expediency to Principle." Rev. of <u>Ornamentalism: How the British Saw</u>
<u>Their Empire</u>, by David Cannadine. <u>Atlantic Monthly</u> Nov. 2001: 126–35.

Kaufman, Stanley. "Polishing a Gem." Rev. of <u>The Blue Angel</u>, dir. Josef von
Sternberg. <u>New Republic</u> 30 July 2001: 28–29.

Lahr, John. "Nobody's Darling: Fascism and the Drama of Human Connection in
<u>Ashes to Ashes</u>." Rev. of <u>Ashes to Ashes</u>, by Harold Pinter. The Roundabout
Theater Co. Gramercy Theater, New York. <u>New Yorker</u> 22 Feb. 1999: 182–83.

Newspaper Article

Henriques, Diana B. "Hero's Fall Teaches Wall Street a Lesson." <u>Seattle Times</u> 27
Sept. 1998: A1+.

Newspaper Editorial

"Dr. Frankenstein on the Hill." Editorial. <u>New York Times</u> 18 May 2002, natl.
ed.:A22.

Letter to the Editor of a Magazine or Newspaper

Tomsovic, Kevin. Letter. <u>New Yorker</u> 13 July 1998: 7.

Print Articles or Books Downloaded from a Database

Because of the difficulty in determining original page numbers for downloaded
articles, citations in this category must begin with complete print information, followed by the electronic information.

General Format for Material from Licensed Databases

Author. "Title." <u>Periodical Name</u> Print publication data including date and
volume/issue numbers: pagination. <u>Database</u>. Database company (if different).
Library information. Date of access <URL of the database service's home page,
if known>.

Note that there is no punctuation between the date of access and the URL; the intended effect is a statement that on that date, the material was found at that location or via that service.

Print Article Retrieved from Licensed Database

Lanza, Robert P., Betsy L. Dresser, and Philip Damiani. "Cloning Noah's Ark."
<blockquote>Scientific American Nov. 2000: 84- . Academic Search Elite. EBSCO. Alexandria (Va.) Lib. 14 Sept. 2003 <http://www.epnet.com/>.</blockquote>

Watanabe, Myrna. "Zoos Act as Sentinels for Infectious Diseases." Bioscience 53
<blockquote>(2003): 792. ProQuest. Raynor Lib., Marquette U. 26 July 2004 <http://www.il.proquest.com/proquest/>.</blockquote>

Follow the formats for print magazines or scholarly journals, as relevant. When the database text provides only the starting page number of a multipage article, insert a hyphen and a space after the number, before the period. Providing only one number (as in the Watanabe citation above) indicates that the article has only one page.

Broadcast Transcript Retrieved from Licensed Database

Conan, Neal. "Arab Media." Talk of the Nation. With Shibley Telhami. 4 May 2004.
<blockquote>Transcript. LexisNexis. Reed Elsevier. Raynor Lib., Marquette U. 31 July 2004 <http://www.lexisnexis.com/>.</blockquote>

The label "Transcript" after the broadcast date shows that a print copy was used.

Reference Material Retrieved from Licensed Database

"Cicada." Encyclopædia Britannica. 2004. Encyclopædia Britannica Online. Raynor
<blockquote>Lib., Marquette U. 31 July 2004 <http://0search.eb.com.libus.csd.mu.edu:80/ eb/article?eu=84788>.</blockquote>

This example uses the MLA citation provided at the end of the Britannica article. The URL is unique to the database license for the academic library through which we accessed it.

"Toni Morrison." American Decades 1990–1999. Ed. Tandy McConnell. Detroit:
<blockquote>Gale Group, Inc., 2001. Biography Resource Center. Seattle Public Lib. 14 Sept. 2003 <http://www.galegroup.com/BiographyRC/>.</blockquote>

Papers and Monographs from an Information Service

Information services such as ERIC (Educational Resources Information Center) or NTIS (National Technical Information Service) provide material to your library on microfiche or online with indexes on CD-ROM or online. Much of the material from these services has not been published in major journals or magazines. Frequently they are typescripts of conference papers or other scholarly work disseminated on microfiche. Cite microfiche copies as you would cite print materials, adding an identifying phrase instead of publication information, and then an accession number at the end.

Coll, Richard K., Sara Tofield, Brent Vyle, and Rachel Bolstad. "Free-Choice Learning at a Metropolitan Zoo." Paper presented at the Annual Meeting of the National Association for Research in Science Teaching, Philadelphia, PA, 23–26 Mar. 2003. ERIC ED 477832.

For electronic versions, follow the format for periodical articles from a licensed database, adding the database information after the descriptive phrase and the accession number.

Coll, Richard K., Sara Tofield, Brent Vyle, and Rachel Bolstad. "Free-Choice Learning at a Metropolitan Zoo." Paper presented at the Annual Meeting of the National Association for Research in Science Teaching, Philadelphia, PA, 23–26 Mar. 2003. ERIC ED 477832. <u>Ovid</u>. Raynor Lib., Marquette U. 26 July 2004 <www.ovid.com>.

E-Book

Hanley, Wayne. <u>The Genesis of Napoleonic Propaganda, 1796–1799</u>. Columbia UP, 2002. <u>Gutenberg-e</u>. 31 July 2004 <http://www.gutenberg-e.org>.

Machiavelli, Niccolo. <u>Prince</u>. [1513.] <u>Bibliomania</u>. 31 July 2004 <http://www.bibliomania.com>.

Information about the original print version, including a translator if relevant and available, should be provided. Use brackets for adding information not provided in the source.

Web and Internet Sources

Because Web and Internet sources vary widely in design and in the ways they approach content, creating citations for them can sometimes be a puzzling process. To help you create useful, accurate citations, we provide a general format followed by some general principles you can apply when creating Web citations; we then devote the rest of this section to model citations for types of sources that students frequently use.

General Format for Web Sources

Author of the page or document, if available. "Title of page or document." Title of
  the overall site, usually taken from the home page. Date of publication online or
  last update of the site, if available. Total range of paragraphs or pages, if they
  are numbered within the site itself (as in a .pdf document). Name of site sponsor, if available and not already stated in the Web site title. Date you accessed
  the site <URL of the specific document>.

Note that the main divisions are separated by periods except that no punctuation
is used between the date of access and the URL.

Here is an illustration that contains nearly all of the elements listed above:

Smith, Anne-Marie. "Advances in Understanding International Peacemaking."
  United States Institute of Peace. 2000. 76 pp. 25 May 2004
  <http://www.usip.org/pubs/summaries/advances.pdf>.

This citation indicates a seventy-six-page .pdf document by Anne-Marie Smith titled "Advances in Understanding International Peacemaking" and published in
2000. It was posted on the Web site of the United States Institute of Peace, which
uses its name as the title of the site. The researcher accessed this document on 25
May 2004 at the URL given.

The next example shows a citation for which not all the information elements
were available:

"Nuclear Power Plant Accidents." Infoplease. Pearson Education. 21 Sept. 2004
  <http://www.infoplease.com/ipa/A0001457.html>.

This citation begins with the article title because there is no named author. We
learned by clicking on the "About Us" link that the Web site Infoplease is sponsored by Pearson Education. There is no entry for the date of the article because
none was provided; also, there is no entry for number of pages because the site
doesn't indicate page breaks. The researcher accessed the site on 21 Sept. 2004 at
the URL given.

Alternatives to Providing a URL

In MLA style, the preferred way to show Web location is to copy the source's URL
directly into the citation. In some cases, however, this is difficult if not impossible.
Some URLs are so long that they are unwieldy and prone to transcription errors,
and some Web sites seek to simplify access by using just a primary URL with internal links that do not appear in the URL window. MLA suggests the following
three alternatives to providing specific URLs:

1. Provide the URL of the site's search page (if available).

> Gidley, Cheryl. "The Best of Both Worlds." <u>Philanthropy News Digest</u> 2004.
>
> The Foundation Center. 15 Aug. 2004 <http://fdncenter.org/pnd/
>
> archives/index.jhtml>.

> (This URL takes you immediately to the site's search box. Enter "Gidley"
> in the search box to locate the source.)

2. Provide the URL of the site's home page.
3. Indicate the sequence of links a reader can follow from the site's home page.

> "Myths and Realities about Antibiotic Resistance." <u>Union of Concerned
>
> Scientists</u>. <http://www.ucsusa.org>. Path: Food and Environment;
>
> Antibiotic Resistance; FAQs.

> (This citation tells the user to start at the UCSUSA home page, click on "Food
> and Environment," then "Antibiotic Resistance," and finally "FAQs.")

Whole Web Site

<u>MyNRA</u>. 2005. National Rifle Association. 3 Aug. 2005 <http://www.mynra.org>.

Documents within a Web Site

Marks, John. "Overview: Letter from the President." <u>Search for Common Ground</u>.

25 June 2004 <http://www.sfcg.org>. Path: About SFCG; Overview.

Bailey, Ronald. "The Impact of Science on Public Policy. Testimony before House

Subcommittee on Energy and Mineral Resources. 108th Congress." <u>Reason

Public Policy Institute</u>. 4 Feb. 2004. 10 pp. 18 Sept. 2004

<http://www.rppi.org/impact.pdf>.

The first example uses the "path method" rather than a URL to indicate Web access. The second includes data about the length of the document, available from a quick check of the .pdf document.

Article from a Newspaper or Newswire Site

Thevenot, Brian. "Once in a Blue Moon." <u>Times Picayune</u> [New Orleans] 31 July

2004. 31 July 2004 <http://www.nola.com/news/t-p/frontpage/index.ssf?/base/

news-1/1091264442208250.xml>.

"Great Lakes: Rwanda Backed Dissident Troops in DRC-UN Panel." <u>IRIN News.org</u>.

21 July 2004. 31 July 2004 <http://www.irinnews.org/advsearch.asp>.

Broadcast Transcript from a Web Site

Michels, Spencer, and Margaret Warner. "The Politics of 9/11." Online NewsHour.
    28 July 2004. Transcript: background and discussion. PBS. 31 July 2004
    <http://www.pbs.org/newshour/bb/terrorism/july-dec04/9-11_7-28.html>.

Article from a Scholarly E-Journal

Welch, John R., and Ramon Riley. "Reclaiming Land and Spirit in the Western
    Apache Homeland." American Indian Quarterly 25 (2001): 5–14. 19 Dec. 2001
    <http://muse.jhu.edu/journals/american_indian_quarterly/v025/25.1welch.pdf>.

E-Mail

Daffinrud, Sue. "Scoring Guide for Class Participation." E-mail to the author. 12 Dec.
    2001.

Use the subject line as the title of the e-mail.

Online Posting to a Listserv, Bulletin Board, Newsgroup, or Blog*

CalEnergyGuy. "Energy Crisis Impacts on the Economy: Changes since 2001." Blog
    posting. 27 July 2004. California Energy Blog. 1 Aug. 2004
    <http://calenergy.blogspot.com/2004_07_01_calenergy_archive.html>.

Follow the format for citing an e-mail, using the appropriate label before the date
of posting. After the posting date, add these elements: name of the forum, your
date of access, and a URL for—in order of preference—an archived version of the
post, the forum home page, or the posting itself. It may be helpful to insert the
name of a sponsoring organization, if available, after the name of the forum.

Miscellaneous Sources

Television or Radio Program

"Lie Like a Rug." NYPD Blue. Dir. Steven Bochco and David Milch. ABC. KOMO,
    Seattle. 6 Nov. 2001.

Film

Shakespeare in Love. Dir. John Madden. Perf. Joseph Fiennes and Gwyneth Paltrow.
    Screenplay by Marc Norman and Tom Stoppard. Universal Miramax, 1998.

---

*Forums for blog entries are not listed in the *MLA Handbook,* so we have interpolated a format based on
the formats given for other types of Internet forums.

Sound Recording

Dylan, Bob. "Rainy Day Woman." <u>Bob Dylan MTV Unplugged</u>. Columbia, 1995.

For sound recordings begin the entry with what your paper emphasizes—for example, the artist's name, composer's name, or conductor's name—and adjust the elements accordingly.

Cartoon, Comic Strip, or Advertisement

Trudeau, Garry. "Doonesbury." Comic strip. <u>Seattle Times</u> 19 Nov. 2001: B4.

Banana Republic. Advertisement. <u>Details</u> Oct. 2001: 37.

Interview

Castellucci, Marion. Personal interview. 7 Oct. 2001.

Lecture, Speech, or Conference Presentation

Sharples, Mike. "Authors of the Future." Conference of European Teachers of
    Academic Writing. U of Groningen. Groningen, Neth. 20 June 2001.

Government Publications

Government publications are often difficult to cite because there are so many varieties. In general, follow these guidelines:

- Usually cite as author the government agency that produced the document. Begin with the highest level and then branch down to the specific agency:

  > United States. Dept. of Justice. FBI
  >
  > Idaho. Dept. of Motor Vehicles

- Follow this with the title of the document, underlined.
- If a specific person is clearly identified as the author, you may begin the citation with that person's name, or you may list the author (preceded by the word "By") after the title of the document.
- Follow standard procedures for citing publication information for print sources or retrieval information for Web sources.

United States. Dept. of Justice. FBI. <u>The School Shooter: A Threat Assessment
    Perspective</u>. By Mary O'Toole. 2000. 16 Aug. 2001 <http://www.fbi.gov/
    publications/school/school2.pdf>.

Formatting an Academic Paper in MLA Style

An example research paper in MLA style is shown on pages 344–350. Here are the distinctive formatting features of MLA papers.

- Double-space throughout including block quotations and the "Works Cited" list.

- Use one-inch margins top and bottom, left and right. Indent one-half inch or five spaces from the left margin at the beginning of each paragraph.

- Number pages consecutively throughout the manuscript including the "Works Cited" list, which begins on a new page. Page numbers go in the upper right-hand corner, flush with the right margin, and one-half inch from the top of the page. The page number should be preceded by your last name. The text begins one inch from the top of the page.

- Do *not* create a separate title page. Type your name, professor's name, course number, and date in the upper left-hand corner of your paper (all double-spaced), beginning one inch from the top of the page; then double-space and type your title, centered, without underlines or any distinctive fonts (capitalize the first word and important words only); then double-space and begin your text.

- Start a new page for the Works Cited list. Type "Works Cited" centered, one inch from the top of the page in the same font as the rest of the paper; do not enclose it in quotation marks. Use hanging indentation for each entry longer than one line, of five spaces or one-half inch, formatted according to the example on page 350.

Student Example of an MLA-Style Research Paper

For an illustration of a student research paper written in MLA style, see Mark Bonicillo's proposal argument on pages 344–350.

Understanding APA Style

In many respects, the APA style and the MLA style are similar and the basic logic is the same. However, the APA style has a few distinguishing features:

- APA style emphasizes dates of books and articles and de-emphasizes the names of authors. Therefore the date of publication appears in parenthetical citations and is the second item mentioned in each entry in the "References" list (the name of the bibliography at the end of a paper).

- Only published or retrievable documents are included in the "References" list. Personal correspondence, e-mail messages, interviews, and lectures or speeches are referenced in text citations only.

- APA style uses fewer abbreviations and spells out the complete names of university presses. However, it uses an ampersand (&) instead of the word *and* for items in a series in the reference list and in text citations.

- APA style uses italics rather than underlines for titles and capitalizes only the first word of titles and subtitles of books and articles. It doesn't place titles of articles in quotation marks.

- APA style uses only an initial for authors' or editors' first names in the "References" citations.

- APA style has a distinctive format for title pages and frequently includes an "abstract" of the paper immediately following the title page.
- Page numbers are placed at the top right-hand margin and are preceded by a "running head" (a short version of the title).
- APA uses block indentation for quotations when they are longer than forty words. Quotations shorter than forty words are worked into your own text using quotation marks as in the MLA system.

APA Method of In-Text Citation

To cite sources in the APA system, you follow procedures very similar to those in the MLA system. When you make an in-text citation in APA style, you place inside the parentheses the author's last name and the year of the source as well as the page number if a particular passage or table is cited. The elements in the citation are separated by commas and a "p." or "pp." precedes the page number(s). If a source has more than one author, use an ampersand (&) to join their names. When the author is mentioned in an attributive tag, you include only the date (and page if applicable). The following examples show parenthetical documentation with and without attributive tags according to APA style.

> The Spanish tried to reduce the status of women who had been able to do business, get divorced, and sometimes become village chiefs (Karnow, 1989, p. 41).
>
> According to Karnow (1989, p. 41), the Spanish tried to reduce the status of women who had been able to do business, get divorced, and sometimes become village chiefs.

Just as with MLA style, readers of APA style look for sources in the list of references at the end of the paper if they wish to find full bibliographic information. In the APA system, this bibliographic list is titled "References" and includes only the sources cited in the body of the paper. If your sources include two works by the same author published in the same year, place an "a" after the date for the first work and a "b" after the date for the second, ordering the works alphabetically by title in the "References" list. If Karnow had published two different works in 1989, your in-text citation would look like this:

> (Karnow, 1989a, p. 41)
>
> or
>
> (Karnow, 1989b, p. 41)

APA style also makes provisions for quoting or using data from an indirect source. Use the same procedures as for MLA style (see the example on pp. 397–398), but in your parenthetical citation use "as cited in" rather than the MLA's "qtd. in." Here is the APA equivalent of the example on page 398:

A Buddhist monk, Thich Nhat Hanh, stresses the importance of inner peace: "If we can learn ways to touch the peace, joy, and happiness that are already there, we will become healthy and strong, and a resource for others" (as cited in Moriwaki, 1995, p. C4).

APA Format for the "References" List

Like the MLA system, the APA system includes a complete bibliography, called "References," at the end of the paper. Entries are listed alphabetically, with a similar kind of hanging indentation to that used in MLA style. If you list more than one item for an author, repeat the author's name each time and arrange the items in chronological order beginning with the earliest. If two works appeared in the same year, arrange them alphabetically, adding an "a" and a "b" after the year for purposes of in-text citation. Here is a hypothetical illustration:

Smith, R. (1995). *Body image in Western cultures, 1750–present.* London: Bonanza Press.

Smith, R. (1999a). *Body image in non-Western cultures.* London: Bonanza Press.

Smith, R. (1999b). Eating disorders reconsidered. *Journal of Appetite Studies, 45,* 295–300.

APA Citations

Books

One Author

Brumberg, J. J. (1997). *The body project: An intimate history of American girls.* New York: Vintage.

Two or More Authors

Dombrowski, D. A., & Deltete, R. J. (2000). *A brief, liberal, Catholic defense of abortion.* Urbana: University of Illinois Press.

Belenky, M., Clinchy, B. M., Goldberger, N. R., & Tarule, J. M. (1986). *Women's ways of knowing: The development of self, voice, and mind.* New York: Basic Books.

APA style uses "et al." only for books with more than six authors.

Second, Later, or Revised Edition

Montagu, A. (1986). *Touching: The human significance of the skin* (3rd ed.). New York: Perennial Press.

Republished Book (For Example, a Paperback Published after the Original Hardback Edition or a Modern Edition of an Older Work)

Hill, C. (1991). *The world turned upside down: Radical ideas during the English revolution.* London: Penguin. (Original work published 1972)

The in-text citation should read: (Hill, 1972/1991).

Wollstonecraft, M. (1995). *The vindication of the rights of woman, with strictures on political and moral subjects.* Rutland, VT: Tuttle. (Original work published 1792)

The in-text citation should read: (Wollstonecraft, 1792/1995).

Multivolume Work

Churchill, W. S. (1956–1958). *A history of the English-speaking peoples* (Vols. 1–4). New York: Dodd, Mead.

Citation for all the volumes together. The in-text citation should read: (Churchill, 1956–1958).

Churchill, W. S. (1957). *A history of the English-speaking peoples: Vol. 4. The great democracies.* New York: Dodd, Mead.

Citation for a specific volume. The in-text citation should read: (Churchill, 1957).

Article in Reference Work

Ling, T. O. (1970). Buddhism in Burma. In S. G. F. Brandon (Ed.), *Dictionary of comparative religion.* New York: Scribner's.

Translation

De Beauvoir, S. (1961). *The second sex* (H. M. Parshley, Trans.). New York: Bantam Books. (Original work published 1949)

The in-text citation should read: (De Beauvoir, 1949/1961).

Corporate Author (a Commission, Committee, or Other Group)

American Red Cross. (1993). *Standard first aid.* St. Louis, MO: Mosby Lifeline.

Anonymous Author

The New Yorker cartoon album: 1975–1985. (1987). New York: Penguin Books.

Alphabetize this entry under "n." The in-text citation should be a shortened version of the title as follows: (*New Yorker cartoon album*, 1987).

Edited Anthologies

Citing the Editor

O'Connell, D. F., & Alexander, C. N. (Eds.). (1994). *Self recovery: Treating addictions using transcendental meditation and Maharishi Ayur-Veda.* New York: Haworth Press.

Citing an Individual Article

Royer, A. (1994). The role of the transcendental meditation technique in promoting smoking cessation: A longitudinal study. In D. F. O'Connell & C. N. Alexander (Eds.), *Self recovery: Treating addictions using transcendental meditation and Maharishi Ayur-Veda* (pp. 221–239). New York: Haworth Press.

The pattern is as follows: Author of article. (Year of publication). Title of article. In Name of editor (Ed.), *Title of anthology* (pp. inclusive page numbers of article). Place of publication: Name of press.

Articles in Scholarly Journals Accessed in Print

Scholarly Journal That Numbers Pages Continuously

Barton, E. L. (1993). Evidentials, argumentation, and epistemological stance. *College English, 55,* 745–769.

The pattern is as follows: Author. (Year of publication). Article title. *Name of Journal, volume number,* inclusive page numbers. Note that the volume number is italicized along with the title of the journal.

Scholarly Journal That Restarts Page Numbering with Each Issue

Pollay, R. W., Lee, J. S., & Carter-Whitney, D. (1992). Separate, but not equal: Racial segmentation in cigarette advertising. *Journal of Advertising, 21*(1), 45–57.

The citation includes the issue number in parentheses as well as the volume number. Note that the issue number and the parentheses are *not* italicized.

Articles in Magazines and Newspapers Accessed in Print

Magazine Article with Named Author

Snyder, R. L. (2001, August–September). A daughter of Cambodia remembers: Loung Ung's journey. *Ms., 12,* 62–67.

Hall, S. S. (2001, March 11). Prescription for profit. *New York Times Magazine,* 40–45,
59, 91–92, 100.

The pattern is as follows: Author. (Year, Month [Day]). Title of article. *Name of
Magazine, volume number [if stated in magazine],* inclusive pages. If page numbers
are discontinuous, identify every page.

Anonymous Magazine Article

Daddy, daddy. (2001, July 30). *New Republic, 225,* 12–13.

Review of Book or Film

Schwarz, B. (2001, November). A bit of bunting: A new history of the British empire
elevates expediency to principle [Review of the book *Ornamentalism: How the
British saw their empire*]. *Atlantic Monthly, 288,* 126–135.

Kaufman, S. (2001, July 30). Polishing a gem [Review of the motion picture *The blue
angel*]. *New Republic, 225,* 28–29.

Newspaper Article

Henriques, D. B. (1998, September 27). Hero's fall teaches Wall Street a lesson.
Seattle Times, pp. A1, A24.

Newspaper Editorial

Dr. Frankenstein on the hill [Editorial]. (2002, May 18). *The New York Times,* p. A22.

Letter to the Editor of a Magazine or Newspaper

Tomsovic, K. (1998, July 13). Culture clash [Letter to the editor]. *New Yorker,* p. 7.

Print Articles or Books Downloaded from a Database

Print Article Downloaded from Licensed Database

Watanabe, M. (2003). Zoos act as sentinels for infectious diseases. *Bioscience, 53,*
792. Retrieved July 26, 2004, from ProQuest database.

Note the commas before and after the year in the retrieval statement.

Broadcast Transcript Retrieved from Licensed Database

Conan, N. (Anchor), & Telhami, S. (Guest). (2004, May 4). Arab media [Radio
transcript]. *Talk of the nation.* Retrieved July 31, 2004, from LexisNexis database.

Reference Material Retrieved from Licensed Database

Cicada. (2004). *Encyclopædia Britannica.* Retrieved July 31, 2004, from Britannica
Online database.

The *Publication Manual of the American Psychological Association,* 5th ed., has no model format for an online reference database, so we followed the manual's advice to adapt the format of similar items.

Papers and Monographs from an Information Service
Information services such as ERIC (Educational Resources Information Center) or NTIS (National Technical Information Service) provide material to your library on microfiche or online, offering indexes on CD-ROM or online. Much of the material from these services has not been published in major journals or magazines. Frequently they are typescripts of conference papers or other scholarly work disseminated on microfiche.

Coll, R. K., Tofield, S., Vyle, B., & Bolstad, R. (2003, March). *Free-choice learning at a metropolitan zoo.* Paper presented at the annual meeting of the National Association for Research in Science Teaching, Philadelphia, PA. (ERIC Document Reproduction Service No. ED477832)

If you retrieve the document online, add a retrieval statement indicating the name of the database and the date retrieved, as in the preceding examples.

Web and Internet Sources

Documents within a Web Site
Provide corporate authors when a document does not list an individual author. Use "n.d." if no publication date is provided.

Marks, J. (n.d.). Overview: Letter from the president. Retrieved June 25, 2004, from the Search for Common Ground Web site: http://www.sfcg.org/sfcg/sfcg_overview.html

United States Institute of Peace. (2000). Advances in understanding international peacemaking. Retrieved May 25, 2004, from http://www.usip.org/pubs/summaries/adv_intl.html

Article from a Newspaper Site
Thevenot, B. (2004, July 31). Once in a blue moon. *Times Picayune* [New Orleans]. Retrieved July 31, 2004, from http://www.nola.com/t-p/

Broadcast Transcript from a Web Site
Michels, S. (Correspondent), & Warner, M. (Anchor). (2004, July 28). The politics of 9/11 [Television transcript]. *Newshour with Jim Lehrer.* Retrieved July 31, 2004, from the Online Newshour Website: http://www.pbs.org/newshour/bb/terrorism/july-dec04/9-11_7-28.html

Because the APA *Manual* doesn't have a model for broadcast transcripts, we modified the format for television broadcasts by adding identifying labels.

Article from a Scholarly E-Journal

Welch, J. R., & Riley, R. (2001). Reclaiming land and spirit in the western Apache homeland. *American Indian Quarterly, 25,* 5–14. Retrieved December 19, 2001, from http://muse.jhu.edu/journals/american_indian_quarterly/v025/25.1welch.pdf

E-Book

Hoffman, F. W. (1981). *The literature of rock: 1954–1978.* Retrieved December 19, 2001, from http://www.netlibrary.com/ebook_info.asl?product_id=24355

The *Publication Manual of the American Psychological Association,* 5th ed., has no example of an E-book. We followed the manual's advice about how to proceed when an unusual case arises.

E-Mail, Interviews, and Personal Correspondence

APA guidelines limit the "References" list to publishable or retrievable information. Cite personal correspondence in the body of your text, but not in the "References" list: "Daffinrud (personal communication, December 12, 2001) claims that. . . . "

Online Posting to a Listserv, Bulletin Board Newsgroup, or Blog

CalEnergyGuy. (2004, July 27). Energy crisis impacts on the economy: Changes since 2001 [Blog posting]. Retrieved August 1, 2004, from the Web site of the California Energy Blog: http://calenergy.blogspot.com/2004_07_01_calenergy_archive.html

We have again followed the APA's advice to interpolate a format from similar models.

Miscellaneous Sources

Television Program

Bochco, S., & Milch, D. (Directors). (2001, November 6). Lie like a rug [Television series episode]. In *NYPD blue.* New York: American Broadcasting Company.

Film

Madden, J. (Director). (1998). *Shakespeare in love* [Motion picture]. United States: Universal Miramax.

Sound Recording

Dwarf Music. (1966). Rainy day woman [Recorded by B. Dylan]. On *Bob Dylan MTV unplugged* [CD]. New York: Columbia. (1995)

Follow this format: Writer of song or copyright holder. (Date of copyright). Title of song [Recorded by artist if different from writer]. On *Title of album* [Medium such as CD, record, or cassette]. Location: Label. (Date of album if different from date of song)

Unpublished Paper Presented at a Meeting

Sharples, M. (2001, June 20). *Authors of the future.* Keynote address presented at Conference of European Teachers of Academic Writing, Groningen, the Netherlands.

Government Publications

O'Toole, M. (2000). *The school shooter: A threat assessment perspective.* Washington, DC: U.S. Federal Bureau of Investigation. Retrieved August 16, 2001, from http://www.fbi.gov/publications/school/school2.pdf

Conclusion

This chapter has shown you how to use sources purposively, how to help readers separate your ideas from those of sources through the use of rhetorically effective attributive tags, and how to work sources into your own writing through summarizing, paraphrasing, and quoting. It has also defined plagiarism and shown you how to avoid it. The last half of the chapter has shown you the nuts and bolts of citing and documenting sources in both the MLA and APA styles. It has explained the logic of parenthetical citation systems, showing you how to match sources cited in your text with those in your concluding bibliography. It has also shown you the documentation formats for a wide range of sources in both MLA and APA styles.

Student Example of an APA-Style Research Paper

We conclude with a sample of a successful effort: Megan Matthews' researched argument on Navy sonar and whales. She uses the APA system for citing and documenting her sources.

Sounding the Alarm:

Navy Sonar and the Survival of Whales

Megan Matthews

English 260

November 1, 2002

Sounding the Alarm:

Navy Sonar and the Survival of Whales

Imagine that you are forced to live in an apartment next to a city freeway   1
with a constant roar of engines and tires against concrete. Cars cruise by on the
surface streets with bass systems so powerful that your windows shake and your
ears hurt. You tolerate the din day after day, but you and your friends have to shout
to be heard. What if you had no alternative place to live?

This scenario is, of course, preposterous. We can move to find the coveted   2
sound of silence. For whales, dolphins, and sea turtles, however, noise is becoming
an inescapable catastrophe that threatens far more than their aesthetic
sensibilities. The incessant rumbling of cargo ships, the loud explosions of
undersea mineral explorations, and the annoying cacophony of the blasting devices
used by fisheries have turned Jacques Cousteau's world of silence into an
underwater freeway. Now, however, a new and more dangerous source of sound
has been approved for use in the oceans—the United States Navy's Low Frequency
Active Sonar System (LFA sonar), which will track enemy submarines. The Navy
claims that the technology is needed to ensure national security, since it detects
submarines at greater distances than previous sonar systems. However, the
potential damage to marine life and to the long-term health of the oceans
themselves outweighs the Navy's questionable claims about national security. The
U. S. Congress should cut funds for further deployment of LFA sonar.

Since the mid-1980s, the Navy has developed and tested LFA sonar systems.   3
LFA is *active* because it does more than just listen for nearby submarines, like our
older systems. With LFA, 18 acoustic transmitters the size of bathtubs act like giant
woofer speakers suspended beneath the ship on cables. The speakers emit bursts
of sound every 6 to 100 seconds. These bursts can be as powerful as 215 decibels,
a sound level equivalent to standing 1 meter away from a departing commercial jet
(National Marine Fisheries Service [NMFS], 2002a, p. 3). The Navy prefers low-
frequency sonar because low-frequency waves travel farther than high-frequency
waves, which is why the bumping bass of a car stereo reverberates after the car
spins around a street corner. In this case, the sonar's sound waves reflect off
objects from hundreds of miles away and alert the ship's crew to the presence of
submarines. In its Environmental Impact Statement, the Navy explains that it needs
LFA sonar because modern submarines are quieter than clunky Cold War versions.
Their ability to run quietly makes the new subs virtually undetectable until they are

close by, leaving the Navy only minutes to respond to a potential submarine threat (Department of the Navy [DON], 2001, p. ES-2). After studying possible solutions, the Navy believes LFA sonar is the only system capable of providing reliable and dependable long-range detection of quieter, harder-to-find submarines (DON, 2001, p. ES-2). Unfortunately, the far-traveling waves that bounce off enemy submarines also can pierce the inner ears of whales and dolphins.

4   To its credit, the Navy has acted to protect marine mammals and other sea life. The Navy studied existing research reports on the levels of sounds that can cause hearing damage to marine mammals and concluded that protecting whales and dolphins from levels above 180 dB would prevent any harm to their hearing and behavior. Based on these studies, the National Oceanic and Atmospheric Administration's National Marine Fisheries Service determined that the Navy's employment of LFA sonar at levels below 180 dB would have no more than a negligible impact on marine mammal species and stocks (National Oceanic and Atmospheric Administration [NOAA], 2002). The Navy therefore plans to use a maximum volume of 180 dB when marine mammals are nearby. As an initial protective measure, the sonar will not be allowed to operate above 180 dB if it is within 12 nautical miles of coastlines and islands to ensure that coastal stocks of marine mammals and sea turtles will be relatively unaffected by LFA sonar (NMFS, 2002b). This measure protects critically endangered species, like northern right whales, who feed in coastal areas. The Navy also plans to avoid damaging whale hearing and behavior by trying to prevent animals from swimming near the ships. The Navy wants to detect animals that wander within 1 kilometer of the vessel, where they might be exposed to sounds of 180 dB or more. The protective monitoring systems will rely on humans and technology to protect sea animals. Sailors who have been trained to detect and identify marine mammals and sea turtles will stand on deck to look for whales and dolphins (Schregardus, 2002, p. 48149). Underwater microphones will also listen for sounds that whales and dolphins make. Finally, the Navy has developed a second active sonar system called the High Frequency Marine Mammal Monitoring Sonar. It will locate and monitor animals who enter the 180 dB area and will run before and during the LFA sonar transmissions. If whales, dolphins, or sea turtles are observed, the crew will turn off the LFA system until the animals move away.

5   These efforts to protect sea life are commendable, but current marine research shows that LFA sonar poses a much higher risk to marine mammals than

the Navy acknowledges. The conclusions drawn by the Navy about potential hearing damage to marine mammals are open to serious doubt, and their measures to protect the sea environment are inadequate.

To begin, biologists generally agree that hearing is the primary sense of marine mammals. No one knows precisely what functions hearing performs, but it is likely that whales depend on sound to avoid predators, to communicate across great distances between pods and prospective mates, and to establish mother-calf bonds. According to a detailed study by the National Resources Defense Council (Jasny, 1999), significant noise interference could threaten individual mammals or entire populations if biologically important behaviors like these are disrupted. Furthermore, like the members of a rock band, whales and dolphins may experience hearing loss after repeated exposure to sounds at the same frequency. In 1996, two sperm whales residing in a heavily trafficked area of the Canary Islands made no apparent efforts to avoid a collision with a cargo ship and were killed. Autopsies revealed damage to their inner ears, which some environmental scientists believe could have been caused by repeated exposure to the sounds of cargo ships (Jasny, 1999). The Navy's tests of different kinds of sonar systems are also suspected to have caused 16 Cuvier's beaked whales to beach and die in the Bahamas. The Navy had been testing midrange active sonar in the area; autopsies of four whales revealed extensive bleeding in the inner ears and around the brain. The conclusions of the Navy and Fisheries Service interim and final reports named the sonar tests as the most likely cause of the beachings (DON and NMFS, 2001). Although the type of sonar was midrange, rather than low-frequency, the link still implies that whales can be harmed or even killed by sonar—and that the effects can be unanticipated. Beachings also occurred after naval sonar exercises in Greece and the Canary Islands. In Greece, sonar is the likely culprit; scientists cannot establish the cause of death, however, because the initial examination of the bodies was not thorough (Jasny, 1999). Finally, according to Jasny, the long-term effects of noise pollution may not be limited to hearing; noise pollution can increase stress levels, which lead to shorter life spans and lower birth rates—effects that humans may not notice for decades. One ping from a low-frequency system may only *harass* whales, to use the term commonly encountered in Navy or Fisheries Service discussions of low-frequency sonar, but if whales are exposed to LFA sound waves repeatedly, the effects may be long-lasting and even irreversible.

7   The importance of hearing to marine mammals means that the effect of LFA sonar on the sea environment needs to be extensively studied. Unfortunately, the studies used by the Navy to demonstrate that LFA sonar poses little threat to marine life are scant, scientifically flawed, and inconclusive. No one actually knows how loud or frequent sounds need to be to cause permanent or temporary hearing loss to whales and sea turtles. Most studies have focused on captive species like seals and some dolphins; the data is extrapolated to estimate the hearing capacities of other species. The Navy uses the findings of several scientific workshops that studied the range where serious hearing problems could occur. Based upon these conclusions, as well as the Navy's own examinations of marine mammal inner ear models and extrapolation from human results, the Navy believes that protecting marine mammals from levels above 180 dB will be sufficient (DON, 2001, p. 14). Yet the Navy itself admits, in its own environmental impact statement, that data regarding underwater hearing capabilities of marine mammals are rare and limited to smaller species that can be studied in laboratories (DON, 2001, p. 11). The Navy has tried to dispel fears that mammals are physically and behaviorally harmed by LFA sonar by releasing the results of three separate tests Navy scientists conducted on baleen whale populations in California and Hawaii; these studies concluded that most whales did not alter any observable aspect of their behavior for more than "a few tens of minutes" (DON, 2001, p. 16). Nevertheless, three tests on baleen whales is hardly adequate to conclude that other species of whales, as well as other marine mammals, would react in the same way as the baleen whale. Moreover, none of these studies examined the long-term effects of repeated exposures, nor were whales exposed to sounds above 155 dB, even though the estimated LFA safety level is 180 dB. One has difficulty understanding how the Navy can set 180 dB as their safety threshold when their own tests did not monitor whales at this level. Moreover, some scientists claim that *less intense* sounds can be harmful. Dr. Marsh Green, the President of the Ocean Mammal Institute and an animal behavior specialist, claims that "a significant body of research show[s] that whales avoid underwater sounds starting at 110 to 120 decibels" (Knickerbocker, 2001). If the scientific community continues to debate this issue, it seems unlikely that the Navy could have indisputable evidence that the sonar will not harm whales.

8   Clearly the Navy's claim that LFA sonar will not hurt marine mammals and other sea life will not survive close scrutiny. Of even greater concern is the

Sounding the Alarm   6

dangerous precedent that the U.S. Navy will set if it deploys LFA sonar on its surface ships. There is a strong possibility that other nations might develop LFA sonar systems in order to keep up with the United States. The nuclear weapons race of the past proves that military powers constantly compete with each other to be prepared for armed conflicts. This often results in a frantic struggle to develop the same technologies worldwide with no regard for environmental and social effects. Already, according to Jasny (1999), NATO countries are investigating their own use of similar LFA systems. If additional countries deploy the technology, whales and dolphins will face much greater risks of meeting sonar systems in open water. In addition, the world's governments have not discussed treaties that would require nations to turn off sonar systems in arctic waters, which the Navy currently plans to do. Whales, dolphins, and sea turtles will have no permanent safe havens if other militaries choose to run their systems worldwide.

The Navy justifies developing LFA sonar for the sake of national security; in   9
light of the September 11, 2001, terrorist attacks, this claim almost guarantees unquestioned public support. Even so, in the age of terrorism, do enemy submarines present significant threats? A confusing array of Navy documents makes it nearly impossible for the general public to find out the facts about potential danger from submarines. The Navy argues that 224 diesel-electric submarines are operated by nonallied nations but never explains who these nations are or how much of a threat they actually pose (Schregardus, 2002, p. 48146). This long-standing anxiety about submarines feels like part of the old Cold War mentality when the nation to fear was the Soviet Union. Perhaps now we should be more concerned about cargo ships than submarines. A large percentage of freight containers are never inspected at our ports, and these seem to be easier targets for terrorists than our Navy ships. Finally, the most recent attack on a Navy ship, the USS *Cole,* came from another boat, not a submarine. The number of terrorists who have sophisticated submarine technology must be smaller than the number who can place a small bomb on a small boat, train, car, or cargo ship.

Moreover long-term national security also depends on healthy oceans.   10
Millions of people incorporate fish into their diet, and oceans provide materials for countless human products. Any changes to the balance of marine life could degrade the entire ecosystem. If the health of the oceans is damaged by LFA sonar, it will be only a matter of time before humans feel the effects. Our national environmental security, which never receives much attention in the media, should be as important

to the United States as our military readiness. The proposed widespread use of LFA sonar on the Navy's surface ships opens up a range of questions about the long-term effects of our underwater activities. When combined with other sources of human noise pollution, LFA sonar poses dangerous threats to marine life. According to Dr. Sylvia Earle, former Chief Scientist at the National Oceanic and Atmospheric Administration, undersea noise pollution is like the death of a thousand cuts (as cited in Jasny, 1999, executive summary, first sidebar). Each time we turn up the volume in the oceans, we make it more difficult for marine animals to communicate with each other. We may even diminish their hearing capacities, endangering their abilities to migrate safely and to avoid countless ships that crisscross their routes. Until more is known about the long-term effects of LFA sonar, the Navy should delay operation of LFA sonar voluntarily. If it does not do so, the U.S. Congress should cut off further funding. The debate over LFA sonar cannot be defined as a simple environment-versus-government battle. It is a discussion about whether or not environmental security and ocean health matter to humans. At its core, it is a debate about our futures.

References

Department of the Navy. (2001). *Executive summary: Final overseas environmental impact statement and environmental impact statement for Surveillance Towed Array Sensor System Low Frequency Active (SURTASS LFA) Sonar.* Retrieved October 5, 2002, from http://www.surtass-lfa-eis.com/docs/EXSUM%20FEIS%201-15.pdf

Department of the Navy and National Marine Fisheries Service. (2001, December 20). *Joint interim report: Bahamas marine mammal stranding event of 15–16 March 2000.* Retrieved October 15, 2002, from http://www.nmfs.noaa.gov/prot_res/overview/Interim_Bahamas_Report.pdf

Jasny, M. (1999, March). *Sounding the depths: Supertankers, sonar, and the rise of undersea noise.* Retrieved October 15, 2002, from the National Resources Defense Council Web site: http://www.nrdc.org/wildlife/marine/sound/sdinx.asp

Knickerbocker, B. (2001, August 20). US Navy plans for loud sonar raises fears for whales. *Christian Science Monitor.* Retrieved October 20, 2002, from http://news.nationalgeographic.com/news/2001/08/0815_wirenavyboom.html

National Marine Fisheries Service. (2002a). *Biological opinion on proposed employment of Surveillance Towed Array Sensor System Low Frequency Active Sonar.* Retrieved October 8, 2002, from http://www.nmfs.noaa.gov/prot_res/readingrm/ESAsec7/7pr_surtass-2020529.pdf

National Marine Fisheries Service. (2002b). *Final determination and rulemaking on the harassment of marine mammals incidental to Navy operations of Surveillance Towed Array Sensor System Low Frequency Active (SURTASS LFA) Sonar.* Retrieved October 5, 2002, from http://www.nmfs.noaa.gov/prot_res/readingrm/MMSURTASS/LFAexecsummary.PDF

National Oceanic and Atmospheric Administration. (2002, July 15). *Strong protection measures for marine mammals tied to operation of Low Frequency Sonar* (NOAA news release 2002–90). Retrieved October 15, 2002, from http://www.publicaffairs.noaa.gov/releases2002/july02/noaa02090.html

Schregardus, D. R. (2002, July 16). *Record of decision for Surveillance Towed Array Sensor System Low Frequency Active (SURTASS LFA) Sonar,* Fed Reg 67 (141), pp. 48145–48154 (2002, July 23). Retrieved October 12, 2002, from http://www.surtass-lfa-eis.com/docs/LFA%20EIS%20ROD.pdf

Appendix One

Informal Fallacies

In this appendix, we look at ways of assessing the legitimacy of an argument within a real-world context of probabilities rather than within a mathematical world of certainty. Whereas formal logic is a kind of mathematics, the informal fallacies addressed in this appendix get embedded in everyday arguments, sometimes making fallacious reasoning seem deceptively persuasive, especially to unwary audiences. We begin by looking at the problem of conclusiveness in arguments, after which we give you an overview of the most commonly encountered informal fallacies.

The Problem of Conclusiveness in an Argument

In real-world disagreements, we seldom encounter arguments that are absolutely conclusive. Rather, arguments are, to various degrees, "persuasive" or "nonpersuasive." In the pure world of formal logic, however, it is possible to have absolutely conclusive arguments. For example, an Aristotelian syllogism, if it is validly constructed, yields a certain conclusion. Moreover, if the first two premises (called the "major" and "minor" premises) are true, then we are guaranteed that the conclusion is also true. Here is an example:

VALID SYLLOGISM

Major premise: All chickens are feathered animals.

Minor premise: Clucko is a chicken.

Conclusion: Therefore Clucko is a feathered animal. (guaranteed conclusion)

This syllogism is said to be valid because it follows a correct form. Moreover, because its premises are true, the conclusion is guaranteed to be true. However, if the syllogism follows an incorrect form (and is therefore invalid), we can't determine whether the conclusion is true or not.

INVALID SYLLOGISM

Major premise: All chickens are feathered animals.

Minor premise: Quacko is a feathered animal.

Conclusion: Therefore Quacko is a chicken. (nonguaranteed conclusion)

In the valid syllogism, we are guaranteed that Clucko is a feathered animal because the minor premise states that Clucko is a chicken and the major premise places chickens within the larger class of feathered animals. But in the invalid syllogism, there is no guaranteed conclusion. We know that Quacko is a feathered animal but we can't know whether he is a chicken. He may be a chicken, but he may also be a buzzard or a duck. The invalid syllogism thus commits a "formal fallacy" in that its form doesn't guarantee the truth of its conclusion even if the initial premises are true.

From the perspective of real-world argumentation, the problem with formal logic is that it isn't concerned with the truth of premises. For example, the following argument is logically valid even though the premises and conclusion are obviously untrue:

VALID SYLLOGISM WITH UNTRUE MAJOR AND MINOR PREMISES

Major premise: The blood of insects can be used to lubricate lawn mower engines.

Minor premise: Vampires are insects.

Conclusion: Therefore the blood of vampires can be used to lubricate lawn mower engines.

Even though this syllogism meets the formal requirements for validity, its argument is ludicrous.

In this appendix, therefore, we are concerned with "informal" rather than "formal" fallacies because informal fallacies are embedded within real-world arguments addressing contestable issues of truth and value. Disputants must argue about issues because they can't be resolved with mathematical certainty; any contestable claim always leaves room for doubt and alternative points of view. Disputants can create only more or less persuasive arguments, never conclusive ones.

An Overview of Informal Fallacies

The study of informal fallacies remains the murkiest of all logical endeavors. It's murky because informal fallacies are as unsystematic as formal fallacies are rigid and systematized. Whereas formal fallacies of logic have the force of laws, informal fallacies have little more than explanatory power. Informal fallacies are quirky; they identify classes of less conclusive arguments that recur with some frequency, but they do not contain formal flaws that make their conclusions illegitimate no matter what the terms may say. Informal fallacies require us to look at the meaning of the terms to determine how much we should trust or distrust the conclusion. In evaluating arguments with informal fallacies, we usually find that arguments are "more or less" fallacious, and determining the degree of fallaciousness is a matter of judgment.

Knowledge of informal fallacies is most useful when we run across arguments that we "know" are wrong, but we can't quite say why. They just don't "sound right." They look reasonable enough, but they remain unacceptable to us. Informal fallacies are a sort of compendium of symptoms for arguments flawed in this way. We must be careful, however, to make sure that the particular case before us "fits" the descriptors for the fallacy that seems to explain its problem. It's much easier, for example, to find informal fallacies in a hostile argument than in a friendly one simply because we are more likely to expand the limits of the fallacy to make the disputed case fit.

In arranging the fallacies, we have, for convenience, put them into three categories derived from classical rhetoric: *pathos, ethos,* and *logos.* Fallacies of *pathos* rest on flaws in the way an argument appeals to the audience's emotions and values. Fallacies of *ethos* rest on flaws in the way the argument appeals to the character of opponents or of sources and witnesses within an argument. Fallacies of *logos* rest on flaws in the relationship among statements in an argument.

Fallacies of *Pathos*

Argument to the People (Appealing to Stirring Symbols)   This is perhaps the most generic example of a *pathos* fallacy. Arguments to the people appeal to the fundamental beliefs, biases, and prejudices of the audience in order to sway opinion through a feeling of solidarity among those of the group. Thus a "Support Our Troops" bumper sticker, often including the American flag, creates an initial feeling of solidarity among almost all citizens of goodwill. But the car owner may have the deeper intention of actually meaning "support our president" or "support the war in _____." The stirring symbol of the flag and the desire shared by most people to support our troops is used fallaciously to urge support of a particular political act. Arguments to the people often use visual rhetoric, as in the soaring eagle used in Wal-Mart corporate ads or images of happy families in marketing advertisements.

Appeal to Ignorance   This fallacy persuades an audience to accept as true a claim that hasn't been proved false or *vice versa.* "Jones must have used steroids to get those bulging biceps because he can't prove that he hasn't used steroids." Appeals to ignorance are particularly common in the murky field of pseudoscience. "UFOs (ghosts, abominable snowmen) do exist because science hasn't proved that they don't exist." Sometimes, however, it is hard to draw a line between a fallacious appeal to ignorance and a legitimate appeal to precaution: "Genetically modified organisms must be dangerous to our health because science hasn't proved that they are safe."

Appeal to Popularity—Bandwagon   To board the bandwagon means (to use a more contemporary metaphor) to board the bus or train of what's popular. Appeals to popularity are fallacious because the popularity of something is irrelevant to its actual merits. "Living together before marriage is the right thing to do because most couples are now doing it." Bandwagon appeals are common in advertising where the claim that a product is popular substitutes for evidence of the product's excellence. There are times, however, where popularity may indeed be relevant: "Global warming is probably caused by human activity because a preponderance of scientists now hold this position." (Here we assume that scientists haven't simply climbed on a bandwagon themselves, but have formed their opinions based on research data and well-vetted, peer-reviewed papers.)

Appeal to Pity   Here the arguer appeals to the audience's sympathetic feelings in order to support a claim that should be decided on more relevant or objective grounds. "Honorable judge, I should not be fined $200 for speeding because I was distraught from hearing news of my brother's illness and was rushing to see him in the hospital." Here the argument is fallacious because the arguer's reason, while evoking sympathy, is not a relevant justification for speeding (as it might have been, for instance, if the arguer had been rushing an injured person to the emergency room). In many cases, however, an arguer can legitimately appeal to pity, as in the case of fund-raising for victims of a tsunami or other disaster.

Red Herring   This fallacy's funny name derives from the practice of using a red herring (a highly odiferous fish) to throw dogs off a scent that they are supposed to be tracking. This fallacy refers to the practice of throwing an audience off track by raising an unrelated or irrelevant point. "Debating a gas tax increase is valuable, but I really think there should be an extra tax on SUVs." Here the arguer, apparently uncomfortable with the gas tax issue, diverts the conversation to the emotional issue of SUVs. A conversant who noted how the argument has gotten off track might say, "Stop talking, everyone. The SUV question is a red herring; let's get back to the topic of a gas tax increase."

Fallacies of *Ethos*

Appeal to False Authority   Arguers appeal to false authority when they use famous persons (often movie stars or other celebrities) to testify on issues about which these persons have no special competence. "Joe Quarterback says Gooey Oil keeps his old tractor running sharp; therefore, Gooey Oil is a good oil." Real evidence about the quality of Gooey Oil would include technical data about the product rather than testimony from an actor or hired celebrity. However, the distinction between a "false authority" and a legitimate authority can become blurred. Consider the Viagra ads by former Vice President Bob Dole during the first marketing years of this impotence drug. As a famous person rather than a doctor, Dole would seem to be a false authority. But Dole was also widely known to have survived prostate cancer, and he may well have used Viagra. To the extent a person is an expert in a field, he or she is no longer a "false authority."

Ad Hominem Literally, *ad hominem* means "to the person." An *ad hominem* argument is directed at the character of an opponent rather than at the quality of the opponent's reasoning. Ideally, arguments are supposed to be *ad rem* ("to the thing"), that is, addressed to the specifics of the case itself. Thus an *ad rem* critique of a politician would focus on her voting record, the consistency and cogency of her public statements, her responsiveness to constituents, and so forth. An *ad hominem* argument would shift attention from her record to features of her personality, life circumstances, or the company she keeps. "Senator Sweetwater's views on the gas tax should be discounted because her husband works for a huge oil company" or "Senator Sweetwater supports tax cuts for the wealthy because she is very wealthy herself and stands to gain." But not all *ad hominem* arguments are *ad hominem* fallacies. Lawyers, for example, when questioning expert witnesses who give damaging testimony, will often make an issue of their honesty, credibility, or personal investment in an outcome.

Poisoning the Well This fallacy is closely related to *ad hominem*. Arguers poison the well when they discredit an opponent or an opposing view in advance. "Before I yield the floor to the next speaker, I must remind you that persons who oppose my plan do not have the best interests of working people in their hearts."

Straw Man The straw man fallacy occurs when you oversimplify an opponent's argument to make it easier to refute or ridicule. Rather than summarizing an opposing view fairly and completely, you basically make up the argument you wish your opponent had made because it is so much easier to knock over, like knocking over a straw man or scarecrow in a corn field. See pages 145–147 for a fuller discussion of the straw man fallacy.

Fallacies of *Logos*

Hasty Generalization This fallacy occurs when someone makes a broad generalization on the basis of too little evidence. Generally, the evidence needed to support a generalization persuasively must meet the STAR criteria (sufficiency, typicality, accuracy, and relevance) discussed in Chapter 6 (pp. 110–111). But what constitutes a sufficient amount of evidence? The generally accepted standards of sufficiency in any given field are difficult to determine. The Food and Drug Administration (FDA), for example, generally proceeds cautiously before certifying a drug as "safe." However, if people are harmed by the side effects of an FDA-approved drug, critics often accuse the FDA of having made a hasty generalization. At the same time, patients eager to have access to a new drug and manufacturers eager to sell a new product may lobby the FDA to quit "dragging its feet" and get the drug to market. Hence, the point at which a hasty generalization passes over into the realm of a prudent generalization is nearly always uncertain and contested.

Part for the Whole   Sometimes called by its Latin name *pars pro toto*, this fallacy is closely related to hasty generalization. In this fallacy, arguers pick out a part of the whole or a sample of the whole (often not a typical or representative part or sample) and then claim that what is true of the part is true for the whole. If, say, individuals wanted to get rid of the National Endowment for the Arts (NEA), they might focus on several controversial programs funded by the NEA and use them as justification for wiping out all NEA programs. The flip side of this fallacy occurs when an arguer picks only the best examples to make a case and conveniently forgets about other examples that might weaken the case.

Post Hoc, Ergo Propter Hoc   The Latin name of this fallacy means "after this, therefore because of this." The fallacy occurs when a sequential relationship is mistaken for a causal relationship. (See Chapter 12, pp. 249–250, where we discuss this fallacy in more depth.) For example, you may be guilty of this fallacy if you say, "Cramming for a test really helps because last week I crammed for my psychology test and I got an A on it." When two events occur frequently in conjunction with each other, we've got a good case for a causal relationship. But until we can show how one causes the other and until we have ruled out other causes, we cannot be certain that a causal relationship is occurring. For example, the A on your psych test may be caused by something other than your cramming. Maybe the exam was easier, or perhaps you were luckier or more mentally alert. It is often difficult to tell when a *post hoc* fallacy occurs. When the New York police department changed its policing tactics in the early 1990s, the crime rate plummeted. Many experts attributed the declining crime rate to the new policing tactics, but some critics proposed other explanations. (See Case 1 on p. 242, where economist Steven Levitt attributes the declining rate to the legalization of abortion in the 1970s.)

Begging the Question—Circular Reasoning   Arguers beg the question when they provide a reason that simply restates the claim in different words. Here is an example: "Abortion is murder because it is the intentional taking of the life of a human being." Because "murder" is defined as "the intentional taking of the life of a human being," the argument is circular. It is tantamount to saying, "Abortion is murder because it is murder." In the abortion debate, the crucial issue is whether a fetus is a "human being" in the legal sense. So in this case the arguer has fallaciously "begged the question" by assuming from the start that the fetus is a legal human being. The argument is similar to saying, "That person is obese because he is too fat."

False Dilemma—Either/Or   This fallacy occurs when an arguer oversimplifies a complex issue so that only two choices appear possible. Often one of the choices is made to seem unacceptable, so the only remaining option is the other choice. "It's my way or the highway" is a typical example of a false dilemma. Here is a more subtle one: "Either we allow embryonic stem cell research, or we condemn persons with diabetes, Parkinson's disease, or spinal injuries to a life without a cure." Clearly, there may be other options here including other approaches to curing these diseases. A good extended example of the false dilemma fallacy is found in sociologist Kai Erikson's analysis of President Truman's decision to drop the A-bomb on Hiroshima. His analysis suggests that the Truman administration prematurely reduced numerous options to just two: Either drop the bomb on a major city, or sustain unacceptable losses in a land invasion of Japan. Erikson, however, shows there were other alternatives.

Slippery Slope   The slippery slope fallacy is based on the fear that once we put a foot on a slippery slope heading in the wrong direction, we're doomed to slide right out of sight. The controlling metaphor is of a slick mountainside without places to hold on rather than of a staircase with numerous stopping places. Here is an example of a slippery slope: "Once we allow medical use of marijuana, we'll eventually legalize it for everyone, after which we're on a slippery slope toward social acceptance of cocaine and heroin." Slippery slope arguments are especially common when individuals request exceptions to bureaucratic rules: "Look, Blotnik, no one feels worse about your need for open-heart surgery than I do. But I still can't let you turn this paper in late. If I were to let you do it, then I'd have to let everyone turn in papers late." Slippery slope arguments can be very persuasive—and often rightfully so because every slippery slope argument isn't necessarily a slippery slope fallacy. Some slopes really are slippery. The slippery slope becomes a fallacy when we forget that we can often dig a foothold into the slope and stop. For example, we can define procedures for exceptions to rules so that Blotnik can turn in his paper late without allowing everyone to turn in a paper late. Likewise, a state could legalize medical use of marijuana without legalizing it for everyone.

False Analogy   In Chapter 13 on resemblance arguments, we explained that no analogy is perfect (see our discussion of disanalogies on p. 272). Any two things being compared are similar in some ways and different in other ways. Whether an analogy is persuasive or false often depends on the audience's initial degree of skepticism. For example, persons opposed to gun control may find the following argument persuasive: "Banning guns on the basis that guns accidentally kill people is like banning cars on the basis that cars accidentally kill people." In contrast, supporters of gun control are likely to call this argument a false analogy on the basis of dissimilarities between cars and guns. (For example, they might say that banning cars would be far more disruptive on our society than would be banning guns.) Just when a persuasive analogy turns into a false analogy is difficult to say.

Non Sequitur   The name of this fallacy means "it does not follow." *Non sequitur* is a catchall term for any claim that doesn't follow from its premises or is supported by irrelevant premises. Sometimes the arguer seems to make an inexplicably illogical leap: "Genetically modified foods should be outlawed because they are not natural." (Should anything that is not natural be outlawed? In what way are they not natural?) At other times there may be a gap in the chain of reasons: "Violent video games have some social value because the Army uses them for recruiting." (There may be an important idea emerging here, but too many logical steps are missing.) At still other times an arguer might support a claim with irrelevant reasons: "I should not receive a C in this course because I currently have a 3.8 GPA." In effect, almost any fallacy could be called a *non sequitur* because fallacious reasoning always indicates some kind of disconnect between the reasons and the claim.

Loaded Label or Definition   Sometimes arguers will try to influence their audience's view of something by creating a loaded label or definition. For example, people who oppose the "estate tax" (which calls to mind rich people with estates) have relabeled it the "death tax" in order to give it a negative connotation without any markers of class or wealth. Or to take another example, proponents of organic foods could create definitions like the following: "Organic foods are safe and healthy foods grown without any pesticides, herbicides, or other unhealthy additives." "Safe" and "healthy" are evaluative terms used fallaciously in what purports to be a definition. The intended implication is that nonorganic foods are not safe and healthy.

For Class Discussion

Working individually or in small groups, determine the potential persuasiveness of each of the following argument cores. If fleshed out with supporting evidence, how persuasive do each of these arguments promise to be? If the arguments seemed doomed because of one or more of the fallacies discussed in this appendix, identify the fallacies and explain how they render the argument nonpersuasive. In your discussion, remember that it is often hard to determine the exact point where fallacious reasoning begins to kick in, especially when you consider different kinds of audiences. So in each case, consider also variations in audience. For which audiences would any particular argument appear potentially fallacious? Which audiences would be more likely to consider the argument persuasive?

1. Either we legalize marijuana or we watch a steady increase in the number of our citizens who break the law.
2. Smoking must cause lung cancer because a much higher percentage of smokers get lung cancer than do nonsmokers.

3. Smoking does not cause cancer because my grandfather smoked two packs per day for fifty years and died in his sleep at age ninety.

4. Society has an obligation to provide housing for the homeless because people without adequate shelter have a right to the resources of the community.

5. Based on my observations of the two renters in our neighborhood, I have concluded that people who own their own homes take better care of them than those who rent. [This arguer provided detailed evidence about the house-caring practices of the two renters and of the homeowners in the neighborhood.]

6. Intelligent Design must qualify as a scientific theory because hundreds of scientists endorse it.

7. If we pass legislation requiring mandatory registration of handguns, we'll open the door to eventual confiscation of hunting rifles.

8. Those who support gun control are wrong because they believe that no one should have the right to defend himself or herself in any situation.

9. Most other progressive nations have adopted a program of government-provided health insurance. Therefore it is time for the United States to abandon its present employer-funded insurance system and adopt federally funded universal health insurance.

10. You should discount Dr. Smith's objections to federally funded health care because as a doctor he may face a loss of some income.

Appendix Two

The Writing Community
Working in Groups

In Chapter 1 we stressed that today truth is typically seen as a product of discussion and persuasion by members of a given community. Instead of seeing "truth" as grounded in some absolute and timeless realm such as Plato's forms or the unchanging laws of logic, many modern thinkers assert that truth is the product of a consensus among a group of knowledgeable peers. Our own belief in the special importance of argumentation in contemporary life follows from our assumption that truth arises out of discussion and debate rather than dogma or pure reason.

In this appendix, we extend that assumption to the classroom itself. We explain a mode of learning often called *collaborative learning*. It involves a combination of learning from an instructor, learning independently, and learning from peers. Mostly it involves a certain spirit—the same sort of inquiring attitude that's required of a good arguer.

From Conflict to Consensus: How to Get the Most Out of the Writing Community

Behind the notion of the writing community lies the notion that thinking and writing are social acts. At first, this notion may contradict certain widely accepted stereotypes of writers and thinkers as solitary souls who retreat to cork-lined studies where they conjure great thoughts and works. But although we agree that every writer at some point in the process requires solitude, we would point out that most writers and thinkers also require periods of talk and social interchange before they retreat to solitude. Poets, novelists, scientists, philosophers, and technological innovators tend to belong to communities of peers with whom they share their ideas, theories, and work. In this section, we try to provide you with some practical advice on how to get the most out of these sorts of communities in developing your writing skills.

Avoiding Bad Habits of Group Behavior

Over the years, most of us have developed certain bad habits that get in the way of efficient group work. Although we use groups all the time to study and accomplish demanding tasks, we tend to do so spontaneously and unreflectively without asking why some groups work and others don't. Many of us, for example, have worked on committees that just didn't get the job done and wasted our time, or else got the job done because one or two tyrannical people dominated the group. Just a couple of bad committee experiences can give us a healthy skepticism about the utility of groups in general. "A committee," according to some people, "is a sort of centipede. It has too many legs, no brain, and moves very slowly."

At their worst, this is indeed how groups function. In particular, they have a tendency to fail in two opposite directions, failures that can be avoided only by conscious effort. Groups can lapse into "clonethink" and produce a safe, superficial consensus whereby everyone agrees with the first opinion expressed in order to avoid conflict or to get on to something more interesting. At the other extreme is a phenomenon we'll call "egothink." In egothink, all members of the group go their own ways and produce a collection of minority views that have nothing to do with each other and would be impossible to act on. Clonethinkers view their task as conformity to a norm; egothinkers see their task as safeguarding the autonomy of individual group members. Both fail to take other people and other ideas seriously.

Successful groups avoid both extremes and achieve unity out of diversity. This means that any successful community of learners must be willing to endure creative conflict. Creative conflict results from an initial agreement to disagree respectfully with each other and to focus that disagreement on ideas, not people. For this reason, we say that the relationship among the members of a learning community is not so much interpersonal or impersonal as *transpersonal,* or "beyond the personal." Each member is personally committed to the development of ideas and does whatever is necessary to achieve that development.

The Value of Group Work for Writers

Because we are basically social animals, we find it natural, pleasurable even, to deal with problems in groups. Proof of this fact can be found on any given morning in any given student union in the country. Around the room you will find many students working in groups. Math, engineering, and business majors will be solving problems together, comparing solutions and their ways of arriving at solutions. Others will be comparing their class notes and testing their understanding of concepts and terms by explaining them to each other and comparing their explanations. Why not ease into the rigors of writing in a similar fashion?

A second major advantage of working on writing in a group is that it provides a real and immediate audience for people's work. Too often, when students write in a school setting, they get caught up in the writing-for-teacher racket, which may distort their notion of audience. Argumentative writing is best aimed either at persons who disagree with you or at a neutral "jury" that will be weighing both sides of a controversy. A group of peers gives you a better sense of a real-world audience "out there" than does a single teacher.

There's danger, of course, in having several audiences consider your writing. Your peer audience may well respond differently to your writing than your instructor. You may feel misled if you are praised for something by a peer and then criticized for the same thing by your instructor. These things can and will happen, no matter how much time you spend developing universally accepted criteria for writing. Grades are not facts but judgments, and all judgments involve uncertainty. Students who are still learning the criteria for making judgments will sometimes apply those criteria differently than an instructor who has been working with them for years. But you should know too that two or more instructors might give you conflicting advice, just as two or more doctors might give you different advice on what to do about the torn ligaments in your knee. In our view, the risks of misunderstanding are more than made up for by gains in understanding of the writing process, an understanding that comes from working in writing communities where everyone functions both as a writer and as a writing critic.

A third advantage to working in writing communities is closely related to the second advantage. The act of sharing your writing with other people helps you get beyond the bounds of egocentrism that limit all writers. By egocentrism, we don't mean pride or stuck-upness; we mean the failure to consider the needs of your readers. Unless you share your writing with another person, your audience is always a "mythical group," a fiction or a theory that exists only in your head. You must always try to anticipate the problems others will have in reading your work. But until others actually read it and share their reactions to it with you, you can never be fully sure you have understood your audience's point of view. Until another reads your writing critically, you can't be sure you aren't talking to yourself.

Forming Writing Communities: Skills and Roles

Given that there are advantages to working in groups, just how do we go about forming writing communities in the classroom? We first have to decide how big to make the groups. From our experience, the best groups consist of either five to seven people or simply two people. Groups of three or four tend to polarize and become divisive, and larger groups tend to be unmanageable. Because working in five- to seven-person groups is quite different from working in pairs, we discuss each of these different-size groups in turn.

Working in Groups of Five to Seven People

The trick to successful group work is to consider the maximum number of viewpoints and concerns without losing focus. Because these two basic goals frequently conflict, you need some mechanisms for monitoring your progress. In particular, it's important that each group member is assigned to perform those tasks necessary to effective group functioning. (Some teachers assign roles to individual students, shifting the roles from day to day. Other teachers let the groups themselves determine the roles of individuals.) That is, the group must recognize that it has two objectives at all times: the stated objectives of a given task and the objective of making the group work well. It is very easy to get so involved with the given task that you overlook the second objective, generally known as "group maintenance."

The first role is group leader. We hesitate to call persons who fill this role "leaders" because we tend sometimes to think of leaders as know-it-alls who take charge and order people about. In classroom group work, however, being a group leader is a role you play, not a fixed part of your identity. The leader, above all else, keeps the group focused on agreed-on ends and protects the right of every group member to be heard. It's an important function, and group members should share the responsibility from task to task. Here is a list of things for the leader to do during a group discussion:

1. Ensure that everyone understands and agrees on the objectives of any given task and on what sort of final product is expected of the group (for example, a list of criteria, a brief written statement, or an oral response to a question).

2. Ask that the group set an agenda for completing the task, and have some sense of how much time the group will spend at each stage. (Your instructor should always make clear what time limits you have to operate within and when he or she expects your task to be completed. If a time limit isn't specified, you should request a reasonable estimate.)

3. Look for signs of getting off track, and ask individual group members to clarify how their statements relate to agreed-on objectives.

4. Actively solicit everyone's contributions, and take care that all viewpoints are listened to and that the group does not rush to incomplete judgment.

5. Try to determine when the task has been adequately accomplished.

In performing each of these functions, the leader must learn diplomatic ways of facilitating a group. Instead of saying to one silent and bored-looking member of the group, "Hey, Irwin, you haven't said diddly-squat here so far," the leader might say, "Irwin, what's your view here? Do you agree with Beth that the paper is disorganized?" By giving Irwin a graceful way to join in, you will be expanding the number of voices in the group while helping this class member feel valued.

A second crucial role for well-functioning groups is that of recorder. The recorder's function is to provide the group with a record of their deliberations so they can measure their progress. It is particularly important that the recorder write down the agenda and the solution to the problem in precise form. Because the recorder must summarize the deliberations fairly precisely, he must ask for clarifications. In doing this, he ensures that group members don't fall into the "ya know?" syndrome (a subset of clonethink) in which people assent to statements that are in fact cloudy to them. (Ya know?) At the completion of the task, the recorder should also ask whether there are any significant remaining disagreements or unanswered questions. Finally, the recorder is responsible for reporting the group's solutions to the class as a whole.*

The rest of the group members, though they have no formally defined roles, have an equally important obligation to participate fully. To ensure full participation, group members can do several things. They can make sure that they know all the other group members by their first names and speak to them in a friendly manner. They can practice listening procedures wherein they try not to dissent or disagree without first charitably summarizing the view with which they are taking issue. Most importantly, they can bring to the group as much information and as many alternative points of view as they can muster. The primary intellectual strength of group work is the ability to generate a more complex view of a subject. But this more complex view cannot emerge unless all individuals contribute their perspectives.

Working in Pairs

Working in pairs is another effective form of community learning. In our classes we use pairs at both the early-draft and the late-draft stages of writing. At the early-draft stage, it serves the very practical purpose of clarifying a student's ideas and sense of direction at the beginning of a new writing project. The interaction best takes place in the form of pair interviews. When you first sit down to interview each other, each of you should have done a fair amount of exploratory writing and thinking about what you want to say in your essay and how you're going to say it. Here is a checklist of questions you can use to guide your interview:

1. "What is your issue?" Your goal here is to help the writer focus an issue by formulating a question that clearly has alternative answers.

2. "What is your position on the issue, and what are alternative positions?" After you have helped your interviewee formulate the issue question, help her clarify this issue by stating her own position and showing how that position differs from opposing ones. Your interviewee might say, for example, that "many of my friends are opposed to building more nuclear power plants, but I think we need to build more of them."

3. "Who is your audience?" Your interviewee might say, "I am addressing this paper to neutral citizens who haven't yet made up their mind about nuclear power."

4. "Can you walk me through your argument step-by-step?" Once you know your interviewee's issue question and intended position, you can best help her by having her walk you through her argument, talking out loud. You can ask prompting questions such as "What are you going to say first?"

---

*There is a debate among experts who study small-group communications about whether the roles of leader and recorder can be collapsed into one job. Your group may need to experiment until it discovers the structure that works best for bringing out the most productive discussions.

"What next?" and so on. At this stage your interviewee will probably still be struggling to discover the best way to support the point. You can best help by brainstorming along with her, both of you taking notes on your ideas. Often at this stage you can begin making a schematic plan for the essay and formulating supporting reasons as *because* clauses. Along the way, give your interviewee any information or ideas you have on the issue. It is particularly helpful at this stage if you can provide counterarguments and opposing views.

The interview strategy is useful before writers begin their rough drafts. After the first drafts have been written, there are a number of different ways of using pairs to evaluate drafts. One practice that we've found helpful is simply to have writers write a one-paragraph summary of their own drafts and of their partner's. In comparing summaries, writers can often discover which, if any, of their essential ideas are simply not getting across. If a major idea is not in the reader's summary, writer and reader need to decide whether it's due to a careless reading or to problems within the draft. The nice thing about this method is that the criticism is given indirectly and hence isn't as threatening to either party. At other times, your instructor might also devise a checklist of features for you to consider, based on the criteria you have established for the assignment.

Another powerful strategy late in the writing process is to read your nearly final drafts aloud, either to your pair partner or to larger groups. Doing so is a chance to share the fruits of your labor with others and to hear finished essays that you may have seen in the draft stages. Hearing everyone else's nearly finished products can also help you get a clearer perspective on how your own work is progressing. Listening to the essays read can both reassure you that your work is on par with other people's and challenge you to write up to the level of the best student writing in your group. Your instructor will explain the process he or she finds most valuable for these late peer reviews.

Many of you might find this process a bit frightening at first. But the cause of your fright is precisely the source of the activity's value. In reading your work aloud, you are taking public responsibility for your words. The word has become deed. If you aren't at least a little nervous about reading an essay aloud, you probably haven't invested much in your words. Knowing that you will take public responsibility for your words is an incentive to make that investment—a more real and immediate incentive than grades.

For Class Discussion

This exercise asks you to participate in a thirty-minute small-group task and then to analyze and evaluate your group's process.

Part One—Small-group task: As a small group, identify a significant problem on your campus that inhibits learning or the quality of student life (total time: thirty minutes). Your goal for this task is not to provide a solution to the problem but simply to understand the problem's causes and context and to persuade your audience that the problem is significant and worth solving. Your recorder should be prepared to present to the whole class your group's consensus answers to the following questions:

- What is the problem?
- What are the stakes in this problem? (For whom is it a problem? Why is it a problem for these persons? Who suffers or what opportunities are lost? Give specific examples.)
- What are the causes of this problem?
- Why hasn't this problem been solved up to this point?
- Who has the power to solve the problem?
- Why is this a significant problem worthy of people's attention?

Part Two—Evaluating your group's process*

a. Working individually (time: five minutes), each student should answer the following questions:

- Overall, how effectively did your group work together on this task? (poorly, adequately, well, extremely well)
- Out of the X members of your group (specify number), how many participated actively most of the time? (none, one, two, three, four, five, six, seven)
- Give one specific example of something you learned from the group or thought about that you probably wouldn't have learned or thought about working alone.
- Give one specific example of something the other group members learned from you or thought about because of your contribution to the discussion.
- Suggest one change the group could make to improve its performance.

b. As a group, share your individual answers to these questions.

c. Reach consensus on one or more things the group could do to improve its performance. Be prepared to report this consensus to the whole class.

Group Project: Holding a "Norming Session" to Define "Good Argumentative Writing"

In this next group task, your problem is to define and identify "good argumentative writing" by creating criteria for evaluating an argument. This is a particularly

---

*The questions for this task are adapted from Elizabeth F. Barkely, K. Patricia Cross, and Claire Howell Major, *Collaborative Learning Techniques: A Handbook for College Faculty* (San Francisco: Jossey-Bass, 2005), 93.

crucial problem for developing writers insofar as you can't begin to measure your growth as a writer until you have some notion of what you're aiming for. For this task you will rank-order five student essays from best to worst according to criteria you establish within your small groups. College professors use this process regularly (often known as a "norming session") to determine criteria for grading student essays for large-scale assessment projects.

Task 1 (Homework): Preparing for the Group Discussion   Read the five student essays on pages 443–449. These essays were written early in an argument course. Students were asked to develop two or three reasons in support of a claim. Students had studied the argumentative concepts in Chapters 1–6 but had not yet studied refutation strategies. Although the students were familiar with classical argument structure, this introductory assignment did not ask them to summarize and respond to opposing views. The instructor's focus was only on students' developing some good reasons in support of a contestable claim.

After you have looked over the five student essays, concentrate for this task on "Bloody Ice" and "Legalization of Prostitution." Which of these two arguments is the better one? Freewrite your reasons for selecting the better argument, focusing on specific details of what you liked in the better essay and what you saw as problems in the weaker essay. (Note: Both essays have strengths and weaknesses, so you aren't trying to argue that one is excellent and the other is totally awful; you are just trying to determine which of the two more nearly meets the criteria for "good argumentative writing.") When you have finished your freewrite, develop a list of the criteria you used to make your judgment. You will be sharing this list with your classmates.

Task 2 (In-Class Group Work): Developing a Master List of Criteria   As a group, share your evaluations of "Bloody Ice" and "Legalization of Prostitution." Then try to reach group consensus on which of these two is the better essay and why. As a group, justify your evaluation by making a list of criteria you used and a rationale for rating some criteria more important than others. For example, does "quality of reasons" rank higher than "organization and development"? Does "use of evidence" rank higher than "lively style"? Your instructor may then ask each group to report its rankings to the whole class. The goal in this case is to create a class consensus about the two essays along with a master list of criteria.

Task 3 (Homework or Individual In-Class Time): Applying the Criteria to All Five Essays   Read again all five of the essays and rank-order them 1 to 5, best to worst, using the criteria developed during the previous discussions. Freewrite your rationale for ranking each essay as you did.

Task 4 (In-Class Group Work): Reaching Consensus on Ranking of Essays
Your goal now is to reach consensus on how you rank the essays and why you rank them the way you do. Feel free to change the criteria you established earlier if they seem to need some modification. Be careful in your discussions to distinguish between evaluation of the writer's written product and your own

personal position on the writer's issue. In other words, there is a crucial difference between saying, "I don't like LeShawn's essay because I disagree with his claim" versus saying, "I don't like LeShawn's essay because he didn't provide adequate evidence to support several of his reasons." As each group reports the results of its deliberations to the whole class, the instructor will highlight discrepancies among the groups' decisions and collate the criteria as they emerge. If the instructor disagrees with the class consensus or wants to add items to the criteria, he or she might choose to make these things known at this time. By the end of this stage, everyone should have a list of criteria for good argumentative writing established by the class.

Bloody Ice

It is March in Alaska. The ocean-side environment is full of life and death. Man 1 and animal share this domain but not in peace. The surrounding iceflows, instead of being cold and white, are steaming from the remains of gutted carcasses and stained red. The men are hunters and the animals are barely six weeks old. A slaughter has just taken place. Thousands of baby Harp seals lie dead on the ice and thousands more of adult mothers lay groaning over the death of their babies. Every year a total limit of 180,000 seals set by the U.S. Seal Protection Act is filled in a terrifying bloodbath. But Alaska with its limit of 30,000 is not alone. Canadians who hunt seals off the coast of Northern Newfoundland and Quebec are allowed 150,000 seals. The Norwegians are allowed 20,000 and native Eskimos of Canada and Greenland are allowed 10,000 seals per year. Although this act appears heartless and cruel, the men who hunt have done this for 200 years as a tradition for survival. They make many good arguments supporting their traditions. They feel the seals are in no immediate danger of extinction. Also seal furs can be used to line boots and gloves or merely traded for money and turned into robes or fur coats. Sometimes the meat is even used for food in the off hunting months when money is scarce. But are these valid justifications for the unmerciful killings? No, the present limit on Harp seal killings should be better regulated because the continued hunting of the seals will lead to eventual extinction and because the method of slaughter is so cruel and inhumane.

The Harp seal killing should be better regulated first because eventual extinc- 2 tion is inevitable. According to *Oceans* magazine, before the limit of 180,000 seals was established in 1950, the number of seals had dwindled from 3,300,000 to 1,250,000. Without these limitations hundreds of thousands were killed within weeks of birth. Now, even with this allotment, the seals are being killed off at an almost greater rate than they can remultiply. Adult female seals give birth once every year but due to pollution, disease, predation, whelping success, and malnutrition they are already slowly dying on their own without being hunted. Eighty percent of the seals slaughtered are pups and the remaining twenty percent are adult seals and even sometimes mothers who try attacking the hunters after seeing their babies killed. The hunters, according to the Seal Protection Act, have this right.

3   Second, I feel the killing should be better regulated because of the inhumane method used. In order to protect the fur value of the seals, guns are not used. Instead, the sealers use metal clubs to bludgeon the seal to death. Almost immediately after being delivered a direct blow, the seals are gutted open and skinned. Although at this stage of life the seal's skull is very fragile, sometimes the seals are not killed by the blows but merely stunned; thus hundreds are skinned alive. Still others are caught in nets and drowned, which, according to *America* magazine, the Canadian government continues to deny. But the worst of the methods used is when a hunter gets tired of swinging his club and uses the heel of his boot to kick the seal's skull in. Better regulation is the only way to solve this problem because other attempts seem futile. For example, volunteers who have traveled to hunting sites trying to dye the seals to ruin their fur value have been caught and fined heavily.

4   The plight of the Harp seals has been long and controversial. With the Canadian hunters feeling they have the right to kill the seals because it has been their industry for over two centuries, and on the other hand with humane organizations fearing extinction and strongly opposing the method of slaughter, a compromise must be met among both sides. As I see it, the solution to the problem is simple. Since the Canadians do occasionally use the whole seal and have been sealing for so long they could be allowed to continue but at a more heavily regulated rate. Instead of filling the limit of 180,000 every year and letting the numbers of seals decrease, Canadians could learn to ranch the seals as Montanans do cattle or sheep. The United States has also offered to help them begin farming their land for a new livelihood. The land is adequate for crops and would provide work all year round instead of only once a month every year. As a result of farming, the number of seals killed would be drastically cut down because Canadians would not be so dependent on the seal industry as before. This would in turn lead back to the ranching aspect of sealing and allow the numbers to grow back and keeping the tradition alive for future generations and one more of nature's creatures to enjoy.

RSS Should Not Provide Dorm Room Carpets

1   Tricia, a University student, came home exhausted from her work-study job. She took a blueberry pie from the refrigerator to satisfy her hunger and a tall glass of milk to quench her thirst. While trying to get comfortable on her bed, she tipped her snack over onto the floor. She cleaned the mess, but the blueberry and milk stains on her brand new carpet could not be removed. She didn't realize that maintaining a clean carpet would be difficult and costly. Tricia bought her own carpet. Some students living in dorm rooms want carpeted rooms provided for them at the expense of the University. They insist that since they pay to live on campus, the

rooms should reflect a comfortable home atmosphere. However, Resident Student Services (RSS) should not be required to furnish the carpet because other students do not want carpets. Furthermore, carpeting all the rooms totals into a very expensive project. And lastly, RSS should not have to provide the carpet because many students show lack of respect and responsibility for school property.

Although RSS considers the carpeting of all rooms a strong possibility, students like Tricia oppose the idea. They feel the students should buy their own carpets. Others claim the permanent carpeting would make dorm life more comfortable. The carpet will act as insulation and as a sound proofing system. These are valid arguments, but they should not be the basis for changing the entire residence hall structure. Those students with "cold feet" can purchase house footwear, which cost less than carpet. Unfortunately carpeting doesn't muffle all the noise; therefore, some students will be disturbed. Reasonable quietness should be a matter of respect for other students' privacy and comfort. Those opposed to the idea reason out the fact that students constantly change rooms or move out. The next person may not want carpet. Also, if RSS carpets the rooms, the students will lose the privilege they have of painting their rooms any color. Paint stains cannot be removed. Some students can't afford to replace the carpet. Still another factor, carpet color, may not please everyone. RSS would provide a neutral color like brown or gray. With tile floors, the students can choose and purchase their own carpets to match their taste.

Finally, another reason not to have carpet exists in the fact that the project can be expensive due to material costs, installation cost, and the maintenance cost caused mainly by the irresponsibility of many students. According to Rick Jones, Asst. Director of Housing Services, the cost will be $300 per room for the carpet and installation. RSS would also have to purchase more vacuum cleaners for the students' use. RSS will incur more expense in order to maintain the vacuums. Also, he claims that many accidents resulting from shaving cream fights, food fights, beverage parties, and smoking may damage the carpet permanently. With floor tiles, accidents such as food spills can be cleaned up easier than carpet. The student's behavior plays an important role in deciding against carpeting. Many students don't follow the rules of maintaining their rooms. They drill holes into the walls, break mirrors, beds, and closet doors, and leave their food trays all over the floor. How could they be trusted to take care of school carpet when they violate the current rules? Many students feel they have the "right" to do as they please. This irresponsible and disrespectful behavior reflects their future attitude about carpet care.

In conclusion, the university may be able to afford to supply the carpets in each room, but maintaining them would be difficult. If the students want carpets, they should pay and care for the carpets themselves. Hopefully, they will be more cautious and value it more. They should take the initiative to fundraise or find other financial means of providing this "luxury." They should not rely on the school to provide unnecessary room fixtures such as carpets. Also, they must remember that if RSS provides the carpet and they don't pay for the damages, they and future students will endure the consequences. What will happen???? Room rates will skyrocket!!!!!

Sterling Hall Dorm Food

1   The quality of Sterling Hall dorm food does not meet the standard needed to justify the high prices University students pay. As I watched a tall, medium-built University student pick up his Mexican burrito from the counter it didn't surprise me to see him turn up his nose. Johnny, our typical University student, waited five minutes before he managed to make it through the line. After he received his bill of $4.50 he turned his back to the cash register and walked away displeased with his meal.

2   As our neatly groomed University student placed his ValiDine eating card back into his Giorgio wallet, he thought back to the balance left on his account. Johnny had $24 left on his account and six more weeks left of school. He had been eating the cheapest meals he could and still receive a balanced meal, but the money just seemed to disappear. No student, not even a thrifty boy like Johnny, could possibly afford to live healthfully according to the University meal plan system.

3   Johnny then sat down at a dirty table to find his burrito only half way cooked. Thinking back to the long-haired cook who served him the burrito, he bit into the burrito and noticed a long hair dangling from his lips. He realized the cook's lack of preparation when preparing his burrito.

4   Since the food costs so much, yet the quality of the food remains low, University students do not get the quality they deserve. From the information stated I can conclude that using the ValiDine service system University students would be jeopardizing their health and wasting their hard-earned money. University students deserve something more than what they have now.

ROTC Courses Should Not Get College Credit

1   One of the most lucrative scholarships a student can receive is a four-year ROTC scholarship that pays tuition and books along with a living allowance. It was such a scholarship that allowed me to attend an expensive liberal arts college and to pursue the kind of well rounded education that matters to me. Of course, I am obligated to spend four years on active duty—an obligation that I accept and look forward to. What I am disappointed in, however, is the necessity to enroll in Military Science classes. Strong ROTC advocates argue that Military Science classes are essential because they produce good citizens, teach leadership skills, and provide practical experience for young cadets. Maybe so. But we could get the same benefits without having to take these courses for credit. Colleges should make ROTC training an extracurricular activity, not a series of academic courses taken for academic credit.

First of all, ROTC courses, unlike other college courses, do not stress inquiry   2
and true questioning. The ROTC program has as its objective the preparation of future officers committed to the ideals and structure of the military. The structure of
the military is based upon obediently following the orders of military superiors.
Whereas all my other teachers stress critical thinking and doing independent analysis, my ROTC instructors avoid political or social questions saying it is the job of
civilian leaders to debate policies and the job of the military to carry them out. We
don't even debate what role the military should play in our country. My uncle, who
was an ROTC cadet during the Vietnam war, remembers that not only did ROTC
classes never discuss the ethics of the war but that cadets were not allowed to
protest the war outside of their ROTC courses. This same obedience is demanded in
my own ROTC courses, where we are not able to question administration policies
and examine openly the complexity of the situation in Iraq and Kuwait.

A second reason that Army ROTC courses do not deserve academic credit is   3
that the classes are not academically strenuous, thus giving cadets a higher GPA
and an unfair advantage over their peers. Much of what a cadet does for academic
credit involves nonacademic activities such as physical training for an hour three
days a week so that at least some of a cadet's grade is based on physical activity,
not mental activity. In conducting an informal survey of 10 upper-classmen, I found
out that none of them has ever gotten anything lower than an A in a Military
Science class and they do not know of anyone who got anything lower than an A.
One third-year cadet stated that "the classes are basic. A monkey coming out of the
zoo could get college credit for a Military Science class." He went on to say that
most of the information given in his current class is a brush-up to 8th grade U.S.
history. In contrast, a typical liberal arts college class requires much thought, questioning, and analysis. The ROTC Military Science class is taught on the basis of "re-
gurgitated knowledge," meaning that once you are given a piece of information you
are required to know it and reproduce it at any time without thought or question. A
good example is in my class Basic Officership. Our first assignment is to memorize
and recite in front of the class the Preamble to the Constitution of the United
States. The purpose of doing so doesn't seem to be to understand or analyze the
constitution because we never talk about that. In fact, I don't know what the purpose is. I just do it because I am told to. Because the "A" is so easy to get in my
ROTC class, I spend all my time studying for my other classes. I am a step ahead of
my peers in the competition for a high GPA, even though I am not getting as good
an education.

Finally, having to take ROTC classes means that I can't take other liberal arts   4
courses which would be more valuable. One of the main purposes for ROTC is to give
potential officers a liberal education. Many cadets have the credentials to get into an
armed forces academy, but they chose ROTC programs because they could combine
military training with a well-rounded curriculum. Unfortunately, by taking Military
Science classes each quarter, cadets find that their electives are all but eaten up by
the time they are seniors. If ROTC classes were valuable in themselves, I wouldn't
complain. But they aren't, and they keep me from taking upper division electives in
philosophy, literature, and the humanities.

5   All of these reasons lead me to believe that Army ROTC cadets are getting shortchanged when they enroll for Military Science classes. Because cadets receive a lucrative scholarship, they should have to take the required military science courses. But these courses should be treated as extracurricular activities, like a work-study job or like athletics. Just as a student on a full-ride athletic scholarship does not receive academic credit for football practices and games, so should a student on a full-ride ROTC scholarship have to participate in the military education program without getting academic credit. By treating ROTC courses as a type of extracurricular activity like athletics, students can take more elective credits that will expand their minds, better enabling them to have the knowledge to make moral decisions and to enjoy their world more fully.

Legalization of Prostitution

1   Prostitution . . . It is the world's oldest profession. It is by definition the act of offering or soliciting sex for payment. It is, to some, evil. Yet the fact is it exists.

2   Arguments are not necessary to prove the existence of prostitution. Rather, the argument arises when trying to prove something must be done to reduce the problems of this profession. The problems which exist are in the area of crime, of health, and of environment. Crime rates are soaring, diseases are spreading wildly, and the environment on the streets is rapidly decaying. Still, it has been generally conceded that these problems cannot be suppressed. However, they can be reduced. Prostitution should be legalized because it would reduce the wave of epidemics, decrease high crime rates, provide good revenue by treating it like other businesses, and get girls off the streets where sexual crimes often occur.

3   Of course, there are those who would oppose the legalization of prostitution stating that it is one of the main causes for the spread of venereal diseases. Many argue that it is interrelated with drug-trafficking and other organized crimes. And probably the most controversial is the moral aspect of the subject; it is morally wrong, and legalizing it would be enforcing, or even justifying, such an existence.

4   These points propose good arguments, but I shall counter each point and explain the benefits and advantages of legalizing prostitution. In the case of prostitution being the main cause for the spread of epidemics, I disagree. By legalizing it, houses would be set up which would solve the problem of girls working on the streets and being victims of sexual crimes. It would also provide regular health checks, as is successfully done in Nevada, Germany, and other parts of the U.S. and Europe, which will therefore cut down on diseases spreading unknowingly.

5   As for the increase of organized crime if prostitution is legalized, I disagree again. Firstly, by treating it like businesses, then that would make good state revenue. Secondly, like all businesses have regulations, so shall these houses. That would put closer and better control in policing the profession, which is presently a

problem. Obviously, if the business of prostitution is more closely supervised, that would decrease the crime rates.

Now, I come to one of the most arguable aspects of legalizing prostitution: the moral issue. Is it morally wrong to legalize prostitution? That is up to the individual. To determine whether anything is "right or wrong" in our society is nearly impossible to do since there are various opinions. If a person were to say that prostitution is the root of all evil, that will not make it go away. It exists. Society must begin to realize that fear or denial will not make the "ugliness" disappear. It still exists.

Prostitution can no longer go ignored because of our societal attitudes. Legalizing it is beneficial to our society, and I feel in time people may begin to form an accepting attitude. It would be the beginning of a more open-minded view of what is reality. Prostitution . . . it is the world's oldest profession. It exists. It is a reality.

A Classroom Debate

In this exercise, you have an opportunity to engage in a variant of a formal debate. Although debates of this nature don't always lead to truth for its own sake, they are excellent forums for the development of analytical and organizational skills. The process for the debate is as follows.

Stage One: Determining Propositions for the Debate   Your debate topics will build upon the "For Class Discussion" exercise on pages 332–333. Your instructor will place on the board the significant campus problems identified by small groups. Small groups will then reconvene, select one of the problems previously developed by the class, and reach consensus on a possible solution to the problem. Your group will then create a debatable proposition in the following form: "Resolved: Our campus [the administration, the library, food services, etc.] should do X [your group's solution] in order to solve the problem of Y [the original problem]." Your instructor will collect and publish the debate propositions.

Stage Two: Forming Debate Teams   After doing the calculations on how many propositions should be debated and how many teams are needed, your instructor will assign students to two- or three-person groups, designating each group specifically as the Affirmative Team or the Negative Team for an assigned proposition. If you are placed on an Affirmative Team, your task is to create the best possible arguments for enacting the proposed solution by showing why the problem is significant and how the benefits of the solution will outweigh the costs. If you are placed on a Negative Team, your task is to create the best possible arguments against the proposed solution by showing that the proposed solution won't work or is too expensive or that the problem itself isn't worth solving or is by its nature unsolvable.

Stage Three: Homework and Preparation Time   Your homework in preparation for the debates is to conduct research (interviewing students, gathering personal examples, polling students, finding data or expert testimony, and so forth) to support your side of your assigned case. Team members should meet to share their findings, create the best arguments for their position, anticipate what the opposing team will say, and prepare for the debates. Each team will have two speakers, each with five minutes maximum. The first speaker presents the best case for the proposal; the second speaker presents a rebuttal of the opposing team's argument.

Stage Four: The Actual Debates   There will be as many debates as there are paired Affirmative and Negative teams. Because each speaker is limited to five minutes, a complete debate typically lasts twenty minutes. The order of speaking is as follows:

FIRST AFFIRMATIVE:	Presents best case for the proposal
FIRST NEGATIVE:	Presents best case against the proposal
SECOND NEGATIVE:	Rebuts argument of First Affirmative
SECOND AFFIRMATIVE:	Rebuts argument of First Negative

Those team members who do not speak will be designated observers. Their task is to take notes on the debate, paying special attention to the quality of support for each argument and to those parts of the opposing argument that were not rebutted. Observers should be prepared to assess what they see as the strengths and weaknesses of each team's arguments and presentation

Stage Five: Analysis and Debriefing   The observers will report to the class on their perceptions of the debates by using their prepared analysis. The instructor will attempt to synthesize the main points of the debates and the most telling arguments for each side.

An Anthology
of Arguments

Source: General Motors Corp. Used with permission, GM Media Archives.

This Chevy Blazer ad, with its focus on the commanding light-house, skillfully responds to its kairotic moment—a world endan-gered by terrorism—by proposing how consumers can keep their families safe. This ad contrasts strikingly with the Saturn VUE ad, discussed on pages 172–173 and shown in Color Plate G, by omitting the common image of the sport-utility vehicle in a forest, mountain, or desert setting.

An Overview of the Anthology

Part Five, an anthology of engaging verbal and visual arguments addressing twelve important issues, will let you put into practice your new skills of reading and analyzing arguments, conducting inquiry, and joining an argumentative conversation. As we discussed in Chapter 3, writers of arguments come from all walks of life and produce arguments from multiple social contexts within many communities in society. They may be ordinary citizens, members of advocacy groups or lobbyists, media commentators, professional staff writers for magazines and newspapers, scholars and academics, or other kinds of stakeholders within workplaces, neighborhoods, or civic or cultural organizations. Motivated by some occasion, these stakeholders write to an audience for a purpose within a genre, their rhetorical situations influencing their decisions about content, structure, and style.

We chose the articles in this anthology to show this rich variety of argumentative occasions, the multisided nature of argument, and the complexity of issues. The arguments you encounter here represent distinctly divergent angles of vision, different ways of conceptualizing controversies, and different argumentative strategies to influence readers' views and to win over decision makers. Passionate in their own ways, these stakeholders also differ in their commitment to persuasion versus truth-seeking, thereby creating differences in style, tone, and treatment of alternative views. In addition, faced with different rhetorical contexts and purposes, these writers create arguments in many genres: short opinion-editorials, academic arguments grounded in research, advocacy Web sites, congressional speeches, white papers to set forth the views and policy proposals of organizations, and a rich array of visual arguments, from public affairs advocacy ads, to poster arguments and fliers, to political cartoons and commercial advertisements.

To help you understand the cultural context for each set of readings, we have provided brief introductions to each unit, headnotes for each article, and a concluding set of discussion questions that urge you to see the complexity of the issue and the consequences of different claims. The introductions to each unit sketch key points of background, provide context, and suggest the cultural significance of the issue. The headnotes to each article give original publication data, identify the genre of the piece, and, in most cases, briefly identify the writer and the political perspective.* We encourage you to continue this contextualizing process by using the guide questions we provide in the next section. Finally, we encourage you to consider the class discussion questions at the end of each unit to help you appreciate the multisided views of stakeholders and to acknowledge the consequences, strengths, and limitations of different claims.

As you read through the arguments in this anthology, note how current topical issues (such as whether the federal government should require labeling of genetically engineered food) touch on broad, enduring questions about cultural values such as the rights of consumers versus the rights of corporations. No matter what the specific issue is, certain recurring patterns of concern keep cropping up, such

---

*For full citation information, see the Credits at the back of the book.

as principles versus consequences, spiritual values versus material values, rights of individuals versus rights of society, duties to self versus duties to others, short-range consequences versus long-range consequences, or tradition versus change. One advantage of an anthology of arguments is that in reading through them you can see for yourself how frequently these large issues recur in different guises.

In creating this anthology, we had in mind two main ways you might approach these readings. First, we invite you to enter these argumentative conversations yourself. After listening to and responsibly weighing the alternative views, you will face the responsibility of synthesizing various perspectives to create your own argument for a new context. Often you will need to do more research in order to clarify your views and take a stand. By eliciting your questions and enlarging your perspective—the process of dissent and synthesis at the heart of argument—the arguments in this anthology can challenge you to speak out on your own on these controversies.

A second way to approach these arguments—and one that can be combined with the first way—is to examine these articles for their wide variety of argumentative strategies to see how they can expand your repertoire as an arguer. In studying these arguments, you should ask questions like these: What works or doesn't work to make this argument persuasive? Why might a given argument be effective for its intended audience but not for some other audience? What can this argument teach me about presenting a positive *ethos,* about treating opposing views, about successful uses of evidence, or about appealing to *pathos?* Learning more about your options can empower you as a writer of arguments.

Guide Questions for the Analysis and Evaluation of Arguments

To help you develop skills at analyzing and evaluating arguments, we provide in this section three handy checklists of guide questions. These questions summarize the key principles of argument we have covered throughout the text.

List 1: Questions for Analyzing and Evaluating a Conversation

Whenever you read two or more arguments addressing the same issue, we recommend that you follow the principles of reading described in Chapter 2.

1. What does each argument say? (Reading as a believer, be able to summarize each argument, stating its main claim and supporting reasons in a single sentence if possible.)
2. How can each argument be doubted? (Reading as a doubter, search for weaknesses in the argument, think about what is left out, and articulate important questions that you would like to raise if you could talk to the author.)
3. How have the rhetorical context and genre shaped each argument?
4. Why do the disputants disagree? (Do they disagree about the facts of the case? Do they differ in the selection or interpretation of the facts or other

data they use for evidence? Do they disagree about values, assumptions, and beliefs?)

5. Which arguments appear to be stronger? (Which arguments seem most persuasive to you? Before you could take a stand on the issue yourself, what further questions would you need to have answered? Which of your own assumptions, values, and beliefs would you have to examine further and clarify?)

List 2: Questions for Analyzing and Evaluating an Individual Argument

The previous questions ask you to examine arguments in the context of the conversations to which they belong. This next set of questions asks you to look closely at a single argument, examining in detail its structure, its argumentative strategies, and its rhetorical force.

1. What is the writer's purpose and audience?
   - Who are the intended readers? What are their values and beliefs?
   - How does the writer hope to change the intended readers' views on the issue?
   - What was the occasion for writing? What motivated the writer to produce this piece?

2. What genre is the piece?
   - Where was this piece published?
   - How does the genre of the piece—or its place of publication—influence its content, point of view, or style?
   - How can certain features of the text be explained by genre?

3. What seems to be the writer's perspective, bias, or angle of vision?
   - What does the text reveal about the author's values and beliefs?
   - What does the author omit?
   - How committed is the author to his or her claim?
   - What views does the author oppose? Why?

4. Does the argument have a strong logical core?
   - What is the writer's claim? Where is it explicitly stated or where is it implied?
   - What are the main reasons in support of the claim? Are the reasons audience-based?

5. How effective is the writer's use of evidence?
   - Is the evidence relevant, sufficient, and appropriately up-to-date?
   - Does the evidence come from reputable sources?

- What kind of evidence is used?
- How is the argument reasonably supported and developed? Are there any obvious flaws or fallacies in the argument?

6. How effective is the writer at making ethical appeals?
   - What *ethos* does the writer project?
   - How does the writer try to seem credible and trustworthy to the intended audience?

7. How effective is the writer at creating pathetic appeals?
   - How effective is the writer at using audience-based reasons?
   - How effective is the writer's use of concrete language, word choice, examples, and analogies for giving the argument emotional presence?

8. How could the writer's argument be refuted?
   - Can the writer's reasons and grounds be called into question?
   - Can the writer's warrants and backing be called into question?

9. If used, how effective are the author's use of images, graphics, or other visuals?
   - Why did the author choose or design these particular images, graphics, or visuals?
   - How do font sizes and styles, the layout of images and text, and the use of color contribute to the effectiveness of the visual?
   - How does the composition of images—such as setting, props, clothing, poses of characters, and so forth—contribute to the effectiveness of the visual?
   - How are graphics used to tell a particular story with numbers? Why does the author focus on this particular story rather than another story?

List 3: Questions for Responding to a Reading and Forming Your Own Views

This final set of questions is designed to help you speak back to a text in order to form your own views.

1. Which of the author's points do you agree with?
2. What new insights has the reading given you?
3. Which of the author's points do you disagree with?
4. What gaps or omissions do you see in the text? What has the author overlooked?
5. What questions or problems does the text raise for you? How has it troubled you or expanded your views?
6. In terms of your own evolving views on this issue, how useful is this reading? How might you use it in your own argument?

FINDING SOLDIERS: THE VOLUNTEER ARMY, RECRUITMENT, AND THE DRAFT

As the United States' involvement in Iraq stretches on, the military is facing critical recruitment problems. In addition, the military is drawing heavily on the National Guard and the Army Reserve, returning troops to Iraq for enlistments of indefinite length and employing a large number of contractors, or mercenaries, to play quasi-military roles in Iraq. The military is also using multiple strategies to find soldiers: lowering its recruitment standards, being more innovative and aggressive in its recruitment campaigns—including trying to interest high school students and get early commitments from them—and offering larger financial incentives and benefits.

Since the Vietnam War and the unpopular draft that supplied soldiers for it, the country has relied on an "all-volunteer Army" and on the principle that a smaller but highly trained, highly technologically equipped fighting force is better than an Army composed of less-skilled draftees. However, the current Army is not designed for prolonged engagements like Iraq, nor is the size of the Army sufficient to handle multiple global conflicts. Although polls show that a majority of Americans are opposed to a draft and the Bush administration has repeatedly said it will not reinstitute conscription, many analysts suggest that a draft is needed. The problem of filling the Army has taken the form of many questions being debated by journalists, analysts, military strategists, policymakers, and citizens: What size Army does the United States need to maintain its global superpower status? Can an all-volunteer Army supplemented with military contractors serve our national security and foreign policy needs, or should the United States reinstate a draft? Who should be in the military for our national security? Citizen soldiers? Professional military? Mercenaries? Drafted soldiers? Should citizens be required to serve their country? What are the fairest and most effective ways to fill military quotas? How can the responsibility of defending the country be equitably spread among classes, ethnic groups, and genders? Which of the present recruitment strategies are the most effective?

The readings in this chapter—in addition to the Armed Forces Day 2005 poster on page 73, the screen captures from the Army's online game, *America's Army*, in Color Plates H and I, and the political cartoon on recruitment on page 315—introduce you to the vigorous controversy about these urgent questions and ask you to consider your values and your own views on these issues.

New Model Army

Donald Rumsfeld

The current secretary of defense for the Bush administration, Donald Rumsfeld, has had a long career of political posts, including U.S. congressman, White House chief of staff, and U.S. ambassador to NATO. He also served as CEO of two Fortune 500 companies. This brief to the Pentagon, expressing his vision for the United States Army, was released on March 15, 2005.

In just 28 months, U.S. forces, with our Coalition partners, have overthrown two terrorist regimes, captured or killed thousands of terrorist leaders and operatives, disrupted terrorist cells on virtually every continent, and undoubtedly prevented a number of additional terrorist attacks. Our troops have performed magnificently—despite the significant increase in operational tempo of the global war on terror, which has increased the demand on the force.

Managing that demand is one of the Department of Defense's top priorities. Doing so means being clear about the problem, and fashioning the most appropriate solutions. Much of the current increase in demand on the force is most likely a temporary spike caused by the deployment of nearly 115,000 troops to Iraq. We do not expect to have 115,000 troops permanently deployed in any one campaign.

Nevertheless, for the moment, the increased demand is real, and over the past two years we have taken a number of immediate actions to alleviate it. We are increasing international military participation in Iraq and Afghanistan. We are accelerating the training of Iraqi security forces—now over 200,000—so Iraqis will increasingly take responsibility for their own security and stability, and we are hunting down those who threaten Iraq's transition to self-government and self-reliance.

Another way of relieving the increased demand on the force is to add more people—and we have done that as well. Using the emergency powers granted to the president by Congress, since September 2001 we have increased active force levels above authorized levels—by 33,000, or more at times. If the situation demands it, we will not hesitate to add still more—whatever is needed. However, the fact that we have to increase force levels at all should give us pause. U.S. Armed Forces currently total about 2.6 million men and women—1.4 million active forces, 876,000 guard and reserve in units, and 287,000 individual ready reserves. Yet despite these large numbers, the deployment of 115,000 troops to Iraq has required that we temporarily increase the size of the force.

That should tell us something. It tells us that the real problem is not necessarily the size of our active and reserve military components, per se, but rather how forces have been managed, and the mix of capabilities at our disposal.

Army Chief of Staff Gen. Pete Schoomaker compares the problem to a barrel of rainwater on which the spigot is placed too high up. The result: when you turn it on, it only draws water off the top, while the water at the bottom is not accessible or used. Our real problem is that the way our total force is presently managed, we have to use many of the same people over and over again. In Gen. Schoomaker's analogy, the answer is not a bigger barrel of more than the current 2.6 million men and women available, but to move the spigot down, so more of the potentially available troops are accessible, usable, and available to defend our nation. The department must promptly reorganize to gain better access to the fine men and women who make up the all-volunteer force, and to ensure we have the skills needed available as and when needed. Clearly, we are not doing so today.

7   Take the Guard and Reserve for example. Since Sept. 11, 2001, we have mobilized roughly 36% of the Selected Reserve. Those mobilizations have concentrated on certain skill sets: installation security forces, air crews, military police, Special Forces, civil affairs, and intelligence officers. Yet even now, we have not mobilized over 60% of the Selected Reserve to fight the global war on terror. Indeed, 58% of the current Guard and Reserve force have not been involuntarily mobilized in the past decade. Clearly they have not been stressed. That suggests that our problem is certainly not too few forces. Rather, it is that we have too few forces with the skill sets that are in high demand, and too many forces with skills that are not in high demand.

8   We are working hard to fix that—by rebalancing skill sets within the Reserve component and between the active and reserve force. In 2003, we rebalanced some 10,000 positions. We expect to have rebalanced a total of 50,000 positions by the end of next year. Simultaneously, the services are transforming to increase combat capability while relieving demand on the forces. For example, the Army has put forward a plan that, when implemented, will use our emergency authorities to bring the Army's temporary strength up by nearly 30,000 troops above its peacetime statutory limit—it is today about 7,000 above that limit. But the proposal is to use that increase, and all the movement in the system during the force deployments and redeployments, to increase the Army's combat power by up to 30%. How? Instead of simply adding more Divisions, the Army is focusing instead on creating a "Modular Army" comprised of smaller, self-contained brigades that would be interchangeable, available to work for any Division.

9   The new more "Modular Army" will be appropriate for the 21st century. In the event of a crisis, the 4th Infantry Division commander, for example, could gather two of his own brigades, combine them with available brigades from, say, the 1st Armored Division and the National Guard, and deploy them together. The result is improved interoperability within the Army, even as the Army is becoming more interoperable with the other services, as we saw in Iraq. This is a bold proposal and the DoD leadership is working with Congress on it.

10   In addition, other initiatives are underway to improve force management and increase capability: We are taking military personnel out of civilian jobs to free them up for military tasks. We are reducing the number of troops and dependents that are constantly being rotated in and out of foreign bases and facilities. And we are fixing the mobilization process to make it more respectful of troops, families, and employers.

11   The key to these initiatives is flexibility—to be able to increase or decrease as demand requires, and to manage the force as the security circumstances permit. Today, with authority granted by Congress, the DoD has the flexibility to adjust troop levels as the security situation requires—and we are doing so. A permanent increase in statutory end-strength, as many are proposing, would significantly reduce flexibility.

12   The president charged us with the responsibility of transforming the department for the challenges our nation faces in this century. The American people expect this: that we maintain the best force in the world, and that we be respectful of the people in that force and of the taxpayers who support it. And that is what we are doing.

The Case for the Draft

Phillip Carter and Paul Glastris

Paul Glastris served as a speechwriter to the Clinton administration from 1998 to 2001 and is currently the editor-in-chief of The Washington Monthly. *He is also a senior fellow at the* Western Policy Center, *a foreign policy institute that focuses on United States policy and action in Eastern Europe. Phillip Carter is a former U.S. Army officer who now writes on national security issues for* The Washington Monthly. *He also practices international and contract law. This article appeared in the March 2005 issue of* The Washington Monthly, *an independent magazine devoted to politics and government.*

The United States has occupied many foreign lands over the last half century— Germany and Japan in World War II, and, on a much smaller scale, Haiti, Bosnia, and Kosovo in the 1990s. In all these cases, we sponsored elections and handed-off to democratic governments control of countries that were relatively stable, secure, and reasonably peaceful.   1

In Iraq, we failed to do this, despite heroic efforts by U.S. and coalition troops.   2
The newly-elected Iraqi government inherits a country in which assassinations, kidnappings, suicide bombings, pipeline sabotages, and beheadings of foreigners are daily occurrences. For the last eight months, the ranks of the insurgency have been growing faster than those of the security forces of the provisional Iraqi government—and an alarming number of those government forces are secretly working for the insurgency. American-led combat operations in Ramadi and Fallujah killed large numbers of the enemy, but at the price of fanning the flames of anti-American hatred and dispersing the insurrection throughout Iraq. Despite nearly two years of effort, American troops and civilian administrators have failed to restore basic services to much of the central part of the country where a majority of Iraqis live. The U.S. military has not even been able to secure the 7-mile stretch of highway leading from the Baghdad airport to the Green Zone where America's own embassy and the seat of the Iraqi government are headquartered.

How we got to this point is by now quite obvious. Even many of the war's   3
strongest supporters admit that the Bush administration grievously miscalculated by invading Iraq with too few troops and then by stubbornly refusing to augment troop numbers as the country descended into violent mayhem after the fall of Saddam.

This analysis, of course, presumes that it was ever possible to invade and   4
quickly pacify Iraq, given the country's religious–ethnic divisions and history of tyranny. But it also presumes that the fault is primarily one of judgment: that the president and key senior military officials made a mistake by accepting Defense Secretary Donald Rumsfeld's theory that a "transformed" American military can prevail in war without great masses of ground troops. That judgment was indeed foolish; events have shown that, while a relatively modest American force can win a stunning battlefield victory, such a force is not enough to secure the peace.

5   But there's a deeper problem, one that any president who chose to invade a country the size of Iraq would have faced. In short, America's all-volunteer military simply cannot deploy and sustain enough troops to succeed in places like Iraq while still deterring threats elsewhere in the world. Simply adding more soldiers to the active duty force, as some in Washington are now suggesting, may sound like a good solution. But it's not, for sound operational and pragmatic reasons. America doesn't need a bigger standing army; it needs a deep bench of trained soldiers held in reserve who can be mobilized to handle the unpredictable but inevitable wars and humanitarian interventions of the future. And while there are several ways the all-volunteer force can create some extra surge capacity, all of them are limited.

6   The only effective solution to the manpower crunch is the one America has turned to again and again in its history: the draft. Not the mass combat mobilizations of World War II, nor the inequitable conscription of Vietnam—for just as threats change and war-fighting advances, so too must the draft. A modernized draft would demand that the privileged participate. It would give all who serve a choice over how they serve. And it would provide the military, on a "just in time" basis, large numbers of deployable ground troops, particularly the peacekeepers we'll need to meet the security challenges of the 21st century.

7   America has a choice. It can be the world's superpower, or it can maintain the current all-volunteer military, but it probably can't do both.

PLOWING A FIELD WITH A FERRARI

8   Before the invasion of Iraq, Army Chief of Staff Eric Shinseki and Army Secretary Thomas White advised Rumsfeld that many more troops would be needed to secure Iraq (something on the order of 250,000 to 300,000). Secretary of State Colin Powell, whose State Department was shut out of the post-war planning process, also privately argued for a bigger force. A RAND Corporation analysis, published in summer 2003, offered a range of estimates for what size force would be necessary in Iraq. Using troops-to-population ratios from previous occupations, RAND projected that, two years after the invasion, it would take anywhere from 258,000 troops (the Bosnia model), to 321,000 (post–World War II Germany), to 526,000 (Kosovo) to secure the peace.

9   None of these figures seems, at first glance, unachievable for a U.S. military comprised of 14 million active-duty troops, 870,900 reservists, and 110,000 individual ready reservists (soldiers who have served their tour of duty and are not training with the reserves but who can by statute still be called up for service). And yet an Iraq deployment that has never exceeded 153,000 ground personnel has put so much stress on the military that a senior Army Reserve official has candidly stated that current rotation policies will lead to a "broken force." How can that be?

10   To answer that question, begin by deducting virtually the entire Navy and Air Force from the head count; the Iraq occupation has been almost exclusively a ground game, hence an Army and Marine operation. Next, consider that the United States sends into combat not individual soldiers but units, complete with unit

equipment sets, unit leaders, and an organizational structure that facilitates command, control, and logistical support. So instead of counting individual soldiers—a meaningless exercise—one must look at how many *units* the United States could theoretically put on the ground if it wanted to mobilize every active and reserve soldier available. And if you do that, you come to a figure of roughly 600,000 troops. That's the total number of deployable soldiers that the United States could theoretically have called upon to man the initial invasion.

In practice, however, the Pentagon would never have sent that many troops to   11
Iraq, for good reasons: It would have left the defense cupboard bare and served as an open invitation to America's enemies to make trouble elsewhere in the world. Massing a 600,000 force would have meant not only pulling nearly all front-line troops out of Korea, but also mobilizing the poorly-resourced divisions of the National Guard, the third-string crew that the president can call on when the first string (active troops) and the second string (the Guard's elite "enhanced" reserve brigades) are depleted.

Given the need to hold troops in reserve for deterrence purposes, the Pentagon   12
had perhaps 400,000 troops available for the invasion. Yet that number includes many troops in specialized fields that are of little or no use in desert warfare or peacekeeping—off-loading equipment in sea ports, for instance. Such troops could have been reshaped into provisional infantry units, as the Army has done with artillery and air-defense formations, but that would've taken time. The number of troops with units that would actually have been of use in Iraq was probably closer to the figures that Gen. Shinseki and Secretary White have suggested: 250,000 to 300,000—in other words, the lower end of what RAND estimated would be required for success.

But even that number is deceptive. It is the size of the force that could have   13
been initially sent into Iraq, not the number that could have realistically been *sustained* there. Because so many soldiers in the all-volunteer military are married with families (compared to conscript armies), and because soldiers must periodically be induced or persuaded to voluntarily reenlist, the Pentagon must rotate its forces in and out of theater every 12 months or so in order to maintain morale and reenlistment. Thus, just as a civilian police department must hire three to four police officers for every one cop on the beat, so too must the U.S. military have three to four soldiers for every one serving in Iraq.

The Pentagon, then, could have realistically kept those initial 250,000 to 300,000   14
troops in place only for a limited time—perhaps a year, certainly not more than two. That might have been enough time to pacify the country, especially if higher troop numbers at the outset would have quelled the early looting and disorder. Then again, a year or two might not have been sufficient time to beat back an insurgency which, we now know, was to some extent planned in advance of the invasion. In that case, keeping 250,000 to 300,000 troops in Iraq for two years or longer would have risked so lowering morale and reenlistment rates as to destroy the all-volunteer force. It would have been like plowing a field with a Ferrari; it could have been done, but only once.

15   Taking the need for rotations into account, then, the U.S. military can comfortably handle something like 80,000 troops in Iraq at any one time. The actual number on the ground has averaged 133,286 for the last two years, and more than 150,000 soldiers are in Iraq now.

16   That's a woefully insufficient number for the task. Yet it is pushing the outside limits of what the current force structure can handle. It has meant imposing "stop-loss" emergency measures to prevent soldiers from exiting the service. It has required deploying nearly every active-duty brigade, including one previously committed elsewhere in Korea. It has meant raiding the seed corn of military readiness by deploying the Army's elite "opposing force" training units—seasoned soldiers who play the enemy in mock exercises to build the skills of greener troops before they are sent into battle. It has necessitated calling up all 15 of the National Guard's enhanced readiness brigades, as well as poorly-resourced National Guard divisions that have not been mobilized *en masse* since the Korean War. It has led the Army Reserve Chief Lt. Gen. James Helmly to write in a recent memo that the Reserve will be unable to meet its commitments without substantial use of the Army's *involuntary mobilization* authorities under federal law. As of Dec. 15, 2004, the Army Reserve retained just 37,515 deployable soldiers out of a total of 200,366—almost no cushion at all. And in the final two months of last year, the Reserves missed their enlistment targets last year by 30 percent—a sign of even greater problems to come.

17   All this for a war that most planners consider to be a medium-sized conflict— nothing like what the United States faced in World War I, World War II, or the Cold War. And while threats of that magnitude aren't anywhere on the horizon, there are plenty of quite possible scenarios that could quickly overwhelm us—an implosion of the North Korean regime, a Chinese attack on Taiwan, worsening of the ethnic cleansing in the Sudan, or some unforeseen humanitarian nightmare. Already we have signaled to bad actors everywhere the limits of our power. Military threats might never have convinced the Iranians to give up their nuclear program. But it's more than a little troubling that ruling Iranian mullahs can publicly and credibly dismiss recent administration saber-rattling by pointing to the fact that our forces are pinned down in Iraq.

STRESS TEST

18   Every 20 years or so for the past century, America has found it necessary, for national security reasons, to send at least half a million troops overseas into harm's way, and to keep them there for years at a time. It did so in World War I, sending 4.1 million doughboys and Marines to Europe. In World War II, it mobilized 16 million for the war effort. America sent more than 3 million grunts to fight in Korea against the North Koreans and Chinese, in the first hot war of the Cold War. It rotated 5.1 million soldiers and Marines through Vietnam over a decade, with 543,400 stationed there at the height of that war in April 1969. And more recently, America sent 550,000 ground troops to eject Saddam's forces from Kuwait, as part of a ground force which totaled 831,500 with allied contributions from dozens of nations. Along the way, the United States military simultaneously

fought small wars in Greece, Lebanon, El Salvador, Somalia, Haiti, Bosnia, and Kosovo, requiring the commitment of thousands more. This ability to deploy large numbers of troops overseas for long periods of time has been the price of America's superpower status—what President John Kennedy alluded to in his inaugural address when he said America would bear any burden to assure the survival and the success of liberty.

There's no reason to think that America will be exempt from paying that price in the future. Even those who don't support the Bush policy of using unilateral force to democratize the Middle East (and we don't), and who prefer to work through military alliances whenever possible (and we do), should understand the need to increase American troop strength. The international community failed to act in Rwanda largely because the United States chose not to send troops; our NATO allies sent soldiers into Bosnia and Kosovo only because we put substantial numbers

19

of ours in, too. The same will hold true for just about any other major war or humanitarian intervention in the future.

20   What we're increasingly learning from Iraq is that the all-volunteer force, as presently built, cannot do that—indeed, it was consciously designed to be incapable of such deployments. Today's force was built for precisely the kinds of wars that Caspar Weinberger and Colin Powell envisioned in their doctrines: wars with explicit purposes, narrow parameters, and clear exit strategies. In other words, it was built for the kinds of wars the military prefers to fight, not necessarily the kinds of wars we have, as a nation, historically fought.

21   The evolution of this force owes much to Vietnam. After that war ended, the nation's senior generals devised a military structure called the "total force" concept to circumvent two of the great moral hazards they identified with Vietnam: the failure to mobilize the nation, with all of its strata and segments, for the war; and the reliance on young American conscripts, who were coerced by the state to kill or be killed.

22   Vietnam had been fought almost entirely by active-duty volunteers and conscripts. A great number of young men, including many from the nation's privileged classes, sought refuge in the reserves as a way out of duty in Vietnam. The total force concept entailed, first of all, the splitting of lay war-fighting and support functions. Henceforth, active-duty troops would perform nearly all the traditional combat roles; reservists would provide most of the support functions, such as logistics and military policing. This ensured that future wars could not be fought without the heavy involvement of the reserves. Army Gen. Creighton Abrams and other leaders felt that this would be a check on the power of presidents to go to war because mass reserve call-ups typically require a great deal of political capital.

23   Second, Pentagon leaders replaced the conscripted military with an all-volunteer force that would recruit enlistees with pay and benefits like the civilian world. This all-volunteer model, they believed, would improve morale for the simple reason that all soldiers would be in the service by choice. It would also improve military effectiveness because if soldiers could be lured to stay longer by reenlisting, they could acquire higher levels of skill. The mantra of the new military became "send a bullet, not a man"; the modern American military came to embrace precision firepower over manpower in what historian Russell Weigley called the "American way of war."

24   This all-volunteer military made good on nearly all these promises. After a rough period in the late 1970s, the U.S. military emerged a leaner, better force in the 1980s, proving itself in the small wars of that decade—Grenada, Libya, and Panama. Then came the first Gulf War—the apothesis of the all-volunteer, total force model. Coming off the Cold War, the Army had 18 divisions on active duty, in comparison to 10 today, and had little in the way of a pressing commission with the imminent collapse of the Soviet Union. By mobilizing seven of these Army divisions and two Marine divisions, in addition to the reserves and ready reserves, military leaders were able to send half a million troops to the Saudi desert. But because that war lasted just months, largely due to U.S. reluctance to invade and occupy Iraq, the system worked. Active-duty soldiers deployed for less than a year, without fear of immediately being sent back to fight; reservists were similarly tapped just once. Desert Storm did not break the all-volunteer force because that war was precisely

the kind that the force had been designed to fight: a limited campaign for limited ends, of limited duration, and with a defined exit strategy.

Unfortunately, national security threats don't always conform to the military's precise specifications. The 1990s brought two wars, in Bosnia and Kosovo, requiring the long-term commitment of U.S. troops for peacekeeping. These were relatively modest-sized deployments. Yet the military leadership complained that they put undo stress on the system, and, indeed, then-Gov. George Bush lambasted the Clinton administration in 2000 for the way it managed military readiness, charging that the Kosovo war put two of the Army's 10 divisions out of action, hurting the nation's ability to respond to threats abroad. In the wake of September 11, the U.S. military mobilized tens of thousands of reservists for homeland security and sent thousands of elite infantrymen and special forces into the mountains of Afghanistan; neither mission conformed to the model of past wars. 25

Then came Operation Iraqi Freedom, and the real stress test began. 26

FIVE BAD OPTIONS

In theory, there are several ways to get out of the military manpower bind we find ourselves in. In reality, there are inherent limits to almost all of them. 27

The first option—at least the one Democrats and moderate Republicans have talked most about—is to convince other countries to share the burden in Iraq. But that's not likely. Even if the security situation in Iraq improves and the Bush administration begins to share decision-making—something it's so far refused to do— European leaders would be extremely wary of trying to sell their citizens on sending troops to keep the peace in a war they expressly opposed. It may be possible to convince the Europeans and other developed nations to be more willing to contribute troops the next time there's an international need. But that, as we've seen, will require more U.S. troops, not fewer. Nor should it be the policy of the United States to have to rely on other countries' troops. We must be prepared to intervene unilaterally if necessary. 28

A second solution to the manpower crisis would be to rely more on private military contractors whose use has exploded in recent years. Currently, more than 40,000 government contractors are on duty in Iraq, working in myriad jobs from security to reconstruction. The advantage of using contractors is that they provide surge capacity; they are hired only for the duration of an engagement. But according to Peter W. Singer, a research fellow at the Brookings Institution, these private armies also create problems. First, all costs considered, they're not necessarily less expensive for the military. Second, private military contractors often compete with the military for personnel, so any growth in these contractors usually results in tension between military retention and contractor recruiting efforts. Third, contractors operate in a legal gray area where their financial and accounting activities are heavily regulated, but their operations are barely looked at. It's one thing to contract for truck drivers; it's another to hire contractors to guard Afghan President Hamid Karzai or work as interrogation linguists in the Abu Ghraib prison because the military has too few commandos or linguists in its own ranks. The military has probably 29 already pushed the contractor concept about as far as it will go; expecting much more surge capacity from private industry is probably unrealistic.

30   A third possibility might be to follow the advice of several cutting-edge military reformers to radically transform today's military. According to these reformers, today's force was drawn up for a bygone age of massed superpower armies; it does not reflect today's threats. These visionaries would downsize the Navy, scrap some of the Army's mechanized divisions, and in these and other ways free up tens of thousands of troops to be redeployed into "soldier centric" units capable of doing everything along the spectrum from humanitarian relief in Banda Aceh to combat patrols in Baghdad. Under pressure from the Iraq mission, the military has taken some steps in this direction—for instance, by retraining and reequipping some army artillery and air defense units into military police units. But such moves have been incremental in nature thus far; the true scope of the problem is orders of magnitude larger than the Pentagon's current solution. And some day, a war may come which requires all kinds of combat power—from large land-based formations to ships capable of sailing through the Taiwan strait to legions of peacekeepers. The military cannot build additional capability simply by playing a shell game with its personnel; at some point, it must genuinely add more soldiers too, and in large numbers.

31   A fourth option, and the most obvious one, would be to simply increase the size of the active-duty force. This too has been discussed. During the 2004 campaign, Sen. John Kerry called for increasing the active-duty force by 40,000 troops. More recently a bipartisan group of hawkish defense intellectuals published an open letter on *The Weekly Standard* Web site calling on Congress to add 25,000 ground troops each year for the next several years. And the Pentagon has announced some money for extra troops in the administration's latest budget. The problem with such proposals is that they underestimate both current manpower needs and the cost of forcing the all-volunteer military to grow.

32   In theory, one can always lure the next recruit, or retain the next soldier, by offering a marginally higher monetary incentive—but in reality, there are practical limits to such measures. The pool of people who might be convinced to join the Army is mainly comprised of healthy young people with high school degrees but no college plans. That pool is inherently limited, especially when the economy is heating up and there's a shooting war on. Last year, despite signing bonuses in the tens of thousands and other perks, military recruiters had to lower entry standards to meet their enlistment goals. The active force met its recruiting targets for 2004, but the reserves have found themselves increasingly struggling to bring enough soldiers in the door.

33   But it's the long-term cost issues that most militate against making the all-volunteer force bigger. Generals today are fond of saying that you recruit a soldier, but you retain their families. One reason the Army has resisted Congress' attempts to raise its end strength is that it does not want to embrace all of the costs associated with permanently increasing the size of the military, because it sees each soldier as a 30-year commitment—both to the soldier and his (or her) family. According to the Congressional Budget Office, each soldier costs $99,000 per year—a figure which includes medical care, housing, and family benefits.

The United States does not necessarily need a massive standing military all the   34
time. What it needs is a highly trained professional force of a certain size—what we
have right now is fine—backed by a massive surge capacity of troops in reserve to
quickly augment the active-duty force in times of emergency. Sure, right now, the
Army is light several hundred thousand deployable ground troops. But over the long
term, the demands of Iraq will subside, the need for troops will decline, and it could
be another decade or two before another mission that big comes along.

The problem is that under the all-volunteer system it's hard to fix the short-   35
term problem (too few troops now) without creating long-term problems (too many
troops later). And so, paying for the salaries and benefits and families of 50,000 or
500,000 extra soldiers on active duty over the course of their careers doesn't, from
a military standpoint, make sense. Politically, it would put the senior military leadership in the position of convincing the American people to keep military budgets
extremely high to pay for a huge standing army that isn't being used and might not
be for years. It might be possible now to convince the public to add another 100,000
soldiers (annual cost: about $10 billion in personnel costs alone, not including
equipment and training). But the generals rightly worry that this support will evap-
orate after Iraq stabilizes. Indeed, Americans have a long tradition dating back to
the writing of Constitution, of refusing to support a large standing military unless
the need is apparent. (The public paid for a much bigger all-volunteer military in the
1970s and 1980s, but only because of the obvious need to deter a massive Soviet
army from threatening Europe; after the Berlin Wall fell, both political parties supported big cuts in troop strength). What we really need is the capability to rapidly
mobilize and deploy a half million troops to project U.S. power abroad, and to be
able to sustain them indefinitely while maintaining a reserve with which to simultaneously engage other enemies.

A fifth option would be to build this surge capacity into the reserves, instead of   36
the active force. Under this plan, which some military personnel planners are already discussing, the army would radically bump up enlistment bonuses and other
incentives to lure vastly more young people directly into the reserves than are being
recruited now. Such a plan would have the advantage of creating the surge capacity
the nation needs without saddling the nation with a large, standing professional
army. But the disadvantages are substantial, too. For such a plan to work, the military would have to make a commitment, which thus far it never has, to fix the leg-
endary resources problems and anemic readiness of the reserves. A great many reservists have gone through the crucible of combat in Afghanistan and Iraq, and yet
still cope with vehicles that lack armor, weapons older than they are, and a pancity
of training dollars. Also, the army would always (and rightly) insist that signing
bonuses for reservists be substantially below those offered by to active-duty recruits. And even if bonuses and other renumeration for both the active-duty and the
reserves were to rise substantially, it is hard to see how the reserves could lure in a
sufficient number of recruits without significantly lowering admissions standards.
The real advantage of the all-volunteer force is its quality. If the military tries to recruit so many soldiers that it must substantially lower its entry requirements, then
the all-volunteer force will lose its qualitative edge. This decrease in quality will

have a cascade effect on discipline within the ranks, degrading combat effectiveness for these units.

A 21ST-CENTURY DRAFT

37   That leaves one option left for providing the military with sufficient numbers of high-quality deployable ground forces: conscription. America has nearly always chosen this option to staff its military in times of war. Today, no leading politician in either party will come anywhere near the idea—the draft having replaced Social Security as the third rail of American politics. This will have to change if the United States is to remain the world's preeminent power.

38   Traditional conscription has its obvious downsides. On a practical level, draftees tend to be less motivated than volunteers. Because they serve for relatively short periods of time (typically two years), any investment made in their training is lost to the military once the draftees return to civilian life. And despite the current manpower shortage, there's no foreseeable scenario in which all 28 million young Americans currently of draft age would be needed.

39   Above all else, there's the serious ethical problem that conscription means government compelling young adults to risk death, and to kill—an act of the state that seems contrary to the basic notions of liberty which animate our society.

40   In practice, however, our republic has decided many times throughout its history that a draft was necessary to protect those basic liberties. Even if you disagreed with the decision to invade Iraq, or think the president's rhetoric is demagogic and his policies disastrous, it is hard to argue that Islamic terrorism isn't a threat to freedom and security, at home and abroad. Moreover, any American, liberal or conservative, ought to have moral qualms about basing our nation's security on an all-volunteer force drawn disproportionately, as ours is, from America's lower socioeconomic classes. And the cost of today's war is being borne by an extremely narrow slice of America. Camp Pendleton, Calif., home to the 1st Marine Expeditionary Force, is also home to approximately one-seventh of the U.S. fatalities from Iraq. In theory, our democracy will not fight unpopular wars because the people who must bear the casualties can impose their will on our elected leaders to end a war they do not support. But when such a small fraction of America shoulders the burden—and pays the cost—of Americas wars, this democratic system breaks down.

41   Nor are the practical considerations of a draft impossible to overcome. A draft lottery, of the kind that existed in the peacetime draft of the 1950s, with no exemptions for college students, would provide the military an appropriate and manageable amount of manpower without the class inequities that poisoned the national culture during Vietnam. Such a system, however, would not avoid the problem of flooding the military with less-than-fully-motivated conscripts.

42   A better solution would fix the weaknesses of the all-volunteer force without undermining its strengths. Here's how such a plan might work. Instead of a lottery, the federal government would impose a requirement that no four-year college or university be allowed to accept a student, male or female, unless and until that stu-

dent had completed a 12-month to two-year term of service. Unlike an old-fashioned draft, this 21st-century service requirement would provide a vital element of personal choice. Students could choose to fulfill their obligations in any of three ways: in national service programs like AmeriCorps (tutoring disadvantaged children), in homeland security assignments (guarding ports), or in the military. Those who chose the latter could serve as military police officers, truck drivers, or other non-combat specialists requiring only modest levels of training. (It should be noted that the Army currently offers two-year enlistments for all of these jobs, as well as for the infantry.) They would be deployed as needed for peacekeeping or nation-building missions. They would serve for 12-months to two years, with modest follow-on reserve obligations.

Whichever option they choose, all who serve would receive modest stipends and GI Bill-type college grants. Those who sign up for lengthier and riskier duty, however, would receive higher pay and larger college grants. Most would no doubt pick the less dangerous options. But some would certainly select the military—out of patriotism, a sense of adventure, or to test their mettle. Even if only 10 percent of the one-million young people who annually start at four-year colleges and universities were to choose the military option, the armed forces would receive 100,000 fresh recruits every year. These would be motivated recruits, having chosen the military over other, less demanding forms of service. And because they would all be college-grade and college-bound, they would have—to a greater extent than your average volunteer recruit—the savvy and inclination to pick up foreign languages and other skills that are often the key to effective peacekeeping work. 43

A 21st-century draft like this would create a cascading series of benefits for society. It would instill a new ethic of service in that sector of society, the college-bound, most likely to reap the fruits of American prosperity. It would mobilize an army of young people for vital domestic missions, such as helping a growing population of seniors who want to avoid nursing homes but need help with simple daily tasks like grocery shopping. It would give more of America's elite an experience of the military. Above all, it would provide the all-important surge capacity now missing from our force structure, insuring that the military would never again lack for manpower. And it would do all this without requiring any American to carry a gun who did not choose to do so. 44

The war in Iraq has shown us, and the world, many things: the bloody costs of inept leadership; the courage of the average American soldier; the hunger for democracy among some of the earth's most oppressed people. But perhaps more than anything, Iraq has shown that our military power has limits. As currently constituted, the U.S. military can win the wars, but it cannot win the peace, nor can it commit for the long term to the stability and security of a nation such as Iraq. Our enemies have learned this, and they will use that knowledge to their advantage in the next war to tie us down and bleed us until we lose the political will to fight. 45

If America wishes to retain its mantle of global leadership, it must develop a military force structure capable of persevering under these circumstances. Fortunately, we know how to build such a force. We have done it many times in the past. The question is: Do we have the will to do so again? 46

Uncle Sam and Aunt Samantha

Anna Quindlen

Anna Quindlen, winner of the 1992 Pulitzer Prize for her column in The New York Times, *is currently a columnist for* Newsweek. *She is also the author of several novels, children's books, and nonfiction books in which she explores themes of American society, women, and motherhood. This article appeared in* Newsweek *on November 5, 2001.*

1   One out of every five new recruits in the United States military is female. The Marines gave the Combat Action Ribbon for service in the Persian Gulf to 23 women. Two female soldiers were killed in the bombing of the USS Cole.

2   The Selective Service registers for the draft all male citizens between the ages of 18 and 25.

3   What's wrong with this picture?

4   As Americans read and realize that the lives of most women in this country are as different from those of Afghan women as a Cunard cruise is from maximum-security lockdown, there has nonetheless been little attention paid to one persistent gender inequity in U.S. public policy. An astonishing anachronism, really: while women are represented today in virtually all fields, including the armed forces, only men are required to register for the military draft that would be used in the event of a national-security crisis.

5   Since the nation is as close to such a crisis as it has been in more than 60 years, it's a good moment to consider how the draft wound up in this particular time warp. It's not the time warp of the Taliban, certainly, stuck in the worst part of the 13th century, forbidding women to attend school or hold jobs or even reveal their arms, forcing them into sex and marriage. Our own time warp is several decades old. The last time the draft was considered seriously was 20 years ago, when registration with the Selective Service was restored by Jimmy Carter after the Soviet invasion of, yep, Afghanistan. The president, as well as the Army chief of staff, asked at the time for the registration of women as well as men.

6   Amid a welter of arguments—women interfere with esprit de corps, women don't have the physical strength, women prisoners could be sexually assaulted, women soldiers would distract male soldiers from their mission—Congress shot down the notion of gender-blind registration. So did the Supreme Court, ruling that since women were forbidden to serve in combat positions and the purpose of the draft was to create a combat-ready force, it made sense not to register them.

7   But that was then, and this is now. Women have indeed served in combat positions, in the Balkans and the Middle East. More than 40,000 managed to serve in the Persian Gulf without destroying unit cohesion or failing because of upper-body strength. Some are even now taking out targets in Afghanistan from fighter jets, and apparently without any male soldier's falling prey to some predicted excess of chivalry or lust.

Talk about cognitive dissonance. All these military personnel, male and female   8
alike, have come of age at a time when a significant level of parity was taken for
granted. Yet they are supposed to accept that only males will be required to defend
their country in a time of national emergency. This is insulting to men. And it is insulting to women. Caroline Forell, an expert on women's legal rights and a professor at the University of Oregon School of Law, puts it bluntly: "Failing to require
this of women makes us lesser citizens."

Neither the left nor the right has been particularly inclined to consider this is-   9
sue judiciously. Many feminists came from the antiwar movement and have let their
distaste for the military in general and the draft in particular mute their response.
In 1980 NOW released a resolution that buried support for the registration of
women beneath opposition to the draft, despite the fact that the draft had been redesigned to eliminate the vexing inequities of Vietnam, when the sons of the working class served and the sons of the Ivy League did not. Conservatives, meanwhile,
used an equal-opportunity draft as the linchpin of opposition to the Equal Rights
Amendment, along with the terrifying specter of unisex bathrooms. (I have seen the
urinal, and it is benign.) The legislative director of the right-wing group Concerned
Women for America once defended the existing regulations by saying that most
women "don't want to be included in the draft." All those young men who went to
Canada during Vietnam and those who today register with fear and trembling in the
face of the Trade Center devastation might be amazed to discover that lack of desire
is an affirmative defense.

Parents face a series of unique new challenges in this more egalitarian world,   10
not the least of which would be sending a daughter off to war. But parents all over
this country are doing that right now, with daughters who enlisted; some have even
expressed surprise that young women in this day and age, are not required to register alongside their brothers and friends. While all involved in this debate over the
years have invoked the assumed opposition of the people, even 10 years ago more
than half of all Americans polled believed women should be made eligible for the
draft. Besides, this is not about comfort but about fairness. My son has to register
with the Selective Service this year, and if his sister does not when she turns 18, it
makes a mockery not only of the standards of this household but of the standards of
this nation.

It is possible in Afghanistan for women to be treated like little more than fe-   11
cund pack animals precisely because gender fear and ignorance and hatred have
been codified and permitted to hold sway. In this country, largely because of the
concerted efforts of those allied with the women's movement over a century of
struggle, much of that bigotry has been beaten back, even buried. Yet in improbable
places the creaky old ways surface, the ways suggesting that we women were made
of finer stuff. The finer stuff was usually porcelain, decorative and on the shelf, suitable for meals and show. Happily, the finer stuff has been transmuted into the right
stuff. But with rights come responsibilities, as teachers like to tell their students.
This is a responsibility that should fall equally upon all, male and female alike. If
the empirical evidence is considered rationally, if the decision is divested of out-
moded stereotypes, that's the only possible conclusion to be reached.

The Return of the Draft
Tim Dickinson

Tim Dickinson, a writer and editor in San Francisco, has contributed regularly to Mother Jones, *an independent nonprofit committed to social justice. This article appeared in* Rolling Stone *magazine, a liberal magazine devoted to music, entertainment, and political news, on January 27, 2005.*

1   Uncle Sam wants you. He needs you. He'll bribe you to sign up. He'll strong-arm you to re-enlist. And if that's not enough, he's got a plan to draft you.

2   In the three decades since the Vietnam War, the "all-volunteer Army" has become a bedrock principle of the American military. "It's a magnificent force," Vice President Dick Cheney declared during the election campaign last fall, "because those serving are ones who signed up to serve." But with the Army and Marines perilously overextended by the war in Iraq, that volunteer foundation is starting to crack. The "weekend warriors" of the Army Reserve and the National Guard now make up almost half the fighting force on the front lines, and young officers in the Reserve are retiring in droves. The Pentagon, which can barely attract enough recruits to maintain current troop levels, has involuntarily extended the enlistments of as many as 100,000 soldiers. Desperate for troops, the Army has lowered its standards to let in twenty-five percent more high school dropouts, and the Marines are now offering as much as $30,000 to anyone who re-enlists. To understand the scope of the crisis, consider this: The United States is pouring nearly as much money into incentives for new recruits—almost $300 million—as it is into international tsunami relief.

3   "The Army's maxed out here," says retired Gen. Merrill McPeak, who served as Air Force chief of staff under the first President Bush. "The Defense Department and the president seem to be still operating off the rosy scenario that this will be over soon, that this pain is temporary and therefore we'll just grit our teeth, hunker down and get out on the other side of this. That's a bad assumption." The Bush administration has sworn up and down that it will never reinstate a draft. During the campaign last year, the president dismissed the idea as nothing more than "rumors on the Internets" and declared, "We're not going to have a draft—period." Defense Secretary Donald Rumsfeld, in an Op-Ed blaming "conspiracy mongers" for "attempting to scare and mislead young Americans," insisted that "the idea of reinstating the draft has never been debated, endorsed, discussed, theorized, pondered or even whispered by anyone in the Bush administration."

4   That assertion is demonstrably false. According to an internal Selective Service memo made public under the Freedom of Information Act, the agency's acting director met with two of Rumsfeld's undersecretaries in February 2003 precisely to debate, discuss and ponder a return to the draft. The memo duly notes the administration's aversion to a draft but adds, "Defense manpower officials concede there are critical shortages of military personnel with certain special skills, such as medical personnel, linguists, computer network engineers, etc." The potentially prohibitive cost of "attracting and retaining such personnel for military service," the memo

adds, has led "some officials to conclude that, while a conventional draft may never be needed, a draft of men and women possessing these critical skills may be warranted in a future crisis." This new draft, it suggests, could be invoked to meet the needs of both the Pentagon and the Department of Homeland Security.

The memo then proposes, in detail, that the Selective Service be "re-engineered"   5
to cover all Americans—"men and (for the first time) women"—ages eighteen to thirty-four. In addition to name, date of birth and Social Security number, young adults would have to provide the agency with details of their specialized skills on an ongoing basis until they passed out of draft jeopardy at age thirty-five. Testifying before Congress two weeks after the meeting, acting director of Selective Service Lewis Brodsky acknowledged that "consultations with senior Defense manpower officials" have spurred the agency to shift its preparations away from a full-scale, Vietnam-style draft of untrained men "to a draft of smaller numbers of critical-skills personnel."

Richard Flahavan, spokesman for Selective Service, tells *Rolling Stone* that   6
preparing for a skills-based draft is "in fact what we have been doing." For starters, the agency has updated a plan to draft nurses and doctors. But that's not all. "Our thinking was that if we could run a health-care draft in the future," Flahavan says, "then with some very slight tinkering we could change that skill to plumbers or linguists or electrical engineers or whatever the military was short." In other words, if Uncle Sam decides he needs people with your skills, Selective Service has the means to draft you—and quick.

But experts on military manpower say the focus on drafting personnel with spe-   7
cial skills misses the larger point. The Army needs more soldiers, not just more doctors and linguists. "What you've got now is a real shortage of grunts—guys who can actually carry bayonets," says McPeak. A wholesale draft may be necessary, he adds, "to deal with the situation we've got ourselves into. We've got to have a bigger Army."

Michael O'Hanlon, a military-manpower scholar at the Brookings Institute, be-   8
lieves a return to a full-blown draft will become "unavoidable" if the United States is forced into another war. "Let's say North Korea strikes a deal with Al Qaeda to sell them a nuclear weapon or something," he says. "I frankly don't see how you could fight two wars at the same time with the all-volunteer approach." If a second Korean War should break out, the United States has reportedly committed to deploying a force of nearly 700,000 to defend South Korea—almost half of America's entire military.

The politics of the draft are radioactive: Polls show that less than twenty per-   9
cent of Americans favor forced military service. But conscription has some unlikely champions, including veterans and critics of the administration who are opposed to Bush's war in Iraq. Reinstating the draft, they say, would force every level of society to participate in military service, rather than placing a disproportionate burden on minorities and the working class. African-Americans, who make up roughly thirteen percent of the civilian population, account for twenty-two percent of the armed forces. And the Defense Department acknowledges that recruits are drawn "primarily from families in the middle and lower-middle socioeconomic strata."

A societywide draft would also make it more difficult for politicians to commit   10
troops to battle without popular approval. "The folks making the decisions are committing other people's lives to a war effort that they're not making any sacrifices for," says Charles Sheehan-Miles, who fought in the first Gulf War and now serves

as director of Veterans for Common Sense. Under the current all-volunteer system, fewer than a dozen members of Congress have children in the military.

11   Charlie Moskos, a professor of military sociology at Northwestern University, says the volunteer system also limits the political fallout of unpopular wars. "Without a draft, there's really no antiwar movement," Moskos says. Nearly sixty percent of Americans believe the war in Iraq was a mistake, he notes, but they have no immediate self-interest in taking to the streets because "we're willing to pay people to die for us. It doesn't reflect very well on the character of our society."

12   Even military recruiters agree that the only way to persuade average Americans to make long-term sacrifices in war is for the children of the elite to put their lives on the line. In a recent meeting with military recruiters, Moskos discussed the crisis in enlistment. "I asked them would they prefer to have their advertising budget tripled or have Jenna Bush join the Army," he says. "They unanimously chose the Jenna option."

13   One of the few politicians willing to openly advocate a return to the draft is Rep. Charles Rangel, a Democrat from New York, who argues that the current system places an immoral burden on America's underprivileged. "It shouldn't be just the poor and the working poor who find their way into harm's way," he says. In the days leading up to the Iraq war, Rangel introduced a bill to reinstate the draft—with absolutely no deferments. "If the kids and grandkids of the president and the Cabinet and the Pentagon were vulnerable to going to Iraq, we never would have gone—no question in my mind," he says. "The closer this thing comes home to Americans, the quicker we'll be out of Iraq."

14   But instead of exploring how to share the burden more fairly, the military is cooking up new ways to take advantage of the economically disadvantaged. Rangel says military recruiters have confided in him that they're targeting inner cities and rural areas with high unemployment. In December, the National Guard nearly doubled its enlistment bonus to $10,000, and the Army is trying to attract urban youth with a marketing campaign called "Taking It to the Streets," which features a pimped-out yellow Hummer and a basketball exhibition replete with free throwback jerseys. President Bush has also signed an executive order allowing legal immigrants to apply for citizenship immediately—rather than wait five years—if they volunteer for active duty.

15   "It's so completely unethical and immoral to induce people that have limited education and limited job ability to have to put themselves in harm's way for ten, twenty or thirty thousand dollars," Rangel says. "Just how broke do you have to be to take advantage of these incentives?" Seducing soldiers with cold cash also unnerves military commanders. "We must consider the point at which we confuse 'volunteer to become an American soldier' with 'mercenary,' " Lt. Gen. James Helmly, the commander of the Army Reserve, wrote in a memo to senior Army leadership in December.

16   The Reserve, Helmly warns, "is rapidly degenerating into a broken force." The Army National Guard is also in trouble: It missed its recruitment goals of 56,000 by more than 5,000 in fiscal year 2004 and is already 2,000 soldiers short in fiscal 2005. To keep enough boots on the ground, the Pentagon has stopped asking volunteer soldiers to extend their service—and started demanding it. Using a little-known provision called "stop loss," the military is forcing reservists and guardsmen to remain on active duty indefinitely. "This is an 'all-volunteer Army' with foot-

notes," says McPeak. "And it's the footnotes that are being held in Iraq against their wishes. If that's not a back-door draft, tell me what is."

David Qualls, who joined the Arkansas National Guard for a year, is one of 40,000 troops in Iraq who have been informed that their enlistment has been extended until December 24th, 2031. "I've served five months past my one-year obligation," says Qualls, the lead plaintiff in a lawsuit challenging the military with breach of contract. "It's time to let me go back to my life. It's a question of fairness, and not only for myself. This is for the thousands of other people that are involuntarily extended in Iraq. Let us go home." 17

The Army insists that most "stop-lossed" soldiers will be held on the front lines for no longer than eighteen months. But Jules Lobel, an attorney with the Center for Constitutional Rights who is representing eight National Guardsmen in a lawsuit challenging the extensions, says the 2031 date is being used to strong-arm volunteers into re-enlisting. According to Lobel, the military is telling soldiers, "We're giving you a chance to voluntarily re-enlist—and if you don't do it, we'll screw you. And the first way we'll screw you is to put you in until 2031." 18

But threatening volunteers, military experts warn, could be the quickest way to ensure a return to the draft. According to O'Hanlon at the Brookings Institute, such "callousness" may make it impossible to recruit new soldiers—no matter how much money you throw at them. And if bigger sign-up bonuses and more aggressive recruitment tactics don't do the trick, says Helmly of the Army Reserve, it could "force the nation into an argument" about reinstating the draft. 19

In the end, it may simply come down to a matter of math. In January, Bush told America's soldiers that "much more will be asked of you" in his second term, even as he openly threatened Iran with military action. Another war, critics warn, would push the all-volunteer force to its breaking point. "This damn thing is just an explosion that's about to happen," says Rangel. Bush officials "can say all they want that they don't want the draft, but there's not going to be that many more buttons to push." 20

Military Service
Louis Caldera

Louis Caldera, the current president of the University of New Mexico, has held a number of political and public service positions, including secretary of the army under the Clinton administration from 1998 to 2001. His opinion piece appeared in the Fall 2002 issue of The Brookings Review, *published by the Brookings Institution, an independent, nonpartisan think tank.*

Military service can be a transformative life experience. It was for me, and it continues to be so for today's young servicemen and women. As young Americans consider their options for national and community service today, however, military service is rarely even on the agenda. What must we do to increase the interest of our young people in serving their country in uniform? 1

2   I volunteered to serve driven by the immigrant spirit to give something back to the country that had given so much to my family and to me. Bookish, shy, a sheltered son of struggling, Spanish-speaking parents, I knew little of the world outside my own cloistered neighborhood. The military, with its emphasis on leadership development, moral and physical courage, and command presence and voice, opened my eyes to the vast possibilities of life. I learned that the world had much more to offer me than I had ever imagined and that no doors were closed to me except the ones I chose not to open. Our mission in the army—to be prepared to defend the nation and to serve wherever called in support of our nation's interests in the world—gave me a deeper appreciation for the forces, events, and people that shape the world we live in. Inchoate notions of duty, service, and citizenship began to become tangible and permanent.

3   Throughout my recent tenure as secretary of the army, I heard young men and women express what service means to them. Often deployed far from home, they would say there was no place they would rather be, because they knew they were making a difference. Whether helping to save lives and leading recovery efforts in Central America after Hurricane Mitch or preventing genocide in Bosnia-Herzegovina, they could palpably feel the gratitude of those for whom their presence and aid meant hope for a better life for themselves and for their children. Standing watch on the world's hot spots or training to deploy there if necessary, they knew that what they were prepared to do was essential to protecting our nation. These young people did not come, by and large, from America's most privileged families. Yet they were the ones who had internalized the sense that we are abundantly blessed as Americans and called, out of our own principles and enlightened self-interest, to lead and to help others in places riven by hatred and calamity.

4   Why does military service not figure more prominently in calls for a renewed commitment to service? In part, it is the benign result of the structure of such service initiatives as AmeriCorps and America's Promise, which address urgent domestic needs. In part, it results from the end of the draft a generation ago: relatively few parents, teachers, and other role models of today have ever worn the uniform of our country. It may also come from misconceptions about the nature of modern military service, discomfort with the fundamental role of the military, lingering suspicion and hostility arising from an antiwar movement that spanned three decades, and unhappiness with current policies toward openly gay service members. Whatever the reasons, few adults challenge today's young people to consider serving their country in uniform.

5   President Bush has included the military in his recent national service proposals, but creating new opportunities for military service that parallel civilian service will not be easy. The military itself has struggled to find ways to embrace the concept of more young people serving shorter tours of duty without compromising the requirements of military cohesiveness and readiness, particularly in the era of the high-tech battlefield. Today's recruitment and training costs are high. Because service members often train for a year or more before arriving at their first unit, the military services prefer four- to six-year enlistment contracts and put a premium on retaining skilled careerists. Moreover, high personnel turnover at the unit level degrades unit cohesiveness. Teams never quite gel as new recruits keep moving in and out of the ranks. Trainers and leaders rarely get to hone higher-order team competencies as they constantly work to rebuild basic ones. So it will not be as simple

as mandating shorter tour options—a proposal that many in the military suspect will bring into the ranks soldiers who are not really committed to the proposition that they must train as if war is imminent and that they will be the ones to fight it.

Despite these difficulties, we should try to create some workable opportunities for shorter-term military service, and we should work with employers, educators, and government leaders to create an enhanced framework of realistic enlistment and reenlistment incentives. Above all, we should make military service an important part of the national conversation about the obligations and benefits of service. Young Americans deserve to know about this opportunity to see firsthand our country's principles put into action, to work with people of all backgrounds and walks of life, to challenge themselves to live by the high standards the military demands of those who respond to the call of duty. For them, as for me and for so many others, military service can be the foundation for a lifelong commitment to public service and the source of a deep appreciation for the importance of civic engagement in a democracy.

6

Weapons of Mass Instruction

Mullen, Agency for the Department of Defense

Part of a recent advertising campaign directed at "influencers, adults who influence potential enlistees"(from www.todaysmilitary.com) this ad, created for the Joint Advertising, Market Research and Studies Program in the Department of Defense, highlights the personal value and character-building dimension of serving in the military. Note how the ad features a woman and spotlights artistic ability and dream fulfillment.

Courtesy of JAMRS.

When Valerie Vigoda's band GrooveLily tours the United States, they encounter new reasons to turn around and go home every day — long hours, bad food, bad weather, homesickness — things that try to convince them that they'd be better off in some 9-to-5 job or just chillin' on the couch.

PERSEVERANCE
- VALERIE VIGODA
U.S. ARMY ROTC/NATIONAL GUARD 1984-1994

What keeps Valerie going? A deep love of music, an addiction to applause and a few qualities that weren't exactly listed in the course guide at Princeton. Stamina. Follow-through. And what she calls "the ability to play the hand you're dealt."

The qualities you acquire while in the Military are qualities that stay with you forever.

TODAY'S MILITARY
See it for what it really is.
1-866-VIEW-NOW
www.todaysmilitary.com
Active • Guard • Reserve

Military Service Can Open the Eyes of Country's 'Elite'
Kathryn Roth-Douquet

Kathryn Roth-Douquet is an attorney and a former aide to the Clinton White House and the Department of Defense. She is a frequent contributor to the popular newspaper USA Today, *in which this piece appeared on January 18, 2005.*

1   I recently went to a dinner party attended by Sen. Hillary Clinton. After the meal, an elegant Manhattanite seated beside me asked the senator about a *military draft.* "Without one," the woman asserted, "they'll never get my educated and talented boys." I'm sure she's right. These days, people of means routinely reject military service.

2   Until a generation ago, the children of presidents, oilmen and bankers regularly saw service. Franklin Roosevelt, Joseph Kennedy, Prescott Bush—all titans—had sons who served.

3   Today, 1% of those serving in Congress have a child in the armed forces—an institution that, according to military sociologist Charles Moskos, is bereft of "children of the privileged." That's too bad. The real losers here are the young and privileged adults themselves.

4   I was, by many measures, a child of privilege, too. I came from a manicured suburb, attended expensive schools—Bryn Mawr, Princeton—and served as an aide in the Clinton White House. I've worked for charitable foundations, a white-glove law firm, and I still raise money for the Democratic Party. From these perches, the military seemed another world.

LIFE WITH A MARINE

5   Then I married a Marine Corps officer and came to see the narrowness of the "us-and-them" view of military service. During my husband's six-month deployments—airlifting aid to East Timor, sorting through the fog of war in Baghdad—and from living with military people, I've learned what military service is about. As one who was weaned on the ideologies of the American left, I've been forced to reconsider some assumptions. I've come to believe that, even for the "haves" of society, the military offers much to admire and emulate.

6   If I could address the country's fortunate young who imagine themselves one day making a difference, this is what I would say: You expect to do well in life. No one you know is in the military. There's a war going on that you think was a mistake or, perhaps, a good idea gone wrong. You think military service is for people without money or skills—not someone like you.

7   Now, consider this proposition: Joining the military may make you a better person and profoundly inform your entire life. Military service nurtures belief, without

irony, in the tenets that founded this country, and a love of country distinct from jingoism. Its every action expresses awe for the noble experiment of liberal democracy.

Servicemembers provide the defense that is a precondition of our pursuit of individual happiness and common good. Service fosters a love of strangers and comrades you hope to keep safe. When this nation, through the voice of its elected leader, asks you to help protect our freedoms, your role has meaning. Answering the call is not a career move, but an act of the heart.   8

NOW MORE THAN EVER

As long as there is an impulse to evil in this intertwined world, an impulse to take advantage, enslave, seize power from the weak; as long as our enemies embrace their cult of death; as long as those passions hold sway in whole regions, we need to be vigilant of our security.   9

Moreover, our military has become an arm of democratic hopes around the world. In the wake of the catastrophic tsunami in South Asia, it is the U.S. military that is providing the most effective relief. America's armed forces build roads and dams in Africa. They conduct diplomacy around the world the way that the State Department, with its tiny budget, simply cannot.   10

I ask political leaders—few of whom served in the military, many of whom will stand in this week's inaugural salute to the troops—to join me in this plea. Enlisting in the military won't make you richer, fatten your resume or bring the material gains that dazzle society. It may make you better, though. And it will bring you closer to the heart of this country. True, there are some who do wrong in that role. You can be one who does right.   11

For your service, you will not only develop values and perspective, you will make this country fairer and stronger. Then in your middle age, you can be part of a new elite: a civilian leader who understands the armed forces. No country can prosper when its leaders lack wisdom on national defense. The service you provide later, as a wise leader, may do our country the greatest good.   12

I Need You
Matt Carmody

Matt Carmody is a freelance editorial cartoonist and the political cartoons editor of Free World Syndicate, a network that encourages political dialogue and the use of the Internet to fight corporate control of information. This cartoon appeared on the Web site "Artizans—the World's Best Cartoons, Caricatures, Graphic Art & Illustrations" (http://zone.artizans/com) for February 25, 2005.

Military Misconceptions

David L. Englin

David L. Englin is an Air Force veteran who frequently contributes to liberal media sources, including The American Prospect, The New Republic, *and* TomPaine.com, *among others. He maintains a blog, www.rippleofhope.net, for "strong progressive voices." This piece appeared on TomPaine.com, a media center for "people who care about the progressive cause," on October 22, 2004.*

1   As Rep. John Conyers and filmmaker Michael Moore reminded me recently, many on the left still think the military is where poor, uneducated minorities go for lack of other options. During the recent, tragically brief flurry of discussion about the bill offered by Conyers and Rep. Charles Rangel, D-NY, to reinstate the draft, Conyers proclaimed that today's military amounts to "an indirect draft of minorities and the poor." In *Fahrenheit 9/11*, Michael Moore presented viewers with a pair of Marine Corps recruiters zealously targeting African-American high school students in an economically struggling community. These are but two manifestations of a liberal zeitgeist about military service that is out of touch with the reality of today's force.

Until recently, I had been associated with the U.S. military for my entire life,   2
from my birth and childhood on U.S. military bases overseas, to my cadet years at
the U.S. Air Force Academy, and through eight years of service as a commissioned
officer. But thanks to my own liberalism, marrying a liberal activist, and the Air
Force sending me to an elite liberal graduate school, I spent my time in uniform
straddling two worlds: the military officer corps and liberal intelligentsia. Now that
our nation is suddenly embroiled in an election-year showdown over which candidate might reinstate the draft, I am more concerned than ever that many of my fellow liberals cling to Vietnam-era misconceptions about the makeup of the military.
Liberal concerns about the draft and military demographics stem mostly from a
laudable sense of justice about who pays the price when America goes to war. While
that moral impulse is correct, Democrats need to get a better handle on the facts if
we expect to bring a credible promise of hope to military men and women suffering
under the Bush administration's mismanagement.

Despite the widely held—and voiced—misconceptions about the military, the   3
most recent Department of Defense population study paints an ethnic picture of
new recruits and officers that looks fairly similar to the civilian population. In the
enlisted force (versus the officer corps) African Americans make up 16 percent of
new recruits, compared to 14 percent of civilians of comparable age (between 18
and 24 years old). Hispanics make up 11 percent of new recruits, compared to 16
percent of comparable civilians. "Other" minority categories make up 6 percent of
new recruits, compared to 5 percent of comparable civilians.

Commissioned officers are required to have college degrees. Many on the left   4
might be surprised to learn that, at 8 percent, the proportion of African-American
commissioned officers is exactly the same as the proportion of African Americans in
the civilian workforce aged 21 to 49 with college degrees. Hispanics make up 4 percent of commissioned officers, compared to 5 percent of comparable civilians.
"Other" minority categories make up 5 percent of commissioned officers, compared
to 8 percent of comparable civilians.

Looking beyond officers and new enlistees to the total enlisted population, 10   5
percent are Hispanic, compared to 14 percent of the civilian workforce aged 18 to
44, but 22 percent are African American, compared to 13 percent of comparable
civilians. This last figure might be the source of lingering misconceptions. While
the number of African Americans who join the military is about the same as the
number of African Americans in the comparable civilian population, more African
Americans stay in the military longer. It could be that this is due to fewer good employment options in the civilian world. However, studies have shown that the military is better racially integrated than any other segment of American society.
Therefore, it is just as likely that African Americans stay in the military because it
is a rare slice of America where merit matters more than race and where Americans
of all ethnic backgrounds are treated fairly.

If we are concerned about who bears the scars of war, we also need to look at   6
who serves in risky combat specialties. Even with a higher proportion of African
Americans in the enlisted ranks, it turns out that only about 12 percent of African
American enlistees serve in direct combat specialties, compared to about 18 percent
of white and Hispanic enlistees. Conversely, only about 12 percent of white enlistees

serve in less-risky functional support and administrative specialties, compared to about 27 percent of African-American and 18 percent of Hispanic enlistees.

7   The military does not track the family incomes of new enlistees, so it is difficult to know whether the people joining the military are indeed poor. However, the military does keep detailed statistics on the levels of education new recruits achieved before joining the service, and we know that a person with less education is more likely to be poor. The National Center for Children in Poverty found that 81 percent of children whose parents have no high school diploma live in low-income families, and that as education increases, the likelihood of poverty decreases. Far from being the dregs of America's schools, new enlistees actually come into the service much better educated than their civilian compatriots. Among new active-duty enlistees, 92 percent had a high school diploma or equivalent before enlisting, compared to 79 percent of comparable civilians. In the Reserve, the figure is 87 percent. Among officers, 95 percent had at least a bachelor's degree before being commissioned, and more than a quarter of all officers have advanced degrees (although the majority of advanced degrees were earned while in uniform.) Additionally, before enlisting, new recruits on average scored higher on standardized tests and read at a higher grade level than their civilian counterparts. Obviously, new recruits are not uneducated compared to their peers, and given the link between education and income, it is clear that the vast majority of them are not poor.

8   Anecdotally, most military men and women come from solidly middle-class backgrounds, but today's military is by no means a direct representation of the American population. Women account for just 17 percent of the military, and a disproportionately high number of new recruits come from the South, whereas a disproportionately low number come from the Northeast. However, it is clear that the Vietnam-era image held by many liberals of a military that serves up poor, uneducated, ethnic minorities as cannon fodder bears no resemblance to today's force.

9   As the Bush administration ambles down a foreign policy road that could eventually lead to the enormous appetite for troops that only a draft could provide, Democrats like Conyers and Rangel are right to want an honest national discussion about who pays the price when America goes to war. The war in Iraq is stretching our military—especially the National Guard and Reserve—to the breaking point, and any long-term solution must include an increase in the size of the force. The discussion ought to include a thoughtful examination of the draft, and it was a sad abdication of leadership for Republicans in Congress to ignore that for months, only to shut down the issue with great fanfare to score campaign points for the president. If we want to save our overstretched forces and fill the void in leadership left by those on the right, Democrats will need to move beyond long-held misconceptions about the face of America's military.

For Class Discussion

1. What different arguments can you sketch out for each of the following positions on the issue of military recruitment and the draft?

- In favor of reinstituting a draft (consider the perspectives of citizen soldiers, military leaders, practical-utilitarian thinkers, liberals, conservative patriots, feminists)
- Against reinstituting a draft (consider the views of military experts, political leaders/Rumsfeld, liberals, feminists)

2. Some of the readings in this chapter and a number of the visuals in this book (the Armed Forces Day 2005 poster, p. 73, the America's Army images in Color Plates H and I, the cartoons on pages 315 and 480, and the "Perseverance" Army ad on p. 477) illustrate U.S. military recruitment strategies and problems. The army is using computer simulation games, offers of free cosmetic surgery to military personnel and their families, and advertising at sports events that attract daring young people. Although the Army claims that America's Army, the free online action game that simulates Army experience and that is one of the top five or six most popular games, is simply a public relations tool, it too clearly has a recruitment agenda. How effective do you find the Army's recruitment strategies? (You may need to do some additional research, such as logging on to America's Army or to DefenseLink News to see the new ad campaign posters.) What values do these recruiting campaigns appeal to? How have the creators of this strategy designed their approach to appeal to specific audiences? Do you think the Army is justified in spending large amounts of taxpayers' money to fund these recruitment venues?

3. Concern about the possibility of a draft has fired up the energy of many advocacy groups. After investigating one of the following Web sites, list what you see as the primary argument this site is making against the draft: www.citizen-soldier.org (Citizen Soldier); www.objector.org (The Central Committee for Conscientious Objectors); or www.nodraft.info (People Against the Draft).

4. A provocative conversation about military recruitment is taking place within the genre of political cartoons. Find a political cartoon and bring it to class. Then, working individually or in groups, sketch out the argument the cartoon makes and discuss how the image and text work to make this cartoon effective. What insight does it contribute to the controversy over recruitment?

5. Choose one of the readings in this unit and analyze it carefully using the List 2 Guide questions on pages 454–455.

OPTIONAL WRITING ASSIGNMENT   Write a letter to your congressman or congresswoman arguing for your informed view on how the United States Army should fill the military. Show that you understand the problems from political leaders' perspectives.

RESPONSES TO TERRORISM: PUBLIC SAFETY AND CIVIL LIBERTIES

With memories of September 11, 2001, still fresh in American minds, with terrorist acts increasing in frequency around the world, and with terrorist leaders still issuing threats against the United States, the national conversation about the war on terrorism and homeland security rages on. A key part of the United States' domestic strategy against terrorism has been the USA PATRIOT (an acronym for "Uniting and Strengthening America by Providing Appropriate Tools Required to Intercept and Obstruct Terrorism") Act, which has given broad new policing powers to the federal government for gathering evidence on suspected terrorists and making arrests. Now many voices are asking, Are the terror-fighting strategies adopted by the U.S. government protecting America, or has the increased surveillance and governmental power jeopardized Americans' civil liberties? In other words, have we lost the balance between maintaining national security and preserving the constitutional rights important in a democracy? Opponents of the PATRIOT Act charge that it—and proposed extensions of it—threaten Americans' freedom of association, information, speech, and freedom from unreasonable searches, as well as our right to legal representation and speedy and public trials. The war on terrorism thus raises a number of questions: Has it pushed us to accept violations of human rights? Is racial profiling justified in the war against terrorism? To what extent are the American people willing to alter their normal behaviors to increase their safety and security? And finally, with serious discussion of the United States' treatment of "enemy combatants" at Abu Ghraib and Guantanamo Bay, what constitutes torture and what treatment of prisoners is justifiable in the war on terrorism?

We begin this unit with former Attorney General John Ashcroft's early defense of the PATRIOT Act and follow with readings that offer various perspectives on civil liberties and racial profiling. We conclude this unit with two pieces that explore ethical questions about the use of torture. The readings in this unit connect also to our examination of the United States' international role and its military might in the next unit, "The United States as Sole Superpower" (pp. 507–534).

Testimony to the Senate Committee on the Judiciary

John Ashcroft

In this speech before the Senate Judiciary Committee, delivered on December 6, 2001, Attorney General John Ashcroft outlines the Bush administration's initial response to terrorism following September 11, 2001. Here he praises and justifies the procedures legalized by the USA PATRIOT Act.

Mr. Chairman, Senator Hatch, members of the Judiciary Committee, thank you 1
for this opportunity to testify today. It is a pleasure to be back in the United States
Senate.

On the morning of September 11, as the United States came under attack, I was 2
in an airplane with several members of the Justice Department en route to
Milwaukee, in the skies over the Great Lakes. By the time we could return to
Washington, thousands of people had been murdered at the World Trade Center.
One hundred eighty-nine were dead at the Pentagon. Forty-four had crashed to the
ground in Pennsylvania. From that moment, at the command of the President of the
United States, I began to mobilize the resources of the Department of Justice toward one single, overarching and overriding objective: to save innocent lives from
further acts of terrorism.

America's campaign to save innocent lives from terrorists is now 87 days old. It 3
has brought me back to this committee to report to you in accordance with
Congress's oversight role. I welcome this opportunity to clarify for you and the
American people how the Justice Department is working to protect American lives
while preserving American liberties.

Since those first terrible hours of September 11, America has faced a choice 4
that is as stark as the images that linger of that morning. One option is to call
September 11 a fluke, to believe it could never happen again, and to live in a dream
world that requires us to do nothing differently. The other option is to fight back, to
summon all our strength and all our resources and devote ourselves to better ways
to identify, disrupt and dismantle terrorist networks.

Under the leadership of President Bush, America has made the choice to fight 5
terrorism—not just for ourselves but for all civilized people. Since September 11,
through dozens of warnings to law enforcement, a deliberate campaign of terrorist
disruption, tighter security around potential targets, and a preventative campaign
of arrest and detention of lawbreakers, America has grown stronger—and safer—
in the face of terrorism.

Thanks to the vigilance of law enforcement and the patience of the American 6
people, we have not suffered another major terrorist attack. Still, we cannot—we
must not—allow ourselves to grow complacent. The reasons are apparent to me
each morning. My day begins with a review of the threats to Americans and
American interests that were received in the previous 24 hours. If ever there were
proof of the existence of evil in the world, it is in the pages of these reports. They
are a chilling daily chronicle of hatred of America by fanatics who seek to extin-
guish freedom, enslave women, corrupt education and to kill Americans wherever
and whenever they can.

The terrorist enemy that threatens civilization today is unlike any we have ever 7
known. It slaughters thousands of innocents—a crime of war and a crime against
humanity. It seeks weapons of mass destruction and threatens their use against
America. No one should doubt the intent, nor the depth, of its consuming, destructive hatred.

Terrorist operatives infiltrate our communities—plotting, planning and waiting 8
to kill again. They enjoy the benefits of our free society even as they commit them-

selves to our destruction. They exploit our openness—not randomly or haphazardly—but by deliberate, premeditated design.

9   This is a seized al Qaeda training manual—a "how-to" guide for terrorists—that instructs enemy operatives in the art of killing in a free society. Prosecutors first made this manual public in the trial of the al Qaeda terrorists who bombed U.S. embassies in Africa. We are posting several al Qaeda lessons from this manual on our website today so Americans can know our enemy.

10   In this manual, al Qaeda terrorists are told how to use America's freedom as a weapon against us. They are instructed to use the benefits of a free press—newspapers, magazines and broadcasts—to stalk and kill their victims. They are instructed to exploit our judicial process for the success of their operations. Captured terrorists are taught to anticipate a series of questions from authorities and, in each response, to lie—to lie about who they are, to lie about what they are doing and to lie about who they know in order for the operation to achieve its objective. Imprisoned terrorists are instructed to concoct stories of torture and mistreatment at the hands of our officials. They are directed to take advantage of any contact with the outside world to, quote, "communicate with brothers outside prison and exchange information that may be helpful to them in their work. The importance of mastering the art of hiding messages is self-evident here."

11   Mr. Chairman and members of the committee, we are at war with an enemy who abuses individual rights as it abuses jet airliners: as weapons with which to kill Americans. We have responded by redefining the mission of the Department of Justice. Defending our nation and its citizens against terrorist attacks is now our first and overriding priority.

12   We have launched the largest, most comprehensive criminal investigation in world history to identify the killers of September 11 and to prevent further terrorist attacks. Four thousand FBI agents are engaged with their international counterparts in an unprecedented worldwide effort to detect, disrupt and dismantle terrorist organizations.

13   We have created a national task force at the FBI to centralize control and information sharing in our investigation. This task force has investigated hundreds of thousands of leads, conducted over 500 searches, interviewed thousands of witnesses and obtained numerous court-authorized surveillance orders. Our prosecutors and agents have collected information and evidence from countries throughout Europe and the Middle East.

14   Immediately following the September 11 attacks, the Bureau of Prisons acted swiftly to intensify security precautions in connection with all al Qaeda and other terrorist inmates, increasing perimeter security at a number of key facilities.

15   We have sought and received additional tools from Congress. Already, we have begun to utilize many of these tools. Within hours of passage of the USA PATRIOT Act, we made use of its provisions to begin enhanced information sharing between the law-enforcement and intelligence communities. We have used the provisions allowing nationwide search warrants for e-mail and subpoenas for payment information. And we have used the Act to place those who access the Internet through cable companies on the same footing as everyone else.

Just yesterday, at my request, the State Department designated 39 entities as   16
terrorist organizations pursuant to the USA PATRIOT Act.

We have waged a deliberate campaign of arrest and detention to remove sus-   17
pected terrorists who violate the law from our streets. Currently, we have brought
criminal charges against 110 individuals, of whom 60 are in federal custody. The
INS has detained 563 individuals on immigration violations.

We have investigated more than 250 incidents of retaliatory violence and   18
threats against Arab Americans, Muslim Americans, Sikh Americans and South
Asian Americans.

Since September 11, the Customs Service and Border Patrol have been at their   19
highest state of alert. All vehicles and persons entering the country are subjected to
the highest level of scrutiny. Working with the State Department, we have imposed
new screening requirements on certain applicants for non-immigrant visas. At the
direction of the President, we have created a Foreign Terrorist Tracking Task Force
to ensure that we do everything we can to prevent terrorists from entering the
country, and to locate and remove those who already have.

We have prosecuted to the fullest extent of the law individuals who waste pre-   20
cious law enforcement resources through anthrax hoaxes.

We have offered non-citizens willing to come forward with valuable information   21
a chance to live in this country and one day become citizens.

We have forged new cooperative agreements with Canada to protect our com-   22
mon borders and the economic prosperity they sustain.

We have embarked on a wartime reorganization of the Department of Justice.   23
We are transferring resources and personnel to the field offices where citizens are
served and protected. The INS is being restructured to better perform its service
and border security responsibilities. Under Director Bob Mueller, the FBI is under-
going an historic reorganization to put the prevention of terrorism at the center of
its law enforcement and national security efforts.

Outside Washington, we are forging new relationships of cooperation with state   24
and local law enforcement.

We have created 93 Anti-Terrorism Task Forces—one in each U.S. Attorney's   25
district—to integrate the communications and activities of local, state and federal
law enforcement.

In all these ways and more, the Department of Justice has sought to prevent   26
terrorism with reason, careful balance and excruciating attention to detail. Some of
our critics, I regret to say, have shown less affection for detail. Their bold declara-
tions of so-called fact have quickly dissolved, upon inspection, into vague conjec-
ture. Charges of "kangaroo courts" and "shredding the Constitution" give new
meaning to the term "the fog of war."

Since lives and liberties depend upon clarity, not obfuscation, and reason, not hy-   27
perbole, let me take this opportunity today to be clear: Each action taken by the
Department of Justice, as well as the war crimes commissions considered by the
President and the Department of Defense, is carefully drawn to target a narrow class
of individuals—terrorists. Our legal powers are targeted at terrorists. Our investigation is focused on terrorists. Our prevention strategy targets the terrorist threat.

28   The advice I give to the President, whether in his role as Commander-in-Chief or in any other capacity, is privileged and confidential. I cannot and will not divulge the contents, the context, or even the existence of such advice to anyone—including Congress—unless the President instructs me to do so. I cannot and will not divulge information, nor do I believe that anyone here would wish me to divulge information, that will damage the national security of the United States, the safety of its citizens or our efforts to ensure the same in an ongoing investigation.

29   As Attorney General, it is my responsibility—at the direction of the President—to exercise those core executive powers the Constitution so designates. The law enforcement initiatives undertaken by the Department of Justice, those individuals we arrest, detain or seek to interview, fall under these core executive powers. In addition, the President's authority to establish war-crimes commissions arises out of his power as Commander-in-Chief. For centuries, Congress has recognized this authority and the Supreme Court has never held that any Congress may limit it.

30   In accordance with over two hundred years of historical and legal precedent, the executive branch is now exercising its core Constitutional powers in the interest of saving the lives of Americans. I trust that Congress will respect the proper limits of Executive Branch consultation that I am duty-bound to uphold. I trust, as well, that Congress will respect this President's authority to wage war on terrorism and defend our nation and its citizens with all the power vested in him by the Constitution and entrusted to him by the American people.

31   Thank you.

Rights in an Insecure World

Deborah Pearlstein

Deborah Pearlstein is the director of the United States Law and Security Program at Human Rights First, an organization dedicated to aiding human rights activists, defending refugees, and promoting justice and peace worldwide. A visiting scholar at Princeton, Stanford, and Harvard, Pearlstein is a leading authority on United States constitutional law. This article was printed in October 2004 in The American Prospect, *a liberal magazine committed to resisting the dominance of conservatism in the United States. In this piece, Pearlstein speaks as a public intellectual attempting to deepen the civic debate about national security and individual freedom.*

1   Almost as soon as the planes crashed into the twin towers, scholars, pundits, and politicians began asserting that our most important challenge as a democracy now is to reassess the balance between liberty and security. As Harvard human-rights scholar Michael Ignatieff wrote in *The Financial Times* on September 12, "As

America awakens to the reality of being at war—and permanently so—with an enemy that has as yet no face and no name, it must ask itself what balance it should keep between liberty and security in the battle with terrorism."

Long before anyone had a clear idea of what went wrong—much less how to make sure it never happened again—public debate began with the assumption that something about the current "balance" was partially to blame for the attacks' success. As the attorney general testified in December 2001, "al-Qaeda terrorists are told how to use America's freedom as a weapon against us." In embracing the USA PATRIOT Act just weeks after the attacks, congressional member after congressional member stood to explain, as then-Senate Majority Leader Trent Lott put it, "When you're at war, civil liberties are treated differently." Minority Leader Dick Gephardt embraced the assumption as well, saying, "[W]e're not going to have all the openness and freedom we have had."

Our open society had made us less secure. The converse was as clear: A less free society would be safer. We had posited a solution before we had identified the problem. And we had based the solution on the premise that liberty and security are a zero-sum game.

While the drive to think about September 11 in terms of its implications for personal liberties was understandable, the balance metaphor is badly flawed. As the commission report itself demonstrates, the fundamental freedoms of our open society were not the primary (or even secondary) reason the terrorists succeeded on September 11. FBI agents in Minneapolis failed to search terrorist suspect Zacarias Moussaoui's computer before the attacks, not because constitutional restrictions against unreasonable searches and seizures prevented them from doing so but because they misunderstood the tools the law provided. The vast majority of the September 11 hijackers were able to enter the United States not because equal protection provisions prevented border officials from targeting Arab and Muslim men for special scrutiny but because, according to the commission, "[b]efore 9/11, no agency of the U.S. government systematically analyzed terrorists' travel strategies" to reveal how terrorists had "detectably exploited] weaknesses in our border security."

It is also not the case that a society less concerned with human rights is *per se* better protected from terrorism. On the contrary, some of our most rights-damaging measures since September 11 have had a neutral or even negative effect on counterterrorism. Most important, it is not the case that enhanced security invariably requires a compromise of human rights.

The balance metaphor has made crafting a security policy response to September 11 easy—and often misguided. It has also made policy unduly prone to undermine human rights. Three years after the fact, both rights and security are the worse for wear.

CAUGHT IN THE BALANCE

The PATRIOT Act became an important first example: It allows the FBI to secretly access Americans' personal information (library, medical, telephone, and financial records, among other things) without needing to show to an independent authority (like a judge) that the target is particularly suspected of terrorist activity. Yet the September 11 commission's report and other studies done since the attacks suggest that our primary intelligence failure on September 10 was not having too little information; our problem was failing to understand, analyze, and disseminate the significant quantity of information we had. For example, Minneapolis FBI agents did not understand what "probable cause" meant (the level of evidence required to obtain a regular criminal search warrant)—so they did not understand that they could have secured a run-of-the-mill search warrant on Moussaoui. This failure is a problem not remedied by the PATRIOT provision that gives the FBI power to trawl secretly through Americans' records. That power is all about gathering more data; it does nothing to address the problem of analysis that we still have. Still, changing the law was fast and easy—far easier than changing culture, competence, or overarching foreign policy. Imposing upon rights could become a policy substitute for enhancing security.

8   A similar approach was evident in the FBI's "voluntary" interview programs in certain immigrant and minority communities—a process that expended enormous resources and deeply alienated the communities whose cooperation in intelligence gathering may be needed most. After September 11, hundreds of foreign nationals in the United States were wrongly detained, unfairly deported, and subject to mistreatment and abuse under government programs, from special registration requirements to voluntary interviews to the detention of those seeking political asylum from a list of predominantly Arab and Muslim countries. Yet an April 2003 Government Accounting Office report on the effects of these interviews revealed that none of the information gathered from the interviews had yet been analyzed for intelligence, and there were "no specific plans" to do so. Indeed, from a security point of view, information overload can make matters worse. Instead of looking for a needle in a haystack, we must now find a needle in a field full of hay.

9   And just as our security needs for more careful intelligence assessments, thorough analysis, and greater information sharing are at their height, the executive-branch impulse has been to crack down on information shared not only with the public but with Congress itself. In 2003, the executive branch classified 25 percent more information (based on the number of executive-agency determinations that certain information should be classified) than the year before, which itself had seen a large rise. The CIA's numbers went up 41 percent, the Justice Department's 89 percent. At the same time, the amount of information being declassified fell to half what it had been in 2000, and one-fifth of 1997 levels. And this is not just about traditionally classified information. Last December, for example, the Defense Department announced a new policy preventing its own inspector general from posting unclassified information that was, in the Pentagon's estimation, "of questionable value to the general public." At the same time, despite repeated congressional requests over a period of years for complete statistics on how the PATRIOT Act has been used by the Justice Department, information available to Congress remains incomplete.

PARADIGMS LOST

Aggressive or humiliating interrogation is the most pointed example of counter- 10
productive policy. If the most important issue we face in the treatment of a suspect
who knows the location of a ticking bomb is "what balance" to keep between security and liberty, of course liberty will lose. Saving the lives of 3,000 innocents
weighs far heavier in the balance than the rights of any one individual.

But how does aggressive interrogation improve security? Set aside the fact that 11
the certainty of the ticking-bomb scenario never exists in the real world. When John
Ashcroft argued that terrorists were trained to "use our freedoms against us," he
pointed to an al-Qaeda training-manual instruction that terrorists, if captured,
should lie in response to questions from authorities. However, neither the manual
nor the attorney general explained how a denial of human rights can overcome the
instruction to lie. Are terrorists less likely to lie if we humiliate them in violation of
Geneva Convention protections—which we are, after all, bound to obey by law?

To the extent that the United States is able to answer this question—and com- 12
pared with the counterterrorism expertise in Israel and the United Kingdom, our
knowledge is limited at best—published accounts point to the opposite conclusion.
As one Army interrogator put it in testimony related to the investigation of Abu
Ghraib, "Embarrassment as a technique would be contradictory to achieving results." That is an important reason why the Army field manual has for decades instructed soldiers to avoid such tactics. They of course violate rights. They also do
not reliably work. On the other hand, the widespread use and public revelation of
such tactics has been powerfully effective in fueling anger and resentment that may
feed anti-American terrorism for some time.

Now compare these tactics with security-enhancing measures that require es- 13
sentially no balancing of security with human rights. For example, a bipartisan
array of counterterrorism experts continues to criticize as inadequate inspection
regimes for the 7 million cargo containers that arrive in U.S. ports each year—yet
all acknowledge the danger of attack through such containers as a significant
ongoing threat. The same may be said for the threat of bioterrorist attack, but the
largely rights-neutral improvement of international public-health surveillance
(which could help identify infectious-disease agents before they enter the United
States) has also taken a backseat. And many in Congress have resisted entirely
rights-neutral programs that would help the former Soviet Union secure stock-
piles of fissile material to prevent it from becoming available on the global black
market. And on and on.

This is not to suggest that balancing security interests against liberty interests 14
is never required. It is to emphasize that taking a stone away from the rights side of
the scale does not necessarily give the security side an advantage any more than
taking a stone away from the security side strengthens rights. It is to underscore
that viewing the issue of security post–September 11 as an exercise where rights
and security are opposed is likely to produce both poor security policy and rights-
damaging results.

THE MORAL EQUIVALENT OF LAW

15   If escaping the balancing framework is important to making good judgments about security policy, it is essential to preserving a regime of human rights under law. The dangers of this have been acutely evident in the new U.S. approach to detention and interrogation. Since early 2002, the White House has insisted that the president has the power to designate American citizens "enemy combatants," and thereby deprive them of the constitutional protections of the U.S. criminal justice system, or, indeed, any legal rights at all. More or less the same position has applied to the U.S. detention of thousands of foreign nationals held indefinitely in a global system from Iraq to Afghanistan to Guantanamo Bay.

16   As White House Counsel Alberto Gonzales put it in a speech defending the combatant-detention policy to the American Bar Association's Standing Committee on Law and National Security, at issue in these cases was "the balance struck by this administration between protecting our country and preserving our freedoms." This balance had to be struck by the chief executive as "a matter of prudence and policy"—not one fixed in some more permanent domestic or international framework of rights, or one unduly constrained by law. "You have to realize," the president's lawyer told the Supreme Court, "that in situations where there is a war . . . you have to trust the executive to make the kind of quintessential military judgments that are involved" in interrogating detainees under U.S. control. This was not just about a particular entitlement—to a lawyer, to confidentiality, or to due process. This was about the idea of rights itself.

17   This argument took center stage this past spring when the Supreme Court heard its first three cases arising in the war on terrorism. In each of these cases—two involving the detention of U.S. citizens as "enemy combatants," one involving the detention of hundreds of foreign nationals beyond U.S. borders—the president argued that we should abandon reliance on law according to standards known to all and fixed in advance (the very definition of the rule of law) and move toward a more "flexible" anti-terrorism system where the rule of the road is not law but (in every case, at any moment) balance. Would an enemy-combatant detainee ever be able to assert his innocence to someone other than his interrogator? one justice asked during oral arguments. "As I understand it," the president's lawyer answered, "the plan on a going-forward basis, reflecting the unique situation of this battle, is to provide individuals like [Yaser Esam] Hamdi, like [Jose] Padilla, with the equivalent" of some review. "We don't know for sure."

18   By most accounts, the Court's decisions in these cases were a victory for human rights. In the case of U.S. citizen Hamdi, eight of the nine justices rejected the White House assertion that the president alone determined what rights Hamdi was entitled to receive. The federal courts will also have a role now in checking presidential power to detain foreign nationals at Guantanamo Bay. And while U.S. citizen Padilla may have to jump through additional procedural hoops, Hamdi's case put the handwriting for him on the wall: There would be no such thing as a rights-less citizen of the United States.

19   Nonetheless, these cases presented questions about government power and law that were staggeringly fundamental. And judging by the United States' ongoing de-

tention of individuals in uncertain status around the world, and its ongoing resistance to allowing Guantanamo Bay detainees to challenge their detention in federal courts, the administration's basic position remains: Rules can be made "going forward"; on any given day, those rules may not be available for consideration by a court; and the rights available in each situation are "unique." In the rush to adjust the balance, we are abandoning the idea at the core of international human-rights law that some measures are fixed.

Conceiving our primary post–September 11 challenge as what balance to keep   20
between liberty and security leaves us prone to see links between liberty and security where they need not exist, and prone to see rights under law as just another weight that can be readily removed from the scale. In fact, the basic balance between liberty and security in U.S. law was established in some detail centuries ago, at a time when the United States as an enterprise had never been more vulnerable or less secure. It included a commitment to the idea that people should be able to know in advance what the law is, and that if circumstances—like pressing new challenges to national security—required the laws to be changed, the people would have a say in how to change them. We have called that commitment the rule of law. And human rights are meaningless without it.

Racial Profiling: A Matter of Survival
Michelle Malkin

Michelle Malkin is a widely syndicated columnist and the author of In Defense of Internment: The Case for "Racial Profiling" in World War II and the War on Terror *(2004). Malkin also contributes to Fox News Channel, a conservative news source. This article was published on August 17, 2004, in* USA Today.

When our national security is on the line, "racial profiling"—or more precisely,   1
threat profiling based on race, religion or nationality—is justified. Targeted intelligence-gathering at mosques and in local Muslim communities, for example, makes perfect sense when we are at war with Islamic extremists.

Yet, last week, the FBI came under fire for questioning Muslims in Seattle   2
about possible terrorist ties. Members of a local mosque complained to Rep. Jim McDermott, D-Wash., who called for a congressional investigation of the FBI's innocuous tactics. The American Civil Liberties Union of Washington accused the agency of "ethnic profiling."

But where else are federal agents supposed to turn for help in uncovering ter-   3
rorist plots by Islamic fanatics: Buddhist temples? Knights of Columbus meetings? Amish neighborhoods?

Some might argue that profiling is so offensive to fundamental American val-   4
ues that it ought to be prohibited, even if the prohibition jeopardizes our safety. Yet many of the ethnic activists and civil-liberties groups who object most

strenuously to the use of racial, ethnic, religious and nationality classifications during war support the use of similar classifications to ensure "diversity" or "parity" in peacetime.

5   The civil-rights hypocrites have never met a "compelling government interest" for using racial, ethnicity or nationality classifications they didn't like, except when that compelling interest happens to be the nation's very survival.

MISSED OPPORTUNITIES

6   Consider what happened in summer 2001, when Phoenix FBI agent Kenneth Williams urged his superiors to investigate militant Muslim men whom he suspected of training in U.S. flight schools as part of al-Qaeda missions.

7   Williams' recommendation was rejected, FBI Director Robert Mueller later said, partly because of concerns that the plan could be viewed as discriminatory racial profiling.

8   Mueller acknowledged that if Williams' Phoenix profiling memo had been shared with the agency's Minneapolis office, which had unsuccessfully sought a special intelligence warrant to search suspected terrorist Zacarias Moussaoui's laptop computer, the warrant might have been granted.

9   If the FBI had taken Williams' advice, the feeling of some Arabs and Muslims might have been hurt. But the Twin Towers might still be standing and 3,000 innocent people might be alive today.

10   Absolutists who oppose national-security profiling often invoke the World War II experience of Japanese-Americans. When asked whether the 12 Muslim chaplains serving in the armed forces should be vetted more carefully than military rabbis or priests, Sarah Eltantawi of the Muslim Public Affairs Council raised the specter of Japanese internment.

11   The analogy is ridiculous. The more extensive screening of 12 military officers is a far cry from the evacuation of 112,000 individuals on the West Coast. The targeted profiling of Muslims serving in sensitive positions is not a constitutional crisis.

12   Some argue that the dismissal of charges against Army Capt. James Yee, a former Muslim chaplain who ministered to enemy combatants at Guantanamo Bay, Cuba, and was initially suspected of espionage, undermines the case for profiling of any kind. Not at all. As the Defense Department has acknowledged, the military's 12 Muslim chaplains were trained by a radical Wahhabi school and were certified by a Muslim group founded by Abdurahman Alamoudi, who was charged in September 2003 with accepting hundreds of thousands of dollars from Libya, a U.S.-designated sponsor of terrorism. These associations cannot be ignored.

13   Unfortunately, the Pentagon caved in to Eltantawi and her fellow travelers. Rather than focus exclusively on the 12 Muslim chaplains, it pressed forward with a review of all 2,800 military chaplains.

14   The refusal to be discriminating was, as Sen. Jon Kyl, R-Ariz., acknowledged, the "height of politically correct stupidity."

SMOKE-AND-MIRRORS ARGUMENTS

In the wake of 9/11, opponents of profiling have shifted away from arguing   15
against it because it is "racist" and now claim that it endangers security because it
is a drain on resources and damages relations with ethnic and religious minorities,
thereby hampering intelligence-gathering. These assertions are cleverly fine-tuned
to appeal to post–9/11 sensibilities, but they are unfounded and disingenuous. The
fact that al-Qaeda is using some non-Arab recruits does not render profiling moot.
As long as we have open borders, Osama bin Laden will continue to send Middle
East terrorists here by land, sea and air. Profiling is just one discretionary investigative tool among many.

Post–9/11, the belief that racial, religious and nationality profiling is never jus-   16
tified has become a dangerous bugaboo. It is unfortunate that loyal Muslims or
Arabs might be burdened because of terrorists who share their race, nationality or
religion. But any inconvenience is preferable to suffering a second mass terrorist attack on American soil.

Losing Liberties

Arsalan Iftikhar

*Arsalan Iftikhar is the national legal director for the Council on American-
Islamic Relations, the nation's largest American Muslim advocacy group in
Washington, committed to promoting justice and understanding. This article
was published on May 19, 2005, on TomPaine.com. This Web site is a liberal
"journal of news, opinions, and alternative views," inspired by Thomas Paine, a
founding father who supported individual liberty and independence from Britain.*

Nearly four years after the 9/11 terror attacks—the greatest tragedy to befall   1
our nation in modern history—our country has learned certain lessons regarding
our role in the global community. But we have more to learn about treatment of our
own citizens—lessons that will hopefully lead us to a stronger, safer and more vi-
brant society for people of all races, faiths and cultures.

Since the 9/11 attacks, the most disturbing legal trend in America has been the   2
growing disparity in how American Muslims are treated under the law.

Recently, the Council on American-Islamic Relations (CAIR), the nation's   3
largest American Muslim civil rights group, reported that it processed a total of
1,522 incident reports of civil rights cases last year—a 49 percent increase in cases
of harassment, violence and discriminatory treatment from 2003. That's the highest
number of Muslim civil rights cases ever reported to CAIR.

4   In addition, CAIR received 141 reports of actual and potential violent anti-Muslim hate crimes, a 52 percent increase from 2003.

5   Overall, 10 states alone accounted for almost 79 percent of all reported incidents of discrimination. These states include California, New York, Arizona, Virginia, Texas, Florida, Ohio, Maryland, New Jersey and Illinois.

6   By far the greatest increase from last year occurred in the area of unreasonable arrests, detentions, unlawful searches/seizures and interrogations. In 2003, complaints concerning suspect law enforcement techniques accounted for only 7 percent of all reported incidents. In 2004, however, these reports rose to almost 26 percent of all reported cases to CAIR.

7   In the months after 9/11, Attorney General John Ashcroft, using his powers under section 412 of the now infamous USA PATRIOT Act, rounded up and imprisoned well over 1,200 Muslim and Arab men based solely on pretextual immigration violations. The most disturbing fact about these mass roundups was the fact that the Justice Department refused to disclose the detainees' identities, give them access to lawyers or allow them to have contact with their families. The inspector general conceded in his official report that they stopped counting the detainees after 1,200 because the "statistics became too confusing."

8   Georgetown University law professor and civil liberties expert David Cole has said that, "Thousands were detained in this blind search for terrorists without any real evidence of terrorism, and ultimately without netting virtually any terrorists of any kind."

9   In June 2002, Ashcroft instituted the National Security Entry-Exit Registration System, more commonly referred to as NSEERS. One of the most ambiguous and publicly debated aspects of NSEERS was known as "Special Registration." Special Registration required all male nationals over the age of 14 from 25 countries to report to the government to be registered and fingerprinted. With the sole exception of North Korea, every single one of the 25 countries on the Special Registration bulletin was Muslim or Arab. The ACLU denounced the plan as "a thinly veiled effort to trigger massive and discriminatory deportations of certain immigrants."

10   In one year alone, the Special Registration program registered 83,310 foreign nationals, placing 13,740 into deportation proceedings.

11   The Justice Department also found it prudent to create high-profile terrorism cases based on the flimsiest evidence. For example, after spending 76 days in solitary confinement and being labeled a "spy" in most media circles by government leaks based on sealed evidence, where can Army chaplain and West Point graduate Captain James Yee go to regain his respectability? Yee was falsely accused of treasonous crimes that could have resulted in the death penalty. Why was it that after the West Point graduate was cleared of all "espionage" allegations, the Army still saw fit to charge him with pornography and adultery charges? Of course, these charges were eventually dropped as well, and Captain Yee is a free man seeking to reclaim the good name that was tarnished by overzealous federal authorities.

12   On March 11, 2004, 10 bombs exploded on four trains in Madrid, Spain. The death toll exceeded 190 people, and at least 1,800 were injured. A partial fingerprint found on a bag containing detonators was analyzed by the FBI, and officials

proclaimed the match to be a "100 percent identification" of American lawyer Brandon Mayfield—a white convert to Islam who was subsequently arrested and jailed as a "material witness" in the 3/11 Madrid bombings.

Of course, all of the evidence was sealed by the government. But it was still conveniently leaked to the press that the FBI may have caught the "American Connection" to the Madrid Bombings.   13

Despite the fact that a Scotland Yard fingerprint expert found any claim of a fingerprint match "horrendous," part of the evidence used to detain Mayfield for two weeks included "miscellaneous Spanish documents" that the FBI found in the home of Mayfield and his Egyptian-American wife. The absurdity of the Justice Department's case was revealed when *The New York Times* reported that these "documents" were later identified as nothing more than his children's Spanish homework.   14

Unfortunately, since the story had already been leaked to the media and many major news outlets were carrying the breaking story of the "American Connection" to the Madrid bombings, the damage to Mr. Mayfield and the American Muslim community had already been done.   15

In addition to the ongoing Iraqi occupation, this upward trend in civil rights violations against American Muslims can also be attributed to Islamophobic rhetoric coming from certain right-wing circles. For instance, when Ann Coulter says that there should be a "forced conversion of Muslims" to Christianity or Pat Robertson states that he would never allow Muslim or Hindu judges on the federal bench, they betray our nation's pluralistic origins. Such seething hatred expressed in mainstream media outlets breeds prejudice and fosters the perpetuation of stereotypes.   16

Dr. Martin Luther King Jr. once said that, "Injustice anywhere is a threat to justice everywhere." Although much of our government's focus today is on "spreading democracy" and "winning the hearts and minds" of people abroad, it is high time that the Bush administration try spreading a little American democracy here—while winning the hearts and minds of Americans by treating all people equally under the law.   17

Civil Liberties Groups Resist Government
Wayne Stayskal

Wayne Stayskal is a nationally syndicated cartoonist who has worked for the Chicago Tribune *and* Chicago American. *This cartoon was published on* Cybercast News Service *at cnsnews.com, an online news source committed to providing balanced news to "fairly present all legitimate sides of a story" (from their Web site).*

To See or Not to See

Patricia J. Williams

Patricia Williams is a law professor at Columbia University and the author of Seeing a Colour-Blind Future: The Paradox of Race *(1997), among other books. This article, a reflective, exploratory argument in Williams's regular column, "Diary of a Mad Law Professor," was published on June 28, 2004, in* The Nation, *a liberal magazine that endeavors to "wage war upon the vices of violence, exaggeration, and misrepresentation" in political writing in an effort to critically discuss political and social issues (http://www.thenation.com/about/).*

1   Boston's Massachusetts Bay Transportation Authority recently announced a new policy of stopping people "randomly" to request identification from those whom police believe to be acting "suspiciously"; they will also be asking to check packages and bags "at random." In New York City, meanwhile, the MTA has instituted a new policy forbidding cameras anywhere in the subway. One angry photographer protesting the ban cited a friend who was questioned by police after taking a picture

of his wife near the Whitestone Bridge. Apparently in response to recent scandals, Donald Rumsfeld has issued a ban on all digital cameras, cell phones with digital cameras and camcorders from all military compounds. And on the planetary line of defense, the Pentagon, having had the foresight to purchase the right to publish satellite photographs of Earth a few years ago, has never disseminated the same— thus removing aerial photos of hotspots like Afghanistan from the public realm. Although the contracts are said to have expired, John Pike of globalsecurity.org says that imaging companies don't want to "gratuitously annoy their biggest customer, the US military. These companies are run by businessmen, not crusading journalists."

Down on the ground, a Pakistani immigrant was detained after he asked a   2
stranger to snap a picture of him amid the fall foliage of upstate New York. The lovely colors were reflected in the lapping pool of a water-treatment plant; the stranger thought he might be casing the joint and called the police. At the borders, it is not only citizens of designated countries who are scrutinized and detained but also artwork, music and books. Curators, conductors and academics are frustrated in their ability to plan for conferences or shows involving work shipped from places like Cuba, Africa, the Middle East.

The flip side to all this banning and blindfolding is that the police have cameras   3
trained on the public all over New York City. Private security firms have cameras guarding every inch of work and shopping space. Antiterrorism measures allow law enforcement to "sneak and peek" into private homes and personal computers based on the suspicions of individual officers, without judicial oversight or accountability. Not that oversight will help in a time of panic: As of this writing, an art professor at the University of Buffalo named Stephen Kurtz awaits the outcome of a grand jury investigation into his series of gallery installations protesting the genetic modification of food. When Kurtz's wife died recently of a heart condition, the paramedic who came to his home saw petri dishes and a DNA extractor used to analyze food for possible genetic alteration. The paramedic reported him to the FBI, who confiscated the extractor, his computer and papers, as well as his wife's body. Although nothing hazardous was found, a grand jury has been convened to consider whether he should be prosecuted under a provision of the "U.S. Biological Weapons Anti-Terrorism Act of 1989," a law recently expanded by the USA Patriot Act to prohibit the possession of "any biological agent, toxin, or delivery system" that has no "prophylactic, protective, bona fide research, or other peaceful purpose."

Perhaps the emergence of this lumbering Panopticon wouldn't be quite so worri-   4
some if we could be sure that there was equality of sneaking and peeking. Given specific events like the upcoming conventions and election, most of us might not mind if guards searched everyone who entered the subway, regardless of race, religion or rank. Since that is obviously impossible—we depend on a transit system that transports rather than grinds to a standstill—most of us also probably would accept random, truly random, searches as a more efficient deterrent. For example, we wouldn't be so bothered if officials were stopping not just brown people "randomly" but, say, every third person through the turnstile, or everyone with a backpack—if, in other words, the winnowing were consistently neutral. But "random" is often employed as

though it were synonymous with the idle suspicions of individual officers—despite history attesting to the manner in which free-floating "suspicion" is too frequently a cipher for ethnic stereotyping, racial voyeurism, unconstitutional animus.

5   Conducting the searches and manning the cameras are so many security guards, private contractors, prison wardens, housing police, sheriffs and regular police. A random sampling of law-enforcement personnel would no doubt reveal ordinary Americans: They pray to God, beat their spouses, pay their taxes, molest their children and love their dogs at approximately the same frequency as everyone else. Some of them are well-trained professionals, some barely more than neglected, out-of-control kids, like Lynndie England. For better or worse, they carry within them the likes, prejudices, violence and ideals of our very complex society. Some of them live next door. Some want to make sure you never get within twenty miles of their neighborhood. Some believe that you are the Antichrist. Some want to marry your daughter.

6   But all that personal preference and human idiosyncrasy is beside the point if they conform to reasonably clear guidelines informed by as broad a range of public input and oversight as possible. If, on the other hand, the network of information gatherers and secret surveillers is allowed to become an ever more closed society and to indulge their own prejudices and paranoia, we will see a very different, if no less human, reaction: the increased conforming of our society to the standards of sober bureaucrats, information analysts so narrowly focused as to be narrow-minded, media rumor-mills and traumatized military men. Our homes, backpacks, offices, pockets and cars will have to be suitably sanitized of books they haven't read, of science they don't understand, of art that unsettles them, of looks that trigger flashbacks and of ideas that are so creative as to seem foreign.

7   We must not cede the power to witness what is happening to us, to know how we are seen, to oversee our own representation. Without that freedom, we must recognize ourselves in the awful words spoken by the despairing family of one Iraqi man who has disappeared into U.S. custody: "It's because they have absolute force. No one sees what they do."

The Case for Torture
Michael Levin

This argument, first published in Newsweek *on June 7, 1982, has achieved a kind of "classic" status as a provocative view of torture. It has gained in relevance with the increase in the frequency, ubiquity, and magnitude of terrorist attacks, leaving governments puzzling over how to fight terrorism. Michael Levin is a controversial professor of philosophy at the City College of New York. He is known for his libertarian views and his outspoken stance on feminism and race. In this piece, he tackles the difficult subject of torture and ethics.*

It is generally assumed that torture is impermissible, a throwback to a more brutal age. Enlightened societies reject it outright, and regimes suspected of using it risk the wrath of the United States.

I believe this attitude is unwise. There are situations in which torture is not merely permissible but morally mandatory. Moreover, these situations are moving from the realm of imagination to fact.

Death: Suppose a terrorist has hidden an atomic bomb on Manhattan Island which will detonate at noon on July 4 unless . . . (here follow the usual demands for money and release of his friends from jail). Suppose, further, that he is caught at 10 A.M. of the fateful day, but—preferring death to failure—won't disclose where the bomb is. What do we do? If we follow due process—wait for his lawyer, arraign him—millions of people will die. If the only way to save those lives is to subject the terrorist to the most excruciating possible pain, what grounds can there be for not doing so? I suggest there are none. In any case, I ask you to face the question with an open mind.

Torturing the terrorist is unconstitutional? Probably. But millions of lives surely outweigh constitutionality. Torture is barbaric? Mass murder is far more barbaric. Indeed, letting millions of innocents die in deference to one who flaunts his guilt is moral cowardice, an unwillingness to dirty one's hands. If *you* caught the terrorist, could you sleep nights knowing that millions died because you couldn't bring yourself to apply the electrodes?

Once you concede that torture is justified in extreme cases, you have admitted that the decision to use torture is a matter of balancing innocent lives against the means needed to save them. You must now face more realistic cases involving more modest numbers. Someone plants a bomb on a jumbo jet. He alone can disarm it, and his demands cannot be met (or if they can, we refuse to set a precedent by yielding to his threats). Surely we can, we must, do anything to the extortionist to save the passengers. How can we tell 300, or 100, or 10 people who never asked to be put in danger, "I'm sorry, you'll have to die in agony, we just couldn't bring ourselves to. . . ."

Here are the results of an informal poll about a third, hypothetical, case. Suppose a terrorist group kidnapped a newborn baby from a hospital. I asked four mothers if they would approve of torturing kidnappers if that were necessary to get their own newborns back. All said yes, the most "liberal" adding that she would like to administer it herself.

I am not advocating torture as punishment. Punishment is addressed to deeds irrevocably past. Rather, I am advocating torture as an acceptable measure for preventing future evils. So understood, it is far less objectionable than many extant punishments. Opponents of the death penalty, for example, are forever insisting that executing a murderer will not bring back his victim (as if the purpose of capital punishment were supposed to be resurrection, not deterrence or retribution). But torture, in the cases described, is intended not to bring anyone back but to keep innocents from being dispatched. The most powerful argument against using torture as a punishment or to secure confessions is that such practices disregard the rights of the individual. Well, if the individual is all that important—and he is—it is correspondingly important to protect the rights of individuals threatened by terrorists. If life is so valuable that it must never be taken, the lives of the innocents must be saved even at the price of hurting the one who endangers them.

8   Better precedents for torture are assassination and pre-emptive attack. No Allied leader would have flinched at assassinating Hitler, had that been possible. (The Allies did assassinate Heydrich.) Americans would be angered to learn that Roosevelt could have had Hitler killed in 1943—thereby shortening the war and saving millions of lives—but refused on moral grounds. Similarly, if nation A learns that nation B is about to launch an unprovoked attack, A has a right to save itself by destroying B's military capability first. In the same way, if the police can by torture save those who would otherwise die at the hands of kidnappers or terrorists, they must.

9   **Idealism:** There is an important difference between terrorists and their victims that should mute talk of the terrorists' "rights." The terrorist's victims are at risk unintentionally, not having asked to be endangered. But the terrorist knowingly initiated his actions. Unlike his victims, he volunteered for the risks of his deed. By threatening to kill for profit or idealism, he renounces civilized standards, and he can have no complaint if civilization tries to thwart him by whatever means necessary.

10   Just as torture is justified only to save lives (not extort confessions or recantations), it is justifiably administered only to those *known* to hold innocent lives in their hands. Ah, but how can the authorities ever be sure they have the right malefactor? Isn't there a danger of error and abuse? Won't We turn into Them?

11   Questions like these are disingenuous in a world in which terrorists proclaim themselves and perform for television. The name of their game is public recognition. After all, you can't very well intimidate a government into releasing your freedom fighters unless you announce that it is your group that has seized its embassy. "Clear guilt" is difficult to define, but when 40 million people see a group of masked gunmen seize an airplane on the evening news, there is not much question about who the perpetrators are. There will be hard cases where the situation is murkier. Nonetheless, a line demarcating the legitimate use of torture can be drawn. Torture only the obviously guilty, and only for the sake of saving innocents, and the line between Us and Them will remain clear.

12   There is little danger that the Western democracies will lose their way if they choose to inflict pain as one way of preserving order. Paralysis in the face of evil is the greater danger. Some day soon a terrorist will threaten tens of thousands of lives, and torture will be the only way to save them. We had better start thinking about this.

Situational Ethics and the Argument for Torture

McQ

This blog was posted by "McQ" on The QandO Blog, a neolibertarian Web page dedicated to "free markets, free people" (from their Web site). Neolibertarianism is a new subset of libertarianism, stemming from the Iraq war. This line of political thought advocates an interventionist foreign policy, "pragmatism" as its ultimate principle, and the rights of individuals. This piece was posted on May 30, 2005.

Last week I talked with Dale, and subsequently with Jon, after they'd again expressed their opinions about torture and abuse of prisoners in our custody by members of the U.S. military. I believe my question was, after a quick chuckle, "are you boys having fun?"   1

As usual, the mention of torture and abuse by members of our military brought responses from both sides of the political spectrum, but particularly from those who lean to the right. Many of the comments were, quite frankly, surprising. The seeming desire to wave it all away with rationalization and excuses was telling, and disappointing. The thread running through many of the comments received was "we're certainly not doing it to the extent that they are" as if numbers of dead due to torture was much more important than the act itself. Completely ignored was the principle involved and invoked. We believe in human rights, therefore we don't torture and abuse prisoners.   2

Others argued that while distasteful, it was necessary in order to acquire vital information, again ignoring principle. Lastly there was the group that considered any criticism of the US military to be out of bounds, distracting and potentially destructive to the morale of those fighting in Iraq.   3

A couple of points before I discuss these basic arguments. I supported and continue to support the war in Iraq. It was and is necessary and in the long term, it will make the world a safer place. Secondly, I'm a veteran of 28 years military service. I criticized the military during those 28 years, when it deserved criticism, and I will criticize it now, when it deserves such criticism. That's my right and duty as an American. That's not to say I think that it is a bad organization. Quite the contrary, I think we have the finest military we and the world has ever seen. But like all large organizations, it has problems and it can be better. Those problems must be surfaced, discussed, criticized and have action taken to correct them.   4

The charges of torture and abuse of prisoners in our custody is one of those problems. In the most recent of the posts, one of our commenters, JWG, summed up the side rationalizing torture and abuse in the following list: 5

1. The terrorists are worse
2. The GC doesn't apply
3. It's not enough deaths to be a problem
4. War is hell
5. People are dying in other parts of the world
6. The anti-war crowd thinks it's bad

"The terrorists are worse." By condoning torture and abuse by our soldiers, it becomes a matter of degree and not principle. Principle is thrown right out of the window with the acceptance that our torture isn't as bad or as widespread as theirs. Because theirs is "worse," ours, apparently, is then acceptable. It's the same sort of rationalization which occurs in other arguments in which people are driven by   6 anger to abandon principle for vengeance. We're upset by what the terrorists do. It's a natural human phenomenon to want vengeance for acts of terrorism. We want to punish and get even with those who perpetrate such atrocities. But then, when we indulge ourselves in such behavior, we abandon the moral high ground for the same fetid pit in which our enemies exist. We become no better than them.

7   "The Geneva Conventions don't apply." Maybe, maybe not . . . but basic principles of human rights do apply, that is if you really believe in such things. And those principles do not lend themselves to torture and abuse of prisoners who are in our custody and essentially defenseless, regardless of their alleged crimes. It's rather difficult to make the argument to the rest of the world that the United States stands and fights for the human rights of everyone when we're found to be violating them among prison populations under our control.

8   Arguments "3," "4" and "5" are simply variations on the rationalization theme found in "the terrorists are worse" argument. The "it's a small percentage" argument is particularly heinous. Compared to Vietnam, our losses in Iraq are a small percentage. Does that mean we shouldn't be concerned with the deaths in Iraq until they reach the proportions of Vietnam? Of course not. Nor should we callously wave off these deaths with a "it's a small percentage" argument. There should be no deaths in our custody due to torture or abuse. None. That speaks to principle, not convenience, vengeance or rationalization.

9   The last argument, "the anti-war crowd thinks its bad" is one of the more interesting arguments. Its premise is "if they think its bad, then it probably isn't because they think everything the military does is bad." Naturally the rationalization begins based on that premise. It becomes more important to win politically than to recognize they may have a valid argument and stand on principle yourself. Politics over principle.

10   A very dangerous corollary to that premise is "our military can do no wrong." Well, it can, and has. What's interesting about the military is it works very hard to correct those things it has done badly or actions it considers to be wrong. Abu Ghraib wasn't "broken" by CBS, it was broken by our military launching an investigation. The abuses we've recently found out about in Afghanistan came from an internal Department of Defense investigation the military conducted. If they know it is wrong to torture and abuse prisoners and have taken the time to investigate and punish those committing such acts, why are there those among us that feel compelled to defend such practices? And why do they think they're doing a favor to the military by doing so?

11   There's one other argument I want to address and it was brought up by commenter Tim Higgins:

> You see, if the argument being made is "look at all the torture and murder going on—we need to do a better job training and disciplining our troops, and identify and punish, if applicable, whoever in the chain of command is responsible for ordering that this take place"—then I would come off as much more sympathetic.

12   Well Tim, that is the argument being made. This blog, from the beginning, has said this sort of behavior by members of our military (not by the military as a whole)

is completely unacceptable and against every principle we as Americans hold dear. We've argued that the occurrences are more than random and speaks to a very apparent lack of leadership or at least emphasis by leadership. That's not an indictment of all of the leaders, or the administration, or even most of the leaders. It's an indictment of those leaders charged with the custody of prisoners in various locales. They've not done the job. And they've either disregarded guidance or ignored it. They've also either been ignorant of the activities or implicitly condoned them. That's unacceptable.

But in a broader argument, we're saying that you can make all the technical arguments you care to make, rationalize torture and murder as some sort of burning necessity upon which our safety is dependent and claim that abuse is fair pay-back for the behavior of our enemies, but we, all of us, reject any argument which tries to legitimize torture and abuse, and we reject it on principle. None of us want to hear bad things about our military. But when it does bad things, it should be criticized. This is an argument about who we are and what we support on principle, not what we can rationalize as appropriate given the current circumstance.   13

The most surprising part about the rationalization seen in the pro-torture (or "who cares," or "they're worse" or "its only a small percentage" or "they aren't covered by the Geneva Conventions") argument are the situational ethics adopted by many on the right in making the arguments. It demonstrates, very well, how successful the left has been in selling this odious concept over the years.   14

For Class Discussion

1. One of the disputes in this unit focuses on the extent to which the United States is abusing human rights in its war on terrorism. Concerning human rights, where do writers in this unit disagree about the facts of the case? Where do they disagree about basic beliefs, values, and underlying assumptions? Where do you stand?

2. Working in small groups or as a whole class, and drawing on the readings in this unit and on your own personal experience and critical thinking, create core arguments (reasons and possible kinds of evidence) for each of the following claims.

   a. The USA PATRIOT Act has/has not led to excesses of police powers that violate civil rights guaranteed by the U.S. Constitution.

   b. Under some/no circumstances, torture is ethically justifiable.

   c. Racial profiling is/is not justified in the war on terrorism.

   d. Instead of increasing its powers over citizens' lives, the U.S. government should be pursuing measures to secure our borders, ports, and likely terrorist targets, such as chemical and nuclear power plants.

3. As a class consider this dilemma: Americans, as members of a free and open society, traditionally value individualism, privacy, freedom of movement, open access to government information, acceptance of diversity and

multiculturalism, welcoming of immigrants (as symbolized by the Statue of Liberty), constitutional protections against unlawful arrest, and constitutional guarantees of free speech, free association, and freedom from governmental invasions of privacy. To what extent are you willing to exchange some of these freedoms for more safety and security against terrorism? How much are you willing to put your tax money into a new Department of Homeland Security as opposed, say, to universal medical coverage or better schools?

4. Choose one of the readings in this unit and analyze it carefully using the List 2 Guide questions on pages 454–455.

OPTIONAL WRITING ASSIGNMENT   From this unit, choose an argument on the U.S. response to terrorism with which you particularly disagree. Then write your own argument in which you summarize fairly the views you oppose, respond to those views, and then present your own perspective supported with reasons and evidence. Unless your instructor provides more specific directions, choose the audience and genre that most fit your rhetorical context.

THE UNITED STATES AS SOLE SUPERPOWER

The concept of "superpower" arose during the Cold War when there were two superpowers—the United States and the Soviet Union. These two nations, restrained from nuclear war by the policy of MAD (mutual assured destruction), coexisted from 1945 through the early 1990s when the Soviet Union collapsed. During the Cold War, the United States used its military might in regional conflicts to ward off communist aggressors (North Korea) or communist revolutionary insurgents (Vietnam). When the Soviet Union collapsed, many Americans hoped that U.S. military spending might be reduced and converted into either tax cuts or domestic programs such as health care, education, and environmental projects. However, despite some reductions in military spending, military preparedness remained a high priority—often for regional police actions (Gulf War during the administration of the first President Bush) or for peacekeeping missions (Balkans, Kosovo under the Clinton administration).

After September 11, 2001, the "war on terrorism" again accelerated military spending, first, for the war against the Taliban in Afghanistan, and then for the war against Iraq. This flexing of military muscle has sparked an international controversy over the U.S. role as the world's sole superpower. With unquestioned military supremacy, how should the United States position itself against other nations? Should the United States seek to remain the world's sole superpower? If so, what kind of superpower should the United States be? To what extent should the United States bind itself by signing treaties? Should the United States act unilaterally to protect its own interests or seek international agreements and cooperation? Should the United States seek military superiority or military dominance? What should be its policy toward putting weapons in space?

The Bush administration's apparent answers to these questions touched off intense debate, as you will see in the readings that follow. President Bush, propelled by his vision of "moral clarity" in the wake of the September 11 attacks, began a series of policies and actions that moved the United States toward unilateralism. The Justice Department suspended the civil rights of persons suspected of ties to terrorism, in apparent violation of international agreements on human rights. The Bush administration withdrew from a Cold War antiballistic missile treaty with Russia in order to proceed with a missile defense system. It also announced its intention not to abide by a nuclear nonproliferation treaty in order to plan possible use of tactical nuclear weapons in its war on terrorism. At a graduation speech at West Point, President Bush proclaimed the policy of "preemptive strike," through which he justified an attack on Saddam Hussein for reasons other than immediate self-defense. During this same period, opposition to the Bush administration's policies arose both within the United States and throughout the world.

The readings in this unit will enable you to see the beliefs and values in conflict in this debate and to understand the general lines of reasoning of disputants who confront the fact of America's military strength and its worldwide political, cultural, and economic hegemony.

Graduation Speech at West Point

George W. Bush

Widely regarded as one of his most important speeches, President Bush's gradu-ation address to the United States Military Academy at West Point on June 1, 2002, was the occasion for announcing the Bush administration's policy of pre-emptive first strikes and providing a supporting rationale for this doctrine. (We omit the first minutes of his speech, where President Bush establishes rapport with the cadets, tells some in-jokes about West Point versus other military acad-emies, and sets the stage for the serious remarks to follow.)

1   . . . Every West Point class is commissioned to the Armed Forces. Some West Point classes are also commissioned by history, to take part in a great new calling for their country. Speaking here to the class of 1942—six months after Pearl Harbor—General Marshall said, "We're determined that before the sun sets on this terrible struggle, our flag will be recognized throughout the world as a symbol of freedom on the one hand, and of overwhelming power on the other." (Applause.)

2   Officers graduating that year helped fulfill that mission, defeating Japan and Germany, and then reconstructing those nations as allies. West Point graduates of the 1940s saw the rise of a deadly new challenge—the challenge of imperial com-munism—and opposed it from Korea to Berlin, to Vietnam, and in the Cold War, from beginning to end. And as the sun set on their struggle, many of those West Point officers lived to see a world transformed.

3   History has also issued its call to your generation. In your last year, America was attacked by a ruthless and resourceful enemy. You graduate from this Academy in a time of war, taking your place in an American military that is powerful and is honorable. Our war on terror is only begun, but in Afghanistan it was begun well. (Applause.)

4   I am proud of the men and women who have fought on my orders. America is profoundly grateful for all who serve the cause of freedom, and for all who have given their lives in its defense. This nation respects and trusts our military, and we are confident in your victories to come. (Applause.)

5   This war will take many turns we cannot predict. Yet I am certain of this: Wherever we carry it, the American flag will stand not only for our power, but for freedom. (Applause.) Our nation's cause has always been larger than our nation's defense. We fight, as we always fight, for a just peace—a peace that favors human liberty. We will defend the peace against threats from terrorists and tyrants. We will preserve the peace by building good relations among the great powers. And we will extend the peace by encouraging free and open societies on every continent.

6   Building this just peace is America's opportunity, and America's duty. From this day forward, it is your challenge, as well, and we will meet this challenge together. (Applause.) You will wear the uniform of a great and unique country. America has no

empire to extend or utopia to establish. We wish for others only what we wish for ourselves—safety from violence, the rewards of liberty, and the hope for a better life.

In defending the peace, we face a threat with no precedent. Enemies in the past 7 needed great armies and great industrial capabilities to endanger the American people and our nation. The attacks of September the 11th required a few hundred thousand dollars in the hands of a few dozen evil and deluded men. All of the chaos and suffering they caused came at much less than the cost of a single tank. The dangers have not passed. This government and the American people are on watch, we are ready, because we know the terrorists have more money and more men and more plans.

The gravest danger to freedom lies at the perilous crossroads of radicalism and 8 technology. When the spread of chemical and biological and nuclear weapons, along with ballistic missile technology—when that occurs, even weak states and small groups could attain a catastrophic power to strike great nations. Our enemies have declared this very intention, and have been caught seeking these terrible weapons. They want the capability to blackmail us, or to harm us, or to harm our friends— and we will oppose them with all our power. (Applause.)

For much of the last century, America's defense relied on the Cold War doc- 9 trines of deterrence and containment. In some cases, those strategies still apply. But new threats also require new thinking. Deterrence—the promise of massive re- taliation against nations—means nothing against shadowy terrorist networks with no nation or citizens to defend. Containment is not possible when unbalanced dicta- tors with weapons of mass destruction can deliver those weapons on missiles or se- cretly provide them to terrorist allies.

We cannot defend America and our friends by hoping for the best. We cannot 10 put our faith in the word of tyrants, who solemnly sign non-proliferation treaties, and then systemically break them. If we wait for threats to fully materialize, we will have waited too long. (Applause.)

Homeland defense and missile defense are part of stronger security, and they're 11 essential priorities for America. Yet the war on terror will not be won on the defen- sive. We must take the battle to the enemy, disrupt his plans, and confront the worst threats before they emerge. (Applause.) In the world we have entered, the only path to safety is the path of action. And this nation will act. (Applause.)

Our security will require the best intelligence, to reveal threats hidden in caves 12 and growing in laboratories. Our security will require modernizing domestic agen- cies such as the FBI, so they're prepared to act, and act quickly, against danger. Our security will require transforming the military you will lead—a military that must be ready to strike at a moment's notice in any dark corner of the world. And our security will require all Americans to be forward-looking and resolute, to be ready for preemptive action when necessary to defend our liberty and to defend our lives. (Applause.)

The work ahead is difficult. The choices we will face are complex. We must un- 13 cover terror cells in 60 or more countries, using every tool of finance, intelligence and law enforcement. Along with our friends and allies, we must oppose proliferation and confront regimes that sponsor terror, as each case requires. Some nations need military training to fight terror, and we'll provide it. Other nations oppose terror, but tolerate the hatred that leads to terror—and that must change. (Applause.) We will send diplomats where they are needed, and we will send you, our soldiers, where you're needed. (Applause.)

14   All nations that decide for aggression and terror will pay a price. We will not leave the safety of America and the peace of the planet at the mercy of a few mad terrorists and tyrants. (Applause.) We will lift this dark threat from our country and from the world.

15   Because the war on terror will require resolve and patience, it will also require firm moral purpose. In this way our struggle is similar to the Cold War. Now, as then, our enemies are totalitarians, holding a creed of power with no place for human dignity. Now, as then, they seek to impose a joyless conformity, to control every life and all of life.

16   America confronted imperial communism in many different ways—diplomatic, economic, and military. Yet moral clarity was essential to our victory in the Cold War. When leaders like John F. Kennedy and Ronald Reagan refused to gloss over the brutality of tyrants, they gave hope to prisoners and dissidents and exiles, and rallied free nations to a great cause.

17   Some worry that it is somehow undiplomatic or impolite to speak the language of right and wrong. I disagree. (Applause.) Different circumstances require different methods, but not different moralities. (Applause.) Moral truth is the same in every culture, in every time, and in every place. Targeting innocent civilians for murder is always and everywhere wrong. (Applause.) Brutality against women is always and everywhere wrong. (Applause.) There can be no neutrality between justice and cruelty, between the innocent and the guilty. We are in a conflict between good and evil, and America will call evil by its name. (Applause.) By confronting evil and lawless regimes, we do not create a problem, we reveal a problem. And we will lead the world in opposing it. (Applause.)

18   As we defend the peace, we also have an historic opportunity to preserve the peace. We have our best chance since the rise of the nation state in the 17th century to build a world where the great powers compete in peace instead of prepare for war. The history of the last century, in particular, was dominated by a series of destructive national rivalries that left battlefields and graveyards across the Earth. Germany fought France, the Axis fought the Allies, and then the East fought the West, in proxy wars and tense standoffs, against a backdrop of nuclear Armageddon.

19   Competition between great nations is inevitable, but armed conflict in our world is not. More and more, civilized nations find ourselves on the same side—united by common dangers of terrorist violence and chaos. America has, and intends to keep, military strengths beyond challenge—(applause)—thereby, making the destabilizing arms races of other eras pointless, and limiting rivalries to trade and other pursuits of peace.

20   Today the great powers are also increasingly united by common values, instead of divided by conflicting ideologies. The United States, Japan and our Pacific

friends, and now all of Europe, share a deep commitment to human freedom, embodied in strong alliances such as NATO. And the tide of liberty is rising in many other nations.

Generations of West Point officers planned and practiced for battles with Soviet 21 Russia. I've just returned from a new Russia, now a country reaching toward democracy, and our partner in the war against terror. (Applause.) Even in China, leaders are discovering that economic freedom is the only lasting source of national wealth. In time, they will find that social and political freedom is the only true source of national greatness. (Applause.)

When the great powers share common values, we are better able to confront se- 22 rious regional conflicts together, better able to cooperate in preventing the spread of violence or economic chaos. In the past, great power rivals took sides in difficult regional problems, making divisions deeper and more complicated. Today, from the Middle East to South Asia, we are gathering broad international coalitions to increase the pressure for peace. We must build strong and great power relations when times are good; to help manage crisis when times are bad. America needs partners to preserve the peace, and we will work with every nation that shares this noble goal. (Applause.)

And finally, America stands for more than the absence of war. We have a great 23 opportunity to extend a just peace, by replacing poverty, repression, and resentment around the world with hope of a better day. Through most of history, poverty was persistent, inescapable, and almost universal. In the last few decades, we've seen nations from Chile to South Korea build modern economies and freer societies, lifting millions of people out of despair and want. And there's no mystery to this achievement.

The 20th century ended with a single surviving model of human progress, 24 based on non-negotiable demands of human dignity, the rule of law, limits on the power of the state, respect for women and private property and free speech and equal justice and religious tolerance. America cannot impose this vision—yet we can support and reward governments that make the right choices for their own people. In our development aid, in our diplomatic efforts, in our international broadcasting, and in our educational assistance, the United States will promote moderation and tolerance and human rights. And we will defend the peace that makes all progress possible.

When it comes to the common rights and needs of men and women, there is no 25 clash of civilizations. The requirements of freedom apply fully to Africa and Latin America and the entire Islamic world. The peoples of the Islamic nations want and deserve the same freedoms and opportunities as people in every nation. And their governments should listen to their hopes. (Applause.)

A truly strong nation will permit legal avenues of dissent for all groups that 26 pursue their aspirations without violence. An advancing nation will pursue economic reform, to unleash the great enterpreneurial energy of its people. A thriving nation will respect the rights of women, because no society can prosper while denying opportunity to half its citizens. Mothers and fathers and children across the Islamic world, and all the world, share the same fears and aspirations. In poverty, they struggle. In tyranny, they suffer. And as we saw in Afghanistan, in liberation they celebrate. (Applause.)

27   America has a greater objective than controlling threats and containing resentment. We will work for a just and peaceful world beyond the war on terror.

28   The bicentennial class of West Point now enters this drama. With all in the United States Army, you will stand between your fellow citizens and grave danger. You will help establish a peace that allows millions around the world to live in liberty and to grow in prosperity. You will face times of calm, and times of crisis. And every test will find you prepared—because you're the men and women of West Point. (Applause.) You leave here marked by the character of this Academy, carrying with you the highest ideals of our nation.

29   Toward the end of his life, Dwight Eisenhower recalled the first day he stood on the plain at West Point. "The feeling came over me," he said, "that the expression 'the United States of America' would now and henceforth mean something different than it had ever before. From here on, it would be the nation I would be serving, not myself."

30   Today, your last day at West Point, you begin a life of service in a career unlike any other. You've answered a calling to hardship and purpose, to risk and honor. At the end of every day you will know that you have faithfully done your duty. May you always bring to that duty the high standards of this great American institution. May you always be worthy of the long gray line that stretches two centuries behind you.

31   On behalf of the nation, I congratulate each one of you for the commission you've earned and for the credit you bring to the United States of America. May God bless you all. (Applause.)

The New Bush Doctrine

Richard Falk

This article, which directly critiques Bush's graduation speech at West Point, appeared in the liberal political commentary magazine The Nation *on July 15, 2002. Richard Falk is an emeritus professor of international law and policy at Princeton University and chairs the Nuclear Age Peace Foundation.*

1   President Bush's June graduation address to the cadets at West Point has attracted attention mainly because it is the fullest articulation, so far, of the new strategic doctrine of pre-emption. The radical idea being touted by the White House and Pentagon is that the United States has the right to use military force against any state that is seen as hostile or makes moves to acquire weapons of mass destruction—nuclear, biological or chemical. The obvious initial test case for pre-emption is Iraq, whose government the United States is continually threatening to overthrow, either on the model of the displacement of the Taliban

in Afghanistan or by some other method. Washington's war plans have evidently not been finalized, and whether the intimations of war—despite the numerous objections voiced by neighboring governments and European allies—are to be taken literally is still unclear.

What is certain, and scary, is the new approach to the use of international force   2 beneath the banner of counterterrorism and in the domestic climate of fervent nationalism that has existed since September 11. This new approach repudiates the core idea of the United Nations Charter (reinforced by decisions of the World Court in The Hague), which prohibits any use of international force that is not undertaken in self-defense after the occurrence of an armed attack across an international boundary or pursuant to a decision by the UN Security Council. When Iraq conquered and annexed Kuwait in 1990, Kuwait was legally entitled to act in self-defense to recover its territorial sovereignty even without any UN authorization. And the United States and others were able to join Kuwait in bolstering its prospects, thereby acting in what international lawyers call collective self-defense.

Back in 1956, when the American commitment to this Charter effort to limit the   3 discretion of states to the extent possible was still strong, the US government surprised its allies and adversaries by opposing the Suez war of Britain, France and Israel because it was a nondefensive use of force against Egypt, despite the provocations associated at the time with Nasser's anti-Israeli, anti-Western militancy. This legal commitment had evolved by stages in the period after World War I, and when the surviving leaders of Germany and Japan were prosecuted for war crimes, "crimes against the peace" were declared to be even worse than atrocities committed in the course of the war. The task of the Charter was to give this concept as clear limits as possible.

Pre-emption, in contrast, validates striking first—not in a crisis, as was done   4 by Israel with plausible, if not entirely convincing, justification in the 1967 war, when enemy Arab troops were massing on its borders after dismissing the UN war-preventing presence, but on the basis of shadowy intentions, alleged potential links to terrorist groups, supposed plans and projects to acquire weapons of mass destruction, and anticipations of possible future dangers. It is a doctrine without limits, without accountability to the UN or international law, without any dependence on a collective judgment of responsible governments and, what is worse, without any convincing demonstration of practical necessity.

It is true that the reality of the mega-terrorist challenge requires some rethink-   5 ing of the relevance of rules and restraints based on conflict in a world of territorial states. The most radical aspects of the Al Qaeda challenge are a result of its non-territorial, concealed organizational reality as a multistate network. Modern geopolitics was framed to cope with conflict, and relations among sovereign states; the capacity of a network with modest resources to attack and wage a devastating type of war against the most powerful state does require acknowledgment that postmodern geopolitics needs a different structure of security.

Postmodernity refers here to preoccupations that can no longer be reduced to   6 territorial dimensions. This contrasts with "modernity," born internationally in 1648 at the Peace of Westphalia with the emergence of the secular sovereign state, and a world politics that could be understood by reference to territorial ambitions and defense. For Osama bin Laden, the focus has been on nonterritorial empowerment via mega-terrorism, with the vision of an Islamic umma replacing the modern, Western-inspired structure of distinct sovereign states. For George W. Bush, the emphasis has been on carrying the retaliatory war to the networked enemy concealed in some sixty countries, and on declaring war against all those nonstate forces around the world.

7   To respond to the threat of mega-terrorism does require some stretching of international law to accommodate the reasonable security needs of sovereign states. Prior cross-border military reactions to transnational terrorism over the years by the United States, India, Israel and others were generally tolerated by the UN and international public opinion because they seemed proportionate and necessary in relation to the threats posed, and the use of force relied upon was in its essence reactive, not anticipatory. International law was bent to serve these practical imperatives of security, but not broken. But the Bush doctrine of pre-emption goes much further, encroaching on highly dangerous terrain. It claims a right to abandon rules of restraint and of law patiently developed over the course of centuries, rules governing the use of force in relation to territorial states, not networks.

8   To propose abandoning the core legal restraint on international force in relations among states is to misread the challenge of September 11. It permits states to use force nondefensively against their enemies, thereby creating a terrible precedent. There is every reason to think that containment and deterrence remain effective ways to approach a state that threatens unwarranted expansion. There is no evidence to suggest that Iraq cannot be deterred, and its pattern of behavior in relation to its war against Iran in the 1980s, as well as its conquest and annexation of Kuwait in 1990, were based on a rational calculation of gains that, when proved incorrect, led to a reversal of policy. Brutal and oppressive as the regime in Iraq is, it was accepted until 1990 as a geopolitical ally of sorts. As a state, it acts and behaves normally, that is, by weighing benefits and costs. It is surrounded and threatened by superior force, and any attempt to lash out at neighbors or others would almost certainly result in its immediate and total destruction. There is no reason whatsoever to think that deterrence and containment would not succeed, even should Baghdad manage to acquire biological, chemical or nuclear weapons. Deterrence and containment succeeded in relation to the Soviet Union for more than four decades, under far more demanding circumstances.

9   What is at stake with pre-emption, as tied to the "axis of evil" imagery, is more hidden and sinister. What is feared in Washington, I think, is not aggressive moves by these countries but their acquisition of weapons of mass destruction that might give them a deterrent capability with respect to the United States and other nations. Since the end of the cold war the United States has enjoyed the luxury of being undeterred in world politics. It is this circumstance that makes Bush's "unilateralism" particularly disturbing to other countries, and it must be understood in relation to the moves of the Pentagon, contained in a report leaked last December, to increase US reliance on nuclear weapons {a variety of strategic circumstances}. At West Point, Bush declared with moral fervor that "our enemies . . . have been

caught seeking these terrible weapons." It never occurs to our leaders that these weapons are no less terrible when in the hands of the United States, especially when their use is explicitly contemplated as a sensible policy option. There is every reason for others to fear that when the United States is undeterred it will again become subject to "the Hiroshima temptation," in which it might threaten and use such weapons in the absence of any prospect of retaliation.

Bush goes further, combining empire with utopia, reminding his West Point audience that "the twentieth century ended with a single surviving model of human progress based on nonnegotiable demands of human dignity, the rule of law, limits on the power of the state, respect for women and private property, and free speech and equal justice and religious tolerance." The clear intention is to suggest that America is the embodiment of this model. And while Bush does concede that "America cannot impose this vision," he does propose that it "can support and reward governments that make the right choices for their own people," and presumably punish those that don't. Not only does the United States claim the right to global dominance but it also professes to have the final answers for societal well-being, seeming to forget its homeless, its crowded and expanding prisons, its urban blight and countless other domestic reminders that ours may not be the best of all possible worlds, and especially not for all possible peoples. 10

This vision of postmodern geopolitics is underwritten by a now-familiar strong message of evangelical moralism. Bush notes that "some worry that it is somehow undiplomatic or impolite to speak the language of right and wrong. I disagree," and adds that "moral truth is the same in every culture, in every time, and in every place." Such moral absolutism is then applied to the current global realities. Bush insists that "we are in a conflict between good and evil, and America will call evil by its name. By confronting evil and lawless regimes, we do not create a problem, we reveal a problem. And we will lead the world in opposing it." Aside from occupying the moral high ground, which exempts America from self-criticism or from addressing the grievances others have with respect to our policies, such sentiments imply a repudiation of dialogue and negotiation. As there can be no acceptable compromise with the forces of evil, there can be no reasonable restraint on the forces of good. We may lament fundamentalism in the Islamic world and decry the fulminations of Osama bin Laden, but what about our own? 11

In contemplating this geopolitical vision for the future, one wonders what happened to candidate Bush's rhetoric about the importance of "humility" in defining America's role in the world. Of course, he was then trying to downsize the humanitarian diplomacy attributed (mostly wrongly) to Clinton/Gore, but the contrast in tone and substance is still striking. One wonders whether the heady atmosphere of the Oval Office has fed these geopolitical dreams, or whether our President, well-known for his lack of foreign policy knowledge, has been manipulated into a crusading mode by bureaucratic hawks who seized the opportunity so tragically provided by September 11. 12

Many influential Americans share this dream of a borderless global empire but adopt less forthright language. For instance, the respected military commentator Eliot Cohen, writing in a recent issue of *Foreign Affairs*, suggests that "in the 13 twenty-first century, characterized like the European Middle Ages by a universal (if problematic) high culture with a universal language, the U.S. military plays an extraordinary and inimitable role. It has become, whether Americans or others like it or not, the ultimate guarantor of international order." To make such an assertion without apology or justification is to say, in effect, that the imperial role of the United States is no longer in doubt, or even subject to useful debate. To acknowledge that it makes no difference whether Americans or others support this destiny is to reveal the fallen condition of democracy and the irrelevance of international public opinion. Along similar lines of presupposition, Stephen Biddle, in the same issue of *Foreign Affairs*, observes in relation to the problems of the Balkans, and specifically Kosovo, that "Americans do well in crusades," but then he cites Cohen and Andrew Bacevich to the effect that "they are not suited . . . to the dirty work of imperial policing to secure second- or third-tier interest." Such an outlook makes the fact of an American global empire a foregone conclusion.

14   But pre-emption and double standards were not the only troubling features of this postmodern geopolitical outlook outlined in the West Point speech. There is first of all the issue of global dominance, a project to transform the world order from its current assemblage of sovereign states in the direction of a postmodern (that is, nonterritorial) global empire administered from Washington. Bush misleadingly assured the graduating cadets that "America has no empire to extend or utopia to establish," and then went on to describe precisely such undertakings. The President mentioned that past rivalries among states arose because of their efforts to compete with one another, but insisted that the future will be different because of American military superiority: "America has, and intends to keep, military strengths beyond challenge, thereby making the destabilizing arms races of other eras pointless, and limiting rivalries to trade and other pursuits of peace." The ambition here is breathtaking and imperial—nothing less than to remind all states that the era of self-help security is essentially over, that America is the global gendarme, and that other states should devote their energies to economic and peaceful pursuits, leaving overall security in Washington's hands. One can only wonder at the reaction of foreign ministries around the world, say in Paris or Beijing, when confronted by this language, which dramatically diminishes traditional sovereign rights, as well as by the reinforcing moves to scrap the ABM treaty, to build a missile defense shield and to plan for the weaponization of space.

15   Whether it is Bush at West Point, or the more sedate writings of the foreign policy elite writing for each other, or for that matter intelligent and progressive criticism, useful analysis must proceed from the postmodern realization that we are addressing a menacing nonstate adversary concealed in a network that is simultaneously everywhere and nowhere. These new circumstances definitely call for new thinking that adapts international law and global security in an effective and constructive manner. But the adjustments called for by Bush do not meet the specific challenge of mega-terrorism, and they unleash a variety of dangerous forces. What is needed is new thinking that sees the United States as part of a global community that is seeking appropriate ways to restore security and confidence, but builds on existing frameworks of legal restraints and works toward a more robust UN, while

not claiming for itself an imperial role to make up the rules of world politics as it goes along. Given the bipartisan gridlock that has gripped the country since September 11, positive forms of new thinking will almost certainly come, if they come, from pressures exerted by the citizenry outside the Beltway. We as citizens have never faced a more urgent duty.

Our "Next Manifest Destiny"

John J. Miller

At the end of the previous article, Richard Falk noted the Bush administration's desire "to build a missile defense shield and to plan for the weaponization of space" (p. 516). In this article, which appeared in the conservative magazine National Review, *John J. Miller presents the conservative argument in favor of military control of space—in Miller's words, "to use space for projecting American power around the globe." John J. Miller is the national political reporter for* National Review *magazine and the author of* The Unmaking of Americans: How Multiculturalism Has Undermined the Assimilation Ethic *(The Free Press, 1998).*

1   On the morning of September 13, 1985, Air Force Major Doug Pearson smashed through the sound barrier in his F-15. Pointed almost directly upward more than seven miles above the Pacific Ocean, he tapped a little red button on the side of his control stick, and released a missile strapped to the belly of his plane. The missile blazed out of sight, leaving the earth's atmosphere quickly and reaching a speed of 13,000 miles per second. Pearson wondered if it would hit anything.

2   The mission was classified, so Pearson had developed a code with the folks back at Edwards Air Force Base: The radioman would tell him to level off at a certain altitude if his missile struck its target, an obsolete scientific probe orbiting 345 miles over Hawaii. As it happened, the code wasn't necessary. When Pearson checked in a few minutes after firing, he could hear cheering in the background from the control room.

3   It was the one time an American pilot had ever destroyed an object in outer space. People still talk about Pearson as the country's first "space ace." He remains its only space ace. A few weeks after the satellite was destroyed, Congress banned further tests. "We had hoped to conduct more," recalls Pearson, now a general. "But politics were what they were, and the nation decided to go another way."

4   Space is the next great frontier of military innovation, but for 17 years the nation has gone another way. It has squandered a remarkable opportunity that may not be available much longer. Rather than move rapidly to build on the success of Pearson and many others involved in the military use of space, the United States has refused to develop technologies that will be essential to national security in the

21st century, from anti-satellite (ASAT) missiles like Pearson's to space-based lasers that can destroy ICBMs right after they've left their launch pads.

5 Democrats ridiculed Ronald Reagan's Strategic Defense Initiative as "Star Wars," and not much has changed: Rep. Dennis Kucinich, Democrat of Ohio, recently introduced the Space Preservation Act of 2002, which would ban weapons from space "for the benefit of all humankind." The language of his bill is so broad that it would effectively reinstate the now-defunct Anti-Ballistic Missile Treaty. It would also block construction of the limited missile-defense system now underway at Fort Greely in Alaska, as well as a sea-based system whose development the Pentagon says it may now accelerate.

6 That's because ABMs that intercept their targets above the atmosphere—all of them, basically—may reasonably be deemed weapons in space. (ICBMs are weapons in space, too, but they don't engage anything until their warheads dive back into the earth.) With the ABM Treaty at last finding its deserved place on the ash heap of history, however, we now have an unprecedented occasion to rethink U.S. military strategy in space. What the country needs is an aggressive commitment to achieving space control—a kind of Monroe Doctrine for the heavens, opening them to the peaceful purposes of commerce and science but closing them to anything that threatens American national security. The United States today is the undisputed leader in space technology, but the gap between our capabilities and those of potential adversaries won't remain so wide forever. The time for bold action is now.

OLD HAT, NEW HAT

7 The military space age arguably began during the Second World War, when 1,400 German V-2 rockets rained down on England. The V-2s did not do an enormous amount of physical damage, but they did terrify the public and highlight the revolutionary potential of space weapons. "The significance of this demonstration of German skill and ingenuity lies in the fact that it makes complete nonsense out of strategic frontiers, mountains, and river barriers," said CBS newsman Edward R. Murrow from London.

8 The Pentagon began to exploit the vast emptiness of space soon after. Military satellites have been in orbit for more than 40 years. In this sense, the militarization of space is old hat. Today, in fact, the armed services rely on space so much that they simply couldn't function as they currently do without access to it. Satellites facilitate communications, monitor enemy activity, and detect missile launches. Their surveillance capabilities are astounding: The KH-11 supposedly can spot objects six inches in size from hundreds of miles up. These functions were critical to the success of American campaigns against Iraq and Serbia in the 1990s, and they are essential to operations in Afghanistan.

9 Even seemingly mundane uses of space have military value. The Global Positioning System is well known to civilian navigators, but it was designed for military navigational purposes, such as helping cruise missiles locate their targets and special-ops units find their rally points. On June 6, 1944, General Eisenhower surely would have appreciated a weather forecast of the type we now routinely get from satellites via local TV and radio broadcasts. On September 11, 2001, it was

the space-enabled transmission of cell-phone signals and instant news that helped Todd Beamer and the other passengers of United Flight 93 prevent an already catastrophic day from turning even worse.

These are all examples of "force enhancement," to use Pentagon parlance. By generating and channeling information, space-based assets help earthbound soldiers, sailors, and pilots improve their performance. Yet the United States will also need tools of "force application"—weapons that act against adversaries directly in and from space, for both offensive and defensive purposes. What our country requires, in short, is the weaponization outer space. 10

This already would have occurred in at least limited form, but for the mulish opposition of arms-control liberals. Reagan's SDI routinely struggled for funding in the 1980s and early 1990s, and then went on life support during the Clinton administration. The budget for ground-based ABMs was slashed by nearly 80 percent in Clinton's first year—defense contractors even had their system-development bids returned to them unopened. The Brilliant Pebbles program, an outgrowth of SDI that would have placed a swarm of maneuverable interceptors in orbit, was eliminated completely. "These actions effectively destroyed the nation's space-based missile-defense options for the following decade," says Henry Cooper, who ran the Strategic Defense Initiative Organization at the Pentagon during the first Bush administration. 11

The budgets of other programs, such as the ASAT technology tested by Pearson in 1985, were essentially trimmed to death. In 1990, Democrats in Congress forbade ASAT laser testing (the Republican majority let the ban lapse in 1995). The Army worked on ground-based ASAT missiles through the 1990s, and by 1997 its tests were starting to show real promise. The next year, however, Clinton had a test of his own to run—the line-item veto, since ruled unconstitutional by the Supreme Court—and he used it against the Army program, "We could have had something online," says Steven Lambakis of the National Institute for Public Policy. "Now we'd be forced to cobble together an emergency response if we really needed to knock out a satellite." 12

The United States soon will have at least a residual ASAT capability—any national missile-defense system that can shoot down ICBMs also can obliterate satellites. What we don't have, however, is a growing architecture of space-based weapons along the lines of what Reagan began to describe in his visionary SDI speech in 1983. This May, Senate Democrats passed big cuts to ground-based missile defense, which is humdrum compared with space-based lasers and the like—and the White House has not yet beaten back even this challenge. 13

UP IN THE BLUE

The wrangling over weapons and budgets stems from a fundamental confusion over what space is and how we should use it. From the standpoint of physics, space begins about 60 miles above sea level, which is roughly the minimum height a satellite must attain to achieve orbit. In this sense, space is just another medium, much like land, water, and air, with its own special rules of operation. For military purposes, however, space is more: It's the ultimate high ground, a flank from above 14 whose importance, for those able to gain access to it, may represent the critical difference in future conflicts.

15   For arms-control fanatics, however, space is a kind of sanctuary, and putting weapons in it poses an unconscionable threat. U.N. secretary general Kofi Annan has called for ensuring "that outer space remains weapons-free." Theresa Hitchens of the Center for Defense Information warns of threats to "global stability" and "the potential for starting a damaging and destabilizing space race." With space, there's always the sense that weapons violate some pristine nature. This is clearly one of the sentiments behind the Kucinich bill. Yet it is exactly wrong—there should be weapons way up there because then there will be fewer of them right down here.

16   Space power is now in its infancy, just as air power was when the First World War erupted in 1914. Back then, military planes initially were used to observe enemy positions. There was an informal camaraderie among pilots; Germans and French would even wave when they flew by each other. Yet it wasn't long before the reality of war took hold and they began shooting. The skies were not to be a safe haven.

17   The lesson for space is that some country inevitably will move to seize control of it, no matter how much money the United States sinks into feel-good projects like the International Space Station. Americans have been caught napping before, as when the Soviet Union shocked the world with Sputnik in 1957. In truth, the United States could have beaten the Soviets to space but for a deliberate slow-down strategy that was meant to foster sunny relations with the world's other superpower.

18   The United States is the world's frontrunner in space, with about 110 military satellites in operation, compared with about 40 for Russia and 20 for the rest of the world. Yet a leadership role in space is not the same as dominance, and the United States today lacks the ability to defend its assets against rudimentary ASAT technology or to deny other countries their own weapons in space. No country appears to be particularly close to putting weapons in orbit, though the Chinese are expected to launch their first astronaut in the next year or two and they're working hard to upgrade their military space capabilities. "It would be a mistake to underestimate the rapidity with which other states are beginning to use space-based systems to enhance their security," says the just-released annual report of the Stockholm International Peace Research Institute. At a U.N. disarmament conference two years ago, Chinese officials called for a treaty to keep weapons out of space—a possible sign that what they really want is some time to play catch-up.

19   The private sector also requires a secure space environment. When the Galaxy IV satellite failed in 1998, paging services shut down, affecting an estimated 44 million customers. Banks and credit-card companies also were affected, along with a few television and radio stations. Saddam Hussein may lack the rocket power to lob a nuclear warhead halfway around the world, but he could mount one on top of a Scud and fire it straight upward. A nuclear explosion in low orbit could disable scores of satellites and wreak havoc on modem economies everywhere—an example of space-age terrorism.

20   Plenty of people inside the government already recognize how much the United States relies on space. There's a U.S. Space Command headquartered in Colorado Springs, and each branch of the military is to some extent involved in space power. In 1999, secretary of defense William Cohen called space power "as important to

the nation as land, sea, and air power." His successor, Donald Rumsfeld, chaired a commission on space and national security right before joining the Bush administration. The panel's report, issued last year, warned of a "Space Pearl Harbor" if the country doesn't develop "new military capabilities."

While Cohen's rhetoric was fine, his boss, Bill Clinton, didn't seem to agree with it. Rumsfeld is friendly to the notion of space power, but President Bush so far hasn't talked much about it. When Bush gave his missile-defense speech at the National Defense University a year ago, he spoke of land-, sea-, and air-based defenses—but made no mention of space. "A lot of us noticed that," says one Air Force officer.   21

The Rumsfeld commission also emphasized defense: how to protect American satellites from foreign enemies. It had almost nothing to say about offense: how to use space for projecting American power around the globe. The commission was a creature of consensus, so this does not necessarily represent Rumsfeld's own thinking. And defense certainly is important. Military satellites are tempting targets because they're so crucial to the United States in so many ways. They are protected by their remoteness, but not much else. Their frail bodies and predictable flight paths are a skeet shoot compared with hitting speedy ICBMs, an ability that the United States is just starting to master. They're also vulnerable to jamming and hacking. Hardening their exteriors, providing them with some maneuverability, and having launch-on-demand replacements available are all key ingredients to national security. Yet defense doesn't win wars. In the future, the mere act of protecting these assets won't be enough to preserve American military superiority in space.   22

ASTRO POLITICS

In addition to an assortment of high-tech hardware, the United States could use an Alfred Thayer Mahan for the 21st century. In 1890, Mahan was a captain in the Navy when the first edition of his book *The Influence of Sea Power on World History* was published. Today it ranks among the classic texts of military theory. Mahan argued that nations achieve greatness only if they dominate the seas and their various geographic "pressure points," holding up the example of the British Royal Navy. One of Mahan's early readers was a young man named Theodore Roosevelt, who began to apply these ideas while working in the Department of the Navy during the 1890s, and later as president. Mahanian principles shook the country loose from its traditional strategy of coastal defense and underwrote a period of national dynamism, which included the annexation of Hawaii, victory in the Spanish-American War, and the construction of the Panama Canal.   23

No writer has clearly become the Mahan of space, though one candidate is Everett C. Dolman, a professor at the Air Force's School of Advanced Airpower Studies, in Alabama. Dolman's new book *Astropolitik* offers a grand strategy that would have the United States "endeavor at once to seize military control of low-Earth orbit" and impose "a police blockade of all current spaceports, monitoring and controlling all traffic both in and out." Dolman identifies low-Earth orbit as a chokepoint in the sense of Mahan—anybody who wants access to space must pass through it. "The United States should grab this vital territory now, when there's no real competition for it," Dolman tells me. "Once we're there, we can make sure the   24 entry cost for anybody else wanting to achieve space control is too high. Whoever takes space will dominate Earth."

25   Dolman would benefit from a political benefactor. Mahan enjoyed the patronage of Roosevelt, who took a scholar's ideas and turned them into policies. Space has a number of advocates within the military bureaucracy, mostly among its younger members. It does not have a political champion, with the possible exception of Sen. Bob Smith, a New Hampshire Republican who has made the subject a personal passion. Smith calls space America's "next Manifest Destiny" and believes the Department of Defense should establish an independent Space Force to serve alongside the Army, Navy, and Air Force. Smith, however, may not stay in the Senate much longer, facing stiff political challenges at home.

26   With the right mix of intellectual firepower and political muscle, the United States could achieve what Dolman calls "hegemonic control" of space. The goal would be to make the heavens safe for capitalism and science while also protecting the national security of the United States. "Only those spacecraft that provide advance notice of their mission and flight plan would be permitted in space," writes Dolman. Anything else would be shot down.

27   That may sound like 21st-century imperialism, which, in essence, it would be. But is that so bad? Imagine that the United States currently maintained a battery of space-based lasers. India and Pakistan could inch toward nuclear war over Kashmir, only to be told that any attempt by either side to launch a missile would result in a boost-phase blast from outer space. Without taking sides, the United States would immediately defuse a tense situation and keep the skies above Bombay and Karachi free of mushroom clouds. Moreover, Israel would receive protection from Iran and Iraq, Taiwan from China, and Japan and South Korea from the mad dictator north of the DMZ. The United States would be covered as well, able not merely to deter aggression, but also to defend against it.

28   National security always has been an expensive proposition, and there is no getting around the enormous costs posed by a robust system of space-based weaponry. It would take a supreme act of national will to make it a reality. We've done it before: Winning the Cold War required laying out trillions of dollars, much of it on machines, missiles, and warheads that never saw live combat. Seizing control of space also would cost trillions, but it would lead to a world made immeasurably safer for America and what it values.

Weapons in the Heavens: A Radical and Reckless Option

Michael Krepon

Michael Krepon is the author of several books on space and national military policy: Space Assurance or Space Dominance? The Case Against Weaponizing Space, *with Christopher Cleary (2004) and* Cooperative Threat Reduction, Missile Defense, and the Nuclear Future *(2003). He is president emeritus of the Henry L. Stimson Center, "a nonprofit, nonpartisan institution devoted to enhancing international peace and security" (from www.stimson.org). This researched policy proposal was posted on the Arms Control Association Web site in November 2004 along with other articles on weapons in space. The Arms Control Association is an advocacy organization seeking "support for effective arms control policies" through education, analysis, media programs, and regular publications.*

1   Of all the risky "transformation" initiatives championed by Secretary of Defense Donald Rumsfeld, the one receiving the least media attention is the weaponization of space. Shortly before arriving for his second tour at the Pentagon, Rumsfeld chaired a commission calling for the U.S. government to vigorously pursue "the option to deploy weapons in space to deter threats and, if necessary, defend against attacks on U.S. interests."[1]

2   The Air Force is now actively implementing Rumsfeld's wishes. As General Lance Lord, commander of U.S. Air Force Space Command, explained, "We must establish and maintain space superiority. Modern warfare demands it. Our nation expects it. Simply put, it's the American way of fighting."[2]

3   Rumsfeld's transformation in U.S. military space policy is driven by worst-case assumptions that the weaponization of space is inevitable; that conflict follows commerce in space, as on the ground; and that the United States must not wait to suffer a "Space Pearl Harbor."[3] Yet, the countries most capable of developing such weapons, such as Russia and China, have professed strong interest in avoiding the weaponization of space. The Bush administration has refused negotiations on this subject.

4   If Rumsfeld's plans to weaponize space are carried to fruition, America's armed forces, economy, and diplomacy will face far greater burdens, while controls over proliferation would be weakened further. Although everybody loses if the heavens become a shooting gallery, no nation loses more than the United States, which is the primary beneficiary of satellites for military and commercial purposes.

5   If the United States leads the way in flight-testing and deploying new anti-satellite (ASAT) weapons, other states will surely follow suit because they have too much to lose by allowing the Pentagon sole rights to space warfare. U.S. programs will cost more and be far more sophisticated than the ASAT weapons of potential adversaries, who will opt to kill satellites cheaply and crudely. The resulting competition would endanger U.S. troops that depend on satellites to an unprecedented degree for battlefield intelligence, communication, and targeting to win quickly and with a minimum of casualties.

6   Space warfare would have far-reaching adverse effects for global commerce, especially commercial transactions and telecommunication services that use satellites. Worldwide space industry revenues now total almost $110 billion a year, $40 billion of which go to U.S. companies.[4] These numbers do not begin to illuminate how much disruption would occur in the event of space warfare. For a glimpse of what could transpire, the failure of a Galaxy IV satellite in May 1998 is instructive. Eighty-nine percent of all U.S. pagers used by 45 million customers became inoperative, and direct broadcast transmissions, financial transactions, and gas station pumps were also affected.[5]

7   Weaponizing space would poison relations with China and Russia, whose help is essential to stop and reverse proliferation. ASAT weapon tests and deployments would surely reinforce Russia's hair-trigger nuclear posture, and China would likely feel compelled to alter its relaxed nuclear posture, which would then have negative repercussions on India and Pakistan. The Bush administration's plans would also further alienate America's friends and allies, which, with the possible exception of Israel, strongly oppose the weaponization of space. The fabric of international controls over weapons of mass destruction, which is being severely challenged by Iran's and North Korea's nuclear ambitions, could rip apart if the Bush administration's interest in testing space and nuclear weapons is realized.

8   This highly destabilizing and dangerous scenario can be avoided, as there is no pressing need to weaponize space and many compelling reasons to avoid doing so. If space becomes another realm for the flight-testing and deployment of weapons, there will be no sanctuary in space and no assurance that essential satellites will be available when needed for military missions and global commerce. Acting on worst-case assumptions often can increase this likelihood. Crafting a space assurance[6] posture, including a hedging strategy in the event that others cheat, offers more potential benefits and lower risks than turning the heavens into a shooting gallery.

CHARTING A DANGEROUS COURSE

9   During the Cold War, no weapons were deployed in space, and the last test of an ASAT weapon occurred almost two decades ago, in 1985. This record of restraint reflects international norms and widespread public sentiment to keep space free of weapons. The 1967 Outer Space Treaty calls on the exploration and use of outer space to be conducted "for the benefit and in the interests of all countries" and mandates that space may not be subject to "national appropriation" by any means. Why, then, would space warriors now seek to chart a different and far more dangerous course? If the weaponization of space were inevitable, it would have occurred decades ago when Washington and Moscow competed intensively in other domains. Indeed, the record of restraint since the Cold War ended suggests that the Outer Space Treaty's injunctions against placing weapons of mass destruction in space could be broadened if they are championed by the United States, China, and Russia.

10   The prediction that warfare follows commerce and that the burgeoning of space-aided commerce will produce hostilities is also suspect.[7] To the contrary, most of the world's strife takes place in poor regions. Space-aided commerce occurs primarily between nations with advanced commercial sectors, which generally have peaceful relations. Moreover, commercial space activities are often collaborative undertakings where risks and costs are shared. No nation that has invested heavily in space-aided commerce stands to gain if these orbital planes are endangered by space weapons debris or space mines. Any country that flight-tests, deploys, or uses space weapons threatens the activities of all other space-faring nations.

11   A third argument for weaponizing space rests on the unparalleled position that the United States now enjoys in terrestrial warfare. Consequently, the Rumsfeld

Commission and space warriors argue that weaker nations will carry out surprise attacks in space to neutralize U.S. nuclear war-fighting advantages. The best way to secure U.S. interests, the proponents say, is to transition from superiority to dominance.

Worries about a surprise attack in space cannot be written off, but there are far   12
easier, less traceable, and more painful ways for America's enemies to engage in asymmetric warfare than by attacking U.S. satellites. Weapons in space and weapons on Earth specifically designed to neutralize or destroy objects in space are being pursued for another reason as well: to help U.S. armed forces win quickly and with a minimum of casualties. This rationale only makes sense if America's adversaries will refrain from fighting back in space. If they return fire, however, U.S. troops are likely to be punished rather than helped because of their greater reliance on satellites.

Similarly, the clear preference of U.S. space warriors is to use nondestructive   13
techniques that disorient, dazzle, or disable an adversary's satellites without producing debris that could destroy the space shuttle, the international space station, and satellites. America's weaker foes, however, have far less incentive to be so fastidious about debris in their approach to space warfare.[8] States possessing nuclear weapons and ballistic missiles could explode a nuclear weapon in space to wreak havoc on satellites.

HAIR TRIGGER IN THE HEAVENS

To prevent adversaries from shooting back, the United States would need to   14
know exactly where all threatening space objects are located, to neutralize them without producing debris that can damage U.S. or allied space objects, and to target and defeat all ground-based military activities that could join the fight in space. In other words, successful space warfare mandates pre-emptive strikes and a preventive war in space as well as on the ground. War plans and execution often go awry here on Earth. It takes enormous hubris to believe that space warfare would be any different. If ASAT and space-based, ground-attack weapons are flight-tested and deployed, space warriors will have succeeded in the dubious achievement of replicating the hair-trigger nuclear postures that plagued humankind during the Cold War. Armageddon nuclear postures continue to this day, with thousands of U.S. and Russian nuclear weapons ready to be launched in minutes to incinerate opposing forces, command and control nodes, and other targets, some of which happen to be located within large metropolitan areas. If the heavens were weaponized, these nuclear postures would be reinforced and elevated into space.

U.S. space warriors now have a doctrine and plans for counterspace operations,   15
but they do not have a credible plan to stop inadvertent or uncontrolled escalation once the shooting starts. Like U.S. war-fighting scenarios, there is a huge chasm between plans and consequences, in which requirements for escalation dominance make uncontrolled escalation far more likely. A pre-emptive strike in space on a nation that possesses nuclear weapons would invite the gravest possible consequences. Attacks on satellites that provide early warning and other critical military

support functions would most likely be viewed either as a surrogate or as a prelude to attacks on nuclear forces.

INTERNATIONAL CONSEQUENCES

16   Even if space weapons are not used, their flight-testing or presence overhead, capable of impairing a country's ability to see, hear, navigate, detect impending danger, and fight, would have profound implications for international relations. The medium of space is not country-specific. The placement of space weapons in low-Earth orbit will be of concern to any country over which the space weapon passes or could pass with orbital adjustments.

17   Washington policymakers do not talk often or publicly about space warfare, and China and Russia continue to seek improved ties to the United States. There is, however, considerable awareness in Moscow and Beijing about the Pentagon's plans and deep skepticism that the Pentagon's interest in space warfare is directed solely at states such as North Korea and Iran. Instead, the Air Force's new counterspace doctrine is widely viewed in the broader context of the Bush administration's endorsement of pre-emptive strikes and preventive wars, open-ended national missile defense deployments, and the integration of improved broad-area surveillance and conventional deep-strike capabilities alongside U.S. nuclear forces, which remain on high states of alert.

18   If U.S. counterspace programs proceed, Russia and China can be expected to forge closer ties, pursuing joint diplomatic initiatives to prevent the weaponization of space, alongside military research and development programs to counter U.S. military options. Instead of engaging in a Cold War-like nuclear arms race with Washington, Moscow and Beijing will compete asymmetrically, using less elaborate and expensive techniques, such as by trailing expensive U.S. space weapons and satellites with cheap space mines.[9]

A BETTER ALTERNATIVE: SPACE ASSURANCE

19   Instead of weaponizing space, a "space assurance" posture would offer a greater likelihood that essential U.S. satellites will be available when needed. Adopting a space assurance posture above all requires the avoidance of dangerous military activities in space, including flight tests that simulate attacks against satellites and the deployment of ASAT and space weapons. Space assurance has many other mutually reinforcing components. One basic element is to maintain superior U.S. conventional military capabilities. Potential adversaries must understand clearly that if they damage, or destroy U.S. satellites, they will not alter the outcome of battle. Rather, they will only suffer more casualties by impairing satellites that improve targeting and reduce collateral damage.

20   A second key element of space assurance is increased situational awareness in space so U.S. military leaders can quickly identify developments that could cause potential harm to satellites. This includes improved monitoring capabilities for objects in space, whether small satellites operated by foreign nations or space debris.

A corollary requirement to improved situational awareness is improved intelligence capabilities relating to the space programs of potential adversaries.

The more U.S. officials know or can find out about space-related activities of potential adversaries, the more they can strengthen deterrence against unwelcome surprises. Another way to strengthen deterrence would be to adopt a hedging strategy against the initiation by others of space warfare flight tests and deployments. One key aspect of a hedging strategy is already in place. In extremis, the United States could use long-range ballistic missiles and lasers designed for other missions to disable or kill satellites. These residual, or latent, space warfare capabilities, which are growing with the advent of missile defense interceptors, have long existed. Rather than leading inexorably to the flight-testing and deployment of weapons specifically designed for space warfare, they have served as an insurance policy while deterring unwelcome surprises. 21

Additional hedges can be taken in the form of research and development programs that stop short of flight-testing. Potential adversaries can be expected to be working on their own space warfare initiatives behind closed doors, as is now the case with the United States. Ongoing research and development programs would shorten the timelines of flight-testing new initiatives if potential adversaries do not emulate U.S. restraint. Not every research and development program is worthy of support, however, particularly kinetic-kill programs that generate space debris. 22

An essential element of space assurance is the strengthening of existing norms against the flight-testing and deployment of space weapons. Many norms for responsible space-faring nations already exist, including prohibiting the placement of weapons of mass destruction in space under the aforementioned Outer Space Treaty, helping astronauts in distress, registering space objects, accepting liability for damage caused by national endeavors in space, and acknowledging that the exploration and use of outer space should be carried out for the benefit of all countries and humankind. 23

The scope of existing norms needs to be expanded if space assurance is to be reinforced. Traditionally, the forum in which international norms are codified is the Conference on Disarmament (CD) in Geneva. This 65-nation body operates by consensus, however, and at best requires many years to reach agreement on treaty texts, which might then be stalled further in the process of ratification, as is now the case with the Comprehensive Test Ban Treaty. This reason is not sufficient to block or reject negotiations in the CD relating to the prevention of space weapons, but it does suggest the wisdom of reinforcing existing norms in quicker ways. 24

The development of a code of conduct establishing agreed "rules of the road" for responsible space-faring nations can expedite international efforts to prevent the weaponization of space. Many codes of conduct already exist in the form of bilateral or multilateral executive agreements. During the Cold War, the United States entered into executive agreements with the Soviet Union to prevent dangerous military practices at sea, on the ground, and in the air. The Bush administration champions codes of conduct to prevent ballistic missile proliferation and terrorism. A similar approach could reinforce space assurance. 25

26   The U.S.–Soviet Incidents at Sea (INCSEA) accord, signed in 1972, has served as a model for comparable agreements signed by more than 30 other sea-faring nations. The INCSEA agreement established important rules, including pledges to avoid collisions at sea, the use of blinding light to illuminate the bridges of passing ships, and interference in the "formations" of the other party. Washington and Moscow subsequently signed the Prevention of Dangerous Military Activities (PDMA) agreement in 1989. The PDMA agreement covers, among other dangerous military activities, "interfering with command and control networks in a manner that could cause harm to personnel or damage to equipment of the armed forces of the other Party." It establishes procedures to deal with boundary incursions and permits the designation of "special caution areas."

27   Space also deserves "rules of the road" to help prevent incidents and dangerous military activities. Such a code of conduct would include provisions against simulated attacks; the flight-testing and deployment of space weapons; dangerous maneuvers in space, except those for rescue, repair, and other peaceful purposes; and commercial interference, as well as requirements to mitigate space debris.[10]

28   The definitions of space warfare, the scope of agreed constraints, and the ability to monitor them have plagued every prior initiative in this field. They will also bedevil efforts to craft a code of conduct. Nonetheless, this effort is worth pursuing. The risks associated with pursuing a code of conduct for responsible space-faring nations are minimal compared to the risks of flight-testing and deploying space weapons.

29   The weaponization of space was avoided during the Cold War, even though both superpowers jockeyed for military advantage on virtually every other front. Space weaponry can also be avoided now, when the United States enjoys unparalleled agenda-setting powers. Existing norms against weaponizing space can be strengthened if Washington exercises restraint, adopts prudent hedges, and joins others in diplomatic efforts to pursue space assurance. The time is ripe to reinforce existing norms in space that have greatly benefited space-aided commerce, scientific exploration, and the U.S. armed forces.

Endnotes

1. "Report of the Commission to Assess United States National Security Space Management and Organization," January 11, 2000, p. xii (hereinafter Rumsfeld Commission report).
2. General Lance W. Lord, "Keynote Address to the National Space and Missile Materials Symposium," Seattle, June 22, 2004.
3. Rumsfeld Commission report, p. 100.

4. Office of Space Commercialization, U.S. Department of Commerce, "Trends in Space Commerce," June 2001.

5. Mike Mills, "Satellite Glitch Cuts Off Data Flow," *The Washington Post*, May 21, 1998.

6. The term "space assurance" was proposed by Douglas Necessary, who participated in a study group convened by the Henry L. Stimson Center to assess U.S. military space policy. For an elaboration of this concept, see Michael Krepon with Christopher Clary, *Space Assurance or Space Dominance? The Case Against Weaponizing Space* (Washington, DC: Henry L. Stimson Center, 2003).

7. See, for example, Rumsfeld Commission report and United States Space Command, "Vision for 2020," August 1997.

8. A recent Federation of American Scientists study, "Ensuring America's Space Security: Report of the FAS Panel on Weapons in Space," greatly underestimated the debris problem created by space warfare by focusing mainly on ballistic missile intercepts in low-Earth orbit that create the fewest problems relating to debris. For a more comprehensive and realistic view of the problem, see Theresa Hitchens, "Space Debris: Next Steps" (presentation, Geneva, March 24–25, 2004), found at http://www.cdi.org.

9. For more on the problem of space mines, see Richard L. Garwin, "Space Weapons: Not Yet" (paper presented at the Pugwash Workshop on Preserving the Non-Weaponization of Space, May 22–24, 2003), found at http://fas.org/RLG/030522-space.pdf.

10. With the help of others, the Henry L. Stimson Center's Space Security Project has drafted a model code of conduct for responsible space-faring nations. See "A Model Code of Conduct for the Prevention of Incidents and Dangerous Military Practices in Outer Space," found at http://www.stimson.org/wos/?SN=WS20040830709.

Keep Space for Peace

Global Network Against Weapons & Nuclear Power in Space

This advocacy poster, showing the monument to the atomic bombing of Hiroshima, Japan in August 1945, is available at www.space4peace.org, the Global Network Against Weapons & Nuclear Power. Seeking to stop a new arms race, this organization, along with The Secure World Foundation, is committed to opposing the plan of the United States Space Command to put weapons in space.

The Great American Myth

Samuel Huntington

Samuel Huntington is especially known for his influential book The Clash of Civilization and the Remaking of World Order *(1996). A political scientist at Harvard University, Huntington is a neoconservative and an outspoken critic of U.S. immigration policies. This piece, presenting Huntington's view of the United States as a global power, comes from his Grano lecture on the subject of the American Empire and was published in the Canadian news commentary magazine* Maclean's, *February 14, 2005.*

My central argument is the American empire doesn't exist. It's a myth. And the   1
fact that people believe in this myth has some not very good consequences. Because of the belief in this myth by both Americans and non-Americans, we are moving in the direction in which, if current trends continue, Iraq will only be the first in a series of incidents with disastrous consequences.

The usual definition of empire is the rule exercised by one nation or people over   2
other peoples. And quite clearly, the United States has not been much of an empire throughout its history. We did have colonies at one time in the Philippines and a few other places, but we didn't exercise direct rule over other people by and large.

More recent theorists and commentators have broadened the definition to in-   3
clude the ability to shape events in other societies in a significant way. One of the astonishing things in the past decade, however, has been the extent to which the concept of America having an empire has been adopted so enthusiastically by people who are labelled neo-conservatives. So we have this peculiar situation in which liberals find it hard to challenge the idea of an American empire because the neo-conservatives say, "We should go out and reform the world, promote democracy and human rights and reshape the world basically in the American image." And the liberals just don't know how to deal with that sort of a conservatism.

With the collapse of the Soviet Union and the end of the Cold War, the power of   4
the United States has declined momentously. Now, people say, "Well, you're the only superpower, and therefore you can do anything you want." But that's simply not the case, because you can only exercise authority and influence over other countries if you can get them to go along; if they need you in one way or another. Countries all over the world now no longer need the United States to provide their security as they did during the Cold War. The idea that the European Union would have evolved in the way in which it has during the past decade or so would have been unthinkable during the Cold War, when the United States was crucial to providing the security for Germany and France. They don't need us now—and control over them, as well as over many other countries, clearly has gone down dramatically.

It is useful to think of global power today in terms of four levels. First, there is   5
the United States, which is indeed the only superpower with overwhelming dominance in virtually every category of power, whether it's military, economic, technological, cultural, diplomatic or what have you.

6   There are, however, at level two, a significant number of major regional powers. These would include the European Union, meaning basically the German and France condominium in Europe; Russia; China; India; Brazil in Latin America; Israel in the Middle East; Iran in the Persian Gulf; Indonesia in Southeast Asia; and probably South Africa in Africa. And these are powers which don't have the same global sweep as the United States, but still like to think that they should exercise influence within their particular region of the world.

7   There are, thirdly, a large number of secondary regional powers. And some of them are clearly very important countries, but they have to orient their attitudes and thinking in terms of their relationship with the major regional powers. These would include the United Kingdom in Europe; Poland, Ukraine, Uzbekistan in the Russian sphere; Pakistan, obviously; Japan; Argentina; various other countries.

8   Then at the fourth level, there is everybody else, some of which are important for one reason or another, but don't quite play the same role in shaping global politics.

9   This four-level structure of global politics is basically a uni-multi-polar world. The United States cannot dictate what goes on all by itself. It needs the cooperation of some of these major regional powers to accomplish anything in world affairs. But, on the other hand, the United States, as the only superpower, is generally able to veto international actions proposed by any coalition of these other major actors.

10   In this new power structure, a natural antagonism exists between the super-power and the major regional powers. The United States thinks it has, and in large part it does have, a significant interest in every part of the world. Each of the major regional powers, however, thinks it should be able to shape what goes on in its part of the world and clearly resents U.S. efforts to do that.

11   There is, however, this third level of actors, what I've called the secondary regional powers. And what are their interests? Well, their basic interest, or at least one underlying basic interest, is not to be dominated by big brother next door, by the major power in their region. And hence, they share an interest in working with the United States against these major regional powers.

12   One can see the significance of these alignments if one looks at the attitudes that governments took towards the launching of the war in Iraq. All of the major regional powers with the notable exception, of course, of Israel, opposed it. Most of the secondary regional powers supported it and sent troops in varying degrees. The principal providers of troops to fight in the war included, of course, Britain, but also Poland and Ukraine, who sent relatively large numbers of troops.

13   Even in the current situation, the United States has not been very successful in achieving its major objectives such as preventing nuclear proliferation. Iran undoubtedly will have nuclear weapons at some point in the next three or four years. It is very natural for any country that considers itself the major power in its region to want nuclear weapons. That's the symbol of your power. Now, I don't think nuclear weapons are going to be used by a state in any war in the future, but it's still a symbol of power. When a major regional power like India gets nuclear weapons, that just encourages Pakistan to go ahead with what it was doing and demonstrate that it has nuclear weapons, too. So if a major regional power in

a region gets it, at least some secondary regional powers are going to want that capability also.

Also, the United States has not been successful in a significant way in the past 14 decade in promoting democratization around the world. It also wasn't successful in lining up meaningful support for the Iraq war, and then there is this much broader feeling of anti-Americanism throughout the world, that the United States is just too powerful and has to be cut down to size. I think that for the United States to export democracy or free markets to other countries is something to be avoided. We can certainly support the groups in those countries which want to move in that direction, but the idea that we're going to be able to impose our rather peculiar view of democracy and of economic liberalism on other countries seems to me to be a very dangerous fallacy.

These factors are at work here as we see efforts to change the structure of 15 global politics from what I have awkwardly called a uni-multi-polar world into a truly multi-polar world. That is the way in which inevitably the world is moving, and both the world and the United States will probably be much better off once we get there.

For Class Discussion

1. Based on the readings in this unit and on your own knowledge and perspectives, sketch out the core arguments for and against each of the following positions:
   - The doctrine of preemptive strikes in the war on terrorism
   - Establishing United States' military dominance of space
   - The policy of space assurance
   - Establishing a multi-polar world
   - Abiding by international law as determined by treaties and the United Nations

2. How would you describe the differences in underlying values, assumptions, and beliefs among Bush, Miller, Huntington, Falk, and Krepon?

3. Note the titles of the two articles about weaponizing space (pp. 517 and 522). What do the titles and their associations—the authors' choice of words with powerful emotional resonance—contribute to the authors' arguments?

4. What are the main differences between Bush's and Huntington's view of the United States' role in global politics?

5. Choose one of the readings in this unit and analyze it carefully using the List 2 Guide questions on pages 454–455.

OPTIONAL WRITING ASSIGNMENT   Using the knowledge and awareness of United States' foreign and military policies gained from the readings in this unit and any reading you have done on your own, write a policy proposal that expresses your citizen's perspective on some issue related to foreign policy, the war on terrorism, the development of the United States' space weapons program, or the United States' status as a superpower. Depending on your instructor's desires, you might write an op-ed piece for your college newspaper, a letter to a congressman, an advocacy poster or newspaper ad, or a researched white paper to be sent to a policymaker.

ENVIRONMENTAL FRIENDLINESS VERSUS MARKET FREEDOM: THE CASE OF THE SPORT-UTILITY VEHICLE

As consumers continue to face higher gas prices and as scientists and analysts become more vocal about the eventual end of the world's oil resources, public controversy continues over the sport-utility vehicle.

Sport-utility vehicles gained sales prominence when car manufacturers responded to the federal government's 1975 regulations on fuel economy—known as CAFE (Corporate Average Fuel Economy—currently set at an average of 20.7 mpg for trucks and 27.5 mpg for cars)—by welding SUV bodies onto truck frames and marketing SUVs as light trucks. With this category of vehicles, car manufacturers tapped into Americans' imagination and desire for space, physical security on the road, and options for an outdoor recreational lifestyle. With grand and mighty names like "Expedition," "Trailblazer," and "Denali," sport-utility vehicles have appeared in greater number on American roads, particularly urban streets, and have become a favorite choice for family vehicles.

The sport-utility vehicle, its owners, and its manufacturers, as well as the government, are now embroiled in multiple contentious issues. With concern growing about available foreign oil supplies, oil as a nonrenewable resource, and global warming, more people are questioning the sense of manufacturing and driving sport-utility vehicles. Why are these vehicles still popular? Environmentalists point to SUVs as gas guzzlers that contribute excessively to global warming, while political economists warn about our dependence on foreign oil. Some public voices are calling on the government to support car manufacturers' efforts to develop green cars, hybrids or hydrogen-fueled cars. Meanwhile, proponents of the automotive industry state that car manufacturers produce what consumers want and cite the cost of developing new technology. So, what should we do about SUVs and the problems they bring and symbolize?

The readings in this unit as well as the ad for the Saturn VUE in Color Plate G and the Chevy Blazer ad on page 451 explore diverse perspectives on sport-utility vehicles.

The American Dream: Why Environmentalists Attack the SUV

John Bragg

John Bragg is a policy analyst for the Center for the Moral Defense of Capitalism and a teacher of world history. This article was posted on May 31, 2001, on the online Capitalism Magazine, *a publication that takes a libertarian perspective, giving priority to individual choice.*

1   The SUV is under attack. Greens say they use too much gas, threaten air quality and contribute pell-mell to the desecration of the environment. So why would
anyone build these horrible engines of death? They build them because SUVs have
advantages in safety, cargo space and power that Americans demand.

2   The large cars from Detroit's heyday have been abolished by environmental regulations of the 1970s. In 1975, Federal fuel efficiency mandates forced car manufacturers to smaller and lighter designs until 1983, when Chrysler adapted the first
minivan. Unlike the once popular station wagon, the minivan fell under the lower
"light truck and van" fuel efficiency regulations, a loophole which allowed companies to build larger, heavier, safer vehicles without falling under the "gas-guzzler"
tax. The SUV, which became popular in the late 80s enjoyed a similar exemption.
The minivan and the SUV gave America the powerful, spacious vehicles that they
had demanded before the regulations—they were our reply to Washington's attempts to force everyone into smaller cars.

3   Yet today there is no symbol of consumption hated more than the SUV. There is
a history behind this hatred: The people attacking SUVs are the same people who
have spent the past thirty years attacking cars and hailing Al Gore's call ten years
ago to abolish the internal-combustion engine. SUVs are attacked because they are
today's foremost examples of what a car is.

4   The chief virtue of the automobile is the personal *independence* it gives the
owner—a car can go anywhere roads go and some places they don't, with a speed
unimaginable in the pre-automobile era. Its secondary virtue is protection—from
the elements and from collision. In both a car and an SUV, passengers are protected
by the vehicle's structure from the wind and rain. But in a collision, the SUV simply
provides more protection than a smaller car does. Larger cars better protect the
people in them—that's why your father wanted you to get a huge, boxy old car
when you were sixteen instead of a little Mustang—so that you would live through
your first accident. Protection is a big advantage.

5   So why then do the greens oppose safer cars? They oppose big cars for the
same reason that they oppose big houses, new highways, new power plants, or basically any wealth-creating or wealth-enjoying endeavor. Wealth means that someone has changed their environment and *improved* it for human use. Most people
want their environment arranged for their benefit—air-conditioned in summer,
heated in winter, ventilated, bug-free and clean. In fact, it is man's ability to adapt
his environment to his own desires that sets him apart from other animals and has
allowed him to prosper.

6   The environmentalists respond that nature is intrinsically valuable, not for anything it does or can do but simply because it is. Since people disturb nature, people
as such are a problem. Moderate environmentalists say that this is a straw man,
that they do not hate people, they just want to protect endangered species and have
clean air, water and food. Endangered species are valuable because, well, they are
endangered—nature put them there. Intrinsic value.

7   Clean air and water benefit people. But if the moderate environmentalists really
wanted people to benefit, then they would support the SUV. The SUV is an example of

people using the best technology available to enhance their lives. Environmentalists attack America's SUVs because Americans like them—Americans like technology and we like the power over our surroundings.

It's appropriate then that the car is the greatest modern symbol of American 8 freedom. If you don't agree, ask any teenager counting the days until his license. He won't need to ask for a ride to his job, to the mall, to school, to a friend's, to anywhere. Even if he has to ask for Mom's keys, he's driving himself—a step towards independence. If he buys his own car, he has his first piece of meaningful property—it has a price, it has economic utility, it has a limited lifespan, there are operating costs, and it must be used with respect for others or there will be consequences.

Cars are such a symbol of Americanism that the Soviets in the 1930s had to 9 cancel propaganda showings of John Steinbeck's "Grapes of Wrath" because Soviet audiences were furious to find that even destitute Americans had pickups to migrate in. Contrary to the environmentalists, cars are a powerful symbol of what makes America the greatest, and the freest, country in the world.

Gas and Gasbags . . . or, the Open Road and Its Enemies

Henry Payne and Diane Katz

This article appeared in the March 25, 2002, issue of the conservative news commentary magazine the National Review. *Henry Payne, an editorial cartoonist for the* Detroit News *and a freelance writer, and Diane Katz, director of science, environment, and technology policy at the Mackinac Center for Public Policy in Michigan, identify problems with raising CAFE standards and with alternative fuel sources such as hydrogen fuel cells.*

Any crisis in the Middle East inevitably prompts Washington to scapegoat the 1 automobile as a threat to national security. The dust had barely settled on lower Manhattan last fall before calls went forth—from pundits and pols across the spectrum—to relinquish our "gas-guzzlers" in the name of energy independence.

But just as the Cassandras will dominate media coverage of energy, so will 2 Middle Eastern oil continue to fuel America's vehicles for the foreseeable future. Simple economics, geography, and consumer choice all demand it.

Since Sept. 11, Washington has mobilized to end our "dangerous addiction" to 3 foreign energy sources. Sens. John Kerry and John McCain are proposing dramatic increases in federal fuel-economy standards. The energy package crafted by majority leader Tom Daschle advocates "biodiesels," and the Natural Resources Defense Council is insisting that we could cut gasoline consumption by 50 percent over ten years—if only the feds would mandate what and where we drove.

4   Even the "oil men" in the Bush administration have advocated doling out millions in research subsidies for hydrogen fuel cells that supposedly would replace the internal-combustion engine. The project, Energy Secretary Spencer Abraham announced in January, is "rooted in President Bush's call to reduce American reliance on foreign oil."

5   In fact, the price of oil has declined since Sept. 11, as it consistently has for decades, and with producers scattered all over the world, no single nation or region can stop the flow.

6   But supporters of a comprehensive energy policy seem undeterred by these realities. "Logic," Robert Samuelson writes in the *Washington Post,* "is no defense against instability. We need to make it harder for [Middle Easterners] to use the oil weapon and take steps to protect ourselves if it is used. Even if we avoid trouble now, the threat will remain."

7   Past efforts to attain a petroleum-free utopia, however, have largely failed. For example, despite three decades of federal fuel-economy standards, oil imports as a share of U.S. consumption have risen from 35 to 59 percent.

8   A market-based solution, such as a gas tax, is the most obvious approach to cutting consumption, but even environmentalists concede that proposing one would spell political suicide. Moreover, gas taxes are an expensive solution and come with no guarantee of energy independence. The European Union, for example, taxes gas up to $4 per gallon—and still imports over half its oil.

9   So instead of enraging consumers at the pump, Washington has largely relied on backdoor taxes.

10   The regulatory regime known as CAFE (Corporate Average Fuel Economy) was hatched in the wake of the oilprice shocks of the early 1970s, when sedans still made up most of the nation's fleet. Instead of the redesigned smaller, lighter, and less powerful vehicles, however, consumers flocked to minivans, small trucks, and sport utility vehicles, which are held to a lower CAFE standard (20.7 mpg versus the 27.5 mpg required for cars).

11   Today, both passenger cars and light trucks are more efficient than ever, having improved 114 percent and 56 percent, respectively, since 1974. But gasoline is so cheap, despite continuing Middle Eastern crises, that on average Americans are driving twice as many miles as in years past.

12   A recent study by H. Sterling Burnett of the National Center for Policy Analysis found that raising CAFE standards by 40 percent—as Kerry and others recommend—would not "reduce future U.S. dependence on foreign oil." CAFE's only function is to keep regulators busy calculating elaborate formulas for determining compliance in which manufacturers then look for loopholes. (CAFE requires that a manufacturer's trucks meet an average standard of 20.7 mpg. Thus DaimlerChrysler AG, for example, designates its popular PT Cruiser as a "truck" in order to offset the low mpg of its large SUVs, such as the Dodge Durango.)

13   Worse, stricter CAFE standards would surely undermine the very economic security that proponents vow to protect. The profits of U.S. automakers—and tens of thousands of UAW jobs—depend on sales of SUVs and light trucks. According to an analysis by Andrew N. Kleit, a professor at Pennsylvania State University, the Kerry

CAFE proposal would reduce the profits of General Motors by $3.8 billion, of Ford by $3.4 billion, and of DaimlerChrysler by $2 billion. Foreign manufacturers, which largely specialize in smaller vehicles, would see a profit increase of $4.4 billion.

Evidently hoping to shield automakers from a CAFE assault—and to win PR   14 points for expanded domestic drilling—the Bush administration has embraced the latest alternative-fuel fad: the hydrogen fuel cell.

The Bush plan replaces the Partnership for a New Generation of Vehicles, Al   15 Gore's vain attempt to produce an affordable, emissions-free family sedan capable of 80 mpg by 2004. Over eight years, Washington pumped more than $1.5 billion into the program—in addition to the $1.5 billion sunk into it by the Big Three. In its annual review of the project last August, the National Research Council judged the super-car goals to be inherently "unrealistic."

The Bush plan has drawn broad political support. Former Clinton chief of staff   16 John Podesta cheers, "The next step is hydrogen-powered fuel-cell vehicles. But the only way to get these vehicles out of the lab and onto the road is with incentives and requirements aimed at producing 100,000 vehicles by 2010, 2.5 million by 2020."

But the 100-year dominance of conventional internal-combustion engines over   17 alternatives is no accident. A quick primer on the complexities of hydrogen power helps explain why.

Hydrogen's status as the new darling of the sustainable-energy movement is   18 understandable. Its promise lies first in its performance: Unlike ethanol, it supplies more energy per pound than gasoline. When used to power an automobile, its only emission is water—making it especially attractive to an industry already under pressure from clean-air and global-warming rules. And hydrogen is one of the most plentiful elements on the planet.

The trouble is, hydrogen always comes married to another element—as in   19 methane gas or water.

Most fuel-cell technology today relies on hydrogen extracted from methane, in a   20 process that emits large quantities of greenhouse gases. And as *Car and Driver* magazine's technical analyst, Patrick Bedard, explains, domestic sources of methane are "[t]oo limited to serve any significant demand for automobiles." A study by the Argonne National Laboratory concluded that the U.S. would have to look to foreign sources—primarily in Russia and Iran, and in other Middle East nations.

Goodbye, oil dependence. Hello, methane dependence.   21

Given these hurdles, attention is turning instead to electrolysis—the extraction   22 of hydrogen from water, which is readily obtainable along America's ample coasts. Electrolysis is, however, the most energy-intensive process of any fuel alternative; studies differ on whether it would consume more carbon-based fuels than the use of hydrogen would save. What is certain, points out Stanford University professor John McCarthy, is that "the advantage of hydrogen, if you have to burn carbon fuels (coal, oil, or gas) to manufacture it, would be negligible."

In other words, McCarthy explains, the unspoken truth about hydrogen is that   23 "it is a synonym for nuclear power."

Leading researchers in the field—including David Scott of the University of   24 Victoria in Canada, Cesare Marchetti of the International Institute for Applied

Systems Analysis, and Jesse Ausubel of Rockefeller University—say that the only way to produce liquid hydrogen in the mass quantities needed for transportation is with a major investment in nuclear power. Says Scott: "[A]pplying the most elementary numeracy, nuclear fission is the only realistic option."

25   Ironically, many of the political voices now embracing hydrogen fuel are the same ones that have prevented the construction of a single new U.S. nuclear plant in 25 years. Ausubel has written in *The Industrial Physicist* magazine that "understanding how to use nuclear power, and its acceptance, will take a century or more."

26   For now, the answer is still gasoline. Compared with the technical barriers to developing alternative fuels, there already exist numerous market mechanisms to mitigate potential oil shortages. As suggested by Donald Losman, a National Defense University economist, these include: stockpiling, futures contracts, diversifying the supplier base, and relaxing the restrictions that currently mandate some 13 different fuel blends in 30 cities. Dramatic improvements in fuel efficiency also could be achieved if Washington allowed automakers to market diesel-powered vehicles. In Germany, for example, Volkswagen mass markets the 80-mpg Lupo, which is powered by a direct-injection diesel engine. But that's anathema to American greens who insist—without evidence—that diesel's particulate emissions are dangerous to public health.

27   All fuels require trade-offs, of course. But politically correct, misguided energy schemes will not make America more independent. Gasoline remains by far the best deal we have.

Gimme an SUV—ASAP: Teenagers Are the Next Big Market for Sport-Utility Vehicles—and the Consequences Could Be Deadly

Keith Bradsher

Keith Bradsher is the author of High and Mighty—SUVs: The World's Most Dangerous Vehicles and How They Got That Way *(2002). This article appeared in the September 28, 2002, edition of the* National Post.

1   Sitting at the wheel of her family's bright red Chevrolet Suburban sport-utility vehicle in a high school parking lot on a bright autumn afternoon in 1999, April reached over to the front passenger seat and grabbed a plastic tiara. Brandishing it out the window, she explained how she had just been chosen as one of five homecoming princesses at her high school in a wealthy Los Angeles suburb partly because of the popularity she enjoyed by driving the biggest vehicle of any student.

2   "I love big trucks because they just look cool and have big tires," she said. "Everybody knows me as the girl who drives the big red truck."

She never needed its four-wheel drive, but the vehicle's high ground clearance 3 had given her the confidence to take occasional shortcuts across medians and lawns. "I'll go behind the bushes and along the railroad tracks," she explained. "I drive it to school every day—I feel safe, I feel like I'm the queen of the road because I'm up high and can see everything for miles." April said she was 5-foot-6, but felt much taller in the SUV. Her father had jacked up the Suburban's suspension by six inches.

"Up here, I'm probably 6-foot-10," she said, staying in the driver's seat. "I love 4 it, it just makes me feel powerful—if someone disses me, I can tailgate the crap out of them."

But as she kept talking, April confessed that the size of her vehicle also fright- 5 ened her. Her voice fell somewhat and her initial bubbly enthusiasm ebbed as she began talking about her concerns of ending another person's life in a crash. These fears had grown ever since she had recently struck her neighbour's parked Chevrolet Astro van.

"I'm worried about if I might kill someone—I hit my neighbour's truck and 6 lifted it up, and I barely hit it," she said. "That's one of my biggest fears, I might kill someone."

It is an appropriate fear, and one that unfortunately seems to dissuade few par- 7 ents from allowing their children to drive SUVs. Of the students who drove their own vehicles to the high school that day in Whittier, Calif., at least a quarter seemed to be in sport utilities. By contrast, I couldn't help noticing there were no SUVs in the section of the parking lot reserved for the teachers, who probably earned less than many of their students' parents.

There are lines of sport-utility vehicles parked these days outside the affluent fra- 8 ternities and sororities at the University of Michigan and other big universities across the United States. High school parking lots are beginning to look the same way. Young people are the next big market for SUVs, especially used SUVs, with alarming consequences for traffic safety. With more than half of U.S. SUVs less than five years old, and with very few SUVs more than 12 years old, their drivers until now have tended to be their first owners—responsible, middle-aged people. Many of the initial owners have been married people who drive in the daytime and early evening, when crashes are less frequent per million miles travelled than late at night.

Automakers' difficulties in keeping up with demand for new SUVs have kept 9 the prices of used SUVs unusually high.

But the high prices for used models have also discouraged their purchase by 10 young people and by hard-core drunk drivers, who tend to buy the oldest, cheapest vehicles on the market.

There are still very few SUVs in the vast pool of older vehicles, but there will be 11 far more over the coming decades. Indeed, SUVs built now may be especially likely to stay on the roads for a long time, and to keep inflicting heavy damage on cars and rolling over at an alarming rate through those years, too. Detroit's SUVs fare better than its cars in reliability surveys by groups such as *Consumer Reports,* possibly because SUVs are of simple, heavy-duty construction and have had a lot of money and managerial attention devoted to them. Even an SUV that has been in a fatal collision, killing a car occupant and injuring its own occupants, can sometimes be in fairly good driving condition, requiring repairs only to the surface metal and passenger compartment, but not to the heavy steel underbody, according to police investigators of crashes. The only thing scarier than a drunk or teenager at the wheel of a shiny, new full-size SUV will be a drunk or teenager at the wheel of a 15-year-old full-size SUV with failing brakes. And the more than 20 million SUVs that have already been built with too little regard for stability and the safety of other road users will be roaming the roads for a very long time.

12   Automakers do not try to attract drunks to SUVs, but they do market SUVs to young people, both as a way to sell them new SUVs and as a way to keep demand strong and prices high for used SUVs. This is a bad idea, although the safety implications have not yet received much attention. The teenaged SUV driver incident that has drawn the most attention so far has not even involved a person as the victim, but a dog. On Jan. 2, 2002, U.S. President Bill Clinton's dog, Buddy, ran into the street in Chappaqua, N.Y., while chasing a contractor's truck and was struck and killed by a high school student driving an SUV. The police ruled the canine death an accident and did not bring charges. But the case highlighted that SUVs have begun to catch on among the segment of the population with the worst driving record.

13   This trend is ominous for three reasons. An unusually large proportion of the American population is in its teens and early 20s, and their ranks are growing daily for demographic reasons. Tastes in automobiles tend to form in the early teens and often last for life. Yet no age group is less suited to drive SUVs than people in their teens and early 20s.

14   Researchers for various automakers and their consulting firms have consistently found that today's young people love the feeling of power of SUVs, and are more likely than people in any other age bracket to prefer SUVs to cars. Indeed, influential market researchers such as Jim Bulin, the long-time Ford strategist, say affection for SUVs varies inversely with age.

15   Men and women who grew up in the Depression or the Second World War very seldom buy sport utilities. Baby Boomers are deeply split in their attitudes toward SUVs, with some preferring cars and minivans while others have embraced four-wheel drive vehicles. Drivers in their 20s and early 30s like SUVs but have had surprisingly little influence on the auto market because their numbers are limited and because they have not yet reached their peak earning years.

16   Teenagers and college students, though, love SUVs with an extraordinary unanimity. (Automakers conduct focus groups with teens as young as 13 with their parents' permission.)

17   According to GM, 90% of teens interviewed in 1999 said they preferred SUVs to any other class of vehicles. That is an alarming figure given that SUVs are still only about 17% of the market.

18   Automotive preferences seem to be a lot like tastes in music: They form early, often in rebellion against parents' tastes, and they last for life. Baby Boomers who came of age in the 1960s have never shaken their love of groups like the Beatles,

the Grateful Dead and Rolling Stones. Some of their younger brothers and sisters retain an incomprehensible love of disco music from the 1970s.

Similarly, men and women who lusted after big cars in the 1930s and 1940s are 19 still buying large cars today. People seem to form their strongest, most enduring attachments to music and to automobiles between the ages of 12 and 15, Ford officials say. The disheartening implication of all this is that people who have entered the auto market since the mid-1980s may go on buying SUVs for life.

Auto market researchers have taken notice of young people's interest in SUVs. 20 "It's surprising, the appeal in younger generations," said Ed Molchany, the Ford brand manager for Explorers. "All of our SUVs are very strong with Generation Y, it's a very popular brand and imagery."

Ford's youth strategy did not get started until late 1997. Through the early and 21 mid-1990s, the Ford factories in St. Louis and Louisville that assembled Explorers could not come close to meeting demand, so they mostly built bigger Explorers with four doors. The four-door models had larger profit margins than two-door models. Ford was building 430,000 Explorers a year, but only 30,000 to 50,000 a year had only two doors.

But the market for four-door, mid-sized sport-utility vehicles had changed by 22 the end of 1997. Chrysler had introduced the four-door Dodge Durango and Mercedes had come out with its four-door M-Class, partly relieving the shortage that had kept Explorer factories working around the clock. A flood of foreign sport-utility vehicles was coming on the market, both truck-based and car-based. Ford itself had introduced the larger Ford Expedition in 1996, and many well-heeled families began choosing Expeditions instead of Explorers.

So Ford introduced a "Sport" options package for the two-door Explorer, with 23 spiffier wheels and other details calculated to attract buyers in their 20s and even younger. It was an instant success. "There was this younger group, more singles, more females," said Douglas W. Scott, Ford's group marketing manager for all sport-utility vehicles, and Molchany's predecessor as the marketing manager just for Explorers. "It was a younger buyer really interested in the look."

The new version was so popular that Ford later labelled it a different model, the 24 Explorer Sport. To go with it, Ford created an Explorer Sport Trac, which has an open, four-foot pickup truck bed in the back. Both were virtually identical to the Explorer beneath the sheet metal, and continued to be made on the same assembly lines. Annual production of two-door versions zoomed to 100,000 a year, as Ford sold fewer four-door models and more two-door models.

With these inexpensive Explorer variants, Ford has succeeded in lowering 25 sharply the overall average age of Explorer buyers. "I'm working really hard to target youth," said Drew Cook, a Ford marketing manager for the Sport Trac and Ranger small pickups. Compared to Ranger pickups, he said, "The Sport Trac is positioned a little bit earlier, firmly entrenched among Gen Xers."

This is particularly important in Detroit. The bane of the domestic industry is 26 that its models are mostly popular with older Americans who may soon buy their last car, as younger Americans have gravitated toward European and Asian models.

The average age for buyers of Buick cars is nearly 70, near the end of their auto-purchasing years. Buyers of Explorer Sport and Sport Trac may be coming back to dealerships for as many as 15 additional vehicles over their lifetimes. "It's a lot of folks just out of college," Scott said.

27   But the goal is only partly to sell more vehicles now. Ford also wants to convince people at as early an age as possible to become interested in Explorers, in the hope they will buy more Explorers of various sizes and configurations throughout their adult lives.

28   "We want to bring people in younger than ever before, and that's driving the product offering," Molchany said. Toward that goal, Ford has used direct-mail campaigns, tapping commercially available databases of prosperous households with young residents, said James G. O'Connor, the president of the Ford brand division. Ford has also provided promotional vehicles of the Explorer, Explorer Sport and Explorer Sport Trac for sports events that cater to younger television viewers.

29   Ford has not been alone in promoting SUVs to younger buyers. Executives at other automakers say the fastest growth in SUVs at the expense of cars over the next decade will come in models that will cost less than US$20,000 and be affordable for young people.

30   "The next inroads we really see in trucks are really here," said Paul Ballew, GM's top market researcher, while adding that Ford was ahead of GM in this area. "A large part of Ford's youth strategy is to leverage their truck strength."

31   Chrysler ran an extensive radio and television advertising campaign in the summer of 1996 aimed at persuading parents and grandparents to buy the small, inexpensive Jeep Wrangler for their children and grandchildren. Chrysler's market research had found that while many teenagers and early twentysomethings loved the Wrangler, they could not afford it and were buying cheap used vehicles instead. But Chrysler noticed that their elders could afford the Wrangler. So Chrysler ditched its previous, long-standing ad campaign, a macho series of television ads that featured Wranglers in fights with bulls and other adventures that nervous parents and grandparents might not want Junior to try.

32   Instead, Chrysler began running ads in which a clean-cut young man sat near a clean-cut young woman at a campfire on a beautiful mountainside while a Jeep Wrangler sat parked nearby in the gathering dusk. The message, Chrysler marketing officials said, was that buying a Wrangler was a good way for parents and grandparents to help young people visit the pristine wilderness. There was no suggestion of sex in the ads to frighten the elders—the young men and women in these ads were not sitting too close together. There were not even any tents in sight, so perhaps the youngsters were supposed to drive back down the apparently roadless mountainside in the dark. Radio ads for the Wrangler were even more carefully tailored to parents, with one ad featuring a young woman who goes for a drive with her mother and has a cheerful chat about the young woman's boyfriend, whom the mother likes.

33   Whether the campaign worked is hard to judge. Statistics on teen ownership of vehicles are highly unreliable, because vehicles are often registered in the names of the teens' parents. There are no publicly available statistics at all on how teens

pay for their vehicles. But whatever the reason, the Wrangler has sold well over the last five years, as have other small sport-utility vehicles, which tend to draw young drivers.

Teens and people in their early 20s may love SUVs, but should they be driving them? A wealth of recent research says parents who really care about the safety of their sons or daughters should not allow them to drive a sport-utility vehicle, and should discourage children from riding in SUVs driven by friends.   34

The death rate for young people in auto accidents has been extraordinary even without the recent rise of SUVs. A third of all death of Americans from ages 15 to 24, about 10,000 deaths a year, occur in motor vehicle accidents. That roughly equals all deaths in this age group from all diseases, and exceeds the number of deaths in this age bracket from homicides and suicides combined.   35

Surprisingly little work has been done on exactly how young people die in crashes. The existing research does show, however, that young people die disproportionately in single-vehicle crashes, apparently because of their inexperience, rather than perishing in collisions with other vehicles. And many of these single-vehicle crashes involve rollovers—the kind of crashes to which SUVs are especially vulnerable, accounting for three-fifths of all deaths in SUVs. Since rollovers appear to be the biggest single cause of paralysis, and since people paralyzed in their teen years lose more years of mobility than those paralyzed later in life, allowing a teen to drive an SUV can be an especially sad mistake.   36

The Insurance Institute for Highway Safety has issued a press release warning parents against allowing young drivers behind the wheel of SUVs: "Don't let your teen drive an unstable vehicle. Sport-utility vehicles, especially the smaller ones, are inherently less stable than cars because of their higher centres of gravity. Abrupt steering manoeuvres—the kind that can occur when teens are fooling around or overcorrecting a driver error—can cause rollovers in these less stable vehicles. A more stable car would, at worst, skid or spin out."   37

Indeed, even auto industry safety officials are wary of recommending SUVs for young people. Helen Petrauskas, the long-time Ford vice-president for safety and environment, said at a retirement lunch with reporters at Henry Ford's Fairlane Estate in the spring of 2001 that she had insisted her own daughter drive a Ford Tempo when she was learning to drive. Petrauskas even insisted that her daughter not choose an exciting colour, like red. Parents should choose cars that look like they would not be very interesting to drive, she suggested.   38

Sue Cischke, her successor, said at the same event that for teens, "probably a mid-sized sedan is good advice—what their image is, and what they want to do, is often different from what their parents want."   39

A few celebrities have taken an interest in what will happen as the next generation of SUV drivers takes over. The most prominent is Paul Newman, an actor who is also a racecar driver and understands the value of nimble steering and excellent brakes.   40

"In 1973, everybody's running around buying Volkswagen diesels," Newman said in 1999. "And now they're buying Expeditions. And this is the thing that I don't   41 understand about the government. As this fad grew, why didn't they insist on certain bumper heights? I mean, it's criminal," Newman said.

42   "And when an Expedition is eight years old and it goes down to 7,000 bucks, there'll be a lot of kids buying them and, unfortunately, it's the younger generation that's responsible for a lot of accidents. So you put a 17-year-old kid behind a 5,500-pound car and have them run into your blue-haired lady driving her Tercel Toyota. You know, it's going to be mayhem."

Environmental Double Standards for Sport Utility Vehicles

This article, written by an advocacy organization, Suv.org, which is a subset of Friends of the Earth, was published on the Web site www.suv.org. Friends of the Earth is a liberal, international environmental organization founded in San Francisco. The suv.org Web site provides information on the harmful emissions and gas consumption of sport utility vehicles and suggests ways to prevent further environmental damage. This scholarly article presents a comprehensive and in-depth argument on the problem of sport-utility vehicles.

WHAT IS WRONG WITH SUVS?

1   SUVs represent a paradox to consumers—television advertisements present them as a way to return to nature, yet they actually accelerate existing environmental problems. Commercials often depict happy families driving on mountain roads, avoiding falling rocks and enjoying the flowered wilderness in leather-seated comfort. The sad truth is that these vehicles are contributing to the destruction of our natural resources.

2   In reality, only 5 percent of SUVs are ever taken off-road,[1] and the vast majority of these vehicles are used for everyday driving. And there are a lot of them on the roads. In 1985, SUVs accounted for only 2 percent of new vehicle sales.[2] SUVs now account for one in four new vehicles sold,[3] and sales continue to climb.

3   Driving an SUV has a much greater impact on the environment than driving other passenger cars. In large part, this is due to double standards set by law and government regulations. For example, current federal regulations allow SUVs to have far worse fuel economy than other vehicles. The federal corporate average fuel economy (CAFE) standards set the fuel economy goals for new passenger cars at 27.5 miles per gallon (mpg). But under the law, SUVs are not considered cars—they are characterized as light trucks. Light trucks only have to achieve 20.7 mpg. It should be noted that this is an average for all light trucks, which is why it is possible to have SUVs on the road that only achieve 12 mpg. In fact, some SUVs, like the

massive Ford Excursion, are so large that they no longer qualify as "light trucks," and are not subject to any kind of fuel economy standards.

When CAFE was instituted in the 1970s, there were few SUVs and light trucks on the road, and they were primarily used for farm and commercial work. Today, however, the demographics of an SUV buyer are quite different. The amount of gasoline burned by a vehicle is important for several reasons. The most crucial is the threat of global warming.

THE THREAT FROM GLOBAL WARMING

Contrary to some rhetoric you may have heard, global warming has been extremely well studied. In 2001, the Intergovernmental Panel on Climate Change (IPCC) issued a report on global warming with many dire predictions. The World Meteorological Organization and the United Nations Environment Programme created the IPCC in 1988 to study the risks associated with global climate change. The IPCC found that about three quarters of the anthropogenic (caused by humans) emissions of carbon dioxide to the atmosphere during the past 20 years is due to fossil fuel burning. The IPCC anticipates higher temperatures and heat waves over the next century, as well as more intense and dangerous storms.[4]

The EPA seconds these concerns. According to the EPA, "increasing concentrations of greenhouse gases are likely to accelerate the rate of climate change. Scientists expect that the average global surface temperature could rise 1–4.5°F (0.6–2.5°C) in the next fifty years, and 2.2–10°F (1.4–5.8°C) in the next century, with significant regional variation. Evaporation will increase as the climate warms, which will increase average global precipitation. Soil moisture is likely to decline in many regions, and intense rainstorms are likely to become more frequent. Sea level is likely to rise two feet along most of the U.S. coast."[5]

According to the U.S. Environmental Protection Agency (EPA), one of the most important things you can do to reduce global warming pollution is to buy a vehicle with higher fuel economy. This is because every gallon of gasoline your vehicle burns puts 20 pounds of carbon dioxide (CO_2) into the atmosphere. Scientific evidence strongly suggests that the rapid buildup of CO_2 and other greenhouse gases in the atmosphere is raising the earth's temperature and changing the earth's climate with potentially serious consequences. Choosing a vehicle that gets 25 rather than 20 miles per gallon will prevent 10 tons of CO_2 from being released over the lifetime of your vehicle.[6] Passenger cars and trucks account for about 20 percent of all U.S. CO_2 emissions.[7]

Today a car that gets approximately 27.5 mpg, like a Volkswagen New Beetle, will emit 54 tons of carbon dioxide (CO_2) from the burning of gasoline over its lifetime. An SUV that gets 14 mpg, like a Lincoln Navigator, will emit over 100 tons of CO_2 over its lifetime.[8] A Harper's Magazine writer took the massive Ford Excursion, the biggest of all SUVs, for a test drive. During a drive around a city, the mighty Excursion was only getting 3.7 miles per gallon. It is estimated the Excursion will produce 134 tons of carbon dioxide during its lifetime.[9] The National Academy of Sciences estimates that if fuel economy had not been improved in the late 1970s, U.S. fuel consumption would be about 2.8 million barrels of oil per day higher than it is. This is about 14 percent of today's oil consumption.[10] However, all of the major fleet-wide improvements in vehicle fuel economy occurred from the middle 1970s through the late 1980s, but it has been consistently falling since then. In fact, average new vehicle fuel economy fell in 2000 to 24 mpg, its lowest level 20 years. The increasing market share of light trucks and SUVs accounts for much of the decline in fuel economy of the overall new light vehicle fleet.[11]

9   Global warming is a real danger that cannot be ignored. However, automakers continue to build fuel-inefficient vehicles. The vehicles we drive are contributing to this problem, but automakers don't seem particularly concerned.

10   The EPA has an excellent website devoted to global warming, which answers many of the common questions about the problem. You can visit the site here: http://www.epa.gov/globalwarming/.

SUVS' SMOG FORMING EMISSIONS

11   SUVs have a significant environmental impact even beyond the problem of global warming. Federal law gives heavy sport utility vehicles permission to emit higher levels of toxic and noxious pollution—carbon monoxide, hydrocarbons, and nitrogen oxides. Sport utility vehicles can spew 30 percent more carbon monoxide and hydrocarbons and 75 percent more nitrogen oxides than passenger cars.[12] These combustion pollutants contribute to eye and throat irritation, coughing, nau-

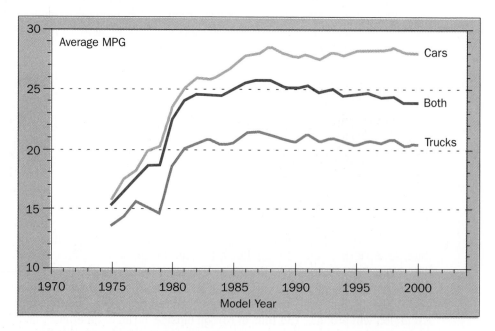

Source: Heavenrich and Hellman.[13]

sea, dizziness, fatigue, confusion and headaches. Hydrocarbons and nitrogen oxides are precursors to ground level ozone, which causes asthma and lung damage.[14]

These pollutants are regulated under the Clean Air Act of 1990. If a region is unable to reduce their emissions these pollutants for these pollutants, the EPA may impose penalties. This is known as reaching "attainment." Many of the large urban areas in the U.S. are in "serious nonattainment." 12

The U.S. EPA and the Department of Energy have teamed up to create a website that lists vehicle fuel economy, and compares vehicles to each other. It also goes a step further by giving each vehicle a score of zero to ten for the amount of smog producing pollution the vehicle emits. Ten is considered a perfect score. Unfortunately, many popular SUVs only rate four or below, with many at zero. This rating system is an excellent tool to help people see the impact of their vehicle choice, and it is a great help for people interested in purchasing a new vehicle. The chart below looks at the fuel economy and emissions scores of some of the most popular 4-wheel drive SUVs. All data is from the U.S. EPA and the Department of Energy. The website can be found here: www.fueleconomy.gov. 13

Manufacturer	Model	Cylinder	Liter	City MPG	Hwy MPG	EPA Rating
Dodge	Durango	8	5.2	12	17	1
Cadillac	Escalade	8	6.0	12	16	*
Ford	Expedition	8	5.4	12	17	1
Jeep	Grand Cherokee	6	4.0	15	20	4
GMC	Yukon	8	5.7	14	16	0
Lincoln	Navigator	8	5.4	12	16	1
Land Rover	Range Rover	8	4.6	12	15	1
Chevrolet	Suburban	8	5.3	14	16	0

*The EPA and DOE have not rated this vehicle.

Unfortunately, increasing numbers of Americans are living in areas with poor air quality from ozone pollution, according to the American Lung Association (ALA). The ALA found that 141 million Americans lived in areas with poor air quality during 1997–1999. This is nine million more people than in the previous two-year period.[15] 14

The Washington, D.C., region has a non-attainment ranking of serious for ozone pollution. As mentioned above, ground level ozone can be a serious problem for many areas. When a region has a "bad air day," it is usually because the levels of ozone in the air have created an unhealthy situation. In the case of Washington, D.C., the EPA is considering cutting off the region's road building funds until the region can come up with a viable solution to the pollution problem. However, standing in the way of any solution is the number of SUVs on the road. 15

The amount of nitrogen oxide in the D.C. region's air is expected to be eight tons per day over the limit of 162 tons by 2005, according to Ronald Kirby of the Metropolitan Washington Council of Governments. In July, Mr. Kirby told the 16

Washington Post that the growth of SUVs on the roads in the past few years has been tremendous, jumping from 15 percent of all vehicles to 25 percent in just three years.[16] In fact, Marsha Kaiser, planning director for the Maryland Department of Transportation, said that her agency predicts the "huge increase" in SUVs on the road will tip the region beyond its limits.[17] All passenger vehicles pollute, but SUVs produce so much more pollution than the average car. In terms of air pollution, one SUV is like two or three cars on the road.

17   This is a very significant development, and it shows the kind of impact that a large amount of polluting SUVs can have on air quality. The Fairfax County government, in Northern Virginia, is concerned enough about this problem to halt purchases of SUVs for official business and replace some of the ones they already own. This step is "more than just symbolic," according to County Supervisor Gerald Connolly, who believes the county needs to change how it approaches car purchases.[18]

18   Many regions still haven't gotten the message, however. Governors attending the National Governors Association meeting in Rhode Island in August 2001 drove SUVs provided free of charge by General Motors. Sixty-five GMC Yukons were shipped up to Rhode Island for the event. Governor Lincoln Almond said the state was appreciative. "We don't take a gesture by GM and tell them what to do," he said.[19] According to the U.S. EPA, various models of the Yukon get between 12 and 17 miles per gallon, and most receive a zero out of ten on the pollution scale.[20]

U.S. DEPENDENCY ON OIL

19   Finally, it is important to note that SUVs are contributing to our dependence on imported oil. The more gasoline we use, the more oil we have to import from other countries. Currently, more than half of the oil we use is imported. This level of dependence on imports is the highest in our history, and will only increase unless we do a better job with conservation and alternative fuels.[21]

20   If current rates of consumption were to continue, the world's remaining resources of conventional oil would be used up in 40 years. The United States uses more than 3 billion barrels of oil per year just on passenger cars and light trucks.[22]

21   Clearly, there are significant problems with SUVs that need to be remedied. The good news is that SUVs can be improved without much effort.

WHAT CAN BE DONE?

22   In July 2001, the National Academy of Sciences (NAS) released a study on fuel economy standards. The NAS found that light trucks, SUVs, minivans, and pickup trucks could reach 28–30 mpg for an additional cost of $1,200–$1,300.[23] Automakers make an average of $10,000 in pure profit on each SUV sold.[24] It shouldn't be too much to ask automakers to sacrifice a small amount of their profits to clean up these vehicles. The NAS study specifically pointed out that safety would not be sacrificed, and actually assumes an increase in vehicle weight, which is associated with certain safety-enhancing features. [25] However, the NAS points out that reducing the weight of the largest SUVs on the roads would make all drivers safer, since the biggest SUVs tend to do the most damage in an accident. [26]

The Union of Concerned Scientists (UCS) has also looked at this issue, and   23
found similar results. The UCS report concluded similar fuel economy levels were
achievable at nearly identical consumer cost—all using existing technologies that
automakers could implement quickly. The excellent UCS report is called "Drilling in
Detroit," and it can be found at http://www.ucsusa.org/vehicles/drill_detroit-
exec.html.

We may wish people who don't need giant vehicles won't buy them, but people   24
will buy whatever they want. The best thing we can do is to ensure prospective vehicle purchasers are educated on their choices, and encourage them to make the
most environmentally sound decisions.

The good news is that SUVs can be improved without much effort, and without   25
sacrificing safety. Automakers have made some baby steps, but they have so far
been unwilling to make a serious effort to improve these vehicles.

In the meantime, we must work to change the federal standards governing these   26
vehicles. SUV drivers are not to blame for the lower fuel economy and emissions
standards that these vehicles enjoy, and SUV drivers are not to blame for automakers' lack of innovation and improvement. Automakers have shown a strong unwillingness over the years to clean up their products, or even to make them safer without a push from the federal government—or from consumers. Therefore, people who
are concerned about these issues must work to educate the public while working to
improve the federal regulations governing SUVs. Only education and improved environmental standards will push automakers into cleaning up these vehicles.

In 2000, Ford Motor Company announced plans to improve their SUV fleet fuel   27
economy by 25 percent by 2005. This is a great first step, and it shows that automakers are capable of improving their vehicles. It also shows that a concerned
public can influence a company like Ford. This is why educated consumers must demand better vehicles, and demand that Congress and the president finally address
the problem with today's fuel economy standards.

But automakers are unlikely to make significant improvements unless they are   28
pushed. William Clay Ford, the chairman of Ford Motor Company, put it best. "The
best way to get the auto industry to stop dragging its feet is to have us race against
each other. We love to do that, and we're good at it." The race will begin as soon as
fuel economy standards are improved to a realistic level.

Endnotes

1. "The Unstoppable SUV," Keith Naughton. *Newsweek*, July 2, 2001.
2. "Bad Sports," Paul Roberts. *Harper's Magazine*. April 2001.
3. *Newsweek*.
4. "Summary for Policymakers: A Report of Working Group I of the IPCC, 2001" (http://www.ipcc.ch/).
5. Environmental Protection Agency's Global Warming website. http://www.epa.gov/globalwarming/climate/index.html.
6. Fuel Economy website. Department of Energy and Environmental Protection Agency (http://www.fueleconomy.gov/feg/climate.shtml).
7. Light-Duty Automotive Technology and Fuel Economy Trends 1975 Through 2000.
8. Union of Concerned Scientists. Policy Framework "Federal Fuel Economy Standards—Past, Present, and Future" (www.ucsusa.org).

9. *Harper's Magazine.*

10. Effectiveness and Impact of Corporate Average Fuel Economy Standards. Division on Engineering and Physical Sciences, Board on Energy and Environmental Systems, Transportation Resource Board. National Research Council, July 2001. Page ES-4

11. Light-Duty Automotive Technology and Fuel Economy Trends 1975 Through 2000. Executive Summary. Robert M. Heavenrich and Karl H. Hellman. Advanced Technology Division, Office of Transportation and Air Quality. U.S. Environmental Protection Agency. Air and Radiation EPA420-S-00-003 (http://www.epa.gov/otaq/fetrends.htm 06 Jan 2001).

12. Motor Vehicle Facts and Figures, 1997. American Automobile Manufacturers Association. pg. 84.

13. Light-Duty Automotive Technology and Fuel Economy Trends 1975 Through 2000.

14. Wagner, Travis. *In Our Backyard: A guide to understanding pollution and its effects.* Van Nostrand Reinhold. New York. 1994. pg. 88–103.

15. "More Americans Breathing Dirty Air, Lung Association Says in 2001 Report," Steve Cook. Daily Report for Executives, Bureau of National Affairs. May 2, 2001. Page A-11.

16. "SUVs Drive Area to Pollution Violations," Katherine Shaver, *Washington Post.* July 8, 2001.

17. "Increase in Trucks Threatens Road Work; Poor Air Quality Could Halt Projects," Katherine Shaver, *Washington Post.* June 23, 2001.

18. "Fairfax to Stop Buying SUVs; Supervisors Set an Example to Help Clean Region's Air," David Cho, *Washington Post.* July 24, 2001.

19. "Governors Get Free SUVs, Gas Money," Ken Maguire, Associated Press. August 3, 2001.

20. Fuel Economy website. Department of Energy and Environmental Protection Agency (http://www.fueleconomy.gov/feg/byclass.htm).

21. Fuel Economy website. Department of Energy and Environmental Protection Agency (http://www.fueleconomy.gov/feg/oildep.shtml).

22. Energy Information Administration, Annual Energy Review 2000. (http://www.eia.doe.gov).

23. Effectiveness and Impact of Corporate Average Fuel Economy Standards. Pages 3-29 to 3-34.

24. *Harper's Magazine.*

25. Effectiveness and Impact of Corporate Average Fuel Economy Standards. Page 3-16.

26. Effectiveness and Impact of Corporate Average Fuel Economy Standards. Page ES-8.

Road Outrage: How Corporate Greed and Political Corruption Paved the Way for the SUV Explosion

Arianna Huffington

Arianna Huffington is a nationally syndicated columnist and author of several books, including the New York Times' *bestseller,* Pigs at the Trough: How Corporate Greed and Political Corruption are Undermining America *(2003) and her latest,* Fanatics and Fools: The Game Plan for Winning Back America *(April 2004). In 2003, she ran for governor as an Independent in California. This article was published on her Web page "Arianna Online," which posts her columns and book information, as well as blogs and forums regarding controversial political issues. Huffington is one of the founders of Americans for Fuel Efficient Cars (AFEC), along with film producer Lawrence Bender, environmental activist Laurie David, and Ariel Emanuel, a movie and television agent.*

This nonprofit organization is "dedicated to decreasing America's reliance on foreign oil" (www.detriotproject.com) and is known for its dramatic anti-SUV television ad campaign, The Detroit Project.

America's automakers have finally sputtered into first gear.   1

Responding to the growing public outcry over its reckless gas-guzzling ways, the   2
auto industry used the Detroit Auto Show this week to unveil a line-up of "coming soon to a showroom near you" hybrid vehicles—including a number of hybrid SUVs.

The question—though I'm willing to bet no one at the car show asked it—is: 3
What took them so long? After all, cars powered by a combination of gas and electricity have been around since 1905, when the Woods Motor Vehicle Co. offered a dual-powered model.

And while Detroit's sudden interest in hybrids after a near-century of neglect is   4
certainly a step in the right direction, given the fact that many of the prototypes on display in the Motor City won't be on showroom floors for years—if ever—it's fair to wonder just how decisive a step it is.

It's one thing to make a big show of rolling out glittering "concept models" in-   5
tended for future production—or to promise, as GM did, to have a million hybrid vehicles for sale by 2007 "if demand is high"—and quite another to commit the marketing resources necessary to create the high demand. Time will tell if the industry has really fallen in love with this new/old kid on the block or if the industry's embrace of hybrid technology is just a one-night stand, a here-today-gone-tomorrow defensive gambit for the PR cameras.

We have ample reason to question the sincerity of the industry's stated inten-   6
tions. Anyone remember the Supercar, that 80 mpg marvel that was supposed to hit the road by 2004 but instead managed to eat up $1.5 billion in taxpayer money before being abandoned on the side of the highway? Or the FreedomCAR, the Bush administration's equally lame "responsible vehicle" partnership with Detroit? Both highly touted programs allowed automakers to look like they were sweating blood to improve fuel efficiency while doing everything in their power to convince consumers to buy more and more fuel-inefficient—and hugely profitable—SUVs.

For a good indication of Detroit's real plans, we need look no further than this   7
week's L.A. Auto Show. (Yes, I'm a regular on the auto show circuit.) There were as many hybrid cars on display as there were rickshaws. And in full-page newspaper ads headlined "What's Up At GM?" the auto giant bragged about having "once again shattered the record for SUV sales, topping the million mark for the second consecutive year—propelled by breakout vehicles like the one-of-a-kind Hummer H2."

The sales deck is clearly stacked in favor of Detroit's beloved behemoths, with   8
billions being spent on SUV advertising and ever-more tempting marketing come-ons, like GM's "Zero, Zero, Zero" program which was introduced in December and offered no-interest financing on 13 of its SUVs for up to 60 months—very tempting in these tough times.

Of course, Washington continues to do its part by holding SUVs to lower fuel ef-   9
ficiency and air pollution standards than passenger cars. Our politicians have even refused to close a deeply misguided tax loophole that rewards buyers of extra large—and extra wasteful—SUVs with extra large tax breaks.

10   Think of that: at a time when our leaders should be touting the importance of reducing our dependence on foreign oil, the people being given a financial incentive to purchase a new vehicle are those buying fuel-chugging SUVs.

11   "I was surprised," said Karl Wizinsky, a health care consultant from Michigan who just bought a giant Ford Excursion even though he admits he doesn't really need it, "that a $32,000 credit on a $47,000 purchase was available in the first year. I mean, it is a substantial credit." Yes, it is. And it's created a substantial—and artificial—demand.

12   It's the kind of lunatic public policy that makes you want to slam on your brakes and scream out your car window: How can this kind of thing happen?

13   The answer is as simple as it is distressing: special interest money has once again trumped the public interest. That's why the auto industry was able to turn its back on hybrid technology for so long, and why our politicians refuse to this day to demand that the auto industry change its hydrocarbon-loving ways.

14   The numbers tell the story: the auto industry spent close to $37 million on lobbying in 2000. And you can bet that money wasn't spent trying to convince Congress to designate a "Windshield Wiper Appreciation Week." Although I'm sure Congress would have been glad to oblige if its deep-pocket pals in Detroit had only asked. After all, the industry has donated over $77 million to federal candidates and the political parties since the 1990 election—with $12.5 million doled out during the 2002 election cycle.

15   It also doesn't hurt to have very good friends in very high places. Before becoming White House chief of staff, Andy Card was an executive at GM, and before that, the chief lobbyist for the Big Three auto makers. And you wondered why the administration has thrown its considerable weight behind GM's efforts to overturn a California law requiring carmakers to put more energy-efficient models on the road?

16   Because of the corporate takeover of our democracy, Washington has remained firmly stuck in the Dark Ages of energy policy. That's why Bill Clinton came charging into office promising to raise fuel efficiency standards to 45 miles per gallon but left without having increased it one inch per gallon. And why George W. Bush can try and score points by proposing to raise the ludicrously low SUV mileage standard by an equally ludicrous 1.5 mpg over the next four years.

17   It's also why the Big Three, once again, have to play catch up with Toyota and Honda, which have been putting out hybrid cars since 1997. How ironic that if American car buyers want to do something truly patriotic, they have to buy Japanese to do it.

18   So Detroit has sensed—belatedly but still ahead of the slowcoaches in Washington—that public opinion is shifting—and has taken some baby steps toward meeting the rising demand for more socially responsible cars.

19   Now it's up to all of us to make sure that the pressure and the demand continue to grow. Otherwise, the auto industry will gladly underfund and under-advertise its hybrid models, allowing them to crash and burn—yet more "proof" that American consumers don't really care about anything other than their precious SUVs.

20   And that would suit those gas-guzzlers in Detroit—and those cash-nuzzlers in Washington—just fine.

Running Out of Oil—and Time
Paul Roberts

Paul Roberts is a contributor to Harper's Magazine, *among others, focusing on the energy industry. He is also the author of* The End of Oil: On the End of a Perilous New World *(2004). First published on March 6, 2004, in the* Los Angeles Times, *this opinion piece was reprinted on the "Common Dreams" Web page, a nonprofit organization promoting "progressive visions for America's future" and resisting corporate intrusion into politics and media (from their Web site).*

The news last month that the vast Saudi oil fields are in decline is a far bigger   1
story than most in the media, or the United States, seem to realize. We may begrudge the Saudis their 30-year stranglehold on the world economy. But even the possibility that the lords of oil have less of the stuff than advertised raises troubling questions. How long will the world's long-term oil supplies last? As important, what will the big importing nations, like the U.S., do the day world oil production hits its inevitable peak?

For more than a century, Western governments have been relentlessly upbeat   2
about the long-term outlook for oil. Whenever pessimists claimed that supplies were running low—as they have many times—oil companies always seemed to discover huge new fields. It's now an article of faith among oil optimists, including those in the U.S. government, that global oil reserves won't run out for at least four decades, which seems like enough time to devise a whole suite of alternative energy technologies to smoothly and seamlessly replace oil.

But such oil optimism, always questionable, is now more suspect than ever.   3
True, we won't "run out" of oil tomorrow, or even 10 years from now. But the long-term picture is grim. In the first place, it's not a matter of running out of oil but of hitting a production peak. Since 1900, world oil production—that is, the number of barrels we can pump from the ground—has risen in near-perfect step with world oil demand. Today, demand stands at about 29 billion barrels of oil a year, and so does production. By 2020, demand may well be 45 billion barrels a year, by which time, we hope, oil companies will have upped production accordingly.

At some point, however, production simply won't be able to match demand. Oil   4
is an exhaustible resource: The more you produce, the less remains in the ground, and the harder it is to bring up that remainder. We won't be "out of oil"; a vast amount will still be flowing—just not quickly enough to satisfy demand. And as any economist can tell you, when supply falls behind demand, bad things happen.

During the 1979 Iranian revolution, the last time oil production fell off signifi-   5
cantly, world oil prices hit the modern equivalent of $80 a barrel. And that, keep in mind, was a *temporary* decline. If world oil production were to truly peak and begin a permanent decline, the effect would be staggering: Prices would not come back down. Any part of the global economy dependent on cheap energy—which is to say, pretty much everything these days—would be changed forever.

6   And that's the good news. The term "peak" tends to suggest a nice, neat curve, with production rising slowly to a halfway point, then tapering off gradually to zero—as if, since it took a century to reach a peak, it ought to take another 100 years to reach the end. But in the real world, the landing will not be soft. As we hit the peak, soaring prices—$70, $80, even $100 a barrel—will encourage oil companies and oil states to scour the planet for oil. For a time, they will succeed, finding enough crude to keep production flat, thus stretching out the peak into a kind of plateau and perhaps temporarily easing fears. But in reality, this manic, post-peak production will deplete remaining reserves all the more quickly, thus ensuring that the eventual decline is far steeper and far more sudden. As one U.S. government geologist put it to me recently, "the edge of a plateau looks a lot like a cliff."

7   As production falls off this cliff, prices won't simply increase; they will fly. If our oil dependence hasn't lessened drastically by then, the global economy is likely to slip into a recession so severe that the Great Depression will look like a dress rehearsal. Oil will cease to be viable as a fuel—hardly an encouraging scenario in a world where oil currently provides 40% of all energy and nearly 90% of all transportation fuel. Political reaction would be desperate. Industrial economies, hungry for energy, would begin making it from any source available—most likely coal—regardless of the ecological consequences. Worse, competition for remaining oil supplies would intensify, potentially leading to a new kind of political conflict: the energy war.

8   Thus, when we peak becomes a rather pressing question. Some pessimists tell us the peak has already come, and that calamity is imminent. That's unlikely. But the optimists' forecast—that we don't peak until around 2035 —is almost as hard to believe. First, oil demand is climbing faster than optimists had hoped, mainly because China and India, the sleeping giants, are waking up to embrace a Western-style high-energy industrialism that includes tens of millions of new cars. Second, even as oil demand is rising, oil discovery rates are falling. Oil can't be produced without first being found, and the rate at which oil companies are locating new oil fields is in serious decline. The peak for world discoveries was around 1960; today, despite astonishing advances in exploration and production technology, the industry is finding just 12 billion new barrels of oil each year—less than half of what we use. This is one reason that oil prices, which had averaged $20 a barrel since the 1970s, have been hovering at $30 for nearly a year.

9   Oil companies, not surprisingly, are getting anxious. Despite the fact that the current high oil prices are yielding massive company profits, companies are finding it harder and harder to replace the oil they sell with newly discovered barrels. On average, for every 10 barrels an oil company sells, its exploration teams find just four new barrels—a trend that can go on only so long. Indeed, most Western oil firms now say the only way to half this slide is to get back into the Middle East, which kicked them out during the OPEC nationalizations of the 1960s and '70s. This has, in fact, become the mantra of the oil industry: Get us back into the Middle East or be prepared for trouble. And the Bush administration seems to have taken the message to heart.

Now, of course, the Middle East is looking less and less like the Promised   10
Land. Western analysts have long feared that the Saudis and other oil-state leaders
are too corrupt, unstable and bankrupt to step up their oil production fast enough to
meet surging world demand. Last week's revelations, in which some Saudis themselves expressed doubt over future production increases, have only heightened
such concerns.

Put another way, we may not be able to pinpoint exactly when a peak is coming,   11
but recent events suggest that it will be sooner than the optimists have been telling
us—perhaps by 2020, or even 2015 if Asian demand picks up as fast as some analysts now expect. What this means is that we can no longer sit back and hope that
an alternative to oil will come along in time. Such complacency all but ensures that,
when the peak does arrive, our response will be defensive, costly and hugely disruptive. Instead, we must begin now, with every tool at our disposal, to find ways to
get "beyond petroleum" if we are to have any hope of controlling the shift from oil to
whatever comes next.

As Toyota Goes . . .

Thomas L. Friedman

*Thomas L. Friedman is the winner of three Pulitzer prizes for his journalism
with* The New York Times *and is especially celebrated for his international reporting in the Middle East. Before becoming the newspaper's foreign affairs
columnist, Friedman served as a White House correspondent and chief economic
correspondent. He has also authored two books on globalization,* The Lexus
and the Olive Tree: Understanding Globalization *(1999) and* The World Is
Flat: A Brief History of the Twenty-First Century *(2005). This op-ed column
was published in* The New York Times *on June 17, 2005.*

So I have a question: If I am rooting for General Motors to go bankrupt and be   1
bought out by Toyota, does that make me a bad person?

It is not that I want any autoworker to lose his or her job, but I certainly would   2
not put on a black tie if the entire management team at G.M. got sacked and was replaced by executives from Toyota. Indeed, I think the only hope for G.M.'s au-
toworkers, and maybe even our country, is with Toyota. Because let's face it, as
Toyota goes, so goes America.

Having Toyota take over General Motors—which based its business strategy on   3
building gas-guzzling cars, including the idiot Hummer, scoffing at hybrid technology and fighting Congressional efforts to impose higher mileage standards on U.S.
automakers—would not only be in America's economic interest, it would also be in
America's geopolitical interest.

4   Because Toyota has pioneered the very hybrid engine technology that can help rescue not only our economy from its oil addiction (how about 500 miles per gallon of gasoline?), but also our foreign policy from dependence on Middle Eastern oil autocrats.

5   Diffusing Toyota's hybrid technology is one of the keys to what I call "geo-green." Geo-greens seek to combine into a single political movement environmentalists who want to reduce fossil fuels that cause climate change, evangelicals who want to protect God's green earth and all his creations, and geo-strategists who want to reduce our dependence on crude oil because it fuels some of the worst regimes in the world.

6   The Bush team has been M.I.A. on energy since 9/11. Indeed, the utter indifference of the Bush team to developing a geo-green strategy—which would also strengthen the dollar, reduce our trade deficit, make America the world leader in combating climate change and stimulate U.S. companies to take the lead in producing the green technologies that the world will desperately need as China and India industrialize—is so irresponsible that it takes your breath away. This is especially true when you realize that *the solutions to our problems are already here.*

7   As Gal Luft, co-chairman of the Set America Free coalition, a bipartisan alliance of national security, labor, environmental and religious groups that believe reducing oil consumption is a national priority, points out: the majority of U.S. oil imports go to fueling the transport sector—primarily cars and trucks. Therefore, the key to reducing our dependence on foreign oil is powering our cars and trucks with less petroleum.

8   There are two ways we can do that. One is electricity. We don't import electricity. We generate all of our needs with coal, hydropower, nuclear power and natural gas. Toyota's hybrid cars, like the Prius, run on both gasoline and electricity that is generated by braking and then stored in a small battery. But, says Luft, if you had a hybrid that you could plug in at night, the battery could store up 20 miles of driving per day. So your first 20 miles would be covered by the battery. The gasoline would only kick in after that. Since 50 percent of Americans do not drive more than 20 miles a day, the battery power would cover all their driving. Even if they drove more than that, combining the battery power and the gasoline could give them 100 miles per gallon of gasoline used, Luft notes.

9   Right now Toyota does not sell plug-in hybrids. Some enthusiasts, though, are using kits to convert their hybrids to plug-ins, but that adds several thousand dollars—and you lose your Toyota warranty. Imagine, though, if the government encouraged, through tax policy and other incentives, every automaker to offer plug-in hybrids? We would quickly move down the innovation curve and end up with better and cheaper plug-ins for all.

10   Then add to that flexible-fuel cars, which have a special chip and fuel line that enable them to burn alcohol (ethanol or methanol), gasoline or any mixture of the two. Some four million U.S. cars already come equipped this way, including from G.M. It costs only about $100 a car to make it flex-fuel ready. Brazil hopes to have all its new cars flex-fuel ready by 2008. As Luft notes, if you combined a plug-in hy-

brid system with a flex-fuel system that burns 80 percent alcohol and 20 percent gasoline, you could end up stretching each gallon of gasoline up to 500 miles.

In short, we don't need to reinvent the wheel or wait for sci-fi hydrogen fuel cells. The technologies we need for a stronger, more energy independent America are already here. The only thing we have a shortage of now are leaders with the imagination and will to move the country onto a geo-green path.

11

Oil and War

Khalil Bendib

Khalil Bendib is an independent cartoonist, originally from Morocco and Algeria. He is also an internationally known Muslim Arab artist and creator of public artworks. He owns his own company, StudioBendib, located in Berkeley, California. His Web site displays these slogans: "The pen is funnier than the sword" and "Cartoons that speak truth to power" (www.bendib.com). As a cartoonist, he is known for his satirical insights on national and global issues.

For Class Discussion

1. The following exercise will help you sort out the multiple-issue questions and varied views on SUVs discussed in this unit's readings. Working individually or in groups, sketch out core arguments representing the following perspectives:

   - the environmental case against SUVs;
   - the automotive manufacturing position in support of SUVs;
   - consumers' arguments for buying SUVs;
   - the libertarian free-market perspective against raising CAFE standards;
   - the political argument rejecting increases in CAFE standards as a viable plan;
   - the pro-government intervention position on gasoline usage, fuel supply, and economic policy;
   - the arguments for and against the safety of SUVs.

   What other stakeholders or angles of vision are involved in this network of issues?

2. Find two current SUV magazine ads that differ in their appeal to consumers. Examining the interplay of visual and textual elements in the ads, reconstruct the particular target audience for each ad and analyze the specific features and imaginative appeals that each ad emphasizes.

3. Find one political cartoon related to SUVs, hybrid cars, global warming, or oil resources and bring it to class. Working individually or in groups, analyze the argument implicit in your cartoon. What dimension of the SUV controversy does each cartoon choose to portray? Which cartoon do you think is the most effective at conveying its point and why?

4. Choose one of the arguments for closer analysis, applying the second set of guide questions on pages 454–455.

OPTIONAL WRITING ASSIGNMENT   Imagine a scenario in which one of your best friends strongly disagrees with you about the ethics of buying and driving SUVs. If you would like to buy an SUV, your friend—a vehement environmentalist—thinks you should buy a car with good fuel economy. If you yourself are opposed to SUVs, your friend is avidly saving to purchase an SUV. Using Rebekah Taylor's Rogerian argument as a model (Chapter 8, pp. 157–159), write a letter that seeks to open your friend's mind to a possible change in views. As Rebekah does, begin by articulating your understanding of your friend's position. Then, perhaps drawing on the reasons and evidence raised in the readings in this unit and any other readings on SUVs, present your own position. Finally, identifying a few common points that you and your friend can agree on, call for some change in your friend's views.

WAL-MART AND THE PUBLIC GOOD

Wal-Mart, the super discount corporation, is the biggest retail company in the world with more than 5,100 stores, more than 1.6 million employees, and annual sales of around $285 billion. In fact, Wal-Mart's profits make it richer than a number of countries. All this growth, wealth, and national and global dominance have put Wal-Mart at the center of a number of heated controversies. On the one hand, Wal-Mart is known for its range of merchandise, its "everyday low prices" affordable by low-income Americans, and its friendly, folksy, American image; on the other hand, Wal-Mart has the reputation of driving other local and smaller retailers out of business, of discriminating against its women employees, of underpaying its workers, of not providing affordable medical coverage, of fiercely preventing unionizing, of driving the wages of other competitor companies lower, and of endlessly expanding—constructing its mammoth concrete stores in more communities around the U.S. and the world. At stake in all these conflicts are Wal-Mart's own employer-employee-consumer relationships; its powerful effect on markets, competitors, and communities; and the influence of its business model as a successful big-box store.

The controversies surrounding Wal-Mart have taken a number of specific concrete forms. Currently, Wal-Mart is engaged in a massive class-action suit involving 1.5 million women, and communities across the country—often galvanized by anti-Wal-Mart and anti-sprawl Web sites—have launched campaigns to prevent Wal-Mart from building new stores. In recent countermoves, Wal-Mart has sought to change its negative image by building up its reputation for social contributions (see its Web site "Wal-Mart Facts" at www.walmartfacts.com) and by sponsoring an environmental program, "Acres for America," in partnership with the National Fish and Wildlife Foundation. (One of Wal-Mart's corporate ads for this program appears in Color Plate F.)

The readings in this unit (as well as the Color Plate ad and the political cartoon on page 315) invite you to explore questions about these conflicting images of Wal-Mart: Is Wal-Mart's economic and social influence on the United States positive or negative? What should Americans do as citizens and consumers to influence Wal-Mart's business practices? Should communities oppose the building of new Wal-Mart stores? Should Americans stop patronizing this super-discount chain?

Wal-Mart Nation: The Race to the Bottom

Floyd J. McKay

Freelance writer Floyd J. McKay is a journalism professor emeritus at Western Washington University. He wrote this op-ed piece, which we found in the Seattle Times *(February 18, 2004), during a time when retail workers in California were organizing to keep Wal-Mart out of California cities.*

Los Angeles is not my kind of town. But the Angelinos are about to take a   1
stand that ought to be applauded across the country.

2   That stand is to say "no" to a Wal-Mart "supercenter" that the retailing giant hopes to open in the city.

3   These superstores are not your father's Wal-Mart; they are monstrous, sprawling over some 25 acres and employing up to 600 workers. Their lure, of course, is lower prices.

4   Wal-Mart, it seems to me, epitomizes the race to the bottom that has the United States by the throat as the 21st century opens.

5   Why do people shop at these behemoths, when they know full well that they are driving out of existence small businesses owned and operated by their neighbors, employing other neighbors?

6   They shop because of price, and they are forced to do so by the declining standard of living we have offered working people for more than a generation. People who work for minimum wage, with little or no benefits, who cannot afford to fix their car or their kids' teeth have no choice but to search out the lowest price.

7   Wal-Mart buys offshore, without apology and for the cheapest possible prices, from companies paying the lowest-possible wages.

8   As jobs in America are lost to foreign sweatshops to feed the Wal-Mart engine, American workers are forced to accept jobs at lower pay, with bad working conditions. They are funneled to Wal-Mart's promise of cheap goods, in effect patronizing the very companies that caused their economic misery.

9   This is a cruel travesty on working people in this country.

10   Wal-Mart is currently being sued in some 40 cases charging various abuses of labor laws, and last fall it was reported the company extensively employs illegal aliens as janitors. Wal-Mart has successfully opposed unionization and frequently pays well below competing stores.

11   All of these practices—alleged abuses of labor laws, hiring illegals, and the low rate of pay and benefits at Wal-Mart—serve to depress the labor market in communities in which the giant is located. That is a major factor in Los Angeles' opposition to the supercenter.

12   We live in a nation in which the real-dollar income of an average family has declined for years, while corporate profits and executive pay have skyrocketed.

13   The gap between rich and poor has widened at an alarming rate in the past 20 years. In 44 states, the gap has increased not only between rich and poor, but between rich and middle-class families. None of the six exceptions is a Northwest state. Oregon has one of the worst gaps, Washington is about average.

14   In some states, the inequity is staggering. In three of the nation's largest states—California, New York and Ohio—families in the lowest 20 percent bracket actually lost real income from 1978 to 2000. In 1999 dollars, the loss was between 5 and 6 percent. In those same states, the real income gain for the top 20 percent of families ranged from 37 to 54 percent.

15   Nationwide, from 1978 to 2000, the lowest 20 percent of families gained only $972 annually, or 7.1 percent; the top 5 percent gained $87,779, or 58.4 percent.

16   These findings, by the nonpartisan Center on Budget and Policy Priorities (www.cbpp.org), were before the Bush tax cuts and the current recession, both of which will further widen the gap.

You can't blame Sam Walton for this disparity, but operations like Wal-Mart 17
feed off the impoverishment of America.

Sadly, there are byproducts in quality of life, often unseen until it is too late. 18

The greatest is the destruction of America's small and mid-sized towns, in- 19
creasingly bereft of small businesses and dominated by big-box retailers—acres of
barren asphalt parking lots, corporate managers on their way to the next-larger
store, employees scrambling to keep low-wage jobs.

My wife's recently deceased aunt could no longer shop in the small Iowa town 20
where she and her late husband ran a feed store. The store is closed, as are the
other small businesses. The elderly woman had to drive—or be driven—past the
empty shops several miles to Wal-Mart, the nearest place to get the basics of life.

Wal-Mart is like a neutron bomb, sucking life out of small towns, leaving build- 21
ings without the essence of civic life.

Those of us fortunate to earn middle-class incomes can make a choice, and 22
shun Wal-Mart. The tragedy is that for an ever-increasing segment of America, the
despicable race to the bottom has left no other choice than to shop for cheap, regardless of the consequences.

Don't Blame Wal-Mart

Robert B. Reich

*Formerly on the faculty of Harvard University's John F. Kennedy School of
Government, Robert B. Reich was the secretary of labor during the presidency of
Bill Clinton. He is the author of ten books on history, politics, economics, and busi-
ness. This op-ed piece appeared in* The New York Times *on February 28, 2005.*

Bowing to intense pressure from neighborhood and labor groups, a real estate 1
developer has just given up plans to include a Wal-Mart store in a mall in Queens,
thereby blocking Wal-Mart's plan to open its first store in New York City. In the eyes
of Wal-Mart's detractors, the Arkansas-based chain embodies the worst kind of economic exploitation: it pays its 1.2 million American workers an average of only
$9.68 an hour, doesn't provide most of them with health insurance, keeps out
unions, has a checkered history on labor law and turns main streets into ghost
towns by sucking business away from small retailers.

But isn't Wal-Mart really being punished for our sins? After all, it's not as if 2
Wal-Mart's founder, Sam Walton, and his successors created the world's largest retailer by putting a gun to our heads and forcing us to shop there.

Instead, Wal-Mart has lured customers with low prices. "We expect our suppli- 3
ers to drive the costs out of the supply chain," a spokeswoman for Wal-Mart said.
"It's good for us and good for them."

4   Wal-Mart may have perfected this technique, but you can find it almost everywhere these days. Corporations are in fierce competition to get and keep customers, so they pass the bulk of their cost cuts through to consumers as lower prices. Products are manufactured in China at a fraction of the cost of making them here, and American consumers get great deals. Back-office work, along with computer programming and data crunching, is "offshored" to India, so our dollars go even further.

5   Meanwhile, many of us pressure companies to give us even better bargains. I look on the Internet to find the lowest price I can and buy airline tickets, books, merchandise from just about anywhere with a click of a mouse. Don't you?

6   The fact is, today's economy offers us a Faustian bargain: it can give consumers deals largely because it hammers workers and communities.

7   We can blame big corporations, but we're mostly making this bargain with ourselves. The easier it is for us to get great deals, the stronger the downward pressure on wages and benefits. Last year, the real wages of hourly workers, who make up about 80 percent of the work force, actually dropped for the first time in more than a decade; hourly workers' health and pension benefits are in free fall. The easier it is for us to find better professional services, the harder professionals have to hustle to attract and keep clients. The more efficiently we can summon products from anywhere on the globe, the more stress we put on our own communities.

8   But you and I aren't just consumers. We're also workers and citizens. How do we strike the right balance? To claim that people shouldn't have access to Wal-Mart or to cut-rate airfares or services from India or to Internet shopping, because these somehow reduce their quality of life, is paternalistic tripe. No one is a better judge of what people want than they themselves.

9   The problem is, the choices we make in the market don't fully reflect our values as workers or as citizens. I didn't want our community bookstore in Cambridge, Mass., to close (as it did last fall) yet I still bought lots of books from Amazon.com. In addition, we may not see the larger bargain when our own job or community isn't directly at stake. I don't like what's happening to airline workers, but I still try for the cheapest fare I can get.

10   The only way for the workers or citizens in us to trump the consumers in us is through laws and regulations that make our purchases a social choice as well as a personal one. A requirement that companies with more than 50 employees offer their workers affordable health insurance, for example, might increase slightly the price of their goods and services. My inner consumer won't like that very much, but the worker in me thinks it a fair price to pay. Same with an increase in the minimum wage or a change in labor laws making it easier for employees to organize and negotiate better terms.

11   I wouldn't go so far as to re-regulate the airline industry or hobble free trade with China and India—that would cost me as a consumer far too much—but I'd like the government to offer wage insurance to ease the pain of sudden losses of pay. And I'd support labor standards that make trade agreements a bit more fair.

12   These provisions might end up costing me some money, but the citizen in me thinks they are worth the price. You might think differently, but as a nation we aren't

even having this sort of discussion. Instead, our debates about economic change take place between two warring camps: those who want the best consumer deals, and those who want to preserve jobs and communities much as they are. Instead of finding ways to soften the blows, compensate the losers or slow the pace of change—so the consumers in us can enjoy lower prices and better products without wreaking too much damage on us in our role as workers and citizens—we go to battle.

I don't know if Wal-Mart will ever make it into New York City. I do know that   13
New Yorkers, like most other Americans, want the great deals that can be had in a rapidly globalizing high-tech economy. Yet the prices on sales tags don't reflect the full prices we have to pay as workers and citizens. A sensible public debate would focus on how to make that total price as low as possible.

Down and Out in Discount America
Liza Featherstone

Liza Featherstone is a freelance writer who has specialized in student and youth activism as well as workers' issues. She is the author or co-author of two influential books: Students Against Sweatshops: The Making of a Movement *(Verso, 2002) and* Selling Women Short: The Landmark Battle for Worker's Rights at Wal-Mart *(Basic, 2004). This article appeared in the liberal magazine* The Nation *on January 3, 2005.*

On the day after Thanksgiving, the biggest shopping day of the year, Wal-Mart's   1
many progressive critics—not to mention its business competitors—finally enjoyed a bit of schadenfreude when the retailer had to admit to "disappointing" sales. The problem was quickly revealed: Wal-Mart hadn't been discounting aggressively enough. Without low prices, Wal-Mart just isn't Wal-Mart.

That's not a mistake the big-box behemoth is likely to make again. Wal-Mart   2
knows its customers, and it knows how badly they need the discounts. Like Wal-Mart's workers, its customers are overwhelmingly female, and struggling to make ends meet. Betty Dukes, the lead plaintiff in *Dukes v. Wal-Mart,* the landmark sex-discrimination case against the company, points out that Wal-Mart takes out ads in her local paper the same day the community's poorest citizens collect their welfare checks. "They are promoting themselves to low-income people," she says. "That's who they lure. They don't lure the rich. . . . They understand the economy of America. They know the haves and have-nots. They don't put Wal-Mart in Piedmonts. They don't put Wal-Mart in those high-end parts of the community. They plant themselves right in the middle of Poorville."

Betty Dukes is right. A 2000 study by Andrew Franklin, then an economist at   3
the University of Connecticut, showed that Wal-Mart operated primarily in poor and

working-class communities, finding, in the bone-dry language of his discipline, "a significant negative relationship between median household income and Wal-Mart's presence in the market." Although fancy retailers noted with chagrin during the 2001 recession that absolutely everybody shops at Wal-Mart—"Even people with $100,000 incomes now shop at Wal-Mart," a PR flack for one upscale mall fumed—the Bloomingdale's set is not the discounter's primary market, and probably never will be. Only 6 percent of Wal-Mart shoppers have annual family incomes of more than $100,000. A 2003 study found that 23 percent of Wal-Mart Supercenter customers live on incomes of less than $25,000 a year. More than 20 percent of Wal-Mart shoppers have no bank account, long considered a sign of dire poverty. And while almost half of Wal-Mart Supercenter customers are blue-collar workers and their families, 20 percent are unemployed or elderly.

4   Al Zack, who until his retirement in 2004 was the United Food and Commercial Worker's vice president for strategic programs, observes that appealing to the poor was "Sam Walton's real genius. He figured out how to make money off of poverty. He located his first stores in poor rural areas and discovered a real market. The only problem with the business model is that it really needs to create more poverty to grow." That problem is cleverly solved by creating more bad jobs worldwide. In a chilling reversal of Henry Ford's strategy, which was to pay his workers amply so they could buy Ford cars, Wal-Mart's stingy compensation policies—workers make, on average, just over $8 an hour, and if they want health insurance, they must pay more than a third of the premium—contribute to an economy in which, increasingly, workers can only afford to shop at Wal-Mart.

5   To make this model work, Wal-Mart must keep labor costs down. It does this by making corporate crime an integral part of its business strategy. Wal-Mart routinely violates laws protecting workers' organizing rights (workers have even been fired for union activity). It is a repeat offender on overtime laws; in more than thirty states, workers have brought wage-and-hour class-action suits against the retailer. In some cases, workers say, managers encouraged them to clock out and keep working; in others, managers locked the doors and would not let employees go home at the end of their shifts. And it's often women who suffer most from Wal-Mart's labor practices. *Dukes v. Wal-Mart*, which is the largest civil rights class-action suit in history, charges the company with systematically discriminating against women in pay and promotions [see Featherstone, "Wal-Mart Values: Selling Women Short," December 16, 2002 [*The Nation*]].

SOLIDARITY ACROSS THE CHECKOUT COUNTER

6   Given the poverty they have in common, it makes sense that Wal-Mart's workers often express a strong feeling of solidarity with the shoppers. Wal-Mart workers tend to be aware that the customers' circumstances are similar to their own, and to identify with them. Some complain about rude customers, but most seem to genuinely enjoy the shoppers.

7   One longtime department manager in Ohio cheerfully recalls her successful job interview at Wal-Mart. Because of her weight, she told her interviewers, she'd be

better able to help the customer. "I told them I wanted to work in the ladies department because I'm a heavy girl." She understands the frustrations of the large shopper, she told them: "You know, you go into Lane Bryant and some skinny girl is trying to sell you clothes.' They laughed at that and said, 'You get a second interview!'"

One plaintiff in the *Dukes* lawsuit, Cleo Page, who no longer works at Wal-Mart, says she was a great customer service manager because "I knew how people feel when they shop, so I was really empathetic." 8

Many Wal-Mart workers say they began working at their local Wal-Mart because they shopped there. "I was practically born in Wal-Mart," says Alyssa Warrick, a former employee now attending Truman State University in Missouri. "My mom is obsessed with shopping. . . . I thought it would be pretty easy since I knew where most of the stuff was." Most assumed they would love working at Wal-Mart. "I always loved shopping there," enthuses *Dukes* plaintiff Dee Gunter. "That's why I wanted to work for 'em." 9

Shopping is traditionally a world of intense female communication and bonding, and women have long excelled in retail sales in part because of the identification between clerk and shopper. Page, who still shops at Wal-Mart, is now a lingerie saleswoman at Mervyn's (owned by Target). "I do enjoy retail," she says. "I like feeling needed and I like helping people, especially women." 10

Betty Dukes says, "I strive to give Wal-Mart customers one hundred percent of my abilities." This sentiment was repeated by numerous other Wal-Mart workers, always with heartfelt sincerity. Betty Hamilton, a 61-year-old clerk in a Las Vegas Sam's Club, won her store's customer service award last year. She is very knowledgeable about jewelry, her favorite department, and proud of it. Hamilton resents her employer—she complains about sexual harassment and discrimination, and feels she has been penalized on the job for her union sympathies—but remains deeply devoted to her customers. She enjoys imparting her knowledge to shoppers so "they can walk out of there and feel like they know something." Like Page, Hamilton feels she is helping people. "It makes me so happy when I sell something that I know is an extraordinarily good buy," she says. "I feel like I've done somebody a really good favor." 11

The enthusiasm of these women for their jobs, despite the workplace indignities many of them have faced, should not assure anybody that the company's abuses don't matter. In fact, it should underscore the tremendous debt Wal-Mart owes women: This company has built its vast profits not only on women's drudgery but also on their joy, creativity and genuine care for the customer. 12

WHY BOYCOTTS DON'T ALWAYS WORK

Will consumers return that solidarity and punish Wal-Mart for discriminating against women? Do customers care about workers as much as workers care about them? Some women's groups, like the National Organization for Women and Code Pink, have been hoping that they do, and have encouraged the public not to shop at Wal-Mart. While this tactic could be fruitful in some community battles, it's unlikely to catch on nationwide. A customer saves 20–25 percent by buying groceries at 13

Wal-Mart rather than from a competitor, according to retail analysts, and poor women need those savings more than anyone.

14   That's why many women welcome the new Wal-Marts in their communities. The *Winona* (Minnesota) *Post* extensively covered a controversy over whether to allow a Wal-Mart Supercenter into the small town; the letters to the editor in response offer a window into the female customer's loyalty to Wal-Mart. Though the paper devoted substantial space to the sex discrimination case, the readers who most vehemently defended the retailer were female. From the nearby town of Rollingstone, Cindy Kay wrote that she needed the new Wal-Mart because the local stores didn't carry large-enough sizes. She denounced the local anti-Wal-Mart campaign as a plot by rich and thin elites: "I'm glad those people can fit into and afford such clothes. I can barely afford Shopko and Target!"

15   A week later, Carolyn Goree, a preschool teacher also hoping for a Winona Wal-Mart, wrote in a letter to the *Post* editor that when she shops at most stores, $200 fills only a bag or two, but at Wal-Mart, "I come out with a cart full top and bottom. How great that feels." Lacking a local Wal-Mart, Goree drives over the Wisconsin border to get her fix. She was incensed by an earlier article's lament that some workers make only $15,000 yearly. "Come on!" Goree objected. "Is $15,000 really that bad of a yearly income? I'm a single mom and when working out of my home, I made $12,000 tops and that was with child support. I too work, pay for a mortgage, lights, food, everything to live. Everything in life is a choice. . . . I am for the little man/woman—I'm one of them. So I say stand up and get a Wal-Mart."

16   Sara Jennings, a disabled Winona reader living on a total of $8,000, heartily concurred. After paying her rent, phone, electric and cable bills, Jennings can barely afford to treat herself to McDonald's. Of a recent trip to the LaCrosse, Wisconsin, Wal-Mart, she raved, "Oh boy, what a great treat. Lower prices and a good quality of clothes to choose from. It was like heaven for me." She, too, strongly defended the workers' $15,000 yearly income: "Boy, now that is a lot of money. I could live with that." She closed with a plea to the readers: "I'm sure you all make a lot more than I. And I'm sure I speak for a lot of seniors and very-low-income people. We *need* this Wal-Mart. There's nothing downtown."

FROM CONSUMERS TO WORKERS AND CITIZENS

17   It is crucial that Wal-Mart's liberal and progressive critics make use of the growing public indignation at the company over sex discrimination, low pay and other workers' rights issues, but it is equally crucial to do this in ways that remind people that their power does not stop at their shopping dollars. It's admirable to drive across town and pay more for toilet paper to avoid shopping at Wal-Mart, but such a gesture is, unfortunately, not enough. As long as people identify themselves as consumers and nothing more, Wal-Mart wins.

18   The invention of the "consumer" identity has been an important part of a long process of eroding workers' power, and it's one reason working people now have so little power against business. According to the social historian Stuart Ewen, in the

early years of mass production, the late nineteenth and early twentieth centuries, modernizing capitalism sought to turn people who thought of themselves primarily as "workers" into "consumers." Business elites wanted people to dream not of satisfying work and egalitarian societies—as many did at that time—but of the beautiful things they could buy with their paychecks.

Business was quite successful in this project, which influenced much early advertising and continued throughout the twentieth century. In addition to replacing the "worker," the "consumer" has also effectively displaced the citizen. That's why, when most Americans hear about the Wal-Mart's worker-rights abuses, their first reaction is to feel guilty about shopping at the store. A tiny minority will respond by shopping elsewhere—and only a handful will take any further action. A worker might call her union and organize a picket. A citizen might write to her congressman or local newspaper, or galvanize her church and knitting circle to visit local management. A consumer makes an isolated, politically slight decision: to shop or not to shop. Most of the time, Wal-Mart has her exactly where it wants her, because the intelligent choice for anyone thinking as a consumer is not to make a political statement but to seek the best bargain and the greatest convenience.

19

To effectively battle corporate criminals like Wal-Mart, the public must be engaged as citizens, not merely as shoppers. What kind of politics could encourage that? It's not clear that our present political parties are up to the job. Unlike so many horrible things, Wal-Mart cannot be blamed on George W. Bush. The Arkansas-based company prospered under the state's native son Bill Clinton when he was governor and President. Sam Walton and his wife, Helen, were close to the Clintons, and for several years Hillary Clinton, whose law firm represented Wal-Mart, served on the company's board of directors. Bill Clinton's "welfare reform" has provided Wal-Mart with a ready workforce of women who have no choice but to accept its poverty wages and discriminatory policies.

20

Still, a handful of Democratic politicians stood up to the retailer. California Assemblywoman Sally Lieber, who represents the 22nd Assembly District and is a former mayor of Mountain View, was outraged when she learned about the sex discrimination charges in *Dukes v. Wal-Mart,* and she smelled blood when, tipped off by dissatisfied workers, her office discovered that Wal-Mart was encouraging its workers to apply for public assistance, "in the middle of the worst state budget crisis in history!" California had a $38 billion deficit at the time, and Lieber was enraged that taxpayers would be subsidizing Wal-Mart's low wages, bringing new meaning to the term "corporate welfare."

21

Lieber was angry, too, that Wal-Mart's welfare dependence made it nearly impossible for responsible employers to compete with the retail giant. It was as if taxpayers were unknowingly funding a massive plunge to the bottom in wages and benefits—quite possibly their own. She held a press conference in July 2003, to expose Wal-Mart's welfare scam. The Wal-Mart documents—instructions explaining how to apply for food stamps, Medi-Cal (the state's healthcare assistance program) and other forms of welfare—were blown up on posterboard and displayed. The morning of the press conference, a Wal-Mart worker who wouldn't give her name

22

for fear of being fired snuck into Lieber's office. "I just wanted to say, right on!" she told the assemblywoman.

23   Wal-Mart spokespeople have denied that the company encourages employees to collect public assistance, but the documents speak for themselves. They bear the Wal-Mart logo, and one is labeled "Wal-Mart: Instructions for Associates." Both documents instruct employees in procedures for applying to "Social Service Agencies." Most Wal-Mart workers I've interviewed had co-workers who worked full time for the company and received public assistance, and some had been in that situation themselves. Public assistance is very clearly part of the retailer's cost-cutting strategy. (It's ironic that a company so dependent on the public dole supports so many right-wing politicians who'd like to dismantle the welfare state.)

24   Lieber, a strong supporter of the social safety net who is now assistant speaker pro tempore of the California Assembly, last year passed a bill that would require large and mid-sized corporations that fail to provide decent, affordable health insurance to reimburse local governments for the cost of providing public assistance for those workers. When the bill passed, its opponents decided to kill it by bringing it to a statewide referendum. Wal-Mart, which just began opening Supercenters in California this year, mobilized its resources to revoke the law on election day this November, even while executives denied that any of their employees depended on public assistance.

25   Citizens should pressure other politicians to speak out against Wal-Mart's abuses and craft policy solutions. But the complicity of both parties in Wal-Mart's power over workers points to the need for a politics that squarely challenges corporate greed and takes the side of ordinary people. That kind of politics seems, at present, strongest at the local level.

26   Earlier this year, labor and community groups in Chicago prevented Wal-Mart from opening a store on the city's South Side, in part by pushing through an ordinance that would have forced the retailer to pay Chicago workers a living wage. In Hartford, Connecticut, labor and community advocates just won passage of an ordinance protecting their free speech rights on the grounds of the new Wal-Mart Supercenter, which is being built on city property. Similar battles are raging nationwide, but Wal-Mart's opponents don't usually act with as much coordination as Wal-Mart does, and they lack the retail behemoth's deep pockets.

27   With this in mind, SEIU president Andy Stern has recently been calling attention to the need for better coordination—and funding—of labor and community anti-Wal-Mart efforts. Stern has proposed that the AFL-CIO allocate $25 million of its royalties from purchases on its Union Plus credit card toward fighting Wal-Mart and the "Wal-Martization" of American jobs [see Featherstone, "Will Labor Take the Wal-Mart Challenge?" June 28 [*The Nation*]].

28   Such efforts are essential not just because Wal-Mart is a grave threat to unionized workers' jobs (which it is) but because it threatens all American ideals that are at odds with profit—ideals such as justice, equality and fairness. Wal-Mart would not have so much power if we had stronger labor laws, and if we required employers to pay a living wage. The company knows that, and it hires lobbyists in Washington to vigorously fight any effort at such reforms—indeed, Wal-Mart has

recently beefed up this political infrastructure substantially, and it's likely that its presence in Washington will only grow more conspicuous.

The situation won't change until a movement comes together and builds the   29
kind of social and political power for workers and citizens that can balance that of Wal-Mart. This is not impossible: In Germany, unions are powerful enough to force Wal-Mart to play by their rules. American citizens will have to ask themselves what kind of world they want to live in. That's what prompted Gretchen Adams, a former Wal-Mart manager, to join the effort to unionize Wal-Mart. She's deeply troubled by the company's effect on the economy as a whole and the example it sets for other employers. "What about our working-class people?" she asks. "I don't want to live in a Third World country." Working people, she says, should be able to afford "a new car, a house. You shouldn't have to leave the car on the lawn because you can't afford that $45 part."

The Price Is Right

Pankaj Ghemawat and Ken A. Mark

Pankaj Ghemawat was the youngest person ever appointed as full professor in Harvard University's School of Business, where he currently holds a distinguished chair. His current teaching and research focus on business strategies in a globalized economy. Ken A. Mark is a business consultant in Toronto. This article appeared as an op-ed piece in The New York Times *on August 3, 2005.*

Nowadays, mighty Wal-Mart's headquarters in Bentonville, Ark., must feel less   1
like a hotbed of retailing than like a war room. The company faces a groundswell of criticism, largely focused on its treatment of workers. From low wages to limited health care coverage, Wal-Mart has some issues to tackle, and it has mostly responded with feel-good television advertisements and denial. But to chalk up Wal-Mart's success simply to the exploitation of its work force, as many of the company's most ferocious critics do, is simply wrong, for two reasons.

First, Wal-Mart hasn't just sliced up the economic pie in a way that favors one   2
group over another. Rather, it has made the total pie bigger. Consider, for example, the conclusions of the McKinsey Global Institute's study of United States labor productivity growth from 1995 to 2000. Robert Solow, a Nobel laureate in economics and an adviser on the study, noted that the most important factor in the growth of productivity was Wal-Mart. And because the study measured productivity per man hour rather than per payroll dollar, low hourly wages cannot explain the increase.

Second, most of the value created by the company is actually pocketed by its   3
customers in the form of lower prices. According to one recent academic study, when Wal-Mart enters a market, prices decrease by 8 percent in rural areas and 5 percent in urban areas. With two-thirds of Wal-Mart stores in rural areas, this

means that Wal-Mart saves its consumers something like $16 billion a year. And because Wal-Mart's presence forces the store's competitors to charge lower prices as well, this $16 billion figure understates the company's real impact by at least half.

4   These kinds of savings to customers far exceed the costs that Wal-Mart supposedly imposes on society by securing subsidies, destroying jobs in competing stores, driving employees toward public welfare systems and creating urban sprawl. Even if these offenses could all be ascribed to Wal-Mart, their costs wouldn't add up to anything like $16 billion.

5   Similarly, the savings to customers also exceed the total surplus the company generates for its shareholders—a surplus that would be wiped out if Wal-Mart's million-plus employees were to receive a $2-per-hour pay increase, modest though that sounds. Such a possibility would be unacceptable to Wal-Mart's shareholders, who include not only Sam Walton's heirs but also the millions of Americans who invest in mutual funds and pension plans. Instead, the more than 100 million Americans who shop at Wal-Mart would most likely just end up paying higher prices.

6   This last point suggests that the debate around Wal-Mart isn't really about a Marxist conflict between capital and labor. Instead, it is a conflict pitting consumers and efficiency-oriented intermediaries like Wal-Mart against a combination of labor unions, traditional retailers and community groups. Particularly in retailing, American policies favor consumers and offer fewer protections to other interests than is typical elsewhere in the world. Is such pro-consumerism a good thing?

7   The answer depends on who these consumers are, and Wal-Mart's customers tend to be the Americans who need the most help. Our research shows that Wal-Mart operates two-and-a-half times as much selling space per inhabitant in the poorest third of states as in the richest third. And within that poorest third of states, 80 percent of Wal-Mart's square footage is in the 25 percent of ZIP codes with the greatest number of poor households. Without the much-maligned Wal-Mart, the rural poor, in particular, would pay several percentage points more for the food and other merchandise that after housing is their largest household expense.

8   So in thinking about Wal-Mart, let's keep in mind who's reaping the benefits of those "everyday low prices"—and, by extension, where the real conflict lies.

The Wal-Martization of America

The New York Times

This New York Times *editorial appeared on November 15, 2003, at the height of grocery workers' protests against Wal-Mart's movement into Southern California.*

1   The 70,000 grocery workers on strike in Southern California are the front line in a battle to prevent middle-class service jobs from turning into poverty-level ones.

The supermarkets say they are forced to lower their labor costs to compete with Wal-Mart, a nonunion, low-wage employer aggressively moving into the grocery business. Everyone should be concerned about this fight. It is, at bottom, about the ability of retail workers to earn wages that keep their families out of poverty.

Grocery stores in Southern California are bracing for the arrival, in February, of 2
the first of 40 Wal-Mart grocery supercenters. Wal-Mart's prices are about 14 percent lower than other groceries' because the company is aggressive about squeezing costs, including labor costs. Its workers earn a third less than unionized grocery workers, and pay for much of their health insurance. Wal-Mart uses hardball tactics to ward off unions. Since 1995, the government has issued at least 60 complaints alleging illegal anti-union activities.

Southern California's supermarket chains have reacted by demanding a two- 3
year freeze on current workers' salaries and lower pay for newly hired workers, and they want employees to pay more for health insurance. The union counters that if the supermarkets match Wal-Mart, their workers will be pushed out of the middle class. Their members are already only a step—or a second family income—from poverty, with wages of roughly $18,000 a year. Wal-Mart sales clerks make about $14,000 a year, below the $15,060 poverty line for a family of three.

Wal-Mart may also be driving down costs by using undocumented immigrants. 4
Last month, federal agents raided Wal-Marts in 21 states. Wal-Mart is facing a grand jury investigation, and a civil racketeering class-action filed by cleaners who say they were underpaid when working for contractors hired by Wal-Mart. Wal-Mart insists that it was unaware of its contractors' practices. But aware or not, it may have helped to deprive legally employable janitors of jobs and adequate pay.

This Wal-Martization of the work force, to which other low-cost, low-pay stores 5
also contribute, threatens to push many Americans into poverty. The first step in countering it is to enforce the law. The government must act more vigorously, and more quickly, when Wal-Mart uses illegal tactics to block union organizing. And Wal-Mart must be made to pay if it exploits undocumented workers.

Unions understand that the quickest way to win this war is to organize Wal- 6
Mart workers. And Wal-Mart's competitors have to strive for Wal-Mart's efficiency without making workers bear the brunt. Consumers can also play a part. Wal-Mart likes to wrap itself in American values. It should be reminded that one of those is paying workers enough to give their families a decent life.

Why Wal-Mart Is Good
Steve Maich

Steve Maich is a business columnist for the Canadian public affairs magazine Maclean's, *which published this article in July 2005. Maich maintains a popular*

Web log "All Business," in which he comments on globalized economics from a Canadian perspective.

1   There's a place on the western edge of Cleveland that encapsulates the story of the city—its proud industrial past, its slow depressing decline, its hopes for a brighter future. But the battle now being waged over that patch of land tells an even bigger tale.

2   It's called the steelyard flats, a 130-acre plot of barren wasteland at the intersection of Interstates 90 and 71, in what was once the heart of Cleveland's thriving steel industry. The site has sat idle since 2000, when LTV Steel went bankrupt. The finishing mill was torn down, and the shells of a few remaining buildings have been crumbling here ever since. The place is now littered with discarded scrap metal, concrete and junk: a dozen old tires here, a shattered TV there.

3   Soon, however, this site will also be a symbol of renewal. In May, work began on what will be the first big-box shopping centre in this city of 500,000 people. It's called Steelyard Commons, and will include a Target store, a Home Depot, a Staples, plus restaurants and smaller businesses. It's expected to bring close to 2,000 jobs to the city identified as the most impoverished urban area in the U.S. in the 2004 census. Unemployment here runs at 11 per cent—roughly double the national average.

4   But there's a problem. Wal-Mart Stores, the world's biggest retailer, will be the anchor tenant of Steelyard Commons, and that has transformed this place into another front in North America's most bitter retail cold war. Wal-Mart's critics say the company destroys local economies, putting small competitors out of business; that it abuses workers with low wages and paltry benefits; and that it drives urban sprawl and all the environmental damage that goes with it. And so, a coalition of labour leaders, activists and city councillors have banded together, vowing to keep Wal-Mart out even if it means killing the whole project.

5   It's a divisive political standoff that's been mirrored in communities throughout North America over the past few years. To the project's advocates in City Hall, this is just the kind of development Cleveland so desperately needs. Aside from precious jobs, the mall will spin off US$3 million in property taxes annually, US$1.8 million of which will go to the city's struggling school system, plus US$700,000 in local payroll tax. It will also give city residents a place to shop near home, rather than travelling to the suburbs. Officials estimate local residents spend US$4 billion a year in retail shops, a third of which currently goes outside the city. If ever there was a Wal-Mart that deserves support, they say, this is it.

6   But that's just the point: Wal-Mart isn't engaged in a series of messy local zoning disputes. It's at war with a well-financed, well-organized opposition, determined to fight it on every front. From Los Angeles to the Saguenay, from Hartford, Conn., to Vancouver, a broad array of activist groups and unions have launched protests, lawsuits and ad campaigns, all aimed at discrediting Wal-Mart, halting its growth, and unionizing its workforce.

7   Like most wars, it's about money and power, and the first casualty is truth. Because even after all the scrutiny and analysis of the Wal-Mart phenomenon, most

of what we've been told—about worker abuse, destroyed small-town economies, crushed suppliers and greedy management—is wrong.

To Carol Foote, it just didn't make sense. It was near the end of the summer of 2000, and most of her neighbours in Miramichi, N.B., were planning to drive to Moncton, an hour and a half away, to buy school supplies for their kids at Wal-Mart. Foote knew that many in town already made regular trips there to buy household goods, clothes and electronics. And she knew every carload took more money from the local economy. But the prices, they said, were just too good to pass up. 8

So, Foote and her friend Paula Beaulieu decided to make it their mission to bring Wal-Mart to Miramichi. They organized a petition, and within six weeks they'd gathered 11,276 signatures in and around the town of about 19,000 residents. "The whole talk of the Miramichi was this petition," Foote remembers. "Lots of people would say, 'I'll sign, but we'll never get one,' and I'd say, 'C'mon, you've got to believe!' " 9

It took almost five years of trying, but last January Wal-Mart finally opened an outlet in Miramichi. Aside from creating dozens of jobs, Foote says the store has brought new life to the town's small commercial district. Pennington's has opened a store, Staples is on the way, and there is talk of a Quizno's sandwich shop. To city dwellers, the arrival of such mass-market brands is no big deal, but in a little town like Miramichi, they represent investment that would've seemed impossible a few years ago. 10

This is how the Wal-Mart revolution was built: on small towns like Miramichi. The numbers are truly staggering. Wal-Mart had sales of US$288.2 billion last year—meaning, if it were a country, it would be the world's 33rd biggest economy, ahead of Sweden, Switzerland and Hong Kong. It has 1.7 million employees worldwide, slightly less than the population of Montreal. The company's stock has risen 79 per cent in the past decade, giving it a market value just north of US$200 billion—more than the total combined value of Canada's Big Five banks. And profit rose 13 per cent last year, to US$10.3 billion, making it the undisputed Goliath of retail. 11

In Canada, the growth is no less impressive. Wal-Mart first arrived here in 1994, buying 122 Woolco stores with about 15 per cent of the department store market. Over the next decade, it more than doubled its number of outlets and increased its market share to about 52 per cent. And while critics portray this as the work of a ravenous invading force, the truth is most communities reached out to Wal-Mart and embraced it. 12

Foote heard lots of grousing about Wal-Mart, but when she looks at what it has brought to her town, she has no regrets. "We weren't trying to hurt our city, we just wanted it to grow," she says. "The stores here charged so much, people had to go to Moncton. And when they did, they'd buy their fuel there, they'd eat there. All our money was leaving town. I thought, 'This has got to stop.'" Rather than Wal-Mart crushing the few local businesses like the critics warned, she suspected the store would invigorate them, because that's just what has happened in hundreds of places across the country. 13

In 2002, Ryerson University completed the first major study on the company's impact on nearby small retailers, and found the opening of a new outlet is generally 14 an economic boon for the whole area—attracting other retailers and driving up sales at nearby stores. In metropolitan areas, a new Wal-Mart was generally followed by an increase of $56.8 million in local sales, and the opening of 12.9 new stores. In rural areas, the commercial boost was $74.1 million and 16.7 new stores on average. Meanwhile, economic growth in areas with Wal-Mart stores far outpaced growth in places without them. The final line of the study said it all: "It is difficult to make the case that a Wal-Mart store actually puts other retailers out of business."

15   That study confirmed what Wal-Mart had long claimed: that its stores are economic generators, not predators. And, it seems, even small-business owners are coming around to that view. A 2004 Canadian Imperial Bank of Commerce survey of more than 1,800 small-business owners across Canada found that just 16 per cent of respondents said they had been hurt by competition from big-box retailers like Wal-Mart and Home Depot. Five percent said the big boxes had actually helped them, while the vast majority claimed little or no impact.

16   Andy Grossman, however, doesn't buy any of that. Grossman is executive director of Wal-Mart Watch, a lobbying and publicity organization that coordinates the efforts of several anti-Wal-Mart groups. In April, it launched a two-week media blitz across the U.S., with full-page ads in major newspapers like the *New York Times* alleging a by-now familiar litany of misdeeds. "Wal-Mart needs to become a better corporate citizen, a better neighbour and a better employer," Grossman says. And at the very top of his list of grievances is Wal-Mart's purported ill-treatment of its workers. But there again, research suggests the criticism is overblown.

17   To be sure, nobody is claiming that being a Wal-Mart associate is a job many would aspire to. It's a low-wage gig, with only moderate opportunity for advancement, and it's not easy. The average full-time Wal-Mart worker in the U.S. makes US$9.68 an hour, which works out to roughly US$17,500 a year before taxes. If that worker is a sole earner trying to support a spouse and child, it puts him only about US$1,500 above the federal poverty line. Labour advocates say that in light of Wal-Mart's US$10-billion profit, the company should pay higher wages. But a closer look at the numbers paints a different picture. Wal-Mart's 2004 profit works out to a little more than US$6,000 per employee, compared to US$54,000 at General Electric, and US$143,000 per employee at Microsoft. Despite mammoth earnings, Wal-Mart doesn't have as much room for generosity as it first appears.

18   Health care is another oft-cited complaint. Only about 48 percent of Wal-Mart's workers buy into the company's health care plan, and critics say that's because it's too expensive: US$40 a month for an individual and US$155 for a family, plus a US$1,000 deductible. A recent study by researchers at the University of California at Berkeley concluded Wal-Mart's wages and benefits are so low that its workers in California rely on about US$86 million in public assistance every year. On the other hand, Wal-Mart points out that only about 36 percent of all retail workers get employee-sponsored health care in the U.S.—meaning its plan is better than most in its industry. And while unions say the company should provide big benefits like

those offered by General Motors, financial analysts point out that skyrocketing health care costs now threaten the stability of GM's business and have contributed to massive layoffs—hardly a model to emulate.

Even in Canada, where the health care issue is largely moot, it would still be difficult to raise a family on an associate's wage. But very few are in that position. While the majority of Wal-Mart employees work full time, the company also employs many students, seniors and people collecting a second income. And Wal-Mart says only seven percent of its staff are supporting a family.   19

Perhaps most telling is the fact that most Wal-Mart workers seem content. Human resources consulting firm Hewitt Associates issues an annual ranking of Canadian employers based largely on worker satisfaction surveys, and for three of the past four years Wal-Mart has been named best retailer, due mainly to incentives like profit sharing and a discounted stock purchase program. And despite union claims of widespread mistreatment, Andrew Pelletier, director of corporate affairs with Wal-Mart Canada, says new stores usually receive between six and 10 applications for every available job.   20

The various campaigns to paint Wal-Mart as an avaricious and abusive employer simply don't hold up to scrutiny, says Elisa Sumanski, a legal analyst with the National Right to Work Legal Defense Foundation, a Virginia-based group that represents workers in disputes with their unions, and which has received grants from Wal-Mart's founding Walton family. "We think it's really pretty simple—if Wal-Mart is such a terrible place to work, then why are so many thousands of people so eager to work there?" she says.   21

But when it comes to Wal-Mart, perception and myth are powerful. In spite of all the evidence to the contrary, the company is still struggling with the consequences of its increasingly tainted image. For much of the past year debate raged in Vancouver's city council over plans to build the city's first Wal-Mart. Opponents complained the store would be an energy-hogging blight on the environment. Wal-Mart responded by designing perhaps the most environmentally progressive big-box store ever—lit with skylights, cooled with shade trees, with rainwater running the toilets, and a geothermal heating system run by wind-turbine power. But nothing could convince the critics. "Big-box stores create traffic congestion, cause air pollution and harm small businesses," said councillor Anne Roberts, who led the anti-Wal-Mart campaign. Last month, city council rejected the plan by eight to three.   22

Shortly after, Wal-Mart received its second B.C. rejection in a week, this time when the town council of the Vancouver Island city of Campbell River voted 7–0 against a rezoning application that would have paved the way for the retailer. More than 300 people spoke against Wal-Mart during three days of hearings, most saying the proposed riverside site should be used for a park. Pushing the development was the Campbell River Indian Band, which was hoping to buy the parcel of land from a logging company and had applied to have its status changed. After being turned down, some band members said racism had played a part in the rejection.   23

As far as Bruce Bartlett is concerned, people who hate Wal-Mart don't understand it.   24

25   Bartlett, a former deputy assistant secretary for economic policy at the U.S. Treasury Department, now serves as senior fellow at the National Center for Policy Analysis, a conservative Washington think tank. Over the past two decades, he has watched the company's astonishing rise with admiration, and the recent public backlash with dismay.

26   His concern is not primarily for the company or its executives. Nor is he worried for the descendants of founder Sam Walton—by far the wealthiest clan in North America. Rather, Bartlett worries about the impact the war on Wal-Mart will have on the poor families who have come to rely on the stores. "The problem with this debate is that there's no one out there representing the people who've benefited from Wal-Mart, which is primarily the poor people," Bartlett says. "If you're stuck with a low income and you can reduce the amount you pay for basic items, then your real income goes up."

27   Those savings are substantial. In 2002, a study by the New England Consulting Group estimated that Wal-Mart's "everyday low prices" on a wide range of groceries and household goods saves U.S. consumers US$100 billion annually, or US$600 a year for the average American family. That's because not only does Wal-Mart sell for less, it forces competitors to cut prices in order to compete. UBS Warburg analysts measured grocery prices in various markets across the country and found that basic food items are 10 to 15 percent cheaper in areas where Wal-Mart competes. So it's far from being an insidious influence: those savings are a godsend for consumers, especially for working-poor families. As W. Michael Cox, chief economist for the Federal Reserve Bank of Dallas, said in 2003: "Wal-Mart is the greatest thing that ever happened to low-income Americans."

28   As Wal-Mart has grown, those savings have sent ripple effects through every corner of the North American economy, even benefiting consumers who've never set foot in one of its stores. In 2002, the consulting firm McKinsey & Co. delved into the so-called "Wal-Mart effect" and found it was the biggest single contributor to the growth of economic productivity across the U.S. between 1995 and 1999. According to McKinsey, Wal-Mart's pioneering approach to computerized inventory management, and analysis of store traffic patterns to better deploy its staff in peak hours, improved the efficiency of thousands of companies. The U.S. National Bureau of Economic Research has found that Wal-Mart's prices have a significant impact on holding down the rate of inflation. That, in turn, helps keep interest rates low, and helps fuel economic growth.

29   All this isn't some happy accident, but a fundamental part of what makes the company tick. Ever since Sam Walton opened his first store in Arkansas in 1962, Wal-Mart has dedicated itself to providing the lowest possible price for people living on a budget. "The underpinning of everyday low prices is a commitment to lowering the cost of living," says Wal-Mart Canada's Pelletier. "That was Sam Walton's vision, and it permeates the company today. The only way we can do that is by driving waste out."

30   Even now, 13 years after Walton died, his obsession with cost is still evident in every aspect of the business. Head offices are spartan and basic. Company officials

fly economy, and stay at bargain hotels. And every person, in every division, is constantly encouraged to look for less expensive ways of doing everything. Critics say this obsession with price has put relentless pressure on suppliers, even driving some out of business as they failed to meet Wal-Mart's demands for efficiency. But the company makes no apologies. It offers suppliers full access to sales data on every item sold, right to the minute and the penny. And every year thousands of small suppliers line up for the chance to get their products on Wal-Mart's shelves.

That helps explain why, for the past several years, Wal-Mart has ranked among   31
the world's most admired companies, according to *Fortune* magazine's annual rankings. This year's survey of thousands of executives and industry analysts put the company first among retailers for innovation, employee talent, quality of management, financial soundness, and second for social responsibility.

So, last year, when Bruce Bartlett saw opponents in his own city of Washington   32
defeat plans for a Wal-Mart, he shook his head. "It's just stupid and frankly insane if you really care about the well-being of your constituents," he says. "They're shooting themselves in the foot, and they're just showing that they really don't care about people at all. They'd rather cater to a few squeaky wheels."

But the wheels turning against Wal-Mart are more than squeaky. They're coor-   33
dinated, tireless, and deeply committed to their cause. For them, defeating Wal-Mart is a matter of life or death.

Tom Robertson is a guy who wears his passions on his sleeve.   34

Sitting in his wood-panelled office near downtown Cleveland, the head of the   35
northern Ohio chapter of the United Food and Commercial Workers union lays out his objections to Cleveland's proposed Wal-Mart, but he finds it hard to contain his contempt. "My mission isn't to organize Wal-Mart when they come to town. My mission is to keep them the hell out of town so they won't drive wages down," he explains, gaining steam as he speaks. "They just fuckin' destroy jobs, period, because they replace high-paying jobs with low-paying jobs."

Robertson is paid to defend the unionized workers at a chain of small local gro-   36
cery stores that will be threatened by Wal-Mart's arrival. But, he acknowledges, this fight is about more than just this city and his roughly 1,600 local members. It's about saving the union movement itself, and that's why so many labour organizations and their political allies have joined the fight. "If Wal-Mart continues to grow and expand based on their terms and conditions, with nobody overseeing the way they treat people and compete, yes—it could destroy the labour movement," Robertson says.

The plight of Robertson's own union illustrates why. Over the past three years, his   37
local has lost 3,000 members—a decline of more than 10 percent—and he says Wal-Mart is the number 1 reason for it. Unionized stores have had to cut staff and wages to compete, and other companies have increased efforts to prevent unionization.

The UFCW's membership crisis is but one example of a larger trend unfolding   38
throughout the continent, as traditionally union-heavy industrial companies downsize, and as mostly non-union sectors like services, technology and retail become a much larger portion of the economy. The same phenomenon is happening in

Canada, where private sector unionization has fallen from 26 percent in the early 1970s to just 18 percent in 2003. In short, organized labour is dying a slow death and its financial strength and political influence are waning as a result.

39   The fight over Wal-Mart is really a fight to halt organized labour's gradual death spiral. If the unions are to turn the tide, they need to be in retail, and if they are going to get into retail, they have to get into Wal-Mart—union leaders themselves acknowledge as much. As Stuart Acuff, organizing director of the AFL-CIO, America's umbrella organization for trade unions, told *Fortune* last year, "If we want to survive, labour has no choice but to organize Wal-Mart."

40   They've spared no expense to do it. For the past five years, the UFCW has sent organizers around Canada and the U.S., trying to get Wal-Mart workers to sign union cards and force certification votes. It waged a four-year effort, at a cost of about US$3 million a year, to certify a single Las Vegas store. But so far, they've had no luck.

41   Wal-Mart has been equally aggressive in keeping the unions out. Managers are encouraged to report union activity, and the UFCW points to dozens of cases in which it accuses the company of firing workers for working on behalf of the union. When the UFCW was able to get a unit certified in Jonquiére, Que., the company responded by shutting down the store. Pelletier insists, however, that this is not a fight over worker rights. "At the end of the day, this campaign is all about money for the union," he says. "The union is looking for dues to finance their operations. If they could collect union dues from our thousands of associates across the country, this would amount to millions of dollars a year into the union and out of the pockets of our workers."

42   Lately, though, the unions and their allies have changed their approach. Efforts to unionize have been stymied, so they've decided to focus on discrediting the company and slowing its growth. Hence Wal-Mart Watch's publicity campaign, and the union-supported zoning fights cropping up everywhere. "It's an effort to destroy Wal-Mart because the company's continued growth and success is really an argument against the need for unionization," Sumanski says.

43   But Andy Grossman says the union fight is only part of the picture. As he sees it, Wal-Mart is driving a vicious cycle: it starts with lower prices, and leads over time to a single player essentially rewriting the economics of the industry for everybody. Pretty soon, there are fewer employers, lower wages, less medical coverage, more poverty—all widening the gap between the rich owners of Wal-Mart stock and the poor who shop and work there. "This is a societal fight," Grossman explains. "Wal-Mart is a symbol, because they're so good at what they do, others have to emulate them. This company's reach is so broad, we need to change the relationship between it and the communities it seeks to do business in, otherwise it's going to continue to destroy our societies."

44   For Grossman, those are the stakes: social destruction. Never mind that most of the research refutes this view. Never mind that millions more consumers vote with their feet and their wallets every year, opting for the financial freedom Wal-Mart affords. The point is that Grossman, and thousands of others, believe with near-religious zeal that Wal-Mart is dangerous. And the war drags on.

Back in Cleveland, Chris Ronayne is still a little baffled by the whole contro-　45
versy. As chief of staff to Democratic Mayor Jane Campbell and former head of the
city planning commission, he knew enough to expect opposition to any plan to bring
Wal-Mart to the city. And he knew his boss would be locking horns with the very
union bosses that helped put her in office in 2001.

Still, he didn't expect the debate to be so nasty. Opponents tried, and failed, to　46
pass a change to zoning laws to keep the company out, and protesters recently tried
to crash Campbell's re-election campaign kickoff. Former supporters have denounced the mayor for selling out to the Great Satan of Corporate America. "We see
this as a first step toward a bigger turnaround, toward making Cleveland into a city
that can attract residents." Ronayne says. "We know these are starter jobs, but this
city has seen a serious erosion of our employment base and a starter job is better
than no job, from our perspective. We need jobs, period."

And while there is certainly a vocal faction, led by the UFCW, vowing to keep　47
fighting Wal-Mart every step of the way, it remains in the minority. With the support
of about 78 percent of residents in a recent poll and with a legal building permit in
hand, it appears Wal-Mart has won this battle. The war, though, is less certain, and
the company knows it. Already it's getting much more difficult and expensive for
Wal-Mart to build stores. It is sued thousands of times every year by local activists,
disgruntled ex-employees, and unions. Thanks to a steady stream of negative press,
thousands of consumers would sooner go barefoot than buy shoes there.

The company, as always, puts a positive spin on things. Pelletier says all the　48
scrutiny will only make Wal-Mart stronger and more responsive. He says it will
keep listening to the complaints, and acting to address what it can. But the one
thing that will not change is Sam Walton's admonition to put the customer first, always. Carol Foote likes it that way. "I think sometimes it's just easier for people to
blame the other guy," she says. "If your customers aren't coming back, maybe you
should look at why they're not coming back rather than trying to point the finger."

But the war on Wal-Mart raises more complicated questions. If the company　49
helps poor families, creates decent jobs and fuels economic growth, what does it
say that so many are so determined to stop it? More important—if Wal-Mart loses
this fight, who wins?

A New World to Conquer

David Horsey

*David Horsey, a nationally syndicated political cartoonist, has won two Pulitzer
Prizes for editorial cartooning (in 1999 and again in 2003). This cartoon, which
we found in the* Seattle Post-Intelligencer, *appeared in newspapers around the
country in January 2004.*

For Class Discussion

1. The readings in this unit (as well as the corporate ad in Color Plate F and the cartoon in Chapter 14, page 315) have looked at Wal-Mart from multiple perspectives. What are some of the main views these articles present on each of the following issues?

   ■ Wal-Mart's labor practices (employee wages, medical insurance, gender equity, compensation insurance, career opportunities)

   ■ Wal-Mart's effect on local businesses

   ■ Wal-Mart's contribution to the appearance of a community

   ■ Wal-Mart's benefits for consumers

2. Which of the views of Wal-Mart that you sketched out in Question 1 do you find most persuasive as an argument? In other words, which argument offers the most compelling and reliable evidence as well as the most effective appeals to *ethos* and *pathos*?

3. Some of the articles in this unit emphasize consumers' responsibility, claiming that Americans' demand for low prices is a major cause of Wal-Mart's success. What points could you offer in support of this idea? What points can you think of against it?

4. Some opponents of Wal-Mart have particularly objected to these statements:

   ■ Wal-Mart is a patriotic, true-American company.

   ■ Wal-Mart is an environmentally conscious company.

   What is the strongest evidence in favor of and against these claims?

5. Some journalists and economic analysts have compared Wal-Mart to other big-box retail chains such as Costco, Home Depot, Lowe's, and Target. In many cases, Costco is said to balance its treatment of its employees, its appeals to customers, and its returns for shareholders more effectively than Wal-Mart. After doing some research on Costco or another big-box retailer, what do you see as the main similarities and differences between it and Wal-Mart?

6. Choose one of the readings in this unit and analyze it carefully using the List 2 Guide questions on pages 454–455.

OPTIONAL WRITING ASSIGNMENT   Write a persuasive letter to a friend in which you urge him or her to give up shopping at Wal-Mart or assuage his or her guilt about shopping at Wal-Mart. Build the most compelling case for this friend by tapping into your friend's values and needs. To gather more evidence for your letter, you might consult Wal-Mart's Web site (www.walmartfacts.com) or some of the anti-Wal-Mart sites (Wal-Mart Versus Women, www.walmartvswomen.com; Sprawl-Busters, www.sprawl-busters.com; or Walmart Watch.com, www.walmartwatch.com).

BIOTECH AGRICULTURE AND THE ETHICS OF FOOD PRODUCTION

If you have eaten any processed foods lately, you have probably eaten food from genetically modified crops. Pervaded by much uncertainty, confusion, fear, and optimism, the multiple controversies surrounding genetically modified foods involve numerous stakeholders. Proponents of biotech agriculture point to its potential to increase crop yield, reduce the need for pesticides and herbicides and thereby reduce the impact of these chemicals on the environment, lower production costs, add nutritional content to foods, and grow crops in formerly unsuitable conditions. Skeptics and opponents, however, consider genetically engineered foods highly experimental, even mutant, and object to the unleashing of new genetic material into the environment, to the rapid commercialization of products that may have unforeseen long-term consequences, and to food growers' and producers' lack of accountability to consumers concerning the ingredients of the food they are buying. Finally, lawmakers, policymakers, businesses, scientists, and public interest groups also argue about the driving forces behind the push for biotech foods, about the control of patents, and about international policy.

The readings in this unit, as well as those in Chapter 2 and the cartoon on page 1, focus primarily on the ethics of biotech foods as they connect to problems of world hunger, the preservation of the environment, the safety of consumers, and the just distribution of knowledge and wealth.

Will Frankenfood Save the Planet?
Jonathan Rauch

This influential article arguing for the humanitarian and environmental benefits of biotech agriculture appeared in The Atlantic *in October 2003. Its author, Jonathan Rauch, is a senior writer and columnist for* National Journal *magazine in Washington and a correspondent for* The Atlantic. *He is the author of several books and many articles on public policy, culture, and economics. He is also a visiting scholar at the Brookings Institution, a leading Washington think tank. In 2005 he received the National Magazine Award for columns and commentary. Note that he is not a scientist. This article is based on his own field research conducted by visiting biotech sites and interviewing scientists and agricultural experts.*

1   That genetic engineering may be the most environmentally beneficial technology to have emerged in decades, or possibly centuries, is not immediately obvious. Certainly, at least, it is not obvious to the many U.S. and foreign environmental groups that regard biotechnology as a bête noire. Nor is it necessarily obvious to people who grew up in cities, and who have only an inkling of what happens on a

modern farm. Being agriculturally illiterate myself, I set out to look at what may be, if the planet is fortunate, the farming of the future.

It was baking hot that April day. I traveled with two Virginia state soil-and-water-conservation officers and an agricultural-extension agent to an area not far from Richmond. The farmers there are national (and therefore world) leaders in the application of what is known as continuous no-till farming. In plain English, they don't plough. For thousands of years, since the dawn of the agricultural revolution, farmers have ploughed, often several times a year; and with ploughing has come runoff that pollutes rivers and blights aquatic habitat, erosion that wears away the land, and the release into the atmosphere of greenhouse gases stored in the soil. Today, at last, farmers are working out methods that have begun to make ploughing obsolete.

At about one-thirty we arrived at a 200-acre patch of farmland known as the Good Luck Tract. No one seemed to know the provenance of the name, but the best guess was that somebody had said something like "You intend to farm this? Good luck!" The land was rolling, rather than flat, and its slopes came together to form natural troughs for rainwater. Ordinarily this highly erodible land would be suitable for cows, not crops. Yet it was dense with wheat—wheat yielding almost twice what could normally be expected, and in soil that had grown richer in organic matter, and thus more nourishing to crops, even as the land was farmed. Perhaps most striking was the almost complete absence of any chemical or soil runoff. Even the beating administered in 1999 by Hurricane Floyd, which lashed the ground with nineteen inches of rain in less than twenty-four hours, produced no significant runoff or erosion. The land simply absorbed the sheets of water before they could course downhill.

At another site, a few miles away, I saw why. On land planted in corn whose shoots had only just broken the surface, Paul Davis, the extension agent, wedged a shovel into the ground and dislodged about eight inches of topsoil. Then he reached down and picked up a clump. Ploughed soil, having been stirred up and turned over again and again, becomes lifeless and homogeneous, but the clump that Davis held out was alive. I immediately noticed three squirming earthworms, one grub, and quantities of tiny white insects that looked very busy. As if in greeting, a worm defecated. "Plant-available food!" a delighted Davis exclaimed.

This soil, like that of the Good Luck Tract, had not been ploughed for years, allowing the underground ecosystem to return. Insects and roots and microorganisms had given the soil an elaborate architecture, which held the earth in place and made it a sponge for water. That was why erosion and runoff had been reduced to practically nil. Crops thrived because worms were doing the ploughing. Crop residue that was left on the ground, rather than ploughed under as usual, provided nourishment for the soil's biota and, as it decayed, enriched the soil. The farmer saved the fuel he would have used driving back and forth with a heavy plough. That saved money, and of course it also saved energy and reduced pollution. On top of all that, crop yields were better than with conventional methods.

The conservation people in Virginia were full of excitement over no-till farming. Their job was to clean up the James and York Rivers and the rest of the Chesapeake Bay watershed. Most of the sediment that clogs and clouds the rivers, and most of the fertilizer runoff that causes the algae blooms that kill fish, comes from farmland. By all but eliminating agricultural erosion and runoff—so Brian Noyes, the local conservation-district manager, told me—continuous no-till could "revolutionize" the area's water quality.

7   Even granting that Noyes is an enthusiast, from an environmental point of view no-till farming looks like a dramatic advance. The rub—if it is a rub—is that the widespread elimination of the plough depends on genetically modified crops.

8   It is only a modest exaggeration to say that as goes agriculture, so goes the planet. Of all the human activities that shape the environment, agriculture is the single most important, and it is well ahead of whatever comes second. Today about 38 percent of the earth's land area is cropland or pasture—a total that has crept upward over the past few decades as global population has grown. The increase has been gradual, only about 0.3 percent a year; but that still translates into an additional Greece or Nicaragua cultivated or grazed every year.

9   Farming does not go easy on the earth, and never has. To farm is to make war upon millions of plants (weeds, so-called) and animals (pests, so-called) that in the ordinary course of things would crowd out or eat or infest whatever it is a farmer is growing. Crop monocultures, as whole fields of only wheat or corn or any other single plant are called, make poor habitat and are vulnerable to disease and disaster. Although fertilizer runs off and pollutes water, farming without fertilizer will deplete and eventually exhaust the soil. Pesticides can harm the health of human beings and kill desirable or harmless bugs along with pests. Irrigation leaves behind trace elements that can accumulate and poison the soil. And on and on.

10   The trade-offs are fundamental. Organic farming, for example, uses no artificial fertilizer, but it does use a lot of manure, which can pollute water and contaminate food. Traditional farmers may use less herbicide, but they also do more ploughing, with all the ensuing environmental complications. Low-input agriculture uses fewer chemicals but more land. The point is not that farming is an environmental crime—it is not—but that there is no escaping the pressure it puts on the planet.

11   In the next half century the pressure will intensify. The United Nations, in its midrange projections, estimates that the earth's human population will grow by more than 40 percent, from 6.3 billion people today to 8.9 billion in 2050. Feeding all those people, and feeding their billion or so hungry pets (a dog or a cat is one of the first things people want once they move beyond a subsistence lifestyle), and providing the increasingly protein-rich diets that an increasingly wealthy world will expect—doing all of that will require food output to at least double, and possibly triple.

12   But then the story will change. According to the UN's midrange projections (which may, if anything, err somewhat on the high side), around 2050 the world's population will more or less level off. Even if the growth does not stop, it will slow. The crunch will be over. In fact, if in 2050 crop yields are still increasing, if most of the world is economically developed, and if population pressures are declining or even reversing—all of which seems reasonably likely—then the human species may at long last be able to feed itself, year in and year out, without putting any additional net stress on the environment. We might even be able to grow everything we need while *reducing* our agricultural footprint: returning cropland to wilderness, repairing dam-

aged soils, restoring ecosystems, and so on. In other words, human agriculture might be placed on a sustainable footing forever: a breathtaking prospect.

The great problem, then, is to get through the next four or five decades with as   13
little environmental damage as possible. That is where biotechnology comes in.

One day recently I drove down to southern Virginia to visit Dennis Avery and   14
his son, Alex. The older Avery, a man in late middle age with a chinstrap beard, droopy eyes, and an intent, scholarly manner, lives on ninety-seven acres that he shares with horses, chickens, fish, cats, dogs, bluebirds, ducks, transient geese, and assorted other creatures. He is the director of global food issues at the Hudson Institute, a conservative think tank; Alex works with him, and is trained as a plant physiologist. We sat in a sunroom at the back of the house, our afternoon conversation punctuated every so often by dog snores and rooster crows. We talked for a little while about the Green Revolution, a dramatic advance in farm productivity that fed the world's burgeoning population over the past four decades, and then I asked if the challenge of the next four decades could be met.

"Well," Dennis replied, "we have tripled the world's farm output since 1960.   15
And we're feeding twice as many people from the same land. That was a heroic achievement. But we have to do what some think is an even more difficult thing in this next forty years, because the Green Revolution had more land per person and more water per person—"

"—and more potential for increases," Alex added, "because the base that we   16
were starting from was so much lower."

"By and large," Dennis went on, "the world's civilizations have been built   17
around its best farmland. And we have used most of the world's good farmland. Most of the good land is already heavily fertilized. Most of the good land is already being planted with high-yield seeds. [Africa is the important exception.] Most of the good irrigation sites are used. We can't triple yields again with the technologies we're already using. And we might be lucky to get a fifty percent yield increase if we froze our technology short of biotech."

"Biotech" can refer to a number of things, but the relevant application here is   18
genetic modification: the selective transfer of genes from one organism to another. Ordinary breeding can cross related varieties, but it cannot take a gene from a bacterium, for instance, and transfer it to a wheat plant. The organisms resulting from gene transfers are called "transgenic" by scientists—and "Frankenfood" by many greens.

Gene transfer poses risks, unquestionably. So, for that matter, does traditional   19
crossbreeding. But many people worry that transgenic organisms might prove more unpredictable. One possibility is that transgenic crops would spread from fields into forests or other wild lands and there become environmental nuisances, or worse. A further risk is that transgenic plants might cross-pollinate with neighboring wild plants, producing "superweeds" or other invasive or destructive varieties in the wild. Those risks are real enough that even most biotech enthusiasts—including Dennis Avery, for example—favor some government regulation of transgenic crops.

What is much less widely appreciated is biotech's potential to do the environ-   20
ment good. Take as an example continuous no-till farming, which really works best

with the help of transgenic crops. Human beings have been ploughing for so long that we tend to forget why we started doing it in the first place. The short answer: weed control. Turning over the soil between plantings smothers weeds and their seeds. If you don't plough, your land becomes a weed garden—unless you use herbicides to kill the weeds. Herbicides, however, are expensive, and can be complicated to apply. And they tend to kill the good with the bad.

21   In the mid-1990s the agricultural-products company Monsanto introduced a transgenic soybean variety called Roundup Ready. As the name implies, these soybeans tolerate Roundup, an herbicide (also made by Monsanto) that kills many kinds of weeds and then quickly breaks down into harmless ingredients. Equipped with Roundup Ready crops, farmers found that they could retire their ploughs and control weeds with just a few applications of a single, relatively benign herbicide—instead of many applications of a complex and expensive menu of chemicals. More than a third of all U.S. soybeans are now grown without ploughing, mostly owing to the introduction of Roundup Ready varieties. Ploughless cotton farming has likewise received a big boost from the advent of bioengineered varieties. No-till farming without biotech is possible, but it's more difficult and expensive, which is why no-till and biotech are advancing in tandem.

22   In 2001 a group of scientists announced that they had engineered a transgenic tomato plant able to thrive on salty water—water, in fact, almost half as salty as seawater, and fifty times as salty as tomatoes can ordinarily abide. One of the researchers was quoted as saying, "I've already transformed tomato, tobacco, and canola. I believe I can transform any crop with this gene"—just the sort of Frankenstein hubris that makes environmentalists shudder. But consider the environmental implications. Irrigation has for millennia been a cornerstone of agriculture, but it comes at a price. As irrigation water evaporates, it leaves behind traces of salt, which accumulate in the soil and gradually render it infertile. (As any Roman legion knows, to destroy a nation's agricultural base you salt the soil.) Every year the world loses about 25 million acres—an area equivalent to a fifth of California—to salinity; 40 percent of the world's irrigated land, and 25 percent of America's, has been hurt to some degree. For decades traditional plant breeders tried to create salt-tolerant crop plants, and for decades they failed.

23   Salt-tolerant crops might bring millions of acres of wounded or crippled land back into production. "And it gets better," Alex Avery told me. The transgenic tomato plants take up and sequester in their leaves as much as six or seven percent of their weight in sodium. "Theoretically," Alex said, "you could reclaim a salt-contaminated field by growing enough of these crops to remove the salts from the soil."

24   His father chimed in: "We've worried about being able to keep these salt-contaminated fields going even for decades. We can now think about *centuries.*"

25   One of the first biotech crops to reach the market, in the mid-1990s, was a cotton plant that makes its own pesticide. Scientists incorporated into the plant a toxin-producing gene from a soil bacterium known as *Bacillus thuringiensis.* With Bt cotton, as it is called, farmers can spray much less, and the poison contained in the plant is delivered only to bugs that actually eat the crop. As any environmentalist can tell you,

insecticide is not very nice stuff—especially if you breathe it, which many Third World farmers do as they walk through their fields with backpack sprayers.

Transgenic cotton reduced pesticide use by more than two million pounds in the United States from 1996 to 2000, and it has reduced pesticide sprayings in parts of China by more than half. Earlier this year the Environmental Protection Agency approved a genetically modified corn that resists a beetle larva known as rootworm. Because rootworm is American corn's most voracious enemy, this new variety has the potential to reduce annual pesticide use in America by more than 14 million pounds. It could reduce or eliminate the spraying of pesticide on 23 million acres of U.S. land. 26

All of that is the beginning, not the end. Bioengineers are also working, for instance, on crops that tolerate aluminum, another major contaminant of soil, especially in the tropics. Return an acre of farmland to productivity, or double yields on an already productive acre, and, other things being equal, you reduce by an acre the amount of virgin forest or savannah that will be stripped and cultivated. That may be the most important benefit of all. 27

Of the many people I have interviewed in my twenty years as a journalist, Norman Borlaug must be the one who has saved the most lives. Today he is an unprepossessing eighty-nine-year-old man of middling height, with crystal-bright blue eyes and thinning white hair. He still loves to talk about plant breeding, the discipline that won him the 1970 Nobel Peace Prize: Borlaug led efforts to breed the staples of the Green Revolution. (See "Forgotten Benefactor of Humanity," by Gregg Easterbrook, an article on Borlaug in the January 1997 *Atlantic*.) Yet the renowned plant breeder is quick to mention that he began his career, in the 1930s, in forestry, and that forest conservation has never been far from his thoughts. In the 1960s, while he was working to improve crop yields in India and Pakistan, he made a mental connection. He would create tables detailing acres under cultivation and average yields—and then, in another column, he would estimate how much land had been saved by higher farm productivity. Later, in the 1980s and 1990s, he and others began paying increased attention to what some agricultural economists now call the Borlaug hypothesis: that the Green Revolution has saved not only many human lives but, by improving the productivity of existing farmland, also millions of acres of tropical forest and other habitat—and so has saved countless animal lives. 28

From the 1960s through the 1980s, for example, Green Revolution advances saved more than 100 million acres of wild lands in India. More recently, higher yields in rice, coffee, vegetables, and other crops have reduced or in some cases stopped forest-clearing in Honduras, the Philippines, and elsewhere. Dennis Avery estimates that if farming techniques and yields had not improved since 1950, the world would have lost an additional 20 million or so square miles of wildlife habitat, most of it forest. About 16 million square miles of forest exists today. "What I'm saying," Avery said, in response to my puzzled expression, "is that we have saved every square mile of forest on the planet." 29

Habitat destruction remains a serious environmental problem; in some respects it is the most serious. The savannahs and tropical forests of Central and South America, Asia, and Africa by and large make poor farmland, but they are the earth's 30 storehouses of biodiversity, and the forests are the earth's lungs. Since 1972 about 200,000 square miles of Amazon rain forest have been cleared for crops and pasture; from 1966 to 1994 all but three of the Central American countries cleared more forest than they left standing. Mexico is losing more than 4,000 square miles of forest a year to peasant farms; sub-Saharan Africa is losing more than 19,000.

31   That is why the great challenge of the next four or five decades is not to feed an additional three billion people (and their pets) but to do so without converting much of the world's prime habitat into second- or third-rate farmland. Now, most agronomists agree that some substantial yield improvements are still to be had from advances in conventional breeding, fertilizers, herbicides, and other Green Revolution standbys. But it seems pretty clear that biotechnology holds more promise—probably much more. Recall that world food output will need to at least double and possibly triple over the next several decades. Even if production could be increased that much using conventional technology, which is doubtful, the required amounts of pesticide and fertilizer and other polluting chemicals would be immense. If properly developed, disseminated, and used, genetically modified crops might well be the best hope the planet has got.

32   If properly developed, disseminated, and used. That tripartite qualification turns out to be important, and it brings the environmental community squarely, and at the moment rather jarringly, into the picture.

33   Not long ago I went to see David Sandalow in his office at the World Wildlife Fund, in Washington, D.C. Sandalow, the organization's executive vice-president in charge of conservation programs, is a tall, affable, polished, and slightly reticent man in his forties who holds degrees from Yale and the University of Michigan Law School.

34   Some weeks earlier, over lunch, I had mentioned Dennis Avery's claim that genetic modification had great environmental potential. I was surprised when Sandalow told me he agreed. Later, in our interview in his office, I asked him to elaborate. "With biotechnology," he said, "there are no simple answers. Biotechnology has huge potential benefits and huge risks, and we need to address both as we move forward. The huge potential benefits include increased productivity of arable land, which could relieve pressure on forests. They include decreased pesticide usage. But the huge risks include severe ecological disruptions—from gene flow and from enhanced invasiveness, which is a very antiseptic word for some very scary stuff."

35   I asked if he thought that, absent biotechnology, the world could feed everybody over the next forty or fifty years without ploughing down the rain forests. Instead of answering directly he said, "Biotechnology could be part of our arsenal if we can overcome some of the barriers. It will never be a panacea or a magic bullet. But nor should we remove it from our tool kit."

36   Sandalow is unusual. Very few credentialed greens talk the way he does about biotechnology, at least publicly. They would readily agree with him about the huge risks, but they wouldn't be caught dead speaking of huge potential benefits—a point I will come back to. From an ecological point of view, a very great deal depends on other environmentalists' coming to think more the way Sandalow does.

Biotech companies are in business to make money. That is fitting and proper.   37
But developing and testing new transgenic crops is expensive and commercially
risky, to say nothing of politically controversial. When they decide how to invest
their research-and-development money, biotech companies will naturally seek products for which farmers and consumers will pay top dollar. Roundup Ready products,
for instance, are well suited to U.S. farming, with its high levels of capital spending
on such things as herbicides and automated sprayers. Poor farmers in the developing world, of course, have much less buying power. Creating, say, salt-tolerant cas-
sava suitable for growing on hardscrabble African farms might save habitat as well
as lives—but commercial enterprises are not likely to fall over one another in a
rush to do it.

If earth-friendly transgenics are developed, the next problem is disseminating   38
them. As a number of the farmers and experts I talked to were quick to mention,
switching to an unfamiliar new technology—something like no-till—is not easy. It
requires capital investment in new seed and equipment, mastery of new skills and
methods, a fragile transition period as farmer and ecology readjust, and an often
considerable amount of trial and error to find out what works best on any given
field. Such problems are only magnified in the Third World, where the learning
curve is steeper and capital cushions are thin to nonexistent. Just handing a peasant farmer a bag of newfangled seed is not enough. In many cases peasant farmers
will need one-on-one attention. Many will need help to pay for the seed, too.

Finally there is the matter of using biotech in a way that actually benefits the   39
environment. Often the technological blade can cut either way, especially in the
short run. A salt-tolerant or drought-resistant rice that allowed farmers to keep
land in production might also induce them to plough up virgin land that previously
was too salty or too dry to farm. If the effect of improved seed is to make farming
more profitable, farmers may respond, at least temporarily, by bringing more land
into production. If a farm becomes more productive, it may require fewer workers;
and if local labor markets cannot provide jobs for them, displaced workers may
move to a nearby patch of rain forest and burn it down to make way for subsistence
farming. Such transition problems are solvable, but they need money and attention.

In short, realizing the great—probably unique—environmental potential of   40
biotech will require stewardship. "It's a tool," Sara Scherr, an agricultural economist with the conservation group Forest Trends, told me, "but it's absolutely not going to happen automatically."

So now ask a question: Who is the natural constituency for earth-friendly   41
biotechnology? Who cares enough to lobby governments to underwrite research—
frequently unprofitable research—on transgenic crops that might restore soils or
cut down on pesticides in poor countries? Who cares enough to teach Asian or
African farmers, one by one, how to farm without ploughing? Who cares enough to
help poor farmers afford high-tech, earth-friendly seed? Who cares enough to agi-
tate for programs and reforms that might steer displaced peasants and profit-seek-
ing farmers away from sensitive lands? Not politicians, for the most part. Not farmers. Not corporations. Not consumers.

42   At the World Resources Institute, an environmental think tank in Washington, the molecular biologist Don Doering envisions transgenic crops designed specifically to solve environmental problems: crops that might fertilize the soil, crops that could clean water, crops tailored to remedy the ecological problems of specific places. "Suddenly you might find yourself with a virtually chemical-free agriculture, where your cropland itself is filtering the water, it's protecting the watershed, it's providing habitat," Doering told me. "There is still so little investment in what I call design-for-environment." The natural constituency for such investment is, of course, environmentalists.

43   But environmentalists are not acting as such a constituency today. They are doing the opposite. For example, Greenpeace declares on its Web site: "The introduction of genetically engineered (GE) organisms into the complex ecosystems of our environment is a dangerous global experiment with nature and evolution . . . GE organisms must not be released into the environment. They pose unacceptable risks to ecosystems, and have the potential to threaten biodiversity, wildlife and sustainable forms of agriculture."

44   Other groups argue for what they call the Precautionary Principle, under which no transgenic crop could be used until proven benign in virtually all respects. The Sierra Club says on its Web site,

> In accordance with this Precautionary Principle, we call for a moratorium on the planting of all genetically engineered crops and the release of all GEOs [genetically engineered organisms] into the environment, *including those now approved*. Releases should be delayed until extensive, rigorous research is done which determines the long-term environmental and health impacts of each GEO and there is public debate to ascertain the need for the use of each GEO intended for release into the environment. [italics added]

Under this policy the cleaner water and healthier soil that continuous no-till farming has already brought to the Chesapeake Bay watershed would be undone, and countless tons of polluted runoff and eroded topsoil would accumulate in Virginia rivers and streams while debaters debated and researchers researched. Recall David Sandalow: "Biotechnology has huge potential benefits and huge risks, and we need to address both as we move forward." A lot of environmentalists would say instead, "*before* we move forward." That is an important difference, particularly because the big population squeeze will happen not in the distant future but over the next several decades.

45   For reasons having more to do with politics than with logic, the modern environmental movement was to a large extent founded on suspicion of markets and artificial substances. Markets exploit the earth; chemicals poison it. Biotech touches both hot buttons. It is being pushed forward by greedy corporations, and it seems to be the very epitome of the unnatural.

46   Still, I hereby hazard a prediction. In ten years or less, most American environmentalists (European ones are more dogmatic) will regard genetic modification as one of their most powerful tools. In only the past ten years or so, after all, environmentalists have reversed field and embraced market mechanisms—tradable emis-

sions permits and the like—as useful in the fight against pollution. The environmental logic of biotechnology is, if anything, even more compelling. The potential upside of genetic modification is simply too large to ignore—and therefore environmentalists will not ignore it. Biotechnology will transform agriculture, and in doing so will transform American environmentalism.

Ten Reasons Why Biotechnology Will Not Ensure Food Security, Protect the Environment, and Reduce Poverty in the Developing World

Miguel A. Altieri and Peter Rosset

This scholarly policy argument appeared first in the academic journal AgBioForum *in 1999 and was subsequently posted on the Web site for that publication. The article has also been published in* Sierra Magazine. *Miguel A. Altieri, Ph.D., teaches agroecology in the Department of Environmental Science, Policy and Management at the University of California at Berkeley and is a technical advisor to the Latin American Consortium on Agroecology and Development in Santiago. Peter Rossett is the executive director of the Institute for Food and Development Policy, www.foodfirst.org.*

Biotechnology companies often claim that genetically modified organisms (GMOs)—specifically, genetically altered seeds—are essential scientific breakthroughs needed to feed the world, protect the environment, and reduce poverty in developing countries. The Consultative Group on International Agricultural Research (CGIAR) and its constellation of international centers around the world charged with research to enhance food security in the developing world echo this view, which rests on two critical assumptions. The first is that hunger is due to a gap between food production and human population density or growth rate. The second is that genetic engineering is the only or best way to increase agricultural production and, thus, meet future food needs. 1

Our objective is to challenge the notion of biotechnology as a magic bullet solution to all of agriculture's ills, by clarifying misconceptions concerning these underlying assumptions. 2

1. There is no relationship between the prevalence of hunger in a given country and its population. For every densely populated and hungry nation like Bangladesh or Haiti, there is a sparsely populated and hungry nation like Brazil and Indonesia. The world today produces more food per inhabitant than ever before. Enough food is available to provide 4.3 pounds for every person every day: 2.5 pounds of grain, 3

beans and nuts, about a pound of meat, milk and eggs and another of fruits and vegetables. The real causes of hunger are poverty, inequality and lack of access to food and land. Too many people are too poor to buy the food that is available (but often poorly distributed) or lack the land and resources to grow it themselves (*Lappe, Collins & Rosset, 1998*).

4   2. Most innovations in agricultural biotechnology have been profit-driven rather than need-driven. The real thrust of the genetic engineering industry is not to make third world agriculture more productive, but rather to generate profits (*Busch et al., 1990*). This is illustrated by reviewing the principle technologies on the market today: (1) herbicide resistant crops, such as Monsanto's "Roundup Ready" soybeans, seeds that are tolerant to Monsanto's herbicide Roundup, and (2) "Bt" (*Bacillus thuringiensis*) crops which are engineered to produce their own insecticide. In the first instance, the goal is to win a greater herbicide market-share for a proprietary product and, in the second, to boost seed sales at the cost of damaging the usefulness of a key pest management product (the *Bacillus thuringiensis* based microbial insecticide) relied upon by many farmers, including most organic farmers, as a powerful alternative to insecticides. These technologies respond to the need of biotechnology companies to intensify farmers' dependence upon seeds protected by so-called "intellectual property rights" which conflict directly with the age-old rights of farmers to reproduce, share or store seeds (*Hobbelink, 1991*). Whenever possible corporations will require farmers to buy a company's brand of inputs and will forbid farmers from keeping or selling seed. By controlling germplasm from seed to sale, and by forcing farmers to pay inflated prices for seed-chemical packages, companies are determined to extract the most profit from their investment (*Krimsky & Wrubel, 1996*).

5   3. The integration of the seed and chemical industries appears destined to accelerate increases in per acre expenditures for seeds plus chemicals, delivering significantly lower returns to growers. Companies developing herbicide tolerant crops are trying to shift as much per acre cost as possible from the herbicide onto the seed via seed costs and technology charges. Increasingly price reductions for herbicides will be limited to growers purchasing technology packages. In Illinois, the adoption of herbicide resistant crops makes for the most expensive soybean seed-plus-weed management system in modern history—between $40.00 and $60.00 per acre depending on fee rates, weed pressure, and so on. Three years ago, the average seed-plus-weed control costs on Illinois farms was $26 per acre, and represented 23% of variable costs; today they represent 35–40% (*Benbrook, 1999*). Many farmers are willing to pay for the simplicity and robustness of the new weed management system, but such advantages may be short-lived as ecological problems arise.

6   4. Recent experimental trials have shown that genetically engineered seeds do not increase the yield of crops. A recent study by the United States Department of Agriculture (USDA) Economic Research Service shows that in 1998 yields were not significantly different in engineered versus non-engineered crops in 12 of 18 crop/region combinations. In the six crop/region combinations where Bt crops or herbicide tolerant crops (HTCs) fared better, they exhibited increased yields be-

tween 5–30%. Glyphosphate tolerant cotton showed no significant yield increase in either region where it was surveyed. This was confirmed in another study examining more than 8,000 field trials, where it was found that Roundup Ready soybean seeds produced fewer bushels of soybeans than similar conventionally bred varieties (*USDA, 1999*).

5. Many scientists claim that the ingestion of genetically engineered food is harmless. Recent evidence, however, shows that there are potential risks of eating such foods as the new proteins produced in such foods could: (1) act themselves as allergens or toxins; (2) alter the metabolism of the food producing plant or animal, causing it to produce new allergens or toxins; or (3) reduce its nutritional quality or value. In the case of (3), herbicide resistant soybeans can contain less isoflavones, an important phytoestrogen present in soybeans, believed to protect women from a number of cancers. At present, developing countries are importing soybean and corn from the United States, Argentina, and Brazil. Genetically engineered foods are beginning to flood the markets in the importing countries, yet no one can predict all their health effects on consumers, who are unaware that they are eating such food. Because genetically engineered food remains unlabeled, consumers cannot discriminate between genetically engineered (GE) and non-GE food, and should serious health problems arise, it will be extremely difficult to trace them to their source. Lack of labeling also helps to shield the corporations that could be potentially responsible from liability (*Lappe & Bailey, 1998*). [7]

6. Transgenic plants which produce their own insecticides closely follow the pesticide paradigm, which is itself rapidly failing due to pest resistance to insecticides. Instead of the failed "one pest-one chemical" model, genetic engineering emphasizes a "one pest-one gene" approach, shown over and over again in laboratory trials to fail, as pest species rapidly adapt and develop resistance to the insecticide present in the plant (*Alstad & Andow, 1995*). Not only will the new varieties fail over the short-to-medium term, despite so-called voluntary resistance management schemes (*Mallet & Porter, 1992*), but in the process may render useless the natural Bt-pesticide which is relied upon by organic farmers and others desiring to reduce chemical dependence. Bt crops violate the basic and widely accepted principle of integrated pest management (IPM), which is that reliance on any single pest management technology tends to trigger shifts in pest species or the evolution of resistance through one or more mechanisms (*NRC, 1996*). In general, the greater the selection pressure across time and space, the quicker and more profound the pests' evolutionary response. An obvious reason for adopting this principle is that it reduces pest exposure to pesticides, retarding the evolution of resistance. But when the product is engineered into the plant itself, pest exposure leaps from minimal and occasional to massive and continuous exposure, dramatically accelerating resistance (*Gould, 1994*). *Bacillus thuringiensis* will rapidly become useless, both as a feature of the new seeds and as an old standby sprayed when needed by farmers that want out of the pesticide treadmill (*Pimentel et al., 1989*). [8]

7. The global fight for market share is leading companies to massively deploy transgenic crops around the world (more than 30 million hectares in 1998) without [9]

proper advance testing of short-or long-term impacts on human health and ecosystems. In the United States, private sector pressure led the White House to decree "no substantial difference" between altered and normal seeds, thus evading normal Food and Drug Administration (FDA) and Environmental Protection Agency (EPA) testing. Confidential documents made public in an on-going class action lawsuit have revealed that the FDA's own scientists do not agree with this determination. One reason is that many scientists are concerned that the large scale use of transgenic crops poses a series of environmental risks that threaten the sustainability of agriculture (*Goldberg, 1992; Paoletti & Pimentel, 1996; Snow & Moran, 1997; Rissler & Mellon, 1996; Kendall et al., 1997; Royal Society, 1998*). These risk areas are as follows:

- The trend to create broad international markets for single products is simplifying cropping systems and creating genetic uniformity in rural landscapes. History has shown that a huge area planted to a single crop variety is very vulnerable to new matching strains of pathogens or insect pests. Furthermore, the widespread use of homogeneous transgenic varieties will unavoidably lead to "genetic erosion," as the local varieties used by thousands of farmers in the developing world are replaced by the new seeds (*Robinson, 1996*).

- The use of herbicide resistant crops undermines the possibilities of crop diversification, thus, reducing agrobiodiversity in time and space (*Altieri, 1994*).

- The potential transfer through gene flow of genes from herbicide resistant crops to wild or semidomesticated relatives can lead to the creation of superweeds (*Lutman, 1999*).

- There is potential for herbicide resistant varieties to become serious weeds in other crops (*Duke, 1996; Holt & Le Baron, 1990*).

- Massive use of Bt crops affects non-target organisms and ecological processes. Recent evidence shows that the Bt toxin can affect beneficial insect predators that feed on insect pests present on Bt crops (*Hilbeck et al., 1998*). In addition, windblown pollen from Bt crops, found on natural vegetation surrounding transgenic fields, can kill non-target insects such as the monarch butterfly (*Losey et al., 1999*). Moreover, Bt toxin present in crop foliage plowed under after harvest can adhere to soil colloids for up to 3 months, negatively affecting the soil invertebrate populations that break down organic matter and play other ecological roles (*Donnegan et al., 1995; Palm et al., 1996*).

- There is potential for vector recombination to generate new virulent strains of viruses, especially in transgenic plants engineered for viral resistance with viral genes. In plants containing coat protein genes, there is a possibility that such genes will be taken up by unrelated viruses infecting the plant. In such situations, the foreign gene changes the coat structure of the viruses and may confer properties, such as changed method of transmission between plants. The second potential risk is that recombination between RNA virus and a viral RNA inside the transgenic crop could produce a new pathogen leading to more severe disease problems. Some researchers have shown that recombination occurs in transgenic plants and that under certain conditions it produces a new viral strain with altered host range (*Steinbrecher, 1996*).

Ecological theory predicts that the large-scale landscape homogenization with   10 transgenic crops will exacerbate the ecological problems already associated with monoculture agriculture. Unquestioned expansion of this technology into developing countries may not be wise or desirable. There is strength in the agricultural diversity of many of these countries, and it should not be inhibited or reduced by extensive monoculture, especially when consequences of doing so result in serious social and environmental problems (*Altieri, 1996*).

Although the ecological risks issue has received some discussion in govern-   11 ment, international, and scientific circles, discussions have often been pursued from a narrow perspective that has downplayed the seriousness of the risks (*Kendall et al., 1997; Royal Society, 1998*). In fact, methods for risk assessment of transgenic crops are not well developed (*Kjellsson & Simonsen, 1994*) and there is justifiable concern that current field biosafety tests tell little about potential environmental risks associated with commercial-scale production of transgenic crops. A main concern is that international pressures to gain markets and profits is resulting in companies releasing transgenic crops too fast, without proper consideration for the long-term impacts on people or the ecosystem.

8. There are many unanswered ecological questions regarding the impact of   12 transgenic crops. Many environmental groups have argued for the creation of suitable regulation to mediate the testing and release of transgenic crops to offset environmental risks and demand a much better assessment and understanding of ecological issues associated with genetic engineering. This is crucial, as many results emerging from the environmental performance of released transgenic crops suggest that in the development of resistant crops not only is there a need to test direct effects on the target insect or weed, but the indirect effects on the plant. Plant growth, nutrient content, metabolic changes, and effects on the soil and non-target organisms should all be examined. Unfortunately, funds for research on environmental risk assessment are very limited. For example, the USDA spends only 1% of the funds allocated to biotechnology research on risk assessment, about $1–2 million per year. Given the current level of deployment of genetically engineered plants, such resources are not enough to even discover the "tip of the iceberg." It is a tragedy-in-the-making that so many millions of hectares have been planted without proper biosafety standards. Worldwide such acreage expanded considerably in 1998 with transgenic cotton reaching 6.3 million acres, transgenic corn reaching 20.8 million acres, and transgenic soybean 36.3 million acres. This expansion has been helped along by marketing and distribution agreements entered into by corporations and marketers (i.e., Ciba Seeds with Growmark and Mycogen Plant Sciences with Cargill), and in the absence of regulations in many developing countries. Genetic pollution, unlike oil spills, cannot be controlled by throwing a boom around it.

13   9. As the private sector has exerted more and more dominance in advancing new biotechnologies, the public sector has had to invest a growing share of its scarce resources in enhancing biotechnological capacities in public institutions, including the CGIAR, and in evaluating and responding to the challenges posed by incorporating private sector technologies into existing farming systems. Such funds would be much better used to expand support for ecologically based agricultural research, as all the biological problems that biotechnology aims at can be solved using agroecological approaches. The dramatic effects of rotations and intercropping on crop health and productivity, as well as of the use of biological control agents on pest regulation have been confirmed repeatedly by scientific research. The problem is that research at public institutions increasingly reflects the interests of private funders at the expense of public good research, such as biological control, organic production systems and general agroecological techniques. Civil society must request for more research on alternatives to biotechnology by universities and other public organizations (*Krimsky & Wrubel, 1996*). There is also an urgent need to challenge the patent system and intellectual property rights intrinsic to the World Trade Organization (WTO) which not only provide multinational corporations with the right to seize and patent genetic resources, but will also accelerate the rate at which market forces already encourage monocultural cropping with genetically uniform transgenic varieties. Based on history and ecological theory, it is not difficult to predict the negative impacts of such environmental simplification on the health of modern agriculture (*Altieri, 1996*).

14   10. Much of the needed food can be produced by small farmers located throughout the world using agroecological technologies (*Uphoff & Altieri, 1999*). In fact, new rural development approaches and low-input technologies spearheaded by farmers and non-governmental organizations (NGOs) around the world are already making a significant contribution to food security at the household, national, and regional levels in Africa, Asia and Latin America (*Pretty, 1995*). Yield increases are being achieved by using technological approaches, based on agroecological principles that emphasize diversity, synergy, recycling and integration; and social processes that emphasize community participation and empowerment (*Rosset, 1999*). When such features are optimized, yield enhancement and stability of production are achieved, as well as a series of ecological services such as conservation of biodiversity, soil and water restoration and conservation, improved natural pest regulation mechanisms, and so on (*Altieri et al., 1998*). These results are a breakthrough for achieving food security and environmental preservation in the developing world, but their potential and further spread depends on investments, policies, institutional support, and attitude changes on the part of policy makers and the scientific community; especially the CGIAR who should devote much of its efforts to the 320 million poor farmers living in marginal environments. Failure to promote such people-centered agricultural research and development due to the diversion of funds and expertise towards biotechnology will forego an historical opportunity to raise agricultural productivity in economically viable, environmentally benign, and socially uplifting ways.

References

Alstad, D. N., and Andow, D. A. (1995). Managing the evolution of insect resistance to transgenic plants. *Science, 268,* 1894–1896.

Altieri, M. A. (1994). *Biodiversity and pest management in agroecosystems.* New York: Haworth Press.

Altieri, M. A. (1996). *Agroecology: The science of sustainable agriculture.* Boulder, CO: Westview Press.

Altieri, M. A., Rosset, P., and Thrupp, L. A. (1998). *The potential of agroecology to combat hunger in the developing world* (2020 Brief No. 55). Washington, DC: International Food Policy Research Institute.

Benbrook, C. (1999). *World food system challenges and opportunities: GMOs, biodiversity and lessons from America's heartland.* Unpublished manuscript.

Busch, L., Lacey, W. B., Burkhardt, J., and Lacey, L. (1990). *Plants, power and profit.* Oxford, England: Basil Blackwell.

Casper, R., and Landsmann, J. (1992). The biosafety results of field tests of genetically modified plants and microorganisms. P. K. Landers (Ed.), *Proceedings of the Second International Symposium Goslar,* pp. 89–97, Germany.

Donnegan, K. K., Palm, C. J., Fieland, V. J., Porteous, L. A., Ganis, L. M., Scheller, D. L., and Seidler, R. J. (1995). Changes in levels, species, and DNA fingerprints of soil microorganisms associated with cotton expressing the Bacillus thuringiensis var. Kurstaki endotoxin. *Applied Soil Ecology, 2,* 111–124.

Duke, S. O. (1996). *Herbicide resistant crops: Agricultural, environmental, economic, regulatory, and technical aspects.* Boca Raton: Lewis Publishers.

Goldberg, R. J. (1992). Environmental concerns with the development of herbicide-tolerant plants. *Weed Technology, 6,* 647–652.

Gould, F. (1994). Potential and problems with high-dose strategies for pesticidal engineered crops. *Biocontrol Science and Technology, 4,* 451–461.

Hilbeck, A., Baumgartner, M., Fried, P. M., and Bigler, F. (1998). Effects of transgenic Bacillus thuringiensis corn fed prey on mortality and development time of immature Chrysoperla carnea Neuroptera: Chrysopidae. *Environmental Entomology, 27,* 460–487.

Hobbelink, H. (1991). *Biotechnology and the future of world agriculture.* London: Zed Books, Ltd.

Holt, J. S., and Le Baron, H. M. (1990). Significance and distribution of herbicide resistance. *Weed Technology, 4,* 141–149.

James, C. (1997). *Global status of transgenic crops in 1997* (ISAAA Briefs No. 5.). Ithaca, NY: International Service for the Acquisition of Agri-Biotech Application (ISAAA). Available on the World Wide Web: http://www.isaaa.org/frbrief5.htm

Kendall, H. W., Beachy, R., Eismer, T., Gould, F., Herdt, R., Ravon, P. H., Schell, J., and Swaminathan, M. S. (1997). *Bioengineering of crops* (Report of the World Bank Panel on Transgenic Crops, pp. 1–30). Washington, DC: World Bank.

Kennedy, G. G., and Whalon, M. E. (1995). Managing pest resistance to Bacillus thuringiensis endotoxins: Constraints and incentives to implementation. *Journal of Economic Entomology, 88,* 454–460.

Kjellsson, G., and Simonsen, V. (1994). *Methods for risk assessment of transgenic plants.* Basil, Germany: Birkhauser Verlag.

Krimsky, S., and Wrubel, R. P. (1996). Agricultural biotechnology and the environment: Science, policy and social issues. Urbana, IL: University of Illinois Press.

Lappe, F. M., Collins, J., and Rosset, P. (1998). *World hunger: Twelve myths.* New York: Grove Press.

Lappe, M., and Bailey, B. (1998). *Against the grain: Biotechnology and the corporate takeover of food.* Monroe, ME: Common Courage Press.

Liu, Y. B., Tabashnik, B. E., Dennehy, T. J., Patin, A. L., and Bartlett A. C. (1999). Development time and resistance to Bt crops. *Nature, 400,* 519.

Losey, J. J. E., Rayor, L. S., and Carter, M. E. (1999). Transgenic pollen harms monarch larvae. *Nature, 399,* 214.

Lutman, P. J. W. (1999). (Ed.). Gene flow and agriculture: Relevance for transgenic crops. *British Crop Protection Council Symposium Proceedings, 72,* 43–64.

Mallet, J., and Porter, P. (1992). Preventing insect adaptations to insect resistant crops: Are seed mixtures or refugia the best strategy? *Proceedings of the Royal Society of London Series B Biology Science, 250,* 165–169.

National Research Council (NRC). (1996). *Ecologically based pest management.* Washington, DC: National Academy of Sciences.

Palm, C. J., Schaller, D. L., Donegan, K. K., and Seidler, R. J. (1996). Persistence in soil of transgenic plant produced bacillus thuringiensis var. kustaki-endotoxin. *Canadian Journal of Microbiology, 42,* 1258–1262.

Paoletti, M. G., and Pimentel, D. (1996). Genetic engineering in agriculture and the environment: Assessing risks and benefits. *BioScience, 46,* 665–671.

Pimentel, D., Hunter, M. S., LaGro, J. A., Efroymson, R. A., Landers, J. C., Mervis, F. T., McCarthy, C. A., and Boyd, A. E. (1989). Benefits and risks of genetic engineering in agriculture. *BioScience, 39,* 606–614.

Pretty, J. (1995). Regenerating agriculture: Policies and practices for sustainability and self-reliance. London: Earthscan.

Rissler, J., and Mellon, M. (1996). *The ecological risks of engineered crops.* Cambridge, MA: MIT Press.

Robinson, R. A. (1996). Return to resistance: Breeding crops to reduce pesticide resistance. Davis, CA: AgAccess.

Rosset, P. (1999). *The multiple functions and benefits of small farm agriculture in the context of global trade negotiations* (IFDP Food First Policy Brief No. 4). Washington, DC: Institute for Food and Development Policy.

Royal Society. (1998, February). Genetically modified plants for food use. *Statement 2/98.* London: Royal Society.

Snow, A. A., and Moran, P. (1997). Commercialization of transgenic plants: Potential ecological risks. *BioScience, 47,* 86–96.

Steinbrecher, R. A. (1996). From green to gene revolution: The environmental risks of genetically engineered crops. *The Ecologist, 26,* 273–282.

United States Department of Agriculture (USDA). (1999). *Genetically engineered crops for pest management.* Washington, DC: USDA Economic Research Service.

Uphoff, N., and Altieri, M. A. (1999). *Alternatives to conventional modern agriculture for meeting world food needs in the next century* (Report of a Bellagio Conference). Ithaca, NY: Cornell International Institute for Food, Agriculture and Development.

Monsantoland

This poster image has appeared on numerous Web sites protesting the major biotech food company, Monsanto. Note the impact of its claim and its powerful appeals to pathos.

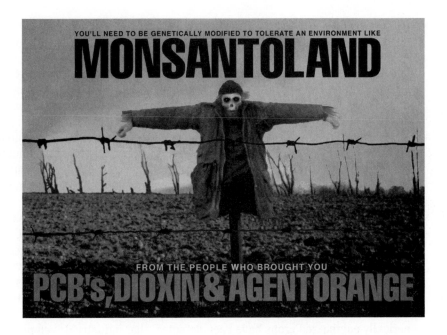

Lessen the Fear of Genetically Engineered Crops

Gregory A. Jaffe

This middle-ground policy argument appeared in the Christian Science Monitor *on August 8, 2001. Gregory A. Jaffe is codirector for the Project on Biotechnology for the Center for Science in the Public Interest.*

Protesters carrying signs stating "Biocide is Homicide" and shouting concerns about the risks of eating genetically engineered foods recently demonstrated outside the biotechnology industry's annual convention. Inside the convention center, the industry extolled the safety of genetically engineered foods and the benefits of future crops like "golden rice."

Neither corporate hyperbole nor radical slogans do much to inform the public. What is needed is the shaping of sensible measures to ensure that genetically engineered foods are safe. The first few engineered crops are already providing remarkable benefits. Cotton modified to kill insects has greatly diminished farmers' use of toxic insecticides, thereby reducing costs, increasing yields, and, presumably, reducing harm to nontarget species. Likewise, biotech soybeans facilitate no-till farming, which reduces soil erosion and water pollution.

3   Despite such benefits, agricultural biotechnology is under siege for reasons good and bad. Activists have burned fields and bombed labs. Farmers will not plant genetically engineered sweet corn, sugar beets, and apples, for fear of consumer rejection. And countries in Europe and Asia refuse to import US-grown genetically engineered crops. Some countries now require labeling of foods containing engineered ingredients. Those requirements have spurred food processors, who want to avoid negative-sounding labels, to eliminate bioengineered ingredients.

4   Buffeted by the polarized debate, many Americans oppose biotech foods, in part because farmers and seed companies get the benefits while consumers bear the risk. If anti-genetically engineered sentiment increases, US farmers may be forced to forgo the advantages of engineered crops. And most public and private investment in agricultural biotechnology would dry up.

5   To reap the benefits of agricultural biotechnology, minimize the risks, and boost public confidence, the US must upgrade its flawed regulatory system. Currently, the Food and Drug Administration (FDA) does not formally approve any genetically engineered crops as safe to eat. Instead, it reviews safety data provided voluntarily by seed companies. That consultation process, which the FDA admits is "not a comprehensive scientific review of the data," culminates with the FDA stating only that it has "no further questions . . . at this time." Although no health problems with genetically engineered crops have been detected, that industry-driven process is weak insurance. The recent FDA proposal requiring a formal notification before marketing a biotech food is an improvement.

6   All biotech foods should go through a mandatory approval process with specific testing and data requirements. The National Academy of Sciences should be commissioned to recommend a precise method of assessment.

7   Genetically engineered crops also raise environmental concerns. They could lead to pesticide-resistant insects and weeds and might contaminate plants that are close relatives of the crops. To safeguard our ecosystem, the current laws need fixing. Congress should close regulatory gaps to ensure that all future applications of biotechnology, ranging from fast-growing fish to corn plants that produce industrial chemicals, receive thorough environmental reviews. Also, the Environmental Protection Agency must enforce restrictions it has imposed on bioengineered crops to help prevent emergence of insecticide-resistant pests.

8   Although strong regulations would minimize environmental and safety risks, nothing would boost public confidence more than engineered products that benefit consumers. No beneficial products currently exist.

9   Worldwide acceptance of biotechnology will only occur when other countries reap benefits from this technology. Instead of spending millions of dollars on feel-good advertising campaigns, the biotech industry should train developing-country scientists and fund research in those countries. Companies—and universities—should donate patented crops and processes to developing countries. Agricultural biotechnology is not a panacea for all agricultural problems here or abroad, nor is it free from risk. But, with adequate safeguards, it could provide tremendous benefits for an ever-populous, pesticide-drenched, and water-deficient globe.

Food Industry Should Modify Its Stance on Altered Food

Froma Harrop

This op-ed piece by nationally syndicated columnist Froma Harrop appeared in newspapers across the United States in November 2002. The immediate context for Harrop's argument was an Oregon referendum—defeated by voters at the polls—to require labeling of genetically modified foods. The presence of the referendum on the Oregon ballot stimulated a corporate advertising blitz by the major growers of genetically modified foods, who outspent their opponents 25 to 1.

My primitive response to genetically modified foods is to ask, "What's wrong with the grub of the last 250,000 years?" Mucking around with genetic material to create new kinds of fruits, vegetables and animals seems somehow unnecessary. Cows have produced pretty good milk over the millennia using their cow genes. So why insert rat genes into a perfectly acceptable cow?

Call me old-fashioned, but given a choice between a traditional tomato and a tomato carrying fish DNA, I will select the former.

Are these genetically modified organisms (GMOs) safe to eat? I don't know. But regardless of the science, I remain an anchor in the stream of progress. I do not want GMOs on my plate for moral, ethical, emotional, religious, aesthetic, sentimental and other reasons I haven't thought of yet.

Monsanto, I'm obviously not your customer. But I'd like to make a deal with you and the other food/biotech companies pushing all this gene splicing. Let me decide whether or not to buy genetically engineered foods at the store. Don't force me onto a farm in the woods where I must sit guard over my organic vegetable patch with a shotgun and a crazed look on my face. In other words, stop fighting proposals to label foods for GMO content.

The biotech-food-industrial complex opposes such labeling for sound business reasons: The world is full of people like me. Polls consistently show Americans objecting to genetically manipulated food by solid majorities. Some 93 percent of the respondents to a poll conducted for ABCNEWS.com wanted mandatory labeling of bio-engineered products.

That's why the complex pounced on a potentially path-clearing referendum in Oregon that would have required labels. Monsanto joined Kraft, Unilever and other opponents to outspend supporters 25-to-1. The proposal was soundly defeated following ludicrous claims that a labeling law would cost the average Oregon family $550 a year. (Similar laws in Europe, Japan and Australia have not noticeably raised the price of food.)

Actually, the U.S. trade representative will soon decide whether to drag Europe before the World Trade Organization over its restrictions on importing genetically modified corn and soybeans. Right now, 34 percent of corn and 75 percent of soybeans in America are grown from genetically manipulated seed.

8   With Europeans already inflamed by U.S. environmental policies, this seems a swell time for the Bush administration to bully them over their food supply, Europe's No. 1 cultural issue. Prince Charles is going around the kingdom condemning genetically engineered food as something that "takes mankind into realms that belong to God and God alone."

9   The Bush administration and Monsanto like each other a great deal, which is why we can't trust our government to give us the straight story on GMOs. Of course, they will never conquer dine-o-saurs like me. But if they want to win over folks concerned only about how GMOs might affect health and the environment, they're going about it the wrong way.

10   A U.S. Food and Drug Administration confident about the safety of these products would not have weighed in so loudly against the Oregon labeling proposal. And what possessed the administration to name Monsanto's former Washington lobbyist for GMOs as second in command at the Environmental Protection Agency?

11   Over at the National Academy of Sciences, a panel sung the praises of federal efforts to regulate genetically engineered foods. It turned out that six of the 12 panel members had ties to the biotech industry.

12   The complex showers the public with rather impressive claims for GMOs. GMO farmers can up food production for a hungry world. GMO crops reduce pesticide use. GMO cows (the ones with rat genes) produce milk that's better for the heart. Hey, they may be right in some cases.

13   All this matters not to me. Others may forge ahead with new culinary traditions. I won't chow down on GMOs and I will echo Prince Charles' call for "strong and sustained pressure from consumers to ensure that they keep the right not to eat them."

14   Our farmers produce beautiful and abundant food without putting moth genes into catfish. Why mess with success?

What Is the FDA Trying to Feed Us?

Sustainusa.org

Using the "piranhaberry" as its main image, Sustainusa.org, a "non-profit organization that promotes a healthy, sustainable environment through innovative communication strategies" (from its Web page), launched a "Keep Nature Natural" campaign against Monsanto and other biotechnology companies. This striking image appeared on the campaign's fliers, posters, postcards, and magazine ads.

Is Genetic Engineering the Answer to Hunger?

Gerald D. Coleman

Our concluding article focuses on differing ethical views of genetic engineering in the light of Roman Catholic social teaching, which calls on people from rich nations to stand in solidarity with the world's poor. It was published in America, *one of the nation's leading Catholic intellectual magazines. Its author, Gerald D. Coleman, is a professor of moral theology at St. Patrick's Seminary and University in Menlo Park, California.*

Both the developed and developing worlds are facing a critical moral choice in the controversial issue of genetically modified food, also known as genetically modified organisms and genetically engineered crops. Critics of these modifications speak dismissively of biotech foods and genetic pollution. On the other hand, proponents like Nina Federoff and Nancy Marie Brown, authors of *Mendel in the Kitchen: A Scientist's View of Genetically Modified Foods* (2004), promote genetically modified organisms (G.M.'s or G.M.O.'s) as "the miracle of seed science and fertilizers."

2   To mark the 20th anniversary of U.S. diplomatic relations with the Holy See, the U.S. Embassy to the Holy See, in cooperation with the Pontifical Academy of Sciences, hosted a conference last fall at Rome's Gregorian University on "Feeding a Hungry World: The Moral Imperative of Biotechnology." Archbishop Renato Martino, who heads the Pontifical Council for Justice and Peace and has been a strong and outspoken proponent of G.M.O.'s, told Vatican Radio: "The problem of hunger involves the conscience of every man. For this reason the Catholic Church follows with special interest and solicitude every development in science to help the solution of a plight that affects . . . humanity."

3   Americans have grown accustomed, perhaps unwittingly, to G.M.O. products. In the United States, for example, 68 percent of the soybeans, 70 percent of the cotton crop, 26 percent of corn and 55 percent of canola are genetically engineered. G.M.O.'s represent an estimated 60 percent of all American processed foods. A recent study by the National Center for Food and Agriculture found that farmers in the United States investing in biotech products harvested 5.3 billion additional pounds of crops and realized $22 billion in increased income. Most of the world's beer and cheese is made with G.M.O.'s, as are hundreds of medications. In an article published last October, James Nicholson, then U.S. Ambassador to the Vatican and an aggressive promoter of U.S. policy in Vatican circles, wrote that "millions of Americans, Canadians, Australians, Argentines and other people have been eating genetically modified food for nearly a decade—without one proven case of an illness, allergic reaction or even the hiccups. . . . Mankind has been genetically altering food throughout human history." And according to its supporters, biotechnology helps the environment by reducing the use of pesticides and tilling.

4   The World Health Association recently reported that more than 3.7 billion people around the world are now malnourished, the largest number in history. To this, opponents of G.M.O.'s reply that the "real problems" causing hunger, especially in the developing world, are poverty, lack of education and training, unequal land distribution and lack of access to markets. The moral point they advance is that distribution, not production, is the key to solving hunger. Another significant moral issue relates to "intellectual property policies" and the interest of companies in licensing potentially valuable discoveries. The Rev. Giulio Albanese, head of the Missionary News Agency, insists that unless the problem of intellectual property is resolved in favor of the poor, it represents a "provocation" to developing countries: "The concern of many in the missionary world over the property rights to G.M. seeds . . . cannot but accentuate the dependence of the poor nations on the rich ones." In response to this concern, a proposal was made recently (reported in *Science* magazine on March 19) that research universities cooperate to seek open licensing provisions that would allow them to share their intellectual property through a "developing-country license." Universities would still retain rights for research and education and maintain negotiating power with the biotechnology and pharmaceutical indus-

tries. Catholic social ethics would support this type of proposal, since it places the good of people over amassing profit. Three moral paths suggest themselves:

1.   Favor the use of G.M.O.'s. Nobel Prize winner Norman Borlaug, who developed the Green Revolution wheat and rice strains, recently wrote: "Biotechnology absolutely should be part of Africa's agricultural reform. African leaders would be making a grievous error if they turn their back on it." Proponents at the Rome conference agreed, arguing that the use of G.M.O.'s decreases pesticide-use, creates more nutrient-filled crops that require less water and have greater drought resistance, produces more food at a lower cost and uses less land. One small-scale South African farmer concluded, "We need this technology. We don't want always to be fed food aid. We want access to this technology so that one day we can also become commercial farmers."
     This position concludes that the use of G.M.O.'s amounts to a moral obligation.

2.   Condemn the use of G.M.O.'s. Many Catholic bishops take an opposing stance. Perhaps the clearest statement comes from the National Conference of Bishops of Brazil and their Pastoral Land Commission. Their argument is threefold: the use of G.M.O.'s involves potential risks to human health; a small group of large corporations will be the greatest beneficiaries, with grave damage to the family farmers; and the environment will be gravely damaged.
     The bishops of Botswana, South Africa and Swaziland agree: "We do not believe that agro-companies or gene technologies will help our farmers to produce the food that is needed in the 21st century." Roland Lesseps and Peter Henriot, two Jesuits working in Zambia who are experts on agriculture in the developing world, state their opposition on principle: "Nature is not just useful to us as humans, but is valued and loved in itself, for itself, by God in Christ. . . . The right to use other creatures does not give us the right to abuse them."
     In a similar but distinct criticism, the executive director of the U.S. National Catholic Rural Conference, David Andrews, C.S.C., feels that "the Pontifical Academy of Sciences has allowed itself to be subordinated to the U.S. government's insistent advocacy of biotechnology and the companies which market it." Sean McDonagh states: "With patents [on genetically engineered food], farmers will never own their own food. . . ." He believes that "corporate greed" is at the heart of the G.M.O. controversy. Biowatch's Elfrieda Pschorn-Strauss agrees: "With G.M. crops, small-scale farmers will become completely reliant on and controlled by big foreign companies for their food supply."
     This position concludes that the use of G.M.O.'s is morally irresponsible.

3.   Approach the use of G.M.O.'s with caution. Two years ago Pope John Paul II declared that G.M.O. agriculture could not be judged solely on the basis of "short-term economic interests," but needed to be subject to "a rigorous scientific and ethical process of verification." This cautionary stance has been adopted by the Catholic Bishops Conference of the Philippines in urging its government to postpone authorization of G.M.O. corn until comprehensive studies have been made: "We have to be careful because, once it is there, how can we remedy its consequences?"

In 2003 the Rural Life Committee of the North Dakota Conference of Churches also called for "rigorous examination" to understand fully the outcomes of the use of G.M.O.'s. This document endorses the "Precautionary Principle" formulated in 1992 by the United Nations Conference on Environment and Development in order to avoid "potential harm and unforeseen and unintended consequences."

This view mandates restraint and places the fundamental burden on demonstrating safety. The arguments are based on three areas of concern: the impact on the natural environment, the size of the benefit to the small farmer if the owners and distributors are giant companies like Bristol-Myers and Monsanto and the long-term effects of G.M.O.'s on human and animal health and nutrition.

This position concludes that the use of G.M.O.'s should be approached with caution.

5   While the "Precautionary Principle" seems prudent, there is simultaneously a strong moral argument that a war on hunger is a grave, universal need. Last year, 10 million people died of starvation. Every 3.6 seconds someone dies from hunger—24,000 people each day. Half of sub-Saharan Africans are malnourished, and this number is expected to increase to 70 percent by 2010. It was a moral disgrace that in 2002 African governments gave in to G.M.O. opponents and returned to the World Food Program tons of G.M.O. corn simply because it was produced in the U.S. by biotechnology.

6   The Roman conference gives solid reasons that G.M.O.'s are useful, healthful and nonharmful. After all, organisms have been exchanging genetic information for centuries. The tomato, corn and potato would not exist today if human engineering had not transferred genes between species.

7   The Catechism of the Catholic Church teaches that we have a duty to "make accessible to each what is needed to lead a truly human life." The very first example given is food. In *Populorum Progressio* (1967), *Sollicitude Rei Socialis* (1987) and *Centesimus Annus* (1991), Paul VI and later John Paul II forcefully insisted that rich countries have an obligation to help the poor, just as global economic interdependence places us on a moral obligation to be in solidarity with poor nations. Likewise, The Challenge of Faithful Citizenship, published by the U.S. bishops in 2004, argues that the church's preferential option for the poor entails "a moral responsibility to commit ourselves to the common good at all levels."

8   At the same time, it is critical that farmers in developing countries not become dependent on G.M.O. seeds patented by a small number of companies. Intellectual knowledge must be considered the common patrimony of the entire human family. As the U.S. bishops have stated, "Both public and private entities have an obligation to use their property, including intellectual and scientific property, to promote the good of all people" (*For I Was Hungry and You Gave Me Food*, 2003).

9   The Catholic Church sees deep sacramental significance in wheat and bread, and insists on the absolute imperative to feed and care for the poor of the world. A vital way to promote and ensure the dignity of every human being is to enable them to have their daily bread.

For Class Discussion

1. The readings in this unit (as well as the readings in Chapter 2 and the cartoon on page 1) reveal a complex network of issues related to the genetic
   engineering of food. Working in small groups or as a whole class, identify
   specific areas of disagreement or controversy among the authors represented in this unit. Then create as many specific issue questions connected
   to the genetic engineering of food as you can.

2. Some of the disagreement about biotech food involves the concept of "natural." When is a food natural as opposed to unnatural or artificial? Do the
   terms "natural/unnatural" have a scientific meaning or a cultural meaning? In written or visual arguments, how do anti-biotech advocates portray biotech food as "unnatural"? How have supporters of biotech foods
   attempted to answer the accusations that GMDs are unnatural?

3. At the end of "Will Frankenfood Save the Planet?" Jonathan Rauch calls on
   Greenpeace, the Sierra Club, and other environmental organizations to
   change their anti-biotech agendas. Examine the Sierra Club's policy statement on genetic engineering as stated on its Web site, http://www.
   sierraclub.org/policy/conservation/biotech.asp. To what extent do you
   think that some of the Sierra Club's policies on genetically modified foods
   should be revised in light of the readings in this unit?

4. Choose one of the arguments for closer analysis, applying the second set of
   guide questions on pages 454–455.

OPTIONAL WRITING ASSIGNMENT   Many of the advocacy Web sites on all sides of
the controversy over biotech agriculture elicit consumer feedback, suggesting that
we tell our lawmakers and also our local supermarkets what we think about the
labeling and the selling of genetically engineered foods. Write a letter to (a) one of
your state's representatives to Congress, (b) the sponsors of an advocacy web site,
or (c) the CEO of the supermarket where you or your family regularly buy groceries. In your letter, take a stand on some aspect of biotech foods and urge them
to adopt your position. If you are writing to your legislator, you might argue for
more rigorous, systematic, and extensive testing of genetically modified products,
for a moratorium on the sale of genetically modified foods, or for government
support of genetic engineering of foods. If you are writing to an advocacy Web
site, you might urge them to change some of their beliefs, policies, or calls to action. If you are writing to the CEO of your favorite supermarket chain, you might
argue that the supermarket change its buying practices, provide more consumer
information about sources of food, or lobby for or against the labeling of genetically modified ingredients in food products.

THE CULTURAL DEBATE ON STEM CELL RESEARCH AND CLONING

To many people, the word cloning conjures up the image of Dolly, the cloned sheep—a being that is an exact genetic copy of another being. Scientists call the process of producing a cloned creature "reproductive cloning." In experiments with animals, reproductive cloning has been successful in only a small percentage of attempts, and it often results in cloned creatures with various kinds of abnormalities. Although scientists have cloned mice, sheep, cows, and some other animals, no cases of human reproductive cloning have been reported. With few exceptions, the general public, ethicists, and scientists are opposed to human reproductive cloning.

Another kind of cloning, linked to the production of stem cells for possible use in genetic therapies to fight certain diseases, is called "therapeutic cloning." Therapeutic cloning (also called "nuclear transplantation") refers to the process of taking a single cell from a human donor (for example, a skin cell from a person suffering from a disease that might be cured through stem cell therapy), removing the nucleus, which contains the individual's genetic blueprint, and merging it with an egg cell that has had its own nucleus removed. Through an electrochemical process, the egg cell begins to grow, replicating the exact genetic structure of the donor nucleus. After about five days of growth, the resulting embryo is harvested for its stem cells, which match the genetic structure of the donor. These stem cells can then be stimulated to grow into different types of tissues that could be used to treat diabetes, Alzheimer's, Parkinson's, cystic fibrosis, and other diseases. Because the stem cells are harvested from a cloned embryo, they can be inserted into the donor with a much lower chance of rejection than if the stem cells had been harvested from a noncloned embryo (such as an embryo left over from a couple seeking in vitro fertilization for infertility).

The scientific community, politicians, and the public at large are divided on the ethics of this process and on the need for government regulation of it. As you will see from the readings in this unit, persons are divided on whether it is ethical to kill an embryo to harvest its stem cells, no matter whether the embryo is cloned or frozen in a fertility clinic's laboratories. They are also divided on the ethics of cloning itself and on the use of genetic engineering to fight diseases. On August 9, 2001, President Bush delivered a policy statement, announcing that the U.S. government would permit therapeutic stem cell research; Bush's proviso was that this experimentation must be limited to the existing stock of embryos left over from reproductive technology procedures and current research projects. He did not directly address therapeutic cloning, but since all kinds of cloning depend on the use of a donor egg, he presumably opposed it. Following up Bush's declaration, the U.S. House of Representatives passed a bill prohibiting the creation of cloned human embryos for stem cell research. As this book went to press, a new bill was in Congress that might expand federal support for therapeutic cloning by allowing the creation of new stocks. Simultaneously, some states, particularly California, began subsidizing genetic research in hope of establishing major research centers as part of the state's economy.

The cloning and stem cell research issue is explosive for many reasons: It entails many definitional issues that have moral and religious implications (Does a cloned "embryo" have the same status as an embryo created by the union of an egg and sperm? Does it have to be inside a woman's body to be considered a living human?). It also touches on other kinds of ethical issues (Are human embryos commercial property to be exploited for financial gain? Will cloning and stem cell research lead to eugenics and "designer babies"?). It profoundly affects certain groups of people such as sufferers from diseases that might be cured through therapeutic cloning research, scientists seeking new knowledge, or medical research companies seeking new patents and avenues of profit. From the perspective of the voting public, it also continues to generate political proposals (Should the United States ban therapeutic cloning completely, establish a moratorium, or legalize open research?).

The readings in this unit probe these questions as they plunge you into the network of issues intertwined with cloning and stem cell research.

It's Worth Copying Canada's Model for Cloning Legislation

Richard Hayes

In this op-ed piece published in the Seattle Times *on June 3, 2002, Richard Hayes, executive director of the nonprofit Center for Genetics and Society in Oakland, California, proposes a compromise course as a way out of currently stalled conflicts between the many groups for and against scientific experimentation on human genetic materials. This article provides a good overview of issues related to cloning.*

Cloning and the new technologies of human genetic modification are among the 1
most powerful and consequential technologies ever developed. If used wisely they offer new ways to prevent and cure disease, but if abused they could usher in an era of high-tech eugenics that would alter the nature of human life and society forever.

Two constituencies dominate the current debate over cloning and genetic modifi- 2
cation: anti-abortion conservatives and biomedical scientists. Not surprisingly, most conservatives want restrictions on these technologies and most scientists don't.

Given this lineup, it's tempting to assume that the current debate is the latest 3
extension of the abortion and embryo research wars. But this is not the case.

Many pro-choice feminists worry about a new eugenics that would commodify 4
and industrialize the process of child-bearing. Environmentalists fear that genetically altered humans would have few qualms about genetically altering the rest of the natural world. Human-rights and civil-rights advocates worry that new eugenic technologies would throw fuel on the flames of racial and ethnic hatred. Disability-rights leaders know that a society obsessed with genetic perfection could regard the disabled as mistakes that should have been prevented. Peace and justice activists fear brutal international conflict as countries race to create genetically superior populations.

For these and other traditionally liberal constituencies, concern over the new 5
technologies of cloning and genetic manipulation is motivated not by beliefs concerning the moment that human life begins but by the profound dangers to human relationships and society that these technologies pose, if misused.

6   These concerns are not fanciful.

7   Technologies that would allow creation of "designer babies" and full-term human clones are close to becoming practicable. Rogue scientists brag about covert efforts underway to create cloned children. Other scientists declare, often with barely disguised delight, that the routine production of human clones and genetically altered children is "inevitable," regardless of the wishes of society as a whole.

8   Current efforts by the U.S. Congress to pass legislation banning human cloning appear unlikely to succeed, as religious conservatives and the biotech industry fight each other to a stalemate. Although both sides support bans on creating cloned children, conservatives also want immediate, permanent bans on the use of cloning techniques that might have research applications, while the biotech industry resists any meaningful regulation whatsoever.

9   It's been suggested as a compromise that Congress enact a ban on creating cloned children while imposing a moratorium, rather than a permanent ban, on research cloning. During a moratorium the many proposed alternatives to the use of clonal embryos for research could be explored. A moratorium would also allow time to establish structures of regulation for any cloning technologies we might decide should be permitted. Unfortunately, neither side has yet been willing to make the first public move towards pragmatic compromises of this sort.

10   To break this deadlock we need a broader range of constituencies considering the full implications of cloning and other new genetic technologies, and helping decide which applications should be allowed and which should not.

11   Fortunately, a model for how this might be done is close at hand. In 1990 Canada established a Royal Commission on the New Reproductive Technologies, which over a period of several years conducted numerous hearings, workshops, surveys and other activities. Over 40,000 Canadians were involved.

12   The commission's final report represented a broad consensus and provided the basis for federal legislation now before the Canadian Parliament.

13   This legislation addresses all the major issues: reproductive and research cloning, genetic screening, animal-human genetic chimeras, inheritable genetic modification, sex selection and more. Importantly, it ensures that laboratories, clinics and private firms doing controversial genetic research be licensed and subject to monitoring and inspection.

14   The United States should take the Canadian experience to heart. A broad and informed debate is essential if we are to realize the best and avoid the worst that the new genetic technologies have to offer. We cannot afford to do less on a matter of such consequence. The future of our common humanity is at stake.

Of Clones and Clowns
Robert A. Weinberg

This article from the June 2002 Atlantic Monthly *exemplifies an argument that is both intellectual and popular (without scholarly documentation) intended for an educated but not scientifically trained audience. Robert A. Weinberg is a professor of biology at the Massachusetts Institute of Technology, winner of the prestigious National Medal of Science (1997), and a member of the Whitehead Institute for Biomedical Research. He is the author of several books on cancer research. In this argument, he exposes the media's distorting role in confusing serious science with sensational bogus science and shows the intersections and conflicts between peer-reviewed scientific research and commercial biotech industry science.*

Biologists have been rather silent on the subject of human cloning. Some others would accuse us, as they have with predictable regularity in the recent past, of insensitivity to the societal consequences of our research. If not insensitivity, then moral obtuseness, and if not that, then arrogance—an accusation that can never be disproved.   1

The truth is that most of us have remained quiet for quite another reason. Most of us regard reproductive cloning—a procedure used to produce an entire new organism from one cell of an adult—as a technology riddled with problems. Why should we waste time agonizing about something that is far removed from practical utility, and may forever remain so?   2

The nature and magnitude of the problems were suggested by the Scottish scientist Ian Wilmut's initial report, five years ago, on the cloning of Dolly the sheep. Dolly represented one success among 277 attempts to produce a viable, healthy newborn. Most attempts at cloning other animal species—to date cloning has succeeded with sheep, mice, cattle, goats, cats, and pigs—have not fared much better.   3

Even the successes come with problems. The placentas of cloned fetuses are routinely two or three times larger than normal. The offspring are usually larger than normal as well. Several months after birth one group of cloned mice weighed 72 percent more than mice created through normal reproduction. In many species cloned fetuses must be delivered by cesarean section because of their size. This abnormality, the reasons for which no one understands, is so common that it now has its own name—Large Offspring Syndrome. Dolly (who was of normal size at birth) was briefly overweight in her young years and suffers from early-onset arthritis of unknown cause. Two recent reports indicate that cloned mice suffer early-onset obesity and early death.   4

Arguably the most successful reproductive-cloning experiment was reported last year by Advanced Cell Technology, a small biotech company in Worcester, Massachusetts. Working with cows, ACT produced 496 embryos by injecting nuclei from adult cells into eggs that had been stripped of their own nuclei. Implanting the embryos into the uteruses of cows led to 110 established pregnancies, thirty of which went to term. Five of the newborns died shortly after birth, and a sixth died several months later. The twenty-four surviving calves developed into cows that were healthy by all criteria examined. But most, if not all, had enlarged placentas, and as newborns some of them suffered from the respiratory distress typical of Large Offspring Syndrome.   5

The success rate of the procedure, roughly five percent, was much higher than the rates achieved with other mammalian species, and the experiment was considered   6 a great success. Some of the cows have grown up, been artificially inseminated, and given birth to normal offspring. Whether they are affected by any of the symptoms associated with Large Offspring Syndrome later in life is not apparent from the published data. No matter: for $20,000 ACT will clone your favorite cow.

7   Imagine the application of this technology to human beings. Suppose that 100 adult nuclei are obtained, each of which is injected into a human egg whose own nucleus has been removed. Imagine then that only five of the 100 embryos thus created result in well-formed, viable newborns; the other ninety-five spontaneously abort at various stages of development or, if cloning experiments with mammals other than cows are any guide, yield grossly malformed babies. The five viable babies have a reasonable likelihood of suffering from Large Offspring Syndrome. How they will develop, physically and cognitively, is anyone's guess. It seems unlikely that even the richest and most egomaniacal among us, intent on re-creating themselves exactly, will swarm to this technology.

8   Biological systems are extraordinarily complex, and there are myriad ways in which experiments can go awry or their results can be misinterpreted. Still, perhaps 95 percent of what biologists read in this year's research journals will be considered valid (if perhaps not very interesting) a century from now. Much of scientists' trust in the existing knowledge base derives from the system constructed over the past century to validate new research findings and the conclusions derived from them. Research journals impose quality controls to ensure that scientific observations and conclusions are solid and credible. They sift the scientific wheat from the chaff.

9   The system works like this: A biologist sends a manuscript describing his experiment to a journal. The editor of the journal recruits several experts, who remain anonymous to the researcher, to vet the manuscript. A month or two later the researcher receives a thumbs-up, a thumbs-down, or a request for revisions and more data. The system works reasonably well, which is why many of us invest large amounts of time in serving as the anonymous reviewers of one another's work. Without such rigorously imposed quality control, our subfields of research would rapidly descend into chaos, because no publicly announced result would carry the imprimatur of having been critiqued by experts.

10   We participate in the peer-review process not only to create a sound edifice of ideas and results for ourselves; we do it for the outside world as well—for all those who are unfamiliar with the arcane details of our field. Without the trial-by-fire of peer review, how can journalists and the public possibly know which discoveries are credible, which are nothing more than acts of self-promotion by ambitious researchers, and which smack of the delusional?

11   The hype about cloning has made a shambles of this system, creating something of a circus. Many of us have the queasy feeling that our carefully constructed world of science is under seige. The clowns—those who think that making money, lots of it, is more important than doing serious science—have invaded our sanctuary.

12   The cloning circus opened soon after Wilmut, a careful and well-respected scientist, reported his success with Dolly. First in the ring was Richard Seed, an el-

derly Chicago physicist, who in late 1997 announced his intention of cloning a human being within two years. Soon members of an international religious cult, the Raëlians (followers of Claude Vorilhon, a French-born mystic who says that he was given the name Raël by four-foot-high extraterrestrials, and who preaches that human beings were originally created by these aliens), revealed an even more grandiose vision of human cloning. To the Raëlians, biomedical science is a sacrament to be used for achieving immortality: their ultimate goal is to use cloning to create empty shells into which people's souls can be transferred. As a sideline, the Raëlian-affiliated company Clonaid hopes to offer its services to couples who would like to create a child through reproductive cloning for $200,000 per child.

13   Neither Seed nor the Raëlians made any pretense of subjecting their plans to review by knowledgeable scientists; they went straight to the popular press. Still, this wasn't so bad. Few science journalists took them seriously (although they did oblige them with extensive coverage). Biologists were also unmoved. Wasn't it obvious that Seed and the Raëlians were unqualified to undertake even the beginnings of the series of technical steps required for reproductive cloning? Why dignify them with a response?

14   The next wave of would-be cloners likewise went straight to the mainstream press—but they were not so easily dismissed. In March of last year, at a widely covered press conference in Rome, an Italian and a U.S. physician announced plans to undertake human reproductive cloning outside the United States. The Italian member of the team was Severino Antinori, a gynecologist notorious for having used donor eggs and *in vitro* fertilization to make a sixty-two-year-old woman pregnant in 1994. Now he was moving on. Why, he asked, did the desires of infertile couples (he claimed to have 600 on a waiting list) not outweigh the concerns about human cloning? He repeatedly shouted down reporters and visiting researchers who had the temerity to voice questions about the biological and ethical problems associated with reproductive cloning.

15   The American member of the team was Panayiotis Zavos, a reproductive physiologist and an *in vitro* fertilization expert at the Andrology Institute of America, in Lexington, Kentucky. "The genie is out of the bottle," he told reporters. "Dolly is here, and we are next." Antinori and Zavos announced their intention of starting a human cloning project in an undisclosed Mediterranean country. Next up was Avi Ben-Abraham, an Israeli-American biotechnologist with thwarted political ambitions (he ran unsuccessfully for the Knesset) and no reputable scientific credentials, who attempted to attach himself to the project. Ben-Abraham hinted that the work would be done either in Israel or in an Arab country, because "the climate is more [receptive to human cloning research] within Judaism and Islam." He told the German magazine *Der Spiegel,* "We were all created by the Almighty, but now we will become the creators."

16   Both Antinori and Zavos glossed over the large gap between expertise with established infertility procedures and the technical skills required for reproductive cloning. Confronted with the prospect of high rates of aborted or malformed cloned embryos, they claimed to be able to weed out any defective embryos at an early stage of gestation. "We have a great deal of knowledge," Zavos announced to the

press. "We can grade embryos. We can do genetic screening. We can do [genetic] quality control." This was possible, he said, because of highly sensitive diagnostic tests that can determine whether or not development is proceeding normally.

17   The fact is that no such tests exist; they have eluded even the most expert biologists in the field, and there is no hope that they will be devised anytime soon—if ever. No one knows how to determine with precision whether the repertoire of genes expressed at various stages of embryonic development is being "read" properly in each cell type within an embryo. Without such information, no one can know whether the developmental program is proceeding normally in the womb. (The prenatal tests currently done for Down syndrome and several other genetic disorders can detect only a few of the thousands of things that can go wrong during embryonic development.)

18   Rudolf Jaenisch, a colleague of mine with extensive experience in mouse reproductive cloning, was sufficiently exercised to say to a reporter at the *Chicago Tribune*, "[Zavos and Antinori] will produce clones, and most of these will die in utero. . . . Those will be the lucky ones. Many of those that survive will have [obvious or more subtle] abnormalities." The rest of us biologists remained quiet. To us, Antinori, Zavos, and Ben-Abraham were so clearly inept that comment seemed gratuitous. In this instance we have, as on other occasions, misjudged the situation: many people seem to take these three and their plans very seriously indeed. And, in fact, this past April, Antinori claimed, somewhat dubiously, that a woman under his care was eight weeks pregnant with a cloned embryo.

19   In the meantime, the biotechnology industry, led by ACT, has been moving ahead aggressively with human cloning, but of a different sort. The young companies in this sector have sensed, probably correctly, the enormous potential of therapeutic (rather than reproductive) cloning as a strategy for treating a host of common human degenerative diseases.

20   The initial steps of therapeutic cloning are identical to those of reproductive cloning: cells are prepared from an adult tissue, their nuclei are extracted, and each nucleus is introduced into a human egg, which is allowed to develop. However, in therapeutic cloning embryonic development is halted at a very early stage—when the embryo is a blastocyst, consisting of perhaps 150 cells—and the inner cells are harvested and cultured. These cells, often termed embryonic stem cells, are still very primitive and thus have retained the ability to develop into any type of cell in the body (except those of the placenta).

21   Mouse and human embryonic stem cells can be propagated in a petri dish and induced to form precursors of blood-forming cells, or of the insulin-producing cells of the pancreas, or of cardiac muscle or nerve tissue. These precursor cells (tissue-specific stem cells) might then be introduced into a tissue that has grown weak from the loss of too many of its differentiated worker cells. When the ranks of the workers are replenished, the course of disease may be dramatically reversed. At least, that is the current theory. In recent months one version of the technique has been successfully applied to mice.

Therapeutic cloning has the potential to revolutionize the treatment of a number of currently untreatable degenerative diseases, but it is only a potential. Considerable research will be required to determine the technology's possibilities and limitations for treating human patients.

Some worry that therapeutic-cloning research will never get off the ground in this country. Its proponents—and there are many among the community of biomedical researchers—fear that the two very different kinds of cloning, therapeutic and reproductive, have merged in the public's mind. Three leaders of the community wrote a broadside early this year in *Science,* titled "Please Don't Call It Cloning!" Call therapeutic cloning anything else—call it "nuclear transplantation," or "stem cell research." The scientific community has finally awakened to the damage that the clowns have done.

This is where the newest acts of the circus begin. President George Bush and many pro-life activists are in one ring. A number of disease-specific advocacy groups that view therapeutic cloning as the only real prospect for treating long-resistant maladies are in another. In a third ring are several biotech companies that are flogging their wares, often in ways that make many biologists shudder.

Yielding to pressure from religious conservatives, Bush announced last August that no new human embryonic stem cells could be produced from early human embryos that had been created during the course of research sponsored by the federal government; any research on the potential applications of human embryonic stem cells, he said, would have to be conducted with the existing repertoire of sixty-odd lines. The number of available, usable cell lines actually appears to be closer to a dozen or two. And like all biological reagents, these cells tend to deteriorate with time in culture; new ones will have to be derived if research is to continue. What if experiments with the existing embryonic-stem-cell lines show enormous promise? Such an outcome would produce an almost irresistible pressure to move ahead with the derivation of new embryonic stem cells and to rapidly expand this avenue of research.

How will we learn whether human embryonic stem cells are truly useful for new types of therapy? This question brings us directly to another pitfall: much of the research on human embryonic stem cells is already being conducted by biotech companies, rather than in universities. Bush's edict will only exacerbate this situation. (In the 1970s a federal decision effectively banning government funding of *in vitro* fertilization had a similar effect, driving such research into private clinics.)

Evaluating the science coming from the labs of the biotech industry is often tricky. Those who run these companies are generally motivated more by a need to please stock analysts and venture capitalists than to convince scientific peers. For many biotech companies the peer-review process conducted by scientific journals is simply an inconvenient, time-wasting impediment. So some of the companies routinely bypass peer review and go straight to the mainstream press. Science journalists, always eager for scoops, don't necessarily feel compelled to consult experts about the credibility of industry press releases. And when experts are consulted about the contents of a press release, they are often hampered by spotty descriptions of the claimed breakthrough and thus limited to mumbling platitudes.

28   ACT, the company that conducted the successful cow-cloning experiment and has now taken the lead in researching human therapeutic cloning, has danced back and forth between publishing in respectable peer-reviewed journals and going directly to the popular press—and recently tried to find a middle ground. Last fall, with vast ambitions, ACT reported that it had conducted the first successful human-cloning experiment. In truth, however, embryonic development went only as far as six cells—far short of the 150-cell blastocyst that represents the first essential step of therapeutic cloning. Wishing to cloak its work in scientific respectability, ACT reported these results in a fledgling electronic research journal named *e-biomed: The Journal of Regenerative Medicine.* Perhaps ACT felt especially welcome in a journal that, according to its editor in chief, William A. Haseltine, a widely known biotech tycoon, "is prepared to publish work of a more preliminary nature." It may also have been encouraged by Haseltine's stance toward cloning, as revealed in his remarks when the journal was founded. "As we understand the body's repair process at the genetic level, we will be able to advance the goal of maintaining our bodies in normal function, perhaps perpetually," he said.

29   Electronic publishing is still in its infancy, and the publication of ACT's research report will do little to enhance its reputation. By the usual standards of scientific achievement, the experiments ACT published would be considered abject failures. Knowledgeable readers of the report were unable to tell whether the clump of six cells represented the beginning of a human embryo or simply an unformed aggregate of dying cells.

30   One prominent member of the *e-biomed* editorial board, a specialist in the type of embryology used in cloning, asked Haseltine how the ACT manuscript had been vetted before its publication. Haseltine assured his board member that the paper had been seen by two competent reviewers, but he refused to provide more details. The board member promptly resigned. Two others on the editorial board, also respected embryologists, soon followed suit. (Among the scientists left on the board are two representatives of ACT—indeed, both were authors of the paper.) Mary Ann Liebert, the publisher of the journal, interpreted this exodus as a sign that "clearly some noses were out of joint." The entire publication process subverted the potentially adversarial but necessary dynamic between journal-based peer review and the research scientist.

31   No one yet knows precisely how to make therapeutic cloning work, or which of its many claimed potential applications will pan out and which will not. And an obstacle other than experimental problems confronts those pushing therapeutic cloning. In the wake of the cloning revolution a second revolution has taken place—quieter but no less consequential. It, too, concerns tissue-specific stem cells—but ones found in the tissues of adults. These adult stem cells may one day prove to be at least as useful as those generated by therapeutic cloning.

32   Many of our tissues are continually jettisoning old, worn-out cells and replacing them with freshly minted ones. The process depends on a cadre of stem cells residing in each type of tissue and specific to that type of tissue. When an adult stem cell divides, one of its two daughters becomes a precursor of a specialized worker cell, able to help replenish the pool of worker cells that may have been damaged

through injury or long-term use. The other remains a stem cell like its mother, thus ensuring that the population of stem cells in the tissue is never depleted.

Until two years ago the dogma among biologists was that stem cells in the bone marrow spawned only blood, those in the liver spawned only hepatocytes, and those in the brain spawned only neurons—in other words, each of our tissues had only its own cadre of stem cells for upkeep. Once again we appear to have been wrong. There is mounting evidence that the body contains some rather unspecialized stem cells, which wander around ready to help many sorts of tissue regenerate their worker cells. 　33

Whether these newly discovered, multi-talented adult stem cells present a viable alternative to therapeutic cloning remains to be proved. Many of the claims about their capabilities have yet to be subjected to rigorous testing. Perhaps not surprisingly, some of these claims have also reached the public without careful vetting by peers. Senator Sam Brownback, of Kansas, an ardent foe of all kinds of cloning, has based much of his case in favor of adult stem cells (and against therapeutic cloning) on these essentially unsubstantiated scientific claims. Adult stem cells provide a convenient escape hatch for Brownback. Their use placates religious conservatives, who are against all cloning, while throwing a bone to groups lobbying for new stem-cell-based therapies to treat degenerative diseases. 　34

Brownback would have biologists shut down therapeutic-cloning research and focus their energies exclusively on adult stem-cell research. But no one can know at present which of those two strategies is more likely to work. It will take a decade or more to find out. Many biologists are understandably reluctant to set aside therapeutic-cloning research in the meantime; they argue that the two technologies should be explored simultaneously. 　35

Precisely this issue was debated recently by advisory committees in the United States and Germany. The U.S. committee was convened by Bruce Alberts, the president of the National Academy of Sciences and a highly accomplished cell biologist and scientific educator. Quite naturally, it included a number of experts who are actively involved in exploring the advantages and disadvantages of stem-cell therapies. The committee, which announced its findings in January, concluded that therapeutic cloning should be explored in parallel with alternative strategies. 　36

For their trouble, the scientists were accused of financial self-interest by Steven Milloy of Fox News, who said, "Enron and Arthur Andersen have nothing over the National Academy of Sciences when it comes to deceiving the public. . . . Enter Bruce Alberts, the Wizard of Oz–like president of the NAS. . . . On his own initiative, Alberts put together a special panel, stacked with embryonic-stem-cell research proponents and researchers already on the taxpayer dole. . . . Breast-feeding off taxpayers is as natural to the NAS panel members as breathing." 　37

The German committee, which reached a similar conclusion, was assembled by Ernst-Ludwig Winnacker, the head of his country's national science foundation. Winnacker and his colleagues were labeled "cannibals" by the Cardinal of Cologne. Remarks like the ones from Steven Milloy and the cardinal seem calculated to make public service at the interface between science and society as unappealing as possible. 　38

President Bush, apparently anticipating the NAS panel's conclusion, has appointed an advisory committee all but guaranteed to produce a report much more to 　39 his liking. Its chairman, Leon Kass, has gone on record as being against all forms of cloning. (Earlier in his career Kass helped to launch an attack on *in vitro* fertilization.)

40   Meanwhile, a coalition of a hundred people and organizations recently sent a letter to Congress expressing their opposition to therapeutic cloning—among them Friends of the Earth, Greenpeace, the Sierra Club, the head of the National Latina Health Organization, and the perennial naysayer Jeremy Rifkin. "The problem with therapeutic cloning," Rifkin has said, "is that it introduces commercial eugenics from the get-go." Powerful words indeed. Few of those galvanized by Rifkin would know that therapeutic cloning has nothing whatsoever to do with eugenics.

41   Usually progress in biology is held back by experimental difficulties, inadequate instruments, poorly planned research protocols, inadequate funding, or plain sloppiness. But in this case the future of research may have little connection with these factors or with the scientific pros and cons being debated earnestly by members of the research community. The other, more public debates will surely be the decisive ones.

42   The clashes about human therapeutic cloning that have taken place in the media and in Congress are invariably built around weighty moral and ethical principles. But none of us needs a degree in bioethics to find the bottom line in the arguments. They all ultimately converge on a single question: When does human life begin? Some say it is when sperm and egg meet, others when the embryo implants in the womb, others when the fetus quickens, and yet others when the fetus can survive outside the womb. This is a question that we scientists are neither more nor less equipped to decide than the average man or woman in the street, than a senator from Kansas or a cardinal in Cologne. (Because Dolly and the other cloned animals show that a complete embryo can be produced from a single adult cell, some biologists have proposed, tongue in cheek, that a human life exists in each one of our cells.) Take your pick of the possible answers and erect your own moral scaffolding above your choice.

43   In the end, politics will settle the debate in this country about whether human therapeutic cloning is allowed to proceed. If the decision is yes, then we will continue to lead the world in a crucial, cutting-edge area of biomedical research. If it is no, U.S. biologists will need to undertake hegiras to laboratories in Australia, Japan, Israel, and certain countries in Europe—an outcome that would leave American science greatly diminished.

What Human Genetic Modification Means for Women

Judith Levine

This article, originally published in the July–August 2002 edition of World Watch, *explores the potentially dangerous connections between human genetic modification and eugenics and argues that such experimentation is especially relevant to women and children. The WorldWatch Institute describes itself as "a*

nonprofit public policy research organization dedicated to informing policymak-
ers and the public about emerging global problems and trends and the complex
links between the world economy and its environmental support system" (from
the "About WorldWatch" link on its Web site). Judith Levine, a well-known jour-
nalist on women's topics, has written for Ms., New York Woman, *and* Salon,
and has recently published the book Harmful to Minors: The Perils of
Protecting Children from Sex *(2002).*

Seduced by the medical promises of genetic science or fearful of losing repro-   1
ductive autonomy, many feminists have been slow to oppose human genetic engineering. But GE is a threat to women, and in the broadest sense a feminist issue.
Here's why. If anyone should be wary of medical techniques to "improve" ordinary
reproduction—as GE purports to do—it's women. History is full of such "progress,"
and its grave results. When limbless babies were born to mothers who took thalido-
mide, the drug was recalled. But the deadly results of another "pregnancy-enhanc-
ing" drug, DES, showed up only years later, as cancer in the daughters of DES
mothers. The high-estrogen Pill was tested first on uninformed Puerto Rican mothers, some of whom may have died from it.

Today's fertility industry takes in $4 billion a year, even though in-vitro fertil-   2
ization (IVF) succeeds in only 3 of 10 cases. Virtually unregulated and highly competitive, these fertility doctors often undertake experimental treatments. Recently,
the Institute for Reproductive Medicine and Science at New Jersey's St. Barnabas
Medical Center announced the success of a new fertility "therapy" called cytoplasmic transfer, in which some of the cellular material outside the nucleus of one
woman's egg is transferred into the egg of another woman who is having difficulty
sustaining embryo survival. The transferred cytoplasm contains mitochondria (or-
ganelles that produce energy for the cell), which have a small number of their own
genes. So the embryo produced with cytoplasmic transfer can end up with two genetic mothers. This mixing, called "mitochondrial heteroplasmy," can cause life-
threatening symptoms that don't show up until later in life. When the Public
Broadcasting Service's *Nova* enthusiastically reported on the procedure, complete
with footage of its cute outcome, Katy, it mentioned no risks.

Didn't these patients give informed consent? Yes and no. Most read warnings   3
and signed their names. But with genetic therapies there's no such thing as "informed," says Judy Norsigian of the Boston Women's Health Collective, "because
the risks can't be known." Adds biologist Ruth Hubbard, the deadliness of DES was
discovered "only because it showed itself in an otherwise very rare condition. If the
effects [of human genetic engineering] are delayed, and if they are not associated
with a particularly unusual pathology, it could take quite a long time to find out." Or
indeed, "we might never know."

"PERFECTING" HUMAN GENETIC MODIFICATION WOULD REQUIRE EXPERIMENTATION ON WOMEN AND CHILDREN.

Scottish biologist Ian Wilmut, the "father" of the famously first-cloned sheep   4
Dolly, provided these statistics in 2001: Of the 31,007 sheep, mice, pig, and other

mammal eggs that had undergone somatic cell nuclear transfer (cloning), 9,391 viable embryos resulted. From those embryos came 267 live-born offspring. In these animals, *The New York Times* reported, "random errors" were ubiquitous—including fatal heart and lung defects, malfunctioning immune systems, and grotesque obesity. In all, "fewer than 3 percent of all cloning efforts succeed." Dolly may be a victim of accelerated aging, another problem in cloned animals. In January, it was reported that she has arthritis, at the unusually early age of five and a half. Mothers of clones are endangered too, since their bodies have trouble supporting the abnormally large fetuses that cloning often produces.

5   It's likely that scientists will get better at cloning animals, and at the more complex procedures required to produce inheritable genetic alterations. Then, as health activists quip, if it works on a mouse, they will try it on a woman. The problem, warns Stuart Newman, a cell biologist at New York Medical College in Valhalla, is that if it works on a mouse, it is likely not to work on a woman: "Every species presents a new set of problems." How might the process be perfected in humans? In clinical trials?

6   "The degree of risk to be taken should never exceed that determined by the humanitarian importance of the problem to be solved by the experiment," reads the Nuremburg Code, drawn up after World War II to forbid future torturous experiments of the sort Nazi "scientists" inflicted on concentration-camp inmates. What is the humanitarian importance of creating a faster 100-meter sprinter? Or even curing a disease with genetic engineering when other options are still untried? The science to find "safe" means of human GE, says Newman, would constitute "an entirely experimental enterprise with little justification." In other words, "We can't get there from here."

WE ARE NOT OUR GENES.

7   When the Human Genome Project finished its map of our DNA, its press releases called it the "blueprint" of humanity, the very Book of Life. The newspapers had already been filling up with reports of the discovery of a "gene for" breast cancer, and a "gene for" gayness. Many people had begun to believe our genes determine who we become.

8   This line of thinking should sound familiar to women. Not long ago, we were told that hormones, not sexism, explained why there has never been a U.S. female president (she might start a nuclear war in a fit of PMS). A decade after that came the notion that gender is "hard-wired" into the brain. Not incidentally, these claims were made just when social movements were proving Simone de Beauvoir's adage that women are not born but made. Now the old determinism is raising its ugly head once again, with genetics. As "non-traditional" families finally bring legitimacy to social parenting, proponents of inheritable genetic modification tell us not only that we can pre-determine the natures of our children, but that cloning is the only means by which gays and lesbians can become real parents. "Real" parental ties, they imply, are biological, genetic.

9   "Genetic determinism" is not biologically accurate. "It is very unlikely that a simple and directly causal link between genes and most common diseases will ever be found," writes Richard Horton, editor of the British medical journal *The Lancet*. If

this is true of disease, it is even more true of musicality, optimism, or sexual orientation. The more complex a trait, the less useful genetics are to explain it. Hubbard writes, "The lens of genetics really is one of the narrowest foci to define our biology, not to mention what our social being is about."

GENETIC MODIFICATION IS NOT A REPRODUCTIVE "CHOICE."

For feminists, one of the most galling aspects of the debate about human genetic manipulation is the way its proponents have hijacked the language of "choice" to sell its products. IVF clinics and biotech research shouldn't be regulated, say the companies that run them, because that would impinge on "choice" (for the paying customers, if not for their unsuspecting offspring). The Book of Life is becoming a "catalogue" of "consumer eugenics," says sociologist Barbara Katz Rothman. 10

Some ethicists, too, have posited a reproductive "right" to prenatal baby design. People decide whether or not to reproduce based on an expected "package of experiences," wrote John Robertson, an influential bioethicist, in 1998. "Since the makeup of the packet will determine whether or not they reproduce . . . some right to choose characteristics, either by negative exclusion or positive selection, should follow as well." Already, selective abortion is widely accepted after prenatal genetic screening uncovers an "anomaly." Although some (notably disability rights activists) critique such "negative eugenics," many people accept this practice for serious medical conditions. In any case, selecting from among a small number of embryos is a far cry from rearranging the DNA of a future child to achieve some preferred traits. 11

What feminists mean by "choice"—the ability to control fertility with safe and legal birth control and abortion—is far more concrete. It confers existential equality on the female half of the human race, which is why women worldwide have sought it for centuries. But genetic engineering designs in inequality: it will artificially confer heritable advantages only on those who can afford to buy them. Performed prenatally, moreover, it affects the new person without that person's prior consent and possibly to her physical or emotional detriment. "Ending an unwanted pregnancy is apples, and mucking around with genes is oranges," says Marcy Darnovsky of the Center for Genetics and Society. "We support abortion rights because we support a right to not have a child—or to have one. But we don't support a woman's right to do anything to that child once it's alive, like abuse it or kill it." Ironically, as Lisa Handwerker of the National Women's Health Network has pointed out, anti-choice, anti-GE forces share with GE's proponents an obsessive focus on the embryo as an independent entity, while they both virtually ignore the pregnant woman and the child she may bear. 12

BANS ON DANGEROUS GENETIC TECHNOLOGIES
DO NOT GIVE FETUSES "RIGHTS."

Some choice advocates fear that any perceived concern about embryos will cede territory to anti-abortionists, who want full legal protection of embryos and fetuses. 13

U.S. Congressman Henry Waxman reflected this confusion when he said at a Congressional hearing, "I do not believe that the Congress should prohibit potentially life-saving research on genetic cell replication because it accords a cell—a special cell, but only a cell—the same rights and protections as a person."

14   But pro-choice opponents of cloning do not propose to give cells rights. Rather, we worry that cloned embryos might be implanted by unscrupulous fertility entrepreneurs into desperate women, where they'll grow into cloned humans. And from cloning, it is not a big step to designing children.

15   For legal, political, and philosophical reasons, University of Chicago medical ethicist Mary Mahowald proposes clarifying the pro-choice position. "It does feminist support for abortion no good to confuse life with personhood," she told me. "We can admit that the embryo is life and therefore afford it respect—the respect, for instance, of not exchanging its genes with those of another cell. But respecting life is not the same as granting rights. Rights are reserved for living persons."

INDIVIDUAL FREEDOM MUST BE BALANCED WITH SOCIAL JUSTICE.

16   "We're against bans," said a member of a coalition of mainstream reproductive-rights groups, explaining why the coalition was reluctant to join a campaign against human cloning. This reaction is not surprising in the United States, where defense of personal freedom can often trump the public interest.

17   Women's liberation means more than personal freedom, though. Rooted in the Left, feminism is a critique of all kinds of domination and therefore a vision of an egalitarian world—racially and economically, as well as sexually.

18   In the case of species-altering procedures, social justice must prevail over individual "choice." Arguing for an international ban on reproductive cloning and regulation of related research, Patricia Baird, chair of Canada's Royal Commission on New Reproductive Technologies, put it this way: "The framework of individual autonomy and reproductive choice is dangerously incomplete, because it leaves out the effects on others and on social systems, and the effects on the child and future generations." The good news is that good public policy protects individuals too. Baird offered the example of overfishing, which might benefit the fisherman in the short run but deplete the fishery for everyone, including that fisherman, in the long run. Regulation sustains his and his children's livelihoods. "We all have a stake in the kind of community we live in," Baird said.

FEMINISTS CAN WORK ALONGSIDE ANTI-ABORTION CONSERVATIVES AGAINST SPECIES-ALTERING PROCEDURES.

19   "We are repelled by the prospect of cloning human beings . . . because we intuit and we feel, immediately and without argument, the violation of things that we rightfully hold dear," wrote Leon Kass, conservative social critic and chair of President Bush's committee to investigate stem-cell research.

20   Not every feminist holds dear what Kass holds dear: the "sanctity" of the family based in God-given, "natural" forms of reproduction. Still, Kass sat beside Judy Norsigian and Stuart Newman to testify before the U.S. Congress against cloning.

The genetic engineering debate has made strange bedfellows. But it has also 21 rearranged the political definitions that made those bedfellows strangers. "Social conservatives believe [genetic engineering] is playing God and therefore unethical, while anti-biotech activists [of the Left] see it as the first step into a brave new world divided by biological castes," writes social critic Jeremy Rifkin. "Both oppose the emergence of a commercial eugenics civilization." Others suggest that the new political landscape divides differently, between libertarians and communitarians. Whether of the Left or the Right, the former would support an individual right to choose just about any intervention on one's own body or one's offspring, whereas the latter esteem public health and social equality and would reject those interventions, including GE, that endanger them.

Choice activists may at first be surprised when they find that their anti-cloning 22 and anti-eugenics sentiments are shared by opponents of reproductive rights. But passionate arguments for the same position from historically sworn enemies can only make a legislator, or any citizen, listen up. Feminists need sacrifice no part of the defense of women's reproductive autonomy when we champion health and social justice for the future human community.

Embryonic Stem Cell Fairy Tales

Jean Swenson

In the following article, Jean Swenson argues that adult stem cells may provide a more effective avenue of research than embryonic stem cells. Swenson is a quadriplegic as a result of a 1980 spinal cord injury. After her injury, she obtained a master's degree in counseling psychology and has been an advocate for spinal cord research for more than twenty years. The following article appeared in The Minnesota Daily *(the newspaper for the University of Minnesota) on July 27, 2005. The University of Minnesota is home to the prestigious Stem Cell Institute referred to in the article.*

We all remember Hans Christian Andersen's fairy tale, "The Emperor's New 1 Clothes," about the emperor who was swindled into believing his new clothing was the finest available. When he paraded through the streets wearing nothing but imaginary apparel, a child cried out, "But he has nothing on at all!"

As a quadriplegic who could possibly benefit from stem cell research, I fear 2 many of us are being sold an imaginary garment of hope—an illusive belief that embryonic stem cells will cure us.

In reality, no such cures exist now or will in the near future. Like the truthful 3 child, we must exclaim, "But there is nothing here at all!"

Stem cells, found in embryos, umbilical cord blood and adults, can change into 4 specialized cell types. Their value lies in replacing diseased or damaged tissues.

The University, with its Stem Cell Institute, can be proud of its leadership role in the field of adult stem cell research. In fact, the University was the first to show adult stem cells with the same flexibility as embryonic stem cells.

5   However, beyond moral objections, embryonic stem cells have serious problems, such as tumor formation, tissue rejection and genetic instability that prevent human use. For more than 20 years, scientists worldwide, using animal embryonic stem cells, have failed to solve these same roadblocks faced by human embryonic stem cell researchers.

6   On the other hand, adult stem cells and cord blood cells are already being used to safely and effectively treat more than 60 conditions (see www.stemcellresearch.org). Yet, most media seem to downplay these successes while elevating embryonic stem cell cure "potential," when embryonic stem cells have yet to provide even one safe and effective human treatment.

7   *The Lancet,* a prestigious British medical journal that favors embryonic stem cell research, recently called such cure headlines "sensationalist" and "hype." In a June 4 editorial, *The Lancet* reported, "No safe and effective stem cell therapy will be widely available for at least a decade, and possibly longer."

8   Cornell University stem cell scientist Shahin Rafii said, "Just injecting stem cells is not going to work. First, you have to be able to differentiate the cells into functional, transplantable tissues. We don't really know how to do this yet."

9   People who want the government to fund embryonic stem cell research are expecting taxpayers to pay for science projects that knowledgeable investors will not. William Haseltine, embryonic stem cell research advocate and chief executive officer of Human Genome Sciences, said, "The routine utilization of human embryonic stem cells for medicine is 20 to 30 years hence. The timeline to commercialization is so long that I simply would not invest. You may notice that our company has not made such investments."

10   Those serious about clinical trials and treatments—not just basic research—are using adult stem cells or cord blood. The Spinal Cord Society, based in Fergus Falls, Minn., has 200 chapters worldwide. The society is on the cutting edge of spinal cord applied research, meaning they're trying to find treatments that really work.

11   The society will be starting human trials using cells from patients' own nasal cavities. Spinal Cord Society's leadership said it would use embryonic stem cells "if they worked for us." But because of embryonic stem cell medical problems, the society is currently pursuing adult stem cells and avoiding embryonic.

12   Russian scientist Dr. Andrey Brykhovetskii has tried both embryonic stem cells and adult stem cells in his quest for spinal cord injury cure. He has concluded that adult cells are much more effective than embryonic stem cells in restoring function.

13   After former President Ronald Reagan died, people were led to believe that embryonic stem cells could cure Alzheimer's disease.

14   Yet, Alzheimer researcher Michael Shelanski said, "The chance of doing repairs to Alzheimer's brains by putting in stem cells is small. I personally think we're going to get other therapies for Alzheimer's a lot sooner."

15   The National Institutes of Health stem cell researcher Ronald D.G. McKay attempted to explain this distortion by telling a *Washington Post* reporter, "To start

with, people need a fairy tale. Maybe that's unfair, but they need a story line that's relatively simple to understand."

We're watching this fairy tale play out. Like the emperor's "tailors," some who   16
want the approval and funding for basic embryonic stem cell research offer misleading promises about nonexistent embryonic stem cell cures. A much happier ending to this story might come by focusing precious resources on adult stem cell and cord blood treatments that already have shown they will work.

Not on Faith Alone

Mario M. Cuomo

The following article appeared as an op-ed piece in The New York Times *on June 20, 2005. Mario M. Cuomo is the former governor of New York. He is a practicing Catholic who often takes a liberal perspective on social issues.*

There is a way to get beyond the religious morass created by President Bush's   1
position on embryonic stem cells.

Most scientists agree that while adult stem cells offer hope of a cure for some   2
of the cruelest diseases and injuries, embryonic stem cells hold even greater and surer promise. As a result, while most scientists welcomed Mr. Bush's August 2001 offer of government resources to advance adult stem cell research, they and millions of other Americans were sorely disappointed by his refusal to consider retrieving any stem cells from the many thousands of unused embryos awaiting destruction. To most scientists, his compromise restricting federal financing only to research that used the 20 or so embryonic stem cell lines that had already been developed was politically clever but insufficient, not least because most of those cell lines are of limited and uncertain potential.

Mr. Bush does not deny the greater potential of embryonic stem cells: he says   3
his decision was compelled by his belief that retrieving stem cells from the embryo destroys it, thereby resulting in the killing of a human being that cannot be justified no matter how vast the potential benefits.

The president did not claim his conclusion was based on biomedical science. He   4
said only that it was an expression of his religious faith. Asked in March 2004 about the stem cell issue, his science adviser, Dr. John H. Marburger III (who headed a fact-finding commission on the Shoreham nuclear plant in 1983 when I was governor), said: "I can't tell when a fertilized egg becomes sacred," and added, "That's not a science issue."

No doubt the president's belief that human life begins with fertilization is   5
shared by millions of Americans, including many Christians and evangelists. But it remains a minority view and one that the president applies inconsistently. Although Mr. Bush believes that destroying an embryo is murder, he refuses to

demand legislation to stop commercial interests that are busily destroying embryos in order to obtain stem cells. If their conduct amounts to murder as the president contends, it is hardly satisfactory for him to say he will do nothing to stop the evil act other than to refuse to pay for it.

6   However well the president has negotiated the political shoals, he has produced a moral and intellectual mishmash that has failed to dissuade Congress from going further than he has in advancing stem cell research.

7   To extricate himself from an untenable position, the president should start by following the successful pattern established in other areas of dealing with the clash of religious and political questions, including the law concerning abortion. The right of true believers to live by their own religious beliefs will be guaranteed: no one will be compelled to use stem cell research or its products, just as no one will ever be compelled to have an abortion. And the nation will respect the right of believers to advocate for changes in our civil law that correspond with their own view of morality.

8   But our pluralistic political system adopts rights that arise out of consensus, not the dictates of religious orthodoxy; and if such rights are adopted—approving abortions or financing stem cell research on leftover embryos—they will be the law of the land, even if religious dissenters, through their tax dollars, end up helping to pay for things that they find anathema. Every day Americans who abhor the death penalty, contraceptives, abortions and war are required to pay taxes used in part for purposes they consider offensive. That is part of the price we pay for this uniquely successful democracy.

9   So far neither Mr. Bush nor religious believers have convinced a majority of Americans that the use of embryonic stem cells inevitably entails the murder of a human being. Most Americans, vividly aware of the millions of tragic victims of Alzheimer's, Parkinson's, cancer and spinal cord injuries, believe that embryonic stem cell research may provide cures. They will demand that Congress act to realize that potential.

10   If the president vetoes a bill that advances that potential, he will have to provide more than sincere religiosity to prove that human life exists as early as fertilization, a proposition that even the Roman Catholic Church and other religions have historically disputed.

11   The best way to test that proposition would be to employ a panel of respected scientists, humanists and religious leaders to consider testimony from bioscience experts describing when consciousness first appears, when viability outside the womb usually occurs, and how other religions treat the subject. They would then provide their conclusions to lawmakers.

12   Such a panel, the Task Force on Life and the Law, has been operating effectively in New York since 1985, devising public policy to address issues like euthanasia, the definition of death, surrogacy births, the withholding and withdrawing of life-sustaining treatment, reproductive technology and other difficult questions generated by rapid advances in medical technology. The panel's decisions on the definition of death, do-not-resuscitate orders and organ and tissue transplants were all adopted by the Legislature.

If indeed such a panel confirms that Dr. Marburger is right and science cannot   13
supply the proof that human life starts at conception, then the president's position
is based only on his particular religious faith. If so, the president would be wrong to
deny the rest of America that does not share his faith the vast potential benefits of
embryonic stem cells.

Stem Cell Simplicities

Mona Charen

*Nationally syndicated columnist Mona Charen is one of the nation's most prolific
conservative writers. During the Reagan administration, she was a speechwriter
for Nancy Reagan and later for Republican presidential hopeful Jack Kemp. She
has also been an editor for the conservative policy magazine* National Review.
*Her weekly syndicated column is published in more than 200 newspapers around
the United States. This op-ed piece on stem cell research appeared in the online
magazine* Jewish World Review *on July 6, 2001.*

Let's use the bodies of condemned criminals for medical research! We could do-   1
nate the eyes and heart of a Timothy McVeigh-type to some worthy medical experiment, and the lungs and livers of other murderers for similar purposes. Well, after
all, the bodies are only going to be buried anyway, at least this way some good will
come of them.

Why do you squirm? Probably for the same reason that no one stood in line to   2
receive "fresh" organs from Dr. Jack Kevorkian when he offered them.

We flinch from using the organs from condemned people for several reasons,   3
but the most important is our well-grounded fear that using the organs of executed
criminals might introduce temptations to the administration of capital punishment
that would be immoral. If the state takes someone's life, it should be for one reason
only—to exact punishment for a heinous crime. Imagine if judges and juries were
also considering how many lives could be saved by making available fresh hearts,
lungs, kidneys and so on?

And yet, in the debate over stem cell research, we are constantly reminded that   4
these embryos are going to be "discarded" anyway. Well, that only shows how much
work we have to do in sensitizing people to the sanctity of life.

Human embryos should never be "discarded." There are other options, like re-   5
ducing the numbers of embryos that are created in the first place, or embryo adoption. But this is a secondary question. The heart of the matter is this: Is an embryo
an entity that deserves special respect?

Newsweek magazine's cover story on the matter emphatically answers that   6
question in the negative. Over a picture of a fuzzy ball of cells the cover proclaims

"There's Hope for Alzheimer's, Heart Disease, Parkinson's and Diabetes. But Will Bush Cut Off the Money?"

7   Inside, one researcher thunders, "Anyone who would ban research on embryonic stem cells will be responsible for the harm done to real, alive, postnatal, sentient human beings who might be helped by this research."

8   Emphasis on *might*. It may be that the miracle cures confidently predicted for Parkinson's, diabetes and such will come to pass, but some caution is certainly in order. Recall that just a few years ago, medical and media circles were abuzz with hopes for the implantation of fetal brain cells into patients with Parkinson's. Then too, as Neil Munro reminds us in the *National Journal, The Washington Post* urged a president named Bush to lift federal bans on such research since it offered "the best hope for progress on curing such diseases as Parkinson's."

9   The federal ban was not lifted, but some scientists went ahead with the procedure anyway. The results were noted (very quietly) just a couple of months ago. The *New York Times* reported that the experimental treatment was a failure, and that some patients suffered side effects described as "absolutely devastating . . . tragic, catastrophic."

10   While results from stem cells may be better, one never hears a scientist asked: What is the marginal benefit of embryonic stem cells versus those found in umbilical cord blood, or those found in adults? Are we five years, or three, or one year away from achieving the same results with less morally comprised tissue?

11   To extract a stem cell from an embryo is to kill it. Now, Utah Sen. Orrin Hatch argues that an embryo in a fertility clinic freezer does not have the same status as a baby in a mother's womb.

12   A thought experiment: Suppose a burglar with a grudge against a couple went to her fertility clinic and methodically smashed the vials containing their frozen embryos. Would their damages be only the value of the broken glass?

13   It is difficult for people with limited imaginations to see an embryo as a human being. They don't look like us. But that is the stupendous miracle of life. Each of us begins as a dot of information smaller than the period at the end of this sentence. We are dust—and yet with the magic of DNA and with time, we become people. And those little clumps of cells, which even *Newsweek* agrees are "a world of potential," cannot ethically be sacrificed—no matter what the hoped-for gain.

Expand Stem Cells Ethically

Charles Krauthammer

The kairotic moment for the following article was the House of Representatives' passage of a controversial bill (President Bush said he would veto it) sponsored by representatives Mike Castle, a Republican from Delaware, and Diana DeGette, a Democrat from Colorado. The Castle-DeGette bill would lift Bush's

2001 ban on federal funding for new research from embryos that had not been destroyed before August 2001. Charles Krauthammer is a nationally syndicated conservative columnist, a medical doctor, and a member of the President's Council on Bioethics. This op-ed piece appeared in newspapers across the country in August 2005.

It is a good idea to expand federal funding of embryonic stem-cell research. It is 1 a bad idea to do that without prohibiting research that uses embryos created specifically to be used in research and destroyed.

What is deeply troubling about the Castle-DeGette stem-cell bill that passed the 2 House and will soon roar through the Senate is that it combines the good with the bad: expansion with no limit.

The expansion—federal funding for stem cells derived from some of the thou- 3 sands of discarded fertility-clinic embryos that are already slated for extinction—is good because the president's sincere and principled Aug. 9, 2001, attempt to draw a narrower line has failed. It failed politically because his restriction—funding only research on stem cells from embryos destroyed before that day—seems increasingly arbitrary as we move away from that date.

It failed practically because that cohort of embryos is a diminishing source of 4 cells. Stem cells turn out to be a lot less immortal than we thought. The idea was that once you create a line, it could replicate indefinitely. Therefore, you would only need a few lines.

It turns out, however, that as stem cells replicate, they begin to make genetic 5 errors and to degenerate. After several generations, some lines become unusable.

In addition, there has been a new advance since 2001. Whereas stem cells in 6 those days had to be grown on mouse feeder cells, today we can grow stem cells on human feeder cells. That makes them far more (potentially) therapeutically usable.

For both of these reasons, the August 2001 policy is obsolete. Accordingly, 7 Congress will soon federally fund research from embryos newly created in IVF clinics.

It simply will not do for opponents of this expanded research to say that the 8 federal government should not force those Americans who find this research abhorrent to support it with their taxes. By that logic, we should never go to war, or impose the death penalty, except by unanimous consent of the entire population. We make many life-or-death decisions as a society as a whole, without being hostage to the sensibilities of a minority, however substantial and sincere.

Nonetheless, Congress' current vehicle for expanding this research, the Castle- 9 DeGette bill, is extremely dangerous. It expands the reach for a morally problematical area of research—without drawing any serious moral lines.

The moral problem for that majority of Americans who, like me, don't believe that 10 a zygote or blastocyst has all the attributes and therefore merits all the rights of personhood, is this: Does that mean that *everything* is permissible with a human embryo?

Don't they understand the real threat? It is not so much the destruction of exist- 11 ing human embryos—God knows, more than a million are already destroyed every year in abortions, thousands doomed to die in IVF clinics. A handful drawn from fertility clinics *where they will be destroyed anyway* alters no great moral balance.

12   The real threat to our humanity is the creation of new human life willfully for the sole purpose of making it the means to someone else's end—dissecting it for its parts the way we would dissect something with no more moral standing than a mollusk or paramecium. The real Brave New World looming before us is the rise of the industry of human manufacture, where human embryos are created not to produce children—the purpose of IVF clinics—but for spare body parts.

13   It is this creation-for-the-purpose-of-destruction that needs to be stopped—and it does not matter whether that creation occurs by joining sperm and egg (as the Jones Institute in Virginia has already done) or by cloning a cell from an adult, turning it into a human embryo, and then destroying it for its stem cells.

14   Both in my writings and as a member of the President's Council on Bioethics, I have advocated this dual policy for years: expand federal funding of stem-cell research by using discarded embryos but couple that with a firm *national ban* on creating human embryos for any purpose other than the birth of a human baby.

15   We finally have a chance to enact this grand compromise—but only if a majority of senators insist that the welcome expansion provided in the Castle-DeGette bill, which will yield a near endless supply of embryonic stem cells, cannot take place unless the door is firmly closed now, while we still have the chance, on the manufacture of human embryos for research and destruction.

For Class Discussion

1. Many of the articles in this unit incorporate causal arguments to speculate about the potential consequences of different courses of action on cloning and stem cell research. Working individually or in groups, choose several of the views represented in this unit and sketch out the causal arguments that the writers use to support their claims. You might choose from among the following views or any others that you think of. What makes each instance of causal reasoning persuasive or weak?

   - Scientists in favor of therapeutic cloning
   - Public policymakers in favor of therapeutic cloning
   - Scientists in favor of a moratorium on therapeutic cloning
   - Spokespeople for conservative religious views against all cloning and stem cell research
   - Spokespeople for conservative religious views in favor of regulated therapeutic cloning and stem cell research
   - Nonreligious spokespeople against therapeutic cloning

2. One of the major rhetorical problems with a subject like cloning and stem cell research is the need to translate scientific ideas into terms that the general public can understand. In rhetorical language, we would say that this is an issue of finding audience-based reasons and presenting evidence that will be meaningful to a nonscientifically trained audience. Which of the ar-

guments in this unit do you find particularly successful at making this scientific subject clear to readers? How do they work?

3. Where and how in the articles in this unit do arguers on these issues bring in the personal human element or other appeals to *pathos*?

4. According to some of the readings in this unit, where does the therapeutic cloning controversy intersect with abortion, reproductive technology (medical technology used to overcome infertility problems), and genetic enhancement (for example, "designer babies") in the search for perfection?

5. Choose one of the readings in this unit and analyze it carefully using the List 2 Guide questions on pages 454–455.

OPTIONAL WRITING ASSIGNMENT   Some of the readings in this unit reject quick closure and call for more informed public debate on therapeutic cloning and stem cell research. After considering the multiple angles of vision reflected in these readings, write a letter to a U.S. senator from your state in which you speak for yourself or your family. Make a case for the way you would like your senator to vote on this controversial issue. What laws and regulations would you like your politician to support and why?

IN SEARCH OF PERFECTION: STEROIDS, BIONIC ATHLETES, AND DESIGNER CHILDREN

Although steroids have been used by bodybuilders since the 1940s—after being developed by German scientists during World War II—they entered the public consciousness when the International Olympic Committee banned their use in 1975. As early as 1956 Russian weight lifters and wrestlers had been suspected of using steroids, but evidence based on urine tests didn't become widely known until prominent Olympic athletes were disqualified from competitions. Most famously, Canadian sprinter Ben Johnson was stripped of his gold medal in the 1988 Olympics after testing positive for steroids. (Johnson later admitted having using steroids since 1981; consequently, his 1987 World Record in the 100-meter dash was also revoked, and he was suspended for life from further competition.) In 1990, the U.S. Congress passed the Anabolic Steroid Enforcement Act, which defined certain classes of steroids as controlled substances which could be obtained legally only through a doctor's prescription, leading to the creation of a huge black market for the drugs.

Recently, public debate about steroids has focused largely on baseball, where some of the sport's most famous sluggers, including Mark McGwire, Jason Giambi, Rafael Palmeiro, and Barry Bonds, are under intense media scrutiny—and in some cases federal investigation—for illegal use of steroids. Called into question are Mark McGwire's record of 70 home runs in 1998 (breaking the long-standing existing record of 61 home runs) and Barry Bonds's current record of 73 home runs in 2001. The steroid scandal in baseball, accelerated by an exposé book by Jose Canseco and by the federal investigation of BALCO (Bay Area Laboratory Co-Operative), which allegedly supplied steroids for Barry Bonds and others, has created an intense public controversy about performance-enhancing drugs—a controversy with deeply philosophic undertones about the search for human perfection.

The readings that follow will introduce you to the far-ranging ramifications of the steroid controversy. At issue are questions like these: How dangerous are steroids? To what extent is steroid use a form of cheating? What is the difference, if any, between gaining competitive advantage through steroids and gaining competitive advantage through better equipment, LASIK surgery, or use of beta blockers to reduce tension? How are athletes taking steroids different from students taking Ritalin to enhance concentration, social introverts taking Paxil to overcome shyness, or parents using genetic screening or gene doping to create "perfect" offspring? Deep down, how is steroid use related philosophically to designer babies and the search for human perfection?

Steroids, Sports and the Ethics of Winning
Michael Dillingham

Michael Dillingham, a strong advocate for prevention of steroid use, is the team physician for the San Francisco 49ers and for Santa Clara University. This article was published online in 2004 by the Markkula Center for Applied Ethics at Santa Clara University.

Why, ethically, does the use of steroids in sports bother us? The medical issues are fairly straightforward. The use of anabolic steroids increases the athlete's chance of getting liver cancer. Heavy or prolonged use can cause psychological and emotional problems—so-called "steroid rage." 1

Men will have testicular atrophy and libido problems, and women will have abnormal periods and changes in their normal hormonal balance. 2

Because steroids enable heavy lifting, tendon tears and osteoarthritis are common ailments. I could tell you about guys who do what their bodies weren't designed to do—such as benching 400 pounds—and by the time they are 35, they cannot lift their arms. 3

So, why do people use them? The answer to that question is also straightforward. They make you bigger, faster, and stronger. And they work perfectly well in anybody who's training heavily. 4

Should athletes be allowed to make this trade-off? Many say, "It hurts only me, so why does society care?" 5

Society cares because steroid use is a form of cheating. Since steroids work so well, they create an unfair advantage for those who take them, and this breaks the social contract athletes have implicitly agreed to: We are going to have a fair contest. There are things we can and cannot do. Even if there were a safe performance-enhancing substance, if it weren't available to everybody, using it would still be cheating. 6

Unfortunately, steroids are still ubiquitous, and one of the problems is that we let people use them. Society loves sports and tends to look the other way when they become dangerous. We tolerate boxing, where you have two guys beating each other's brains out; we tolerate sports that have severe lifetime side effects like some elements of track and field. 7

The conspirators in this are everywhere—coaches, institutions, even some parents. We see parents who are in complete denial when their kids—college athletes with eating disorders—have stress fractures of their tibias or patellas because their bones are fragile from anorexia. The parents are living through the children's achievements, so it's very difficult to break this pattern. 8

Steroid use is part of this whole youthful delusion that says, "If I just do this for a period of my life, I'll be fine. I'll smoke until I'm older; I'll only binge drink in college; I'll be anorexic or bulimic so I can run, and then I'll stop being that way and I'll go on and have a wonderful life." 9

10   That's playing Russian roulette, which is not a game I think we want to encourage.

11   The only things that work to discourage doping are testing and penalties. You can talk about personal responsibility until you're blue in the face, but to stop steroid use, testing is necessary. Cocaine and steroids have ceased to be big problems in professional football because of testing.

12   In most other professional sports, the inmates are running the asylum. There is no effective testing, and the penalties are pitiful. If Congress pushes this issue, and if professional sports and unions stop obstructing, and if some of the professionals get busted, we may get somewhere. I'm hopeful.

Steroids and Sports: A Provocative Interview with Norm Fost, M.D.

Rick Collins

In this interview, Rick Collins, an attorney, bodybuilder, and nationally acclaimed legal expert on steroids and the law, discusses steroid use with Dr. Norm Fost, a professor of pediatrics and director of the Program in Medical Ethics at the University of Wisconsin. As the interview shows, Dr. Fost is skeptical of many claims made against steroids. Rick Collins is the author of the book Legal Muscle, *which opposes current laws that criminalize steroid use. This interview was published in 2004 in* Muscular Development *magazine and is also available on Rick Collins's Web site www.steroidlaw.com.*

1   By the time the torch was extinguished and the dust of Athens had settled at the end of the summer Olympics, a total of 24 athletes had been thrown out of the Games for cheating by the use of performance-enhancing drugs, double the previous record of 12 from the Los Angeles Games in 1984. And the testing process on other samples still isn't finished.

2   As the commanding general leading the war against performance-enhancing drugs in sports, World Anti-Doping Agency president Dick Pound snared more headlines than most of the athletes. Sometimes it seemed like the war waged on cheating athletes overshadowed the events themselves. Perhaps more than by any other measure, a competitor's strength of character is now defined by the purity of his or her urine.

3   Under IOC rules, anabolic steroid use is cheating. That steroid use in sports is dangerous, immoral and unethical is the principle that underlies its prohibition. This principle is so entrenched that it would seem unthinkable to hear someone seriously challenge it.

4   That's where Norman Fost, M.D., comes in. This man has big cujones, which might seem to be an atypical descriptive term to stumble across when you're read-

ing an article concerning steroids, but it's apt here. In this age of stifling political correctness and "same thinking," it takes big, brass ones to reject the popular military drumbeat and march in the opposite direction.

Dr. Fost isn't short on gray matter, either. A graduate of Princeton (A.B.), Yale (M.D.) *and* Harvard (M.P.H.), he's not only a practicing pediatrician, but also an expert in medical ethics. In fact, he's been the Professor of Pediatrics and Director of the Program in Medical Ethics at the University of Wisconsin since 1973. He's Chairman of the Hospital Ethics Committee, heads the Child Protection Team, and is also a past-Chairman of the American Academy of Pediatrics Committee on Bioethics. Last year he received the William G. Bartholome Award for Excellence in Ethics from the American Academy of Pediatrics. His views are generating increasing mainstream media attention, and he has recently appeared on television and radio broadcasts including ESPN, CBS Evening News, NPR Morning Edition, and C-SPAN.

My personal views on the subject of steroids in competitive sports are fully spelled out in my book, *Legal Muscle,* and won't be the focus here. Dr. Fost has his own take on the topic, and, right or wrong, what he has to say must seem like high treason to anti-steroid soldiers like Dick Pound. I had the opportunity to speak with Dr. Fost in a remarkable, no-holds-barred interview recently, and here are the highlights.

RC: The outcry over steroids in sports has always had two components. One is the potential health danger and the other is the "unfair advantage" issue. Let's start with the health risks.

NF: First, I think we need to separate children and adults. I think absolutely they should be banned for children. Steroids can have permanent effects on growth and other metabolic effects, and children are in no position to be making choices about risks. Of course, there are also risks to competent adults. Many of them are reversible or cosmetic such as hair growth, hair loss, or voice changes. Infertility is an extremely common phenomenon in men and women, usually reversible. Certain oral steroids were associated with liver cancer, but to the best of my knowledge that has not been shown with contemporary injectable steroids. Steroid use does change blood lipids undesirably, and if sustained over many years or decades could increase one's risk for heart disease, but I'm not aware of any studies showing an increase in heart disease among athletes who use them.

RC: So, there isn't any scientific proof that the short-term changes that are common with intermittent steroid cycles are connected to heart disease?

NF: Correct, and the cardiologists that I have talked with think that it's unlikely that it would be. Many steroid risks have been wildly exaggerated or misstated in the press. Take the famous interview with Lyle Alzado, the NFL player who developed a brain tumor and claimed, "See? This is what happens when you use anabolic steroids for too long." Nowhere in the article was there a single reference or scientific source for any connection between steroids and brain tumors, because there is none. These stories appear in the leading journalistic media, creating the false impression that the claims are somehow supported by scientific studies.

RC: Have the media fairly put the risks in perspective of other risks that athletes voluntarily assume?

NF: No, not at all. For example, playing in the NFL for three years or more risks an extremely high rate—80 to 90% in one study—of permanent disability. That's unfortunate, but it goes with the territory and nobody says this is a reason to ban professional football. It's something that competent adults decide to do in exchange for the money, glory and pleasure that they get out of it. We don't think, in America, that people's liberty to take risks like that should be interfered with, just so long as they are not harming anyone else. Whatever the risks of steroids, even the most extravagant view of the risks isn't remotely in that category in terms of potential for permanent disability or even death. There have been dozens of deaths attributed to playing football. I'm not aware of any football players who have died because of steroid use.

RC: Steroid use for athletic performance is banned as "doping" in many sports, so somebody who breaks the rule should be punished, right?

NF: First, this whole idea of calling it "doping" bothers me. The noun "dope" typically refers to illicit narcotics. There's a pejorative tone that is too widely accepted by constantly using the word "anti-doping." It pre-judges the issue, and I think it ought not to be used. Regardless, sports have rules and you have to play by them. If you don't, there are penalties and you suffer the consequences.

RC: Canadian sprinter Ben Johnson seems like the original poster child for that.

NF: To me, the moral issue that is most troubling about the Ben Johnson affair is the way that the press and the public treated this, not just as a breaking of the rule, but as a fundamental moral problem of enormous proportions. We don't make moral judgments about people who commit fouls on the basketball court. It's the claim that Ben Johnson was doing something immoral just because he broke the rule that astonishes me. On the same day that he was discovered to be steroid positive and had his medal taken away from him, American swimmer Janet Evans was holding a press conference about her greasy swimsuit which American technology had developed and kept secret from the East Germans, and which had unequivocally, in her view, shaved seconds off her time and contributed to her victory. Here you have a very clear case of unfair competition and yet this is hailed as a great triumph of American ingenuity. And on the other side you have Ben Johnson—who used something that while banned is universally accessible—being condemned as some sort of moral moron. It's the disconnect between those two events that first got me interested in this and struck me as the most incoherent.

RC: If in a particular sport the rules are silent, you don't see anything inherently unethical in using steroids? You don't see it as an unfair advantage?

NF: It would strike me as one of a thousand things that athletes do to try to gain an advantage over competitors. It is not considered immoral to try to gain a competitive advantage. I would put steroids in the long list of things that athletes do to try to win. Better shoes, better equipment, better training, better coaching than the opponent has. If such advantages were not available to all competitors, then the advantage would be unfair. The usual solution to that is to equalize access. It is remarkable how people brag about manifestly unfair advantages, such as better training facilities, greasy swimsuits, or even superior coaches, and then express outrage about a drug that is generally available to anyone who wants it.

RC: But, doesn't there have to be a line drawn somewhere, however subjective and arbitrary?

NF: Yes, but I don't think steroids are anywhere near it.

RC: What about the claim that steroid use in sports coerces other athletes to use?

NF: "Coercion" is another one of those inflammatory scare words. Coercion in the dictionary means "the use or threat of force." There is no claim that anyone in the United States is being forced into using steroids. You don't have to use them to be successful in the NFL or Track and Field. There are users and non-users. But even if it were true that you couldn't win at the elite level without them, that's part of the cost of playing at that level. There are many risks and deprivations you have to undergo to be a football player—most of them involving far more risk than steroids—or a track star or a gymnast. And if you don't want to do it because it's just too risky, then don't do it. No one is forcing you to do anything, at least not in this country. If they were, that would be wrong.

RC: You're a pediatrician. What about the argument that condoning athletic steroid use among adults sends the "wrong message" to the children?

NF: Again, children should not be using these drugs. I am in favor of whatever it takes, including education and involuntary testing, to make sure children don't use them. There's very disturbing data about middle school children, boys mainly, using anabolic steroids as part of weight lifting programs. According to one study, it's not football players for the most part, but boys who are doing it to make themselves more attractive to girls. The role models aren't athletes. I am more worried about other role modeling in athletics, which I know occurs on a widespread basis and causes much more harm.

RC: What role modeling are you referring to?

NF: The role modeling of hurting people; causing injury; getting the quarterback out of the game; injuring the wide receiver. Look at hockey, where mayhem is mimicked at a very young age. There are articles about the development of youth hockey programs in Canada, in which it's an explicit part of the youth league to teach violence—intimidating and hurting people—because it's viewed that this sort of pit bull training is what it takes to succeed.

RC: If that sort of thing occurs here in the United States, President Bush isn't taking time out of the State of the Union address to talk about it, and Government officials aren't conducting any grand jury investigations into it, as they are into steroid use.

NF: Nor is it even criticized. Or generally reported in the sports pages the way steroids are. Yet I see it all around me. Even the coaches talk about it, "You got to take that guy out of the game." It is widespread and pernicious. As far as I can tell, the use of steroids as role modeling in sports is minuscule compared to that.

RC: What are your thoughts about non-competing adult bodybuilders who elect to use steroids purely for cosmetic reasons?

NF: Whatever ethical issues there are in the use of steroids in competitive sports, which, as I've said, I don't think are worth the attention they receive, they disappear with non-competing personal use. We are not talking about unfair competition, we're not talking about coercion, and we're not talking about undermining the integrity of sport. This is pure personal choice, right up there with smoking, drinking, bungee jumping—that is, choices people make in life which they should be free to make.

RC: Anabolic steroids were placed under the Controlled Substances Act in 1990, limiting the scope of physician prescribing with the threat of criminal penalties. Do steroids belong there?

NF: Whatever the arguments about our regulatory system for narcotics and marijuana and so on, they simply don't apply to steroids. This is not a source of violent criminal activity, school dropouts and all the social problems of illicit drugs. So putting this in that category strikes me as bizarre. If the government is really concerned about safety, if that is really the issue, the steroid situation screams for regulating the drugs through the FDA, and facilitating supervision by doctors. By driving this behavior underground, we have increased whatever risks exist by ensuring that safety studies are not performed, either short or long term. We have also lost control of manufacturing processes, so the user has no way of knowing what, in fact, he is using. The policy of a ban, coupled with criminal penalties, is even more incoherent if safety is the argument.

RC: You've hit on a key theme explored in *Legal Muscle*. But do you think that steroid administration for the purpose of building muscle in healthy adults could be safely accomplished under the supervision of physicians?

NF: There's no drug in the world that has zero risks. The issues are whether the risks are manageable, whether they are in the same ballpark as other drugs that are widely prescribed—and I think they are—and whether the risks can be reduced to an acceptable level. I think the risks are most reduced under a knowledgeable doctor's supervision. No question, there will always be adverse effects, but the life-threatening or irreversible and disabling adverse effects are likely to be low, and risks a competent adult may choose to take on even if properly informed. If the risks are greater than present evidence shows, the most efficient way to learn about that is through well-designed studies, as we do for other regulated drugs.

RC: Critics would argue that if physicians could prescribe steroids for non-medical reasons, some might begin catering to overly ambitious bodybuilders, pushing the envelope further into more dangerous territory.

NF: Generally most doctors practice medicine in a rational, sensible way and we do have corrective measures for people who practice medicine irresponsibly. We have lawsuits and licensing boards to limit, though not prevent, the possibility of that. Besides, slippery slope arguments are not a reason for prohibiting a technology. All technologies have unanticipated harmful effects, but the possibility of that or even the certainty of that has never before been thought to be a reason for prohibition.

RC: What about critics who argue that the adverse effects of steroids won't be seen or known for years, decades, or even generations?

NF: That's an argument that can be made about any drug, any food, or any device that uses a new technology. It's a reason why we have regulations; why we have an FDA that requires careful testing, and NIH funding for long-term studies. It's a reason to do continuous monitoring of drugs' effects, for having an adverse event reporting system, and for having people using these drugs under medical supervision. Everything has unknown risks. Steroids are no different. The mere fact that there are unknown risks is not a reason to prohibit something.

RC: Thanks, Doctor. Provocative stuff, to say the least.

7   Obviously, the existing rules against performance-enhancing drugs in sports must be enforced, and cheaters must be identified and punished for as long as the rules remain in effect. Personally, I have no sympathy for cheaters. But Dr. Fost might ask, looking ahead. "Are we winning the war against drugs in sports?" As

drug-enhanced athletes become increasingly sophisticated and the specter of gene doping looms on the horizon (if it isn't here already), do victory cries from Dick Pound and International Olympic Committee president Jacques Rogge seem to ring hollow?

Whatever our personal views on the ethics of steroids in competitive sports, the   8
civilian casualties of this war are piling up *outside* the stadiums. The war intended to level the playing field in sports spawned criminal laws to facilitate it, yet those ensnared by these laws have been almost exclusively *non*-participants in the Olympics or any other professional or elite athletics. The arrest and prosecution of these non-participating civilians—mostly recreational bodybuilders, and my clients—will continue to be this war's collateral damage.

Doping Scandal: Stop Testing and Legalize All Drugs
Ellis Cashmore

Ellis Cashmore is a professor of culture, media, and sport at Staffordshire University in Great Britain. He is an expert on sports psychology and has also published books on racism and class. In this article, which was published in 2003 in the London newspaper The Observer, *Cashmore uses his insights as a sociologist to question the rationality of banning steroids from sports.*

The crusade against dope by sport's governing bodies is expensive, ineffective,   1
futile and a denial of the reality of contemporary sport.

It is time sport liberalised its policies: it should drop the banned substances list   2
and allow athletes to make informed and intelligent choices as to whether or not they wish to take performance-enhancing substances.

Athletes from across the spectrum have made their intentions signally clear: 3
they will continue to defy the most stringent tests and stay ahead of the curve, always leaving testers lagging in their quest to eliminate doping.

While the governing bodies continue to outlaw pharmaceutically produced sub-   4
stances, athletes are forced to engage in clandestine arrangements, procuring dope from unknown sources and taking it in amounts and for periods that may prove detrimental to their health. An honest policy would permit doping, but invite athletes to disclose whatever substances they have used. Sports organisations could then commission research and advise athletes on what is most effective and in what quantities and at what intervals it can safely be ingested. After all, anti-doping policies were initially designed to protect the health of athletes.

The deaths of cyclists Tommy Simpson and Knut Jensen in the 1960s alerted us   5
to the possible dangers of taking supplements to sustain exhausted bodies during competition. Over the years, the inventory of proscribed substances lengthened and the purpose of the policy shifted from safeguarding the welfare of the competitors to extirpating cheating.

6   But there are no moral absolutes in sport. Definitions of cheating and fair play have changed throughout history. Today's athletes use air-inflated soles on their spikes, rather than flats; they run on fast artificial surfaces, not cinders; they wear aerodynamic body suits rather than baggy shirts. And, of course, they train; this would have been tantamount to cheating in the early nineteenth century. Many of the services popularly used by athletes would have been decried in earlier times: acupuncture, hypnotism, diets, even deep-tissue massage.

7   We happily allow, even recommend, these types of aid to today's athletes, yet instantly condemn them if traces of a banned substance are detected. Yet the inconsistencies multiply. If an Olympic archer uses contact lenses to assist his or her performance, we let it pass. If they take a betablocker to steady their nerves, we suspend them.

8   The hypocrisy of track and field, in particular, is apparent every season when athletes are given huge cash incentives to break records or remain unbeaten on the grand-prix circuit, yet denied the right to maximise their athletic effort. The kind of dope favoured by athletes is not some sort of magic potion. It enables them to train harder and for longer and so become more adept at a discipline.

9   Were sport able to turn back the clock to the 1970s when it was designing its dope policies, it would surely have sought a way of distinguishing the illegal recreational substances that have little or no relevance to sport from the performance-enhancing materials that were thought to promote athletic performance. Instead, it continued to lump them together under the rubric of "drugs"—a term that evokes images of crack-addicted mothers who sell their babies and heroin-ravaged *Trainspotting* types. Athletes are typically highly motivated young men and women striving to challenge the frontiers of physical endeavour. Their preparedness to take dope suggests how single-minded they are in their quest for excellence. It is a fallacy that they are just trying to get an edge. More often, they are trying to re-establish conditions of fair competition. An athlete who has trained diligently for 10 years only to clinch fourth place time and again may strongly suspect—or perhaps know—that the medals consistently go to competitors who use dope. What is he or she to do? Resign themselves to being an also-ran?

10   Doping of some kind has been commonplace since the inaugural Olympics of 776 B.C. It was probably going on during the early twentieth century, an age about which many rhapsodise. But the chariots of fire have long since bolted. The joy of competing for competition's sake has ceded place to a winner-takes-all mentality, nurtured by professionalism. This has been made possible by corporate sponsorship on a scale that makes the World Bank envious. One of the reasons the sponsors turned to sport was because rock stars and movie actors were too prone to embarrassing transgressions. Sports performers, by contrast, were considered clean and wholesome. When sports governing bodies resolve to clamp down harder on drug users, it is for the benefit of their sponsors more than fans. So reliant are many sports on the largess from sponsors, that a withdrawal could be ruinous.

11   Brands such as Kodak or Coca-Cola pay mightily to have their names associated with a pursuit that resonates health, cleanliness and purity. How would they

react if sport allowed "drugs"? That must be a question that weighs heavily on the minds of sport's administrators.

Somehow, they must persuade sponsors and the public that the pharmaceutical materials typically taken by athletes are not drugs, at least not in the way they are popularly conceived.   12

The alternative is to persist in the self-defeating search for ever more sophisticated and comprehensive tests to detect substances that probably do not even have a name at the moment. Already, the costs of detection are punishingly high. There will come a point at which the kind of surveillance and inspection required to monitor athletes will be just too expensive; the corporations will have to be persuaded that radical change is the only way forward.   13

This provides little comfort to idealists who still hark after the amateur ideals. They may abominate the prospect of their children aspiring to achieve in a profession in which doping is extensive. I sense that parents today are no longer dissuading their kids from going into sport. The lure of lucre has made it appear a viable and rewarding career. Would they think twice if they anticipated their offspring would soon be using performance enhancers, if only to remain competitive in an environment in which athletes have carte blanche?   14

My feeling is that it would not make any difference. After all, the only reason we regard performance enhancement as "dirty" is because we have rarely been encouraged to question the present policies. Many of the products on the banned list are available over the counter and most are accessible with a prescription. They are no dirtier than the kind of products the nation is habituated to taking every day.   15

Those parents who insist they would not, need to remind themselves that the future they deplore is actually already with us. Sanctimoniously denying it by claiming "we are winning the war on drugs" remains a deception. This is no white flag, only an acknowledgement that, like every other feature of culture, sport changes and develops. Resisting change leads only to stasis.   16

This Is Your Country on Drugs

Carl Elliott

Carl Elliott has both a Ph.D. in philosophy and a M.D. in pediatrics. He is an associate professor at the Center for Bioethics at the University of Minnesota. This article appeared as an op-ed piece in The New York Times *on December 14, 2004.*

Jacques Barzun famously said that to understand America, one must first understand baseball. Never has his remark been more accurate. Professional baseball players may be the most vilified Americans using performance-enhancing drugs, but   1 they are by no means alone. Performance-enhancing drugs have become a part of ordinary American life.

2   College students take Ritalin to improve their academic performance. Musicians take beta blockers to improve their onstage performance. Middle-aged men take Viagra to improve their sexual performance. Shy people take Paxil to improve their social performance. The difference is that if athletes want to get performance-enhancing drugs they go to the black market. If the rest of us want performance-enhancing drugs, we go to our family doctors.

3   The athletes get no sympathy, of course. This is understandable. A scandal makes headlines only when it involves a star, and professional athletes are stars whose income and status most people can only envy. Many people secretly want to see stars fail—and when they do, these fans revel in it. In the case of baseball, they can revel guiltlessly, because the players have cheated. They have broken the rules of the game. In the rest of America, of course, we have simply changed the rules.

4   Don't steroids carry dangers? Of course they do. But so do the enhancement drugs we get from our doctors. Fen-Phen, the popular weight-loss drug that was linked to pulmonary hypertension and heart disease, has killed and harmed so many people that Wyeth, its manufacturer, has put aside more than $16 billion to compensate victims. Hormone replacement therapy, promoted in the 1960s as an anti-aging drug for women, has been linked to an increased risk of heart disease, strokes, pulmonary emboli and breast cancer. Antidepressants like Prozac, Paxil and Zoloft were described as "cosmetic psychopharmacology" a decade ago, today they are embroiled in a public controversy over their links to suicide and homicide.

5   Perhaps this is the inevitable result of turning our medical system over to the market, where making sick people well is often less profitable than making well people better than well. Procter & Gamble, for example, has decided that the profit margins of its ordinary consumer items like Crest toothpaste and Tide laundry detergent are not nearly as appealing as the enormous profit margins of prescription drugs.

6   So the same week that newspapers reported that Barry Bonds of the San Francisco Giants and Jason Giambi of the Yankees used testosterone supplements, P&G was asking an advisory committee of the Food and Drug Administration for permission to market its new testosterone patch for women. (The panel later said no.) The medical problem it was being used to treat? Decreased libido. Laboratories like Balco, where Bonds and Giambi were clients, market testosterone to underperforming men; P&G hopes to market it to underperforming women.

7   The rest of the world often marvels at the enthusiasm with which Americans consume drugs and procedures for medical enhancement. Antidepressants are one of America's most profitable classes of drugs. America has turned cosmetic surgery into a multibillion dollar industry. The United States produces and consumes more than 85 percent of the world's supply of Ritalin. Perhaps only in the United States is Botox a brand name as familiar as Kleenex or Pampers.

8   Yet enthusiasm may not be the right word. Working up the requisite outrage over Barry Bonds and Jason Giambi may be easy enough. But what about all the other, less gifted athletes who have turned to steroids in fear and desperation? Like

the rest of us, athletes are caught up in a pharmaceutical arms race where to refuse to take drugs is to risk being left behind. This may be less about the desire to succeed than the desire to avoid shame and humiliation.

America's appetite for stimulants, antidepressants and Botox injections looks   9
less like enthusiasm and more like fear. It is the look of a Little Leaguer stepping up to the plate in the bottom of the ninth with two outs and the bases loaded, terrified that he is going to strike out.

The Beam in Your Eye: If Steroids Are Cheating, Why Isn't LASIK?
William Saletan

Using argument from resemblance as its dominant claim-type, William Saletan explores distinctions between performance-enhancing drugs and performance-enhancing surgery and in the process exposes inconsistencies in many anti-steroid arguments. William Saletan is a national correspondent for the e-zine Slate, *where this article was posted on April 17, 2005.*

And why beholdest thou the mote that is in thy brother's eye, but considerest not the   1
beam that is in thine own eye?

—Matthew 7:3   2

A month ago, Mark McGwire was hauled before a congressional hearing and   3
lambasted as a cheater for using a legal, performance-enhancing steroid precursor when he broke baseball's single-season home run record.

A week ago, Tiger Woods was celebrated for winning golf's biggest tournament,   4
the Masters, with the help of superior vision he acquired through laser surgery.

What's the difference?   5

At the steroid hearing on March 17, numerous members of the House   6
Committee on Government Reform, led by Chairman Tom Davis, R-Va., denounced performance-enhancing drugs. They offered three arguments: The drugs are illegal, they're harmful, and they're cheating. But illegality doesn't explain why a drug should be illegal, and the steroid precursor McGwire took, andro, was legal at the time. The director of the National Institute on Drug Abuse conceded at the hearing that steroid precursors weren't banned until last year, that steroids "do, in fact, enhance certain types of physical performance," that some are "prescribed to treat body wasting in patients with AIDS and other diseases that result in loss of lean muscle mass," and that "not all anabolic steroid abusers experience the same deleterious outcomes."

7   Don't get me wrong. If you buy a steroid off the street or the Internet today just to bulk up, you're taking a stupid risk. But much of that risk comes from your ignorance and the dubious grade of steroid you're getting. A star player with access to the best stuff and the best medical supervision isn't taking the same degree of risk. Furthermore, steroids are a crude, early phase of enhancement technology. Chemists are trying every day to refine compounds and doses that might help pro athletes without bad side effects.

8   Already the medical objection to doping has holes. At the hearing, lawmakers displayed a supposedly damning list of "Performance Enhancing Substances Not Covered by Baseball's New Testing Program." The first item on the list was human growth hormone. But the Food and Drug Administration has approved human growth hormone for use in short, healthy children based on studies showing its safety and efficacy. The National Institutes of Health says it's "generally considered to be safe, with rare side effects" in children, and the American Association of Clinical Endocrinologists has found the same pattern in adults.

9   That leaves one comprehensive complaint: cheating. At the hearing, I heard six lawmakers apply this term to performance-enhancing drugs. They compared the drugs to corking bats, deadening baseballs, and sharpening spikes. "When I played with Hank Aaron and Willie Mays and Ted Williams, they didn't put on 40 pounds of bulk in their careers, and they didn't hit more homers in their late thirties than they did in their late twenties," said Sen. Jim Bunning, R-Ky. "What's happening now in baseball isn't natural, and it isn't right." Rep. Mark Souder, R-Ind., chairman of the House subcommittee on drug policy, recalled that baseball had harshly punished players who threw games. He asked why such punishment didn't apply to "players today who systematically cheat through steroids and performance-enhancing drugs to alter the games." Davis, who presided at the hearing, announced that he would co-chair "Zero Tolerance: The Advisory Committee on Ending the Use of Performance-Enhancing Drugs in Sports."

10   Zero tolerance? Wait a minute. If the andro that helped McGwire hit 70 home runs in 1998 was an unnatural, game-altering enhancement, what about his high-powered contact lenses? "Natural" vision is 20/20. McGwire's custom-designed lenses improved his vision to 20/10, which means he could see at a distance of 20 feet what a person with normal, healthy vision could see at 10 feet. Think what a difference that makes in hitting a fastball. Imagine how many games those lenses altered.

11   You could confiscate McGwire's lenses, but good luck confiscating Woods' lenses. They've been burned into his head. In the late 1990s, both guys wanted stronger muscles and better eyesight. Woods chose weight training and laser surgery on his eyes. McGwire decided eye surgery was too risky and went for andro instead. McGwire ended up with 70 homers and a rebuke from Congress for promoting risky behavior. Woods, who had lost 16 straight tournaments before his surgery, ended up with 20/15 vision and won seven of his next 10 events.

12   Since then, scores of pro athletes have had laser eye surgery, known as LASIK (Laser-Assisted *In Situ* Keratomileusis). Many, like Woods, have upgraded their vision to 20/15 or better. Golfers Scott Hoch, Hale Irwin, Tom Kite, and Mike Weir have hit the 20/15 mark. So have baseball players Jeff Bagwell, Jeff Cirillo, Jeff

Conine, Jose Cruz Jr., Wally Joyner, Greg Maddux, Mark Redman, and Larry Walker. Amare Stoudemire and Rip Hamilton of the NBA have done it, along with NFL players Troy Aikman, Ray Buchanan, Tiki Barber, Wayne Chrebet, and Danny Kanell. These are just some of the athletes who have disclosed their results in the last five years. Nobody knows how many others have gotten the same result.

Does the upgrade help? Looks that way. Maddux, a pitcher for the Atlanta 13 Braves, was 0–3 in six starts before his surgery. He won nine of his next 10 games. Kite had LASIK in 1998 and won six events on the Champions Tour over the next five years. Three months after his surgery, Irwin captured the Senior PGA Tour Nationwide Championship.

According to *Golf Digest,* Woods aimed for 20/15 when he signed up for LASIK. 14 This probably didn't strike Woods as enhancement, since he was already using contacts that put him at 20/15. Now ads and quotes offering 20/15 are everywhere. One LASIK practice takes credit for giving Irwin 20/15 vision. Another boasts of raising Barber to 20/15 and calls the result "better than perfect." Other sellers promise the same thing and offer evidence to back it up. Last year, they report, 69 percent of traditional LASIK patients in a study had 20/16 vision six months after their surgery, and new "wavefront" technology raised the percentage to 85. Odds are, if you're getting LASIK, you're getting enhanced.

The medical spin for LASIK, as opposed to the entrepreneurial spin, is that it's 15 corrective. Your eyesight sucks, you go in for surgery, you hope for 20/20. Maybe you get it, maybe you don't, and that's that. But it isn't that simple. If you don't like the results, your doctor might fire up the laser for a second pass. In the business, this is literally called an "enhancement." Hoch, the golfer, got four enhancements in 2002 and 2003. He ended up 20/15 in one eye, 20/10 in the other.

16   Nor do you need poor vision to find a willing doctor. Most states think you're fine to drive a car without corrective lenses as long as your eyesight is better than 20/40. Cirillo, then a third baseman for the Seattle Mariners, was 20/35 in one eye and 20/30 in the other when he went in for LASIK two years ago. He came out 20/20 and 20/12. Cruz, an outfielder for the Toronto Blue Jays, was 20/30 when he went for an eye exam. Five days later, he was under the beam. "The doctor kind of talked me into it," Cruz told the *Toronto Star.* He came out 20/15. According to the *Orange County Register,* Gary Sheffield, then an outfielder for the Los Angeles Dodgers, had eyesight *better* than 20/20 when he asked for laser surgery to raise his batting average. His doctor talked him out of it.

17   Why risk surgery for such small increments? "Every little half-centimeter counts," Cruz told the *Star.* Last year, the *Seattle Times* reported that Troy Glaus, a power hitter for the Anaheim Angels, had gotten LASIK because he "felt his contacts were sufficient, just not always ideal. A windy day or a wave of dust could tip the advantage back to the pitcher." Often, coaches play a role. The Minnesota Twins training staff successfully encouraged several players to get LASIK. Maddux told the *Atlanta Journal and Constitution* that the Braves gave him "a little push" to get LASIK in 2000. Meanwhile, the Braves' manager, having talked to the same doctor about getting LASIK, in his own words "chickened out."

18   This is the difference between therapy and enhancement. You don't need bad vision to get the surgery. Wavefront, if you've got the bucks for it, reliably gives you 20/16 or better. If your vision ends up corrected but not enhanced, you can go back for a second pass. Players calculate every increment. Pro golfers seek "to optimize any competitive advantage," a LASIK surgeon told the *Los Angeles Times.* "They're already tuned in to the best clubs, the best putter, the best ball. . . . Clearly having great vision is one of the best competitive advantages you can have." Eyes are just another piece of equipment. If you don't like 'em, change 'em.

19   The sports establishment is obtuse to this revolution. Leagues worry about how you might doctor bats, balls, or clubs. They don't focus on how you might doctor yourself. Look at the official rules of Major League Baseball: A pitcher can't put rosin on his glove, but he can put it on his hand. A batter can't alter the bat "to improve the distance factor," but the rules don't bar him from altering his body to get the same result. Baseball now has a dope-testing policy, but it isn't in the rules; the players negotiate it. That's why it's weak.

20   At last month's hearing, baseball commissioner Bud Selig testified that in 1998 and 1999 he sent his executive vice president to Costa Rica to check out reports that juiced-up baseballs were causing an epidemic of home runs. Selig was looking for the wrong kind of juice. The U.S. Golf Association's Rules of Golf share the same blind spot: You can't use a device to warm the ball, but you can use it to warm your hands. You can't use a device to measure distance or "gauge the slope of the green," but you can get the same powers through LASIK. In the age of biotechnology, you *are* the device.

Read the testimonials. At 20/15, Kanell can read the eyes of defensive backs.   21
Tom Lehman, who will lead the U.S. golf team in next year's Ryder Cup, says LASIK
improved his ability to "judge distances"—a common benefit, according to the technology's purveyors. Woods says he's "able to see slopes in greens a lot clearer."
Woods' eye surgeon told the *Los Angeles Times,* "Golfers get a different three-dimensional view of the green after LASIK." They "can see the grain" and "small indenta-
tions. It's different. LASIK actually produces, instead of a spherical cornea, an as-
pherical cornea. It may be better than normal vision."

Just ask Tom Davis. "I was in and out in less than one hour," the congressman   22
reports in a testimonial for the Eye Center, a Northern Virginia LASIK practice. "I
was reading and watching television that evening. My reading was not impaired and
my distance vision was excellent."

Good for you, Tom. Now, about that committee you've established for zero toler-   23
ance of performance enhancement. Are you sure you're the right guy to chair it?

The New Eugenics

George Neumayr

George Neumayr is executive editor of The American Spectator, *a conservative
current affairs journal devoted to politics and culture. In this article, Neumayr
explores the current trend toward aborting fetuses with Down syndrome and
other genetic defects and raises ethical issues about gene doping and our desire
for perfect babies. The title "The New Eugenics" depends on the reader's understanding of the "old" eugenics, a discredited social philosophy devoted to improving the human species through selective breeding and other means. This article appeared in* The American Spectator *in June 2005.*

Each year in America fewer and fewer disabled infants are born. The reason is   1
eugenic abortion. Doctors and their patients use prenatal technology to screen unborn children for disabilities, then they use that information to abort a high percentage of them. Without much scrutiny or debate, a eugenics designed to weed out the
disabled has become commonplace.

Not wishing to publicize a practice most doctors prefer to keep secret, the med-   2
ical community releases only sketchy information on the frequency of eugenic abortion against the disabled. But to the extent that the numbers are known, they indicate
that the vast majority of unborn children prenatally diagnosed as disabled are killed.

Medical researchers estimate that 80 percent or more of babies now prenatally   3
diagnosed with Down syndrome are aborted. (They estimate that since 1989, 70
percent of Down-syndrome fetuses have been aborted.) A high percentage of fetuses
with cystic fibrosis are aborted, as evident in Kaiser Permanente's admission to the

New York Times that 95 percent of its patients in Northern California choose abortion after they find out through prenatal screening that their fetus will have the disease.

4   The frequent use of eugenic abortion can also be measured in dwindling populations with certain disabilities. Since the 1960s, the number of Americans with anencephaly and spina bifida has markedly declined. This dropping trend line corresponds to the rise of prenatal screening. Owing to prenatal technology and eugenic abortion, some rare conditions, such as the genetic disorder Tay-Sachs, are even vanishing in America, according to doctors.

5   "There really isn't any entity that is charged with monitoring what has been happening," says Andrew Imparato, head of the American Association of People with Disabilities (AAPD), "A lot of people prefer that that data not be collected. But we're seeing just the tip of the iceberg. This is a new eugenics, and I don't know where it is going to end."

6   "I think of it as a commercial eugenics," says Andrew Kimbrell, executive director of the International Center for Technology Assessment. "Whenever anybody thinks of eugenics, they think of Adolf Hitler. This is a commercial eugenics. But the result is the same, an intolerance for those who don't fit the norm. It is less open and more subtle. Try to get any numbers on reproductive issues. Try to get actual numbers on sex-selection abortions. They are always difficult to get. If you are involved in that commerce, do you really want people to go: So you aborted how many disabled children? That's the last piece of information people want out there."

7   Indeed, intellectual arguments in favor of eugenic abortion often generate great public outcry. Princeton professor Peter Singer drew fire for saying, "It does not seem quite wise to increase any further draining of limited resources by increasing the number of children with impairments." Bob Edwards, the embryologist who created the first test-tube baby through in vitro fertilization, has also drawn protests for predicting that "soon it will be a sin of parents to have a child that carries the heavy burden of genetic disease. We are entering a world where we have to consider the quality of our children."

8   But these comments, far from being unthinkable, reflect unspoken mainstream attitudes and practice. Only through political gaffes (and occasional news stories) is eugenic abortion ever mentioned, such as the time in 2003 when a blundering Hillary Clinton objected to a ban on partial-birth abortion because it didn't contain an exemption for late-term abortions aimed at the disabled. Women should not be "forced" to carry a "child with severe abnormalities," she said.

9   In an interview with TAS, Senator Rick Santorum of Pennsylvania recalled his 2003 exchange with Hillary Clinton on the Senate floor in which she endorsed eugenic abortion. "It was pretty revealing. She was saying there had to be an exemption for disabled children being aborted as opposed to healthy children being aborted," he says. "When she realized what she was advocating for, she had to put in the general niceties. But I don't think you can read her comments and come to any other conclusion than that the children with disabilities should have less constitutional protection than children who are healthy."

10   He added that "the principal reason the Democrats defended the partial-birth abortion procedure was for pregnancies that have 'gone awry' which is not about

something bad happening to the life of the mother but about their finding out the child is not in the condition that they expected, that it was somehow less than wanted and what they had hoped for."

What Hillary Clinton blurted out is spoken more softly, though no less coldly, in   11 the privacy of doctors' offices. Charles Strom, medical director of Quest Diagnostics, which specializes in prenatal screening, told the *New York Times* last year that "People are going to the doctor and saying, 'I don't want to have a handicapped child, what can you do for me?'" This attitude is shared by doctors who now view disabled infants and children as puzzling accidents that somehow slipped through the system. University of Chicago professor Leon Kass, in his book *Life, Liberty and the Defense of Dignity,* writes that "at my own university, a physician making rounds with medical students stood over the bed of an intelligent, otherwise normal ten-year-old boy with spina bifida. 'Were he to have been conceived today,' the physician casually informed his entourage, 'he would have been aborted.'"

The impulse behind prenatal screening in the 1970s was eugenic. After the *Roe*   12 *v. Wade* decision, which pumped energy into the eugenics movement, doctors scrambled to advance prenatal technology in response to consumer demand, mainly from parents who didn't want the burdens of raising children with Down syndrome. Now prenatal screening can identify hundreds of conditions. This has made it possible for doctors to abort children not only with chronic disabilities but common disabilities and minor ones. Among the aborted are children screened for deafness, blindness, dwarfism, cleft palates, and defective limbs.

In some cases the aborted children aren't disabled at all but are mere carriers   13 of a disease or stand a chance of getting one later in life. Prenatal screening has made it possible to abort children on guesses and probabilities. A doctor speaking to the *New York Times* cited a defect for a eugenic abortion that was at once minor and speculative: a woman suffering from a condition that gave her an extra finger asked doctors to abort two of her children on the grounds that they had a 50–50 chance of inheriting that condition.

The law and its indulgence of every conceivable form of litigation has also advanced the new eugenics against the disabled. Working under "liability alerts" from   14 their companies, doctors feel pressure to provide extensive prenatal screening for every disability, lest parents or even disabled children hit them with "wrongful birth" and "wrongful life" suits. In a wrongful birth suit, parents can sue doctors for not informing them of their child's disability and seek compensation from them for all the costs, financial and otherwise, stemming from a life they would have aborted had they received that prenatal information. Wrongful life suits are brought by children (through their parents) against doctors for all the "damages" they've suffered from being born. (Most states recognize wrongful birth suits, but for many states, California and New Jersey among the exceptions, wrongful life suits are still too ridiculous to entertain.)

In 2003, Ob-Gyn Savita Khosla of Hackensack, New Jersey, agreed to pay $1.2   15 million to a couple and child after she failed to flag Fragile X syndrome, a form of mental retardation caused by a defective gene on the X chromosome. The mother felt entitled to sue Khosla because she indicated on a questionnaire that her sibling was mentally retarded and autistic, and hence Khosla should have known to perform prenatal screening for Fragile X so that she could abort the boy. Khosla settled, giving $475,000 to the parents and $750,000 to the child they wished that they had aborted.

16   Had the case gone to court, Khosla would have probably lost the suit. New Jersey has been notoriously welcoming to wrongful birth suits ever since the *Roe v. Wade* decision, after which New Jersey's Supreme Court announced that it would not "immunize from liability those in the medical field providing inadequate guidance to persons who would choose to exercise their constitutional right to abort fetuses which, if born, would suffer from genetic defects."

17   According to the publication *Medical Malpractice Law & Strategy,* "court rulings across the country are showing that the increased use of genetic testing has substantially exposed physicians' liability for failure to counsel patients about hereditary disorders." The publication revealed that many wrongful birth cases "are settled confidentially." And it predicted that doctors who don't give their patients the information with which to consider the eugenic option against disabled children will face more lawsuits as prenatal screening becomes the norm. "The human genome has been completely mapped," it quotes Stephen Winnick, a lawyer who handled one of the first wrongful birth cases. "It's almost inevitable that there will be an increase in these cases."

18   The combination of doctors seeking to avoid lawsuits and parents seeking burden-free children means that once prenatal screening identifies a problem in a child the temptation to eugenic abortion becomes unstoppable. In an atmosphere of expected eugenics, even queasy, vaguely pro-life parents gravitate towards aborting a disabled child. These parents get pressure from doctors who, without even bothering to ask, automatically provide abortion options to them once the prenatal screening has diagnosed a disability (one parent, in a 1999 study, complained of a doctor showing her a video depicting the rigors of raising an afflicted child as a way of convincing her to choose abortion), and they feel pressure from society at large which having accepted eugenic abortion looks askance at parents with disabled children.

19   The right to abort a disabled child, in other words, is approaching the status of a duty to abort a disabled child. Parents who abort their disabled children won't be asked to justify their decision. Rather, it is the parents with disabled children who must justify themselves to a society that tacitly asks: Why did you bring into the world a child you knew was disabled or might become disabled?

20   Andrew Kimbrell points out that many parents are given the complicated information prenatal screening yields with little to no guidance from doctors. "We're leaving parents with complete confusion. Numerous parents are told by doctors, 'We think there is some fault on the 50th chromosome of your child.' A number of polls have shown that people don't understand those odds."

21   "There is enormous confusion out there and nobody is out there to help them," he says. "This is a huge tangle. And it leads people to abort out of confusion: 'I guess I better abort, because I don't know. It sounds really bad and I don't know what the percentages mean.'"

The new eugenics isn't slowing down but speeding up. Not content to wait to   22
see if a child is fit for life, doctors are exploring the more proactive eugenics of
germline genetic engineering (which tries to create desirable traits in an embryo)
and Preimplantation Genetic Diagnosis (PGD), which is used to select the most desirable embryos after extensive genetic testing has been done before they are implanted in mothers' wombs.

"The next stage is to actually start tinkering genetically with these embryos to   23
create advantages such as height," says Kimbrell. PGD is a "gateway technology"
that will advance the new eugenics to the point "where children are literally selected and eventually designed according to a parent's desires and fears," he says.
(Meanwhile, doctors are simultaneously reporting that children born through in
vitro fertilization are experiencing higher rates of birth defects than the average
population, suggesting that for every problem scientists try to solve through dubious means they create multiple new ones.)

Many countries have banned PGD. But American fertility clinics are offering it.   24
Two-thirds of fertility clinics using PGD in the world are in the U.S., says Kimbrell.
"Reproductive technology is an unregulated Wild West scenario where people can
do pretty much anything they want and how they want it," he says.

Charles Darwin's cousin, Francis Galton, coined the term eugenics in the   25
1880s. Sparking off his cousin's theory of evolution, he proposed improving the human race through eugenics, arguing that "what nature does blindly, slowly, and
ruthlessly, man may do providently, quickly, and kindly." As eugenics passes
through each of its stages—from sterilizing the enfeebled at the beginning of the
20th century to aborting the disabled at the end of it and the beginning of the
21st—man is indeed playing God but without any of his providence or care.

Andrew Imparato of AAPD wonders how progressives got to this point. The   26
new eugenics aimed at the disabled unborn tell the disabled who are alive, "disability is a fate worse than death," he says. "What kind of message does this send to
people living with spina bifida and other disabilities? It is not a progressive value to
think that a disabled person is better off dead."

What's Wrong with Enhancement

Michael J. Sandel

*Michael J. Sandel is a professor of government at Harvard University. A former
Rhodes scholar, he is a member of the President's Council on Bioethics, which,
according to its mission statement, "advise[s] the President on bioethical issues
that may emerge as a consequence of advances in biomedical science and technology." The following article is a white paper presented to the council for discussion at its December 2002 meeting. The article was posted on the Council's
Web site at www.bioethics.gov.*

1   We have considered a number of practices that aim at enhancement—athletes' use of performance-enhancing drugs and genetic interventions; parents' use of sperm-sorting or pre-implantation genetic diagnosis to choose the sex of their children; cosmetic psychopharmacology; the search for techniques to improve memory or extend the human lifespan. Each of these practices gives rise to a certain unease that we have struggled to articulate. As we grope to explain what makes at least some of these practices objectionable, we often find ourselves reaching for familiar terms of moral argument. The most familiar is the safety objection: Using steroids to gain an edge in sports, or Ritalin to do better on the SAT, or cloning techniques to produce a designer child, or botox injections to cure a furrowed brow, are troubling because they seek improvements at the cost of incurring medical risk. The safety argument is the least controversial and least interesting objection. It leaves open the question whether these practices are troubling in themselves.

2   Beyond safety, we sometimes couch our objections in familiar arguments about means: Objections in the name of fairness and non-discrimination are one instance of this reflex; objections in the name of respecting the human embryo are another. Confronted with the chilling ratios of excess boys to girls in China, some worry about the gender discrimination the ratios reflect, and others worry about the discarded female embryos. These objections are weighty and legitimate. But they are not the only reasons that sex selection and other forms of genetic engineering are morally troubling. Some sex selection and much genetic engineering does not involve killing embryos, and many instances of enhancement involve no unfairness or discrimination.

3   I would like to explore the intuition that enhancement and genetic engineering are objectionable for reasons that go beyond safety, fairness, and embryos. Consider baseball: Imagine that steroids, or some other performance-enhancing drug, were safe and available to all players who wished to use them, so that none had an unfair advantage. What, if anything, would be wrong with using them? Or suppose that a version of Prozac was found to pose no long-term health risks, and was cheap enough to be accessible even to those of modest means. Would our worries about the non-therapeutic use of mood-brightening drugs be wholly assuaged? Or imagine that sperm-sorting technologies were perfected to the point where parents could choose the sex of their children without killing any embryos. And imagine that such technologies were employed in a society that did not favor boys over girls, and that wound up with a balanced sex ratio. Would sex selection under those conditions be unobjectionable? What about selecting for height, eye color, and other physical characteristics?

4   In each of these cases, it seems to me, something morally troubling persists. The trouble resides not only in the means but in the ends being aimed at. It is commonly said that enhancement, cloning, and genetic engineering pose a threat to human dignity, or point us toward a post-human existence. But we still need to know *how* these practices diminish our humanity. What aspects of human freedom or human flourishing do they threaten?

5   One aspect of our humanity that might be threatened by enhancement and genetic engineering is our capacity to act freely, for ourselves, by our own efforts, and

to consider ourselves responsible—worthy of praise or blame—for the things we do and for the way we are. It is one thing to hit 70 home runs as the result of disciplined training and effort, and something else, something less, to hit them with the help of steroids or genetically-enhanced muscles. Of course the role of effort and enhancement will be a matter of degree. But as the role of the enhancement increases, our admiration for the achievement fades. Or rather, our admiration for the achievement shifts from the player to his pharmacist. This suggests that our moral response to enhancement is a response to the diminished agency of the person whose achievement is enhanced. The more the athlete relies on drugs or genetic fixes, the less his performance represents *his* achievement. At the extreme, we might imagine a robotic, bionic athlete who, thanks to implanted computer chips that perfect the angle and timing of his swing, hits every pitch in the strike zone for a home run. The bionic athlete would not be an agent at all; "his" achievements would be those of his inventor. According to this account, enhancement threatens our humanity by eroding human agency. Its ultimate expression is a wholly mechanistic understanding of human action at odds with human freedom and moral responsibility.

Though there is much to be said for this account, I do not think that the main 6 problem with enhancement and genetic engineering is that they undermine effort and erode human agency. The deeper danger is that they represent a kind of hyperagency, a Promethean aspiration to remake nature, including human nature, to serve our purposes and satisfy our desires. The problem is not the drift to mechanism but the drive to mastery. And what the drive to mastery misses and may even destroy is an appreciation of the gifted character of human powers and achievements.

To acknowledge the giftedness of life is to recognize that our talents and powers are not wholly our own doing, nor even fully ours, despite the efforts we expend to develop and to exercise them. It is also to recognize that not everything in the world is open to any use we may desire or devise. An appreciation of the giftedness of life constrains the Promethean project and conduces to a certain humility. It is, in part, a religious sensibility. But its resonance reaches beyond religion.

It is difficult to account for what we admire about human activity and achievement without drawing upon some version of this idea. Consider two types of athletic achievement untainted by pharmacological or genetic enhancement: We admire players like Pete Rose, who are not blessed with great natural gifts but who manage, through effort and striving, grit and determination, to excel in their sport. But we also admire players like Joe DiMaggio whose excellence consists in the grace and *effortlessness* with which they display their natural gifts. Now suppose we learn that both players took performance-enhancing drugs. Whose turn to drugs do we find more deeply disillusioning? Which aspect of the athletic ideal—effort or gift— is more deeply offended? Some might say effort; the problem with the drug is that it provides a short-cut, a way to excel without effort and striving. But effort and striving are not the point of sports; excellence is. The attempt to "improve" athletic performance by pharmacological means is the ultimate expression of the ethic of willfulness, effort, and striving. The ethic of willfulness and the biotechnological powers it now enlists are both arrayed against the claims of giftedness.

9   The moral problem with enhancement lies less in the perfection it seeks than in the human disposition it expresses and promotes. It might best be described as the hubris objection. Unlike accounts that emphasize the loss of human powers and the erosion of human agency, the hubris objection can explain our moral hesitation to embrace certain genetic alterations of animals. Chickens like to roam, but most egg-laying hens are confined, frustrated, in small battery cages. Suppose we could alter the gene that makes chickens want to run free. The chickens, now content to be confined, would suffer less frustration, and egg production would improve. Or suppose we found a way to dumb down cows to eliminate the fear they experience on their way to the slaughter chute. Or to engineer pigs without hooves, snouts, and tails. Is there anything troubling about altering animals in these ways? Let's assume that by reducing their capacities for our convenience we do not increase the animals' suffering, and may even relieve it. If these animal enhancements give us pause, it cannot be for reasons connected to the erosion of human agency. To the contrary, the genetic improvement of animals represents the ultimate human dominion. If such alterations are troubling, the reason must draw on the idea that life (even animal life) is a gift not subject without limit to our mastery or dominion.

10   When we discussed reproductive cloning, Bill May described what parents lose or override when they seek to specify the physical traits of their children. He spoke of "the openness to the unbidden." This resonant phrase points to a quality of character and heart closely akin to what I have been calling an appreciation of life as gift. It helps us understand the deepest moral objection to the use of embryo selection and other techniques that parents might employ to create designer children. The problem is not that the parents usurp the autonomy of the child they design. (It is not as if the child could otherwise *choose* her gender, height, and eye color for herself.) The problem lies in the hubris of the designing parents, in their drive to master the mystery of birth. Even if this disposition does not make parents tyrants to their children, it disfigures the relation of parent and child, and deprives the parent of the humility and enlarged human sympathies that an "openness to the unbidden" can cultivate.

11   Bill elaborated this insight with a distinction between two aspects of parental love: accepting love and transforming love. Accepting love affirms the being of the child, whereas transforming love seeks the well-being of the child. He observed that, these days, ambitious parents are prone to get carried away with transforming love—promoting and demanding all manner of accomplishments from their children, seeking perfection. "Sometimes," he said, "we act like the ancient Gnostics who despised the given world, who wrote off the very birth of the world as a catastrophe." He drew a parallel between parental love and modern science, which engages us in beholding the world, studying and savoring it, and also in molding the world, transforming and perfecting it.

12   Bill's distinction between molding and beholding corresponds to the contrast I have drawn between the project of mastery and the sense of gift. I want to suggest that what is troubling about enhancement is that it represents the triumph in our time of willfulness over giftedness, of dominion over reverence, of molding over beholding. If something like this is true, then the philosophical stakes in the debate

over enhancement and genetic engineering are higher than we are accustomed to think. Sorting out the ethics of enhancement will force us to reopen questions that have been largely ignored since the 17th century, when the mechanist picture of nature came to prominence in moral and political philosophy. From the start, the project of mastery and the mechanist picture have gone hand in hand. The discovery that nature was not a meaningful order but a morally inert arena for the exercise of human will gave powerful impetus to the project of mastery, and to a vision of human freedom unfettered by the given. We may now have to choose between shaking off our unease with enhancement and finding a way beyond mechanism to the re-enchantment of nature.

For Class Discussion

1. What different arguments can you sketch out for each of the following positions on issues connected to steroids or the search for human perfection?

   - In favor of keeping steroids illegal and banning steroid use from competitive sports
   - In favor of legalizing steroids for adults and permitting them in competitive sports
   - Philosophically supportive of most attempts to improve human performance or beauty through drugs, surgery, gene doping, or other means of genetic enhancement
   - Philosophically troubled by most attempts to improve human performance or beauty through drugs, surgery, gene doping, or other means of genetic enhancement

2. Many of the arguments in this unit attempt to undermine opposition to steroids by comparing steroid use to other kinds of enhancement that we tend to accept or endorse: better equipment, including the "greasy swim" suit used by U.S. swimmer Janet Evans; special contact lenses or LASIK surgery; expensive coaches and equipment that give unfair advantage to wealthy competitors; or use of Ritalin, anti-depressants, Botox, Viagra, and other drugs to enhance human performance or beauty outside of athletics. To what extent could you refute these arguments by showing that steroid use is fundamentally different from these other forms of enhancement?

3. The final two readings in this unit focus on issues connected to our desire for human perfection—issues that may at first seem only tangentially connected to steroids. Michael J. Sandel, the author of the final article in this unit, begins by listing different kinds of practices that aim at enhancement—steroid use in athletes; sperm sorting or genetic diagnosis to predetermine the sex of a fetus; the use of drugs to enhance appearance or promote happiness; and the search for techniques to improve memory or lengthen lifespan. He then states that "[e]ach of these practices gives rise to

a certain unease that we have struggled to articulate." To what extent do you share this unease? Why or why not?

4. Examine the cartoon on page 181, which makes a visual argument against steroid use. How does this argument make its case? Also examine the "goals" page of the "Athletes Against Steroids" Web site shown in Color Plate J. How might some of the writers in this unit object to the "argument" of the baseball cartoon or the Athletes Against Steroids Web site?

5. Choose one of the readings in this unit and analyze it carefully using the List 2 Guide questions on pages 454–455.

OPTIONAL WRITING ASSIGNMENT   Choose one of the hypothetical instances posed by Michael J. Sandel in paragraph 3 (p. 654) of his article "What's Wrong With Enhancement." (He poses hypothetical cases about totally safe steroids, totally cheap and safe Prozac, easy ways to choose the sex of a child, and ways to select height, eye color, or other physical characteristics of a designer baby). Write a short white paper, suitable for discussion at a conference on the ethics of enhancement, in which you set forth your views on the use of enhancement technology in your chosen case. Show that you understand the problem from a variety of perspectives.

MARRIAGE AND FAMILY IN THE NEW MILLENNIUM

You can get a quick overview of the central issues of this unit by looking at two Web sites: the National Marriage Project (http://marriage.rutgers.edu) and the Alternatives to Marriage Project (http://www.unmarried.org). The National Marriage Project, headed by sociologists David Popenoe and Barbara Defoe Whitehead, is a research organization housed at Rutgers University. According to its Web site, its mission is "to strengthen the institution of marriage" through research and analysis aimed at influencing public policy. In contrast, the Alternatives to Marriage Project, founded in 1998 by Marshall Miller and Dorian Solot in response to the National Marriage Project, celebrates a variety of social arrangements that fall outside the pattern of traditional marriage and family. The "About Us" link on their Web site says that the Alternatives to Marriage Project, although supportive of those who choose to marry, "advocates for equality and fairness of unmarried people, including people who choose not to marry, cannot marry, or live together before marriage."

At issue, then, is what vision we should project for marriage and family in the new millennium. The Bush administration, influenced by the National Marriage Project as well as by conservative think tanks such as the Heritage Foundation, has instituted federal policies to discourage cohabitation and premarital sex and to encourage traditional families as foundations of a stable society. Social conservatives also tend to oppose gay marriage and to value moms' staying at home with their children. Social liberals, on the other hand, tend to support more diverse kinds of families and believe that better day care facilities will make it easier for women and men alike to combine family and career. Meanwhile, many young persons today are avoiding or delaying marriage (see the discussion and tables in Chapter 9, pp. 186–190).

The readings in this unit will help you join this national conversation as well as think through your own views of marriage and family.

Restoring a Culture of Marriage: Good News for Policymakers from the Fragile Families Survey

Patrick Fagan and Jennifer Garrett

This white paper from the Heritage Foundation provides an overview of the Bush administration's social policies for promoting marriage. It also shows how sociological research conducted by universities, as well as by public or private think tanks, can enter the public arena to influence government policy. Patrick Fagan is a research fellow in family and cultural issues at the Heritage Foundation. Jennifer

Garrett, who holds a masters degree in public administration and policy, is a research associate in domestic and economic policy at the Heritage Foundation. This white paper was posted on the foundation's Web site on June 13, 2002.

1   President George W. Bush has taken the first bold step in reshaping federal policy to address the root cause of many of society's ills: the breakdown of the married, two-parent family. Specifically, he has requested nearly $300 million a year in the reauthorization of the Temporary Assistance for Needy Families (TANF) Act for efforts that promote marriage.

2   Though critics of the proposal claim that most single parents do not have strong desires or the wherewithal to marry, most of their assertions are to a large extent unfounded. As recently released data from an ongoing longitudinal survey of new parents show, a majority of unwed mothers and fathers not only have a strong desire to marry, but also believe the chances are good that they will. What these new parents need is more encouragement and preparation to realize their hopes.

3   The first round of data from the Fragile Families and Child Wellbeing Study[1]— a four-year project of Princeton University's Center for Research on Child Wellbeing and Columbia University's Social Indicators Survey Center—already shows the promising potential for federal-state efforts to reduce out-of-wedlock births, especially among the poor. For example, according to the survey:[2]

- Contrary to public opinion, the overwhelming majority of children born out of wedlock have parents who are living together or who are romantically involved or seeing each other on a regular basis; they are not born to single mothers with absentee fathers.
- Moreover, a majority of unwed mothers say they are interested in marrying the father and believe they have a 50 percent chance of doing so, and an even greater percentage of these fathers believe their chances to be the same.

4   Thus, there exists within fragile families a very large group of parents who are likely to participate in programs that would prepare them for marriage.

5   Members of Congress should study these survey data carefully in considering the President's request for marriage-related funding in the reauthorization of TANF. As the authors of the preliminary national report on the findings suggest, policymakers could use the data to "design programs that encourage—rather than undermine—the efforts of new parents to raise healthy children, maintain self-sufficiency, and make productive contributions to their communities."[3] By funding initiatives that educate people on the benefits of marriage and encourage unwed parents to acquire the skills for stable marriages, Congress can jump start the process of rebuilding a culture of marriage in America and improving the prospects for millions of America's most fragile families.

WHAT THE FRAGILE FAMILIES SURVEY SHOWS

6   The Fragile Families and Child Wellbeing Study is designed to provide longitudinal data on the conditions and capabilities of new unmarried parents and the con-

sequences of these factors on their children's well-being.[4] The survey, which follows a cohort of newborn children over the first four years of life, finished conducting the baseline interviews on a nationally representative sample of almost 5,000 mothers and 4,000 fathers in 20 cities—including a group of married parents in each city for comparison—by the fall of 2000.[5]

As the Fragile Families Study Web site explains, the survey's findings can address three primary issues of great interest today: out-of-wedlock childbearing, welfare reform, and the role of fathers in a child's well-being.[6] As many studies point out, many children who are born out of wedlock and spend some time on welfare with little support from their fathers experience behavioral problems and do poorly in school. Clearly, policymakers have reason to examine not only the causes of family breakdown that impose such heavy costs on children and society, but also the very policies they enact that actually undermine the formation of two-parent families.

KEY FINDINGS ON MARRIAGE AND COMMITMENT

One of the most significant findings in the preliminary report on the first follow-up interviews is that many of the unwed parents of the children in the study are committed to each other.[7] Specifically:

- 83 percent of unwed mothers reported being romantically involved with the father at the time of their child's birth and are either cohabiting (50 percent) or seeing each other frequently each week (33 percent).[8]
- 73 percent of unmarried mothers and 88 percent of the fathers of their children believed they had a 50-50 chance of marrying each other.[9]
- 64 percent of the unmarried mothers and 73 percent of the fathers agreed or strongly agreed that marriage is better for children.[10]
- 84 percent of the unmarried mothers and 93 percent of the fathers said they put the father's name on the child's birth certificate.[11]
- 79 percent of the unmarried mothers and 89 percent of the fathers said the child would use the father's surname.[12]
- 93 percent of the unwed mothers reported that they wanted the father involved in raising their child.[13] Furthermore, all of the cohabiting fathers and 96 percent of fathers romantically attached to the mothers but not living with them said they intended to stay involved with their child.[14]
- A majority of the unmarried mothers (65 percent) identified "showing love and affection to the child" as the most important quality the father could offer the child. Nearly half of the fathers ranked this quality first (49 percent), and only 12 percent of these couples said that providing financial support was the most important contribution the father could make to the child.[15]

The pattern of positive attitudes toward marriage that emerges for these parents is encouraging. The majority intended to marry and believed marriage is important for the welfare of their child. Of particular interest, and contrary to common rhetoric, is the fact that fathers were even more likely to report a positive outlook on marriage than the mothers were.

KEY FINDINGS ON DOMESTIC VIOLENCE

10   There is good news in these initial data on the incidence of domestic violence in fragile families, which also suggests that these unmarried parents are more likely to marry:

- Only 5 percent of unmarried mothers said that the child's father was violent, and only 6.7 percent said that the fathers had drug or alcohol problems.[16]
- The rate of reported abuse was lowest among those who intended to marry and who did not cohabit (1.6 percent).[17]
- The rate of abuse was the same among parents cohabiting with an intention of marrying (2.2 percent) as among those parents in the control group who did marry (2.3 percent).[18]
- The rate of abuse is more than four times higher among those who cohabit and do not intend to marry or who think it is unlikely they will marry (9.3 percent) than among those who cohabit and intend to marry (2.2 percent).[19]
- Among romantically involved ("visiting") couples who do not intend to marry and who do not live together, the rate of abuse is more than four times higher (7.4 percent) than among those who are romantically involved and intend to marry (1.6 percent).[20] There is no significant difference between the rates for cohabitors and visitors with plans to marry and married parents.

KEY FINDINGS ON EMPLOYMENT, EARNINGS, AND EDUCATION

11   There is also good news in the data with regard to the earnings potential of fragile families—a factor that could contribute to a decision to marry. For example:

- 66 percent of the fathers and 63 percent of the unwed mothers had a high school education or more.[21]
- 98 percent of the fathers had worked in the previous year, and 72 percent had worked in the week prior to the survey.[22]
- The fathers who were living with the baby's mother earned on average $3,000 more per year than the romantically involved fathers who were not living with the baby's mother.[23]

THE POTENTIAL FOR MARRIAGE

12   Based on various reports of the Fragile Families survey data posted on the study's Web site, it is possible to summarize factors that indicate which unwed parents would be more likely to marry. These factors include the following:

- The unwed parents intend to marry and either live together or are romantically involved.
- The father's last name is on the child's birth certificate.
- Both parents want the father to remain involved with his child.
- Both parents believe the father's most important contribution is to show the child his affection.

- Both the father and mother have completed high school.
- The father is working.

The more these factors are present in a couple, the more likely it is that they will be good candidates for marriage preparation or support programs. The number of those who are clearly not good marriage prospects—couples with fathers who are abusive to their mates or who use drugs—is actually relatively small. 13

ARE EXPECTATIONS TOO HIGH?

Although the majority of unmarried parents surveyed for the Fragile Families Study believe that marriage is most advantageous for their children, various researchers report that their expectations for marriage frequently are not borne out by what actually occurs. For example, while 46 percent of mothers interviewed before their child's birth intended to marry the father, only about 24 percent did. And whereas only 28 percent of mothers had intended to cohabit with the father after the child's birth, 35 percent actually did.[24] 14

These findings should be seen not as discouraging, but as confirming the need to address the impact of federal and state policies so that they provide encouragement and skills training rather than act as a hindrance to the poor who want to marry. The President's proposals would help to fill this need. 15

LESSONS FROM WELFARE REFORM

Social policy matters. Perhaps the best example of how bad social policy encourages the kinds of behaviors it is meant to eliminate is the old system of welfare that Congress wisely reformed in 1996. Following the success of Wisconsin's reforms that tied welfare benefits to work, Temporary Assistance for Needy Families funding allowed the states to focus on those people on the rolls who were most likely to find and hold a job. In Wisconsin, this approach had quickly reduced caseloads by about one-third;[25] after that initial success, Wisconsin was able to focus resources on those who needed more help to move from dependency to work. 16

A similar approach makes sense for restoring a culture of marriage among unwed parents in fragile families, most of whom are likely to be receiving some government benefits. As the findings from the Fragile Families Study demonstrate, it is possible to identify which unwed parents are most marriageable in order to focus resources on programs that would help them acquire the skills and support they need for a successful marriage.[26] 17

THE PRESIDENT'S PROPOSALS

Because he recognizes the benefits of stable unions for parents, children, and the nation, President Bush hopes to make rebuilding a culture of marriage a focus of national policy. His current initiative requests nearly $300 million in federal and state TANF money to target state-level programs that promote marriage and marriage skills, particularly among fragile families. 18

19   The initial findings of the Fragile Families Survey indicate that not only do most unwed mothers have a strong desire to marry the father of their child, but they believe they have a fair chance of doing so.[27] The President's proposals would provide the encouragement many of these parents need. It specifically requests funds for:[28]

- Public advertising campaigns on the value of marriage and the skills that increase marital stability and health.
- High school education on the value of marriage, relationship skills, and budgeting.
- Marriage and relationship skills programs that include parenting skills, financial management, conflict resolution, and job and career advancement for non-married pregnant women and non-married expectant fathers.
- Premarital education and marriage skills training for engaged couples and couples interested in marriage.
- Marriage enhancement and marriage skills training programs for married couples.
- Divorce reduction programs that teach relationship skills.
- Marriage mentoring programs that use married couples as role models and mentors in at-risk communities.
- Programs to reduce the disincentives to marriage in means-tested aid programs if offered in conjunction with any activity described above.

20   President Bush's proposal also would enable the U.S. Department of Health and Human Services, as well as the states, local governments, and private organizations, to better understand how public policy can promote families in which children's well-being is secure.

HOW CONGRESS CAN HELP

21   The findings of the Fragile Families Survey shatter the myths that most unwed mothers and fathers are uninvolved and that most unwed fathers do not care about their children's well-being. More important, the data show that the majority of these unmarried parents are romantically involved, are interested in marriage, consider their chances of getting married good, and agree that a two-parent married family is better for their child than a single-parent family.

22   Congress clearly has an opportunity, in reauthorization of the Temporary Assistance for Needy Families Act, to use this research to fund programs that support marriage. The need for such action is further indicated by a May 6 Opinion Research Corporation poll, which found that Americans overwhelmingly believe that out-of-wedlock births harm children, families, and communities.[29]

23   To jump start the process of rebuilding fragile families, Congress should:

- **Approve** the President's request for $300 million per year in TANF funding for initiatives that encourage and support marriage.
- **Disregard** the straw-man objection that the President's proposal would lead to an increase in domestic violence. The Fragile Families findings indicate

that the incidence of domestic violence is minimal among unwed parents who intend to marry.

- **Seek** to reduce the penalties on marriage that remain in means-tested federal welfare programs. These include penalties in the Earned Income Tax Credit (EITC) and on the receipt of food stamps and public housing and other programs that reduce benefits according to household income, thereby discouraging couples from marrying.[30]

CONCLUSION

Members of Congress should recognize from the wealth of social science research that the most effective way to reduce child poverty and increase child wellbeing is to increase the number of stable two-parent married families. The findings of the Princeton University and Columbia University Fragile Families and Child Wellbeing Study show that many unwed mothers have high expectations for the future of their children and their own chances of marrying their child's father. The findings show that a majority of unwed fathers want to be involved in their child's life and also have hopes for marriage.

It is time for Congress to implement policies and programs that would help such couples make a permanent commitment to each other and their children, and begin reaping the emotional, health, educational, social, and economic benefits of marriage. In reauthorizing the TANF Act, Congress should include the $300 million per year for marriage-based programs that meet the President's standards.

Notes

1. The Fragile Families Survey and the reports based on it and cited here can be found at the Center for Research on Child Wellbeing Web site, http://crcw.princeton.edu/fragilefamilies/index.htm. The term "fragile families" underscores the fact that unmarried parents and their children are at greater risk for poverty and behavioral problems than are two-parent married families. The survey follows newborns and their parents over four years. Data reported here reflect baseline interviews on these children and their parents that were completed by the fall of 2000.
2. See Sara McLanahan, Irwin Garfinkel, Nancy E. Reichman, Julien Teitler, Marcia Carlson, and Christina Norland Audigier, The Fragile Families and Child Wellbeing Study Baseline Report: The National Report, Center for Research on Child Wellbeing, August 2001, reporting their "preliminary national estimates," Table 2. Cited hereafter as National Report.
3. Ibid.
4. Ibid., Table 1. For additional information on this subject, see also Robert Rector, Kirk A. Johnson, Ph.D., and Patrick F. Fagan, "The Effects of Marriage on Child Poverty," Heritage Foundation Center for Data Analysis Report No. CDA02-04. April 15, 2002, at www.heritage.org/library/cda/cda02-04.html.
5. Baseline interviews for the Fragile Families and Child Wellbeing Study have been conducted in 75 hospitals in 20 cities across the United States: Austin, Corpus Christi, and San Antonio, Texas; Baltimore, Maryland; Boston, Massachusetts; Chicago, Illinois; Detroit, Michigan; Indianapolis, Indiana; Jacksonville, Florida; Milwaukee, Wisconsin; Nashville, Tennessee; Newark, New Jersey; New York, New York; Norfolk and Richmond, Virginia; Oakland and San Jose, California; Philadelphia and Pittsburgh, Pennsylvania; and Toledo, Ohio.

6. See Fragile Families Survey, "Study Design," at http://crcw.princeton.edu/fragilefamilies/index.htm.

7. See McLanahan et al., National Report, p. 3. The authors report the survey findings for interviews of 2,670 unmarried couples in 16 cities.

8. Ibid., Table 2. The findings reflect the level of cohabiting depending on who was being interviewed: mothers alone, mothers in the company of the fathers, or fathers alone.

9. Ibid.

10. Ibid.

11. Ibid., Table 3.

12. Ibid.

13. Bendheim-Thoman Center for Research on Child Wellbeing and Social Indicators Survey Center, "Dispelling Myths about Unmarried Fathers," Fragile Families Research Brief No. 1, May 2000.

14. Bendheim-Thoman Center for Research on Child Wellbeing and Social Indicators Survey Center, "Father Involvement, Maternal Health Behavior and Infant Health," Fragile Families Research Brief No. 5, January 2001.

15. McLanahan et al., National Report, Table 4.

16. Bendheim-Thoman Center for Research on Child Wellbeing and Social Indicators Survey Center, "Dispelling Myths about Unmarried Fathers."

17. Cynthia Osborne, "A New Look at Unmarried Families: Diversity in Human Capital, Attitudes and Relationship Quality," Center for Research on Child Wellbeing Working Paper No. 02-02-FF, April 2002, Table 4, p. 25. Cited with permission. "Abuse" here includes both physical and emotional abuse. Later studies intend to separate these data.

18. Ibid. These data are similar to findings from the 1999 National Crime Victimization Survey, in which women with children under 12 years of age experienced domestic violence at a rate of 3.8 per 1,000, compared with 32.9 per 1,000 for their never-married peers. See Patrick F. Fagan and Kirk Johnson, Ph.D., "Marriage: The Safest Place for Women and Children," Heritage Foundation Backgrounder No. 1535, April 10, 2002, at http://www.heritage.org/library/backgrounder/bg1535.html.

19. Osborne, "A New Look at Unmarried Families."

20. Ibid.

21. McLanahan et al., National Report, Table 1.

22. Ibid.

23. Bendheim-Thoman Center for Research on Child Wellbeing and Social Indicators Survey Center, "Unwed Fathers, the Underground Economy and Child Support Policy," Center for Research on Child Wellbeing Fragile Families Research Brief No. 3, January 2001.

24. Ronald B. Mincey and Allen T. Dupree, "Can the Next Step in Welfare Reform Achieve PRWORA's Fourth Goal? Family Formation in Fragile Families," Center for Research on Child Wellbeing Working Paper No. 00-23-FF, December 2000.

25. Robert E. Rector and Sarah E. Youssef, "The Determinants of Welfare Caseload Decline," Heritage Foundation Center for Data Analysis Report No. CDA99-04, May 11, 1999, at http://www.heritage.org/library/cda/cda99-04.html.

26. Recent reports that the welfare reforms have discouraged marriage do not tell the whole story. See, for example, Nina Bernstein, "Strict Limits on Welfare Benefits Discourage Marriage, Studies Say," *The New York Times* (regional edition), June 3, 2002. It should be noted that the studies reported by the article did not take into account the effects of the stringent penalties in current means-tested programs that couples face if they marry while on welfare.

27. McLanahan et al., National Report, Table 2.

28. As described in H.R. 4737, Section 103, Promotion of Family Formation and Healthy Marriage. The bill, which was passed by the House, was referred to the Senate on May 16, 2002; see http://thomas.loc.gov/cgi-bin/query/D?c107:3:./temp/~c107qCks1C:e18472.
29. As reported in Maggie Gallagher, "Marriage Polls and Pols," at http://www.townhall.com/columnists/maggiegallagher/mg20020515.shtml.
30. See C. Eugene Steuerle, Senior Fellow, Urban Institute, testimony before the Subcommittee on Human Resources, Committee on Ways and Means, U.S. House of Representatives, 107th Cong., 1st Sess., May 22, 2001, at http://waysandmeans.house.gov/humres/107cong/5-22-01/5-22steu.htm.

Statement Regarding Hearing on Welfare and Marriage Issues

Alternatives to Marriage Project

This white paper from the Alternatives to Marriage Project was submitted to the House Committee on Ways and Means, Subcommittee on Human Resources, held May 22, 2001. The purpose of the white paper is to oppose the Bush administration's proposal to use Temporary Assistance to Needy Families (TANF) funds to promote marriage and discourage "illegitimacy."

1   As a national organization for unmarried people, we believe that the use of Temporary Assistance to Needy Families (TANF) funds to promote marriage and discourage "illegitimacy" is not in the best interests of Americans who live in poverty.

2   One family form is marriage, and we agree that marriage should be supported. We believe, however that a marriage-promoting agenda does real damage in a nation whose strength is rooted in diversity and tolerance. We believe that the well-being of children is critical to our nation's future, and that to that end, all families should be valued and all committed relationships supported. We do not believe it is possible for public policy to promote marriage without simultaneously stigmatizing people who are divorced, withholding resources from single parents, shaming unmarried couples, and ignoring the needs of gay, lesbian, and bisexual people for whom marriage is not an option. Such policies disadvantage the children growing up in such families, and deepen social inequality.

3   The American family is indeed in profound transition. Although divorce rates have receded from their 1981 peak, marriage is not gaining ground. Between 1990 and 2000, the number of families maintained by women without legally married partners in the home increased three times faster than did married-couple families. "Cohabitation is the fastest-growing living arrangement in modern society," observes Johns Hopkins sociologist Andrew Cherlin. It is far from a childless state: scholars Larry Bumpass and Hsien Hen Lu of the University of Wisconsin note that, "a large share of children born to supposedly 'single' mothers today are born into two-parent households." These mothers are legally single, but are living and parenting together with an unmarried partner.

4   Although much of the testimony delivered at your subcommittee meeting paints a bleak portrait of these families, in reality there are millions of happy, healthy, unmarried families whose members are neither "illegitimate" nor a threat to the social fiber of our country. The notion that somehow compelling them to marry as a social cure-all is simplistic and unrealistic. Longer lifespans, the economic independence of women, and later ages at marriage have all contributed to reducing the importance of marriage in everyday life. This is true in nearly every industrial nation, not just the United States.

5   "Under these circumstances, putting all our eggs in the leaky basket of a campaign to reinstitutionalize marriage is a risky strategy and may even backfire," writes family historian Stephanie Coontz in *Newsday* (5/27/01, page B8). Abundant research shows that the children of teen moms who marry the father after birth often do worse than those whose marital status remains unchanged, probably because the basis for the marriage is not a sound one. Researchers overwhelmingly agree that high-conflict marriages can do more damage to children than divorce. Promoting marriage is an appealing quick fix that ignores the deep complexity of family quality and process, which turn out to be far more important to children's well-being than family form.

6   The real question here is what do real-world American families need in order to thrive? We believe that the first item on the agenda should be to reduce the economic stresses that contribute far more than any other factor to family instability. Consider the Minnesota Family Investment Program (MFIP), which allowed parents on welfare to continue to collect benefits as long as their earnings did not go over 40% of the poverty threshold, or about $18,200 for a family of three. An unexpected outcome of the pilot program was that MFIP clients were more likely to get and remain married than people enrolled in the standard welfare system. One place to start is with the minimum-wage, currently averaging $5.15 per hour, or $10,712 per year. According to the Department of Labor, if minimum wage had kept up with inflation over the last thirty years, it would be $7.80 an hour today. We encourage the Ways and Means Committee to promote an hourly wage or annual income that enables an individual to meet his or her family's basic needs.

7   Helping adults become gainfully employed is another legitimate way to foster stable two-parent households. Not surprisingly, women are three times as likely to want to marry the father of their child if he holds a job. Job-training programs, affordable quality child care, health care, transportation and paid parental leave are all crucial ingredients of a stable family life. Higher drop-out rates and more health problems among children are the negative effects of poverty, not marital status.

8   In addition to a living wage and basic benefits, we believe that other laws and policies should be available to the full range of American families. These include domestic partner benefits, family and medical leave, hospital visitation rights, and survivors' benefits. Like public assistance, health care and benefits should not be contingent on one's relationship status, marital status, or sexual orientation. Although such policy changes will take time to effect, they are essential if TANF block grant requirements are to address the heart of economic and social injustice.

Given today's diversity of family forms, it is morally problematic and logistically 9
difficult to restrict social and economic support to families headed by married couples. It ignores the forces of history and the complex reality of American family life, and it penalizes those who most need the assistance of fair and enlightened government policies.

Ultimately, diverting welfare money to programs that promote marriage denies 10
basic services to millions of American children. Programs to promote marriage disregard the fact that marriage is not always the best choice, and may actually do harm, especially to women who are experiencing domestic violence. We hope the committee shares our support of principles that work toward creating healthy, loving relationships and families for all people, married and unmarried.

11

The Alternatives to Marriage Project (www.unmarried.org) is a national organization for unmarried people, including people who choose not to marry, cannot marry, or live together before marriage. We work for greater understanding and acceptance of unmarried people.

Here Comes the Groom: A (Conservative) Case for Gay Marriage
Andrew Sullivan

Andrew Sullivan is the former editor of The New Republic, *a centrist intellectual magazine, and a pioneering writer on gay rights. Holding a doctorate in political science from Harvard, Sullivan is a prolific political commentator who appears regularly on* Nightline, CBS Evening News, *National Public Radio's* Fresh Air, *and* Larry King Live. *As a practicing Catholic whose writing has a strong conservative following, Sullivan here presents an argument for gay marriage. This article, which appeared in* The New Republic *in August 1989, helped initiate the national conversation on gay marriage.*

Last month in New York, a court ruled that a gay lover had the right to stay in 1
his deceased partner's rent-control apartment because the lover qualified as a member of the deceased's family. The ruling deftly annoyed almost everybody. Conservatives saw judicial activism in favor of gay rent control: three reasons to be appalled. Chastened liberals (such as the *New York Times* editorial page), while endorsing the recognition of gay relationship, also worried about the abuse of already

---

*For an additional argument on same-sex marriage—one addressed to a gay rather than straight audience—see student writer Sam Isaacson's essay on pages 308–310.

stretched entitlements that the ruling threatened. What neither side quite contemplated is that they both might be right, and that the way to tackle the issue of unconventional relationships in conventional society is to try something both more radical and more conservative than putting courts in the business of deciding what is and is not a family. That alternative is the legalization of civil gay marriage.

2   The New York rent-control case did not go anywhere near that far, which is the problem. The rent-control regulations merely stipulated that a "family" member had the right to remain in the apartment. The judge ruled that to all intents and purposes a gay lover is part of his lover's family, inasmuch as a "family" merely means an interwoven social life, emotional commitment, and some level of financial interdependence.

3   It's a principle now well established around the country. Several cities have "domestic partnership" laws, which allow relationships that do not fit into the category of heterosexual marriage to be registered with the city and qualify for benefits that up till now have been reserved for straight married couples. San Francisco, Berkeley, Madison, and Los Angeles all have legislation, as does the politically correct Washington, D.C., suburb, Takoma Park. In these cities, a variety of interpersonal arrangements qualify for health insurance, bereavement leave, insurance, annuity and pension rights, housing rights (such as rent-control apartments), adoption and inheritance rights. Eventually, according to gay lobby groups, the aim is to include federal income tax and veterans' benefits as well. A recent case even involved the right to use a family member's accumulated frequent-flier points. Gays are not the only beneficiaries; heterosexual "live-togethers" also qualify.

4   There's an argument, of course, that the current legal advantages extended to married people unfairly discriminate against people who've shaped their lives in less conventional arrangements. But it doesn't take a genius to see that enshrining in the law a vague principle like "domestic partnership" is an invitation to qualify at little personal cost for a vast array of entitlements otherwise kept crudely under control.

5   To be sure, potential DPs have to prove financial interdependence, shared living arrangements, and a commitment to mutual caring. But they don't need to have a sexual relationship or even closely mirror old-style marriage. In principle, an elderly woman and her live-in nurse could qualify. A couple of uneuphemistically confirmed bachelors could be DPs. So could two close college students, a pair of seminarians, or a couple of frat buddies. Left as it is, the concept of domestic partnership could open a Pandora's box of litigation and subjective judicial decision-making about who qualifies. You either are or are not married; it's not a complex question. Whether you are in a "domestic partnership" is not so clear.

6   More important, the concept of domestic partnership chips away at the prestige of traditional relationships and undermines the priority we give them. This priority is not necessarily a product of heterosexism. Consider heterosexual couples. Society has good reason to extend legal advantages to heterosexuals who choose the formal sanction of marriage over simply living together. They make a deeper commitment to one another and to society; in exchange, society extends certain benefits to them. Marriage provides an anchor, if an arbitrary and weak one, in the

chaos of sex and relationships to which we are all prone. It provides a mechanism for emotional stability, economic security, and the healthy rearing of the next generation. We rig the law in its favor not because we disparage all forms of relationship other than the nuclear family, but because we recognize that not to promote marriage would be to ask too much of human virtue. In the context of the weakened family's effect upon the poor, it might also invite social disintegration. One of the worst products of the New Right's "family values" campaign is that its extremism and hatred of diversity has disguised this more measured and more convincing case for the importance of the marital bond.

The concept of domestic partnership ignores these concerns, indeed directly attacks them. This is a pity, since one of its most important objectives—providing some civil recognition for gay relationships—is a noble cause and one completely compatible with the defense of the family. But the decision to go about it is not to undermine straight marriage; it is to legalize old-style marriage for gays.   7

The gay movement has ducked this issue primarily out of fear of division. Much of the gay leadership clings to notions of gay life as essentially outsider, anti-bourgeois, radical. Marriage, for them, is co-optation into straight society. For the Stonewall generation, it is hard to see how this vision of conflict will ever fundamentally change. But for many other gays—my guess, a majority—while they don't deny the importance of rebellion 20 years ago and are grateful for what was done, there's now the sense of a new opportunity. A need to rebel has quietly ceded to a desire to belong. To be gay and to be bourgeois no longer seems such an absurd proposition. Certainly, since AIDS, to be gay and to be responsible has become a necessity.   8

Gay marriage squares several circles at the heart of the domestic partnership debate. Unlike domestic partnership, it allows for recognition of gay relationships, while casting no aspersions on traditional marriage. It merely asks that gays be allowed to join in. Unlike domestic partnership, it doesn't open up avenues for heterosexuals to get benefits without the responsibilities of marriage, or a nightmare of definitional litigation. And unlike domestic partnership, it harnesses to an already established social convention the yearnings for stability and acceptance among a fast-maturing gay community.   9

Gay marriage also places more responsibilities upon gays: it says for the first time that gay relationships are not better or worse than straight relationships, and that the same is expected of them. And it's clear and dignified. There's a legal benefit to a clear, common symbol of commitment. There's also a personal benefit. One of the ironies of domestic partnership is that it's not only more complicated than marriage, it's more demanding, requiring an elaborate statement of intent to qualify. It amounts to a substantial invasion of privacy. Why, after all, should gays be required to prove commitment before they get married in a way we would never dream of asking of straights?   10

Legalizing gay marriage would offer homosexuals the same deal society now offers heterosexuals: general social approval and specific legal advantages in exchange for a deeper and harder-to-extract-yourself-from commitment to another human being. Like straight marriage, it would foster social cohesion, emotional   11 security, and economic prudence. Since there's no reason gays should not be allowed to adopt or be foster parents, it could also help nurture children. And its introduction would not be some sort of radical break with social custom. As it has become more acceptable for gay people to acknowledge their loves publicly, more and more have committed themselves to one another for life in full view of their families and their friends. A law institutionalizing gay marriage would merely reinforce a healthy social trend. It would also, in the wake of AIDS, qualify as a genuine public health measure. Those conservatives who deplore promiscuity among some homosexuals should be among the first to support it. Burke could have written a powerful case for it.

12   The argument that gay marriage would subtly undermine the unique legitimacy of straight marriage is based upon a fallacy. For heterosexuals, straight marriage would remain the most significant—and only legal—social bond. Gay marriage could only delegitimize straight marriage if it were a real alternative to it, and this is clearly not true. To put it bluntly, there's precious little evidence that straights could be persuaded by any law to have sex with—let alone marry—someone of their own sex. The only possible effect of this sort would be to persuade gay men and women who force themselves into heterosexual marriage (often at appalling cost to themselves and their families) to find a focus for their family instincts in a more personally positive environment. But this is clearly a plus, not a minus: gay marriage could both avoid a lot of tortured families and create the possibility for many happier ones. It is not, in short, a denial of family values. It's an extension of them.

13   Of course, some would claim that any legal recognition of homosexuality is a de facto attack upon heterosexuality. But even the most hardened conservatives recognize that gays are a permanent minority and aren't likely to go away. Since persecution is not an option in a civilized society, why not coax gays into traditional values rather than rail incoherently against them?

14   There's a less elaborate argument for gay marriage: it's good for gays. It provides role models for young gay people who, after the exhilaration of coming out, can easily lapse into short-term relationships and insecurity with no tangible goal in sight. My own guess is that most gays would embrace such a goal with as much (if not more) commitment as straights. Even in our society as it is, many lesbian relationships are virtual textbook cases of monogamous commitment. Legal gay marriage could also help bridge the gulf often found between gays and their parents. It could bring the essence of gay life—a gay couple—into the heart of the traditional straight family in a way the family can most understand and the gay offspring can most easily acknowledge. It could do as much to heal the gay-straight rift as any amount of gay rights legislation.

15   If these arguments sound socially conservative, that's no accident. It's one of the richest ironies of our society's blind spot toward gays that essentially conservative social goals should have the appearance of being so radical. But gay marriage is not a radical step. It avoids the mess of domestic partnership; it is humane; it is conservative in the best sense of the word. It's also practical. Given the fact that we already allow legal gay relationships, what possible social goal is advanced by framing the law to encourage those relationships to be unfaithful, undeveloped, and insecure?

Marriage Still Matters to Washington's Children

Jeff Kemp and Harvey Drake, Jr.

Jeff Kemp, a former professional football quarterback and the son of Jack Kemp, a former congressman and vice-presidential candidate, is an inspirational speaker devoted to the preservation and strengthening of traditional family values. The Rev. Harvey Drake, Jr., is president of Emerald City Outreach Ministries, whose mission, according to its Web site, has "a specific focus on rebuilding the health and strength of African American families." This article appeared as an op-ed piece in the Seattle Times *in October 2004 following rulings by judges in several Washington counties that Washington's Defense of Marriage Act was unconstitutional.*

It is the birthright of every child to be raised by their mother and father. To redefine marriage is to rob children of that birthright.   1

Yet, a small group of activist lawyers and judges is putting marriage under siege in the state of Washington. While gays, lesbians and most Americans seek an end to bigotry and hatred, something different is at stake here. The full-court press to legally redefine marriage carries societal implications that are vast and damaging to children and future generations.   2

The two of us join many of all races, religions and creeds who are alarmed by recent court rulings in King and Thurston counties overturning Washington's Defense of Marriage Act (DOMA).   3

We are linking arms as Allies for Marriage and Children to appeal to the vast numbers of Washingtonians troubled by the redefinition of marriage, as well as the decades-long decay of marriage and absence of a common-sense voice defending it. We will work with the state Legislature to find a constitutional solution to preserve marriage as the union of one man and one woman.   4

Some would have you believe this effort is an attack on gays and lesbians. They are wrong. We believe that all people deserve respect. The marriage movement recognizes people's freedom to choose their relationships and will never dictate what other people should believe.   5

However, we will be working to educate the public and legislators on why marriage matters and why it must be strengthened rather than permanently altered and further compromised. We will work to protect marriage and reinvigorate an institution that has already been depleted by social changes such as no-fault divorce.   6

In addition to the rights of children, there are other very practical considerations.   7

Thirty years of scientific research demonstrates that the ideal situation for children is to be raised in a healthy family with their mother and father. The research shows that, in general, every other kind of family arrangement has higher incidences of childhood poverty, drug abuse, school failure, mental-health problems, emotional and physical problems, and teen pregnancy.   8

9   People on the other side of this debate point out, correctly, that men and women have made a hash of marriage already. But that is only another argument for strengthening, not altering, marriage. Increasing respect between men and women recognizes the unique contributions of both in parenting. In other words, men and women bring qualities unique to them that are essential to the total development of children.

10   Changing marriage sends both boys and girls the message that a mom or a dad isn't necessary. Lawyers and judges will have made a whole new parenting structure the legal norm. Are we really prepared to send the message that women— moms—are not necessary in a child's life? Or that dads are no longer needed?

11   Children are confused enough about where they fit in society. If they come from homes missing one gender or the other, and society tells them this is ideal, it is more difficult for them to learn what it means to be a good mother or father, or what it takes to be a good spouse. No small group has the right to dictate to government, society, children and future generations that marriage has changed, or what should be taught to our children in sex-education classes.

12   The judges who ruled in the cases in King and Thurston counties cited research they thought favorable to the idea of raising children in a same-sex home. The truth of the matter is that very little longitudinal research has been undertaken and that the research that does exist is fatally flawed.

13   After reviewing the available literature, noted University of Virginia sociologist Dr. Steven Nock said, "Not a single one of those studies was conducted according to generally accepted standards of scientific research."

14   Two other researchers have written, "The methods used in these studies are so flawed that the studies prove nothing."

15   Yet, it was with those flawed studies in mind that two judges in Washington ruled against the state's marriage laws.

16   Before altering the family landscape for all time, we ought to have a vigorous but respectful dialogue, and take time to reflect on the comprehensive and long-term consequences of removing male-female bonds as the essence of marriage.

17   Washington's constitution places individual rights on a very high plateau.

18   It should. But the triumph of individual adult rights cannot be allowed to trump the rights of children.

19   Redefining marriage sends a message to society "that children don't necessarily need or deserve a mother and a father."

20   Nearly every child would honestly disagree.

Gay, Straight: What's the Deal?
Froma Harrop

A common argument in support of gay marriage is that gays are denied legal rights and benefits available to heterosexuals through marriage. In the following op-ed piece, which appeared in national newspapers in July 2004, syndicated columnist Froma Harrop speaks for single persons, who don't share in the "deal" given to married couples.

The U.S. Senate has blocked the proposed constitutional amendment that would ban gay marriage. In doing this, the senators have earned my gratitude—though for reasons not directly related to gay rights. Rather, the move will spare us all some of the repetitive back-and-forth that has characterized this debate. It has gotten boring, and both sides of the argument irritate me. About 82 million unmarried American adults will know of what I speak.

Gay advocates always note the thousand-plus federal rights and benefits that are available to married heterosexuals and not to committed same-sex couples. The guardians of traditional values then counter that marriage has always been a man-and-woman thing—letting gay couples in on the deal would harm whatever is left of the American family.

What really rankles me, though, is "the deal" itself. That hit home in a news story around the time that Massachusetts started recognizing gay marriages. The day after a lesbian couple wed, the women filed a medical-malpractice lawsuit. One of them suffered from advanced breast cancer, which the suit claimed, a doctor had failed to detect. The other wanted to collect for "loss of consortium." In other words, the doctor's alleged negligence was depriving her of the love and companionship of a mate, and she wanted monetary compensation for her pain.

You can't read this without thinking about similar hurts being felt all the time in non-marital relationships. People develop intense connections with old friends, neighbors and grandmothers. Why can't they sue for loss of companionship, also?

Quickie marriages get more legal respect than friendships lasting decades. An hour after Britney Spears gets hooked to her next husband, the federal government will shower her with all sorts of rights and benefits not available to the man who has spent eight years caring for a mother with Alzheimer's.

So here is the point: The push toward gay marriage doesn't threaten hetero marriages as much as it threatens "the deal." It puts light on the illogic behind handing a variety of goodies to certain people because some civil authority issued them marriage certificates.

There is a potent political issue here, which could complicate matters for candidates. They must do more than just choose between advocates of gay rights and those of so-called traditional values. They must consider the lot of single Americans, who could cause a ruckus if they ever woke up.

So much attention is paid to married couples that most of the public—including single people themselves—thinks of unmarried adults as a marginal minority. Actually, they account for half of America's grownups. Households headed by single people are now the majority in 13 states and 113 congressional districts.

These districts are wildly diverse. Some include the poorest black inner cities, while others are wealthy and mostly white. In the nation's richest congressional district—located on Manhattan's East Side—more than 70 percent of the households are headed by unmarried adults.

10   Government should have no interest in a citizen's marital status. It certainly has no business sending a bigger tax bill to cohabiting sisters than to a man-and-wife team reporting the same income and deductions as the sisters.

11   Marriage is a fine institution and a very important stabilizing force for the raising of children. Some purists will argue that even child tax credits are a kind of social engineering. Using the tax code to help people pay for child expenses seems OK to me. But giving tax breaks to Larry King and his seventh wife—and in the name of helping children—is outrageous.

12   Of course, stereotypes underpin these unfair policies. Married couples are seen as the moral backbone of America. Singles, on the other hand, are regarded as questionable citizens and possibly misfits. In truth, single America includes everything from 21-year-old serial daters and bachelor playboys to widowed grandfathers and divorced parents. And whose business is it, anyway?

13   Perhaps the diversity of the group helps explain why unmarried adults haven't made common cause. They should, and when they do, the whole conversation will change. The real issue will no longer be whether gays should get in on the same marriage deal as heterosexuals, but why the deal exists in the first place.

Who Needs a Husband?

Hila Colman

In this op-ed piece that appeared in The New York Times *on July 17, 2002, Hila Colman, a widow after 40 years of happy marriage, explains why she doesn't want another husband—unlike the typical older widower, who really wants a wife. Hila Colman is a writer of adolescent fiction.*

1   When I was a girl, a long time ago, nice girls (and weren't we all?) wanted to get married. We were primed and indoctrinated by our mothers on how best to attract and capture a suitable young man into marital bliss for a happy life forever after. It worked. For better, and as often for worse, we got married.

2   But what I see now among my friends and peers in their 70s, 80s and 90s is a strange reversal in the man-woman thing. From where I sit (I claim no statistics to back me up), the roles have been switched: older widows do not want another marriage while older widowers do, often fervently. This is not to say that an older woman does not want a man in her life. Of course we do, I do. But not a husband 24 hours a day.

3   The reasons to me are quite obvious. I had a good marriage, I loved my husband dearly for over 40 years. I was devastated when I lost him. But by now I have built a life of living alone. It was not easy; it was hard work and took an emotional toll, but I found it had its perks. My widow friends know them, too: we are not responsible for another person's comfort, we come and go as we please, eat when and what

we like, we are not vulnerable to someone else's moods. As one friend put it bluntly: "I never want to do laundry for a man again."

What we dream about, my friends and I, is to meet a man with whom we can have a relationship—not an affair or a marriage. You could call it a commitment, two consenting adults who can share the same pleasures: dinner and a movie, a concert, ball games, trips—whatever—but each being in his and her own digs. 4

But the men in our age group seem to want something quite different. They want a wife. They want what they had before, a woman in the house to do all the things that a wife is supposed to do—which is, to wrap it up under one big label, To Take Care of Them. 5

Of course it's the fault of my own generation. We grew up when a wife catered to her husband. But if we old ladies can take care of ourselves, why can't the old men? 6

Surely men, who have been running the world for so long, can learn to adapt to managing a household for one and can have an intimate relationship with a woman (albeit a faithful one) without the sanction of a license. 7

Companionship is always the best part of any marriage. So why not go for that and leave out the cumbersome baggage that two older people carry from their previous lives? 8

The Hearth Defended: A Review of Home-Alone America: The Hidden Toll of Day Care, Wonder Drugs, and Other Parent Substitutes *by Mary Eberstadt*

Myrna Blyth

The previous readings in this unit have examined the institution of marriage from the perspective of single persons, gays, and supporters of traditional marriage. The concluding two articles switch the focus to what has been called the "Mommy Wars"—or the conflict between working and stay-at-home moms. The following article is a book review that appeared in the conservative political and cultural journal National Review *in 2004. The book being reviewed,* Home-Alone America: The Hidden Toll of Day Care, Wonder Drugs, and Other Parent Substitutes, *is by Mary Eberstadt, a research fellow at Stanford's Hoover Institute. Eberstadt's book has been influential among cultural conservatives, who are most apt to stress the value of a stay-at-home parent. The gist of Eberstadt's reasoning is conveyed in this appreciative book review by Myrna Blyth, who was the editor-in-chief of* Ladies Home Journal *from 1981 to 2002.*

It's one of history's oldest questions: "What's a mother to do?" And, in this provocative new book, Mary Eberstadt of the Hoover Institution offers a simple and 1 straightforward answer: *stay home with the children.* She has concluded that most of the problems of today's youngsters—from biting toddlers to depressed middle-schoolers to out-of-control teenagers—can be blamed on out-of-the-house moms and absentee dads. "Divorce and dual income, dual income and divorce," she writes. "The refrain hums like a mantra through the literature" of dysfunctional youth.

2   When a female author writes a book criticizing mothers for not being focused enough on their children—and, perhaps, being too focused on their careers—she must explain how she herself managed to accomplish her writing without short-changing her brood. In her introduction, Eberstadt does so, at considerable length:

> I am an at-home mother of four whose "fieldwork" consists mostly of fifteen years or so spent around sandboxes, schools, carpools, baseball games, and the like and whose in-tellectual work is conducted by fits and starts and at odd hours in the basement, one wall over from the washing machine and another removed from the Nintendo set-up. I haven't had a "real" office in more than twelve years. Until very recently motherhood also meant that I did very little writing apart from the occasional essay or review. Today things are different. Three of my children are at school all day long and the youngest is on the verge of it, so there is more time for reading and writing than there has been for most of the last fifteen years. I have a part-time paid baby sitter who is upstairs while I am down, a husband who often works at home, and older children who also help with the youngest one. Thus the "how" of the book.

3   Oh, dear. Would any father, even the most devoted, writing a book about America's children ever have to explain his work habits so exhaustively? The fact that Eberstadt is so compelled confirms how intense the decades-old moms-at-home-vs.-moms-at-work debate remains—and how controversial Eberstadt's chal-lenging book could turn out to be. Sheila Wellington, former head of Catalyst, an or-ganization that supports professional women, and now a professor at NYU's Stern School of Business, told me, "I still spend much of my time talking about the work-and-home balance. That's what my female MBA students still want to hear about."

4   Yet Eberstadt's focus, she makes clear, is not on mothers and how their career choices affect them, but rather on how these choices affect their children. The book is not about the search for balance by today's women—a subject we read about ad nauseam in women's magazines—but rather about how lonely, unsupervised, and unbalanced millions of our children's lives have become. Eberstadt says the goal of her book is to "put children and adolescents front and center [and] to ask what the empirical and extra-empirical record shows so far about this relatively new and un-known world in which many parents, children, and siblings spend many or most of their waking hours apart."

5   If you are a working mom and don't want to feel guilty, stop now. Eberstadt is very effective in making her case that as "more and more children have spent con-siderably less time in the company of their parents . . . the fundamental measures of their well being" have scandalously declined. For example, in the first anecdote in the book's first chapter—about day care, which children now attend while still in their diapers—she sympathetically describes a sick toddler, who should be home in bed, spending all day at a daycare center plaintively calling for his mommy. Child-

care workers report that parents who are unable or unwilling to miss a day at work often dose such youngsters with Tylenol to bring down their fevers before dropping them off at day care. Eberstadt also describes angry two- and three-year-olds who act out their aggression, and wonders about the mental state of "babies and toddlers who take up biting as a habit."

The author notes the callousness of some of day care's defenders, such as feminist writers Susan Faludi and Susan Chira, who acknowledge that very small children may get sick more often because of the time they spend away from home but contend that they "are hardier when they are older." Eberstadt comments that "the real trouble with day care is twofold . . . It increases the likelihood that kids will be unhappy, and the chronic rationalization of that unhappiness renders adults less sensitive to children's needs." Point taken.

Eberstadt documents other harmful effects of today's parents' lack of involvement in their children's well-being. In her chapter on "Why Dick and Jane Are Fat," she maintains it is not the oversized portions, the increase of sweets in our diets, or the lack of exercise that is to blame for our supersized kids: "Today's child fat problem is largely the result of adults not being there to supervise what kids eat." That may be a considerable oversimplification, but one cringes with guilt when she cites some telling examples of how missing parents bribe kids with food: "Mom won't be there for dinner so why don't you treat yourself to pizza and those horrible cinnamon things you like." Or "Sorry I missed your game/play/assembly this morning. How about an ice cream to celebrate?" I doubt there is a working mother who hasn't tried that maneuver.

Eberstadt is also provocative on a subject she has written about knowledgeably before: the overmedicating of our troubled or, should we say, troublesome children, whom harried or self-involved parents just can't handle. In recent years there has been an explosion in the number of children diagnosed with an alphabet of ailments such as ADD or ADHD (attention-deficit/hyperactivity disorder) and other "conduct" disorders such as ODD (oppositional defiant disorder), SAD (separation anxiety disorder), and OCD (obsessive compulsive disorder). Daniel Patrick Moynihan coined the phrase "defining deviancy down" to describe how social pressures were leading to the redefinition—the normalization—of behavior once seen as pathological. "In the case of the juvenile mental problems," Eberstadt writes, we are doing the opposite: "We are defining deviancy up so that children who would have been considered normal a quarter century ago are now judged to have intrinsic 'brain problems' and are treated accordingly."

Because of this, our children are being dosed with behavior-modifying drugs at a startling rate. Friends have told me that in some private schools in Manhattan, more than half the children receive their daily meds at lunchtime from the school nurse. Over the past decade the production of Ritalin, the most frequently prescribed of these drugs, has increased 700 percent. In fact, the drug's manufacturer created a seven-inch Mr. Potato Head look-alike toy called "Ritalin Man" to "help the medicine go down," a marketing ploy that should make us all cringe.

Yet Eberstadt claims that she doesn't want her book to make parents feel guilty, not exactly. "The purpose of these pages is not to ask what any one woman or man has decided to do. It is rather to ask what the accumulation of many millions of such decisions is doing to the children and adolescents of this society." Her hope is "to replace our current low moral bar regarding nurture with a more humane standard acknowledging that individuals and society would be better off if more parents spent more time with children."

11   That may indeed be happening, and not merely because mothers are once more becoming appropriately dutiful. I hope Eberstadt watched and was cheered by a recent *60 Minutes* segment, reported by Lesley Stahl, which featured a group of highly educated women who had chosen to stay home full-time with their children. Their choice made a feminist who was interviewed during the segment furious, and seemed, to some degree, to confuse Stahl, a working-woman icon. But the mothers were sensible and tough-minded about what they had lost by making this choice and what they had gained. They didn't want their kids home alone, most of all because they wanted to be with them. They recognized the benefit not only for their children but for themselves. It is an argument Eberstadt never makes but one that would surely enhance her important, thought-provoking book.

Moms on the Front Lines of America's Culture Wars
Lynne K. Varner

In this op-ed piece published in the Seattle Times *in November 2004, award-winning journalist Lynne K. Varner looks at Mary Eberstadt's book from the perspective of a working mom whose own mother, grandmother, and great-grandmother were also working moms. (Varner's great-grandmother worked "for free as a slave.") Her views on the "mommy wars" differ significantly from Mary Eberstadt's.*

1   In the aftermath of an election that solidified divisions in America's culture wars, I'm predicting who's next in the cross-hairs: working moms.

2   The war between stay-at-home mothers and those with careers is old news. But lately the battle has escalated beyond coffee-klatch sniping to the public-policy arena, where studies routinely make provocative pronouncements about day care's effect on children. Scores of books have emerged taking one side or the other. Mothers who work are either great role models for their children or guilty of all but abandoning them.

3   Last week, more than 62 million women went to the polls. They supported President Bush in higher numbers than in 2000. The issue for many was values. Take a peek under the values tent and you'll find a battlefield with stay-at-home moms on one side and working mothers on the other.

4   The presidential campaign got caught up in the mommy wars. Teresa Heinz Kerry wandered into the crossfire when she questioned whether Laura Bush had

ever held a job. The Bush campaign returned the salvo, pointing out that the first lady holds a master's degree and is a former librarian. The context of Heinz Kerry's words—she was outlining the differences between two women who've led dramatically different lives—was lost. The issue of whether she had dismissed stay-at-home moms became the campaign's defining one for many women. Certainly, it cost John Kerry votes.

Call me paranoid, but lately I've heard people refer to working mothers with as much disdain as religious conservatives refer to gay unions.   5

Gratuitous nods are made toward single moms and poor families that rely on a woman's income. But for the woman who dares to work for reasons other than economic necessity, judgment rains down like a hailstorm. Lately, that judgment is joined by a direct call for a return to traditional values and back to a time when moms stayed at home.   6

I keeping wondering whose mom they're talking about? My mother worked all of her life, starting out as a clerk-typist and retiring as a top manager from the federal government at age 70. She juggled PTA meetings with night school. She stretched out maternity leaves, but when they were up she donned her good suit and headed out of the house without a backward glance.   7

Her mother—my grandmother—toiled in the homes of women who didn't work in the home or outside of it. And my great-grandmother? She worked too, initially for free as a slave and for not much money afterwards.   8

A new book, "Home-Alone America," ignores this part of history and moves directly to warning women about the perils of not mothering full-time. You can get the book's point without cracking it open. Just check out the cover. There's mom in a power suit and high heels striding out the door as Junior slides along the floor clinging forlornly to a silk stockinged-leg.   9

The author, Mary Eberstadt, is a mix of contradictions. She is an educated, affluent woman who advocates women give up their professions to raise children. But in her own life, Eberstadt simply moved her profession to her home and her children to another room with the sitter.   10

Eberstadt describes day-care centers as places where teachers ply children with sugary treats and then let them tear around the room unsupervised. No, that would be home when your child has asked for the 100th time for access to his Halloween stash.   11

The author takes social problems facing adolescents today—from obesity to early sexual activity to a growing dependence on psychotropics—and plants them firmly on the shoulders of moms. The message is, these moms work while their children wither. Despite how many psychiatrists and social scientists warn that there are too many variables in a child's life—from school to parents to home environment—to single out any one culprit, Eberstadt's words sting.   12

The other day, I found this frightening pronouncement from a stay-at-home mom writing for the Institute on Religion and Public Life's Web site: "If our society is to be revitalized, the committed, religious, stay-at-home mother will have to be at the forefront."   13

I'm not sure what I, the committed, religious working mom, ought to do? Pack my handbasket for that trip to hell?   14

15   I shouldn't joke. The reality is, I'm uncomfortable with the strict lines being drawn in our society under the pretense of a return to values. We're getting close to passing the kind of judgments and challenging the kinds of freedoms that made the Puritans leave England.

16   Well, I'm not leaving. Nor am I willing to conform to someone else's notion of values. I can see how cultural wars begin.

For Class Discussion

1. Analyze and evaluate the differences among the writers in this unit concerning issues of traditional versus alternative families, the social utility of state-provided rights and benefits for married couples, and the benefits to children of a stay-at-home parent. How do you account for these different views? Do the writers disagree about the facts of the case? About definitions? About values, beliefs, and underlying assumptions?

2. The tables and graphics in Chapter 9 (pp. 185–190) show that young people are delaying marriage until later in life. What is your explanation for such delay? Working in small groups or as a whole class, make a bulleted list of reasons why the age of first marriage has risen so dramatically since 1960.

3. Working in small groups or as a whole class, draw on the readings from this unit, as well as on your own experiences and critical thinking, to make a bulleted list of reasons

   a. for and against getting married

   b. for and against legalizing gay marriage

   c. for and against what Froma Harrop calls "the deal" for married couples

   d. for and against one parent's staying at home with the kids

4. Choose one of the readings in this unit and analyze it carefully using the List 2 Guide questions on pages 454–455.

Optional Writing Assignment   As the junior staffer for Senator Murk, you've been asked to help the senator determine an appropriate position on one of the following issues: (1) The Bush administration's plan to use welfare dollars for programs to promote marriage and discourage cohabitation and premarital intercourse; (2) a proposal by a coalition of single persons to eliminate state-provided rights and benefits for married couples; (3) a constitutional amendment to define marriage as a union between one man and one woman; or (4) a proposal to provide substantial tax deductions to help defray lost income when a parent decides to stay at home with children.

THE MEDIA AND PUBLIC RESPONSIBILITY: WHAT COUNTS AS NEWS AND WHO DECIDES?

On July 7, 2005, when terrorist bombs exploded in the London subway, Britain and the world experienced what the British newspaper the *Guardian* has called "the democratisation of the news process, the true birth of the 'citizen reporter.' " The public watched live coverage from the scene through mobile phone pictures and video clips sent by nonjournalists. Text messaging and blogging (informal Web journals) also helped to shape the professional news coverage of the crisis. Similarly, news and images sent by soldiers from Iraq or posted on the Web have also influenced the world's understanding of this war, as have the gruesome videos on the Web of beheadings posted by terrorists. Although the United States' government sought initially to censor the now famous flag-draped coffin photo and photos of prisoner abuse in Abu Ghraib, these images have circulated widely, thereby affecting peoples' view of the war. The fact that images can easily be digitally altered and manipulated in terms of presentation and context further complicates the power of visual images to shape viewers' understanding of events.

In addition to these new problems, the media itself is conducting heated discussions of challenges facing the media and journalists—problems such as corporate control and bias in news media; journalistic credibility; reporters' use of confidential sources versus full disclosure of their sources; the proliferation of news venues from which people get their news; political advertising; and shallowness versus in-depth coverage of critical issues.

This chapter asks you to focus on two major media issues: problems with visual images and the problems created by selective news coverage in a democracy that depends on an informed and engaged public. The readings in this chapter explore such issue questions as, How is the selection and use of visual images, made possible by new technology, influencing people's views of events? What ethical problems do these images pose? Should the government and the news media censor graphic images of war, terrorist acts, and disasters? Are the American media strengthening or weakening democracy? What is the influence of corporate ownership and politics on the news media? As you read the articles in this unit, consider your own media habits—your favorite newspapers, television news programs, and radio stations.

Not a Pretty Picture

Sydney H. Schanberg

Best known for his coverage of the war in Cambodia, Sydney H. Shanberg won a Pulitzer Prize for international reporting in 1976 for his contributions to The New York Times. *He now writes regularly for* The Village Voice, *a liberal, New York–based publication, where this article appeared on May 17, 2005.*

1   "History," Hegel said, "is a slaughterhouse." And war is how the slaughter is carried out.

2   If we believe that the present war in Iraq is just and necessary, why do we shrink from looking at the damage it wreaks? Why does the government that ordered the war and hails it as an instrument of good then ask us to respect those who died in the cause by not describing and depicting how they died? And why, in response, have newspapers gone along with Washington and grown timid about showing photos of the killing and maiming? What kind of honor does this bestow on those who are sent to fight in the nation's name?

3   The Iraq war inspires these questions.

4   The government has blocked the press from soldiers' funerals at Arlington National Cemetery. The government has prevented the press from taking pictures of the caskets that arrive day after day at the Dover Air Force Base military mortuary in Delaware, the world's largest funeral home. And the government, by inferring that citizens who question its justifications for this war are disloyal Americans, has intimidated a compliant press from making full use of pictures of the dead and wounded. Also worth noting: President Bush's latest rationale for the war is that he is trying to "spread democracy" through the world. He says these new democracies must have a "free press." Yet he says all this while continuing to restrict and limit the American press.

5   There's a huge disconnect here.

6   More than 1,600 American soldiers have died in this war that began a little over two years ago. Wounded Americans number about 12,000. No formal count is kept of the Iraqi civilian dead and wounded, but it is far greater than the military toll. But can you recall the last time your hometown newspaper ran a picture spread of these human beings lying crumpled at the scene of the slaughter? And when was the last time you saw a picture of a single fallen American soldier at such a scene?

7   Yes, some photos of such bloodshed have been published at times over the span of this war. But they have become sparser and sparser, while the casualty rate has stayed the same or, frequently, shot higher. At the moment, five GIs die every two days.

8   Some readers may object to my use of the word slaughter. I do respect other points of view. But I served in the military, and as a reporter I covered several wars—in India, Vietnam, and Cambodia. I came away persuaded that whether one considers a particular war necessary or misguided, the military goal in armed combat is always to kill and thus render helpless those on the other side. That being the case, what is a government's basis for depriving the public of candid press coverage of what war is all about? How else can voters make informed decisions about a war their government has led them into? The true reason why a government—in this case, the Bush administration—tries to censor and sanitize coverage is to prevent a public outcry against the war, an outcry that might bring down the administration.

9   The photographs that accompany this piece are not gratuitously violent. They are merely real. All but one were taken by David Leeson, a highly regarded photographer at *The Dallas Morning News.* He and his *Morning News* colleague Cheryl Diaz Meyer were awarded the 2004 Pulitzer Prize in breaking-news photography "for their eloquent photographs depicting both the violence and poignancy of the war with Iraq."

I realize there are other sides to the story. One is the government's side.   10
President Bush says that none of the government's actions can be characterized as censorship or intimidation of the press. He says he is merely honoring the fallen by protecting the privacy of their families in their time of grief. A *New York Times* columnist—his name is not needed; the issue is what's important—offered another slant a week ago. He called for less coverage of the war's violence because the press was "frantically competing to get gruesome pictures and details for broadcasts and front pages" at a time when there is "really nothing new to say." He seemed to think the use of these "gruesome pictures" was on the rise—though others in the media-watching industry, such as Howard Kurtz of *The Washington Post*, have been recording a decline. The *Times* columnist said the press was, wittingly or not, assisting the "media strategy" of the suicide bombers and their leaders.

A columnist, of course, is permitted to offer up pretty much any opinion he or   11
she chooses, but still it's very odd to see a journalist—since we historically have always pressed for transparency—recommending that information be left out of stories. He insisted he was "not advocating official censorship" but simply asking the media for "a little restraint." Also, he cited the press controls used by former New York mayor Rudolph Giuliani as a model for achieving "restraint." Giuliani, the column said, had told his police department "to stop giving out details of daily crime in time for reporters' deadlines," in order to keep "the day's most grisly crime" off the 11 o'clock television news.

I don't hold much esteem for the usual crime-and-catastrophe formula on most   12
late-news shows, but I have even less for contentions that withholding information from the public is good for them. Because we are a country of diverse culture groupings, there will always be differences of view, about war photographs and stories, over matters of taste and "shock" issues. But, while the reporter or photographer must consider these impact and shock issues his primary mission has to be one of getting the story right. And getting it right means not omitting anything important out of timidity or squeamishness. When I would return from a war scene, I always felt I had to write the story first for myself and then for the reader. The goal was to come as close as possible to make the reader smell, feel, see, and touch what I had witnessed that day. "Pay attention," was my mental message to the reader. "People are dying. This is important."

A generation later, the photographer David Leeson, whom I talked with on the   13
phone, has similar passions.

He said: "I understand the criticisms about blood and gore. I don't seek that.   14
When I approach a body on the ground after a battle, I'm determined to give dignity to that person's life and photograph him with respect. But sometimes, as with my pictures of child victims, the greatest dignity and respect you can give them is to show the horror they have suffered, the absolutely gruesome horror." Leeson went on: "War is madness. Often when I was in it, I would think of my work as dedicated to stopping it. But I know that's unrealistic. When I considered the readers who would see my photos, I felt I was saying to them: 'If I hurt inside, I want you to hurt too. If something brings me to tears, I want to bring you to tears too.'"

I don't see any place for "restraint" in this picture.   15

Digital Technology in the Age of Terror
Floyd J. McKay

A professor of journalism at Western Washington University known for his lib-
eral views and incisive editorials, Floyd J. McKay is a frequent contributor to the
Seattle Times *editorial pages. This op-ed piece appeared in the* Seattle Times
on May 6, 2004.

1   Historians will someday rank digital technology with the printing press and television as landmark inventions affecting the news media. We are already seeing in Iraq the evidence of this revolution.

2   Every American has seen photos of prisoner abuse inside the notorious Abu Ghraib prison, and perhaps millions have logged onto Internet sites to witness the horrific beheading of Nicholas Berg.

3   There are hundreds—perhaps more—of additional digital images floating around in the hands of soldiers and others, and many will find their way onto the Internet.

4   One of my students is a Marine Corps reservist. He reports that his buddies back from Iraq have loads of digital images, including some of combat situations. Everyone has a digital camera, his friends tell him.

5   Soldiers have always taken photos to send or bring home, but the prospect of instant public circulation raises entirely new issues of credibility, sensitivity and privacy.

6   Digital images can go directly to the Internet without passing scrutiny of editors and photographers who are knowledgeable about the use of software to alter the original images.

7   On the one hand, this is a powerful weapon for transparency, not only in the case of the military but also in the case of any secretive public or private bureaucracy. A whistle-blower with a digital camera or even a camera phone has a voice amplified many times over.

8   Exposure of the Abu Ghraib abuses came only after the photos were released. Earlier warnings by the Red Cross and other human-rights groups got little attention at higher levels. The amateur photos, taken by soldiers showing off, quickly got the attention of our political leaders.

9   So did the video of Berg's murder, raising a whole new set of ethical issues. Did showing the horror play into the hands of Berg's killers, who are obviously trying to scare civilians out of Iraq? Or was it a service to reveal the naked brutality of terrorism?

10   No one has suggested the prison images or the murder video are not genuine, and they show no sign of being altered.

11   But the rush to beat the competition with even-more-sensational images tempts legitimate media into making bad judgments. The prisoner-abuse scandal has brought out at least two of these cases.

The editor of the *Daily Mirror,* the London tabloid, was forced to resign when his 12 newspaper published staged pictures of a British soldier supposedly abusing an Iraqi. The *Boston Globe,* one of this country's leading newspapers, was caught running a photo of alleged sexual abuse of an Iraqi woman; the photo was discovered to have been taken from a pornography Web site.

This illustrates a downside of this new technology. A skilled amateur can use 13 modern software to alter a digital image in ways only an expert can detect. In the hurry of the news cycle, with a cry for new and more-graphic images, more editors will be caught off guard.

Even more tantalizing, and dangerous, is the advance of camera-phone technology. 14

Lawmakers are all aflutter at the possibility that a voyeur will shoot up-skirt or 15 down-blouse pictures of women, and they will go over the Internet. That's a serious concern, but only one of several.

Camera phones have already been used on broadcast television, in the hands of 16 professionals, but technology will soon place top-quality camera phones in the hands of amateurs.

"This just in" takes on a whole new meaning in this context. Feverish for live 17 shots to give them a competitive edge, producers will be sorely tempted to use camera-phone shots from people they don't know and whose agenda is unclear.

Even if regular news channels exercise caution, that does not prevent reckless 18 use of digital images on Internet sites circulated throughout the world. If an irresponsible gossip columnist such as Matt Drudge can become a source of news for millions, a quick shot from a camera phone can affect an important issue for better or for worse, without any professional examining the image.

Some editors have taken a middle way, reserving the most-shocking visuals for 19 a separate Web page with the idea—probably mistaken—that young readers or viewers will not be exposed. But traffic to the Berg-beheading Web site shows millions want more blood and gore.

It was important that someone expose mistreatment of prisoners in our charge. 20 But Abu Ghraib and similar instances open a door that will let in much more than light, and the prospect is daunting.

News Judgment and Jihad
Mark Bowden

Mark Bowden is a journalist, author, and screenwriter and is perhaps best known for his book (and eventual screenplay) Black Hawk Down: A Story of Modern War, *which was a National Book Award finalist, a* New York Times *bestseller, and a successful movie. He contributes regularly to* The Atlantic Monthly, *a Boston-based literary, cultural, and political magazine, where this article appeared in December 2004.*

1   As I write this, three more Western workers have been kidnapped and beheaded by insurgents in Iraq. The pattern is by now sadly familiar. Foreigners are taken hostage. Videotapes are released of the captives kneeling before their masked, armed captors, and demands are made. As the deadline approaches, new videotapes are released of the captives pleading with their governments, often tearfully, to meet the kidnappers' demands. Then comes video of the grisly beheadings.

2   The first time this happened, it was horrifying and startling. Now it has become horrifying and predictable. Yet many of America's newspapers and TV networks continue to treat these criminal atrocities as the most important news of the day. Newspapers play the wrenching stories on the front page, often above the fold, and the networks feature them prominently, often as lead news items. Good taste has, thank goodness, banished the videos of the beheadings to obscure regions of the Internet, where those who must see such things can find them, but editors and producers have yet to display any equivalent exercise of judgment.

3   It is time for American journalism to voluntarily adopt more sensible and prudent standards for covering all acts of terror. When I started working as a newspaper reporter, thirty years ago, editors at least claimed to weigh the relative importance of a day's stories before deciding where to run them in the newspaper. Most sober papers, like *The New York Times,* prided themselves on resisting sensationalism. The steady erosion of this standard has long concerned traditionalists. In today's news world whatever grabs the most attention leads. In general I have no problem with this: people can usually sort out for themselves how the Scott Peterson murder trial stacks up against uranium enrichment in Iran, and nowadays they can readily get more information about either. What disturbs me is the way terrorists use sensationalism to vastly amplify their message. They know that horror and drama capture the media's attention, so they manufacture them. This is why instead of merely executing their victims, they cut off their heads on camera and broadcast the videos. When that gets old, which it will, they will come up with something even more awful.

4   Must we help them? Granted, the murder of a worker or a soldier allied with the American war effort in Iraq is newsworthy. It speaks to the danger of the place, and to the pain and difficulty of subduing the continuing insurgency. But the emphasis on the recent beheadings has largely been driven by the availability of appalling video. The news business is not a monolith (fortunately), and it has no governing body and no way of imposing or enforcing rules. But shouldn't editors and producers weigh the public interest along with news and shock value? Would some larger journalistic principle be lost if they decided to deny these killers center stage?

5   There is plenty of precedent for self-restraint in presenting the news. Most newspapers and networks voluntarily withhold the names of rape victims or juveniles charged with crimes. Newspapers routinely withhold the names of sources and restrict quotations from children. Responsible people have long advocated that television networks withhold tallies and projections on Election Day until polling places on the West Coast have closed. Over the years reputable news organizations have even withheld advance knowledge of U.S. military actions, in order to preserve the element of surprise.

6   Leading the news with acts of terrorism is often both journalistically unwarranted and—assuming that decent people everywhere would like to see such acts

cease—tragically self-defeating. In a democracy, policy is ultimately set by the people, so anybody can alter it by scaring enough of them. Theoretically, a handful of depraved and determined men with a video camera can make the strongest army in the world back down. But to prevail they need journalism's help—and until the world's media stop giving it to them, they will continue killing and videotaping.

Most deaths, at home or abroad, have little real significance beyond the immediate personal tragedy—and, sadly, there is no shortage of that in the world. The slaying of a soldier or a foreign worker in Iraq has a certain local impact: it frightens those in the vicinity and is likely to prompt improvements in security procedures. But it doesn't significantly alter the facts on the ground. The occupying army still controls the same neighborhoods and roads, and still vastly outnumbers and outguns those who oppose it. This past September, in the same week that two Americans were beheaded, more than 3,000 people were killed in Haiti by Tropical Storm Jeanne. On average more than a hundred Americans are killed every day in auto accidents. None of these deaths is any less final than a beheading—an act that makes political sense only if it can be made to influence public policy. But graphic news coverage, tearful vigils with family members, high-visibility funerals, commentary, and analysis can make any tragedy influential.

Without a doubt, the recent beheadings in Iraq were newsworthy and deserved to be widely reported. The American press should never be in the business of censoring or burying bad news, or of becoming a propagandist for the government or military. It is also true that as such sadistic acts have frightened us, they have better acquainted us with the nature of the insurgency. Sensible people recoil. One might argue that giving such stories prominence isolates violent Islamist extremism, which, like the Ebola virus, is too deadly to spread all that far.

But those beheadings were not the most important events in the world on the days they occurred. Nor were they even the most important developments in the region, where American soldiers and volunteers for the Iraqi police force continued to be targeted, and where officials were wrestling over when to hold national elections. The beheadings led the news in so many places strictly because they were so terrible and because they were on videotape, a medium that so vividly conveys the horror.

They led because the cold men behind them wanted them to. I think we should consider the consequences of continually giving those men their way.

No Picture Tells the Truth. The Best Do Better than That

Daniel Okrent

Daniel Okrent became the public editor of The New York Times *in October 2003, and as such is responsible for providing commentary on and defending the* Times' *journalistic practices, as he does in this op-ed piece from the January 9, 2005, issue of* The New York Times.

1   Two Mondays ago, the scale of the Indian Ocean catastrophe was just emerging from the incomplete earlier reports (from a *Times* article the day before: a tidal wave had "killed more than 150 people in Sri Lanka"). By the 4:30 Page 1 meeting, picture editors had examined more than 900 images of devastation to find the one that would stretch across five columns and nearly half the depth of Tuesday's front page. Into a million homes came a grieving mother crouched beside the lifeless bodies of tiny children, and perhaps more horrifying, three pairs of feet extending from beneath a white sheet in an upper corner, suggesting the presence beyond the frame of row upon awful row of the tsunami's pitiless toll.

2   Many readers and at least a few members of *The Times*'s newsroom staff considered the picture exploitative, unduly graphic, and by its size and placement, inappropriately forced upon the paper's readers. Some felt it disrespectful of both the living and the dead. A few said *The Times* would not have published it had the children been white Americans. Boaz Rabin of Weehawken, N.J., wrote, "Lead with letters the size of eggs, use any words you see fit, but don't put a nightmare on the front page."

3   I asked managing editor Jill Abramson why she chose this picture. She said in an e-mail message that after careful and difficult consideration, she decided that the photo "seemed to perfectly convey the news: the sheer enormity of the disaster, as we learned one-third of the casualties are children in a part of the world where more than 50 percent of the population is children. It is an indescribably painful photograph, but one that was in all ways commensurate to the event." When I spoke with director of photography Michele McNally, who believes the paper has the obligation "to bear witness" at moments like this, she had a question for me: "Wouldn't you want us to show pictures from Auschwitz if the gates were opened in our time?"

4   The surpassing power of pictures enables them to become the permanent markers of enormous events. The marines planting the flag at Iwo Jima, the South Vietnamese general shooting his captive at point-blank range, the young John F. Kennedy Jr. saluting his father's passing coffin: each is the universal symbol for a historical moment. You don't need to see them to see them.

5   But in every case, someone needs to choose them. Photo editors (*The Times* employs 40) and their colleagues make hundreds of choices a week. Stories may whisper with nuance and headlines declaim in summary, but pictures seize the microphone, and if they're good, they don't let go. In most cases, a story gets a single picture; major stories may get more, but usually only one on the front page itself—and that becomes the picture that stands for the event.

6   This won't make every reader happy. From last year's mail: "The picture hardly reflects the regular Turkish population." "I have never been a particular [fan] of Richard Grasso, but *The Times* should not prejudge his lawsuit by publishing photos that portray him as a monster." "I find it appalling and disgusting that you would print an Iraqi holding up the boots of one of our dead soldiers." "Why are we shown the pictures of tragically mutilated U.S. civilian contractors but not slain Iraqi children?" One reader felt that a picture of a smiling Jesse Jackson next to George W. Bush made it appear that Jackson had endorsed the president. Another believed

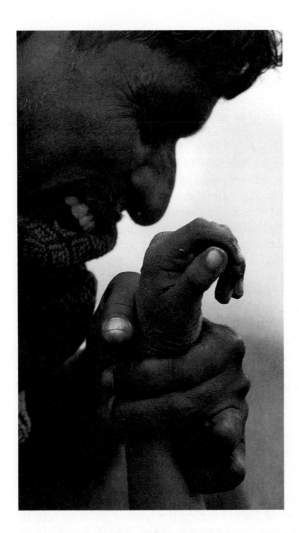

The picture above that appeared on the front page of The Times on December 28 shocked or offended many readers; ombudsmen and public editors at papers that ran the one at left reported receiving very few objections.

that a photo of a dead Palestinian child in the arms of a policeman looked staged, as if to resemble the Pietà. (I've posted a slide show of all the pictures mentioned in this column at www.nytimes.com/weekinreview.)

Richard Avedon once said: "There is no such thing as inaccuracy in a photo-graph. All photographs are accurate. None of them is the truth." In this Age of Fungible Pixels, when not every publication, political campaign, or advocacy orga-nization follows the *Times* policy prohibiting manipulation of news photographs, I'm not even sure about the accuracy part. But the untruth—or, at least, imperfect truth—of any single photograph is inescapable. Some readers object to the way a picture is cropped, arguing that evidence changing its meaning has been sliced out

7

of the frame. But meaning is determined long before that. A photographer points the camera *here,* then turns three inches to the left and snaps again: different picture, maybe a different reality. A photo editor selects from the images the photographer submits (should the subject be smiling? Frowning? Animated? Distracted?). The designer wants it large (major impact) or small (lesser impact). The editor picks it for Page 1 (important) or not (not). By the time a reader sees a picture, it has been repeatedly massaged by judgment. But it's necessarily presented as fact.

8   Last May, for an article considering whether Brazilian President Luiz Inácio Lula da Silva had a drinking problem, editors selected a seven-month-old file photo showing the president hoisting a beer at an Oktoberfest celebration. It may have been a sensible choice; drinking was the subject, and a picture of the president standing at a lectern would have been dull and disconnected. But any ambiguity in the article was steamrolled by visual evidence that may have been factual (da Silva once had a beer), but perhaps not truthful.

9   Even in the coverage of an event as photographically unpromising as a guy in a suit giving a speech, pictures convey judgment. When George J. Tenet resigned as C.I.A. director in June, a front page shot showed him looking down, biting his lip, possibly near tears; according to Bruce Mansbridge of Austin, Tex., at other moments during the broadcast of Tenet's speech, "he appeared quite upbeat." When Donald H. Rumsfeld visited Abu Ghraib in May, *The Times* showed him flanked by soldiers, striding through the grounds of the prison, as if (wrote Karen Smullen of Long Island) "Karl Rove must have said, 'What we really need now is a photo of [Rumsfeld] leading soldiers and looking earnest and determined and strong.' " Did Rumsfeld pause at any point and laugh at a joke told by a colleague, or bark at a reporter who asked him a difficult question?

10   Did any of these pictures tell the whole story, or just a sliver of it?

11   Mix a subjective process with something as idiosyncratic as taste and you're left with a volatile compound. Add human tragedy and it becomes emotionally explosive. The day *The Times* ran the picture of the dead children, many other papers led with a photograph of a grief-racked man clutching the hand of his dead son. It, too, was a powerful picture, and it's easy to see why so many used it. But it was— this is difficult to say—a portrait of generic tragedy. The devastated man could have been in the deserts of Darfur, or in a house in Mosul, or on a sidewalk in Peoria; he could have been photographed 10 years ago, or 10 years from now. His pain was universal.

12   But the picture on the front page of *The Times* could only have been photographed now, and only on the devastated shores of the Indian Ocean. My colleague David House of *The Fort Worth Star-Telegram* says. "In this instance, covering life means covering death." The babies in their silent rows were as real, and as specific, as the insane act of nature that murdered them. This picture was the story of the Indian Ocean tsunami of December 2004—not the truth, but a stand-in for the truth that will not leave the thoughts of those who saw it. *The Times* was right to publish it.

The Massless Media

William Powers

A former reporter for The Washington Post, *William Powers is currently a regular columnist for* The National Journal, *a magazine committed to nonpartisan, reliable reporting. His chosen subject matter centers on the media, politics, and culture, as does this article from the January/February 2005 edition of* The Atlantic Monthly.

One day last June, as a hot political summer was just warming up, a new poll was released. This one wasn't about which candidate voters favored for the White House. It was about which news channels they were choosing with their TV remotes. 1

"Political polarization is increasingly reflected in the public's news viewing habits," the Pew Research Center for the People and the Press reported. 2

Since 2000, the Fox News Channel's gains have been greatest among political conservatives and Republicans. More than half of regular Fox viewers describe themselves as politically conservative (52%), up from 40% four years ago. At the same time, CNN, Fox's principal rival, has a more Democrat-leaning audience than in the past. 3

It's no surprise, of course, that Fox News viewers are more conservative than CNN viewers. But it is rather surprising that even as the network's audience is growing in sheer numbers, it is also growing increasingly conservative. The months following the poll offered further evidence of the ideological sorting of cable-news viewers. During the Democratic National Convention, in July, CNN came in first in the cable ratings, prompting a Fox spokesman to say, "They were playing to their core audience." Weeks later, during the Republican National Convention, Fox News played to its core audience and scored ratings that beat not only CNN and the other cable channels but even the broadcast networks—a historical first. When election day came around and George Bush won, it wasn't hard to predict that Fox News would again be the cable ratings victor: the conservative candidate took the prize, and so, naturally, did the news channel favored by conservatives. 4

Committed partisans on the left and the right have always had ideological media outlets they could turn to (*The Nation* and *National Review,* for example), but for most Americans political affiliation was not the determining factor in choosing where they got their news. The three national networks, CBS, NBC, and ABC, offered pretty much the same product and the same establishment point of view. That product was something you shared with all Americans—not just friends, neighbors, and others like you but millions of people you would never meet, many of them very unlike you. 5

For some time now Americans have been leaving those vast media spaces where they used to come together and have instead been clustering in smaller units. The most broad-based media outlets, the networks and metropolitan newspapers, have been losing viewers and readers for years. But lately, thanks to the proliferation of 6 new cable channels and the rise of digital and wireless technology, the disaggregation of the old mass audience has taken on a furious momentum. And the tribalization is not just about political ideology. In the post-mass-media era audiences are sorting themselves by ethnicity, language, religion, profession, socioeconomic status, sexual orientation, and numerous other factors.

7   "The country has atomized into countless market segments defined not only by demography, but by increasingly nuanced and insistent product preferences," *BusinessWeek* reported last July, in a cover story called "The Vanishing Mass Market." To survive in this environment even old mass-media companies have had to learn the art of "niching down." Though national magazines have produced targeted subeditions for years, the slicing grows ever thinner. Time, Inc., the grand-daddy of print media for the masses, has launched a new women's magazine just for Wal-Mart shoppers. Radio now has satellite and Web variants that let listeners choose their taste pods with exceptional precision. The fast-growing XM Satellite Radio has not just one "urban" music channel but seven, each serving up a different subgenre twenty-four hours a day.

8   Some niches are so small they're approaching the vanishing point. There are now hundreds of thousands of bloggers, individuals who publish news, commentary, and other content on their own idiosyncratic Web sites. Some boast readerships exceeding those of prestigious print magazines, but most number their faithful in the double and triple digits. Find the one who shares your tastes and leanings, and you'll have attained the *ne plus ultra* of bespoke media: the ghostly double of yourself.

9   To sensibilities shaped by the past fifty years, the emerging media landscape seems not just chaotic but baleful. Common sense would suggest that as the vast village green of the broadcast era is chopped up into tiny plots, divisions in the culture will only multiply. If everyone tunes in to a different channel, and discourse happens only among like minds, is there any hope for social and political cohesion? Oh, for a cozy living room with one screen and Walter Cronkite signing off with his authoritative, unifying "That's the way it is."

10   It's instructive to remember, however, that the centralized, homogeneous mass-media environment of Cronkite's day was really an anomaly, an exception to the historical rule. For two centuries before the arrival of television America had a wild, cacophonous, emphatically decentralized media culture that mirrored society itself. And something like that media culture seems to be returning right now.

11   When primitive newspapers first appeared in seventeenth-century London, they were just official bulletins about the doings of the monarchy. Royally sanctioned and censored, they had no ideology other than that of the throne. The first real American newspaper, the *Boston News-Letter,* came straight from this mold. It was put out by an imperial official, the postmaster of colonial Boston, and stamped with the same seal of governmental approval worn by its British predecessors: "Published by Authority."

12   That timid approach didn't last long in America, however. In 1721 a Boston printer named James Franklin, older brother of Benjamin, founded a paper called the *New England Courant,* which brashly questioned the policies of the colony's ruling elite. The very first issue attacked Cotton Mather and other worthies for their

support of smallpox inoculations. The paper was on the wrong side of that argument, but the real news was that it made the argument at all. The *Courant* was "America's first fiercely independent newspaper, a bold, antiestablishment journal that helped to create the nation's tradition of an irreverent press," Walter Isaacson writes in his recent biography of Benjamin Franklin (whose first published writings appeared in his brother's paper).

Franklin's paper set the tone for the evolution of the media in this country. 13 Outspoken newspapers played a crucial role in the Revolutionary War, and when it was over the leaders of the young republic consciously used public policy to nurture a free press. As the Princeton sociologist Paul Starr notes in his recent book, *The Creation of the Media: Political Origins of Modern Communications*, the United States dispensed with the European tradition of licensing papers and policing their content. Congress even granted American publishers lower rates for postal delivery, a valuable subsidy that made starting up and running a paper more economical.

Such policies, combined with the freewheeling ethos that had already taken 14 root in the press, set off a wild journalistic flowering in the nineteenth century. By the 1830s newspapers were everywhere, and they spoke in a myriad of voices about all manner of issues. Alexis de Tocqueville, who was accustomed to the reined-in newspapers of France, marveled at all the variety.

The number of periodical and semi-periodical publications in the United States 15 is almost incredibly large It may readily be imagined that neither discipline nor unity of action can be established among so many combatants, and each one consequently writes under his own standard. All the political journals of the United States are, indeed, arrayed on the side of the administration or against it; but they attack and defend it in a thousand different ways.

In this the media reflected the political scene. The nineteenth century was a 16 time of intense national growth and fervent argument about what direction the country should take. Numerous political parties appeared (Democratic, Whig, Republican, Free Soil, Know-Nothing), and the views and programs they advocated all found expression in sympathetic papers. In fact, the parties themselves financially supported newspapers, as did the White House for a time. Starr notes that according to a U.S. Census estimate, by the middle of the nineteenth century 80 percent of American newspapers were avowedly partisan.

This partisanship was not typically expressed in high-minded appeals to read- 17 ers' better instincts. As Tocqueville wrote, "The characteristics of the American journalist consist in an open and coarse appeal to the passions of his readers; he abandons principles to assail the characters of individuals, to track them into private life and disclose all their weaknesses and vices." When Martin Chuzzlewit, the central character of the Dickens novel by the same name, arrives in the New York City of the early 1840s, he is greeted by newsboys hawking papers with names like the *New York Stabber* and the *New York Keyhole Reporter.* "Here's the *New York Sewer!*," one newsie shouts. "Here's the *Sewer*'s exposure of the Wall Street Gang, and the *Sewer*'s exposure of the Washington Gang, and the *Sewer*'s exclusive account of a flagrant act of dishonesty committed by the Secretary of State when he was eight years old."

18   Yet even though the media of this period were profuse, partisan, and scandalously downmarket, they were at the same time a powerful amalgamator that encouraged participatory democracy and forged a sense of national identity. Michael Schudson, a professor of communication and sociology at the University of California at San Diego and the author of *The Sociology of News* (2003), says that the rampant partisanship displayed by newspapers "encouraged people to be attentive to their common enterprise of electing representatives or presidents." Commenting that "politics was the best entertainment in town in the middle of the 19th century," Schudson compares its effect to that of sports today. "Professional baseball is an integrative mechanism even though it works by arousing very partisan loyalties," he says. In other words, newspapers helped pull the country together not by playing down differences and pretending everyone agreed but by celebrating and exploiting the fact that people didn't. It's the oldest American paradox: nothing unifies like individualism.

19   We tend to think of the rise of the modern mass media as primarily a function of technology: the advent of television, for example, enabled broadcasters to reach tens of millions of Americans, but the cost of entry was high enough to sharply limit the number of networks. However, technology was only one of several factors that determined the character of the media establishment that arose in the United States after World War II. Beginning in the nineteenth century the idea of objectivity began to cross over from science into business and popular culture. As the historian Scott Sandage notes in his new book, *Born Losers: A History of Failure in America,* a whole new industry rose up in nineteenth-century New York when a handful of creative entrepreneurs discovered they could gather "objective" information about businesses and people (the precursor of modern-day credit ratings) and sell it to other businesses for a profit. Soon journalists, including the muckrakers of the Progressive Era, were embracing a similar notion of objective, irrefutable fact. When the Washington journalist Walter Lippmann wrote in the 1920s that "good reporting requires the exercise of the highest of scientific virtues," and called for the founding of journalistic research institutes, he was, as Starr notes, codifying a standard of disinterested inquiry that would influence generations of journalists to come.

20   At the same time, a federal government that had once used policy to encourage the growth of a free press now faced a very different challenge. Unlike newspapers, the public airwaves were a finite resource, and someone had to decide how to dole it out. The solution was a federal regulatory structure that sought to ensure fairness but could never offer the ease of access or the expressive freedom of the press. (Not that the networks necessarily wanted the latter; in order to pull in the large audiences that ad buyers demanded, all strove for a safe neutrality that offended no one.) For these reasons, although the broadcast media reached more people, the range of content they offered was actually more constricted than that of the print media that preceded them.

21   Finally, the political culture of the 1940s and 1950s discouraged extremism. The two major political parties of that period certainly had their differences, but they shared a basic set of beliefs about the country's priorities. Politics hewed to the center, and the media both reflected and reinforced this tendency. The centrist,

"objective" networks and large newspapers didn't just cover the political establishment; they were an essential part of it. The anchormen who appeared on television and the columnists of the great papers were effectively spokesmen for the ruling postwar elite. (On occasion literally so: Lippmann, the great proponent of objectivity, worked with his fellow reporter James Reston on a famous speech by Senator Arthur Vandenberg; both journalists then turned around to write about the speech for their respective papers.)

That establishment consensus exploded in the 1960s and 1970s, with Vietnam   22
and Watergate, but the mass media hung on for a few decades, a vestigial reminder of what had been. The Reagan era and the end of the Cold War dealt the old politico-media structure the final blows. In the 1990s partisan politics really took hold in Washington, and again the news media followed suit. The demise of the postwar consensus made the mass media's centrism obsolete. Long-simmering conservative resentment of the mainstream media fueled the rise of Rush Limbaugh and Fox News. Their success, in turn, has lately inspired efforts on the left to create avowedly liberal radio and cable outlets.

Socially, too, our fragmented media are to this era what James Franklin's news-   23
paper was to the 1720s and the CBS evening news was to the 1950s. The cultural sameness and conformity that prevailed after World War II—the era of Father Knows Best and Betty Crocker—have been replaced by a popular pursuit of difference and self-expression. In explaining why McDonald's has shifted a significant portion of its advertising into niches, an executive of the company told *BusinessWeek,* "From the consumer point of view, we've had a change from 'I want to be normal' to 'I want to be special.' " In a mass-media world it's hard to be special. But in the land of niches it's easy. What is blogging if not a celebration of the self?

The "Trust us, we know better" ethos that undergirded the broadcast era today   24
seems increasingly antique. If red and blue America agree on anything, it's that they don't believe the media. To traditionalists worried about the future of news, this attitude reflects a corrosive cynicism. But in another way it's much like the skepticism that animates great journalism. As the media have become more transparent, and suffered their own scandals, the public has learned to think about the news the same way a good journalist would—that is, to doubt everything it's told.

Although network ratings continue to plummet, there's still evidence else-   25
where of an enduring demand for the sort of connectedness that only broad-based media can offer. For the six months that ended last September 30 many of America's largest newspapers saw the now customary declines in circulation. But among those that saw increases were the only three with a national subscriber base: *The New York Times, The Wall Street Journal,* and *USA Today.* The presidential debates last year drew impressive audiences to the broadcast networks, suggesting that although Americans no longer go to mass outlets out of habit, they will go by choice when there's good reason. In one of those debates Senator John Kerry cracked a Tony Soprano joke, and it was safe to assume that most viewers got the allusion. When we rue the passing of mass togetherness, we often forget that the strongest connective tissue in modern culture is entertainment—a mass medium if ever there was one.

26 Moreover, for all the pointed criticism and dismissive eye-rolling that niche and mass outlets direct each other's way, the two are becoming more and more symbiotic. Where would the Drudge Report and the blogging horde be without *The New York Times*, CBS News, and *The Washington Post*? Were it not for the firsthand reporting offered by those media dinosaurs, the Internet crowd would have nothing to talk about. Conversely, where would the Web versions of mass outlets be without the traffic that is directed their way by the smaller players? If there's a new media establishment taking form, it's shaped like a pyramid, with a handful of mass outlets at the top and innumerable niches supporting them from below, barking upward.

27 Whenever critics of the new media worry about the public's clustering in niches, there's an unspoken assumption that viewers watch only one outlet, as was common thirty years ago—that is, that there are Fox people and CNN people, and never the twain shall meet. But the same Pew poll that showed the increasingly ideological grouping of cable audiences revealed that most Americans watch the news with remote at the ready, poised to dart away at any moment. Pew also detected an enormous affinity for "inadvertent" news consumption: a large majority of Internet users from almost all demographic groups say that while online they encounter news unexpectedly, when they aren't even looking for it. "Fully 73% of Internet users come across the news this way," Pew reported, "up from 65% two years ago, and 55% as recently as 1999." Thus it appears that one of the great joys of newspaper reading—serendipitous discovery—lives on.

28 And although much changes in the media over time, there are some eternal truths. Most outlets crave two things, money and impact, and the easiest path to both is the old-fashioned one: grow your audience. Ambitious niches will always seek to become larger, and in so doing to attract a more diverse audience. It's only a matter of time before the first mass blog is identified, celebrated, and showered with minivan ads.

29 Finally, there's no substantive evidence yet that the rise of the niches is bad for democracy. The fractious, disunited, politically partisan media of the nineteenth century heightened public awareness of politics, and taught the denizens of a new democracy how to be citizens. Fast forward to the present. The United States just held an election that was covered by noisy, divisive, often thoroughly disreputable post-broadcast-era media. And 120 million people, 60 percent of eligible voters, showed up to cast their ballots—a higher percentage than have voted in any election since 1968. Maybe we're on to something.

Why Media Ownership Matters: The More You Watch, the Less You Know

Amy Goodman and David Goodman

Amy Goodman is the News Director and Morning Show host of Democracy Now, *a left-wing New York City–based radio show. Her brother, David Goodman, is a journalist for* Mother Jones, *a liberal news commentary magazine. This article appeared in the* Seattle Times *on April 3, 2005.*

George Bush must have been delighted to learn from a recent Washington Post-ABC News poll that 56 percent of Americans still think Iraq had weapons of mass destruction before the start of the war, while six in 10 said they believe Iraq provided direct support to the al-Qaida terrorist network—notions that have long since been thoroughly debunked by everyone from the U.S. Senate Intelligence Committee to both of Bush's handpicked weapons inspectors, Charles Duelfer and David Kay.

Americans believe these lies not because they are stupid, but because they are good media consumers. Our media have become an echo chamber for those in power. Rather than challenge the fraudulent claims of the Bush administration, we've had a media acting as a conveyor belt for the government's lies.

As the Pentagon has learned, deploying the American media is more powerful than any bomb. The explosive effect is amplified as a few pro-war, pro-government media moguls consolidate their grip over the majority of news outlets. Media monopoly and militarism go hand in hand.

When it comes to issues of war and peace, the results of having a compliant media are as deadly to our democracy as they are to our soldiers. Why do the corporate media cheerlead for war? One answer lies in the corporations themselves—the ones that own the major news outlets.

At the time of the first Persian Gulf War, CBS was owned by Westinghouse and NBC by General Electric. Two of the major nuclear weapons manufacturers owned two of the major networks. Westinghouse and GE made most of the parts for many of the weapons in the Persian Gulf War. It was no surprise, then, that much of the coverage on those networks looked like a military hardware show.

We see reporters in the cockpits of war planes, interviewing pilots about how it feels to be at the controls. We almost never see journalists at the target end, asking people huddled in their homes what it feels like not to know what the next moment will bring.

The media have a responsibility to show the true face of war. It is bloody. It is brutal. Real people die. Women and children are killed. Families are wiped out; villages are razed. If the media would show for one week the same unsanitized images of war that the rest of the world sees, people in the U.S. would say no, that war is not an answer to conflict in the 21st century.

But we don't see the real images of war. We don't need government censors, because we have corporations sanitizing the news. A study released last month by American University's School of Communications revealed that media outlets acknowledged they self-censored their reporting on the Iraq invasion out of concerns about public reaction to graphic images and content.

The media organizations in charge of vetting our images of war have become fewer and bigger—and the news more uniform and gung ho. Six huge corporations now control the major U.S. media: Rupert Murdoch's News Corporation (FOX, HarperCollins, New York Post, Weekly Standard, TV Guide, DirecTV and 35 TV stations), General Electric (NBC, CNBC, MSNBC, Telemundo, Bravo, Universal Pictures and 28 TV stations), Time Warner (AOL, CNN, Warner Bros., *Time* and its 130-plus magazines), Disney (ABC, Disney Channel, ESPN, 10 TV and 72 radio stations), Viacom (CBS, MTV, Nickelodeon, Paramount Pictures, Simon & Schuster and 183 U.S. radio stations), and Bertelsmann (Random House and its more than 120 imprints worldwide, and Gruner + Jahr and its more than 110 magazines in 10 countries).

10   As Phil Donahue, the former host of MSNBC's highest-rated show who was fired by the network in February 2003 for bringing on anti-war voices, told "Democracy Now!," "We have more [TV] outlets now, but most of them sell the Bowflex machine. The rest of them are Jesus and jewelry. There really isn't diversity in the media anymore. Dissent? Forget about it."

11   The lack of diversity in ownership helps explain the lack of diversity in the news. When George W. Bush first came to power, the media watchers Fairness and Accuracy in Reporting (FAIR) looked at who appeared on the evening news on ABC, CBS and NBC. Ninety-two percent of all U.S. sources interviewed were white, 85 percent were male, and where party affiliation was identifiable, 75 percent were Republican.

12   In the run-up to the invasion of Iraq, there was even less diversity of opinion on the airwaves. During the critical two weeks before and after Colin Powell's speech to the United Nations where he made his case for war, FAIR found that just three out of 393 sources—fewer than 1 percent—were affiliated with anti-war activism.

13   Three out of almost 400 interviews. And that was on the "respectable" evening news shows of CBS, NBC, ABC and PBS.

14   These are not media that are serving a democratic society, where a diversity of views is vital to shaping informed opinions. This is a well-oiled propaganda machine that is repackaging government spin and passing it off as journalism.

15   For the media moguls, even this parody of political "diversity" is too much. So as Gen. Colin Powell led the war on Iraq, his son, Michael Powell, chairman of the Federal Communications Commission (FCC), led the war on diversity of voices at home.

16   In the spring of 2003, Michael Powell tried to hand over the airwaves and newspapers to fewer and fewer tycoons by further loosening restrictions on how many media outlets a single company could own. Powell tried to scrap 30-year-old rules that limited the reach of any television network to no more than 35 percent of the national population, and limits on cross-ownership that, for example, prevented newspapers from buying television or radio stations in the same city. The new rules would have allowed a broadcast network to buy up stations that together reached 45 percent of the national population.

17   The attack on the existing media-ownership rules came from predictable corners: Both Viacom, which owns CBS, and Rupert Murdoch's conservative FOX News Channel were already in violation, and would be forced to sell off stations to come into compliance with the 35-percent limit. The rule change would enable Murdoch to control the airwaves of entire cities. That would be fine with Bush and the Powells, since Murdoch is one of their biggest boosters.

Murdoch declared in February 2003 that George W. Bush "will either go down   18
in history as a very great president or he'll crash and burn. I'm optimistic it will be
the former by a ratio of 2 to 1." Murdoch leaves nothing to chance: His FOX News
Channel is doing all it can to help.

It looked like Powell, backed by the Bush White House and with Republican   19
control of Congress, would have no trouble ramming through these historic rule
changes. The broadcast industry left nothing to chance: Between 1998 and 2004,
broadcasters spent a boggling $249 million lobbying the federal government, in-
cluding spending $27 million on federal candidates and lawmakers.

This would normally be called bribery. At the FCC, it's just business as usual.   20

You would think that FCC deregulation, affecting millions of Americans, would   21
get major play in the media. But the national networks knew that if people found
out about how one media mogul could own nearly everything you watch, hear and
read in a city, there would be revolt. The solution for them was simple: They just
didn't cover the issue for a year. The only thing the networks did was to join together—and you thought they were competitors?—in a brief filed with the FCC to
call for media deregulation.

And then, something remarkable happened: Media activists—an unlikely coali-   22
tion of liberals and conservatives—mounted a national campaign to defeat Powell
and stop the corporate sell-off. The FCC received 2 million letters and e-mails, most
of them opposing the sell-off. The Prometheus Radio Project, a grass-roots media
activism group, sued to stop the sale of our airwaves, and won in federal court last
June. These are hopeful signals that the days of backroom deals by media titans are
numbered.

Powell announced his resignation as chairman of the FCC in January. Arguably   23
the worst FCC chairman in history, Powell led with singular zeal the effort to auc-
tion off the public airwaves to the highest corporate bidder. In so doing, he did us all
a favor: For a brief moment, he pulled back the covers on the incestuous world of
media ownership to expose the corruption and rot for all to see.

Kevin Martin, Bush's newly appointed FCC chairman, will, according to an FCC   24
insider, be even worse than Powell. Leading conservative and right-wing religious
groups have been quietly lobbying the White House for Martin to chair the FCC.
Martin voted with Powell on key regulations favoring media consolidation, and in
addition has been a self-appointed indecency czar. The indecency furor conveniently
grabs headlines and pushes for the regulation of content, while Martin and the media moguls plan sweetheart deregulation deals to achieve piecemeal what they
couldn't push through all at once. This is the true indecency afflicting media today.

The major media conglomerates are among the most powerful on the planet.   25
The onrush of digital convergence and broadband access in the workplaces and
homes of America will radically change the way we work, play and communicate.
Fiber-to-the-premise (FTTP) from the regional Bells, Voice over IP (VoIP) telephony,
bundled services from cable companies, and increased capacity in satellite and
wireless technologies will transform the platforms on which we communicate.

Who owns these platforms, what is delivered over them and, fundamentally, in   26
whose interest they work are critical issues before us now. Given the wealth of the

media companies and their shrewd donations into our political process, the advocates for the public interest are in far too short a supply.

27   A blow against media ownership consolidation—now or in the future—will have far-reaching implications, as critical information gains exposure to a caring, active public. Instead of fake reality TV, maybe the media will start to cover the reality of people struggling to get by and of the victories that happen every day in our communities, and in strife-torn regions around the globe.

28   When people get information, they are empowered. We have to ensure that the airwaves are open for more of that. Our motto at "Democracy Now!" is to break the sound barrier. We call ourselves the exception to the rulers. We believe all media should be.

What to Do When News Grows Old Before Its Time

Jack Rosenthal

Jack Rosenthal has worked for The New York Times *since 1969, and won the Pulitzer Prize for editorial writing in 1982. A former employee of the State Department during the mid-1960s, he built his career around urban affairs and politics. He currently serves as the president of the New York Times Company Foundation. This commentary appeared in the* Times *on August 8, 2004.*

1   Dan Okrent, an outsider to *The Times,* has brought energetic reporting and insight to readers' concerns about how the paper covers events in the news. My perspective as an insider draws me to a broader topic: news, period.

2   Our generation is witnessing a relentless rise in the number of news outlets, the frequency of news reports and the media's clamor for every scrap of new information, consequential or not. In this all-news all-the-time environment, society is immersed first in a flood of facts and then in a rush of opinion. Inescapably, the public's interest is soon saturated. Too soon.

3   Not many years ago, news came but twice a day. There were two news cycles, one for A.M.'s, morning papers delivered to your door, and one for P.M.'s, for afternoon papers on the newsstands and the evening TV news. Then, in 1961, a radio pioneer named Gordon McLendon, aiming for the Los Angeles market, turned XETRA in Tijuana into the first all-news station. In 1965, WINS in New York adopted and enlarged the format, becoming one of the most listened-to stations in America.

4   In 1980, Ted Turner brought America's eyes into the picture with CNN, all-news cable television. TV kept evolving with the arrival of Fox as a fourth network, more cable networks and satellites that enabled local stations to report from distant

places. In the mid-70s, there were 617 members of the Senate's TV and radio press gallery. Today, there are 3,031.

So much for the quaint concept of two news cycles. Now, in the electronic era, there's just one, instant and constant. Continuous News is what *The Times* calls the department that serves *The Times* on the Web. And the cable networks, not content with reporting just one subject at a time, send headlines crawling over and over across the bottom of the screen. The meatloaf, once cut in half each day for A.M.'s and P.M.'s, is now sliced so thin that mere morsels are flaunted as Exclusive Reports! 5

"The wires" were for decades a staple of every newsroom—the teletype machines that clacked out A.P. and U.P.I. reports from around the world. Now, clack has yielded to click. Every computer user can call up unlimited news—real and rumored—without any media go-between. When the 9/11 commission posted its report online last month, the Web site quickly experienced 8 million hits and 2.7 million downloads of some or all of the 567-page report. 6

The combination of all these new sources of news has had a pronounced, interlocking effect on newsmakers, the media and the public. 7

Consider, for instance, the phenomenon of news leaks. They used to be surreptitious. In 1967, when *The Washington Post* reported that he was about to nominate Fred M. Vinson Jr. to a federal appeals court, President Johnson angrily canceled the nomination. Today, leaking is officially sanctioned. Indeed, major stories are hardly taken seriously unless they are leaked days in advance. 8

Leaks can be trial balloons. Newsmakers can play on the hunger of the media herd by doling out bits of a story, turning one into four or five days of headlines. With so many reporters clamoring for news, sources can orchestrate the release of information ever more to their advantage. 9

Consider also the acceleration of news reporting. In the 1992 campaign, the Clinton forces devised what has become a staple of modern political practice, the War Room, where every charge or claim of the opposition is heard and answered immediately. Now, the Bush campaign includes a 24-hour operation with a core staff of eight, plus interns, that starts work each day at 5 a.m. 10

The ever increasing need for speed creates other secondary effects. As recently as the 1992 conventions, the nominees would make their big speeches on Wednesday and Thursday, and the *Times* editorial page would respond with quick comments the next morning. But the editors would gradually develop more considered views for the prized platform of the week, the lead editorial on Sunday. Today, any such delay is inconceivable. By Sunday, the subject is tattered and torn. 11

It is even necessary on occasion to editorialize *ahead* of the news. Last month, so much was already known about the 9/11 commission report that *The Times* editorialized about it hours before it was released. Had the editors waited even a day, their views would have been swamped by the torrent of commentary in other media. 12

Much more news and much faster news: it has created a kind of widespread attention deficit disorder. When news events cycled in and out of the spotlight more slowly, they stayed in the public mind longer. People could pay attention until issues of moment were resolved. Now, we are surrounded by news—on the TV at the 13 gym, on the AOL home page, on the car radio on the way to work. To pass through Times Square is to be enveloped by no fewer than four electronic zippers flashing headlines day and night.

14   With such saturation coverage, news gets used up faster, decaying rapidly into what Russell Baker calls "the olds." Public curiosity, let alone the public interest, is exhausted, and the mass media are quick to look for some new sensation even if that means leaving important issues unresolved. News grows old before its time.

15   Consider anthrax. Three years ago, white powder sent in the mail caused deaths, injuries and the closing of government buildings, igniting widespread fear. Apart from sporadic suspicions, what has happened since? Do even the most attentive readers know?

16   Last spring, disclosures of prisoner abuse from Abu Ghraib shocked consciences around the world. Apart from another general's report blaming a few enlisted personnel, like Pfc. Lynndie England, what has happened?

17   Last winter, *The Times* reported that Thomas Scully, then the head of Medicare, threatened to fire the program's chief actuary if he gave Congress an accurate estimate of the cost of the drug bill about to be enacted—at least $100 billion more than the White House had claimed. The bill passed narrowly. An internal investigation later confirmed Scully's threat. So? Has the administration offered a reasonable explanation or apology? What have members of Congress done to ensure that they get honest answers in the future?

18   Saturation coverage now seems inevitably to exhaust the public and leave the media eager to move on. But that means the spotlight goes dark even when the wrongs endure. That, in turn, suggests that this all-news environment is creating a new responsibility for *The Times* and other serious media: systematically to look back, recall and remind.

19   *The Times* does publish a weekly column called Following Up, but it treats its topics as archival curiosities. In a time of saturation plus attention deficit, is it not possible to find a serious, formal way to return the spotlight to unfinished business?

20   The idea of a systematic follow-up raises obvious objections. Editors will say, we do follow up on individual stories from time to time. Or, don't blame us if you missed the sequel. Or, we can't be expected to revisit a story every day. A substantial news follow-up would risk sounding relentlessly sanctimonious. How often is it possible to report that the New York Legislature has failed to do anything substantive without becoming an impossible nag? The selection of which issues to revive could be uncomfortably subjective.

21   One answer might be to perform the follow-up function on *The Times*'s editorial or Op-Ed pages. Another would be to ask readers what *they* want to know more about.

22   In this time of masses of mass media, the public is engulfed by reporting, if not of the serious then surely of the sensational. The examples multiply: O.J., JonBenet, Elián, Chandra, Michael, Kobe, Laci. It's not likely that the electronic media can be relied on to look back and flag unfinished public business. That responsibility falls to serious news institutions, notably this one. In response to the new news technology, *The Times* has created high-quality Web and cable TV operations. A systematic response to the new news cosmology is equally in order.

Too Narrow a Focus

Amotz Asa-El

Current executive director of the Jerusalem Post, *Israeli-born Amotz Asa-El is a former correspondent for the* San Francisco Chronicle. *His editorials often cover Israeli and Middle Eastern Affairs and here parts of Africa. This op-ed piece appeared in the* Seattle Post-Intelligencer *on August 8, 2004.*

With United Nations Secretary-General Kofi Annan personally visiting the   1
Darfur region where thousands of Sudanese have been slaughtered, raped and displaced by their own countrymen, and with world powers threatening to sanction Khartoum for its alleged responsibility for that catastrophe, it is tempting to conclude that while one part of the world is sick, the world beyond it is not.

If only it were so.   2

The disaster in Sudan did not begin this year and is not confined to the Darfur   3
region, which is now in the headlines. The recent deaths of 30,000 Sudanese are but a subchapter in a conflict that has been raging for more than two decades and has taken the lives of more than 1.2 million people.

The tragedy in Sudan brings together all that is ill about post-colonial Africa on   4
the one hand and the dictatorial Middle East on the other.

Here too, as they did in Iraq and Lebanon, European map drawers maneuvered   5
hostile populations into political cohabitations that bred endless civil wars, in this case between Arab Muslims in the north and black Christians in the south.

In 1983, the northerners imposed Islamic law on the entire country, including   6
millions of Christians. Though that decree has since been tempered, it touched off the massive bloodshed whose aftermath the world is now witnessing. Meanwhile, as the Sudanese government fought its people, much of the country ended up in the throes of severe famine.

While all this raises many harsh questions—where, for instance, were the   7
Vatican, the United Nations, the Arab League and the Organization of African Unity—one seems even more perplexing: Where was the media?

Where was everybody while a few hours' flight south of Rome, the largest   8
African country's air force was bombarding civilian populations in an ongoing campaign that resulted in the biggest mass murder anywhere since the Khmer Rouge genocide in Cambodia?

The Sudanese War, after all, involved many more people than the mere 10 mil-   9
lion involved in the massively covered, current round in the Israeli-Arab conflict, whose combined death toll from both sides totals hardly 4,000 people.

Couldn't some of the media armadas that converged on Jerusalem throughout   10
those years have been directed, at least occasionally or even just momentarily, to Sudan?

In Israel, there are "normally" nearly a thousand foreign journalists, who are   11
reinforced by several hundred more whenever the situation heats up. Couldn't at

least some of this personnel, and just a fraction of the numerous inches and endless airtime that were dedicated throughout those years to the Arab-Israeli conflict, been allocated to the Sudanese catastrophe?

12   Apparently not.

13   First of all, it is more pleasant to be stationed in Jerusalem or Tel Aviv than in Khartoum, even before the imposition there of Shari'a law, not to mention hell holes such as Darfur.

14   Secondly, Africa—even when it comes to slave trade, murderous racism and unabashed fundamentalism including the basest persecution of Christians—is, for the Western media, not a story.

15   During the Cold War, Africa would still get, occasionally, its moment in the sun, as part of the media's score keeping while the superpowers were locking horns across the Third World. Since 1989 even that quasi-relevance has disappeared. For the American media, the biggest story of the '90s was not the butchery of thousands of Sudanese but the sexual misdemeanors of the leader of the free world.

16   Yet Sudan is relevant.

17   Sudan is relevant morally, because it has been the stage of wholesale murder of innocents; Sudan is relevant politically, because in the post-9/11 world any attempt to impose Shari'a law, anywhere, can no longer be seen as anecdotal; and Sudan is relevant journalistically, because just like the West Bank, it is the stage of a major clash between antagonistic tribes and competing faiths.

18   As far as the media are concerned, the Middle East is Israel and Palestine.

19   Yet in reality the Middle East is well more than a quarter-of-a-billion Arabs who populate a vast landmass between the Atlantic and Indian oceans.

20   These ignored masses are so politically oppressed and so frequently destitute that their plight ultimately generates religious wars in Africa, festering slums in Europe and terror attacks in America. Yet their stories remain untold.

21   Dissidents rotting in Arab jails do not win even a tenth of the attention accorded to freedom fighters like Andrei Sakharov or Alexander Solzhenitsyn during the Cold War. Evils such as the oppression of the Arab woman—by far the world's least emancipated and employed female—remain largely ignored, as are Arab leaders' squandering of their people's petrodollars or the jailing of gays by Egypt.

22   Why?

23   Because when it comes to budgeting foreign coverage, news organizations see Israel as indispensable, and its neighbors as a curiosity at best, a waste of resources at worst. That, coupled with its accessibility, freedom and comfort, is why tiny Israel is host to more than twice as many Western correspondents than the entire Arab world.

24   That disproportionate scrutiny is also why Israel is fingered even when killing the guilty, while its neighbors get away even with killing the innocent. And that is also why whenever asked whether there is anything wrong with how the media covers the Jewish state I say there isn't; what's wrong is how the Arab states are not covered.

For Class Discussion

1. Daniel Okrent writes that photographic images often function as powerful "permanent markers of enormous events." Think of images from the last three years that have profoundly influenced people's view of an event or issue. How did these images of war, disasters, terrorist attacks, scientific discoveries, or famous people achieve this importance? What did they contribute to the *kairos* of the arguments that they accompanied?

2. A number of the readings in this chapter focus on the issue of sensationalizing events. What values and assumptions underlie the arguments of Schanberg, McKay, Bowden, and Okrent? What views do they hold of "candid press coverage," "gratuitously violent" images, photography and truth, and digital altering of images?

3. What are the similarities and differences between the following writers' main claims about the way that changes in news media are affecting democracy and global citizenship: Schanberg, Powers, the Goodmans, Rosenthal, and Asa-El?

4. Most of the readings in this unit have been written by experienced journalists. How do these writers use appeals to *ethos*? Which writers make the most effective rhetorical use of their professional authority, knowledge, and experience?

5. Choose one of the arguments for closer analysis, applying the List 2 Guide questions on pages 454–455.

OPTIONAL WRITING ASSIGNMENT

Option A

Write an op-ed piece for your local, regional, or university newspaper in which you argue for a position on the censorship of images of war. Consider what information should be withheld from the public, what reasoning the Bush administration, journalists, and citizens have given for censoring war photos, and what reasoning some of the writers in this unit have given for using graphic images. You might want to research the influence of photos in other wars such as World War II and the Vietnam War.

Option B

A number of the readings in this unit discuss how technology and its use in reporting news have outstripped regulations and ethics. Based on these articles in this chapter, write a policy proposal in which you put forth what you think are the most ethical and rational principles for governing the media's use of photos in a democratic society. Consider the problems of the potential for altering images, the blurred lines between amateur and professional journalists/photographers, and inevitable selectivity. Write your proposal from a citizen's perspective for the journalists of your favorite newspaper and television news stations.

GENDER AND TECHNOLOGY IN ADVERTISING

In 1979, Erving Goffman, an influential sociologist, theoretician, and author of the book *Gender Advertisements*, argued that advertisements often depict women in frivolous, childlike, sexual, or silly poses that would be considered unacceptable and unbecoming for men. The effect of these depictions is to make women decorative and irrelevant, removed from serious power and serious attention. Even in advertisements that seem to depict women in a positive light, Goffman found that subtle details—such as body position, gesture, and setting—undermined women's power and independence and reinforced women's subordination. Although styles of advertising have changed, some cultural critics continue to find images of women in advertising problematic.

In this unit, we direct your attention to one of the biggest new areas of consumer goods—business technology and computers. How do advertisers market products related to office equipment, computers, information technology, and communication? Is there a difference between the way men and women are portrayed in the advertisements for these products? Are women depicted positively as serious professionals and competent users, or do these ads subtly undermine women's power and importance, as Goffman observed in earlier advertising? To help you with your examination of the persuasiveness of these ads, you may want to refer to the principles for using type, layout, and color and the questions for analyzing a photograph or drawing discussed in Chapter 9, "Conducting Visual Arguments."

This Is Automatic Xerography

Haloid Xerox

This ad for Haloid Xerox proclaims the speed, capabilities, and low cost of an early generation of copy machines. What features of the images and the composition of this ad suggest the business world of the 1950s?

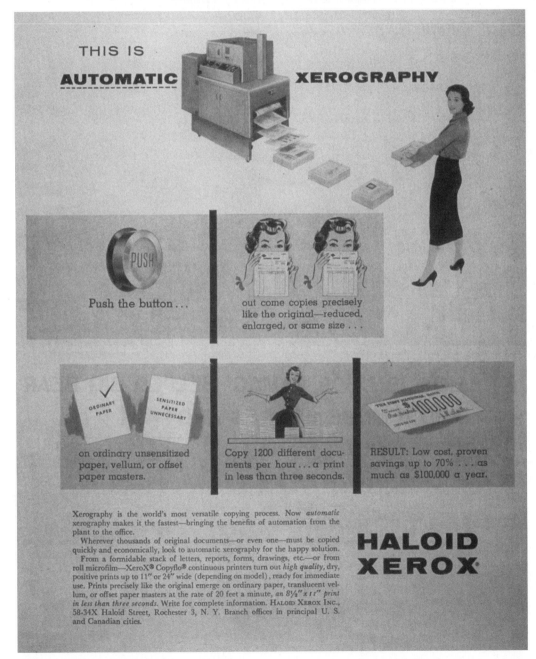

Like Magellan, Grady Has Pioneered a Global Network and Maria Hates Computers

FedEx Express

Part of a larger campaign that is currently popular and that has been appearing in magazines like Newsweek, *the next two ads strike a personal note while they seek to inspire complete confidence in the product. What are the narrative strategies they use to appeal to a range of people?*

Even globetrotting pioneers need an inside scoop. Psssst. Check out **FedEx Global Trade Manager,**[SM] powerful web-based tools that help you ship confidently all over the planet. Get important trade and embargo updates. Estimate duties and taxes. Download important customs forms and documents. Suddenly, the whole world seems to want you. Just try not to get a big head. Seeking safe passage around the world? **Don't worry. There's a FedEx for that.**[SM]

fedex.com

So you're not exactly a digital mastermind, right? Not a problem. With **fedex.com**, your computer skills need hardly apply. Track packages. Prepare shipping labels and access critical shipping info. Store up to 1000 addresses and check account specific rate quotes. All with the greatest of ease. See? That wasn't so hard. Looking to simplify your shipping? **Don't worry. There's a FedEx for that.**[SM]

fedex.com

Try a MIT's Magazine of Innovation
Technology Review *Digital Subscription*
Technology Review

This ad for a digital subscription to Technology Review *features a man dressed casually and working on his laptop, most likely reading his digital subscription. How does this ad convey self-confidence and competence with technology?*

Spacious Corner Office, Redefined
Siemens Corporation

This ad for Siemens, a company producing state-of-the-art business communication systems, appeared in Fortune *magazine on October 28, 2002 (original publication date of ad, 2001). Like many effective ads featuring the latest technology for business, this one plays with the idea of redefining work spaces. What is the dominant impression the image of the woman in this ad projects?*

For Class Discussion

1. Working individually or in groups, compare the following aspects of each of the ads: descriptions of the product; settings (room or scene) and objects in this scene; position, clothing, and appearance of the model in the ad; and the explicit or implicit relationship between the model and his/her use of the product. For help in examining the details of each ad, you might refer to the principles of visual design and points for analyzing images in Chapter 9, pages 162–176.

2. Commercial ads, like full-text arguments, make appeals to *logos, ethos,* and *pathos.* Choose several of the ads in this unit and compare the verbal-visual textual strategies they use to convey their argument, portray the company or product's reliability and quality, and tap the emotions and imagination of readers/viewers. (The core of the argument in each case will be some variant of "X product is excellent or superior and you should buy it because . . .). What role particularly does *pathos* play in each ad?

3. Rank these ads according to the degree of technological competence and business status/professionalism that they ascribe to the person featured in the ad. Which person in which ad comes across as most knowledgeable about his/her work and most competent with the technological equipment? Which seems least? Do any of these ads exemplify Goffman's theory that ads often subtly undermine women's status and power?

4. Scholars and organizations like the American Association of University Women Educational Foundation claim to have discovered a gender gap regarding technology—that is, that boys and men are assumed to be, and often are, more comfortable with digital technologies than girls and women and that the percentage of men holding high-tech jobs far exceeds that of women. Do you think the ads in this unit validate these claims? Additionally, do you think these ads help perpetuate the technology gap? On your own, find several ads for business equipment and computer technology in business and news commentary magazines, and determine whether they reinforce these claims or counter them.

OPTIONAL WRITING ASSIGNMENT   The AAUW's Commission on Technology, Gender, and Teacher Education concluded in its study *Tech-Savvy: Educating Girls in the New Computer Age* (2000) (see www.aauw.org) that girls' lack of interest in computer technology may derive in part from computer games and software that either ignore girls' interests (by featuring violent, "high-kill" elements) or fall into the category of "pink software" (by featuring games exclusively and stereotypically for girls). Research on your own the kinds of computer software or computer games marketed specifically for girls. (You might use the keywords "girls," "technology," and "computer games" with your favorite search engine to find sites like

Mattel, Girl Tech, and Her Interactive.) What gender images do the games produced by these companies convey? To what extent do these games develop critical thinking, technical skills, and interest in computer technology? To what extent do they encourage action and independence versus superficiality and passivity? After analyzing a site or a specific computer game, write an evaluation argument intended for a popular family magazine in which you argue that this site or specific game is or is not helpful in encouraging girls' competence and engagement with technology.

INTERNET CONTROVERSIES: BLOGS, HATE SITES, AND SPAM

The Internet has brought tremendous benefits, including vast resources for information and communication. Through blogs—short for "Web log" or online journals, many posted daily—individuals around the world can offer personal and political commentary, and in fact, since 1999, the "blogosphere" has burgeoned from a meager number of blogs to about ten million blogs. Because they defy all spatial boundaries, blogs offer a huge uncensored arena for individual expression. This growth in popularity has drawn journalists, policymakers, analysts, and scholars to begin to study the potential blogs have for changing the media and politics.

However, in addition to opportunities, the Internet has created new challenges and problems. On the Internet, people can hide their identities and act without accountability. The Internet provides a cyberspace world for online pornography, hate sites, and spam and other junk e-mail. Just as the Internet makes people more dependent on technology, it has also inspired new kinds of crime, from identity theft to the disruptive spread of computer viruses that clog up and stall out users' computers, interfering with valuable business and corrupting important files.

The readings in this unit ask you to think about these issue questions: How are blogs influencing political expression and political freedom? How is the Internet breaking down national barriers and connecting the global community? Will blogs change the mainstream media? Should e-mail hate speech, stalker messages, death threats, and computer-virus writing be protected by free speech? How can young people be taught responsible use of this new technology? Your analysis of the readings in this unit will be enriched by your self-reflections on your own use of the Internet.

Web of Influence

Daniel W. Drezner and Henry Farrell

Daniel W. Drezner is an assistant professor of political science at the University of Chicago, a regular contributor to The New York Times, *the* Wall Street Journal, Foreign Policy, Foreign Affairs, *and* The New Republic Online, *and author of many scholarly articles, including a forthcoming book on globalization. Henry Farrell is an assistant professor of political science at Elliott School of International Affairs at George Washington University. He has written numerous scholarly articles and has written and taught courses on politics and the Internet. This article exploring the effect of blogs on media and politics appeared in the November/December 2004 issue of* Foreign Policy. *This magazine bridges the academic world and the general public and bills itself as "the premier, award-winning magazine of global politics, economics, and ideas" with the mission to "explain how the world works—in particular, how the process of global integra-tion is reshaping nations, institutions, cultures, and, more fundamentally, our daily lives" (from About FP, www.foreignpolicy.com).*

Every day, millions of online diarists, or "bloggers," share their opinions with a global audience. Drawing upon the content of the international media and the World Wide Web, they weave together an elaborate network with agenda-setting power on issues ranging from human rights in China to the U.S. occupation of Iraq. What be-gan as a hobby is evolving into a new medium that is changing the landscape for journalists and policymakers alike.

It was March 21, 2003—two days after the United States began its "shock and awe" campaign against Iraq—and the story dominating TV networks was the rumor (later proven false) that Saddam Hussein's infamous cousin, Ali Hassan al-Majid ("Chemical Ali"), had been killed in an airstrike. But, for thousands of other people around the world who switched on their computers rather than their television sets, the lead story was the sudden and worrisome disappearance of Salam Pax.

Otherwise known as the "Baghdad Blogger," Salam Pax was the pseudonym for a 29-year-old Iraqi architect whose online diary, featuring wry and candid observa-tions about life in wartime, transformed him into a cult figure. It turned out that technical difficulties, not U.S. cruise missiles or Baathist Party thugs, were respon-sible for the three-day Salam Pax blackout. In the months that followed, his reader-ship grew to millions, as his accounts were quoted in the *New York Times,* BBC, and Britain's *Guardian* newspaper. If the first Gulf War introduced the world to the "CNN effect," then the second Gulf War was blogging's coming out party. Salam Pax was the most famous blogger during that conflict (he later signed a book and movie deal), but myriad other online diarists, including U.S. military personnel, emerged to offer real-time analysis and commentary.

Blogs (short for "weblogs") are periodically updated journals, providing online commentary with minimal or no external editing. They are usually presented as a set of "posts," individual entries of news or commentary, in reverse chronological order. The posts often include hyperlinks to other sites, enabling commentators to draw upon the content of the entire World Wide Web. Blogs can function as per-sonal diaries, political analysis, advice columns on romance, computers, money, or all of the above. Their number has grown at an astronomical rate. In 1999, the total number of blogs was estimated to be around 50; five years later, the estimates range from 2.4 million to 4.1 million. The Perseus Development Corporation, a con-sulting firm that studies Internet trends, estimates that by 2005 more than 10 mil-lion blogs will have been created. Media institutions have adopted the form as well, with many television networks, newspapers, and opinion journals now hosting blogs on their Web sites, sometimes featuring dispatches from their own correspon-dents, other times hiring full-time online columnists.

Blogs are already influencing U.S. politics. The top five political blogs together attract over half a million visitors per day. Jimmy Orr, the White House Internet di-rector, recently characterized the "blogosphere" (the all-encompassing term to de-scribe the universe of weblogs) as instrumental, important, and underestimated in its influence. Nobody knows that better than Trent Lott, who in December 2002 resigned as U.S. Senate majority leader in the wake of inflammatory comments he made at Sen. Strom Thurmond's 100th birthday party. Initially, Lott's remarks received little attention in the mainstream media. But the incident was the subject of intense online commentary, prodding renewed media attention that converted Lott's gaffe into a full-blown scandal.

6   Political scandals are one thing, but can the blogosphere influence global politics as well? Compared to other actors in world affairs—governments, international organizations, multinational corporations, and even nongovernmental organizations (NGOs)—blogs do not appear to be very powerful or visible. Even the most popular blog garners only a fraction of the Web traffic that major media outlets attract. According to the 2003 Pew Research Center for the People and the Press Internet Survey, only 4 percent of online Americans refer to blogs for information and opinions. The blogosphere has no central organization, and its participants have little ideological consensus. Indeed, an October 2003 survey of the blogosphere conducted by Perseus concluded that "the typical blog is written by a teenage girl who uses it twice a month to update her friends and classmates on happenings in her life." Blogging is almost exclusively a part-time, voluntary activity. The median income generated by a weblog is zero dollars. How then can a collection of decentralized, contrarian, and nonprofit Web sites possibly influence world politics?

7   Blogs are becoming more influential because they affect the content of international media coverage. Journalism professor Todd Gitlin once noted that media frame reality through "principles of selection, emphasis, and presentation composed of little tacit theories about what exists, what happens, and what matters." Increasingly, journalists and pundits take their cues about "what matters" in the world from weblogs. For salient topics in global affairs, the blogosphere functions as a rare combination of distributed expertise, real-time collective response to breaking news, and public-opinion barometer. What's more, a hierarchical structure has taken shape within the primordial chaos of cyberspace. A few elite blogs have emerged as aggregators of information and analysis, enabling media commentators to extract meaningful analysis and rely on blogs to help them interpret and predict political developments.

8   Under specific circumstances—when key weblogs focus on a new or neglected issue—blogs can act as a focal point for the mainstream media and exert formidable agenda-setting power. Blogs have ignited national debates on such topics as racial profiling at airports and have kept the media focused on scandals as diverse as the exposure of CIA agent Valerie Plame's identity to bribery allegations at the United Nations. Although the blogosphere remains cluttered with the teenage angst of high school students, blogs increasingly serve as a conduit through which ordinary and not-so-ordinary citizens express their views on international relations and influence a policymaker's decision making.

THE TIES THAT BIND

9   University of Michigan history Professor Juan Cole had a lot to say about the war on terror and the war in Iraq. Problem was, not many people were listening.

Despite an impressive résumé (he's fluent in three Middle Eastern languages), Cole had little success publishing opinion pieces in the mainstream media, even after Sept. 11, 2001. His writings on the Muslim world might have remained confined to academic journals had he not begun a weblog called "Informed Comment" as a hobby in 2002. Cole's language proficiency allowed him to monitor news reports and editorials throughout the region. "This was something I could not have been able to do in 1990, or even 1995," he told a Detroit newspaper, referring to the surge of Middle Eastern publications on the Internet. "I could get a level of texture and detail that you could never get from the Western press."

Fellow bloggers took an interest in his writings, especially because he ex-   10 pressed a skepticism about the U.S. invasion and occupation of Iraq that stood apart from the often optimistic mainstream media coverage following the successful overthrow of the Baathist regime. Writing in the summer of 2003, Cole noted: "The Sunni Arabs north, east and west of Baghdad from all accounts hate the U.S. and hate U.S. troops being there. This hatred is the key recruiting tool for the resistance, and it is not lessened by U.S. troops storming towns. I wish [the counterinsurgency operation] well; maybe it will work, militarily. Politically, I don't think it addresses the real problems, of winning hearts and minds."

As a prominent expert on the modern history of Shiite Islam, Cole became   11 widely read among bloggers—and ultimately journalists—following the outbreak of Iraqi Shiite unrest in early 2004. With his blog attracting 250,000 readers per month, Cole began appearing on media outlets such as National Public Radio (NPR) and CNN to provide expert commentary. He also testified before the Senate Foreign Relations Committee. "As a result of my weblog, the *Middle East Journal* invited me to contribute for the Fall 2003 issue," he recalls. "When the Senate staff of the Foreign Relations Committee did a literature search on Moktada al-Sadr and his movement, mine was the only article that came up. Senate staff and some of the senators themselves read it and were eager to have my views on the situation."

Cole's transformation into a public intellectual embodies many of the dynamics   12 that have heightened the impact of the blogosphere. He wanted to publicize his expertise, and he did so by attracting attention from elite members of the blogosphere. As Cole made waves within the virtual world, others in the real world began to take notice.

Most bloggers desire a wide readership, and conventional wisdom suggests   13 that the most reliable way to gain Web traffic is through a link on another weblog. A blog that is linked to by multiple other sites will accumulate an ever increasing readership as more bloggers discover the site and create hyperlinks on their respective Web pages. Thus, in the blogosphere, the rich (measured in the number of links) get richer, while the poor remain poor.

This dynamic creates a skewed distribution where there are a very few highly   14 ranked blogs with many incoming links, followed by a steep falloff and a very long list of medium- to low-ranked bloggers with few or no incoming links. One study by Clay Shirky, an associate professor at New York University, found that the Internet's top dozen bloggers (less than 3 percent of the total examined) accounted for approximately 20 percent of the incoming links. Some link-deprived blogs may become rich over time as top bloggers link to them, which helps explain why new bloggers are not discouraged.

15   Consequently, even as the blogosphere continues to expand, only a few blogs are likely to emerge as focal points. These prominent blogs serve as a mechanism for filtering interesting blog posts from mundane ones. When less renowned bloggers write posts with new information or a new slant, they will contact one or more of the large focal point blogs to publicize their posts. In this manner, poor blogs function as fire alarms for rich blogs, alerting them to new information and links. This self-perpetuating, symbiotic relationship allows interesting arguments and information to make their way to the top of the blogosphere.

16   The skewed network of the blogosphere makes it less time-consuming for outside observers to acquire information. The media only need to look at elite blogs to obtain a summary of the distribution of opinions on a given political issue. The mainstream political media can therefore act as a conduit between the blogosphere and politically powerful actors. The comparative advantage of blogs in political discourse, as compared to traditional media, is their low cost of real-time publication. Bloggers can post their immediate reactions to important political events before other forms of media can respond. Speed also helps bloggers overcome their own inaccuracies. When confronted with a factual error, they can quickly correct or update their post. Through these interactions, the blogosphere distills complex issues into key themes, providing cues for how the media should frame and report a foreign-policy question.

17   Small surprise, then, that a growing number of media leaders—editors, publishers, reporters, and columnists—consume political blogs. *New York Times* Executive Editor Bill Keller said in a November 2003 interview, "Sometimes I read something on a blog that makes me feel we screwed up." Howard Kurtz, one of the most prominent media commentators in the United States, regularly quotes elite bloggers in his "Media Notes Extra" feature for the *Washington Post*'s Web site. Many influential foreign affairs columnists, including Paul Krugman and Fareed Zakaria, have said that blogs form a part of their information-gathering activities.

18   For the mainstream media—which almost by definition suffer a deficit of specialized, detailed knowledge—blogs can also serve as repositories of expertise. And for readers worldwide, blogs can act as the "man on the street," supplying unfiltered eyewitness accounts about foreign countries. This facet is an especially valuable service, given the decline in the number of foreign correspondents since the 1990s. Blogs may even provide expert analysis and summaries of foreign-language texts, such as newspaper articles and government studies, that reporters and pundits would not otherwise access or understand.

19   Even foreign-policy novices leave their mark on the debate. David Nishimura, an art historian and vintage pen dealer, emerged as an unlikely commentator on the Iraq war through his blog, "Cronaca," which he describes as a "compilation of news concerning art, archaeology, history, and whatever else catches the chronicler's eye, with the odd bit of opinion and commentary thrown in." In the month after the fall of Hussein's regime in April 2003, there was much public hand-wringing about reports that more than 170,000 priceless antiques and treasures had been looted

from the Iraqi National Museum in Baghdad. In response to these newspaper accounts, a number of historians and archaeologists scorned the U.S. Defense Department for failing to protect the museum.

Nishimura, however, scrutinized the various media reports and found several inconsistencies. He noted that the 170,000 number was flat-out wrong; that the actual losses, though serious, were much smaller than initial reports suggested; and that museum officials might have been complicit in the looting. "Smart money still seems to be on the involvement of Ba'athists and/or museum employees," he wrote. "The extent to which these categories overlap has been danced around so far, but until everything has been properly sorted out, it might be wise to remember how other totalitarian states have coopted cultural institutions, enlisting the past to remake the future." Prominent right-of-center bloggers, such as Glenn Reynolds, Andrew Sullivan, and Virginia Postrel, cited Nishimura's analysis to focus attention on the issue and correct the original narrative.

As the museum looting controversy reveals, blogs are now a "fifth estate" that keeps watch over the mainstream media. The speed of real-time blogger reactions often compels the media to correct errors in their own reporting before they mushroom. For example, in June 2003, the *Guardian* trumpeted a story in its online edition that misquoted Deputy U.S. Secretary of Defense Paul Wolfowitz as saying that the United States invaded Iraq in order to safeguard its oil supply. The quote began to wend its way through other media outlets worldwide, including Germany's *Die Welt*. In the ensuing hours, numerous bloggers led by Greg Djerijian's "Belgravia Dispatch" linked to the story and highlighted the error, prompting the *Guardian* to retract the story and apologize to its readers before publishing the story in its print version.

Bloggers have become so adept at fact-checking the media that they've spawned many other high-profile retractions and corrections. The most noteworthy was CBS News' acknowledgement that it could not authenticate documents it had used in a story about President George W. Bush's National Guard service that bloggers had identified as forgeries. When such corrections are made, bloggers create the impression at times that contemporary journalism has spun out of control. Glenn Reynolds of "Instapundit" explained to the *Online Journalism Review* that he sees parallels between the impact of the blogosphere and Russia's post-Soviet glasnost. "People are appalled, saying it's the decline of journalism. . . . But it's the same as when Russia started reporting about plane crashes and everyone thought they were just suddenly happening. It was really just the first time people could read about them." Media elites rightly retort that blogs have their own problems. Their often blatant partisanship discredits them in many newsrooms. However, as Yale University law Professor Jack Balkin says, the blogosphere has some built-in correction mechanisms for ideological bias, as "bloggers who write about political subjects cannot avoid addressing (and, more importantly, linking to) arguments made by people with different views. The reason is that much of the blogosphere is devoted to criticizing what other people have to say."

The blogosphere also acts as a barometer for whether a story would or should receive greater coverage by the mainstream media. The more blogs that discuss a particular issue, the more likely that the blogosphere will set the agenda for future news coverage. Consider one recent example with regard to U.S. homeland security. In July 2004, Annie Jacobsen, a writer for Womens WallStreet.com, posted online a first-person account of suspicious activity by Syrian passengers on a domestic U.S. flight: "After seeing 14 Middle Eastern men board separately (six together, eight individually) and then act as a group, watching their unusual glances, observing their bizarre bathroom activities, watching them congregate in small groups, knowing that the flight attendants and the pilots were seriously concerned and now knowing that federal air marshals were on board, I was officially terrified," she wrote. Her account was quickly picked up, linked to, and vigorously debated throughout the blogosphere. Was this the preparation for another September 11-style terrorist attack? Was Jacobsen overreacting, allowing her judgment to be clouded by racial stereotypes? Should the U.S. government end the practice of fining "discriminatory" airlines that disproportionately search Arab passengers? In just one weekend, 2 million people read her article. Reports soon followed in mainstream media outlets such as NPR, MSNBC, *Time,* and the *New York Times,* prompting a broader national debate about the racial profiling of possible terrorists.

24   Some bloggers purposefully harness the medium to promote wider awareness of their causes. With the assistance of experts including Kenneth Roth, the executive director of Human Rights Watch, and Samantha Power, the Pulitzer Prize-winning author of *"A Problem from Hell": America and the Age of Genocide,* cyberactivist Joanne Cipolla Moore set up a blog and Web site, "Passion of the Present," devoted to collecting news and information about genocide in Sudan. Moore sought out dozens of elite bloggers to link to her site and spread the word about Sudan. The blog of Ethan Zuckerman, a researcher at Harvard Law School's Berkman Center for Internet & Society, not only links to Moore's site but has issued a call to arms to the entire blogosphere: "Blogs let us tell offline media what we want. When blog readers made it clear we wanted to know more about Trent Lott's racist comments, mainstream media picked up the ball and dug deeper into the story. . . . What sort of effort would it take to choose an important issue—say the Sudanese government's involvement in Darfur—and get enough momentum in the blogosphere that CNN was forced to bring a camera crew to the region?"

25   In all of these instances, bloggers relied on established media outlets for much of their information. However, blogs also functioned as a feedback mechanism for the mainstream media. In this way, the blogosphere serves both as an amplifier and as a remixer of media coverage. For the traditional media—and ultimately, policymakers—this makes the blogosphere difficult to ignore as a filter through which the public considers foreign-policy questions.

RAGE INSIDE THE MACHINE

26   Blogs are beginning to emerge in countries where there are few other outlets for political expression. But can blogs affect politics in regimes where there is no thriving independent media sector?

27   Under certain circumstances, they can. For starters, blogs can become an alternative source of news and commentary in countries where traditional media are un-

der the thumb of the state. Blogs are more difficult to control than television or newspapers, especially under regimes that are tolerant of some degree of free expression. However, they are vulnerable to state censorship. A sufficiently determined government can stop blogs it doesn't like by restricting access to the Internet, or setting an example for others by punishing unauthorized political expression, as is currently the case in Saudi Arabia and China. The government may use filtering technologies to limit access to foreign blogs. And, if there isn't a reliable technological infrastructure, individuals will be shut out from the blogosphere. For instance, chronic power shortages and telecommunications problems make it difficult for Iraqis to write or read blogs.

Faced with various domestic obstacles, bloggers inside these countries (or expatriates) can try to influence foreign blogs and the media through indirect effects at home. Political scientists Margaret Keck of Johns Hopkins University and Kathryn Sikkink of the University of Minnesota note that activists who are unable to change conditions in their own countries can leverage their power by taking their case to transnational networks of advocates, who in turn publicize abuses and lobby their governments. Keck and Sikkink call this a "boomerang effect," because repression at home can lead to international pressure against the regime from abroad. Blogs can potentially play a role in the formation of such transnational networks. 28

Iran is a good example. The Iranian blogosphere has exploded. According to the National Institute for Technology and Liberal Education's Blog Census, Farsi is the fourth most widely used language among blogs worldwide. One service provider alone ("Persian Blog") hosts some 60,000 active blogs. The weblogs allow young secular and religious Iranians to interact, partially taking the place of reformist newspapers that have been censored or shut down. Government efforts to impose filters on the Internet have been sporadic and only partially successful. Some reformist politicians have embraced blogs, including the president, who celebrated the number of Iranian bloggers at the World Summit on the Information Society, and Vice President Muhammad Ali Abtahi, who is a blogger himself. Elite Iranian blogs such as "Editor: Myself" have established links with the English-speaking blogosphere. When Sina Motallebi, a prominent Iranian blogger, was imprisoned for "undermining national security through 'cultural activity,'" prominent Iranian bloggers were able to join forces with well-known English-language bloggers including Jeff Jarvis ("BuzzMachine"), Dan Gillmor ("Silicon Valley"), and Patrick Belton ("OxBlog") to create an online coalition that attracted media coverage, leading to Motallebi's release. 29

An international protest campaign also secured the freedom of Chinese blogger Liu Di, a 23-year-old psychology student who offended authorities with her satirical comments about the Communist Party. Yet, even as Di was released, two individuals who had circulated online petitions on her behalf were arrested. Such is life in China, where an estimated 300,000 bloggers (out of 80 million regular Internet users) uneasily coexist with the government. Bloggers in China have perfected the art of self-censorship, because a single offensive post can affect an entire online community—as when Internet censors temporarily shut down leading blog sites such as Blogcn.com in 2003. Frank Yu, a Program Manager at Microsoft Research 30

Asia's Advanced Technology Center in Beijing, described this mind-set as he pro-filed a day in the life of a fictional Chinese blogger he dubbed "John X": "After read-ing over his new posting, he checks it for any politically sensitive terms which may cause the government to block his site. . . . Although he is not concerned as much about being shut down, he does not want all the writers that share the host server with him to get locked out as well.

31   "Living in China, we learn to pick the battles that we feel strongly about and let the host of other indignities pass through quiet compliance." Text messaging is a much safer medium for the online Chinese community. Some bloggers, however, do manage to push the envelope, as when Shanghai-based Microsoft employee Wang Jianshuo offered candid, firsthand accounts (including photos) of the SARS and Avian Flu outbreaks.

32   North Korea is perhaps the most blog-unfriendly nation. Only political elites and foreigners are allowed access to the Internet. As might be expected, there are no blogs within North Korea, nor any easy way for ordinary North Koreans to access foreign blogs. However, even in that country, blogs may have an impact. A former CNN journalist, Rebecca MacKinnon, has set up "NKZone," a blog that has rapidly become a focal point for North Korea news and discussion. As MacKinnon notes, this blog can aggregate information in a way that ordinary journalism cannot. North Korea rarely allows journalists to enter the country, and when it does, it assigns government minders to watch them constantly. However, non-journalists can and do enter the country. "NKZone" gathers information from a wide variety of sources, in-cluding tourists, diplomats, NGOs, and academics with direct experience of life in North Korea, and the blog organizes it for easy consumption. It has already been cited in such prominent publications as the *Asian Wall Street Journal* and the *Sunday Times* of London as a source for information about North Korea.

BLOGO ERGO SUM

33   The growing clout of bloggers has transformed some into "blog triumphalists." To hear them tell it, blogging is the single most transformative media technology since the invention of the printing press. Rallying cries, such as "the revolution will be blogged," reflect the belief that blogs might even supplant traditional journalism. But, as the editor of the Washington, D.C.-based blog "Wonkette," Ana Marie Cox, has wryly observed, "A revolution requires that people leave their house."

34   There remain formidable obstacles to the influence of blogs. All bloggers, even those at the top of the hierarchy, have limited resources at their disposal. For the moment, they are largely dependent upon traditional media for sources of informa-tion. Furthermore, bloggers have become victims of their own success: As more mainstream media outlets hire bloggers to provide content, they become more inte-grated into politics as usual. Inevitably, blogs will lose some of their novelty and im-mediacy as they start being co-opted by the very institutions they purport to cri-tique, as when both major U.S. political parties decided to credential some bloggers as journalists for their 2004 nominating conventions.

35   Bloggers, even those in free societies, must confront the same issues of censor-ship that plague traditional media. South Korea recently blocked access to many

foreign blogs, apparently because they had linked to footage of Islamic militants in Iraq beheading a South Korean. In the United States, the Pentagon invoked national security to shut down blogs written by troops stationed in Iraq. Military officials claimed that such blogs might inadvertently reveal sensitive information. But Michael O'Hanlon, a defense specialist at the Brookings Institution, told NPR that he believes "it has much less to do with operational security and classified secrets, and more to do with American politics and how the war is seen by a public that is getting increasingly shaky about the overall venture."

One should also bear in mind that the blogosphere, mirroring global civil society as a whole, remains dominated by the developed world—a fact only heightened by claims of a digital divide. And though elite bloggers are ideologically diverse, they're demographically similar. Middle-class white males are overrepresented in the upper echelons of the blogosphere. Reflecting those demographics, an analysis conducted by Harvard University's Ethan Zuckerman found that the blogosphere, like the mainstream media, tends to ignore large parts of the world.   36

Death by a Thousand Blogs
Nicholas D. Kristof

Nicholas D. Kristof is a well-known columnist for the liberal newspaper The New York Times. *He is an expert on China, and he and his wife, Sheryl WuDunn, have written several books on China's recent social, economic, and political development:* China Wakes *(1995) and* Thunder from the East *(2001). This op-ed piece was published on May 24, 2005, in* The New York Times.

The Chinese Communist Party survived a brutal civil war with the Nationalists,   1
battles with American forces in Korea and massive prodemocracy demonstrations at Tiananmen Square. But now it may finally have met its match—the Internet.

The collision between the Internet and Chinese authorities is one of the grand   2
wrestling matches of history, visible in part at www.yuluncn.com.

That's the Web site of a self-appointed journalist named Li Xinde. He made a   3
modest fortune selling Chinese medicine around the country, and now he's started the Chinese Public Opinion Surveillance Net—one of four million blogs in China.

Mr. Li travels around China with an I.B.M. laptop and a digital camera, investi-   4
gating cases of official wrongdoing. Then he writes about them on his Web site and skips town before the local authorities can arrest him.

His biggest case so far involved a deputy mayor of Jining who is accused of steal-   5
ing more than $400,000 and operating like a warlord. One of the deputy mayor's victims was a businesswoman whom he allegedly harassed and tried to kidnap.

Mr. Li's Web site published an investigative report, including a series of pho-   6
tos showing the deputy mayor kneeling and crying, apparently begging not to be

reported to the police. The photos caused a sensation, and the deputy mayor was soon arrested.

7   Another of Mr. Li's campaigns involved a young peasant woman who was kidnapped by family planning officials, imprisoned and forcibly fitted with an IUD. Embarrassed by the reports, the authorities sent the officials responsible to jail for a year.

8   When I caught up with Mr. Li, he was investigating the mysterious death of a businessman who got in a financial dispute with a policeman and ended up arrested and then dead.

9   All this underscores how the Internet is beginning to play the watchdog role in China that the press plays in the West. The Internet is also eroding the leadership's monopoly on information and is complicating the traditional policy of "nei jin wai song"—cracking down at home while pretending to foreigners to be wide open.

10   My old friends in the Chinese news media and the Communist Party are mostly aghast at President Hu Jintao's revival of ideological slogans, praise for North Korea's political system and crackdown on the media. The former leaders Jiang Zemin and Zhu Rongji are also said to be appalled.

11   Yet China, fortunately, is bigger than its emperor. Some 100 million Chinese now surf the Web, and e-mail and Web chat rooms are ubiquitous.

12   The authorities have arrested a growing number of Web dissidents. But there just aren't enough police to control the Internet, and when sites are banned, Chinese get around them with proxy servers.

13   One of the leaders of the Tiananmen democracy movement, Chen Ziming, is now out of prison and regularly posts essays on an Internet site. Jiao Guobiao, a scholar, is officially blacklisted but writes scathing essays that circulate by e-mail all around China. One senior government official told me that he doesn't bother to read Communist Party documents any more, but he never misses a Jiao Guobiao essay.

14   I tried my own experiment, posting comments on Internet chat rooms. In a Chinese-language chat room on Sohu.com, I called for multiparty elections and said, "If Chinese on the other side of the Taiwan Strait can choose their leaders, why can't we choose our leaders?" That went on the site automatically, like all other messages. But after 10 minutes, the censor spotted it and removed it.

15   Then I toned it down: "Under the Communist Party's great leadership, China has changed tremendously. I wonder if in 20 years the party will introduce competing parties, because that could benefit us greatly." That stayed up for all to see, even though any Chinese would read it as an implicit call for a multiparty system.

16   So where is China going? I think the Internet is hastening China along the same path that South Korea, Chile and especially Taiwan pioneered. In each place, a booming economy nurtured a middle class, rising education, increased international contact and a growing squeamishness about torturing dissidents.

17   President Hu has fulminated in private speeches that foreign "hostile forces" are trying to change China. Yup, count me in—anybody who loves China as I do would be hostile to an empty Mao suit like Mr. Hu. But it's the Chinese leadership itself that is digging the Communist Party's grave, by giving the Chinese people broadband.

You Wanna Take This Online?

Jeff Chu

Text messaging, instant messaging, and Web journals are shaping today's youth in drastic and unanticipated ways, according to this feature article, which appeared in the August 8, 2005, edition of Time, *a weekly news commentary magazine for a general readership. Jeff Chu writes regularly for* Time.

What does 13-year-old Taylor Hern ❤? Lots of things: the actor Ewan McGregor, the color pink, the band My Chemical Romance, her boyfriend Alex. You would know all that if you visited her Xanga, a blog-home-page hybrid that is the modern teen's public and interactive equivalent of a diary. You could even leave a comment on her Xanga or send her an "eProp" if, say, you ❤ Ewan McGregor too.

On April 18, Taylor, who is about to enter eighth grade at Lost Mountain Middle School in Kennesaw, Ga., got an instant message (IM) from her friend Sydney Meyer that said, "OMG [Oh, my God] OMG OMG go to your xanga." Someone using the screen name Immsgirlsgot2hell had left Taylor a comment that read, "Go to my Xanga, bitch." Taylor did—and found a List of Hos. Her name was on it. The list was hurtful, but Taylor says she wasn't as bothered as other girls. "A bunch of the cheerleading chicks spazzed," she says. "Me and all my friends thought it was stupid. Who would actually make time in their schedule to do something like that?"

Turns out, many of her peers would. Technology has transformed the lives of teens, including the ways they pick on one another. If parents and teachers think it's hard to control mean girls and bullying boys in school, they haven't reckoned with cyberspace.

Cyberbullying can mean anything from posting pejorative items like the List of Hos to spreading rumors by e-mail to harassing by instant message. It was experienced in the preceding two months by 18% of 3,700 middle schoolers surveyed by researchers at Clemson University. Their study is scheduled to be presented at this month's American Psychological Association meeting. The phenomenon peaks at about age 13; 21% of eighth-graders surveyed reported being cyberbullied recently. And incidents of online bullying are like roaches: for every one that's reported, many more go unrecorded. "Our statistics are conservative," says Clemson psychologist Robin Kowalski. "Part of the problem is kids not recognizing that what's happening is a form of bullying."

Online bullying follows a gender pattern that's the opposite of what happens offline, the Clemson study found. On playgrounds and in school hallways, boys are the primary perpetrators and victims; online, girls rule. Nearly a third of the eighth-grade girls surveyed reported being bullied online in the previous two months, compared with 10% of boys; 17% of the girls said they had bullied online, but only 10% of the boys said they had. Such stats get an eye roll from teens. "Girls make up stuff and sooooooo much drama," Taylor said (by IM, of course). "Drama queens."

6   On the Internet, you can wear any mask you like—and that can be harrowing for the victim of a cyberbully. A few weeks after the List of Hos was posted, Taylor's classmate Courtney Katasak got an IM from someone using the screen name ToastIsYummy. Courtney thought it might be a friend with a new screen name, so she asked, WHO IS THIS? ToastIsYummy responded with teasing lines and a link to a porn site. "Then they kept sending me these inappropriate messages," she says. "I blocked the screen name so they couldn't talk to me, but I didn't know who this person was or what they were trying to do. It freaked me out."

7   "Anonymity emboldens the person doing it—and it increases the fear factor for the victim," says Kowalski. Parry Aftab, founder of an online nonprofit called WiredSafety.org, says teens "are exploring who they are—and they role-play by being mean, horrible and hateful in ways they would never be offline." Aftab recalls meeting a New Jersey 13-year-old with a preppie-perfect appearance—khakis, button-down shirt, penny loafers complete with pennies—and a creepy hobby of making online death threats against strangers. He would gather information from chat rooms or people's websites, then threaten them as if he knew them. Says Aftab: "He said to me, 'I would never do anything in real life. I'm a good kid. But I can do it online because it doesn't matter.'"

8   Actually, it does. When a cyberbully lashes out, it can be a sign of emotional or psychological problems. And cyberbullying is viral. The Clemson study found that kids who are victimized "seem to be heavily involved in bullying others," says psychologist Sue Limber. In the real world, physical intimidation may keep those who are bullied from retaliating, but that's not a problem online. "Cyberbullying can also lead to other forms of victimization," Limber says. If someone insults a classmate on a Xanga, the effects could include ostracization at school. "Passing notes or writing on lockers was nothing," says Limber. "This takes public to a whole other level."

9   It can be especially embarrassing since cyberbullying often has sexual overtones. "It's raging hormones, and 13 is the heart of it," says Aftab. "We tell adults they can't operate heavy machinery under the influence. These kids are under the influence of hormones 24/7."

10   A parent's instinctive response may be to apply an electronic tourniquet, cutting off a teen's access. But experts agree that severing online links is not the solution. "The Internet is no longer just an advantage. A child is at a disadvantage not having it," says Brittany Bacon, an FBI-trained WiredSafety.org volunteer. She says teens need to learn boundaries and manners in cyberspace just as they must in other venues of society.

11   It's also the parents' responsibility to be aware of a child's life online. "Kids know so much about the computer that some parents just throw up their hands," says Patti Agatston, a counselor with Cobb County Schools' prevention-intervention program in Georgia. "Don't do that," she says. Instead, parents should keep their eyes open. "Parents are totally clueless that some of this even exists," Aftab says.

12   Taylor Hern's mother Caryn counts herself in that number. "I am absolutely an idiot when it comes to that kind of stuff," she says. But Taylor's cyberbullying experience convinced Hern that she had to get Netsavvy. She has signed up for lessons from an expert: her son David, who is 19. "You read about what kids do to other

kids, but you don't think it's going to happen to yours," she says. "Who knows what happens online after I go to bed at 10? I need to find out."

Sarah, It's That Bloke . . .
Adey Bryant

Adey Bryant is a cartoonist and artist living in the United Kingdom. His cartoons have appeared in dozens of publications, including The Times Metro Magazine, Punch, The Daily Mirror, The Weekly News, *and* Readers Digest, *as well as publications in other European Union countries. This cartoon was posted on www.cartoonstock.com.*

Source: www.CartoonStock.com

"Sarah. It's that bloke you've been chatting to on the computer."

Hate Speech Conviction Outlaws Email
Kenneth Lake

Journalist Kenneth Lake, publishing on the Web site of Internet Freedom, a British advocacy group "opposed to all forms of censorship and content regulation on the Net" (from its home page), outlines the dangers to free speech posed by the Machado decision in the United States. This Web opinion piece was posted on February 13, 1998.

In this article, Kenneth Lake refers to the widely publicized e-mail hate case involving Richard Machado, who became the first person in the United States convicted of e-mail crime. On September 20, 1996, student Richard Machado, on academic probation for low grades, sent obscenity-laced death threat e-mails to Asian students at the University of California at Irvine.

1   "I personally will make it my life career to find and kill every one of you personally" signed Asian Hater.

2   The words of an email message that is to have serious consequences for Internet freedom. They were written by Richard Machado, a Los Angeles man who was convicted last Tuesday (10/2/98) of sending racist death threats to 59 Asian students.

3   The email accused Asians for all the crimes on campus, and suggested that Machado would personally "find," "hunt down" and "kill" them if they did not leave the University of California at Irvine. The email was sent from a campus computer and signed "Asian Hater." Machado, a newly naturalised US citizen from El Salvador, was originally charged with 10 counts of civil rights violations. In November, however, a mis-trial was declared after the jury deadlocked and a re-trial was ordered by judge Alice Marie Stolter for the 27th January 1998. For this Machado was to be charged with only two counts: sending the threat based on the recipients' race or ethnicity and "interfering" with their right to attend the University.

4   The case sets a precedent because it puts email on an equal legal footing with telephone calls and postal mail, and introduces the legal category of hate crimes to the online world.

5   Barry Steinhardt, associate director of the American Civil Liberties Union (ACLU), commented that whilst non-specific comments are protected as free speech, a specific threat against an individual is not. Professor Eugene Velokn of the ACLU School of Law added "if you threaten somebody's life in a way that a typical listener will think you're serious, that's constitutionally unprotected." In contrast, Mr Machado's defence attorney has argued that the federal law being used to prosecute his client is in effect criminalising email. However the director of San Francisco's public defenders office has stated that the Internet has no special immunities or special privileges because speech occurs on it.

6   Machado is surely a crackpot racist but his conviction has serious consequences for free speech generally. For some time there has been an authoritarian shift in the focus of criminal law from deed to word to thought. It is clear in this

case that part of the rationale for the charge was the fact that Machado's threat was racially motivated. This is also the reasoning behind Jack Straw's introduction of an offence of racially motivated violence in the UK. But the determination of criminal liability essentially concentrates upon an act and whether the defendant intentionally, recklessly or knowingly committed it. A murder may be motivated by anger, misogyny, political conviction or mercy, but all the court wants to know, in order to convict, is whether there was a murder and whether it was committed intentionally by the defendant.

In Machado's case the only "act" was the sending of a threatening email. The   7
criminalisation of email indicates the continuing expansion of the category of mental crime. In the UK in 1936 the Public Order Act banned "threatening, abusive or insulting words or behaviour" which "might provoke a breach of the peace." In 1986 "breach of the peace" was replaced by "harassment, alarm or distress." In 1997 the Protection from Harassment Act created a further offence of "a course of conduct" (including speech) amounting to harassment of another. The trajectory is to make words as well as deeds much more susceptible to prosecution.

It is difficult to see how Machado could have actually intended to carry out his   8
threat to assassinate 59 students. It is far more likely that Machado's racist comments, like much speech among news groups and mailing lists, were simply an idle threat. Any experienced user will know that abusive messages and flames are commonplace on the Net.

The conviction of Machado means that not only will we have to watch what we   9
say on the Net, but also with the criminalisation of motive we will have to watch why we think it. Before now it had never been a crime to hate anyone. Now it seems that there is an ever expanding category of thoughts that could put you in the clink.

For those who value free expression it is worth remembering that sticks and   10
stones may break your bones but emails will never hurt you.

Internet's Hate Sites Can Be Hidden, But They Can't Be Ignored

Lawrence J. Magid

A serious dilemma for educators and parents is the problem of hate sites. Here Lawrence J. Magid, writing for the Web site of the Online Safety Project, gives his own views on how to approach hate sites. Lawrence J. Magid is a syndicated columnist, broadcaster, and author of numerous articles about online safety. In 1999 he and his colleagues were called "high tech heroes" by Time *magazine for work in developing online strategies for finding missing children. This article was published on safeteens.com on July 19, 1999.*

1   When I agreed to write a column about hate sites on the Internet, I knew that it would be an unsettling experience. But I had no idea just how disturbing it would be.

2   When I researched this topic about three years ago, I found some pretty unsavory sites. But this time I found a lot more, and some, frankly, were nauseating.

3   One was operated by the Church of the Creator, the group that 21-year-old Benjamin Smith was part of until shortly before he embarked on a killing spree in the Midwest that ended when he took his own life. That site was bad enough, but there are hundreds more like it. The Los Angeles-based Simon Wiesenthal Center (http://www.wiesenthal.org), which tracks hate sites, identified more than 1,400 "problematic" Web sites as of March—twice as many as it found the year before. Even that number may be conservative. Rabbi Abraham Cooper, the center's associate dean, estimates that there may be as many as 2,100.

4   I'm not going to go into vivid detail about what I found after looking at about 20 of these sites, but even I was shocked—and I have pretty thick skin. I expected to find Web sites that ridicule African Americans, Jews, gays, immigrants and others, but some took it a few steps further by combining bigotry with articles about guns, bombs and other implements of violence.

5   Others were designed deliberately to shock, with displays of swastikas, burning crosses and nooses. One site mixes hate with stories and photographs that celebrate sex and violence in the most extreme way imaginable.

6   What's most disturbing about these sites is that they're very easy to find. Unlike most pornography sites, the people who run hate sites don't usually put up even a feeble effort to keep out children. On the contrary, some overtly invite children and teens to participate. The Church of the Creator Web site had a children's section complete with puzzles and a coloring book. Another site has a "kids page" that is reportedly maintained by a 10-year-old. Many have music graphics and rhetoric designed to appeal to teens.

7   What can we do about this? We can't ban hate sites because it's impossible to take away the 1st Amendment rights of bigots without jeopardizing the free speech rights of the rest of us. Some people argue that we should place limits on free speech, but even if we could agree on where to draw the line, many of the subtler and seemingly reasonable sites would slip through. In fact, some of the most dangerous sites don't even look like hate sites. They contain what appear to be reasonable—albeit misguided—scientific and historical arguments that, if believed, could lead young people and others to conclude that target groups really are inherently inferior or dangerous.

8   I don't think the government can or should do anything to ban these groups from the Internet, but there are things that individuals and groups can do to shield or inoculate children from them.

9   One option for parents is to install a filtering program that blocks sites advocating hate or violence. Most of the programs designed to keep kids away from pornography can also be configured to keep them out of known hate sites. The Anti-Defamation League (http://www.adl.org) has teamed up with the Learning Company to produce a special version of CyberPatrol called the ADL HateFilter, which blocks hate sites and "encourages parents to teach their children about the

nature of bigotry and the hatemongers who promote it." The program, which runs on Windows, costs $29.95. A seven-day free trial version can be downloaded from ADL's Web site.

With or without filters, it's important for parents to talk with their kids about   10 hate sites and bigotry in general. David Lehr, Pacific Southwest regional director of the Anti-Defamation League, recommends that parents "sit with your kids and point out the logical inconsistencies and danger of hate." He suggests that you "use these sites as teachable moments."

Rabbi Cooper agrees. Because kids are more Net-savvy in many cases than   11 grown-ups, they may actually be more likely to know about hate sites than their parents. "Ask the kids to take a half-hour to show you the stuff," he suggests. "It's a good point of departure to sit down with your child to talk about these issues." You also can use this time to talk about music and other media that celebrate violence or degrade women, gays, minorities and others.

I agree with Lehr and Cooper. But even if you are 100% successful in inoculat-   12 ing your own kids from the influence of these sites, a lot more work has to be done. Not all parents will bother teaching their kids about the dangers of hate, and some even encourage it. Even those of us who believe we can help keep our kids from becoming bigots can't necessarily prevent them from becoming victims of bigotry.

After spending three days wallowing in other people's racist, sexist, homopho-   13 bic, anti-Semitic, anti-Catholic and anti-immigrant propaganda, I've come to the conclusion that the only way to drown out this type of hate speech is through a massive education campaign that encourages our society—especially our youth— to think critically and question anyone who blames their problems on people who look, act, speak or think differently. Web sites operated by ADL and the Wiesenthal Center are a good starting point for ideas.

This is one area in which we all have responsibility for everyone's children.   14 Schools, religious organizations, civic groups, the media and political leaders of all persuasions—and even computer columnists—have a moral obligation to teach tolerance.

The Constitution Does Not Protect Spamming
Adam Cohen

This op-ed piece appeared in The New York Times *on May 12, 2002. Writer Adam Cohen challenges the contention that the First Amendment protects commercial speech and thus makes unconstitutional any attempts to censor or restrict junk e-mail—often called spam. People complain that spam overloads e-mail servers and reduces worker productivity.*

1   There's a new television commercial that pulls viewers in with a flurry of poignant phrases: "I love you" . . . "I felt the baby move" . . . "It's benign." The voice-over is a salute to free speech. "All words are created equal," it says. "The power to use them is our right as humans." Has the First Amendment gone out and gotten itself an advertising strategy? Not quite. The ad is for a phone company. The freedom it celebrates is in a calling plan that says "local and long distance calls are unlimited." Not exactly what James Madison had in mind when he gave the First Amendment top billing in the Bill of Rights.

2   Conflating the right to call for the overthrow of tyranny with the right to call at bargain rates seems harmless enough. But it is emblematic of a troubling trend in constitutional law: the erasing of the line between commercial and noncommercial speech. A campaign is under way, led primarily by conservatives like Supreme Court Justice Clarence Thomas, to make advertising the equal of political advocacy. If it succeeds, which a Supreme Court decision last month seems to make more likely, it could become more difficult for the government to protect people from being harmed, in small ways and large, by corporations.

3   Commercial speech was once given no First Amendment protection at all. In 1942, the owner of a former Navy submarine docked in the East River was told that he could not hand out fliers advertising his boat as a tourist attraction because they littered the streets. He sued, citing his free speech rights, and the Supreme Court threw out the case, saying the Constitution does not protect "purely commercial advertising."

4   Over time, the court wisely backed away from that absolutist approach. It created a new category of commercial speech, which has been protected, but less than other speech. The court has held that the government can punish false or misleading claims about a product in a way that it cannot go after politicians or journalists for saying things that are untrue.

5   In commercial speech cases, courts balance the value of the speech against the government's interest in regulating it. Applying that test, the Supreme Court held that the speech rights of lawyers were not violated when a state disciplined them for misleading advertising.

6   Lately, however, corporations and their supporters, on the Supreme Court and off, have taken to calling the commercial speech doctrine a "contrived distinction," and they have been urging that advertising be accorded the same protection as political speech. At the same time, judges sympathetic to that point of view have been applying the current test in an increasingly aggressive manner to strike down worthy government regulations. Last month, for example, a court struck down a federal law banning junk faxes and affirmed the right of a company called American Blast Fax to continue to blast away.

7   If other courts push corporate free speech to this illogical limit, laws against spam e-mail may suffer the same fate, as judges elevate the right to send e-mail ads for get-rich-quick schemes and Internet pornography sites to a constitutional imperative.

8   More troubling, courts have been increasingly willing to overturn, on First Amendment grounds, laws aimed at protecting public health.

Last month, by a 5-to-4 vote, the Supreme Court struck down a federal law bar-   9
ring pharmacies from advertising "mixed to order" drugs, pharmaceuticals that have not gone through the usual safety screening. The largely conservative major- ity was more concerned about pharmacies' right to market these products than the government's interest in protecting the public from drugs that, as the dissenters noted, "can, for some patients, mean infection, serious side effects or even death."

In his dissenting opinion, Justice Stephen Breyer, writing for four members of   10
the court, suggested that the majority's reasoning could return the country to the dark days of the early 20th century, when the Supreme Court routinely overturned important health and safety laws as a violation of the due process rights of corpora- tions. In the Lochner era—named for *New York v. Lochner,* a case striking down a maximum-hours law for bakers—the courts threw out laws limiting the hours em- ployees could be made to work, minimum wage laws and laws barring companies from making workers promise not to join a union as a condition of employment.

The Lochner era is in some ways a distant mirror of our own times. The   11
Supreme Court's aggressive championing of corporations then is finding more and more parallels in the antiregulation decisions of today's court. What the Lochner- era justices did with their wildly expansive reading of the due process clause, today's court may wind up doing through an expansive reading of the First Amendment.

Commercial speech obviously has value, and the courts have been right to pro-   12
tect it when the government's interests in restricting it are minimal or the law being challenged is truly excessive in scope. The restrictions on commercial speech most offensive to the First Amendment are those that actually aim at speech, at stopping companies from contributing information and opinions to the marketplace of ideas.

But in most of the recent commercial speech cases, the government was curb-   13
ing advertising in an effort to prevent physical harm. When laws protecting the pub- lic from floods of junk faxes, dangerous drugs and other corporate mischief collide with companies' desire to market products, the Supreme Court should continue to use its sensible balancing test, and it should be more willing to find that the balance tips in favor of the people.

Distributing Viruses

Sarah Gordon

Sarah Gordon, a senior research fellow at Symantec Security Response, a major corporation that provides cutting-edge technology and services to help "individuals and enterprises protect and manage their digital assets" (www.symantec.com/corporate/), writes extensively on cybersecurity. She is also technical director of the European Institute for Computer Anti-Virus

Research. This piece was posted in May 2002 on the former New Architect Magazine *site (www.newarchitectmag.com).*

1   While most computer viruses are spread deliberately and actively, others are distributed more passively, through virus exchange Web sites. Many virus writers support exchange sites, and often cite research or the constitutional right to free speech as a reason to let these sites exist. Those who use the sites explain that they don't intend to harm, but to provide information that will help researchers better understand how viruses proliferate (and perhaps how they can be stopped). These arguments, however, fall apart under scrutiny.

2   It's true that the scientific community encourages research, but only when it's conducted within the ethical boundaries of a given discipline. It's unethical to make viruses available for (relatively) anonymous distribution to persons of unknown ability or motive. It's also bad science. How a virus replicates isn't hard to understand; in fact it's fairly common knowledge among researchers. We don't need to see the replication mechanism to figure out what makes viruses "work." The argument doesn't hold up once you understand that viruses are, for the most part, trivial programming exercises.

3   The United States Constitution protects free speech, but virus writing and subsequent distribution aren't pure speech. Rather, they're speech plus action. The U.S. Supreme Court has recognized that speech and action, while closely intertwined, aren't one and the same. Thus, the act of putting virus code on the Internet isn't necessarily protected.

4   Many virus writers contend that they're simply sharing information and can't be held responsible for the damage caused by their virus if someone else uses it to do harm. However, this isn't entirely accurate. Existing U.S. laws let victims of accidental injury seek compensation for losses caused by another's negligence. These laws become even more applicable when you consider the damage that can be done, whether negligible or intentional. Hence, virus writers may in fact be legally responsible—even if they abdicate moral responsibility.

CONSEQUENCES

5   So, what is the answer? Should it be illegal to place virus code on a Web site? Would this help solve the problem? While some voices have argued for a stronger legal remedy, research I've conducted over the last decade (at www.badguys.org/papers.htm) has shown that fear of the law isn't a major deterrent for many virus writers. While most virus writers understand that it's unacceptable to deliberately hurt someone, they don't make the connection that, by creating and/or deploying viruses, they're harming people.

6   Herein lies our greatest challenge, one that isn't simply limited to malicious code. The virtual environment tends to make us depersonalize an interaction. Have you ever written something in e-mail or in a chat room that you would never say in person? If so, you've seen first hand that computers tend to depersonalize interactions, altering the way in which we communicate. We can counter depersonalization

through education and policy. In this way, we can shape a world-view of acceptable and unacceptable cyberspace behavior. Education is likely to be far more effective than the law in the long term.

We have already made some significant strides. For instance, some software developers state clearly in their licensure that their packages may not be distributed from any sites that permit virus distribution. Likewise, some ISPs now have acceptable-use policies that forbid the distribution of viruses. And the acceptability of publicly available viruses has dropped in some populations of young, technically savvy people. Virus distribution may not be illegal, but more and more people are agreeing that it isn't right.

ACTIONS

This is an ongoing battle. We need to continue to let service providers know that allowing viruses to be placed on Web sites for educational purposes is unacceptable. We need to encourage educators to teach which behaviors are acceptable and which are not in the realm of computer use. And these lessons should start as soon as children become aware of computers.

I've been listening to both sides of this argument for more than ten years now. I have concluded that people need to stop thinking they can do whatever they want simply because it's not illegal. Many things aren't illegal, but that doesn't make them responsible or morally right. Making viruses publicly available on the World Wide Web for research or educational purposes? That's nonsense. Call it your constitutional right, but the truth is that it's morally wrong.

For Class Discussion

1. Working individually or in groups, make a list of the ways that you use the Internet (for example, source of news, primary means of communication with friends, purchasing clothing from online catalogs, downloading music, etc.). Think about the cartoon on page 729 and the article on teen cyberbullying as well as your own experiences. In what specific ways do you think that the Internet is affecting interpersonal relationships?

2. According to Daniel Drezner, Henry Farrell, and Nicholas Kristof, what are some of the positive political consequences of blogs? What case can you make for the national and international political power of the Internet?

3. In the anthology unit "The Media and Public Responsibility: What Counts As News and Who Decides?" various writers speculate on forces that are transforming the media. Using the readings in this unit and your own experience, list ways that blogs are affecting "what counts as news and who decides."

4. In the trial of Richard Machado, defense lawyers argued that a hate message sent to fifty-nine different Asian-Americans is much less of a personal threat

than would be a single message sent to one person. They also argued that obscenity-laced hate messages are quite common when somebody gets "flamed" in a chat room. In other words, they argued that a hate message is a genre of Internet discourse that carries less physical threat than would, say, a handwritten death threat attached to a brick and thrown through a window. Do you agree? Should Machado have been sentenced to a year in prison?

5. The Direct Marketing Association, which represents the interests of e-mail advertisers, argues that a complete ban on e-mail advertising would be an unconstitutional denial of free speech. This association wants to distinguish between "legitimate and responsible" e-mail advertising and the truly "junk advertising" that we normally call spam. In your use of e-mail, what experiences have you had with spam? How would you define the difference between spam and responsible e-mail advertising? Do you think spam and/or e-mail advertising should be made illegal?

6. Choose one of the readings in this unit and analyze it carefully using the List 2 Guide questions on pages 454–455.

OPTIONAL WRITING ASSIGNMENT   Using hate sites on the Internet, sending hate e-mails, writing slanderous blogs, and posting computer virus code are highly antisocial behaviors, in some cases fostered by the anonymity of the Internet. Some people argue that these activities are protected by the constitutional right of free speech, or that these are the unavoidable downside of the amazingly powerful and beneficial Internet. Both Jeff Chu and Sarah Gordon mention the need to train young people in computer etiquette and social responsibility, yet neither elaborates on this idea. How would you propose to educate Internet users in responsible behavior? You might want to research such online organizations as WiredSafety.org and Teenangels (www.teenangels.org) and write a researched proposal directed at young people and their families or an op-ed piece for a newspaper in which you argue for the need to tolerate, prohibit, control, or change this behavior.

Credits

Text

Page 5. Wilfred Owen, "Dulce et Decorum Est" from *The Complete Poems and Fragments of Wilfred Owen,* ed. Jon Stallworthy (New York: W. W. Norton, 1984).

Page 15. Sara Jean Green, excerpt from "Mosh Pits: It's Not All Fun, Music" from *The Seattle Times,* June 4, 2002, pp. A1, A9.

Page 15. Excerpt from "Homeless Hit the Streets to Protest Proposed Ban." Reprinted by permission of the Associated Press.

Page 17. Gordon F. Adams, "Petition to Waive the University Math Requirement." Reprinted with the permission of the author.

Page 25. Lisa Turner, "Playing with Our Food," *Better Nutrition,* Vol. 62, No. 6, June 2000, pp. 56–59. Copyright © 2000 Lisa Turner. Reprinted by permission of the author.

Page 41. "Biotech Labeling" from www.whybiotech.com. Courtesy of the Council for Biotechnology Information.

Page 126. David Langley, "'Half-Criminals' or Urban Athletes? A Plea for Fair Treatment of Skateboarders." Reprinted with the permission of the author.

Page 132. Bobbi Buchanan, "Don't Hang Up, That's My Mom Calling," *The New York Times,* December 8, 2003, p. A31.

Page 147. John Tierney, "Recycling Is Garbage," *New York Times Magazine,* June 30, 1996, p. 28. Copyright © 1996 John Tierney. Used with permission.

Page 150. Marybeth Hamilton, from "First Place: A Healing School for Homeless Children." Reprinted with the permission of the author.

Page 153. Ellen Goodman, "Minneapolis Pornography Ordinance," *The Boston Globe.* Copyright © 1985 The Washington Post Writers Group. Reprinted with permission.

Page 157. Rebekah Taylor, "A Letter to Jim." Reprinted with the permission of the author.

Page 205. Aaron Friedman, "All that Noise for Nothing," *The New York Times,* December 11, 2003. Copyright © 2003 New York Times Company, Inc. Used with permission.

Page 231. "Low Carb Diets Unhealthy Trend." This content has been reproduced with the permission of HealthAtoZ.

Page 234. Kathy Sullivan, "Oncore, Obscenity, and the Liquor Control Board." Reprinted with the permission of the author.

Page 236. Charles Krauthammer, "This Isn't a 'Legal' Matter, This Is War," *The Seattle Times,* September 13, 2001, p. B6. Copyright 2001, The Washington Post Writers Group.

Page 239. Eugene Volokh, "You Can Blog, But You Can't Hide," *The New York Times,* December 2, 2004. Copyright © 2004 New York Times Company, Inc. Used with permission.

Page 259. Daeha Ko, "The Monster That Is High School," *University of Washington Daily,* May 9, 1999. Copyright © 1999 by the *University of Washington Daily.* Reprinted with permission of the publisher.

Page 263. Olivia Johnson. "Different But Probably Equal," *The New York Times,* January 23, 2005. Copyright © 2005 New York Times Company, Inc. Used with permission.

Page 266. Carlos Macias, "The Credit Card Company Made Me Do It." Reprinted with the permission of the author.

Anthology

Page 484. John Ashcroft, testimony to the Senate Committee on the Judiciary, December 6, 2001.

Page 488. Deborah Pearlstein, "Rights in an Insecure World," *The American Prospect,* Volume 15, Number 10, October 1, 2004. The American Prospect, 11 Beacon Street, Suite 1120, Boston MA 02108. All rights reserved. Reprinted by permission.

Page 493. Michelle Malkin, "Racial Profiling: A Matter of Survival." *USA Today,* August 17, 2004. Copyright © 2004 Michelle Malkin. Reprinted by permission of Creators Syndicate.

Page 495. Arsalan Iftikhar, "Losing Liberties." TomPaine.com, May 19, 2005.

Page 498. Patricia J. Williams, "To See or Not to See," from the June 28, 2004 issue of *The Nation.* For subscription information, call 1-800-333-8536. Portions of each week's Nation magazine can be accessed at http://www.thenation.com.

Page 500. Michael Levin, "The Case for Torture." *Newsweek,* June 7, 1982. Copyright © 1982 Michael Levin. Used with permission.

Page 502. McQ, "Situational Ethics and the Case for Torture." The QandO Blog, May 30, 2005.

Page 508. George W. Bush, "Remarks by the President at the 2002 Graduation of the U.S. Military Academy at West Point." June 1, 2002.

Page 512. Richard Falk, "The New Bush Doctrine," from the July 15, 2002 issue of *The Nation.* Copyright © 2002. For subscription information, call 1-800-333-8536. Portions of each week's Nation magazine can be accessed at http://www.thenation.com.

Page 517. John Miller, "Our 'Next Manifest Destiny.'" *National Review,* July 15, 2002. Copyright © 2002 by National Review, Inc., 215 Lexington Avenue, New York, NY 10016. Reprinted by permission.

Page 522. Michael Krepon, "Weapons in the Heavens: A Radical and Reckless Option." *Arms Control Today,* 2004. Copyright © 2004. Reprinted by permission.

Page 531. Samuel Huntington, "The Great American Myth." *Maclean's,* February 14, 2005. Copyright © 2005 Samuel Huntington. Used with permission.

Page 535. John Bragg, "The American Dream: Why Environmentalists Attack the SUV." *Capitalism,* May 31, 2001. Copyright © 2001 The Center for the Advancement of Capitalism. Used with permission.

Page 537. Henry Payne and Diane Katz, "Gas and Gasbags . . . or, the Open Road and Its Enemies." *National Review,* March 25, 2002, Vol. 54, Issue 5, pp. 45–56. Copyright © 2002 National Review. Used with permission.

Page 540. Keith Bradsher, "Gimme an SUV—ASAP." *National Post,* September 28, 2002. Copyright © 2002 Keith Bradsher. Reprinted by permission.

Page 546. "Environmental Double Standards for Sport Utility Vehicles." SUV.org.

Page 552. Arianna Huffington, "Road Outrage: How Corporate Greed and Political Corruption Paved the Way for the SUV Explosion." Copyright © 2005 Arianna Huffington. Used with permission. www.ariannaonline.com.

Page 555. Paul Roberts, "Running Out of Oil—and Time." *Los Angeles Times,* March 7, 2004. Copyright © 2004 Paul Roberts. Used with permission.

Page 557. Thomas Friedman, "As Toyota Goes . . ." *New York Times,* June 17, 2005. Copyright © 2005 New York Times Company, Inc. Used with permission.

Page 561. Floyd McKay, "Wal-Mart Nation: The Race to the Bottom." *Seattle Times,* February 18, 2004. Copyright © 2004 Floyd McKay. Used with permission.

Page 563. Robert Reich, "Don't Blame Wal-Mart." *New York Times,* February 28, 2005. Copyright © 2005 New York Times Company, Inc. Used with permission.

Page 565. Liza Featherstone, "Down and Out in Discount America." *The Nation,* January 3, 2005. For subscription information, call 1-800-333-8536. Portions of each week's *Nation* magazine can be accessed at http://www.thenation.com.

Page 571. Pankaj Ghemawat and Ken A. Mark, "The Price is Right." *New York Times,* August 3, 2005. Copyright © 2005 New York Times Company, Inc. Used with permission.

Page 735. Sarah Gordon, "Distributing Viruses." *New Architect,* May 2002. Copyright © 2002 Sarah Gordon. Used with permission.

Images

Page 24. Courtesy of Sustain USA.

Page 73. U. S. Department of Defense.

Page 137. Left, AP/Wide World Photos.

Page 137. Right, Getty Images.

Page 166. Courtesy of the Seattle Field Division of the Drug Enforcement Administration and NW-HIDTA, and *The Seattle Times* (ad design).

Page 167. Courtesy of Common Sense for Drug Policy, Lancaster, PA.

Page 175. Top left and top right, AP/Wide World Photos.

Page 175. Bottom, Reuters/CORBIS.

Page 178. Courtesy DeVito/Verdi, New York, NY.

Page 193. AP/Wide World Photos.

Page 262. Courtesy of United Way of King County and Copacino+Fujikado, Photography by Darrell Peterson.

Page 351. Courtesy of The Mount Sinai Center for Children's Health and the Environment and Fenton Communications.

Page 385. Ken Balcomb, Center for Whale Research.

Page 530. Courtesy of Global Network Against Weapons & Nuclear Power in Space.

Page 601. Courtesy of gatheredimages.com.

Page 605. Courtesy of Sustain USA.

Page 691. Left, Arko Datta/Reuters/CORBIS.

Page 691. Right, AP/Wide World Photos.

Page 709. The Advertising Archive Ltd.

Page 712. Courtesy of Technology Review.

Page 713. Courtesy of Siemens Corporation.

Color Plates

COLOR PLATE A   Courtesy of the Council for Biotechnology Information.

COLOR PLATE C   Alex Quesada/Polaris Images.

COLOR PLATE D   Courtesy of Save the Children.

COLOR PLATE E   Courtesy of Earthjustice.

COLOR PLATE F   Courtesy of WAL*MART.

COLOR PLATE H   © 2005 Army Game Project. Used by Permission.

COLOR PLATE I   © 2005 Army Game Project. Used by Permission.

Index

READINGS AND VISUAL ARGUMENTS BY GENRE

Unless otherwise indicated, the readings or visual arguments appear in the Anthology.